Made in ITALY

A SHOPPER'S GUIDE TO FLORENCE, MILAN, ROME & VENICE

BY ANNIE BRODY
& PATRICIA SCHULTZ

PHOTOGRAPHS BY ENRICO RAINERO

MAPS BY ARNOLD BOMBAY

WORKMAN PUBLISHING, NEW YORK

Library of Congress Cataloging-in-Publication Data
Brody, Annie.   Made in Italy.
   Includes index.   1. Shopping—Italy—Guide-books.
2. Restaurants, lunch rooms, etc.—Italy.
I. Schultz, Patricia.
II. Title.
TX337.I8B76 1988   381'.45'002545   87-27415   ISBN 0-89480-305-0

Workman Publishing Company, Inc.
708 Broadway
New York, New York 10003
Manufactured in the United States of America
First printing April 1988
10   9   8   7   6   5   4   3   2   1

Cover painting: "Triumph of Venus" by Francesco del Cossa,
SCALA/Art Resource, New York.

Front cover photographs: (top) Beltrami; (bottom) Eric Carle,
Shostal Associates. Marble background courtesy Associated Marble Industry, Inc.

Back cover photographs: (top) David Forbert, Shostal Associates;
(bottom) Marty Reichenthal, The Stock Market.

For their love, support and encouragement,
we dedicate this book to our parents

Cecelia and (in loving memory) Benjamin
and
Mary and Leonard

And to two very special friends

Paul
and
Giovanni

CONSULTANTS TO <u>MADE IN ITALY</u>

Fashion: Barbara J. Friedman

Food & Wine: Faith Heller Willinger

Additional Research: Luca Barbero, Simone Bargellini, Rosanna Cirigliano, Barbara Falanga, Barbara J. Friedman, Alessandra Manassei, Alberto Morelli, Rosamaria Rinaldi, Patricia Scarzella, Lisa Selden, Kate Singleton and Anne Zwack

---

Editor: Sally Kovalchick
Book design: Susan Aronson Stirling with Barbara Scott-Goodman
Photo research: Elena Dunbar Lucchetti and Rona Beame
Photography: Enrico Rainero
Maps: Arnold Bombay
Translation: Paula Segurini and Richard Dunbar
Copy editor: Marjorie Flory
Proofreader: John Kremitske
Production: Wayne Kirn, Jacques Williams, Ludvik Tomazic, and Catherine Mayer
Index: Catherine Dorsey

Appreciative thanks to Ciga Hotels, the Italian Shoe Board, the Italian Trade Commission and the many shops that generously supplied photographs.

Any guidebook with inaccurate information is extremely frustrating, especially when you're traveling and time is of the essence. Having experienced this ourselves, we went to great lengths to confirm all the information we included in this book—particularly addresses, telephone numbers, days closed, etc.; however, Italy's major cities, though timeless in appearance, are constantly changing and such information is always subject to alteration. We encourage you to take advantage of the telephone numbers given for restaurants and *trattorie* not only to reserve, but to confirm that the weekly day of *riposo* has not been changed. We invite your comments and suggestions for future editions.

Because the dollar's rate of exchange is always fluctuating, we have categorized establishments as inexpensive, moderate, expensive or very expensive rather than giving fixed prices.

Mille Grazie

A book such as this one ends up being a giant collaboration of the energy, insight and resources of innumerable people. Thus it is only fitting that they be acknowledged here, for surely this book would not have been realized without them. We are deeply grateful for having benefited from so many extraordinary talents.

Our thanks go first to our publisher, Peter Workman, for his singular and steadfast commitment to quality in every aspect of the publishing process out of his enormous love for books—we couldn't have asked for a finer publishing "home." To Sally Kovalchick, our editor, for her understanding, enthusiasm, coaching and enormous expertise in the making of good books—for insisting in her genial and jovial way that we bring forth our very best. To Marjorie Flory for her very thorough and precise copy-editing, which has immeasurably enhanced our writing. To Susan Aronson Stirling for the beautiful and handy design of a book that kept growing and expanding and for her diligence in bringing it all together visually. To Andrea Bass for her energetic and enthusiastic support of the book. To Bob Gilbert for reliably and cheerfully helping with all the unending and unglamorous tasks and details that go on behind the scenes and that quietly hold the pieces together of a project like this. And to Arnold Bombay, who rose to the challenge of our map-making needs with consummate skill and charm.

No less important to the book's production were the countless hours of conversation, advice, ideas, assistance and encouragement from friends and friends of friends, on both sides of the ocean, who cheerfully came forth to share their love for Italy: especially Giancarlo Alhadeff, Paula Atkins, Barbara and Henry Bolan, Donatella Bucci, Barbara J. Friedman, Bird and Tim Smith, Armando Verde, Faith Heller Willinger, Suzanna Zevi and Anne Zwack. We thank them wholeheartedly.

Special heartfelt thanks, too, to our many Italian friends who helped enlighten us in the ways of their country and who generously opened their hearts and their homes to us: in particular, Luca Barbero, Stefano Terrabuio and his parents, Elvio and Gabri, Rossella Meucci and Francesco Reale, Gigi and Federica Marangoni, Daniele Mordini, Elena Lucchetti and Richard Dunbar. Their meaningful friendship and welcoming encouragement was an honor and privilege that brought us the experience of the real Italy.

Finally, our loving thanks and appreciation to two very dear friends, Leah Komaiko and Debora Tiernan, for always being there with their special insight and humor—for seeing us through some of the darker moments of what seemed to be an unending project with their practical wit and for being with us to celebrate the happy moment of its conclusion. Their presence, too, is throughout this book.

With sincere appreciation to all of you,

Annie Brody and Patricia Schultz
March 1988

Contents

Made in Italy

*C*enturies before the splendor of the Renaissance, Italy had been a glorious mecca for traveling pilgrims and romantic adventurers. Today it remains one of the most visited destinations in Europe, offering that perfect sojourn where the treasures and pleasures of travel and shopping are delightfully and inextricably linked.

A celebration of all things Italian, *Made in Italy* is a guide to shopping for the best in Italian fashion, food and design. Rare is a nation as spontaneously loved as Italy, and it was because of our own fascination and love for the Italian people, their unrivaled excellence in design, and their almost reverential respect for the quality of artisanal workmanship that we decided to write *Made in Italy.*

From our first experiences meandering through the quiet, cobble-stoned streets of Brera, observing the colorful morning market in Rome's Campo dei Fiori, and savoring the heady aroma of a small leather workshop in Florence grew our own lifelong love affair with Italy, and our desire to create a book that would share with everyone the chance to visit and understand Italy through shopping.

We handpicked over 800 stores in Italy's four principal cities that offer everything from sleek espresso coffee-makers to feather-light racing bicycles, from artistically arranged food stores to caches of delicately hand-embroidered linens. Recommendations came from well-traveled friends, savvy Italians, fashion and design professionals—and often simply from our own exploration.

The possibilities were so staggering that we eventually limited our selections to those which best represented each city's specialties and expressed the sense of Italianness that we wanted to stress throughout the book. In choosing each entry, we kept in mind (not always in this order) quality and variety of merchandise, originality, craftsmanship, display, ambiance, personality, service and sense of taste—what the Italians call *buon gusto.*

Some listings, such as for Rome's Mondo Antico, where you'll find charming hand-painted miniature theater and opera sets, or Milan's La Casa del Cinghiale, which offers a remarkable range of bags and accessories made exclusively of pigskin, were natural choices for their very uniqueness. Our premise is that buying is only an incidental part of shopping; many memorable stores were included just for the experience of seeing and enjoying the show.

Monomania is a charming characteristic that we came across with some regularity: many a store specializes in one kind of item, such as antique watches or terra-cotta cookware, reflecting the passion of the owner. The diversity and imagination shown in a single-product shop are especially helpful if that specialty is just what you're looking to buy. You'll also notice that in Italy, perhaps more than anywhere else, each store is a mirror of the taste and point of view of its owner and therefore manifests its own distinctive personality.

The listings for world-renowned fashion designers, whose outlets are usually located in each city's downtown area, have been grouped together in a directory for your convenience. In their home towns (Valentino in Rome or Gucci in Florence, for example) personality profiles have been included. For ubiquitous chain stores, we generally mention only the flagship store in the chain's home town, for instance, the Città del Sole toy store in Milan and Richard-Ginori in Florence.

We were not insensitive to the allure of a bargain or the promise of value for your money. However, this book is not for bargain basement shoppers pressed to find the cheapest deal in town; it is for those who want to find the best products available at prices they can afford. We have tried not to overlook anyone—not the lover of classic, avant-garde, trendy or modern styles; nor the food fancier, culture buff, music enthusiast or antiques hunter. When time is an element, we hope to help you quickly locate the object of your search—be it the latest in home furnishings or the most traditional herbal panaceas based on medieval recipes. We also list conveniently located cafés and choice eating places (under Sustenance) to restore you between shops.

Made in Italy explores both the sleek world of showrooms and the colorful realm of characteristic artisanal *botteghe*. The artisan, Italy's living national treasure, has played an honored part in the history of the country. In the halcyon days of the Renaissance, his skills were elevated to an art form, and his awe-inspiring creations garnered international prestige. Today, virtuoso Italian craftsmen with an innate love for beauty, practice skills that are rare if not extinct elsewhere and continue to produce one-of-a-kind works of art. They are also vital to the conservation and restoration of art from the past. Italy's master leather workers, furniture makers, textile weavers, furriers, glass blowers, tailors and fashion designers are arguably the best in the world. Their techniques are remarkably similar to those of their ancestors. Some world-class gold-smiths and jewelers use an ancient method of granulation originated by the Etruscans some 28 centuries ago.

Although modern industry has squeezed out much of Italy's artisanal community, many entrepreneurs have simultaneously discovered a natural compatibility with traditional craftsmen. Artisans seeking to bring their ancient skills into the 21st century are often called upon to be both technicians and artists. In an age of volume production, their handcrafted industrial prototypes ensure end products of impeccable distinction. Nurturing the evolution of Italy's artisanal heritage even further is a recent movement of *nuovi artigiani* (new or contemporary artisans), who fuse tradition with modern inspiration, reinventing and reinterpreting age-old crafts and marketing them in sophisticated ways.

Pride in all things Italian is a fundamental part of the national character and has done much to maintain the quality of "Made in Italy" products. This guide will help shoppers realize that they need not depend on designer name brands or high-priced glamour for beautifully made merchandise. Small family enterprises have always occupied a key position in the mosaic of the national economy, and still abound in both manufac-turing and retailing. The family is everyone's first loyalty; dedication and individualistic pride are passed down from generation to generation. To uphold the family legacy is the artisan's and shopkeeper's inherited duty; from this familial zeal grew enormously successful dynasties, from the Benettons and Bulgaris to the Fendis and Ferragamos.

A country of only modest natural resources, Italy has always relied upon its skills and creativity to compete in the world market. Today, a unique sense of design and style continues to be the country's major export—ubiquitous in the curve of a Ferrari Testarossa, the line of Venetian mouth-blown glass, the intricately inlaid stone mosaic of a jewelry box, or even the aesthetic arrangement of food on a plate. Such artistic imagination results in a sense of daring and a novel approach to problem solving. Originality transcends the boundaries of traditionally established professions: it is not unusual for an architect to channel his talents into fashion design (Gianfranco Ferrè) or for a world-class car designer to invent a new shape of pasta (Fiat designer Giorgetto Giugiaro).

Ultimately, the "Made in Italy" trademark signifies quality. Since they live in cities that are nothing less than magnificent al fresco museums surrounded by sensual, inspiring landscapes, it is no surprise that all

Italians are artists at heart. As artists they uphold high standards of quality while feeling compelled to beautify everything they create. Since Leonardo's day they have transformed the practical and functional into the decorative and aesthetic: vaulted ceilings were elaborately frescoed, and bare walls ennobled with clever *trompe-l'oeil* murals; today, even their letter openers and water pitchers win places in the world's museums of modern art.

Each beautiful product is meant to endure; this is evident both in the country's wealth of august architecture and in its simplest decorative object—a burnished leather box hand-tooled in gold or an exquisite hand-carved cameo made from a conch shell. The tendency to shape, embellish and create from even the most common materials, imbuing everything with the romantic Italian spirit, has not faded over the centuries. In a time of predictable mass-market mediocrity, things "Made in Italy" still stand out for their reliable attention to detail in design and their painstaking workmanship.

For us, shopping in Italy is above all an enjoyable pastime that provides a gateway to the country, its people and culture. You will glimpse something of the legendary Italian spirit in small artisans' *botteghe* or in bustling open-air *mercati*. Across each store's threshold lie humble and grand samplings of the Italian sensibility. Whether you have a lifetime or only a weekend to shop there, *Made in Italy* will enrich your love for all things Italian.

ORGANIZATION

Each city's general introduction unfolds in a rich historical framework, helping you to understand and appreciate the unique nature and importance of each city and to familiarize yourself with its particular shopping personality. In addition to general how-to shopping guidelines, a list of specialties indigenous to that city highlights both their origins and their role in the contemporary marketplace. The variety, quality and authenticity of these specialties are bound to be at their best when purchased in the cities or regions from whence they come. We have divided each city into shopping neighborhoods; a general orientation map offers a bird's-eye view of their location.

Every shopping neighborhood represents a distinctive flavor or appeal. You can choose from genteel high-class or big-name shopping, a foray through the artisanal and bohemian section of town, or an exploration of upscale residential areas. The introduction to each neighborhood will give you an idea of its character and the shopping it offers, as well as a detailed area map whose numbers correspond to the location code numbers of the store entries in the text. Circles are stores; squares are sustenance stops. We do not expect you to visit every shop in numerical order, although in some cases that may prove helpful; rather, the number sequence will help you locate shops of interest to you and chart your course.

At the end of each city chapter, you'll find an index of all local stores arranged by product category, a special bonus if you're looking for particular kinds of things. A joint men's and women's category for fashion and shoes is included so that the couple who prefer to shop together can find one-stop locations. The product index includes sustenance listings arranged by type of establishment and are grouped by neighborhood.

For those who would rather shop than eat, stores generally open during lunch are marked with an asterisk in each city's Index to Stores Listed by Product.

SUSTENANCE SELECTION

Eating establishments, or "sustenance stops," were chosen in keeping with the feel and character of the neighborhood. The exclusive, stylish appeal of downtown or centralized shopping spills over to its restaurants, bar-cafés and wine bars, which are usually on the same grand scale. All *ristoranti* and *trattorie* are open for lunch and dinner unless otherwise noted. Where the wine list is exceptional, it has been mentioned. In the cuisine section of each city introduction, you'll find specific suggestions for fine local or regional wines. These are not inexpensive wines. Often limited in quantity and doled out only to discerning restaurants, they are worth keeping an eye out for, especially if you are an avid eonophile.

Some great discoveries, for shopping and sustenance alike, were technically outside neighborhood boundaries (and not shown on the maps) but couldn't be overlooked. Designated "Taxi Away," they are well worth the foray and will provide a glimpse of some parts of town usually hidden from foreign eyes.

HOW TO READ EACH ENTRY

Headings include general category of store, type of product, and selection, style or noteworthy feature; however, in some instances, only one or two of these designations are necessary.

HOME

GLASS

Contemporary Design

32 VENINI ⌂⌂⌂⌂

Via Montenapoleone 9
*Tel. 70.05.39
Open during lunch
Expensive; credit cards accepted

General category

Type of product

Specialty, style, or noteworthy feature

Map location code

Establishment name

This is our equivalent of a four-star rating—our subjective, overall evaluation based on quality, style, value and ambiance. If money were no object, you'd walk out with four bags full. These are stores you shouldn't miss, even if just to browse or window-shop.

**Address

*Local telephone number

If credit cards are accepted, you can generally expect that American Express, MasterCard (sometimes referred to as Eurocard), and Visa are all taken.

Price category to give you a relative idea ("moderate" can sometimes be thought of as reasonable).

*Note on telephone numbers: If calling from another city within Italy, you must dial the following city codes first: for Milan, 02; Rome, 06; Florence, 055; Venice, 041.

**The ground floor of a large palazzo may house more than one store, all with the same address. Also note that a street name may change every few blocks even though the street itself is continuous.

Shopping Italy with Know-How

*F*irst-time visitors will be surprised to find that although relatively small in size, Italy varies greatly from region to region and sometimes from city to city. That is because for most of its history Italy was a geographical area comprised of many small and completely independent city-states. It was not until 1860 that it became a unified country. The inhabitants of each region are still fiercely proud of their distinctive heritage, so regional differences continue to color many aspects of daily life.

You'll notice these differences most readily in architectural styles, dialects, accents and cuisines. With closer observation you'll find that the character of the people themselves varies according to the region. All of this is reflected in the style and ambiance of shopping and in the local specialties offered for sale.

From the shopper's viewpoint, Milan is unbeatable for its diversity of choice, efficiency, contemporary high-fashion style and modern design. Its hidden beauty and cultural offerings enhance its inherent Italian character, and its role as a gateway to Europe and the most cosmopolitan and European city on the Italian peninsula.

Our other favorite shopping city is Florence, which is less overwhelming and smaller in scale. Downtown Florence is exceptionally easy to navigate. Its compact size places almost all of our listings within walking distance. A centuries-old reputation for quality and artisanal craftsmanship guarantees not only fine traditional purchases, but outstanding avant-garde ones as well.

The Oriental-bazaar-like meanderings of Venice may prove frustrating to the organized shopper with limited time. If you're accustomed to giving a town the once-over before returning to purchase, the rambling, pedestrian layout of Venice's alleyways and labyrinthine back streets will not encourage you. For its historic specialties, however, such as glass, lace, Orientalia and exquisite fabrics, the city is unrivaled. Nor will you find a shortage of top designer clothing or shoes in your roaming.

Serious shoppers may find Rome principally a tourist destination, but there is fine and accessible shopping to satisfy you there. Rome's appeal to the shopper is ancient in origin, and its classic allure and imperial grandeur pervade every piazza, shop and café in town. You'll see why this is where southern Italy, with its sense of *la dolce vita,* unofficially begins.

WHEN YOU GO

Every tourist and shopper should know that June can be lovely in Italy, but July is often unpleasantly hot. In August, *"Chiuso per Feria"* (closed for vacation) signs appear everywhere, unapologetically taped to steel shutters pulled down over storefronts. Summer heat and a nationwide lack of air-conditioning are responsible for retail shops, food stores, bars and restaurants closing down for two to five weeks, some beginning as early as mid-July; even Milan bends to this age-old custom. Surprisingly, Venice is the one exception; there the constant stream of tourism drops only in the dank winter months, encouraging most merchants to stay open during the summer and close in December or January, with everything back in full swing for the late winter arrival of Carnival.

For the shopper, however, fall and spring are the best times to visit Italy. Fall-winter clothing and footwear generally arrive in the stores in September. Holiday fashion appears in early December, with the spring collections showing up around February. Spring's big push is around Easter, and summer clothes arrive just after.

Huge savings in fashion are available during two major sale periods. Some stores start their winter merchandise sales just after Christmas Day, although most wait until January 2. Savvy Italian and foreign shoppers can then clean out the marketplace with savings of up to 50 percent on superior wools, leather, knitwear and silks. Summer merchandise is offered at the same discount in July, when stores prepare for their August closing. During sales, there is slightly more room for bargaining.

Splashy signs in store windows read *"Liquidazione"* (liquidation); *"Saldi," "Svendita"* or *"Occasioni"* (sales); *"Fine stagione"* (end of the season); or *"Sconti"* (discounts). Discounts are also available in designers' stores, although their window advertisements are more discreet.

OPENING AND CLOSING

All banks, offices and shops in Italy are closed on the national holidays listed below.

January 1—*Capodanno or Primo dell'Anno* (New Year's Day)
April 25—*Festa della Liberazione* (Liberation Day)
May 1—*Festa del Lavoro* (Labor Day or May Day)
August 15—*Ferragosto* (Assumption Day)
November 1—*Ognissanti* (All Saints' Day)
December 8—*Festa della Madonna Immacolata* (Immaculate Conception)
December 25—*Natale* (Christmas Day)
December 26—*Santo Stefano* (Saint Stephen's Day)

On the eve of such important holidays as Assumption Day, Christmas and New Year's, some stores close for the day at 1:00 P.M. and banks close at 11:30 A.M. Easter is a floating holiday; shops often close on Good Friday (*Venerdì Santo*) and Easter Monday (*Pasquetta*). Additional information particular to each city, including feast days honoring the local patron saint, is in the introduction to that city.

Retail stores generally stay open from 9:00 A.M. to 1:00 P.M. and from 3:30 or 4:00 to 7:30 or 8:00 P.M. Stores in the north, such as those in Milan, tend to have shorter lunch breaks. Local chambers of commerce regulate the "high season," which runs from May or June to September or October (to November in Venice only), when stores may choose to stay open during lunch, although their policy may vary from year to year. Such stores are marked with an asterisk in the Index to Stores Listed by Product for each city.

Food stores always close one afternoon a week; this differs from city to city and is discussed in the introduction to each city. Italians generally do their food shopping early in the morning, and all other shopping in the late afternoon. If you can avoid these crowded hours, you'll find the sales help less harried and more courteous. Use the long lunch breaks to shop the open-air markets and department stores that do not close, during lunch. Siestas and evenings can be spent window shopping for familiarization and inspiration.

MONEY MATTERS

The lira (abbreviated as "£" or "lit.") is Italy's monetary unit. Italians generally use a decimal point where we would use a comma: 700,000 lire becomes 700.000 lire. A visitor's biggest puzzlement is the number of zeros in the price of even the most inexpensive object. A pocket calculator is an indispensable travel accessory; just as helpful is a home-made index card with the current dollar equivalents of £5,000, 10,000, 15,000, etc.

Traveler's checks are still the safest form of currency. Italian shops and restaurants will give you change in lire, calculating from the day's

official rate found in the local papers. Surprisingly, this rate can often be marginally higher than what the banks offer you, and even at banks the rate of exchange for traveler's checks is often slightly more favorable than that for cash, the reason being the additional cost of security for guarding currency (traveler's checks, which become functionally worthless after they've been countersigned, need not be so carefully watched.)

Don't count on using your personal checks drawn on American banks, but bring them along for the exceptions that exist. Large items such as antiques that will be shipped can often be paid by check, presumably because the shop owner has time to clear your check before releasing your goods for shipment. Small shops that honor overseas checks have been noted in the text. If you are an American Express cardholder, you can cash a personal check (or countercheck) in any American Express office, using your credit card as collateral.

Credit cards are now widely accepted in the shops and restaurants of Italy's major cities. Generally, if an establishment accepts one, it will accept them all. MasterCard International is in partnership with Eurocard in Europe. Therefore, wherever you see the Eurocard logo, it means MasterCard is accepted. (Always remember to ask for a discount if paying with cash; vendors will often deduct the percentage they would otherwise pay to the credit card company.) It is important to know that the exchange rate used to bill you is not the one in effect on the day of your transaction, but rather on the day the charge is actually posted to your account. You cannot control the day the shop owner submits the credit-card slip for payment to his local bank, nor when the bank will submit the slip to the credit-card company. If the dollar were to plummet during such an interval, this could be costly to the purchaser. Also check the credit-card slip for correct prices before signing, particularly on an expensive purchase. Since a corporation name and not the individual store name often appears on the slip, it is recommended that you pen in on your copy what you have purchased and where. This is useful for future reference and customs declaration.

The Italian automated bank machines cannot be activated by American cards. You can, however, get a cash advance against your Visa card at banks affiliated with Bank of America, namely, branches of La Banca d'America e d'Italia; these addresses are listed at the beginning of each city chapter.

Banks in Italy are open Monday through Friday from 8:30 A.M. to 1:30 P.M.; an occasional few reopen one hour after lunch, from 2:45 to 3:45 P.M. They are generally closed all day Saturday and Sunday and on national and local holidays. Any exceptions to this rule are noted in each city chapter. Minimal fluctuations in exchange rates from one bank to another are too slight to warrant shopping around. However, official places of exchange are more favorable than hotels, which often charge a small premium. If you do not spend all the money you have changed before you leave the country, you'll need the original bank transaction receipt to convert the lire back into dollars.

There is no limit to the amount of foreign currency you can bring into Italy, but if you're carrying a large

Concern for quality is respected.

amount, you should declare the amount you are carrying (traveler's checks not included) when you enter so that, if need be, you may carry the same amount back into the United States without complication. To bring the equivalent of a million lire in or out of Italy, you *must* fill out a V2 declaration form at your point of entry. Import or export of Italian currency may not exceed 400,000 lire, in denominations of 50,000 lire or less.

Prices in shops are fixed and always include value-added tax, or VAT (called "IVA" in Italy). In a recent policy change, there is now a system for refunding the value-added tax (which ranges from 18 percent for a dress to as high as 38 percent for jewelry) on purchases made in Italy by citizens or residents of countries outside the European Community. To qualify, you must make a minimum purchase of 520,000 lire in one of the over 3000 establishments that have agreed to participate (they are supposed to display a sign), and you must pay by credit card and request an invoice. When you leave Italy (at present this is operative only at airports), a customs officer examines the merchandise and stamps the invoice, which you then mail back to the seller

SHOPPER'S GLOSSARY

SHOPS

Italy has always been a land of specialization. Here we list each *negozio* (store) or *bottega* (workshop) and describe what it means:

(*negozio d'*) *abbigliamento*—clothing store
antiquario—antique dealer
(*negozio di*) *articoli sportivi*—sporting-goods store
(*negozio di*) *biancheria*—lingerie store
cartoleria—stationery store
casalinga—housewares
(*negozio di*) *dischi*—record and music store
erboristeria—herb shop
farmacia—drugstore
(*negozio di*) *giocattoli*—toy store
gioielleria—jewelry store
giornalaio (or *edicola*)—newsstand
grande magazzino—department store
libreria—bookstore
merceria—notions store, selling cotton undergarments, shoulder pads and other miscellaneous items
(*negozio di*) *mobili*—furniture store
oreficeria—gold jewelry store
pelleteria—leathergoods store
pelliceria—furrier
profumeria—perfume shop, also selling cosmetics and costume jewelry
(*negozio di*) *regali*—gift shop
(*negozio di*) *scarpe*—shoe store
tabaccaio—tobacco store
(*negozio di*) *tessuti*—store selling fabrics for *abbigliamento* (clothing) or *per la casa* (for the home)
ufficio postale—post office

FOOD STORES

alimentari—grocery store
confetteria—candy shop
drogheria—general food store
enoteca—wine shop
gastronomia—gourmet shop
latteria—store selling dairy products
macelleria—butcher
mesticheria—hardware/housewares store
ortolano or *negozio di frutta e verdura*—vegetable and fruit market
panetteria or *forno*—bread shop
pasticceria—pastry shop
pescheria—fish store
pizzicheria—grocery store
salumeria—delicatessen
supermercato—supermarket
vinaio or *vini ed olii*—wine or wine/oil seller merchant

Fruits, vegetables, and other non-packaged items are almost always priced *per etto* (100 grams) or *per chilogramma* (kilogram).
Per portare via means "to take out."

STORE SIGNS

a misura or *su misura*—made-to-measure
artigianale and *fatto a mano*—handmade

nostra produzione, produzione propria or *lavorazione propria*—the shop's own production, often made right on the premises
giorno di riposo settimanale—weekly closing day for bars and restaurants
entre libero or *ingresso libero*—you're invited to come in and just look
prezzo fisso—fixed price
in restauro—under restoration
chiuso per feria—closed for vacation

If you are looking for a specific item, the following terms will be useful.

JEWELRY

bracelet—*braccialetto*
brooch—*spilla*
cameo—*cammeo*
chain—*catena* or *catenina*
charm or small pendant—*ciondolo*
cigarette lighter—*accendino*
cuff links—*gemelli*
earrings—*orecchini*
necklace—*collana*
pendant—*pendente*
pin—*spillo*
ring—*anello*
   engagement ring—*anello di fidanzamento*
   wedding ring—*fede nuziale*
tie clip—*fermacravatta*
watch—*orologio*

CLOTHING AND ACCESSORIES

bathing suit—*costume da bagno*
bag—*borsa* (pocketbook)
belt—*cintura*

blouse or shirt—*camicia*
boots—*stivali*
bra—*reggiseno* or *reggipetto*
briefs—*mutande*
coat—*cappotto*
dress—*vestito*
evening dress—*abito da sera*
garment/suit (generic)—*abito*
gloves—*guanti*
jacket—*giacca*
jeans—*jeans*
nightgown—*camicia da notte*
panties—*mutandine*
pantyhose—*collant*
raincoat—*impermeabile*
sandals—*sandali*
scarf—*sciarpa* (wool), *foulard* (silk)
shirt—*camicia*
shoes—*scarpe*
shoulder pads—*spalline*
skirt—*gonna*
socks—*calzine*
stockings—*calze*
suit (men's & women's)—*completo*
sweater—*maglione*
tie—*cravatta*
trousers—*pantaloni*
tuxedo—*smoking*
wallet—*portafoglio*

LEATHER

calfskin—*vitello*
crocodile—*cocodrillo*
elephant—*elefante*
kidskin—*capretto*
lambskin—*pecora*
ostrich—*struzzo*
pigskin—*cinghiale*
snake—*serpente*
suede—*camoscio*

An extensive railroad system gets you there.

in a pre-stamped, pre-addressed envelope before you leave the country. The
tax refund is credited by the card
company to your account.

GETTING AROUND

Our maps are designed to complement those issued free by the tourist
boards and show the location of the
stores mentioned, which are keyed by
number. For additional information,
particularly on obscure side streets
and suburbs, see the highly detailed
"Tutta Città" directory, which has a
comprehensive street index and di-
vides each city into a series of helpful
maps; it can be found in most bar-
cafés and at your hotel. If you have
time on your hands, ask at your hotel
for some particularly interesting bus
routes, but don't be surprised if you
get lost.

Taxis are everyone's best bet for
getting from one neighborhood to
another; prices are comparable to
American rates, except in Venice

where water taxis are very costly. You
can't always flag down cabs, but
you'll find taxi stands along the main
streets and in important piazzas. Any
restaurant or shop owner can call you
a cab, which will arrive within minutes; you'll be expected to pay from
the point from which the taxi started,
usually the nearest taxi stand. Be
ready, too, to pay supplements at
night and on Sundays and holidays,
as well as for luggage and airport
trips. (See more specific taxi information in each chapter.)

ETIQUETTE

Whenever you enter or leave a shop,
the owner will greet you with *"Buon
giorno"* (Good morning) or *"Buona
sera"* (Good evening)—used upon entering or leaving anytime after lunch.
Any attempt at response will be
warmly received. Only if you are
greeted with the informal *"Ciao"* or
"Salve" should you return the same.

Dress for success if you want
attentive sales help. Shops are generally not self-service, and a reverence
for display and merchandise quality
discourages hands-on browsing. Italians love to rely on shopkeepers' gen-
erations-old expertise regarding the
ripeness of a melon or the authenticity of an antique engraving; it will be
to your advantage to follow this tradition. Salespeople in fine stores are
usually professional, savvy and multilingual. In better clothing boutiques,
they will outfit you from top to toe if
you explain what you're looking for —
evening, business or weekend wear.

SHOPPING TIPS

Antiques and Works of Art: For
any object or piece of furniture or

jewelry over 100 years old, the dealer must supply you with a bill of sale, a government permit allowing you to take it out of the country, and a certificate of authenticity; the latter will be needed at U.S. customs to qualify you for duty exemption. All antique dealers selected for this book are respected in their field and should be able to answer your questions on age, provenance, and workmanship. Always ask if the price is final.

Electrical Appliances: Italian products, from lamps to espresso makers, use AC current, 50 cycles and usually 220 voltage; they will need to be used with a transformer or rewired for use in the States. Some shops catering to tourists carry a limited selection of 110-voltage models for American use; some will even do necessary wiring for you themselves. Allow a few days.

Department and Chain Stores: They are not very plentiful, but for the best in quality and variety in a self-service atmosphere, look for any of the Coin and Rinascente stores. Standa and Upim are lower end of the market, but are undergoing image changes and can offer some good values in novelty items.

Jewelry: All jewelry made in Italy for sale there is supposed to be 18k gold, indicated by an obligatory government regulation *timbro,* or stamp, on each piece. The "18k" stamp can also appear as "750," meaning that there are 750 grams of gold in a kilo or that the alloy is three-quarters gold. (Never, ever buy "hot" gold from shady sidewalk characters who stalk tourists, promising remarkable savings.) Silver is similarly marked "800," "835" or "925," reflecting the number of grams of pure silver in a kilo. (The internationally recognized standard for sterling is 925, while 800 is common in jewelry.)

Linens: Measure your mattress before you leave against the following American sizes. Fitted sheets are only now slowly making an appearance in Italy; you'll need to buy flat sheets (if you purchase them at Pratesi or Frette, you can have them fitted at any of their American locations). Depending upon fabric patterns and decorative borders, you can make slight alterations: you usually must buy an entire set and cannot mix and match different size pillowcases. The Italian *matrimoniale* size is commonly sold for both double and queen-size beds; king size is a recent and rarely found concession to American request.

You will not find standard washcloths. The Italian hand towel, called *viso* or *ospite*, is somewhat smaller than the American, as are the bath towel (*asciugamano*) and the bath sheet (*telo da bagno*).

American	Italian
Single (Twin) 66"w x 96"l	1 *piazza* 71"w x 118"l or 180 cm x 300 cm
Double (Full) 81"w x 96"l	1½ *piazze* 82"w x 118"l or 210 cm x 300 cm
Queen 90"w x 102"l	2 *piazze*/ *matrimoniale* 94"w x 118"l or 240 cm x 300 cm
King 108"w x 102"l	King (if found) 106"w x 118"l or 270 cm x 300 cm

Household Goods: If you plan on buying anything for your home, an invaluable tip is to measure every-

Continued on page 20

SIZE CHART

Sizing is not as standardized in Italy as it is in America; different manufacturers (and designers) will offer slightly different interpretations of the same size. This explains the contradictions you'll find in comparing size conversion charts.* The following charts are as close as you'll come to reality and will at least give you someplace to start.

WOMEN'S CLOTHING
(Dresses, Coats, Suits, Skirts):

USA	ITALY
6	34, 36, 38
8	36, 38, 40
10	38, 40, 42
12	40, 42, 44
14	42, 44, 46
16	44, 46, 48
18	46, 48, 50
20	48, 50, 52

WOMEN'S BLOUSES:

USA	ITALY
30	38
32	40
34	42
36	44
38	46
40	48
42	50
44	52

WOMEN'S HOSIERY:

USA	ITALY
petite	1
petite/medium	2
medium/tall	3
queen	4

WOMEN'S SWEATERS:

USA	ITALY
34	40
36	42
38	44
40	46
42	48
44	50

WOMEN'S SHOES:

USA	ITALY
5½	35
6½	36
7	37
7½	38
8	38½
8½	39
9	40
9½	41

JUNIORS' CLOTHING
(Dresses, Coats, Suits, Skirts):

USA	ITALY
7	34–36
9	36–38
11	38–40
13	40–42

MEN'S CLOTHING
(Jackets, Suits, Coats):

USA	ITALY
32	42, 44, 46
34	44, 46, 48
36	46, 48, 50
38	48, 50, 52
40	50, 52, 54
42	52, 54, 56
44	54, 56, 58
46	56, 58, 60

MEN'S SHIRTS— NECK SIZE:

USA	ITALY
14	36
14½	37
15	38
15½	39
15¾	40
16	41
16½	42
17	43
17½	44
18	45

SLEEVE LENGTH:

USA	ITALY
29 inches	74 centimeters
30	76
31	79
32	82
33	84
34	86
35	88

MEN'S SWEATERS:

USA	ITALY
small	44
medium	46–48
large	50
extra large	52–54

MEN'S SHOES:

USA	ITALY
6	39
6½	40
7	40½
7½	41
8	41½
8½	42
9	42½
9½	43
10	43½
10½	44–44½
11	45
11½–12	46

MEN'S SOCKS:

Same as Italian shoe sizes.

MEN'S & WOMEN'S GLOVES:

Same as American sizes. Trace your friends' hands if you'd like to buy gifts but don't know sizes.

CHILDREN'S CLOTHING:

USA	ITALY
1 yr.	35–40
2	40–45
3	45–50
4	50–55
5	55–60
6	60–65
7	65–70
8	70–75
9	75–80
10	80–85
11	85–90
12	90–95
13	95–100
14	100

INFANT & CHILDREN'S SHOES:

USA	ITALY
4	20
5	21
6	22
7	23
8	24
9	25
10	26
10½	27
11	28
12	29
13	30
1	31
2	32
3	33
4	34
5	35
6	36
7	37

*For a perfect fit, ask if the store offers alteration (alterazioni), a professional and often complimentary service extended to customers.

Continued from page 17
thing you might conceivably think of adorning (windows, tables, etc.) in both inches and centimeters before you go. Then bring along a pocket-size inches/centimeters tape measure so you won't have to agonize over conversions.

READING LABELS

Names of materials that will come in handy are *cotone* (cotton), *seta* (silk), *lino* (linen), *lana* (wool), *pizzo* (lace), and *pelle* or *cuoio* (leather). *Non si stira* means wash-and-wear, but other garment care labels are not always so easy to decipher. The most commonly found symbols are the following (if they are crossed out, the procedures are *not* recommended):

[50°C] —machine wash, warm

⚠ —do not bleach

⊟ —warm iron

Ⓟ —dry-clean

⊠ —do not tumble dry

MADE-TO-MEASURE

Just about anything can be made up to your individual specifications. An exceptionally tall or a large-footed shopper, or one with highly individualistic demands or inclinations, will thrill at the quality of work available. If you are leaving town and must have your goods shipped, however, you are running a risk. While we have selected only establishments of good reputation, if you are not around for the necessary fittings and for final approval, we cannot guarantee the results. Once your measurements are put on file, future orders can be placed by letter or telex and paid for by credit card. American Express has a claims policy should there be complications with your purchase.

SHOPPERS' SUSTENANCE

We have incorporated "sustenance" stops for weary shoppers so that relief and people-watching are never more than a cappuccino away. These places of respite have been divided into the following:

bar-caffè: Far from the American institutions of the same name, Italian bars offer all types of alchohol, coffee and tea, soft drinks and snacks such as breakfast pastries and *panini* (sandwiches). They generally open before breakfast and stay open through lunch and dinner, often till midnight when they are centrally located. If you sit at a table, you'll pay double for the joy of lingering and should leave a 10 to 15 percent tip. If you plan to stand at the bar, you'll need to pay at the *cassa* (cash register) and hand the attendant a *scontrino* (receipt) before you order; leave a few coins at the bar as a tip. (Credit cards are generally not accepted.)

All of the types of eating places listed below are possibilities for lunch or dinner. Lunch is served from 1:00 to 2:30 P.M.; after 3:00 P.M. you'll be hard-pressed to find anyone still serving. Dinner is generally served between 7:30 and 10:00, and if you've chosen a *ristorante*, it's always best to call ahead and reserve a table. Most close one or two days a week, and many take off the entire month of July or August. (They generally accept credit cards.)

enoteca: Loosely translated as a "wine library," this is a place where

Espresso breaks keep you going.

you can browse through prodigious wine collections before purchasing by the bottle or glass. An *enoteca* offers snacks at the bar, usually stand-up fashion, and is far more enjoyable than a retail wine shop selling bottles only.

gelateria: An ice-cream bar, usually open till at least 9 P.M. to serve the after-dinner crowd. Cones and different-size cups *(coppe)* are on display, and local connoisseurs say that for fruit flavors the more pastel (light-colored) the creamy ice cream appears, the more likely it is that the flavor comes from all-natural ingredients.

osteria: An establishment serving simple food in what is generally a casual, rustic setting like that of an inn from which the name originated.

pasticceria: A fresh pastry shop that often, but not always, offers the chance of a chair and coffee.

pizzeria: An informal place where delicious pasta-plus-pizza is an accepted combination, a favorite of most Italians, usually ordered as first and second courses. Pizzerias are open for lunch and usually stay open later than most *trattorie* for dinner.

ristorante: Usually a more refined restaurant, offering some of the country's finest cuisine, from traditional to nouvelle. Where there is an exceptional wine list, we encourage wine lovers to splurge with a few extra dollars to experience Italy's finest vintages. Specific recommended wines are found in the Cuisine sections of each city.

tavola calda: Literally, a "hot table" buffet, where you can pick and choose from an array of possibilities. Sometimes self-service.

trattoria: Often a mom-and-pop operation, low on pretension and high on home cooking. House wines can be quite good and interesting. Generally, it is safe to order regional wines such as Chianti while in Tuscany and Frascati when in Rome. Although reasonably priced, even *trattorie* can run on the expensive side.

GETTING IT ALL HOME

U.S. Regulations: Every individual is allowed to bring up to $400 worth of goods into the country duty-free; this includes items acquired as gifts. For the next $1000, a flat 10 percent duty tax must be paid; for amounts exceeding this, the precise rate of duty will be assessed by the customs official at the time of declaration. There is no limit to what a U.S. tourist can bring back so long as the appropriate duty is paid. Keep all your receipts together to make your customs check free of hassles. You can send duty-free gift parcels (marked "gift enclosed") home to friends or relatives, providing that the total value shipped to one person on one day does not exceed $50. For everything over this amount, the U.S. Postal Service will collect duty and a handling charge upon delivery. If you mail home any personal items you've brought with you from the States, mark the package "American goods returned."

Antiques certified to be at least 100 years old are admitted into the States duty-free, as are paintings, sculptures, and other works of art if certified as original. The authorization needed from the Italian government will be taken care of by the dealer or shop owner with whom you've done business; for Italy, this is primarily an attempt to prevent the removal of pieces of exceptional artistic and historical value from the country. Any respected dealer will expedite this formality.

Brokers and Craters: If you plan to do a lot of shopping, check into American customhouse brokers before you leave. Ask for specific information about sending packages from Italy, their procedure once the goods have arrived at an American port, and whether they have Italian contacts in the cities you plan to visit.

A number of reliable packers and shippers, such as Fracassi in Florence, are suggested in the individual city chapters; they will pick up your purchases at the store or your hotel, pack, crate and ship your goods home. The professional shippers that we've listed all have English-speaking agents who can give you a price estimate on the phone if you tell them weight, size, content, value and destination. If you're shipping by boat, they will consolidate your goods with others to fill a container; air freight is based on volume as well as weight. Some shippers arrange truck service to group goods you've purchased in different cities so that they may be shipped together from the same port. They will handle all export documents, will arrange for an American customs broker if you don't already

have one and, upon request, will insure goods until their destination.

Mailing Parcels: You can mail small packages yourself from the post office. The hours for this particular service will vary from post office to post office. The bureaucratic regulations about wrapping and sending packages of different dimensions and weights are so complicated that it is well worth searching out someone qualified to do it for you. Not everyone is authorized to wrap your package for insurance *(pacco di valore),* using a special red wax sealer. Due to customs regulations, you can't send packages valued at more than 1,000,000 lire through the post office. Be aware that if you want to trace or claim insurance for a package that has never arrived, you must appear in person with your receipt at the Italian post office from which it was sent; it cannot be done from abroad. Airmail takes at least one week, but after one kilogram (2.2 lbs) it becomes very expensive. Mail by sea takes 4 to 8 weeks and requires a special, heavier wrapping paper. Books can be shipped at the less expensive book rate but must weigh less than 2 kg per package.

Some stores may offer to ship your goods home for you. Determine if they will be mailed by air or sea. Print your name and address clearly, and keep your receipt until goods are received. When possible, pay with a major credit card: Visa will investigate packages never received and, if not satisfied, will remove the item from your bill; American Express has a similar policy, and will credit an item already paid for should it never arrive. If there is any question about the professionalism of the merchant, arrange to ship the item yourself.

FLORENCE
Firenze

Florence is the capital of Tuscany and perhaps the best shopping city in the Western world. Compact and manageable, it invites you to explore its history by wandering down narrow medieval streets and through neighborhoods full of character. Taxis and public transportation will often take twice as long as going on foot. Strolling, window-shopping and browsing in the lively open-air markets will make your visit to Forence an incomparably exciting experience.

One cannot think of Florence without its fine leathergoods or the store windows of the Ponte Vecchio laden with gold, but many other high-quality items fill out its impressive spectrum of centuries-old specialties: beautiful men's and women's fashion, exquisite hand-embroidered linens and lingerie, and prestigious porcelain and rustic ceramics, to name but a few. Florence is a microcosm of Italy's best, from the traditional to the avant-garde, from the authentic antique to the impeccable reproduction. Many world-renowned flagship stores are here: Gucci, Ferragamo and Pucci are all celebrated sons of Florence. Their ultra-elegant boutiques in the Centro Storico are filled with beautifully designed articles, representing generations of excellence, whose prices are usually as high as their quality. You'll find the same pride of creation and often a comparable level of workmanship in the smaller, independent family-run shops for more modest prices. Even in the touristy San Lorenzo street market, beneath the brassy veneer there's a feeble hint of the famed Florentine knack for imaginative fashion in the colorful knits and silk ties.

Italy is arguably the best-dressed country in Europe, and Florence is its *arbiter elegantarium.* Although Milan has recently stolen much of the limelight, Florence remains a mecca for serious buyers. Young designers, too, come from all over the world for its timeless inspiration. The prominent fabric and yarn factories of nearby Prato and the leather tanneries of Santa Croce sull'Arno have been known for their premier products since the eighth century.

In Florence, men's fashion tends to be more classic than women's, with fine wools and cottons made into handsomely tailored collections. Women's fashion can be equally conservative, but more often combines classic refinement with the influence of today's fantasy and innovation, the bold and creative design energy for which Italy is famous. The two modes, aristocratic chic and contemporary trendy, cohabit well. During the day you'll see elegantly turned-out men and women striding along the dignified Via Tornabuoni. Towards the hour of the ritualistic *passeggiata* or stroll, the main shopping streets of Calimala and Calzaiuoli that connect the Piazza della Signoria with the Duomo will be filled with attractive young Florentines who have an uncanny flair for throwing together striking wardrobes with daring imagination and slim budgets.

Conservatism in fashion taste reflects the inundation of the British who converged upon Florence beginning in the late 19th century to rediscover the magic of the Renaissance. For Shelley, it was the most beautiful city he had ever seen. Lord Byron made it his home, as did the Brownings, D.H. Lawrence, E.M. Forster, Thomas Hardy and Dylan

Arcaded walkway near the Uffizi Gallery leads to the Ponte Vecchio.

Thomas. "*Gli inglesi,*" as all northern Europeans came to be known here, bought up the hilly countryside surrounding Florence, and the well-heeled local society imitated their understated and traditional styles. It was a confluence of tastes still referred to as "Anglo-florentine." The Via Tornabuoni still boasts an English Drugstore and English Bookstore and, just a block away, the Old English Stores. An English Bakery was located on the Via della Vigna Nuova until recently, when it was purchased by Naj Oleari, the noted producer of decorative cottons. Some Englanders decided to stay for eternity; the English Cemetery in Piazza Donatello is home to a roll call of poets and artists who found creative fullfillment here in an adopted land.

The British disdain for outward displays of consumption is not alien to the Florentines' character. Despite the inclination toward unbridled opulence seen during much of their history, today they consider gaudiness gauche, frown upon waste, and believe that good taste means not luxury so much as the golden mean. The Marchese Emilio Pucci arrives every morning at his 16th-century Palazzo Pucci on his battered bicycle. Some of Florence's most prominent citizens get around town by bus—not always with the honor-system ticket required. Fierce individualism is a national characteristic in a country that has never quite accepted Italian unity, but the Florentines seem to have written the book.

Ever since Florence-born Dante established his local vernacular as the true spoken Italian (prior to that, bastardizations of Latin were haphazardly used everywhere), the Florentines have regarded themselves, with some justification, as the most civilized and enlightened of all Italians, and perhaps of all men. A 14th-century Pope observed that the world was made up of earth, wind, fire and the Florentines. They continue to bask in the glory of their resplendent past, when Florence was home to the Renaissance and, as D.H. Lawrence described it, "Man's perfect center of the Universe." The Medici family died out well over 200 years ago, but a little of the Medici lives on in each native-born Florentine.

The Medici, the wealthy banking dynasty that seemingly master-minded the Renaissance, were the guiding force behind much of the magnificent art and architecture you see today. The lordly, fortress-like palazzos that line the piazzas and stone-paved streets were built by merchant families that flourished under the Medicis' shrewd commercial acumen. The Florentines are sharp businessmen with an almost reverential respect for craftsmanship—qualities inherited over the centuries from Lorenzo dei Medici, called the Magnificent, quintessential patron of artists and artisans. He brought them into his sumptuous courts, financially supported them, gave them free rein, and released an avalanche of artistic and intellectual genius such as the world has never known before or since.

By the 14th-century, the eve of the Renaissance, Florence was already one of Europe's richest and most powerful free city-states. It was officially governed by its merchants' and craftsmen's guilds, progressive associations or unions that organized everyone from butchers, bakers, and silk-spinners to moneylenders (who were to become known as the first bankers of Europe, having invented the international letter of credit and established the first stable international currency, the 13th-century gold florin). Guild members' consummate craftsmanship would later be elevated to art when the Medici called upon them to embellish their princely lives. Master gold- and silversmiths appointed lavish, banquet tables, textile merchants draped the court habitués with silk brocades and hand-stitched damasks that rivaled those of the Orient, jewelers adorned crowned heads and ladies' delicate throats with precious stones, and leather artisans custom-saddled regal steeds and shod aristocratic feet.

It is extraordinary that even today, in a time that breeds volume production, Florentine artisans can maintain the same high level of originality, painstaking craftsmanship and attention to detail. Many operate third- or fourth-generation family concerns in small workshops or *botteghe* in the Oltrarno quarter across the river from the Duomo. Such enterprises, characteristic of Italy in general, form the basic economic structure in Tuscany, where few large industries exist. Each family operates as a team, with parents, children and in-laws all taking pride in the merchandise that upholds the family's name. They often integrate artisanal methods with sophisticated mechanical techniques. Shopping in these family-owned stores is a pleasant experience that offers high-quality merchandise.

Much of the city, particularly the Oltrarno neighborhood, still hums with an atmosphere of creativity, love of labor and apprenticeship. Traditional artisans believe that the splendor of Italy is in its matchless history; they use their ancestors' skills to prolong the past, reproducing antique objects and styles whose beauty, they feel, modern man could never surpass. They reproduce with such fidelity that experts and amateur shoppers alike marvel at their remarkable results. With a little patient hunting, you will be able to find them making and repairing everything from delicate lace fans to ornately carved choir stalls.

The others, the new artisans, are equally concerned with preserving their ancient skills. They, too, keep alive the spirit of five, and sometimes

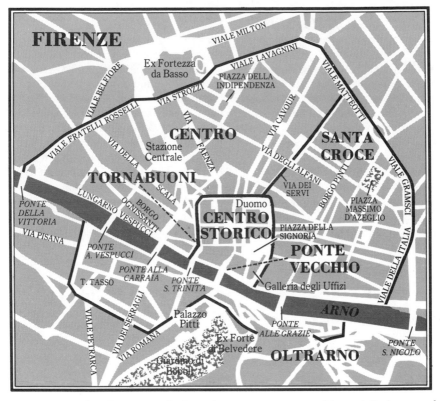

more, centuries but use their talents to express this spirit in novel contemporary ways. You will find their imaginative interpretations in *trompe l'oeil,* semiprecious stone inlay, and marbleized papergoods. They are innovators who keep Florence vibrating today. Whether your taste is traditional or modern, perhaps nowhere else in the 20th-century world can you buy, or even find, the hand labor of such superbly skilled artisans in such delightful profusion.

Florence's august palazzos and characteristic streets are the perfect showcase for its countless imaginative creations. Today's successors of the Medici are the Florentine merchant aristocracy, and you'll understand something of their ingrained self-esteem after just a few hours of wandering through the beauty of the city. As you shop the different neighborhoods, you'll sense the ongoing compulsion to beautify which is an integral part of the Florentine spirit, and which at one time made Florence not only the richest, but the most aesthetic city in the world.

Be sure to consult the Designer Boutique Directory to Florence on page 65 for a complete listing of designer boutique addresses.

Shopping in Florence

STORE HOURS. The winter schedule is generally 9:00 A.M. to 1:00 P.M. and 3:30 P.M. to 7:30 P.M., but stores are closed Sunday and on Monday mornings. In summer, shops usually keep the same morning schedule but take a longer lunch break; they reopen at 4:00 P.M. and close at 8:00 P.M. Most also close on Saturday afternoon but stay open Monday morning. However, throughout the year most jewelry shops are closed all day Monday, and food stores are closed on Wednesday afternoon.

A number of stores which cater to tourists stay open during lunch. See the list on page 137. In addition to the national holidays (see page 11), all shops in Florence are closed on June 24 in honor of the feast of San Giovanni (Saint John the Baptist), the city's patron saint.

BANK HOURS. Banks are open from Monday through Friday, 8:20 A.M. to 1:20 P.M. and 2:45 to 3:45 P.M. (2:30 to 3:30 P.M. on Friday afternoons). One exception to the rule is the Amercian Service Bank, Via della Vigna Nuova 2r at the corner of Via Tornabuoni, which is open Saturday mornings as well. You can draw cash in lire against a Visa credit card at the Banca d'America e d'Italia, Via Por Santa Maria 50r, and with an American Express card, you can cash personal checks on your U.S. bank at their office, Via Guicciardini 49r (Monday through Friday, 9:00 A.M. to 5:30 P.M., non-stop, and Saturday, 9:00 A.M. to 1:00 P.M.) Telephone 27.87.51.

An exchange office at Intertravel, Via dei Lamberti 39/41r is open through lunch, 9:00 A.M. to 6:30 P.M.; in summer, it is open on Sunday mornings as well, 9:00 A.M. to 1:00 P.M. A convenient, little-known alternative is the "Wallet Doctor" near the Uffizi at Via della Ninna 9r. Don't be misled by his miniscule quarters; Signor Carlo Alunno is an authorized agent of the Banca d'Italia and will exchange money at the official rate Monday through Saturday, 9:00 A.M. to 7:30 P.M., with no lunch break. He's also open on Sunday from 9:00 A.M. to 2:00 P.M.

SHOPPING ETIQUETTE. By centuries-old tradition, proud Florentine merchants do not encourage wild bargaining. They are used to a foreign clientele, however, and gentle coaxing and civilized banter have been known to elicit an occasional *sconto* (discount) or *gentilezza* (kindness). This is especially true if you purchase more then one article or are a long-time customer. Artisan stores and workshops may be more informal, but if you bargain, take into consideration the cost of the materials and the time and skill involved. Anyone who bothers to post a *prezzi fissi* (fixed prices) sign usually means it.

Open-air markets call for a different approach to bargaining. See page 35.

SHIPPING SERVICES. Don't risk wrapping your own packages for shipping home; chances are they won't meet Italy's complex postal requirements. Oli-Ca, at Borgo SS. Apostoli 27r (telephone 29.69.17), can supply you with a box as well as efficient wrapping for a nominal cost and is open during regular store hours.

Signor Filippo Piccone's personalized parcel-wrapping service at Vicolo dei Cavallari 6r (telephone 21.19.12) is just 20 yards from the main post office, off the small Piazza dell'Olio. He is authorized to wrap parcels for insured mailing, which requires a special seal. He will consult with you on the most economical or efficient means of shipping and works closely with a number of reputable shippers when the post office becomes too expensive for your needs. He follows the post office's schedule on weekdays (see below) and is open Saturday mornings until noon.

If you need to ship your purchases by boat or air, Fracassi is a very reliable shipping office that will also pick up and will crate or box large items, taking special care with fragile pieces, insuring them for you as well. It is located at Via Santo Spirito 11 (telephone 28.35.97). They are English-speaking and are your best bet for large or valuable shipments. Fracassi also will arrange to consolidate purchases from other cities so that everything can be shipped together. Ask for Signor Massimo Fracassi.

The Central Post Office is located at Via Pelliceria 8, near the Piazza della Repubblica (telephone 21.71.22). It accepts properly wrapped packages for overseas weighing less then one kilo, and is open Monday through Friday, 8:15 A.M. to 1:30 P.M. and 3:00 to 6:30 P.M., and Saturday morning until 1:00 P.M. For packages over one kilo, you'll have to go to the branch at Piazza Davanzati 4 (telephone 21.81.56); they follow the same schedule.

INCIDENTALS. *Taxis.* In addition to the numerous taxi stands scattered about town at most large piazzas (you cannot flag down a cruising cab), you can order a taxi from Chiamata Taxi (telephone 47.98 or 43.90). If you are encumbered with bags and boxes that won't fit in the average taxi, call Taxi Merci (telephone 29.62.30 or 21.03.21); there's room for two persons in the front and your belongings in the back.

Bicycles. If you'd like your own wheels for the day, the bicycle rentals that appear erratically in the Piazza Santa Croce could meet your need. More reliable is the Ciao & Basta bike rental company near the Ponte Vecchio at Costa dei Magnoli 24 (telephone 29.33.57). Another bike rental service, Bicicittà, on Via Alamani near the main train station, operates every day from 8:00 A.M. to 8:00 P.M., including Sundays and holidays. In summer only, you'll find other Bicicittà locations at Piazza Pitti and Fortezza di Basso.

Tourism office. The Tourism Office boasts a most prestigious address: Via Tornabuoni 15 (telephone 21.65.44 or 21.65.45). They'll supply you with maps and information on special events and exhibitions, and help you with other inquiries.

Pharmacies. Two pharmacies in Florence are open 24 hours, including Sundays. Farmacia Molteni is just a block from the Piazza Signoria at Via Calzaiuoli 7r (telephone 26.34.90). The other is located at the main train station, Comunale No. 13 (telephone 26.34.35).

English-Language Publications. Welcome to Florence, Florenscape and *Firenze City* are weekly or monthly publications printed in English and available at newsstands. *Weststuff,* a quarterly magazine of art, fashion and music for Italy and Europe, originates in Florence. *Florence Concierge* is available free at your hotel; at times you'll have to ask for it. All these periodicals include practical information about the city. *Firenze Spettacoli,* an Italian-language newspaper, lists all concerts, events, and exhibitions with useful dates, telephone numbers and addresses.

One-Hour Photo Service. The compulsive photographer who cannot wait until he gets home to see the results of his artistic endeavors, can have his color prints in just one hour. The service is on the expensive side, but both convenient locations take credit cards; they also sell film and batteries and do simple repairs. They are Foto Levi, Vicolo dell'Oro 12/14r, near Ponte Vecchio (tel. 29.40.02); and Fotoexpress, Via Lambertesca 9r (tel. 28.47.63).

THE LILY WHICH IS NOT

The lily became the prized symbol of Florence in ancient times. Although referred to as *il giglio* (the lily), it actually depicts an iris, like the pale blue irises that still grow wild in the fields and gardens of Tuscany, and perhaps explain the city's original Roman name: Florentia, the Flowering One.

The iris (or lily impersonator) was engraved on all public coats-of-arms, building facades and for centuries distinguished the gold florin coin, named after its heraldic image. As Florence became the commercial and banking capital of Renaissance Europe, so did the florin become the most prestigious and respected of currencies in circulation. The image of St. John the Baptist, patron saint of the city, graced the obverse side of the coin, a warranty of utmost purity and exact weight. The Florentine iris is often confused with the similar French fleur-de-lis symbol. The fleur-de-lis does appear on the shield of Florence's powerful Medici family, but only because the privilege of displaying the French symbol was granted to Cosimo the Elder, grandfather of Lorenzo il Magnifico, for his role in maintaining a steadfast political alliance between France and Florence.

Originally, the iris of the Florentine coat-of-arms was white on a red field. When the Guelphs (the political faction supporting the Pope) took over Florence in the 13th century, the colors were reversed, and since then the iris has always been red on a white field. Every Spring, the Florentine Iris Garden awards an international prize to the iris of the brightest red, although nothing ever comes close to the vibrancy of the city's symbol.

Florentine Specialties

FASHION

Typically Florentine in its high quality and self-assured good taste, fashion here is a compatible marriage of the aristocratic and the contemporary. For such a small city, the spectrum of fashion shopping is surprisingly extensive; the fine men's haberdashers are juxtaposed with neon-lit, avant-garde boutiques in the Centro Storico or Centro; together they accommodate every individual's style and whim. Elegant and imaginative window displays reflect Florence's strong sense of stylistic individualism. Europe has looked to Florence for direction since the continent first copied the social manners, erudite salons, and deluxe fabrics of its grand ducal courts. Today, Florence acknowledges Milan's preeminent role in Italy's fashion industry, but it remains in contention as a trend forecaster; Florence's annual Pitti fashion trade shows for men, women and children continue to draw discerning buyers from all over the world. Florence and Milan are Italy's two best fashion-shopping cities.

LEATHER

The tanning and crafting of leather is an ancient Tuscan specialty, and Florence has reigned as the world's leather capital since the early Middle Ages. Today, modern technology combines with ancient methods of curing, dyeing and coloring hides and reptile skins which are brought in from around the globe. The town of Santa Croce sull'Arno, 20 miles from Florence, is devoted almost entirely to tanning leather. Florence's supreme talent is the designing, cutting and sewing of leather articles and garments. In the city, you'll find both the deluxe flagship stores of well-known designers and myriad smaller family- or artisan-operated shops offering an unrivaled range of gloves, shoes, bags, luggage, belts, bound books and small souvenirs.

EMBROIDERED LINENS AND LINGERIE

Delicate hand-embroidered table and bed linens can still be purchased in Florence, although such painstaking diligence commands a justifiably high price. Sumptous ladies' lingerie is made in silk, linen or cotton, exquisitely embroidered and trimmed with lace. Infants' baptismal gowns, baby outfits, little girls' smocks and Lord Fauntleroy detachable collars become instant heirlooms. Far more economical are the machine-made goods that have now flooded the market, and todays's sophisticated, hand-operated machines produce such intricate results that even the knowledgeable eye is sometimes tested. Many well-to-

Hand and machine embroidery at the mercato.

do European families adhere to tradition, however, and settle for nothing less than the hand creations of the old established Florentine concerns for a daughter's trousseau.

BOOKBINDING AND ENDPAPERS

In the tradition of Florence's celebrated Renaissance printing presses, a number of professional bookbinders are still rebinding precious old tomes with gold-tooled leather covers and decorative endpapers. Appreciation for these beautiful endpapers has recently spawned a successful revival of marbleized-paper production. Believed to have been imported from Western Asia during the time of the Crusades, the marbleization process is still carried out only by hand. A gel-like vegetable substance is sprinkled on a bed of water with drops of tempera colors and then raked to create a spiral, wavy pattern; a single sheet of paper is then lightly laid upon the liquid mixture, guaranteeing the uniqueness of the design it absorbs. The resulting decorative papers are used to cover gift items large and small, as are papers with such motifs as the Florentine lily and reproductions of old calligraphy.

JEWELRY

Florence is synonomous with the finest in gold jewelry. You'll find the bold and extravagant, the refined and traditional. Gold is almost always 18 karat, and most of the simple pieces without stones are weighed upon purchase and priced to reflect the daily rates. The busy medieval Goldsmiths' Guild Hall still stands near the Ponte

Exquisite Florentine workmanship.

Vecchio, testimony to Florence's centuries of excellence in gold and jewelry design. The Ponte Vecchio itself groans under the weight of 30-some jewelry stores, selling pieces made with silver and precious and semiprecious stones as well as gold.

SEMIPRECIOUS STONE INLAY

Although called "Florentine mosaic," this meticulous technique utilizes not glass bits or tile squares but semiprecious stones inlaid into a black or neutral background. Each stone is skillfully cut to maximize its variegation and brilliance of color: jasper, lapis lazuli, malachite, agate, rock crystal, alabaster and various colored marbles. At first glance, the results appear to be paintings depicting fruits or flowers, landscapes or geometric designs. They are most commonly used for tabletops, cabinet panels or wall hangings. The technique, inspired by ancient Roman models, was first revived in the 16th century by Ferdinando dei Medici, who commissioned artists to cover entire friezes, floors and tables. The school he founded, now a museum, houses a valuable collection of mosaics using stones far more precious than those used today. Museum: Orefício delle Pietre Dure, Via degli Alfani 78 (near the Piazza Annunziata).

ANTIQUES AND REPRODUCTIONS

Florence offers a profusion of priceless antiques and the expert artisans needed to repair them in the manner they deserve. Elegant antique shops are clustered around the Via Maggio in the Oltrarno area and the Via dei Fossi and Borgognissanti section of the Centro. They specialize in authentic period furniture (mainly Italian Renaissance and Tuscan provincial), statuary and sculpture, majolica from the potteries of central and northern Italy, paintings and objets d'art. You'll also find artisans who will reproduce just about anything, with skills extinct outside Florence. Rookie collectors may not always spot the difference between their impeccable reproductions and the real thing. Many of these artisans' workshops, or *botteghe,* are still located in the back streets of the Oltrarno neighborhood where they first sprang up to be at the beck and call of the Medici Grand Dukes in the nearby Pitti Palace.

INTERNATIONAL HANDICRAFTS EXHIBITION

Although primarily designed for professional buyers from around the world, this extensive artisan fair held in Florence's Fortezza del Basso during the last two weeks of April is open to the public and draws an ever-increasing number of interested visitors. Shoppers can buy many of the beautiful handicrafts at established prices somewhere between wholesale and retail (no credit cards accepted). The merely curious will find it just as rewarding to drop by and take a look at this complete panorama of Italian artisan production under one Renaissance roof.

The Florence location of what is surely one of the largest and most impressive exhibitions of its kind in the world is no coincidence. Florentine and Tuscan crafts play a role of natural supremacy, reflective of a strong sense of individualism and a rich history of artisanship that began well before the guilds of the Renaissance. Tuscany may be the most fertile terrain for handicrafts, but a quick tour of the exhibition confirms that all of Italy remains a country of superb artisans.

You'll see the traditional and the modern in mosaics and leather, jewelry, lace, glassware, weaving, furniture, embroidery, ceramics and more from each of Italy's regions.

Florence's Street Markets

LOCAL COLOR

Florence is the place to experience Italy's colorful markets. While some of the open-air markets have come to cater almost exclusively to tourists, others retain their local clientele and authenticity and offer an invaluable glimpse of everyday life *all'italiana,* if you don't mind the jostling and hawking. Here we describe the markets frequented mostly by the local Florentines. Beginning on the next page, you will find those that thrive on tourism alone. In both types of market, due to low overhead, prices are generally lower than in an average shop.

Easy-to-shop, fun-to-browse open-air markets.

MERCATO DELLE CASCINE
Cascine Park
Tuesday only, 7:00 A.M.–1:00 P.M.

This weekly market is like a cross between a traveling circus and an open-air discount department store. Umbrellaed stands line both sides of a mile-long runway parallel to the Arno River. The stands are coordinated into sections, beginning with those selling vegetables, fruits and flowers, which are grouped alongside those selling kitchen gadgets and home utensils. One section blends into the next: children's and adults' clothing are close together; near them are secondhand clothing and linens, followed by costume jewelry, belts, bags and shoes. There are even occasional live rabbits and chicks. Bargaining for clothing is commonplace, especially if you're dressed like an Italian and can speak some of the language. The pickings are best the earlier in the season you go; true clothing bargains can be found for winter in February and March, and for summer in August and September. Don't get so involved with the show that you forget to watch your pocketbook.

MERCATO CENTRALE DI SAN LORENZO
Piazza del Mercato Centrale
Monday–Saturday, 7:00 A.M.–1:00 P.M.;
4:00 P.M.–7:30 P.M.

This landmark 19th-century cast-iron building is the largest covered food market in Florence—and in Europe. The first floor offers an eye-opening anatomy lesson, with skinned carcasses of cows, lambs, rabbits, wild boar, chickens and every edible part of them (tripe, intestines, spleen, brains, liver and tongue) proudly hung above the white marble counters. There are dozens of cheese varieties, fresh pastas, and bottles of extra-virgin olive oil.

The second floor has over 100 stalls selling nothing but fresh vegetables, fruits and flowers: salad greens in dozens of crisp variations, red Sicilian oranges, white aubergines, and black grapes the size of plums.

Local color at daily food markets.

MERCATO SANT'AMBROGIO
Piazza Ghiberti
Monday–Saturday 7:00 A.M. to 1:00 P.M.

A miniature version of the Mercato Centrale food *emporio,* this is a lively neighborhood market that makes up in character what it lacks in size. Vendors sing, chat, shout, joke, flirt and tout their tomatoes to be the most beautiful in the world. The flavor is that of a simple, middle-class *quartiere,* but many of Florence's best chefs do their daily marketing here. It's only a five-minute walk from Piazza Santa Croce.

TOURIST MARKETS

These are the tourist markets that have been inundated by visitors for decades. The vendors now know that their customers would be paying twice the price for the same wares back home, so your carefully rehearsed bargaining often falls on deaf ears. You'll be more successful if you're buying more than one item, preferably many; if you're paying with cash or traveler's checks (keep abreast of current exchange rates); or if it's near the end of the day and business has been slow. Don't bargain too aggressively; if you're tempted to walk away when the sweater man won't come down any further, consider how insignificant the savings may be when compared to prices at home. Credit cards are frequently accepted, mostly Visa and American Express, although they eliminate any bargaining possibilities; in fact, vendors often charge an additional five to seven percent to cover what they would otherwise lose in the transaction.

MERCATO DELLE PULCI
Piazza dei Ciompi
Tuesday–Saturday, 8:00 A.M.–1:00 P.M.; 3:30–7:00 P.M. and last Sunday of every month

There's not much of interest to a serious collector in this small flea market, but browsing is free and enjoyable. You'll see sepia photos, postcards of Florence in bygone days and amusing bric-a-brac.

MERCATO NUOVO (STRAW MARKET)
Logge del Mercato Nuovo
Daily, 9:00 A.M.–5:00 P.M.

This was officially named the New Market (Mercato Nuovo) to distinguish it from the Old Market in the nearby Piazza della Repubblica that was cleared away in 1890. Built in 1547, the Mercato Nuovo was the center of business for wool and silk manufacturers and bankers; a marble marker still indicates the spot where shamed, bankrupt merchants were publicly spanked before being sent off to jail.

Today it is more commonly known as the Straw Market, from the days when fine straw items were locally produced. Centrally located, it is great for Sunday shopping when the rest of the city sleeps. Although some straw products (now machine-made) can still be found, such as pocketbooks, hats, dolls and place mats, most stands sell leather bags, wallets, umbrellas, jewelry, table linens and tourist paraphernalia. Some vendors try to pass off ersatz Louis Vuitton, Fendi and Gucci bags as the real thing, but poor quality and subtle variations in the signature motifs give them away. The big bronze wild boar that stands guard at the market has conferred upon it the unoffical name of "Mercato del Porcellino." All merchants here speak English. They are not all amenable to bargaining, but try it.

MERCATO SAN LORENZO
Piazza San Lorenzo
Daily, 8:00 A.M–8:00 P.M.

The narrow, pedestrian-only Borgo San Lorenzo (lined with a number of inexpensive shoe stores) leads you from the Piazza del Duomo to the biggest of Florence's markets, the Mercato San Lorenzo. The only Italians in this outdoor bustle are the ones scurrying through on their way to the covered Mercato Centrale. The multilingual vendors are mostly Persian, but the goods are mostly Italian. If you're in the mood, insist on bargaining, as prices are sometimes not much lower than what you'd pay in a store. Many articles, however, such as

The straw market's Porcellino *stands guard.*

soft woolen mufflers in dozens of shades, colorful shawls, cashmere-lined gloves, trendy sunglasses, silk ties and bijoux jewelry, make great souvenirs at reasonable rates, even when posted as *prezzo fisso* (fixed price).

You'll find sweaters in big, fashionable shapes and in angora (check the percentage blend), argyle and mohair. Leather jackets and skirts can be mediocre in quality, but may be worth buying for a season. There are pocketbook stands by the legion, but check carefully on seams, reinforcements, linings and leather quality. Louis Vuitton and Gucci imitations will most often be poorly made, although with patience you can sometimes find high-quality reproductions. The market pours onto adjacent side streets, where lots of fun, secondhand and re-dyed men's shirts and denim clothing can be found.

FACTORY OUTLETS

The Tuscan-based factory for I.V.V. (Industria Vetraria Valdarnese) is located 45 minutes outside Florence. This glassware company is known for its contemporary, lightweight items, all mouth-blown and of a sleek design. The vases, plates and glasses here are either closeouts or over-production.

I.V.V.
Lungarno Guido Reni 60.
P.O. Box 60
52027 San Giovanni Valdarno (AR)
Tel. (055) 94.44.44
(Directions: Take the autostrada toward Arezzo, getting off at the exit for San Giovanni Valdarno.)

I Pellettieri d'Italia are manufacturers for such high-quality accessories labels as Granello, Pitti, Prada and Basile. Pickings here are erratic and unpredictable, but you'll find everything from bags, shoes and umbrellas to a tray of small articles such as wallets and keycases, usually kept hidden under the cash register.

I Pellettieri d'Italia
Località Levanella
52025 Montevarchi (AR)
Tel. (055) 97.89.188
(Directions: Same as for the I.V.V. factory, which is not far away.)

Eagle-eye quality control lets seemingly perfect linens wind up in Pratesi's factory outlet at substantial reductions. See Pratesi listing in Florence Centro (page 87).

Pratesi
Via Montalbano-Casalguidi
Località Ponte Stella
Tel. (0573) 72.72.33
(Directions: Take the autostrada Firenze-Mare toward the coast, getting off at the exit for Pistoia. Follow the signs for the locality of Ponte Stella, about 30 minutes from Florence.)

Florence has grown to incorporate Sesto Fiorentino into its city limits. It's a nice outing here to the Richard-Ginori porcelain factory and museum, both of which follow regular store hours. The factory outlet sells both seconds and regular-merchandise closeouts at a big discount, and will pack and ship your fragile purchases. See Richard-Ginori listing in Florence Centro Storico (page 71).

Richard-Ginori
Viale Giulio Cesare 19
Sesto Fiorentino
Tel. (055) 42.10.472
(Directions: If you're intent upon buying, the 15-minute cab ride is well worth the investment. If you have your own car, follow the signs to this northwest suburb of Florence. You can also take bus No. 28, which leaves from the train station; ask the driver to make sure you get off at the right stop.)

Florentine Cuisine

Elegant and refined as the shopping may be in Florence, dining tends to be rustic and simple. That is not to say it will not be delicious or a gastronomic delight, however; Florentines assert their cuisine to be the finest and most genuine in all of Italy, the way they regard all things Florentine.

For much of its history, Tuscany was agriculturally poor, and from its frugal peasant hearth came the *cucina povera* ("poor man's cooking") that is found in Florence today. It is a healthy and resourceful cuisine, where everything is fresh and nothing is wasted. Only during the Renaissance was Florence noted for elaborate cuisine; the French authority Escoffier admitted that French cuisine was but a refined variation of the Tuscan feasts introduced by Catherine dei Medici when she married the future Henry II of France.

Florence's cuisine heavily emphasizes grilled meats (fish is a rarity); its culinary glory is *bistecca alla fiorentina*. Crusty bread is generally made without salt and is used to thicken soups. Vegetables and meats, however, can be a bit too salted (ask for *senza sale,* or without salt, if you'd rather salt them yourself). Leafy salads and humble haricot beans are dressed with extra-virgin olive oil from the surrounding hills, said to be the best in the world. From the same hills comes the game (*caccia*) loved by the Florentines: wild boar (*cinghiale*), hare (*lepre*), rabbit (*coniglio*) and pheasant (*fagiano*). Tuscany also excels in the processing of the full-flavored *pecorino* cheese made from sheep's milk; the most famous is produced in and around Siena.

Wine has been important in Tuscan cuisine since the Etruscans first started making it 3000 years ago. Everyone knows Chianti, Tuscany's most famous red wine. Rating a DOCG (*denominazione di origine controllata e garantita*), it is made of specific grape varieties from a limited geographical area. Top producers are Castello di Ama, Castello di Volpaia, Badia a Coltibuono, and Vecchie Terre di Montefili. From outside the Chianti region and south of Siena comes the exquisite Brunello di Montalcino, a rich world-class red wine, also a DOCG. Look for Altesino, Tenuta Caparzo, and Villa Banfi. The reds Vino Nobile di Montepulciano (Avignonesi) and Carmignano (Villa di Capezzana) are also fine. Tuscan white wines have gained stature, especially Vernaccia di San Gimignano (Ponte a Rondolino, Guicciardini-Strozzi) and Montecarlo (Fattoria di Buonamico), both smooth and dry. The sometimes hard-to-find dessert wine Vin Santo (Avignonesi, Castellare, and Capezzana) is made from semi-dried grapes and is loft-aged in small wooden barrels for at least three years. It is Tuscany's dessert wine, served with *cantucci* or *biscotti di Prato,* hard almond-studded cookies.

FLORENTINE CUISINE GLOSSARY

Antipasto (Appetizer)
Crostini–Chicken-liver pâté spread on crusty bread.
Pinzimonio–Raw vegetables, traditionally fennel, celery and artichokes, with a rich olive oil for dipping.

Primo Piatto (First Course)
Ribollita–Hearty winter vegetable soup thickened with bread.
Panzanella–Summer salad of tomatoes, basil, cucumber, onion and bread dressed with oil and vinegar.
Pappa al pomodoro–Tomato soup thickened with bread.
Pappardelle sulla lepre–Homemade pasta with wild rabbit sauce.
Penne strascicate–Quill-shaped pasta with a meat sauce.
Pasta alla carrettiera–Pasta with a sauce of tomato, garlic, chili, pepper and parsley.
Tortelli–Spinach and ricotta ravioli.

Secondo Piatto (Entrée)
Carne (Meat):
Bistecca alla fiorentina–T-bone steak at least 2 inches thick, charcoal grilled.
Arista–Roast pork loin with garlic and rosemary.
Spiedini di maiale–Pork-loin cubes and pork liver spiced with fennel and grilled on a skewer with bread and bay leaves.
Fritto misto–Mixed fried foods,

usually chicken, rabbit or lamb chops with vegetables such as peppers, zucchini and potatoes.
Pollo al mattone–Chicken flattened with a brick, then grilled with herbs.
Trippa alla fiorentina–Tripe with tomato sauce served with cheese.

Pesce (Fish):
Baccalà alla fiorentina–Salted cod cooked with tomatoes and herbs.
Fagioli con tonno–White beans, tuna and red onion.

Contorno (Vegetable)
Fagioli all'uccelletto–White beans cooked with tomatoes, garlic and sage.

Formaggio (Cheese)
Pecorino–Sheep's milk cheese, aged or eaten fresh in the spring.

Dolce (Dessert)
Castagnaccio–A baked, unleavened cake made of chestnut flour with raisins, walnuts and rosemary; an acquired taste.
Bongo–Filled cream puffs with chocolate sauce.
Schiacciata alla fiorentina–A simple cake covered with powdered sugar made during Carnival time.
Tiramisu–Literally, "Pick-Me-Up." A creamy, light pudding made with espresso-soaked cake in a whipped *mascarpone* cheese, dusted with chocolate.

Since the Renaissance, Florence's shopping and cultural possibilities have been unmatched.

GASTRONOMIC OUTINGS

A pleasant respite from museum-going or "shoppingitis" is a jaunt into hidden places in Tuscany to discover the true pleasures of the Italian table. Organized by Faith Heller Willinger and her small and efficient operation Cucina Toscana, these day-trips (or longer) can be custom-tailored to indulge your every culinary or oenophile whim.

Or you can join one of her already scheduled food and wine tours that feature memorable eight-course and four-wine lunches in idyllic settings and in fine company.

For more information contact:
Cucina Toscana,
Via della Chiesa 7,
50125 Florence
Tel. (055) 22.70.14.

Centro Storico

*T*he Centro Storico is the very heart of Florentine shopping. Shops here are not about to cower in the shadow of the Duomo; Florence's most impressive palazzos, once private bastions of merchant bigwigs, are now elegant boutiques and flagship stores, which open their massive portals and vaulted chambers to incredulous shoppers who never dreamed of such splendid settings nor such fine merchandise.

The Centro Storico is easy to negotiate, and if you have only one day to shop in Florence, you can spend it here pleasantly and productively. Prices are generally high, since the district's main customers are tourists (i.e., any non-Florentine) who are as curious to shop its renowned stores as to see the Uffizi Galleries.

This historic neighborhood consists of three major piazzas. The Piazza del Duomo is the oldest; the religious center of the city, it is dominated by Brunelleschi's magnificent dome, commissioned to be made *il più bello che si può* ("as beautiful as possible"). The Piazza della Signoria was the center of the political and social life of the Florentine Republic, where major events have always taken place; today, it is the scene of outdoor concerts and of the annual *Calcio in Costume* (the re-creation of a historic soccer game in Renaissance livery). This piazza is one of the most noble squares in Italy, and there is no more perfect spot for a relaxing Campari than in the shadow of the copy of Michelangelo's David. The Piazza della Repubblica offers a wider choice of old-world bar-cafès and a summertime orchestra that plays old tunes. It's hard to believe that this was once the site of the Roman Forum, later of the Jewish ghetto, and then, until the end of the 19th century, of the open-air market. In order to reach the Palazzo Vecchio from their Pitti Palace residence on the south bank of the Arno River, the Grand Dukes' carriages circumvented this entire eyesore, following the then-new and elegant streets we've used as the perimeters of the Centro Storico neighborhood (Via dei Cerretani, Via Proconsolo and Via Tornabuoni). Every city has its elegant Fifth Avenue, and Florence boasts its Via Tornabuoni; we treat this artery, with its lavish concentration of designer boutiques, as an independent neighborhood.

Centro Storico is a microcosm of virtually everything Florence has to

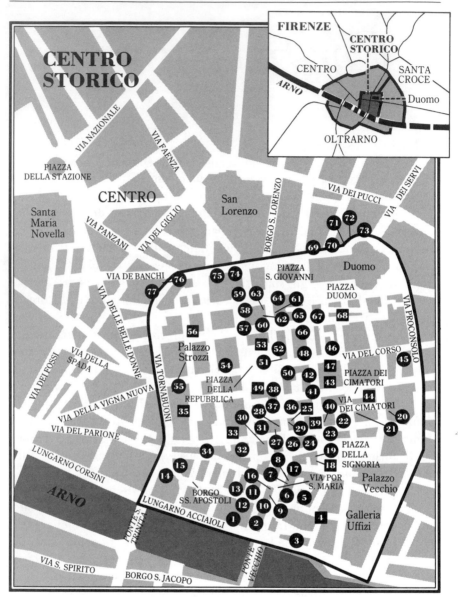

flagship stores and open-air markets. There are even surprising little contemporary shops tucked away in such cobblestoned back streets as Borgo SS. Apostoli, Via Porta Rossa and Via del Corso. The only missing ingredient is the artisan; high rents have traditionally kept all but a few Florentine craftsmen out of this area and located in the nearby, less expensive Oltrarno neighborhood.

GIFTS

HOME ACCESSORIES & JEWELRY

Semiprecious-Stone Inlay

1 G. UGOLINI
Lungarno Acciaioli 66–70r
Tel. 28.49.69
Expensive; credit cards accepted

The overwhelming quantity of fine mosaic workmanship on display makes Ugolini's appear more like a museum than a store. But the hand-laid stone mosaic dining- and coffee-table tops, the framed wall pieces from postcard to mural size, and the small but equally detailed brooches, rings and pendants are all for sale.

The oldest workshop of its kind in Florence, Ugolini's has the most extensive selection of this *pietra dura* art anywhere. It includes traditional still-life compositions and Tuscan landscapes as well as portraits and scenes depicted in a more contemporary style. You'll understand the painstaking precision of detail and the time involved in producing each piece if you peer into the back workshop, where everything on the premises is created.

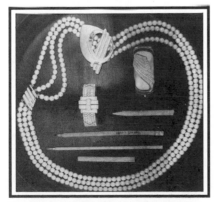

Fine jewelry workmanship at Bijoux Cascio.

COSTUME JEWELRY

TOP-QUALITY IMITATIONS

2 BIJOUX CASCIO 🔔🔔🔔🔔
Via Por Santa Maria 1r
Tel. 29.43.78
Moderate; credit cards accepted
Open during lunch

Bijoux Cascio takes the tradition of Florentine gold-working a step further: its artisans create some of the most convincing imitation jewelry in the world. They cast each costume piece with the same precision and care usually devoted to the real thing. The results are excellent alternatives to precious gems and solid gold, with far lower price tags. After a bedazzling stroll across the Ponte Vecchio, it is ironic to find this boutique, the first on the Via Por Santa Maria, since its windows look like a continuation of what you've just left behind.

The style is generally clean and bold: gold-plated chokers with ersatz pavé diamonds, chains plain or with "jewel" inlays, and pendant earrings with colored stones and pearls. Even cognoscenti of established jewelry names like Bulgari and Van Cleef will have to stare long and hard before detecting an impostor. A second location is at Via Tornabuoni 32r.

LINENS & LINGERIE

TRADITIONAL FLORENTINE HAND EMBROIDERY

3 BRUNA SPADINI
Lungarno Archibusieri 4–6r
Tel. 28.77.32
Expensive; credit cards accepted
Open during lunch

The legendary Bruna Spadini's daughter and son-in-law, an amiable elderly couple, now run this store and are as in love with their exquisite embroidered goods as are their faithful customers. A Rita Hayworth-type nightgown always displayed in the window is the only touch of pizazz; tradition otherwise sets the tone. Elaborately hand-worked table linens and special-occasion double-sheet sets whose prices border on folly are the stuff of which heirlooms are made. Diligent women spend years creating these articles for a small, discerning market. If you're interested in investment linen but have limited funds, various bed and table linens that have required fewer hours of labor are far more affordable. Lovely hand-embroidered handkerchiefs are perfect gifts.

SUSTENANCE

RISTORANTE/TRATTORIA

4 ANTICO FATTORE
Via Lambertesca 1–3
Tel. 26.12.25
Inexpensive to moderate; no credit cards
    accepted
Closed Saturday, Sunday, Monday

Antico Fattore translates as "The Old Farmer," and the restaurant's bohemian, informal though charming setting, with communal tables, suggests its rustic history. Provincial Tuscan food is the order of the day. The pastas are not always as good as the other menu choices, so opt for the hearty homemade soups *(zuppe)* or the raw *pinzimonio* for your first course. Fare is generally on the simple side, fresh and delicious. The atmosphere is convivial.

JEWELRY

5 MATASSINI
Via Lambertesca 20r
Tel. 21.28.97
Expensive; credit cards accepted

The significance of Matassini's move to a new location next door to its old address (18r) is that it's finally gone retail after 60 years of wholesaling to Italy's leading jewelry stores. Now, with no middleman, substantial savings are evident in astounding Bulgari, Marina B. and Cartier look-alikes that emulate general styles rather than copying certain pieces. Other items range from classic tiny gold earrings for little girls to large, bold diamond-encrusted bracelets. The two Matassini sisters are a jovial and enthusiastic pair who clearly love being able to provide fine jewelry to their customers at a savings.

LINENS, LINGERIE & CHILDREN'S WEAR

TRADITIONAL FLORENTINE HAND EMBROIDERY

6 CIRRI
Via Por Santa Maria 38–40r
Tel. 29.65.93
Moderate; credit cards accepted

Cirri's is an outstanding practitioner of the traditional Florentine art of hand embroidery. The dainty white embroidered collars and linen handkerchiefs trimmed with lace displayed in the windows are just a preview—there are said to be more than 10,000 collars and handkerchiefs inside. Baptismal gowns that take a month to be individually embroidered, elegant table and bed linens, delicate infants' sheets and pillowcases, and lace-

A best-selling sailor dress from Cirri.

trimmed ladies' lingerie all come in fine cottons, silks and linens. There are also unique creations for girls from infancy to age 14: cotton batiste blouses and party dresses with scallop embroidery, skirts of hand-folded pleats, and the best-sellers—sailor dresses in white or navy gabardine. The roster of titled customers is as impressive as the handwork.

JEWELRY

Huge Selection

7 C.O.I.
Via Por Santa Maria 8
Tel. 28.39.70
Moderate; credit cards accepted
Open during lunch

The Commercio Oreficeria Italiana (C.O.I.) has no display window because it occupies the second floor (first floor by Italian standards). It's specialty is gold, enormous quantities of it, shaped into bangles and baubles of every variety. The atmosphere is that of a busy gold market, with mul-

tilingual sales assistants tirelessly weighing and calculating each customer's demands. If you have only a general idea of what you'd like, they'll gladly show you their entire collection, usually making your choice twice as difficult. Besides bracelets in every link, chains in every length, trays and trays of loop earrings, rings, and charms, there's an array of precious and semiprecious-stone rings and necklaces. The impression may be of high-volume business, but C.O.I. (pronounced "coy") offers an attractive selection at prices said to be under the daily gold rate. A slight discount is automatic if you pay with cash or traveler's check.

JEWELRY

8 FRATELLI COPPINI
Via Por Santa Maria 78r
Tel. 21.60.55
Expensive; credit cards accepted

Neither the Coppini brothers nor their descendants are with us these days, but their name and tradition have been carried on in their atelier for over 200 years. The small retail shop offers a wide range of fine gold jewelry in an elegant and classic style. Pieces tend to be small and discreet, underlining the Florentine dislike for showiness. The Coppini establishment has always been known for good workmanship and reliable quality.

LINENS, LINGERIE & CHILDREN'S WEAR

EMBROIDERY

9 TAF
Via Por Santa Maria 22r
Tel. 21.31.90
Moderate; credit cards accepted

This is a prime competitor of Cirri's across the street, but the embroidery here is generally somewhat less elaborate, so the prices are lower. Taf's colors depart from traditional pastels and pure whites; embroidered bath sets and tablecloths with matching place mats usually strike a brighter, more contemporary note. Most of the embroidery is done by hand-operated machines—a skill whose end product is not to be scoffed at. If you have any doubts regarding what has been done by hand, the price is usually a giveaway, but don't be shy about asking the salespeople. Another Taf store directly across the street at No. 17r features infants' and children's clothing in linens and cottons. Appliqués, hand-stitching and embroidery brighten up playsuits, dresses and coordinates for the special children in your life.

LEATHERGOODS

BAGS & ACCESSORIES

Classic & Elegant

10 ATHOS
Borgo SS. Apostoli 6r
Tel. 26.28.96
Expensive; credit cards accepted

Anna Maria Baldini has been keeping an illustrious and titled clientele happy for over 25 years, first as a saleswoman and now as the proud owner of Athos. Her selection of leathergoods is classic and elegant, with many Chanel-, Hermès- and Céline-style handbags and wallets at much less than the price of the real thing, but with no compromise in quality. Fancy crocodile and reptile evening bags come with gold chains and exquisite clasps. Athos also ac-

commodates requests for custom-made attaché cases, should their handsome stock not meet your precise needs. They'll happily show you the sketch Larry Hagman drew for his customized version—carefully glued in their guest book along with enthusiastic comments from other notable clients. Anna and her son Enrico are committed to the customer's satisfaction. They will stamp your initials in gold on any leather article if desired and deliver it to your hotel.

JEWELRY

WORKSHOP/STUDIO

Unusual Contemporary Designs

11 GATTO BIANCO
Borgo SS. Apostoli 12r
Tel. 24.03.56
Moderate; credit cards accepted

This postmodern gallery/workshop is the perfect showcase for the bold, contemporary jewelry handmade by Carla and Walter Romani. Most striking are their unusual combinations of precious and common materials: gold, silver, copper, brass, leather, plexiglass and stainless steel, together with such gems as jade, coral

Precious and common materials at Gatto Bianco.

and pearl. Carla and Walter create their pieces like collages in modern forms with primitive overtones. The mountings themselves are often ingenious; many pieces come apart like children's puzzles, offering the owner a chance to wear a single piece in different ways. Each piece is an exclusive design by these two inventive artists, offering the individualist a very distinctive look.

GIFTS

CUSTOM-MADE BOXES

Gift Wrapping & Packing

12 OLI-CA
Borgo SS. Apostoli 27r
Tel. 29.69.17
Inexpensive; no credit cards accepted

Although Oli-Ca specializes in cardboard boxes, as a traveling shopper you'll be more appreciative of its professional boxing and wrapping service for mailing your packages overseas. Signor Caramelli cannot insure, but, for a nominal fee, he will save you a lot of unnecessary frustration if you're not familiar with the various postal regulations. While he's busy wrapping away, browse about the shelves full of pretty paper-covered boxes, which range from the small and dainty to the large storage size. Big round hatboxes are made with an antique machine in the back. Oli-Ca will also wrap presents with your choice of colorful ribbons and beautiful papers, but be forewarned if you expect to bring these through customs: agents may request that you open them to examine the contents. With your parcel wrapped and ready to go, you have a mere two blocks' walk to the main post office.

One of Dodo's whimsical air-brushed motifs.

GIFTS

HAND-PAINTED ACCESSORIES

Fun & Whimsy

13 DODO
Borgo SS. Apostoli 32r
Tel. 28.20.22
Moderate; credit cards accepted

Dodo is a world of childlike fantasy. The spacious, postmodern store is a "must-see" for its displays and ambiance alone. Featured throughout is the Dodo signature—an array of cats with big, amusing grins, fancifully outfitted in lace pinafores and big bow ties. The designs are airbrushed on wooden chairs and tables, cut-out hangers and mirror frames. There is even a four-foot "cocktail cat" holding a serving tray. All of these items are for sale. More diminutive collectibles include wooden pins, earrings, necklaces and hair accessories featuring the same whimsical cats along with butterflies, rabbits and pigs.

The novelty and refinement of Dodo's feline motif immediately made it a hallmark, an easily identifiable designer accessory for young Florentines. Today's teenage following is as devoted as ever, although the Dodo creations know no age limit. Beguiling greeting cards and stationery are new additions, as is a small collection of fun clothes whose Dodo images are reproduced by handpainting or silkscreen printing. The cotton knitwear, including T-shirts, sweatshirts, pajamas and boxer shorts, is the latest innovation. Everything is produced and displayed with artistry, imagination and attention to detail.

HOME

ACCESSORIES & HOUSEWARES

Focus on Design

14 PROFORMA 🍶🍶🍶🍶

Borgo SS. Apostoli 47r
Tel. 26.30.94
Moderate; credit cards accepted

Proforma offers a stunningly beautiful collection of the latest in both modern and classic household furnishings, housewares, kitchen and table accessories, and lamps. The shop's two young, gracious owners, Bona Tondinella and Flavia Gilberti, travel continuously throughout Europe to acquire eclectic goods, choosing judiciously according to their own impeccable tastes rather than succumbing to industry trends.

In addition to the big names of Italian houseware design (Alessi stainless, Guzzini plastics, IVV glassware), Bona and Flavia introduce new and original lines, such as unusual-shaped

Eclectic home design at Proforma.

gray- and pink-flecked ceramicware that resembles granite, from Baldelli of Umbria; slate and marble table tops and decorative objects by a Tuscan firm; and the latest in Italy's witty, hi-tech table lamps. They also feature the work of Bona's husband, Gianfranco, who designs the famous Panpaloni line of silver: postmodern tabletop accessories such as Romancolumn candlesticks. Many of Gianfranco's designs have been featured in Tiffany's of New York but can be bought here for substantially less. Proforma is a personable store where you'll feel welcome to browse and admire its merchandise at leisure.

FABRICS

FURNISHING

Contemporary

15 DEANGELIS

Piazza Santa Trinità 3r
Tel. 28.46.77
Moderate to expensive; credit cards
   accepted

What holds the beautiful DeAngelis fabrics well apart from the rest is that artists, not textile designers, create their patterns. This recognized Milan-based firm reinterprets classic styles for the contemporary home. Marbleized designs, patterns of Roman columns, and sophisticated Italian provincial themes are all printed or woven in 100-percent cotton. There are coordinated wallpapers, hand-loomed wool area rugs in pastel-colored geometric designs and goose-down quilts that can be made to order from your favorite fabrics.

Ask to see the portfolio of DeAngelis' newest venture, an unusual collection appropriately called *cose mobili* (furniture things). It's witty, modern wood furniture that began as an experimental collaboration of five young Italian sculptors and painters.

FASHION

MEN'S

Intimatewear

16 SOTTO SOTTO

Via delle Terme 7r
Tel. 29.60.26
Moderate; credit cards accepted

One of the few shops of its kind, Sotto Sotto specializes exclusively in men's underwear and intimatewear. Owned by a young woman, this small store offers men—and the women who shop for them—a surprisingly extensive variety of boxer shorts, briefs, bikinis, undershirts and sleepwear.

If it's basics you want, T-shirts and briefs of fine-combed cottons are offered in a number of styles and colors that change with the season. Undergarments of pure silk are more novel, though limited, and the ubiquitous licensed labels of Valentino, Ar-

mani and Coveri can be found here as well.

Prices are reasonable for the assortment of fine pajamas and night-shirts in solid and print cottons. You'll also find coordinating light-weight terry-cloth robes that are particularly practical for traveling.

FASHION

MEN'S

Contemporary/Trendy

17 OLIVER ⌂⌂⌂⌂

Via Vaccherecccia 15r
Tel. 29.63.27
Moderate to expensive; credit cards accepted

Oliver's attractive décor is all glass and polished wood. The casually displayed Italian clothing can dress a fashion-conscious man from hat to shoes in just one visit. Relaxed sportswear is the store's trademark, and the wide, carefully marketed selection can accommodate any individual's style. Owner Roberto Ottanelli knows his customer—a savvy and easygoing individual, be he the young Florentine or the American businessman in town for the prestigious Pitti fashion trade shows.

Italian knitwear and outerwear from Iceberg and Byblos, the fun, quality shirts by Henry Cottons and a great collection of wool or cotton trousers of Oliver's own production are the mainstay. Also available are coordinated socks, ties and woolen scarves to finish each season's look. Unlike the majority of Italian clothing stores, Oliver's makes a point of getting winter merchandise into the store by late summer, and summer stock by March or April.

SUSTENANCE
BAR-CAFFÈ

18 RIVOIRE
Piazza della Signoria 5
Tel. 21.44.12
Expensive; no credit cards accepted
Closed Monday

If there's the slightest hint of chill in the air, you must rush to sample the sublime, pudding-rich hot chocolate with fresh whipped cream for which this recently proclaimed historical landmark is renowned. From its small outdoor tables you can absorb the best view in town—the stately beauty of the Palazzo Vecchio and the entire Piazza della Signoria with its statue inhabitants. The Piemontese owner (hence the French-sounding name) originally operated a sweet shop here. He was the first in town to concoct rich chocolate products and confectioner's delicacies. His recipes have not changed over time. A fresh selection of small sandwiches and light salads is also available, and the ambiance is as Old World inside as out.

GIFTS
STATIONERY
Fine Papers & Engraving

19 PINEIDER
Piazza della Signoria 13
Tel. 28.46.55
Expensive; credit cards accepted

No self-respecting upper-class Florentine would consider corresponding on any stationery other then Pineider's elegant notes and traditional papers. They are produced in a range of weights and finishes: *Satinata* (smooth); *Telata* (woven finish); and *Vergata* (laid). Paper is either straight-edged or deckle-edged—in an imitation of the old-fashioned manner of cutting by hand. Heavyweight writing cards come with coordinated lined envelopes in over a dozen colors, from bold primaries to subdued pastels. Business and visiting cards that offer the same aura of prestige and refinement can be made up and, if necessary, shipped in three weeks.

Pineider also makes exquisite leather items such as portfolios, desktop accessories, photo albums and agendas in a variety of different skins, including pigskin and embossed suedes.

BOOKS
GRAPHIC ARTS

20 LIBRERIA DELLA SIGNORIA
Via dei Magazzini 3r
Tel. 21.92.77
Moderate; credit cards accepted

Everyone is welcome to come in and browse through this graphic-arts bookstore located on a side street near Palazzo Vecchio. Due to the enthusiasm and knowledgeability of its owner, Vicenzo Iacono, it has become an established reference point for those seeking particular art posters and books.

There are always newly arrived exhibition posters from all over the world and a wide range of beautiful, color-plated books on art history, antiques, the arts and photography. Much of the stock is in English, and anything you may be searching for and can't find, Signor Iacono will order for you. If a certain art subject interests you, he'll make suggestions and research your needs.

COSTUME JEWELRY
DESIGNER COLLECTION

21 L'OCA BIANCA
Via dei Cerchi 12r
Tel. 21.91.97
Moderate; credit cards accepted

All that glitters is costume jewelry at the Oca Bianca (White Goose). Just two blocks from the Piazza della Signoria along a charming and narrow medieval side street, this small but modern boutique is a storehouse for the best faux jewelry Italy has to offer: Angela Caputi, Carlo Zini, Valentino and Ugo Correani, among others. Most is high-styled and bold, some more discreet and classic. The Oca Bianca produces a line of its own bijoux, as well as small evening bags and belts with unusual buckles.

JEWELRY
CONTEMPORARY SILVER

22 VANZI
Via della Condotta 22r
Tel. 28.70.29
Moderate to expensive; credit cards
   accepted

Vanzi is famous for its contemporary sterling silver and silver-plate jewelry. The clean, open-spaced gallery itself is an architectural showcase, but the bold, striking jewelry steals the show. A young brother-and-sister team design and produce the glitzy silver necklaces and bracelets with matching earrings and rings, as well as a winning collection of sleek silver watches with faces made of shiny onyx, rich lapis lazuli and other semiprecious stones.

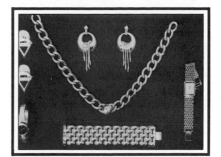

Bold silver jewelry, a Vanzi specialty.

FASHION
MEN'S

Avant-Garde

23 HOMBRE
Via Calzaiuoli 6r
Tel. 21.00.00
Moderate; credit cards accepted

The latest music pouring out of this small shop will draw you inside. The simple décor is a foil to the interesting colors and fabrics of the men's clothing on display. Pants, sports jackets and shirts that can be mixed and matched will please you if you have a strong sense of self and design. As an alternative, pick out a single item or two that will blend with your more conservative wardrobe while adding a little pizzaz. The fashion here is striking and fun, handpicked from a number of small Italian firms.

SHOES
WOMEN'S

Young & Trendy

24 FRANCO RIZZO
Via Calzaiuoli 3r
Tel. 28.48.81
Moderate; credit cards accepted

Originality is the driving inspiration behind Franco Rizzo's fashionable shoe collection. It attracts a young-minded, comfort-conscious wearer who appreciates a well-made shoe and has a contemporary sense of fun. Rizzo keeps up to the minute with original themes and the season's newest colors in his wearable flats and low-heeled creations. No high-heeled elegance here.

SUSTENANCE

BAR-CAFFÈ

25 CAFFÈ MANARESE
Via Arte della Lana 12r
Tel. 21.89.34
Moderate; no credit cards accepted
Closed Sunday

Locals swear that the coffee here is the best in town and don't mind the rather plain setting. For those so inclined, there is also a rich decaffeinated mix that won't let you taste the difference. Both are ground and, more importantly, roasted on the premises upstairs. There's a simple indoor tearoom, and the handful of outdoor tables is just yards from the delicate Gothic 14th-century Orsanmichele church, which was originally built as a granary. Pizzas, grilled sandwiches and other snacks are also available.

COSTUME JEWELRY

DISCREET QUALITY IMITATIONS

26 MARIELLA INNOCENTI
Logge del Mercato Nuovo 3r
Tel. 29.85.31
Moderate; credit cards accepted

Directly across the street from the covered straw market, Mariella Inno-

The Centro Storico, an open-air museum.

centi's windows sparkle with rubies, diamonds, emeralds and sapphires, of which some are real but most are not—and only the price tags tell the difference. These are not the fun and chunky bijoux that are so lavish they could be nothing but costume pieces. Mariella Innocenti's collection imitates the classic and refined precious jewelry whose styles vary with the season. Most pieces are small and dainty, and good, colorful imitation "stones" are liberally used to accentuate cocktail rings, earrings, necklaces and bracelets. The workmanship is admirable, as is the imagination.

FASHION

JUNIORS

Sportswear

27 BENETTON
Via Calimala 68r
Tel. 21.48.78
Moderate; credit cards accepted

Following company policy, this is one of many Benetton boutiques in town, with another just a block away at Via Por Santa Maria 68r (telephone 28.71.11). See Benetton (page 181) for further information.

SHOES, MEN'S & WOMEN'S FASHION

Elaborately Worked Styles

28 BELTRAMI, JUNIOR

Via Calimala 9r
Tel. 21.22.88
Expensive; credit cards accepted

The wares of this Florence-based chain of high-fashion shoe boutiques are best seen here at their "Junior" location. The Beltrami look in both footwear and leather clothing features elaborate styles, combinations of skins, decorative appliqués, innovative trimmings and borders of exotic skins or fur. It seems a bit too showy to be Florentine, but the quality of workmanship and leather is insurpassable and the design imaginative. The boots are the real highlight, extraordinary accessories that will draw compliments for years. Consider the splurge.

The two beautifully appointed Beltrami stores at Via Calzaiuoli 31 and 44r are the original locations. Another large Beltrami is in Piazza dell'Olio just near the Duomo. Prices at Beltrami Junior are no lower than at these other locations, but the fashion seems more interesting and wearable.

Footwear becomes art at Pollini.

SHOES

High Style & Classic

29 POLLINI

Via Calimala 12r
Tel. 21.47.38
Moderate to expensive; credit cards
    accepted

The four Pollini—Vittorio, Alberto, and their sisters Lucia and Lidia— are renowned throughout Italy. They combine class, elegance and refinement with fresh and colorful interpretations. Pollini appeals to both the young and the more conservative, and its store windows are a traditional stop on any Florentine's window-shopping excursion. The men's collections tend to be classic, with loafers and moccasins inspired by British designs, while the women's styles exemplify all that is novel and sophisticated in Italian footwear. Interesting detail and a pinch of fantasy add a distinctive Pollini flavor to whatever ornamentation is currently in vogue. The choice of leathers is up to the minute as well, be they stenciled, stamped, perforated or metallicized. Well over a dozen boutiques in Italy and abroad have secured Pollini's position as front-runners in their field.

FASHION
MEN'S

Contemporary/Trendy

30 GABBANINI FIRENZE
Via Porta Rossa 31r
Tel. 28.34.68
Moderate to expensive; credit cards
  accepted

Gabbanini is a fusion of tradition and style—accent on the latter. Many of the shop's fine-quality separates of handsome Italian fabrics will appear forever classic when worn with other classics. Gabbanini's selection of shirts, sweaters and trousers also enable the young-minded customer to create a modern, up-to-date look. They are perfect for mixing and matching. There's a particular emphasis on sports jackets whose plaids, checks and fabric textures typify fine Italian taste.

Gabbanini has a second location at Via Calzaiuoli 19r (telephone 21.41.28).

FASHION
MEN'S & WOMEN'S

Designer Boutique

31 EMPORIO ARMANI
Via Pellicceria 34r
Tel. 21.20.81
Expensive; credit cards accepted

Here you'll find casual clothing from the new ready-to-wear division of the great Armani for considerably less than his high-fashion collection.

See Milan listing (page 185) for further information and the flagship store.

SPORTS GEAR
MEN'S, WOMEN'S & CHILDREN'S ACTIVE SPORTSWEAR

Accent on Fun Fashion

32 UNIQUE
Via Porta Rossa 57r
Tel. 21.35.05
Moderate; credit cards accepted

It's only to be expected that Italy could produce a sports-clothing store with so much fashion appeal. Unique is modern, spacious and impressively filled with coordinated outfits to keep you looking good while you're having fun at active sports. You'll find each season's best ski, tennis and swimwear from Ellesse, Fila, Valentino, Ungaro, Anzi, Besson and Coveri. The whole family can shop here, as the stock is extensive for both children and adults. The fashion is all as comfortable and practical as it is colorful and stylish—a combination that athletic Italians demand. There's no basic equipment, but not to be overlooked are the ski goggles, sports watches, socks and headbands.

SUSTENANCE
RISTORANTE/TRATTORIA

Late-Night

33 LA BUSSOLA
Via Porta Rossa 58r
Tel. 29.33.76
Moderate; credit cards accepted
Closed Monday; open after midnight

The newly renovated La Bussola is one of the precious few full-service restaurants open after midnight. There's a good selection of typical antipastos (stuffed tomatoes and zucchini, fried peppers, roasted strips of eggplant, cold rice salad) that you can choose yourself. Good light one-course meals such as pasta, pizza or salad can be ordered at the counter-bar or at tables until approximately 2:00 A.M.

FASHION
WOMEN'S
Contemporary

34 ROSSI & ROSSI
Via Porta Rossa 69r
Tel. 21.39.97
Expensive; credit cards accepted

Women executives or those who dress with subtle, sophisticated dash will find Rossi & Rossi's an appealing collection. The salespeople are very knowledgeable in helping you put together a look from a wide selection of separates from the leading labels they carry—Calla, Alberta Ferretti, and Mondrian, the knitwear line by Gian-franco Ferrè, to name but a few. There are smart suits, casual and sophisticated dresses and, in winter, a flurry of warm, stylish coats.

SUSTENANCE
BAR-CAFFÈ
Late-Night

35 CAFFÈ STROZZI
Piazza Strozzi 16r
Tel. 21.25.74
Moderate; no credit cards accepted
Closed Monday; open after midnight

In a pretty, new postmodern setting, you'll find the perfect late-night seat for watching the most stylish local inhabitants. There's a piano bar and video area in the marble-walled inte-rior, but the young set up camp after midnight at the outdoor tables when the season permits. There are only light canapés to munch on, but you're just a few blocks from La Bussola if hunger calls.

FASHION
MEN'S & WOMEN'S
Very Traditional

36 ZANOBETTI
Palagio Arte della Lana
Via Calimala
Tel. 21.06.46
Expensive; credit cards accepted

This splendid medieval palazzo built in 1308 was the seat of the powerful Wool Guild. It could today be home to no finer occupant. Since the beginning of this century, Zanobetti's goal has been not to create a fashion but

The Zanobetti palazzo and classic fashion.

to invent a taste that is timeless in appeal. Now in its fourth generation, Zanobetti proudly maintains its tradition of conservative, classic apparel for men and women.

Its own line of shoes and leather clothing (labeled "Arfango") is still produced according to 14th-century tanning formulas that result in excellent softness, elasticity and durability. Men can find high-quality tweed and cashmere suits and sweaters, as well as shirts, hats, socks, ties and gloves from some of the best Italian and British firms such as Brioni, Aquascutum, Burberry's and Briggs. The selection is less extensive for women, but features dresses, coats and suits from equally distinguished European houses.

FASHION

NOTIONS

Great Assortment

37 QUERCIOLI & LUCHERINI
Via Calimala 13r
Tel. 29.20.35
Inexpensive; no credit cards accepted

In the middle of all the Centro Storico's designer and high-fashion bustle is this charming marriage of an ultra-practical notions store and an old-fashioned haberdasher. The archetypal *merceria* boasts a crowded store window of colorful ribbons, embroidered bands, blazer badges, cords and buttons. Amusingly enough, the real pull here is a great selection of shoulder pads *(spalline),* particularly the big, rounded "Valentino" type, which are hard to come by and can revolutionize a dated silhouette.

CENTRO STORICO BAR-CAFÉS

While there are thousands of bars in Florence, only a handful rank as historical landmarks, living testimony to a vivid past when they were the site of rendezvous for the famous and illustrious who came to discover the city. Today's young and elderly Florentine bon-vivants may not be as celebrated as those patrons of the past, but they are still interesting to watch as you restore your strength with a stiff espresso or a freshly squeezed *spremuta.* Much of the romance of these bar-cafés lives on in their handsome belle-époque décor. You will find them in the Centro Storico listings (Gilli, page 61, Giubbe Rosse, page 60 and Rivoire, page 50).

Florence has few outdoor cafés, other than those in the open squares such as Piazza della Repubblica, where the strains of the summertime orchestra at Caffè Paszkowski also reach the tables of its five neighboring rivals. In most bars, food tends to be simple or limited; one goes primarily to watch and gracefully loaf.

FASHION
MEN'S & WOMEN'S
Young & Avant-Garde

38 PARISOTTO
Via Calimala 33–35r
Tel. 21.45.98
Moderate; credit cards accepted

Elbow your way through the young crowds to see the offbeat window displays of this small avant-garde boutique on the corner of the Piazza della Repubblica. The owner guarantees that no classic garment will ever be permitted within, and that only the strangest and newest looks will grace the racks. Parisotto tries to keep its prices reasonable by buying from the less-established Italian lines but also carries a representation of the most forward-looking English labels, including Katherine Hammet, Body Map and English Eccentrics.

SUSTENANCE
GELATERIA

39 BAR FIORENZA, GELATERIA POMPOSI
Via Calzaiuoli 9r
Tel. 21.66.51
Inexpensive; no credit cards accepted
Closed Sunday

This shiny chrome bar is best known for its fresh, creamy ice cream sold directly to passersby on the pedestrian-only street linking the Piazza della Signoria with the Duomo. For 25 years, owner Signor Pomposi has stayed up the better part of every night peeling fruit for the small but excellent production of *gelato*, which he oversees personally. If you're a kiwi lover, you'll find the best ice-cream interpretation of it here. Pomposi is one of the few bar-cafés in town that don't presweeten their summertime iced coffee, and you can also pick up to go the best *zuppa inglese* in town ("English soup," better known as trifle).

FASHION
WOMEN'S
Stylish Fashion for Large Sizes

40 MARINA RINALDI
Via Calzaiuoli 14r
Tel. 29.23.60
Moderate; credit cards accepted

Attractive styles, new colors and attention to detail—qualities usually found only in high-fashion clothing—are seen here in *taglie comode* (comfortable sizes), a pleasant Italian expression for what Americans call half sizes. This is a new, highly successful retail venture launched by Max Mara, one of Italy's leading ready-to-wear manufacturers. Outstanding fashion in virtually every category, from eveningwear to jeans, from knitwear to coordinates and from bathing suits to coats—all on a conservative, stylish note. The Marina Rinaldi label graces the colorful, impeccably tasteful line of accessories as well.

FASHION
CHILDREN'S
Sportswear

41 BENETTON 012
Via Calzaiuoli 37r
Tel. 28.47.50
Moderate; credit cards accepted

Small, but the most centralized of the Benetton 012 outlets in Florence, for children up to 12 years of age. See Milan listing (page 217) for further information.

LEATHERGOODS
BAGS & SHOES
Young & Imaginative Styling

42 SERGIO BAGS
Via Calzaiuoli 45r
Tel. 29.20.83
Moderate; credit cards accepted

For young and adventurous tastes, Sergio has an outstanding collection of imaginative, sporty bags, belts and shoes, all styled with touches of fantasy. Bags are made of lace, plastic, netting, leather, fur, canvas and other oddities and are as beautifully made as they are unconventional. Most of the shop's merchandise is Sergio's own production, but he also carries other accessories by such fashion leaders as Yien, Piero Guidi and Felizi. The mock-nautical theme of the store's wooden interior adds to the sense of fun.

SUSTENANCE
RISTORANTE/TRATTORIA

43 PAOLI
Via Tavolini 12r
Tel. 21.62.15
Expensive; credit cards accepted
Closed Tuesday

Save this unusual *trattoria* for a special evening when a theatrical atmosphere counts more than the menu. The restaurant is set in the cavernous storerooms of a stately 14th-century palazzo. Imitation Gothic frescoes, gleaming mahogany tables and wrought-iron lamps evoke the 19th century, when Paoli first opened. The Tuscan menu changes every two days, with exceptions such as the permanent *osso buco con riso* (veal shank with rice).

SUSTENANCE
RISTORANTE/TRATTORIA

44 DA GANINO
Piazza dei Cimatori 4r
Tel. 21.41.25
Moderate; no credit cards accepted
Closed Sunday

Set in a tiny piazza off the Via dei Cerchi, Da Ganino has an informal *osteria,* or tavern-like, atmosphere that does little to foretell the excellence of its simple Tuscan fare. Rustic, communal tables seat the artists with the film stars, all cognoscenti of the light *crostini di fegatini,* the variety of dishes made with truffle *(tartufo),* the homemade pasta (in the Spring, try the *tagliatelle* with wild asparagus), the thin-sliced raw beef *(carpaccio)*, and the delicious light desserts made on the premises. In the summer, tables move into the *piazzetta*, and reservations are almost always a must.

SHOES
MEN'S & WOMEN'S
Bargains

45 EUSEBIO
Via del Corso 5r
Tel. 21.37.80
Inexpensive; no credit cards accepted

This is a brand-new location for the cheapest shoe store in town. Spacious

Florence provides a theatrical backdrop.

rooms let you wander and help your-self from displays grouped by size and color, in styles that vary from sporty to punk, from stylish to simple and classic. The findings can be erratic, but for these prices there's usually at least one nice buy to be had. It goes without saying that quality is not great, but some of the treated or stamped synthetics look like real leather and suede to the uncritical eye.

FASHION

WOMEN'S

Sophisticated Knitwear

46 LUISA IL CORSO
Via del Corso 54–56r
Tel. 29.43.74
Moderate to expensive; credit cards
　　accepted

A spin-off of the ultra-fashionable Luisa Via Roma (page 64) just down the block, this small boutique concentrates on exclusive knitwear. Whether summertime cotton knits or winter wool and silk knits crowd the racks, it is easy to mix and match with color-coordinated pieces that are Luisa's own production. Prices are far lower than those of the designer collections at the sister store, but the sophisti-

cated fashion input of young owner Andrea Panconesi is evident in the new venture. A small collection of Luisa's private-label footwear comple-ments each season's new arrivals.

SUSTENANCE

GELATERIA

47 FESTIVAL DEL GELATO
Via del Corso 75r
Tel. 29.43.86
Inexpensive; no credit cards accepted
Closed Monday

The Festival is always a lively spot, with a healthy sound system, a young crowd and 100 flavors. Those who thrive on variety will thrill at the range, from the unique (rice or rose) to the wonderfully refreshing (canta-loupe and mint) and the unusually combined (yogurt-banana, liqueur-flavored mint-chocolate-chip).

PERFUME & COSMETICS

Big Brand-Name Selection

48 PROFUMERIA ALINE
Via Calzaiuoli 53r
Tel. 21.52.69
Moderate; credit cards accepted
Open during lunch

Centrally located and exceptionally well stocked, Aline's supplies men and women with every imaginable cosmetic necessity and luxury. All ma-jor European and American brands are represented in this modern chrome and mirrored boutique. Ladies will find Clinique, Lauder, Lancôme, Chanel, Orlane, Dior, Guerlain, Valentino and Armani, and for men there are Aramis, Burberry,

Hermès, Gucci, Paco Rabanne, Ted Lapidus, Lagerfeld and Cerruti. Affiliated with the renowned Diego della Palma Makeup Studio of Milan, the *profumeria* holds makeup lessons once a month. You can make an appointment for free makeup (20 to 30 minutes), with the understanding that you'll buy some of the products afterwards. Facial treatments using Clinique products are also available.

As in most Italian *profumerie,* there are coincidental assortments of designer bijoux, hair combs and ornaments, cosmetic bags and vanity paraphernalia. There's no self-service; you'll have to direct your request to one of the many multilingual sales assistants.

SUSTENANCE

BAR-CAFFÈ

49 GIUBBE ROSSE
Piazza della Repubblica 13–14
Tel. 21.22.80
Expensive; no credit cards accepted
Closed Thursday; open after midnight

Across the piazza from Gilli's, this 100-year-old establishment is named after the traditional red jackets worn by the waiters. Once the command post for avant-garde artists and intellectuals, it has lightened its atmosphere considerably and today is most appreciated by Americans for its breakfast menu. Eggs prepared as you like them, jam and toast, juice and American coffee can be had outdoors in pleasant weather every morning until 11:00. An ex-German beer hall, Giubbe Rosse is more a bar-restaurant than a *bar-caffè,* with a limited though fine menu of hot selections. Both bar and kitchen stay open until 1:30 A.M.

LEATHERGOODS

SHOES, MEN'S & WOMEN'S FASHION
Big Selection of Fine Footwear

50 MARAOLO/CARRANO
Via Roma 6–10r
Tel. 21.38.16
Moderate; credit cards accepted
Open during lunch

This spacious and elegant boutique carries its own fine fashion designs in both men's and women's shoes, and also features the well-known Andrea Carrano label. Styles range from classic to contemporary and from casual to dressy. In addition to shoes and boots, Maraolo carries wonderful bags, belts and separates from the leading Italian houses: Erreuno, Ginochietti, Coveri, Emporio Armani, Cornelliani and Panchetti. The service is untiringly patient and friendly.

LEATHERGOODS

SHOES & CLOTHING
Elaborate Florentine Styling

51 ROMANO
Piazza della Repubblica
    (corner Via Speziali)
Tel. 21.65.35
Expensive; credit cards accepted

The Florentine leather firm of Romano has five fine shops in town, but this is the largest and undoubtedly the most spectacular. The store itself is as elegant as the merchandise, with gilded reliefs and frescoed ceilings. For women, Romano cultivates a highly feminine look with a splash of fantasy in the elaborate workmanship of shoes, boots, bags and leather clothing. Decorative stitching, appli-

Romano's elegant goods in a setting to match.

qués, contrasting combinations of leathers and skins, and an unexpected sense of originality keep Romano one step ahead of the competition.

Not all the merchandise is Romano, although everything is guaranteed to be of the same quality of workmanship and design concept. You'll find interesting Braccialini handbags, Andrea Pfister footwear for women, and Pancaldi and Valentino leather clothing for men and women. Men's shoes are typically more conservative, although often with a subtle flair. Be forewarned that the service can be snooty at times.

SHOES

MEN'S & WOMEN'S

52 FRATELLI ROSSETTI
Piazza della Repubblica 43–45r
Tel. 21.66.56
Expensive; credit cards accepted

This cool, clean setting is home for Rossetti's elegant and fashionable shoe collections that boast top-of-the-line quality and comfortable fit.

SUSTENANCE

BAR-CAFFÈ

53 GILLI
Piazza della Repubblica 39r
Tel. 29.63.10
Expensive; no credit cards accepted
Closed Tuesday

Here is the quintessential grand bar with chandeliers, brass ceiling fans, stained-glass windows and marble-topped tables, all framed in a setting of heavy wooden moldings, mirrors and 19th-century charm. Home to the affluent and aspiring, a place where deals are made and hearts are broken, Gilli has been in existence in various renditions since 1733. The interior rooms are cool in summer, but the people-watching is best outdoors in the warm Tuscan sun. Light lunches of sandwiches and salads (chef's, chicken and tuna) are available, but Gilli's is mostly known for its rainbow cocktails, especially the Gilli Cooler made with gin and fruit juices and topped with a miniature Italian flag. If you come for tea, you'll see pink and green (rose- and mint-flavored) sugars to sweeten your brew in addition to the usual white and brown.

HOME

CHINA, GLASS, & SILVER

54 UGO POGGI
Via Strozzi 26r
Tel. 21.67.41
Expensive; credit cards accepted

High quality—a prerequisite at Ugo Poggi.

Ugo Poggi is a gleaming showcase of traditional, modern and avant-garde opulence in silver, porcelain, crystal and glass. The modern and avant-garde schools are represented by the much-sought-after Italian silversmiths Ricci and Sabattini, for whom Ugo Poggi is Tuscany's sole agent. Ricci's silver-plated flatware designs (dishwasher-safe) are inspired by and named for various artists or artistic movements, such as Braque, Modigliani, Manet and art deco. Sabattini (see page 196) made a quantum leap in the molding of silver so that its shiny brilliance and pure form could be spectacularly functional. His vases, fish platters, breadbaskets, pitchers and bowls are collectors' items, having won awards and been displayed as silver sculpture in art museums. You might find limited selections of such articles abroad, but their cost is greatly reduced on home territory. Tradition is also on hand at Ugo Poggi in Royal Crown Derby, Royal Doulton, Minton and Mason

porcelain, as well as St. Louis and Murano (Carlo Moretti) crystal.

FASHION

MEN'S, WOMEN'S & CHILDREN'S

The Classic Anglo-Florentine Look

55 PRINCIPE
Via Strozzi 21–29r
Tel. 21.68.21
Moderate to expensive; credit cards accepted

Principe is the exemplification of a Florentine department store. Over generations, the Doni family steadily expanded it until the entire five-floor Palazzo Mattei was theirs. It stands independent, princely, its 14 arched window displays chock-full of the smart fashion that awaits within.

The Principe look is "Anglo-Florentine," a classic British style for children, men and women interpreted with Italian flair and imagination. A quirky exception is the small room devoted to Missoni knitwear, for which Principe has the exclusive in town. But most of the rest of the clothing is made exclusively for Principe with the finest Italian and British fabrics. On the second floor, a man can also choose from bolts of fabric, match his selection with any of the suits displayed and have it made up in a few days.

In case you left your imagination at home, clever floor displays pair textures with rich colors in casual layerings of separates and accessories. Accessories run a complete range from ties and socks to belts and scarves. Principe offers a delightful Florentine experience in refined shopping, with a uniformed staff that is both courteous and attentive.

RISTORANTE/TRATTORIA

56 AL CAMPIDOGLIO
Via Campidoglio 8r
Tel. 28.77.70
Expensive; credit cards accepted
Closed Thursday

As Italian standards go, this large, old-fashioned restaurant is somewhat on the formal side, with crisp white linen and professional though friendly service. The menu is simple and delicious. It goes beyond the typical Tuscan specialties to include the best of other regions. Al Campidoglio is fully air-conditioned in summer, something not as easily found as the tourist would expect.

CHILDREN'S

57 PRÉNATAL
Via Brunelleschi 22r
Tel. 21.30.06
Moderate; credit cards accepted

Fun and fashionable active clothing and accessories for children up to eight years old. See Milan listing (page 282) for more information.

WOMEN'S

Contemporary/Trendy

58 MAX MARA ⛊⛊⛊⛊
Via Brunelleschi 28r
Tel. 28.77.61
Moderate; credit cards accepted

If limited time forces you to choose just one clothing store from the trea-sure trove that Florence provides, go directly to Max Mara, just one block from the Duomo. It is a pleasure to browse through six spacious, air-conditioned rooms that offer reams of high-quality Italian fashion. Max Mara's customers can have tastes that range from the timelessly classic to the chic contemporary or the fun and avant-garde. And nowhere else will you find such value in fabric, style and workmanship.

All the stunning collections are of Max Mara's own design and production, much of which is not yet widely exported. Everything is grouped to facilitate your selection: separates and sweaters to mix or layer; casual or elegant dresses; tailored or boldly cut suits, coats and raincoats. An array of selectively coordinated leather accessories, from big belts to shoes, also runs the gamut from the casually sporty to the very sophisticated.

FASHION

Designer Collection

59 CASA DEI TESSUTI
Via dei Pecori 20–24r
Tel. 21.59.61
Moderate; credit cards accepted

A half century of experience in dealing with Europe's finest textiles has earned the Casa dei Tessuti a respected reputation. Although there are some French and British interlopers, fabrics are predominantly of Italian origin. Don't miss the exquisite designer creations of Armani, Saint-Laurent, Dior, Krizia, Valentino, Lancetti, Coveri and Balestra. There are bolts and bolts of gleaming taffeta and crepe-de-Chine silks, soft cashmeres and alpacas, and often the same print design comes in both silk and wool. The Romoli brothers, owners of the establishment, will gladly show you their unsurpassable collection of bridal fabrics that would have thrilled Catherine dei Medici.

FASHION
JUNIORS
Sportswear

60 STEFANEL
Via Roma 15r
Tel. 29.48.73
Moderate; credit cards accepted
Open during lunch

Big, youthful wardrobes on small budgets is the motto for Stefanel, a serious family-run contender to the Benetton dynasty.

See Milan listing (page 181) for more information.

FASHION
MEN'S
Updated Classic

61 EREDI CHIARINI ☖☖☖☖
Via Roma 18–22r
Tel. 28.44.78
Expensive; credit cards accepted

Owned by the two young Chiarini brothers, Marco and Andrea, this is a tiny two-story department store for men. The updated Chiarini style is obvious in a wide range of fashion necessities and incidentals, right down to blazer buttons, Oxfords and after-shaves. Jackets, suits, trousers and sweaters amalgamate English classicality, American practicality and

distinct Italian taste—a combination that draws a loyal clientele of young professionals with a sense of style.

FASHION
MEN'S & WOMEN'S
International Designer Collection

62 LUISA VIA ROMA ☖☖☖☖
Via Roma 19–21r
Tel. 29.21.30
Expensive; credit cards accepted
Open during lunch

Grandson of the original Luisa (a French milliner), young owner Andrea Panconesi has created one of Italy's premier fashion boutiques. Luisa Via Roma is home to the best in bold, provocative international fashion, the kind that anticipates trends and follows the mercurial tastes of the young and daring. An uncluttered, modern-art-gallery décor is the backdrop for the "art" of fashion, with individual areas showcasing each of the great designers of the minute.

Trends appear first at Luisa Via Roma.

Believing that fashion is also a cultural phenomenon, Panconesi is an insatiable seeker of the new and emerging and is often the first to sponsor the debut collections of striking new talents.

DESIGNER BOUTIQUE DIRECTORY

The following designer boutiques in Florence are listed in alphabetical order by last name, and the shopping neighborhood is highlighted in italics. All take credit cards and follow store hours.

Giorgio Armani (Men's & Women's)
Via Tornabuoni 35-37r
Tel. 21.38.19
Tornabuoni

Laura Biagiotti (Women's)
Via Calimala 27r
Tel. 29.60.72
Centro Storico

Enrico Coveri (Men's & Women's)
Via della Vigna Nuova 27-29r
Tel. 26.17.69
Centro

Fendi (Women's)
Via Tornabuoni 27r
Tel. 28.77.57
Tornabuoni

Salvatore Ferragamo (Men's & Women's)
Via Tornabuoni 16
Tel. 29.21.23
Tornabuoni

Gianfranco Ferrè (Men's & Women's)
Via Strozzi 24r
Tel. 21.22.14
Centro Storico

Gucci (Men's & Women's)
Via Tornabuoni 57-59r
Tel. 26.40.11
Tornabuoni

Gucci (Leathergoods)
Via Tornabuoni 73r
Tel. 26.40.11
Tornabuoni

Emilio Pucci (Women's)
Via dei Pucci 6r
Tel. 28.30.61
Centro

Trussardi (Men's & Women's)
Via Tornabuoni 34-36r
Tel. 21.99.02
Tornabuoni

Valentino (Women's)
Via della Vigna Nuova 47r
Tel. 29.31.42
Centro

Mario Valentino (Men's & Women's)
Via Tornabuoni 67r
Tel. 26.13.38
Tornabuoni

Gianni Versace (Men's & Women's)
Via Tornabuoni 13-15r
Tel. 29.61.67
Tornabuoni

FASHION

MEN'S & WOMEN'S, SHOES & LEATHERGOODS

Contemporary, Sporty, Florentine Chic

63 RASPINI 🗋🗋🗋🗋
Via Roma 25–29r
Tel. 21.30.77
Expensive; credit cards accepted

The Raspini name has become synonymous with beautiful Florentine leathergoods. There are no outlets abroad, only three stylish stores in Florence, of which the Via Roma location is by far the largest. On the ground floor is Raspini's own outstanding production of men's and women's high-style shoes, belts and bags. You can also peruse the work of prestigious Italian shoe designers Maud Frizon, Guido Pasquali, Prada, Linea Lydia, Banfi, Diego della Valle, Cesare Paciotti and Granello.

The second floor is devoted to men's wear: Sicom, C.P. Company, Riccardo Bini, Iceberg, Kenzo, Jean-Paul Gaultier and other labels selected for their compatible styling and quality. On the third floor, women will find the allure of Krizia, Genny, Maison Blu, Iceberg, Moschino and others. The Raspini store on Via Martelli is geared to younger tastes and also features collections for 4- to 14-year-olds by Valentino, Ferrè, Moschino, Coveri and Armani.

JEWELRY

ANTIQUE STYLES

64 CAGLIOSTRO
Piazza San Giovanni 5r
Tel. 28.38.62
Moderate; credit cards accepted

One of many al fresco "drawing rooms."

If you like antique styles, Cagliostro has an interesting mix of everything from Etruscan to art-deco pieces that look like the real thing but cost much less. An offbeat and individual collection also includes African and Oriental silver, ivory and jade curiosities; trading beads; sculpture-like earrings and necklaces inspired by Arnaldo Pomodoro; and a striking number of baroque-design pieces from Rome-based Diego Percossi-Papi (see Rome listing, page 367). A favorite item is the Etruscan-designed good-luck pin, a small silver horn that was meant to carry a flower bud but can be worn alone. Store owner Loretta Malori herself designs many of the art-deco pieces (mostly pins and earrings), which are made up by local artisans.

FASHION

CHILDREN'S & JUNIORS

Trendy & Fun

65 LA RAGAZZERIA
Via Tosinghi 12r
Tel. 28.77.20
Moderate; credit cards accepted

A large, fun boutique of sporty clothing and accessories for youngsters 10 to 16 years old.

See Milan listing (page 174) for more information.

A flower market adds color to this arcade.

LEATHERGOODS

BAGS

Contemporary & Casual

66 LA FURLA
Via Tosinghi 5r
Tel. 29.34.08
Moderate; credit cards accepted

Furla, a bags and accessories company based in Bologna, is always the first to pick up on a trend. Attention-getting leather bags are avant-garde and exciting, done up in good-quality leathers often stamped or colored according to the demands of the season—and available at non-investment prices. The dramatic modern interior also highlights a striking collection of big belts and fashion jewelry.

WINES

67 ALESSI PARIDE
Via delle Oche 27–29r
Tel. 21.49.66
Moderate; credit cards accepted

Tour Italy's bountiful wine country in the prodigious cellars of Alessi Paride. Heavy wooden racks lined with the best vintages and varieties take you through region after region. An entire room is stocked with Chianti alone. Signor Alessi's joy is introducing appreciative oenophiles to the little-known, exceptional wines usually overlooked. On the ground floor is an exposition of his prized stock of wines from 1935 to 1942, along with some elite vintage liquors such as cognac and whiskeys. The pampered palate will thrill at the wealth of European chocolates, marmalades and honeys, and at sweet breads such as the Sienese *panforte* and the traditional Christmas *panettone*.

SUSTENANCE

RISTORANTE/TRATTORIA

68 OTTORINO
Via delle Oche 12–16
Tel. 21.87.47
Expensive; credit cards accepted
Closed Sunday

Recently refurbished, this spacious and elegant eatery is on the ground floor of one of Florence's most beautiful medieval towers. The menu is unusually extensive, with typical Tuscan dishes as well as a good selection of fresh fish. Originality manifests itself in the *torta di verdura,* a kind of quiche made with leeks and swiss chard in a pastry shell, and in a highly un-Tuscan chicken curry dish.

Other specialties include wild mushrooms, asparagus and truffles in season.

SPORTS GEAR

ACTIVE SPORTSWEAR & SPORTS EQUIPMENT

Huge Selection for All Sports

69 LO SPORT

Piazza Duomo 7-8r
Tel. 28.44.12
Moderate; credit cards accepted

Imagine the widest selection of leading Italian and foreign makes of sports equipment and active sportswear under one roof, then multiply it by two. Lo Sport could not boast a more centralized location for its impressive stock of the best in tennis, soccer, swimming, running, sailing, golfing, horseback riding and rollerskating gear. And there's less active, more refined sportswear for the Italian "preppy"—an ample selection of loden coats, shetland sweaters, stylish kilts and corduroy trousers. The salespeople are extremely knowledgeable about all the sports equipment they carry.

Another, smaller "Lo Sport Due" is just two blocks away in the Piazza dell'Olio at No. 5. There is a nice selection of classic, sporty clothing for men and women, including Fila and Missoni Sport.

JEWELRY

Especially Good for Men's Accessories

70 TORRINI

Piazza Duomo 9-10r
Tel. 28.45.07
Expensive; credit cards accepted

Old-world charm in a local piazza.

They may not be Italian-made, but an ample selection of Rolex watches for men and women at a savings is a star attraction at Torrini's. A large sampling of men's fine jewelry and accessories may solve gift dilemmas: cuff links, lapel pins, key chains, bracelets, smoking and desk accessories, and a colorful line of enameled jewelry with flag insignias for yachting fans.

No gift of gold could be more Florentine than Torrini's handmade reproduction of the famous gold *fiorino* coin, once the most powerful and prestigious currency in Renaissance Europe. One side is cast with the image of San Giovanni (St. John), the city's patron saint, and the other with the lily, symbol of Florence (see page 30). Both Torrini and the gold florin go back some 600 years.

JEWELRY

Engraving Specialists

71 FRATELLI FAVILLI
Piazza Duomo 13r
Tel. 21.18.46
Moderate; credit cards accepted

The Favilli brothers are Florence's finest engravers of gold and semiprecious stones. Signet rings are among their specialties, and they can custom-make one to your specifications if necessary. You can request decorative motifs, initials, coats-of-arms or any other designs that particularly interest you. Glass showcases give testimony to the Favilli's careful, skilled etching on gold and semiprecious stones. Old Florentine families would never have their family crests carved anywhere else. If you're not interested in custom work, you can choose from a selection of traditional pieces of etched gold jewelry.

MUSIC

RECORDINGS

Complete Classical Collection

72 SETTECLAVIO
Piazza Duomo 16r
Tel. 28.70.17
Moderate; credit cards accepted

For the *appassionato* of classical music, Setteclavio is one of the few shops of its kind in Europe. It carries over 50,000 instrumental and opera titles distributed among records, cassettes and compact discs imported from all over the world. The friendly salespeople can advise you on the validity of an artist's or orchestra's interpretation and can help you find a rare edition or a collector's item. Settecla-

vio (which means the seven musical keys) has also started a club you can join by mail to exchange ideas and gain access to a catalogue featuring out-of-the-ordinary store offerings.

GIFTS

STATIONERY & ACCESSORIES

Marbleized papergoods

73 IL PAPIRO
Piazza Duomo 24r
Tel. 21.52.62
Expensive; credit cards accepted
Open during lunch and on Sundays

Credit goes to Il Papiro for launching the revival of handcrafted marbleized paper and using it to fashion elegant stationery and decorative objects. In this pleasant, wood-paneled shop you'll find a profusion of beautifully made paper-covered gifts—boxes in all shapes, sizes and colors, picture frames, scrapbooks, notebooks, diaries, address books, pencil holders with coordinated pencils, entire desk sets, paperweights, and even file folders and art portfolios with grosgrain ribbon closings.

Bright paper-covered gifts at Il Papiro.

LINGERIE

74 BOUTIQUE MARCELLA
Via Cerretani 7r
Tel. 21.63.52
Moderate; credit cards accepted

Let them peek into the cool marble-and-brass interior of this small boutique, and even the uninterested will find themselves surrendering to the soft loveliness of its Italian lingerie. The silk and satin confections are mostly sensuous, often lacy and all finely designed. The well-known La Perla and Malizia are the primary collections from which to choose, with delicate bras, panties, garter belts, stockings and pantyhose, and some light cotton and woolen nightgowns and dressing gowns.

SHOES

MEN'S & WOMEN'S

Casual & Contemporary

75 DIVARESE
Via Cerretani 32–34
Tel. 21.31.68
Moderate; credit cards accepted

Recently purchased by the fabled Benetton family and infused with a new sense of contemporary design, this established shoe manufacturer is back on an upswing. You'll find both sleek, modern styles and fun casualwear that complement the Benetton viewpoint on fashion. Prices are affordable as well. The recent introduction of a special line by Giuliana Benetton offers a slightly dressier look. A second, somewhat smaller Divarese location can be found at Via Calzaiuoli 58r (telephone 21.25.27).

Leather seal confirms Bojola's tradition.

LEATHERGOODS

BAGS & ACCESSORIES

Sporty Yet Refined

76 BOJOLA
Via Rondinelli 25r
Tel. 21.155
Moderate; credit cards accepted

A combination of canvas or other durable fabric with natural calfskin, branded with the family's insignia, is today's recognizable Bojola style. There are sporty, young-looking handbags, weekend bags and travel accessories, and a range of luggage pieces in canvas trimmed with leather. The neatly chic fabric-leather combination is carried over to a series of smaller items such as wallets, eyeglass cases and notebooks.

Perhaps no one else, however, makes such beautiful canes and wooden-handled umbrellas. They are a throwback to the days of Felice Bojola, who came to Florence in 1861 when it was the capital of Italy. He was already famous for his hand-carved walking sticks and elegant ladies' parasols. Today, his great-grandchildren fuse their contemporary flair with the family's reverence for quality.

HOME

CHINA, GLASS & SILVER

Classic Italian Porcelain

77 RICHARD-GINORI
Via Rondinelli 17r
Tel. 21.00.41
Moderate to expensive; credit cards
    accepted

Francesco dei Medici was responsible for the development of porcelain in Europe, but it was another enterprising Tuscan, the Marquis Carlo Ginori, who became the first in Italy and one of the first in Europe to set up porcelain production on a commercial scale over 250 years ago.

The quiet dignity of this beautiful flagship store is the setting for 18th-, 19th- and 20th-century classic patterns that embellished the dining rooms of every noble European family and made Richard-Ginori famous. They are still being produced with the perfected technology of today and a level of refinement unchanged since the 18th century. Blue flowers, gold highlights, plaited ribbons, little bouquets, fruit and flower garlands, and Oriental motifs grace the delicate white porcelain of coffee and tea sets, demitasse cups and table settings. A few creative concessions to modern times have been made with art-

An aristocratic Richard-Ginori setting.

nouveau-inspired designs and the award-winning creations of Ginori art directors Gio Ponti and Giovanni Garibaldi. A recent signature silverware collection has been introduced to complement the porcelain place settings. The store also sells Murano glass; Waterford, St. Louis and Orrefors crystal; Lalique knickknacks; Berlin and Villeroy & Boch porcelain.

As a shipbuilder, Carlo Ginori sent one of his vessels off to the Orient to load up with precious porcelain, most of which was broken by the time it arrived. Ginori then started experimenting with Italian clays to obtain optimal opacity and whiteness. He hired Viennese painters and Italian sculptors to labor over the first prototypes. Within just a few years he was producing on an industrial level, and later was a major force behind establishing Italy as a prominent manufacturer of fine porcelain.

The Richard-Ginori factory in nearby Sesto Fiorentino is still active and prosperous today after two and a half centuries. The factory outlet at Viale Giulio Cesare 19 is well worth the 20-minute ride for the substantial discounts it offers on Ginori seconds and closeouts (telephone 42.10.472). See box on Factory Outlets for further information, page 37. While you're there, the adjacent Ginori Museum, at Viale Giulio Cesare 50, exhibits a superb collection of 18th- to 20th-century fine porcelains. (Telephone 44.10.451. Hours: 9:30 A.M. to 1:00 P.M., 3:30 to 6:30 P.M. Closed Sunday and Monday.)

By the way, Richard-Ginori is not and never was a person; ''Richard'' is the renowned Milanese ceramic firm that merged with Ginori in 1896.

Via Tornabuoni

*T*he elegant Via Tornabuoni is a natural dividing line between the Centro Storico and Centro; we have opted to treat it independently, listing its prestigious stores and boutiques below. It offers Florence's *crème de la crème* in shopping, joining with Rome's Via Condotti and Milan's Via Montenapoleone to be the most celebrated of boutique addresses in Italy.

A continuation of the Via Maggio, with its expensive antique stores, and the graceful Ponte Santa Trinità, Via Tornabuoni extends for a few short but eventful blocks perpendicular to the Arno River. Here, Roman

Via Tornabuoni's stately palazzos are home to small and elegant shops.

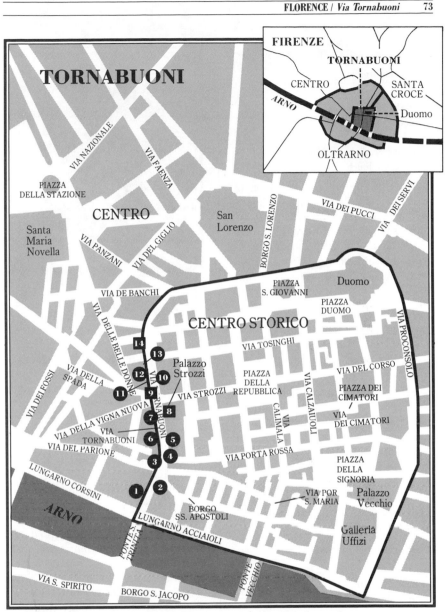

visitors entered the city, then known as Florentia, through a western gate that no longer exists. In its stead today is the busy intersection of the Vias Tornabuoni and Strozzi, marked by the stalwart 17th-century Palazzo Strozzi. Just beyond this point lies the Renaissance Palazzo Antinori, still owned by the Antinori family whose wines grace the world's tables.

You'll find modern glass frontages displaying Italian and European fashion for big spenders and wishful window-gazers alike.

LINENS, LINGERIE & CHILDREN'S WEAR

Delicate Embroidery

1 BARONI

Via Tornabuoni 9r
Tel. 21.05.62
Expensive; credit cards accepted
Open during lunch

Each delicately embroidered item is more beautiful than the next. Choose among *biancheria intima* (personal linen), such as nightgowns, robes, and ladies' blouses in cotton, silk or linen, little girls' dresses, or *biancheria di casa* (house linen), such as tablecloths, place mats, bedspreads, sheets, bath and dish towels. Baroni maintains exacting standards of excellence on the embroidery of each article in the store, whether the work is done by hand or by machine; it is often hard to believe that the latter items are not handmade.

Baroni is headed by the mother-daughter team of Laura and Emanuela, who will work with you on special orders for an odd-sized tablecloth or a blouse with an embroidered design of your own imagination.

FASHION

MEN'S & WOMEN'S

Designer Flagship Boutique

2 FERRAGAMO

Via Tornabuoni 16r
Tel. 29.21.23
Expensive; credit cards accepted

This stately flagship store is by far the most beautiful of all the world's Ferragamo outlets. The historic site, a fortress-like palazzo constructed in 1215, is known to historians as the Palazzo Feroni-Spini, but to Floren-

Ferragamo's flagship store.

tines it is the Palazzo Ferragamo. A series of vaulted ground-floor rooms with stained-glass windows and archways is an appropriate setting for the beautiful, sophisticated footwear that has brought international fame to Salvatore Ferragamo.

A relative newcomer to ready-to-wear, Ferragamo now also creates a high-fashion clothing line. Elegant, conservative outerwear, suits, dresses and separates for men and women are complemented by bold-colored silk scarves and ties and handsome bags and belts. But the prize items remain his men's and women's shoes. These award-winning designs result from his early study of the anatomy of the foot and the mechanics of walking. His dress shoes are as comfortable as his more casual daywear; the common denominators are fit, careful workmanship and beauty. Shoe sizes are American, and most models come in numerous widths to accommodate "problem feet" complaints.

FERRAGAMO

Salvatore Ferragamo was born in Bonito, near Naples, but it was in Florence, with its ancient tradition of leather crafts, that he established himself as perhaps the world's finest creator of elegant and comfortable shoes. Almost single-handedly, he awakened the world to the importance of the shoe as fashion.

One of 14 children, the young Ferragamo found life arduous. As a 9-year-old, he decided he had a talent for shoemaking, a calling that even his *contadino* father felt was far too lowly. On the eve of his sister's first communion, when the family had no money to buy Sunday shoes to replace her wooden clogs, Salvatore created a pair out of scraps of white canvas and cardboard given to him by the local cobbler. Only then did his parents allow him to apprentice. At 11 he moved to Naples, and at 14 he was on his way to America.

It was the golden age of Hollywood. Ferragamo found work in a shoe factory and was lucky enough to be asked to create cowboy boots for westerns; soon he was designing Roman gladiator sandals for Cecil B. DeMille's colossal epics.

Word spread that this earnest Italian cobbler made shoes like no one else; he was dubbed "Shoemaker to the Stars." He made comfortable loafers for Douglas Fairbanks, cork heels studded with pearls for Gloria Swanson, and platform shoes for Theda Bara. His shoes became a status symbol, but he could not keep up with the demand. He returned to Italy to find the skilled helpers he needed to set up large-scale production. In Florence he soon had an army of 600 artisans producing the first handmade shoes to be exported in quantity to the United States.

In America Ferragamo had studied the anatomy of the foot at a podiatry institute and learned that the whole weight of the body is borne by the arch. His education helped him create shoes of unprecedented comfort, while his fantasy led him to use a wide variety of materials: satin, hummingbird feathers, glass, seaweed, cellophane and the skins of ostrich, kangaroo, leopard, python and water snake.

The Shoemaker to the Stars had become the "Shoemaker of Dreams," as Ferragamo described himself in his autobiography. He was one of the forerunners of the "Italian look" that became the rage in the 1950s. Many of his early models have only today come into their own. Even when forced to turn to machine production, he was diligent in maintaining high quality. He died still young in 1960, but his wife Wanda and his children carry on the family enterprise, true to Ferragamo's axiom that "high fashion and comfort are not incompatible."

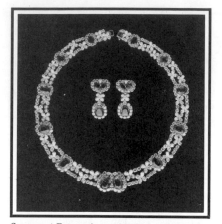

Settepassi-Faraone's jewelry fit for royalty.

JEWELRY
TOP-NAME

3 SETTEPASSI-FARAONE
Via Tornabuoni 25r
Tel. 21.55.06
Expensive to very expensive; credit cards accepted

Since the time of the Medici, Settepassi has been creating lavish jewelry for the world's wealthiest families and the crowned heads of Europe. Settepassi was the most famous and expensive shop on the Ponte Vecchio until, feeling that the bridge had become too touristy, it relocated at this even more prestigious spot.

In the late 19th century, Carlo Settepassi supplied Margherita of Savoy, queen of Italy, with her tiaras and cascades of Oriental pearls. Today, Settepassi is the only Italian jeweler that still works with real Oriental pearls, and prominent debutantes will settle for nothing less than a precious Settepassi strand. You'll find extravagant gold necklaces studded with diamonds, rubies, sapphires and emeralds, with matching earrings—and matching prices. Cuff links for every occasion, ivory objects, and a selection of necklaces, bracelets and earrings in a more accessible, though still high, price range fill out the treasure chest.

In addition, there are choice pieces of antique English silver and a handsome assortment of contemporary silver articles such as picture frames, key rings and even staplers—an elegant touch for the well-appointed desk.

LEATHERGOODS
BAGS & BRIEFCASES

4 DESMO
Via Tornabuoni 18r
Tel. 28.48.36
Expensive; credit cards accepted

Desmo is one of the front-runners in high-quality, high-fashion leather manufacturing. Bags are produced by weaving strips of fine calfskin and stamped leather together (a look made famous by Bottega Veneto), which increases their durability. For women, handbag styles range from the casual, soft, pouchy shoulder bags to elegant evening bags in special skins such as lizard and ostrich, with particular emphasis on precious crocodile in several fashionable and fun colors. Men will be taken by the handsome and practically designed overnight and travel bags and attaché cases. Shoes, wallets and accessories are joined by a small coordinated line of innovative leather clothing for men and women.

LEATHERGOODS

GLOVES & MEN'S ACCESSORIES

5 UGOLINI

Via Tornabuoni 20–22r
Tel. 21.66.64
Expensive; credit cards accepted

The classic and the exotic in men's and women's high-quality gloves can be found here. Gloves for every day, for sports or for formal wear come in suede, silk-lined kid, wild boar, deer, puma and elephant. The Ugolinis once gloved the hands of the Italian royal family and have not compromised their quality since. Other fine-quality accessories include refined silk paisley ties and scarves and creamy cashmere mufflers in a range of solid colors and plaids.

SHOES

WOMEN'S

High-Heeled Comfort & Elegance

6 CASADEI 👜👜👜👜

Via Tornabuoni 33r
Tel. 28.72.40
Expensive; credit cards accepted

For the woman who dreams of finding high-heeled shoes that are as comfortable as they are elegant, Casadei should be the end to a long search.

While the rest of the commercial shoe industry faithfully follows the seasonal ups and downs of the heel's ephemeral status, Casadei has never stopped making its striking and sophisticated high-heeled footwear. The Casadei heel ranges from the squat to the stiletto in both shoes and boots, and the manufacturers maintain that their very wearable high-heeled models are just as comfortable as

Ugolini, a tradition in quality accessories.

their flats. All are beautifully made, with distinct innovations such as combining leathers and suedes or reptile skins.

SHOES

MEN'S & WOMEN'S

Sturdy Classics

7 TANINO CRISCI

Via Tornabuoni 43–45r
Tel. 21.46.92
Expensive; credit cards accepted

Tanino Crisci's shoes are well-sculpted models of classicism that the traditionalist will enjoy season after season. Women's pumps, men's loafers or casualwear and boots for both are sturdy, long-wearing and always in style. The great-grandfather of the current owner imposed standards for high-quality, hand-finished shoes that are still adhered to today. For the lady in cashmere and pearls and the country squire—or anyone with similar tastes.

SUSTENANCE
BAR-CAFFÈ

8 PROCACCI
Via Tornabuoni 64
Tel. 21.16.56
Expensive; no credit cards accepted
Closed Monday

There's no real place to sit and relax, but that is a small price to pay for the light, exquisite truffle-roll sandwiches for which this small bar is world-famous. Old-fashioned Procacci is filled to the brim with bottled and packaged gourmet delicacies, pre-serves and unusual liqueurs that are hard to find elsewhere and that make nice gifts for connoisseurs. The bar has no espresso machine, but that's of no concern for those who come for the truffled delights.

SUSTENANCE
BAR-CAFFÈ

9 GIACOSA
Via Tornabuoni 83
Tel. 29.62.26
Expensive; no credit cards accepted

This elegant corner bar-tearoom is the perfect place to observe Florence's handsome young elite as they linger over their daily *aperitivi* or cappuccinos. A tempting assortment of miniature pastries, canapés and sandwiches makes great appetizers or can serve as a quick lunch at the bar or at one of the few tables. The Negroni cocktail, now an Italian classic, was invented here by the local Count Camillo Negroni in the 1920s. It is made with one-third gin, one-third bitter Campari and one-third Martini & Rossi sweet vermouth.

BOOKS
GENERAL

10 LIBRERIA INTERNAZIONALE SEEBER
Via Tornabuoni 68r
Tel. 21.56.97
Moderate; credit cards accepted

Florence's oldest bookstore has an exhaustive stock of general hardback and paperback literature. A quaint, old-fashioned air hangs about the place, first established to serve the foreign community in the 1860s. An entire room at Seeber's is devoted to foreign (mainly English) books, many of which dwell on Tuscan or Italian themes such as art, architecture and cuisine.

FASHION
MEN'S & WOMEN'S
Designer Flagship Boutique

11 GUCCI
Via Tornabuoni 57–59r
Tel. 26.40.11
Expensive; credit cards accepted

This is the newer and the splashier of Florence's two deluxe Gucci flagship boutiques, accommodating their ever-growing collection of men's and women's ready-to-wear. Under the direction of the new Gucci generation and with the cooperation of some of Milan's top design talents, the fashion collection is, at times, less stereotyped than one might expect. Some items (scarves, blouses, etc.) are inevitably distinguished by the Gucci colors and the logo of interlocking G's. Most garments are more discreet, their fine-quality design and tailoring being the only visible Gucci trademark. These are separates and sportswear that you can pull together with Gucci accessories which are available in limited quantity here, but in delightful profusion at the original Gucci boutique just a few doors down on Tornabuoni. A favorite item for the shopper who has everything is the Gucci sneaker with little GG's stamped into its sole (and green and red laces, of course), which will ennoble your private tennis court.

JEWELRY
TOP-NAME

12 MARIO BUCCELLATI
Via Tornabuoni 71r
Tel. 29.65.79
Expensive; credit cards accepted

In this elegant shop, once the carriage house for the famous Caffè Doney across the street, Mario Buccellati houses his exquisitely designed and handcrafted jewelry and his hand-hammered sterling silver objects for the table.

See Milan listing (page 208).

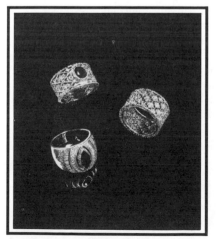

Buccellati's hand-crafted jewelry.

LEATHERGOODS
Designer Flagship Boutique

13 GUCCI
Via Tornabuoni 73r
Tel. 26.40.11
Expensive; credit cards accepted

This Gucci accessories boutique is the birthplace of all those interlocking G's, the most-copied trademark in the world. Gucci is the status symbol from Peking to Paris, but you may have forgotten why if you have recently been inundated by a wave of inferior look-alikes. A brief visit to this elegant flagship store will renew your appreciation for the classic design, high-quality materials and exquisite workmanship of the real thing. You'll also learn that the theme repeated on all Gucci merchandise varies from year to year, though it usually includes the family's initial or the famous red and green striped ribbing. You'll see rooms and rooms of leather and canvas bags, silk scarves, beautifully made leather luggage, loafers and shoes for men and women, home accessories, umbrellas and small, less expensive leathergoods such as wallets and key cases that make perfect gifts.

SUSTENANCE
RISTORANTE/TRATTORIA

14 CANTINETTA ANTINORI
Piazza Antinori 3
Tel. 29.22.34
Moderate; no credit cards accepted
Closed for Saturday and Thursday dinner

Adjoining the regal courtyard of the Palazzo Antinori, this elegant bar-restaurant is always crowded because it guarantees the choicest customers in town, as well as the unrivaled wines, oils, breads and cheeses from the Antinori estates. Six hundred years of wine production have made the Antinoris titans in their field. You can stand at the bar and leisurely sip an award-winning vintage or sit and have a light but memorable meal of an omelet and fresh salad. More rustic fare like *pappa al pomodoro* or warm chickpea-and-pasta soup is perfect for a winter afternoon.

GUCCI

Florentine master saddler Guccio Gucci (from whose name come those two immortally interlocked Gs) opened his little leather workshop and store on Via della Vigna Nuova in 1904, supplying Florence's aristocracy and the local British community with the finest saddles and harnesses they had ever seen. So was born the internationally recognized dynasty of leather design that has become synonymous with "Made in Italy" quality. When Aldo Gucci, grandson of the founder, visited the White House, John F. Kennedy greeted him as the first Italian ambassador of fashion.

Today Aldo and the two other Gucci grandsons, Roberto and Giorgio, head an empire still dedicated to impeccable quality despite the volume production that success has demanded. The prestigious Gs, which triggered a rash of signed designer accessories when they first appeared, have become smaller, but the Gucci collection grows ever larger. Over 6000 articles fill the family's catalogue. Classic items appear time and again: the bags in fine leather or in special G-covered canvas (introduced after World War II when quality leathers were hard to find), all with characteristic red and green ribbing, which have made Gucci the most copied trademark in the world. But biannual collections constantly introduce new models and interpretations in everything from golf bags to silk scarves. And the influence of the fourth generation of Gucci grandchildren is reflected in new ready-to-wear collections and fresh marketing strategies. They've come a long way since Guccio Gucci first designed a sturdy leather walking shoe, a woman's loafer decorated with a horse's bit, which was later to be given a place of honor in the Metropolitan Museum's Costume Institute.

The Ponte Vecchio

*L*inking the north and south banks of the Arno River at its narrowest point, the Ponte Vecchio (the Old Bridge) has long been the heart and symbol of Florence, a landmark as recognizably Florentine as Brunelleschi's Duomo or Michelangelo's David. It retains its 1345 appearance, having been destroyed numerous times before that by fires and floods. Unlike its five neighboring bridges, it was spared by the Germans in World War II, some say because Hitler admired it. It also withstood the devastating flood of 1966, although most of its precious merchandise was swept away by the powerful currents. It seems, in fact, almost immortal, and it is hard to imagine the stunning view from the nearby Piazzale Michelangelo without this gem as its focal point.

For the last 400 years the goldsmiths and jewelers of Florence have held the Ponte Vecchio as their exclusive domain. Prior to that there were butchers, blacksmiths and greengrocers, later followed by the noisy and smelly workshops of tanners and leather workers who soaked their animal skins in the Arno below for as long as eight months.

When the powerful Medici family moved their sumptuous courts to the Pitti Palace on the southern bank of the Arno, they were so affronted by the stench of these "vile arts" that the Grand Duke Ferdinando dei Medici issued a decree that all shops on the Ponte Vecchio be restricted to the guild of goldsmiths and jewelers; he immediately installed 41 of these more genteel craftsmen—and collected twice the royal rent to boot. That was in 1593, and very little has changed since.

If you're in the market for jewelry or merely window cruising, you'll enjoy a stroll across this narrow, centrally located bridge. Thirty-eight small, handsome jewelry stores line both sides of the pedestrian-only crossing, proudly boasting an art handed down to them over the generations. Traditionally specializing in gold craftsmanship, they also offer vast arrays of precious and semiprecious gem settings, antique watches, coral and cameo collections, and tiny Renaissance objects.

Today's shop owners meet ever-increasing demand from waves of tourists by contracting skilled local artisans to supplement their production. But as you stroll along the Ponte Vecchio, look into the small back rooms and you will still see an occasional goldsmith or gem setter keeping alive an ancient art.

Italian gold is rarely less than 18k, but ask to see the government-regulated stamp that must appear on each article, confirming its karat count. Gold jewelry may have a more pinkish or yellowish cast than usual, due to its blend of alloys; this is no reflection of its gold content.

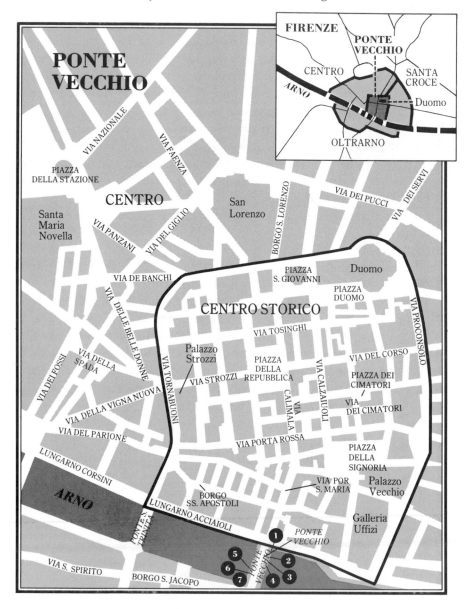

JEWELRY

1 T. RISTORI

Ponte Vecchio 1–3r
Tel. 21.55.07
Expensive; credit cards accepted

Ristori's jewelry is bought as much for its contemporary fashion as for investment. Perfectly cut precious and semiprecious stones set in new interpretations of traditional designs are the boutique's hallmark, appealing to a young and sophisticated clientele. Many of the shapes are large and bold, and the use of striking semiprecious stones keeps the prices less prohibitive than those of neighboring Ponte Vecchio shops. Ristori has taken over the enviable corner location where Settepassi stood until just recently, and the unusually spacious quarters provide an impressive showcase for its collections.

JEWELRY

2 U. GHERARDI

Ponte Vecchio 5
Tel. 21.18.09
Expensive; credit cards accepted

No one dares challenge Gherardi's collection of coral, known to be the most extensive and exquisite in Florence. Between the less expensive corals, simply engraved and set, and the elaborately designed pieces that are works of art in precious settings, Gherardi's accommodates the tastes and finances of all coral lovers. There's also a good selection of cultured pearls, hand-carved cameos and tortoiseshell objects.

The Ponte Vecchio, domain of goldsmiths.

JEWELRY

3 FRATELLI PICCINI

Ponte Vecchio 23r
Tel. 29.47.68
Expensive; credit cards accepted

Piccini's features large, flawless stones, unusually cut and set in unique gold pieces of contemporary design. In addition to its own designs, the shop carries a number of sleek Patek Philippe quartz watches in gold cases. Professional salespeople will also help you decide the new setting for family heirlooms or loose stones. Upstairs is a rarified collection of antique, hand-wrought silver tea services, candelabras, goblets and other precious objects, which the owners are almost reluctant to sell. When the future Queen Elena married Vittorio Emanuelle III in the early 1900s, Piccini created her gem-studded crown. Ever since, the establishment has maintained its reputation as one of the finest jewelers in Italy.

JEWELRY

4 RAJOLA
Ponte Vecchio 24
Tel. 21.53.35
Expensive; credit cards accepted

Rajola's small and elegant boutique was the first to adapt a contemporary bijoux look to fine jewelry, and loyal customers who once selected traditional jewelry merely by the value of the stones forever changed their buying habits. Unusual cuts and unique settings for both semiprecious and precious stones are characteristic of Rajola's singular collection. Many of the chunky, heavy gold chains are made by hand—a rarity these days; others are equally striking, though machine-made and hand-finished.

ANTIQUE JEWELRY

5 MELLI
Ponte Vecchio 44–46r
Tel. 21.14.13
Expensive; credit cards accepted

In contrast to all the shimmering gold displayed nearby, Melli's tiny window is full of antique jewelry and objets from epochs past. Signor Melli's collection is as interesting as a museum. You will probably find handmade chains, elaborate earrings, coral brooches, hand-painted porcelain plates and handsome working clocks. Viennese and English silver pieces, tea services and table settings are among the other rarities that the affable Signor Melli unearths, as his grandfather did before him, during his frequent European treasure hunts.

JEWELRY

6 BURCHI
Ponte Vecchio 54r
Tel. 28.73.61
Expensive; credit cards accepted

A sister company to the two Della Loggia shops, Burchi's design is far more conservative, using large precious stones, fewer semiprecious stones, and almost exclusively gold settings. Burchi's customer is generally an older woman interested in beautifully made pieces. One of the largest jewelry stores on the Ponte Vecchio, Burchi's has a polished wood interior furnished with glass display cases and Tiffany lamps that gracefully set off its stunning collection of classic jewelry.

JEWELRY

7 DELLA LOGGIA
Ponte Vecchio 52r
Tel. 29.60.28
Expensive; credit cards accepted

You'll find only very special contemporary pieces here, for Della Loggia is the least conservative in design among the Bridge's resident jewelers. It helped to initiate the use of precious and semiprecious stones together in the same setting, something for which the shop is still known. Della Loggia was also responsible for the unprecedented combination of steel and gold which continues to dominate its windows in the shape of bijoux-like earrings and necklaces.

A second Della Loggia boutique is just down the street as you walk toward the Duomo, at Via Por Santa Maria 29r.

Centro

*T*ime was when visitors to Florence had no reason to venture beyond the confines of the Centro Storico, the center stage of town. Today, its handsome stores and the crowds they attract have expanded to embrace what is comprehensively called "centro"—a section that spreads north of the Duomo and west of Via Tornabuoni. As you stroll past the gleaming windows of the designer boutiques of Via della Vigna Nuova or Via del Parione, you'll sense the same pulse as that of the Centro Storico; with the exception of some streets, the Centro has taken on much of the air and character once attributed to the Centro Storico alone.

West of Via Tornabuoni, antique-lovers will want to explore the historic Via dei Fossi and Borgo Ognissanti. Serious antique showrooms house precious Italian and European pieces that are finds for their rarity—something reflected in their handsome prices. By contrast, in the unassuming back streets of Via del Moro and Via della Porcellana (Street of the Porcelain Makers) is one of Florence's woodworking quarters. Small workshops pour out onto the sidewalk, where craftsmen are busy restoring and reproducing.

Students take a break near the Accademia.

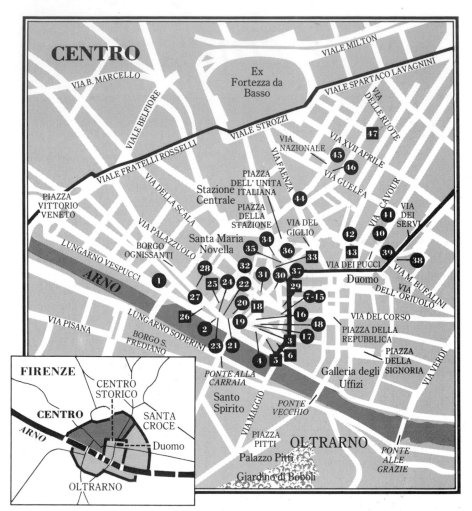

By the time you reach the area around the train station, barely a semblance of the Centro Storico glamour is left. The fast-food outlets and cheap boutiques here are best avoided. The heavily trafficked Via dei Panzani that runs from the station to the Duomo has its share of fun and fashionable boutiques, not necessarily high in quality but moderate in price. The busy Borgo San Lorenzo is a good street for inexpensive shoes. North of this main artery is the famous San Lorenzo market, the largest daily outdoor market of its kind in Italy.

FASHION

MEN'S & WOMEN'S

Made-to-Measure

1 TRIPODI & ROSI SARTORIA
Lungarno Amerigo Vespucci 34r
Tel. 29.80.07
Moderate to expensive; credit cards
    accepted

In a city known for its serious approach to high-quality apparel, Tripodi & Rosi is one of the most prestigious tailor-ateliers. An enterprising pair who have joined skilled forces just recently, Tripodi and Rosi create classic fashion for both men and women from the finest European fabrics. A man's suit takes approximately ten days to make up, a woman's suit or dress a little longer. Depending upon your schedule, they will do the first fitting a day or two after having taken your measurements, and prefer a second fitting before completion. If obligations hurry you on, they will airmail your garments, insured, to your home address. A complete line of leather, silk, wool and cashmere accessories allows you to complete that ultimate look.

LINENS, LINGERIE, & CHILDREN'S WEAR

Embroidery

2 PRATESI
Lungarno Amerigo Vespucci 8–10r
Tel. 29.23.67
Expensive; credit cards accepted

This is the ultra-deluxe mother store for the Tuscan-based Pratesi chain. Maker of some of the most luxurious sheets in the world, Pratesi has filled the linen closets of the Vatican and of

Luxury linens surround Athos Pratesi and wife.

Princess Grace of Monaco. The simple white Egyptian cotton sheets and pillowcases are classics, but you can get fancy with satin quilts, cashmere blankets, creamy silk sheets in romantic colors, and Jacquard tablecloths.

Pratesi linens are noted for their subdued, soothing colors, small floral prints and delicate embroidered trim. The work was once done only by hand, but Pratesi's international market now demands the use of highly sophisticated machinery, whose production is said to be more refined than ever. A very fine thread is used, resulting in an exceptionally high thread count per square inch and an incomparably soft feel. Exquisite infants' sheets, children's clothes and women's lingerie complete the collection.

Take heart if articles with such luxurious prices are but a dream. The family's factory outlet, located about 30 minutes west of Florence, sells "imperfects" whose flaws are usually microscopic. The selection is erratic, but at prices below wholesale, you may eagerly accept certain compromises. (Via Montalbano-Casalguidi, Località Ponte Stella, Pistoia. Telephone (0573)72.72.33. Closed Saturday afternoon and Monday morning.) See Factory Outlets, page 37.

SUSTENANCE

RISTORANTE/TRATTORIA

3 SILVIO
Via del Parione 74r
Tel. 21.40.05
Moderate; no credit cards accepted
Closed Sunday

Tucked away just beyond the Via Tornabuoni, the charming and rustic Silvio's has nonetheless managed to be discovered and patronized by a discerning local following. Quality ingredients are simply prepared: the fresh egg pasta is served with uncomplicated traditional sauces, the soups are simple and delicious—*pasta e ceci* (with garbanzo beans) and *ribollita*, for example. Although Silvio is one of the very few restaurants in Florence to prepare fresh fish (on Tuesday and Thursday), there are also quality meat cuts grilled or roasted. Try the *pecorino* cheese here to taste it at its best, and the fresh *ricotta* if available—a rich, creamy cheese that has nothing to do with the skim-milk excuse you may have known.

LEATHERGOODS

BAGS & ACCESSORIES

4 IL BISONTE
Via del Parione 35A/r
Tel. 21.57.22
Expensive; credit cards accepted

The small Il Bisonte (The Bison) boutique, in what was once the 15th-century home of the Corsini family, smells of the *vachetta,* or natural-hide leather, for which it is so widely known. This durable leather (in both natural and dyed earth colors) is mixed with canvas, straw and fur trimmings to produce dozens of styles, sizes and shapes of sturdy coach-type shoulder bags, soft suitcases and portfolios that will last a lifetime. Each article is stamped with the bison trademark.

Something of a *bisonte* himself, owner and designer Wanny di Filippo is a fun-loving romantic who adores beautiful things. He was the first to produce simple, unlined, oversize bags that looked as if they were fresh from the tannery at a time when everyone else was making constructed handbags. He is flattered by the major trend he launched and indifferent to those who copy his style. He has since branched out into wallets, agendas, key cases, belts and the like. Wanny's wife, Nadia, designs the distinctive sheepskin jackets and coats also displayed in the store.

Sturdy and stylish leathergoods at Il Bisonte.

RISTORANTE/TRATTORIA

5 COCO LEZZONE
Via del Parioncino 26r
Tel. 28.71.78
Moderate; no credit cards accepted
Closed Saturday, and Sunday in summer

Coco Lezzone, a miniscule *trattoria* serving excellent home cooking, has been discovered by chic and demanding Florentines. They sit elbow to elbow at long communal tables, delighting in the copious and authentic dishes, including simple but delicious vegetable *minestrone* and *pappa al pomodoro*. The meats are of uncompromisingly good quality: marvelous *arista* with herbs, *polpette* (meatballs) made with ground steak, stewed beef and the all-time glory, *bistecca alla fiorentina*. No one seems to mind that the menu never changes—even for Prince Charles and Princess Diana, who stopped at Coco Lezzone during a visit to Florence.

Alimentari

6 ALIMENTARI
Via Parione 19r
Tel. 21.40.67
Inexpensive; no credit cards accepted
Closed Wednesday afternoon

This unpretentious grocery store doubles as a great sandwich bar. Since it's always packed to the brim at lunchtime, you'll appreciate it more if you go a little before the stores and offices let out, or in the quieter afternoon hours. You can create your own sandwich with the help of friendly Mariano Orizi behind the counter, who takes endearing pride in his *panini*. There's a variety of fresh breads and rolls, on top of which you can lavish *bresaola* (cured beef sliced paper-thin), *prosciutto* (cured ham), fresh buffalo-milk *mozzarella* cheese with tomatoes, tongue and roast beef, *mortadella* (a kind of bologna), smoked salmon that is best with the soft *stracchino* cheese, and anything else displayed in his glass case. A few upside-down barrels serve as seats, or you can elbow in at the bar with everyone else to enjoy a glass of Chianti with the best *panino* in town.

DESIGNER COLLECTION

7 FILPUCCI STUDIO TRICOT
Via della Vigna Nuova 14r
Tel. 21.54.71
Moderate; credit cards accepted

If you're a serious knitter, or know one, this colorful little boutique can supply you with gorgeous yarns designed and used by Versace and Enrico Coveri, allowing you to mimic their high-spirited, high-fashion knitwear at a fraction of the cost. Each season, Filpucci, Italy's largest and most prestigious yarn manufacturer, produces new collections of yarns to keep savvy knitters ahead of the fashion scene. Their yarn factories in Florence and nearby Prato also wholesale their quality yarns to leading designers, whose creations made with Filpucci yarns are soon parading down the runways of the world's fashion capitals. In this Filpucci retail shop, you can choose from dozens of multi-hued and solid yarns, available in wool, mohair, cashmere, cotton, flax and silk.

LEATHERGOODS
BAGS & BELTS

8 FANTASIA
Via della Vigna Nuova 16r
Tel. 28.29.61
Moderate; credit cards accepted

An exception to the pricey stores that line the Via della Vigna Nuova, Fantasia is a small shop that offers consistently good buys in leather bags and belts for women. Belts are big and novel, have bold buckles, come in both classic and fashion colors and in both smooth and stamped leathers. Sporty shoulder bags are big and roomy, often coordinating with the belt collection and equally moderate in price. Both are made with close attention to detail and finishing. There is a similarly impressive offering for men in brief cases and leather accessories.

FASHION
WOMEN'S

Designers' Collections

9 ALEX 🎒🎒🎒🎒
Via della Vigna Nuova 19r
Tel. 21.49.52
Expensive; credit cards accepted

This boutique offers a hand-picked selection of the season's best in top European fashion for women, from Byblos, Romeo Gigli, Alaïa, Jean-Paul Gaultier, Claude Montana, Thierry Mugler, Complice and Genny. The atmosphere is relaxed, and no one seems to mind extended browsing. A few doors down at No. 5 is a smaller Alex shop, which is more classically stocked with just Basile and les Copains.

FASHION
MEN'S, WOMEN'S & CHILDREN'S

Designer Flagship Store

10 ENRICO COVERI
Via della Vigna Nuova 27–29r
Tel. 26.17.69
Expensive; credit cards accepted
Open during lunch

Tuscan-born Enrico Coveri has been influencing first local and then international fashion for over a decade. Ignoring the national tendency to move north to Milan, the fashion seat, Coveri has set up headquarters in his hometown, and this is his brand-new flagship store. Five spacious rooms are filled with his sophisticated yet sporty designs for those who view fashion as fun. Color is a key word at Coveri, and original seasonal themes are carried through every aspect of the wardrobe, for men, women and children alike. Those with a more conservative bent often find that Coveri's polychromatic sense of humor works best with the children's clothes. Enrico oversees the design of every accessory that bears his name, and there are many: belts, bags, shoes, sunglasses and fun costume jewelry.

The Florentine lily graces a medieval palazzo.

Today's Naj Oleari was once an English bakery.

GIFTS

FABRICS & ACCESSORIES

11 NAJ OLEARI
Via della Vigna Nuova 35r
Tel. 21.06.88
Expensive; credit cards accepted

On the site of what was once the English Bakery (the sign remains over the entrance) is a great source for status gifts for adults and children alike. The colorful printed cottons of Naj Oleari cover everything from umbrellas to teddy bears, from desk diaries to lampshades. Coming upon the bright, whimsical windows of this shop is one of the treats of walking the Via della Vigna Nuova. See Milan listing (page 247).

BOOKS

PHOTOGRAPHY & PRINTS

Of Historical Interest

12 ALINARI PHOTO/BOOKSTORE
Via della Vigna Nuova 46–48r
Tel. 21.89.75
Moderate; credit cards accepted

Alinari is a name inextricably linked with the history of Italian photography. Between 1852 and 1920, various members of this Florentine family photographed artwork, famous personalities, and everyday life *all'italiana* in cities and provinces throughout the country. The result is a priceless archive documenting national treasures. The spacious, modern Alinari Photo/Bookstore continues to reproduce these Alinari prints, offered for sale here mounted or not. Alinari also publishes books, catalogues, calendars, postcards and posters with images from its archives.

The store is part of the Alinari Brothers History of Photography Museum, located in the beautiful 15th-century palazzo of the Rucellai family, textile and dye magnates in the time of the Medicis.

JEWELRY

Private Showroom

13 ALOISIA
Via della Vigna Nuova 18
Tel. 29.89.23
Very expensive; credit cards accepted

Serious jewelry connoisseurs can arrange for a private showing of the prestigious collection designed by the late Contessa Aloisia Rucellai and shown by her handsome son Simone. The comfortable yet intimate setting is an imposing palazzo built by the Rucellai family in 1446, the first full-scale Renaissance urban mansion in Italy. Despite this association with the elaborate Renaissance epoch, the design of the jewelry is clean, contemporary and of utmost refinement. Exquisite precious stones and masterly workmanship produce a limited number of pieces worn by members of Europe's well-to-do. Call between 9:00 and 1:00 P.M. to set up an appointment. Personal checks are accepted.

FASHION
MEN'S & WOMEN'S ACCESSORIES
Big Stylish Hosiery Selection

14 MINETTA
Via della Vigna Nuova 68r
Tel. 28.79.84
Moderate; credit cards accepted

This is Florence's best-stocked shop for high-quality fashion hosiery. Minetta boasts a wide selection of Italian and French brands, many of them not found in the States, in the very latest of styles. Pattern, fit and color are attended to by courteous and patient sales help, who will show you box after box until you've found exactly the right item. For men, there are a fine assortment of leather and wool gloves and a rainbow selection of woolen socks in a number of sophisticated patterns, presented with the same personalized service.

FASHION
MEN'S

15 AMERINI
Via della Vigna Nuova 77r
Tel. 21.15.53
Moderate; credit cards accepted

This small, modern boutique offers a well-chosen collection of men's casual sportswear separates at good prices. Leaning toward the conservative, Amerini's caters to the Italian male or the foreigner who would like to pass as one—in his attire at least. Particularly noteworthy are the bulky and lightweight patterned wool sweaters, conveniently stocked year round. This store is family-owned and -operated and offers courteous service.

Unusual stationery products at Edizioni &c.

GIFTS
STATIONERY
Contemporary Design

16 EDIZIONI &C. 🗒🗒🗒🗒
Via della Vigna Nuova 82r
Tel. 21.51.65
Moderate; credit cards accepted

The stationery products here are so unusual that some, such as the *bi-gliettone*, a geometric self-folding note of rough "poor paper," are actually patented. Others have been featured in the catalogue of New York City's Museum of Modern Art. Everything is designed and produced by Florentine architect/artist/designer Marco Baldini, who continually comes up with unprecedented uses for handsome papers.

Edizioni &c. is an artisan's *bottega* as well as a gallery. Most of the papers shown are handmade, such as a special paper of pure cotton with ragged edges in rich earth tones watermarked "&c." Elegant handbound diaries, guest books and blank books, covered with kidskin leather or precious parchment, are art objects in their own right. Industrially produced papers show no compromise in quality, and desk sets, refillable notebooks, photo albums and portfolios are of stunning high-tech design. Stationery can be personalized with your name and address. Handsome business cards of equally high-quality paper can be made up in two weeks and shipped home to you if you're not around to collect them.

FABRICS

FURNISHINGS

Antique Patterns

17 ANTICO SETIFICIO FIORENTINO
Via della Vigna Nuova 97r
Tel. 28.27.00
Expensive; credit cards accepted

The small Antico Setificio Fiorentino (Antique Florentine Silk Mill) has splendid interior decorating fabrics —silks, velvets, satins, taffetas, damasks, brocades, linens and the borders and fringes to finish them off. If you need at least ten yards, any color or style of fabric can be handmade to order; using methods that first made Florentine silk famous during the Renaissance.

The 550-year-old workshop where these exquisite fabrics are made is located just across the river in the San Frediano section of the Oltrarno. The operation was revived several years ago by Emilio Pucci and other Florentine nobles anxious to keep alive an important element of local history. Today there are 15 skilled silk weavers working on 17th-century hand looms. If you would like to visit the workshop (Via Bartolini 4, telephone 21.38.61), you will be welcomed by director Aldo Marzucchi; but call first for an appointment.

SUSTENANCE

RISTORANTE/TRATTORIA

18 GARGA
Via del Moro 9
Tel. 29.88.98
Moderate; no credit cards accepted

Sharon, a Canadian, and Giuliano, a native of Florence, are the amiable owners of this tiny but noteworthy restaurant. They serve reliably wonderful pasta and other creative dishes. Start with the *scamorza* cheese-anchovy toast appetizer, and continue with delicious fresh *guanciale di spinaci* (spinach-stuffed pasta with Gorgonzola sauce), or *pasta Lorenzo il Magnifico* (pasta with mint and parmesan sauce) or *alla vigliacca* (with its very spicy tomato sauce). Then try tender lamb with pink peppercorns, or filet with tarragon, followed by Sharon's un-Italian, but very delicious cheesecake.

LEATHERGOODS

BAGS & ACCESSORIES

19 SACCARDI
Piazza Goldoni 8/9/10r
Tel. 29.88.33
Moderate; credit cards accepted

Saccardi caters to the Florentines' inclination for classic, high-quality handbags. The tailored, handsomely constructed, finely detailed bags are locally produced and shipped domestically and abroad. The prices are moderate for articles that will last many years and withstand the tides of seasonal fashion. Saccardi is perfect for one-stop shopping, with a practical selection of men's and women's briefcases, shoes and accessories.

FABRICS

FURNISHINGS

Antique Patterns

20 LISIO TESSUTI D'ARTE
Via dei Fossi 45r
Tel. 21.24.30
Expensive; no credit cards accepted

If the magnificent hand-woven damasks and brocades at Lisio's look familiar, it is because you have seen their models in Renaissance frescoes and paintings by Botticelli and Ghirlandaio. Master Lisio rediscovered the tradition of hand-weaving luxury fabrics at the turn of this century, and his rare textiles of antique design are still being produced by hand on ancient wooden looms. A number of more contemporary patterns are also offered. Lisio's exclusive selections have decorated some of the world's most discerning homes. A client may arrive with fabric swatches in hand, hoping to reupholster a priceless antique piece. If Lisio doesn't have the right pattern, no one will, and the firm's craftsmen will gladly make it to order in their workshop/weaving institute in the Tuscan hills outside Florence.

BOOKS

ENGLISH-LANGUAGE

Full Assortment

21 BM BOOKSHOP
Borgo Ognissanti 4r
Tel. 29.45.75
Moderate; no credit cards accepted
Open Sunday

The BM Bookshop is the best and most comprehensive English-language bookstore in Florence. Its impressive collection of over 38,000 titles in both hardcover and paperback deals with culture, history, travel, literature, science, the fine arts, gardening, cooking and crafts. There are children's books and translations of such Italian authors as Dante, Machiavelli, Umberto Eco and Moravia. The shop is home not only to tourists passing through, but to the city's extensive American and English community.

LINENS & LINGERIE

Luxurious Hand Embroidery

22 LORETTA CAPONI ⌂⌂⌂⌂
Borgo Ognissanti 12r
Tel. 21.36.68
Expensive; credit cards accepted

For decades, Loretta Caponi has been famous for her luxury bed and table linens as well as for her exquisite silk lingerie. She has draped the regal dining tables of Europe, and time was when noble daughters could not marry until their delicate trousseaux had arrived from Loretta Caponi.

As a young schoolgirl, Loretta worked furiously at the embroidery she was required to do, in order to have more time for play. Years later, word-of-mouth established her as the *ricami* queen, a perfectionist who brought the fine art of Florentine embroidery beyond its traditionally conservative confines. She believes that, to feel like a beautiful woman, you sometimes have to help nature, and she expresses her philosophy in designs for sexy silk nightgowns and peignoirs, sophisticated bed jackets and baby-doll pajamas. Ideally, these should be worn between her unrivaled

19th-Century European

23 FALLANI BEST

Borgo Ognissanti 15r
Tel. 21.49.86
Expensive; no credit cards accepted

This is one of the best lit and least cluttered of antique stores. Burgundy velvet on the walls and floor forms a theatrical setting to show off the handsome 19th-century European collection. Few women antique dealers in Italy are as respected as Signora Fallani. Her carefully selected paintings, sculptures, furniture and knickknacks conjure up the character of a period that attracts an appreciative foreign following and is her own personal preference.

17th- to 19th-Century Italian

24 PAOLO ROMANO ANTICHITÀ

Borgo Ognissanti 20r
Tel. 29.32.94
Expensive; no credit cards accepted

Big, smiling Paolo Romano represents the third generation of a Florentine family widely known for premier antique dealing. Signor Romano's expertise has been in Italian furniture, paintings and sculpture of the 17th, 18th and 19th centuries. He believes it is important to buy antiques in their country of origin because it gives the acquisition an inextricable flavor.

Signor Romano's grandfather acquired a priceless collection of medieval sculptures and artifacts, which he later donated to the city for a museum near Santo Spirito.

Loretta Caponi inspects her deluxe linens.

crepe-de-Chine bed sheets with delicately embroidered trim. There are also piles of decorative white linen boudoir pillows with dainty lace and tiny embroidery, and table linens that can be embroidered to match your china pattern.

In the bright, sunlit laboratory behind the shop, ten ladies, some of whom have been embroidering for well over half a century, execute Loretta Caponi's intricate designs and fill orders from all over the world. There is little that they cannot do in the custom-order department, although the customer will pay accordingly. Signora Caponi encourages personalized orders. Her favorite comes from an Italian noble family: a collection of bed linens and matching bath towels embroidered to reflect the seasonal changes of flowers and fruits in the garden of their country villa.

SUSTENANCE

RISTORANTE/TRATTORIA

25 SOSTANZA
Via della Porcellana 25r
Tel. 21.26.91
Moderate; no credit cards accepted
Closed Sunday and Saturday dinner

Foreigners go crazy over this old-fashioned workingman's *trattoria,* and so do the Florentines. Everyone is seated together in a small, narrow dining area where it is impossible for the diners not to enter into high-decibel competition with the noisy kitchen in the back. The experience is informal and delightful, as fashion buyers from New York sit elbow to elbow with local bankers. Newcomers and habitués alike usually go for one of two home-cooked specialties on the never-changing menu: the thick and juicy *bistecca alla fiorentina* or the plump chicken breasts that arrive in a casserole of bubbling butter. This is the spot to sample such honest Tuscan fare as *trippa alla fiorentina* or *piccioni arrosti* (roast pigeons). You must save room for dessert—the very best meringue in town or the delicate and tiny wild strawberries in red wine. English-speaking Mario, who has been here for 50 years, is always ready with counsel.

SUSTENANCE

RISTORANTE/TRATTORIA

26 IL CESTELLO DELL'HOTEL EXCELSIOR
Piazza Ognissanti 3
Tel. 29.43.01
Expensive; credit cards accepted
Open 7 days

High dining at Ciga's Hotel Excelsior.

The deluxe, Ciga-managed Excelsior Hotel offers a pleasant terrace restaurant, white-jacketed waiters of great finesse and discretion, a refined menu of both Tuscan and international dishes, and a panorama to end all panoramas. You can eat lightly among a number of innovative salads and nouvelle temptations, such as the *insalata di mare alla viareggina* (mixed fresh seafood). Pastas are light and imaginative, including *quadruccelli alla Caterina* (tiny square noodles with chicken livers), *rigatoncini del cestello* (small macaroni with buttermilk curd, tomato and basil), and especially the small ravioli with truffles flambé. For the main course, there's poached, broiled, grilled and fried fish fresh from the coast and a choice of fine-quality meats roasted or grilled. A royal spread of desserts rivals the view.

LEATHERGOODS

BAGS, SHOES & ACCESSORIES

27 GIOTTI (Bottega Veneta)
Piazza Ognissanti 3-4r
Tel. 29.42.65
Expensive; credit cards accepted

This spacious, modern store is Florence's only Bottega Veneta franchise and claims to have the biggest collection in Italy of the prestigious line of handsome leathergoods. The classic woven-leather shoulder bags are joined by new seasonal models in leather of deep, rich colors. Shoes come in normal and narrow widths. The selection of beautiful Bottega luggage is the most extensive around, and the belts, wallets and other small items make lovely gifts.

Giotti also offers its own line of sophisticated men's and women's leather clothing and does excellent quality custom leather work.

See Venice listing (page 469) for Bottega Veneta's flagship store.

ANTIQUES

Art Nouveau

28 PIERO BETTI GALLERIA
Borgo Ognissanti 46r
Tel. 28.77.25
Expensive; no credit cards accepted

The turn-of-the-century style called "Liberty" in Italian is perhaps at its finest in its French incarnation, art nouveau. That Piero Betti thinks so is obvious in this specialty antique shop where, apart from the Italian glasswork, almost everything is French. The store is laid out as if it were a belle-époque home, with beautiful, curvilinear art-nouveau objects displayed in an entrance, living room and study.

SUSTENANCE

RISTORANTE/TRATTORIA

29 BELLE DONNE
Via delle Belle Donne 16
Tel. 26.26.09
Moderate; no credit cards accepted
Closed Saturday and Sunday

It's typical of the understated character of this small, informal *trattoria* that there's no sign outside. The blackboard menu offers an opportunity to eat lightly, mixing and matching from dishes such as salads of mixed greens with fresh mozzarella, chestnut soup, pasta sauced with seasonal vegetables, perfectly cooked salmon with fresh olive-oil mayonnaise, or beans with scampi. The fresh fruit tarts for dessert are perfection, joined by chestnut pudding, fruit bavarians or, if you can handle it, the best chocolate cake in town. It's crowded at lunch, usually with regulars from the fashion business, so try and arrive before the 1 P.M. crunch.

BOOKS

ART & ESOTERICA

30 FRANCO MARIA RICCI
Via delle Belle Donne 41r
Tel. 28.33.12
Expensive; credit cards accepted

The elite publisher of exquisite tomes that couple the sacred with the profane, Franco Maria Ricci has added a new dimension to the Italian publishing scene. Books with beautiful color plates and rich handmade papers are shown in an appropriately luxurious setting. See Milan listing (page 183).

LEATHERGOODS

BAGS, FINE LUGGAGE & ACCESSORIES

Handcrafted Elegance

31 CELLERINI
Via del Sole 37r
Tel. 28.25.33
Expensive; credit cards accepted

Master artisan Silvano Cellerini and wife.

To those in the know, Silvano Cellerini is one of the finest leather craftsmen in Florence, a city where masters come with the territory. Each article in his elegant store is handmade and double-stitched in the workshop above, where Signor Cellerini and his wife have been working leather with meticulous care for over 30 years. The pride of their production is bags and suitcases, and they carry a limited selection of men's and women's shoes and belts as well. Cellerini's versatility is indicated by the 2500 different models of handbags he has designed and created to date (many still sported by wealthy Americans and European blue bloods). There is also a collection of classic Hermès look-alikes. A new addition to Cellerini's line of exquisite leather luggage is an all-leather baby carrier —a Rolls-Royce of infant travel.

Cellerini's products are made from the world's finest skins: French reptile, crocodile from Singapore, Italian and German calfskin, and pigskin from England. All the handbags are fully lined in leather, and handsome solid-brass buckles are made to Cellerini's own design by a fellow artisan. For such top-of-the-line quality, Cellerini's prices, while not cheap, are unbeatable.

PHARMACY & HERB SHOP
Natural Remedies

32 L'OFFICINA PROFUMO-
FARMACEUTICA DI SANTA
MARIA NOVELLA
Via della Scala 16
Tel. 21.62.76
Moderate; no credit cards accepted

This sanctum sanctorum is worth a visit just to experience the once-hallowed atmosphere and admire the beautifully restored heavy wood paneling and vaulted frescoed ceilings in what was formerly the chapel of a Renaissance monastery. Once inside, you'll swoon from the wonderful aroma of the potpourri for which the *farmacia* is famous. Although it is not reflected in its name, the Officina is also an *erboristeria* (see page 100) that still produces natural remedies from formulas dating back to the 14th century. Among the more peculiar is *crema all'olio di lumaca* (cream of snail's oil), for treating dry skin, while *latte vergine* (virgin milk) clears up acne and freckles. *Pomata di vete d'albero* (pomade of new tree shoots) is said to prevent baldness, and there are shampoos for every type of hair and scalp in existence.

People come from all over the world to stock up on such items as anti-hysteriums (smelling salts once used as anti-plague bodyrubs), and on digestive liqueurs such as Liquore Medici, said to have kept everyone in the Renaissance courts smiling. Also displayed in the ancient oak cabinets are fragrances made from many blossoms, from jasmine to ylang-ylang, as well as one scent reminiscent of freshly cut hay, or *fieno.* The pomegranate soap is for delicate skin, and the mint soap keeps mosquitos at bay. That potent potpourri is made from ten different herbs, berries and dried flowers, aged in terra-cotta containers and then sold in satin sachets or jars. Fragrances for the room come in non-flammable rings to be placed on top of light bulbs, where they suffuse an aroma of stephanotis, sandalwood or verbena.

SUSTENANCE

GELATERIA

33 GELATERIA BANCHI
Via dei Banchi 14r
Tel. 21.37.76
Inexpensive; no credit cards accepted
Closed Sunday

Two blocks from Santa Maria Novella is this no-frills, no-pretensions neighborhood *gelateria,* which produces its own rich ice cream daily. Banchi's is also the only place in Florence that makes real *granite,* shaved ice drowned in dense coffee or fresh fruit juices (strawberry, orange, grapefruit, blueberry and lemon). "Eaten" with a straw, the concoction is especially refreshing in summertime. There are a few round, marble-topped tables where you can put down your shopping bags, but no table service as such.

A creamy gelato *or* granita *break at Banchi's.*

PERFUME & COSMETICS

Self-Service

34 PROFUMERIA ALICE
Piazza dell'Unità Italiana 13r
(entrance on Via dei Panzani)
Tel. 21.45.07
Moderate; credit cards accepted
Open during lunch

This perfume and cosmetics store scores three major points with traveling shoppers: for its wide selection of European brand-name cosmetics and fragrances for both men and women; for being open during lunch; and, best of all, for its self-service setup. You needn't know in advance what you want or if you want anything at all. You can browse to your heart's content among the beautifully packaged Italian shampoos, bath toiletries, hair-grooming accessories and cosmetics. Fragrance testers are on display to let you sample the new and exotic.

FASHION

MEN'S

Contemporary Sweaters

35 MARCO 2
Via Panzani 33r
Tel. 21.02.05
Moderate; credit cards accepted
Open during lunch

Marco's carries a good selection of men's sportswear, but bulky Italian knit sweaters are its chief attraction. There are pullovers, some with leather or suede finishings, in handsome color combinations and patterns. During the summer months, the sweaters are not always on display, so ask to see them.

THE ERBORISTERIA

Today, every street or neighborhood has an *erboristeria,* as it has a stationer or fruit vendor. The history of these shops goes back to the darkest period of the Middle Ages. Medicinal herbs had always been recognized for their curative powers. During the Middle Ages hygienic conditions were particularly abominable and plagues and epidemics ran rampant. A bewildered populace looked to the abbeys and monasteries for potions and lotions, tinctures and pomades to cure malfunctions of the body often believed to be punishments from God, and medieval monks grew in reputation for their expertise in herbal medicine.

Thriving monasteries were not only the site of spiritual enlightenment but also centers for advanced studies of science, philosophy and the arts. Each monastic community had an obligatory herbal or botanical garden and a resident alchemist. It was not surprising that the common folk came to regard these earthly vicars of Christ almost as divine saviors in times of desperate illness or imminent death.

The vast majority of these natural vegetable- and mineral-based remedies were highly effective in treating simple maladies, and there was little they did not profess to cure, from *mal di luna* (a condition brought about by a full moon) to swollen gums. Today's revival of holistic medicine and organic self-cures has reconfirmed the timeless appeal of these natural medicines. They are widely used for such mundane contemporary ailments as indigestion, insomnia and dandruff.

Erboristerie and *farmacie* were once one and the same store. They have long since gone their separate ways, showing little or no sign of reconciliation. Present-day *erboristerie* still retain a somewhat hallowed atmosphere, often keeping the centuries-old décor of wooden apothecary cabinets housing pestles, scales, glass decanters of colorful essences, and large porcelain jars of dried herbs. Herbal liqueurs are also displayed; once distilled under the comforting pretense that they had medicinal powers, they kept many a monk warm during damp and arduous winters. They are still being brewed today, often in these same medieval cloisters by the remnants of monastic communities. Honeys from a variety of blossoms abound, too, as do endless mixtures of *tisane* (teas) that are guaranteed to cure love pangs, sluggishness and the blues.

MEN'S ACCESSORIES

Ties

36 LEONARDO
Via Panzani 28r
Tel. 21.21.53
Moderate; credit cards accepted

Ties, ties, ties—over 2000 of them in pure silk or 100-percent fine wool, all tastefully designed by Florentine Leonardo Poldi-Allai and produced in his workshop nearby. A few vari-colored women's silk scarves are included in this well-stocked specialty shop, the only place in Florence where its Leonardo label is sold. Leonardo designs are available at prestigious retail outlets in the United States, but at twice the price.

MEN'S & WOMEN'S

Discount Bargains

37 BELTRAMI (Discount Outlet)
Via Panzani 1–11r
Tel. 21.26.61
Moderate; credit cards accepted

The discount outlet is a rather new concept to the Italians, so this one is a real find for those who don't mind a bargain-basement atmosphere. Tables are stacked high with discontinued or overstocked models of the prestigious Beltrami line of shoes and boots for men and women (see page 53), at a fraction of what they'd cost in more elegant surroundings. There is an erratic selection of Beltrami bags and also leather or suede coordinates at equally reduced prices.

A timeless corner and a moment's reflection.

HOUSEWARES

Complete Range

38 DINO BARTOLINI
Via dei Servi 30r
Tel. 21.18.95
Inexpensive to moderate; no credit cards
        accepted

Signor Bartolini runs a traditional Florentine housewares store *(casa-linghi)* with no pretensions to high design or trendiness. Instead, you'll find a huge, functional store stocked with every household and kitchen necessity imaginable. There are espresso coffee makers, in every size, cookware, cutlery, flatware, glassware, fine china and porcelain, pasta makers, and endless other gadgets and gizmos. Every item is conveniently displayed, a welcome benefit if your Italian is not up to par or if you stop in just to see the ingenious equipment Italian housewives use to whip up those fabulous meals.

FASHION

WOMEN'S

Designer Boutique

39 EMILIO PUCCI
Palazzo Pucci
Via dei Pucci 6r
Tel. 28.30.61
Expensive; credit cards accepted

This stately Renaissance palazzo has belonged to the family of designer Emilio Pucci for centuries. On the ground floor as you enter is a small boutique of accessories. It acts as an introduction to the elegant boutique upstairs. Between the two of them, a woman can dress in colorful Pucci silks from head to toe. Pucci's trademark turquoise or pink silk *foulard* (scarf) in floral or geometric patterns is a classic accessory that will never age, for his style does not change drastically with the seasons. The clear colors and patterns flow over into his entire collection—blouses, dresses, *palazzo* pajamas, bathing suits, bags, wallets and small gift items. A highlight remains the simple and elegant silk jersey dress that is ideal for traveling and continues to fill out the wardrobes of Europe's well-to-do ladies. All silks are designed by and made exclusively for Pucci in the celebrated silk factories of Como; there are silk crepes, chiffons, twills and jerseys. Fresh summer cottons are also available.

　　The Pucci wine store is just around the corner at Via Ricasoli 20. Fine red, white and rosé wines, elegantly packaged, come from the Chianti area estate first owned by the Pucci family in the 13th century. You can also reach the accessories boutique from the Via Ricasoli entrance.

GIFTS

HOME ACCESSORIES

Focus on Design

40 VICE VERSA
Via Ricasoli 53r
Tel. 29.82.81
Moderate; credit cards accepted
Open during lunch

The accent here is on modern objects for the home with clean, "high" design as well as with a pinch of the whimsical. Attractive displays feature Officina Alessi, a prestigious, hard-to-find collection of stainless steel and silver-plated tea and coffee services created by noted architects and manufactured under the premier Alessi name. There are also pens by Paraphernalia; wooden toys and puzzles; hand-painted ceramic Aquilone figurines; postmodern table clocks sold in signed, limited editions; and the amusing Avant de Dormir tote bags—peculiar, kitschy objects floating in water sealed into the bags' clear plastic linings.

GIFTS

NOVELTIES

Self-Service

41 CALAMAI
Via Cavour (corner of Via degli Alfani)
Tel. 21.44.52
Inexpensive; credit cards accepted
Open during lunch

Five colorful Calamai shops spruce up Florence's shopping scene, but this one has the widest selection of merchandise. It's a cross between an upbeat stationery or party-goods store and an Italian five-and-dime.

EMILIO PUCCI

His address is easy to remember: Marchese Emilio Pucci, Palazzo Pucci, Via dei Pucci. And his profile is unforgettable, that of a proud Florentine *condottiere*, or military lord. He is, indeed, a Renaissance man, a member of one of Florence's oldest merchant and banking families who had a brilliant career as an Air Force officer before becoming a designer. Since then, his creativity and passion for color have altered the nature of Italian fashion, and indeed of the international scene.

Pucci came to the fashion limelight almost by accident. During a 1947 ski trip, a *Harper's Bazaar* photographer was taken by his orig-

Marchese Pucci in Renaissance costume.

inal ski apparel, which she later discovered he had designed himself. He was soon designing sportswear, a field until then neglected by European couturiers, in colorful interpretations.

He made Pucci prints the rage of the 1950s and silk "palazzo" pajamas the rage of the 1960s. He offered women the "total look," a coordinated wardrobe that included hats, head scarves and ball gowns, as well as the indispensable little silk dress that every well-heeled woman bought in a range of delicious patterns. His now-classic turquoise-and-blue, pink-and-purple combinations brightened the world's best parties and resorts. He designed the uniforms for the flight attendants of a number of airlines and for Florence's traffic policewomen. He even designed the banner that was brought to the moon by the Apollo 15 crew.

Pucci's silks are produced exclusively for him in the celebrated Como mills. He spends much of his time in his stately palazzo, site of his flagship boutique and offices. But he seems most at ease every June when he slips into his elaborate velvet Renaissance costume and rides his spirited white horse in the historical pageant, *Calcio in Costume* (Soccer in Costume).

Outdoor cafés offer theater-in-the-round.

The ground floor has big boxes and bins of amusing stationery, school supplies and party items that make inexpensive gifts for children and teenagers. Downstairs, plastic is king: you'll find a large housewares section with well-designed, inexpensive accessories in endless colors for both kitchen and bath.

FABRICS
TRIMMINGS

42 PASSAMANERIA TOSCANA
Piazza San Lorenzo 12r
Tel. 21.46.70
Moderate; credit cards accepted

The *passamaneria* (from the French *passamanerie*) is a singular European institution specializing in trimmings for home furnishing and other accessories: braids, cording, tassels, fringes, and borders of all kinds, as well as doilies, plain and embroidered curtain material, pillows, even tapestries. The Passamaneria Toscana has a huge selection of these things, the best in Florence. Strangely enough, Americans buy a terrific number of cord tassels. In Europe these colorful decorations are tied onto the keys of free-standing armoires, but Americans (happy owners of door-knobbed closets) have created their own ingenious uses for them, including Christmas-tree ornamentation.

SUSTENANCE
RISTORANTE/TRATTORIA

43 GOZZI
Piazza San Lorenzo 8r
No telephone
Inexpensive; no credit cards accepted
Closed Sunday

Smack in the middle of the bustling outdoor San Lorenzo Market is this typical neighborhood workingman's *trattoria*. Décor is old-fashioned, and service at the small wooden tables is fast and friendly. All the simple, traditional Tuscan dishes are here, including thick and wonderful homemade minestrone, followed by roast veal and pork. Being just across the street from the Mercato Centrale guarantees fresh ingredients. This is a lively and interesting show, and you can wash it all down with a decent house *vino rosso.*

SHOES
MEN'S & WOMEN'S
Trendy & Very Affordable

44 VALENTINA
Via Nazionale 98r
Tel. 28.49.80
Inexpensive; credit cards accepted
Open during lunch

If you want to pick up some trendy, casual shoes and boots that will last the season, Valentina is a centrally located stop that offers low-priced selections. It does not carry well-known names and the quality is average, but Valentina has a knack for picking good up-to-the-minute styles of flats and heels in colorful assortments from a number of small Italian manufacturers.

SPORTS GEAR

BICYCLES

Custom-Order Racing Bikes

45 GIUSEPPE BIANCHI
Via Nazionale 130r
Tel. 21.69.91
Moderate; no credit cards accepted

Florence's oldest and largest bicycle manufacturer and outfitter was founded over 100 years ago by Giuseppe Bianchi, a cycling champion. Bianchi's specialty is custom-order racing bikes, using the world-renowned gear assemblies of Campagnolo. Its own Giuseppe Bianchi line of travel and touring bikes is joined by stock models from Cinelli, Bottechia, Colnaga and Scapi. There are children's bikes as well. The store will not ship, however, and advises you to take your bike (unassembled) with you. Salespeople are all well-seasoned cyclists and can answer your every question. If you forgo the bike, settle for such Italian biking accoutrements as bags, baskets, racing sweaters, caps or shoes.

COLLECTIBLES

FANS

Restoration & Framing

46 ARTE CORNICI
Via Guelfa 88r
Tel. 49.94.52
Moderate; credit cards accepted

This may be the only shop of its kind in Italy. Owners Caterina Carola and her husband specialize in restoring and mending antique fans and creating equally beautiful frames in which to display them. They work with a fastidious care born of their passion

A stern look from the statue of Neptune.

for these delicate fashion accessories of a luxurious past. The couple use the same traditional methods which during the Renaissance called upon the talents of many specialized fan artisans.

Signora Carola's private collection of extraordinary fans is on display, and if you show enough enthusiastic appreciation, she may with some reluctance sell you one.

SUSTENANCE

RISTORANTE/TRATTORIA

47 CENTRO VEGETARIANO FIORENTINO
Via delle Ruote 30r
Tel. 47.50.30
Moderate; no credit cards accepted
Closed Monday and Saturday

This is one of the very few strictly vegetarian restaurants in town. It's perfect for when you can't look another *bistecca alla fiorentina* in the face. The menu follows the season of fresh vegetables, with interesting soufflés and casseroles, quiche-type pies, salads and fresh or seasoned cheeses. The atmosphere is warm and informal. When you've made your selection from a large blackboard, you pay at the cash register and bring your receipt to the kitchen to pick up your own dinner.

Santa Croce

*T*he residential neighborhood of Santa Croce spreads east of the Centro Storico from the busy Via Proconsolo. You'll want to visit the splendid 13th-century church of Santa Croce, the sole reason that tourism has ever managed to penetrate this area. Santa Croce is a kind of Florentine Pantheon, where Michelangelo, Galileo and other Italian greats are buried. Although close to the center of town, the Santa Croce area seems refreshingly far from the madding crowd; even though shopping is limited, it is pleasant to stroll here among small neighborhood stores and artisans' boutiques. Fine *trattorie,* elegant restaurants and characteristic bars and cafés are surprisingly abundant.

The contrast between Santa Croce and the Centro Storico is dramatic. You'll leave elegance behind for the working-class air of an authentic neighborhood that must be walked at leisure to be appreciated. Amble down Via dei Neri, crowded with grocery stores and pastry shops. Search out Piazza San Piero, a small and colorful morning marketplace that is the perfect backdrop for a spontaneous production of opera in the streets. Just beyond, the *volta* (archway) protects a flower vendor, a fruit-and-vegetable stand, and a *friggitoria* that sells deep-fried everything. Once all farmland outside the city walls, during the Renaissance this area developed into a messy suburb where the wool- and silk-dyeing business was located—out of town so that the acrid smell of the chemical dyes might not offend any upper-class noses. It still seems a bit detached; you'll roam the winding back streets where the Roman amphitheater once stood, and where Michelangelo played as a child, and feel that you've discovered another Florence.

Commercial rents in this area are generally lower, allowing a growing community of young designers and boutique owners to set up business and making shopping affordable and adventuresome. There's a sense of emerging creativity whose originality makes up for an occasional compromise in quality. Many of these small operations come and go with the seasons, so you'll do best just to walk the neighborhood, happening upon the modest new shop of a budding designer or artisan.

If you prefer a respite from shopping, pull up a park bench in the shady Piazza Massimo d'Azeglio, just beyond the early-19th-century

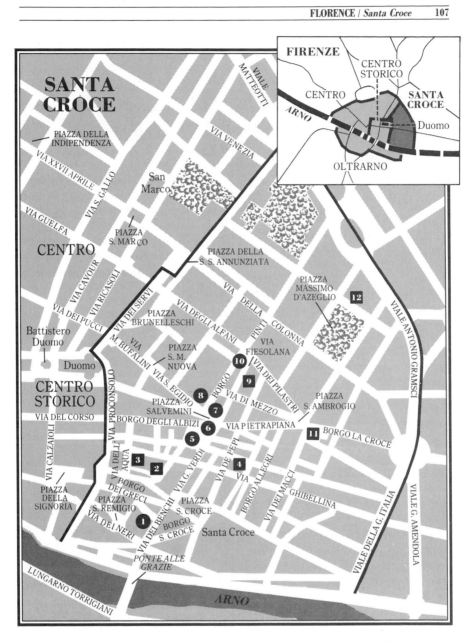

FIRENZE

CENTRO
STORICO

CENTRO

SANTA
CROCE

ARNO

Duomo

OLTRARNO

SANTA
CROCE

PIAZZA DELLA
INDIPENDENZA

VIA XXVII APRILE

VIA S. GALLO

VIA GUELFA

San
Marco

VIA VENEZIA

VIALE MATTEOTTI

PIAZZA
S. MARCO

CENTRO

PIAZZA DELLA
S. S. ANNUNZIATA

VIA CAVOUR

VIA RICASOLI

VIA DEI PUCCI

VIA DEI SERVI

VIA DELLA COLONNA

PIAZZA
MASSIMO
D'AZEGLIO

12

VIA DELLA PINTI

VIALE ANTONIO GRAMSCI

Battistero
Duomo

PIAZZA
BRUNELLESCHI

VIA DEGLI ALFANI

VIA
M. BUFALINI

PIAZZA
S. M.
NUOVA

VIA
FIESOLANA

Duomo

VIA S. EGIDIO

BORGO

10

9

VIA DEI PILASTRI

CENTRO
STORICO

8

VIA DI MEZZO

PIAZZA
S. AMBROGIO

VIA DEL CORSO

PIAZZA
SALVEMINI

7

BORGO DEGLI ALBIZI

6

VIA PIETRAPIANA

11

BORGO LA CROCE

VIA PROCONSOLO

5

VIA CALZAIOLI

3

2

VIA DELL'
AQUA

VIA DE' PEPI

4

VIA

BORGO ALLEGRI

VIA DEI MACCI

GHIBELLINA

VIALE DELLA G. ITALIA

VIALE G. AMENDOLA

PIAZZA
DELLA
SIGNORIA

BORGO
DEI GRECI

PIAZZA
S. REMIGIO

PIAZZA
S. CROCE

VIA G. VERDI

VIA DEI NERI

1

VIA DEI BENCHI

BORGO
S. CROCE

Santa Croce

PONTE ALLE
GRAZIE

LUNGARNO TORRIGIANI

ARNO

Sephardic synagogue. It is the only green square in a city whose broad,
open piazzas have otherwise been turned into parking lots. Treat yourself
to a leisurely picnic—a loaf of fresh bread hot from a nearby *forno* and
some Tuscan *pecorino* cheese that you've picked up at the morning fruit-
and-vegetable market in the Piazza Sant'Ambrogio—and recharge your
energies for an afternoon spree.

CERAMICS
Made in Florence

1 MIGLIORI
Via dei Benci 39
Tel. 28.36.81
Moderate; no credit cards accepted

This well-stocked store features ceramics mostly from Florence and the Tuscan region, with a smattering of Umbrian pieces. There are myriad gift ideas for collectors: Della Robbia-style decorative plates, terra-cotta masks of the four seasons, oil and vinegar sets, artichoke dishes, tureens, pots, vases and much more. If you worry about the frailness of these items, Migliori can pack them, and they'll arrive safely whether with you or by mail.

SUSTENANCE
GELATERIA

2 VIVOLI
Via Isola delle Stinche 7r
Tel. 29.23.34
Inexpensive; no credit cards accepted
Closed Monday

Piero Vivoli's claims are twofold: not only is his ice cream the best in the world, but also he can make ice cream from anything. Buckets of fresh strawberries and cases of melons and bananas go into the 1000 quarts of ice cream he dishes out daily in over two dozen flavors. Six members of his family, the third generation in the business, work in the recently updated *gelateria*, where regular *gelati* team up with *semifreddi*, cold confections made with whipped cream instead of milk and whipped by hand.

SUSTENANCE
RISTORANTE/TRATTORIA
Late-Night

3 AQUA AL DUE
Via dell'Aqua 2
Tel. 28.41.70
Moderate; no credit cards accepted
Closed Monday

Even with reservations you may have to wait, but without them you'll be turned away, as this is one of the busiest eateries in town. The *secondo piatto* (entrée) is indeed secondary here, the prime reason for coming being the delicious sampling of first-course pasta dishes called an *assaggio di primi*. Pasta with different cheese, cauliflower, eggplant and tomato sauces will arrive at your table one at a time, and must be shared by two or more people. In the event that there's still room for dessert, a similar sampling (*assaggio di dolci*) lets you taste a number of fruit tortes, trifles, cakes, and other sweets made on the premises. There are English-speaking waitresses and a young, informal crowd of Florentine denizens.

SUSTENANCE
RISTORANTE/TRATTORIA

4 ENOTECA PINCHIORRI
Via Ghibellina 87
Tel. 24.27.57
Very expensive; credit cards accepted
Closed Sunday, and Monday lunch

Florence's most celebrated restaurant offers you a theatrical evening of *nouvelle gastronomie* and a wine cellar stocked with over 70,000 bottles of Italy's and France's finest wines. In both the beautifully appointed open-air courtyard of this 15th-century palazzo and the elegant inside dining room, owner and consummate sommelier Giorgio Pinchiorri has created a serene environment of crystal, candlelight and exotic flowers. The sophisticated cuisine of his genial wife Annie Feolde reflects her French origin. Portions tend to be small and light; homemade raviolis come in pairs, and tender, boned lamb chops are the size of silver dollars. Among her specialties are such nostalgically traditional dishes as broad *pappardelle* noodles with a savory duck sauce. To experience it all, try the recommended *menu di degustazione*, which consists of eight courses with sorbet entremets.

BOOKS

ART

5 SALIMBENI
Via Matteo Palmieri 14–16r
Tel. 29.20.84
Moderate to expensive; no credit cards
    accepted

For half a century Salimbeni has been one of the largest and best-stocked art bookstores in Florence. Printed predominantly in Italian, beautiful hardbound color-photography books on theater, architecture and history crowd the tables and shelves. The sales help is understandably particular about how you handle the expensive volumes on medieval abbeys, for example, while perusing their rich color plates. Salimbeni, a small though prestigious publisher for the last 20 years, offers titles concerned with the history and culture of Italy, often specifically of Tuscany.

CERAMICS

6 AL TEGAME
Piazza Salvemini 7
Tel. 24.80.568
Moderate; credit cards accepted

There's a country-store air about Al Tegame that evokes the proper setting for its rustic wares. Simple but beautiful hand-painted designs decorate ceramics from such notable regions as Puglia, Emilia Romagna (Faenza) and various parts of Tuscany. In the colorful profusion of its table settings, planters, water pitchers, wall plates, and mugs, you should be able to find the perfect gift. Reliable shipping for these fragile objects is available.

MASKS

WORKSHOP/STUDIO

7 I MASCHERERI
Borgo Pinti 18r
Tel. 21.38.23
Moderate; credit cards accepted

Traditional and modern masks at I Maschereri.

You may have no immediate plans to attend Carnival in Venice, but these beautiful handmade masks of papier-mâché are commonly used as dramatic wall ornaments. You'll recognize the theatrical masks of traditional 16th-century *commedia dell'arte* characters like Arlecchino (Harlequin) and Pulcinella (Punch), and there's even a mask of Michelangelo's David. But the main interest of the two young artisans who have opened this workshop is in their ever-expanding line of original masks, including colorful representations of the sun and the moon and fantastic creatures that spring from their own imaginations. They also make special masks on request for theatrical groups or individuals. The shop's name, I Maschereri, refers to the Renaissance guild of mask makers whose dying art has been reinvigorated by Cristini Bini and Sandro Becucci.

CERAMICS

8 SBIGOLI TERRECOTTE
Via Sant'Egidio 4r
Tel. 24.79.713
Moderate; credit cards accepted

The artistry of Italian earthenware is here in all its shapes, sizes and glory.

Rustic terra cotta and ceramicware at Sbigoli.

The largest, oversized plant holder gets the same hand-painted attention as the smallest demitasse. Oven-proof terra-cotta casseroles and stockpots join a more decorative range of pottery representing various Italian designs, the Tuscan yellow-bird motif being the most prominent. Many of the items are made by the store's owner in a workshop around the corner. Your luggage may accommodate a rustic honey pot or water jug, but if you indulge in an entire table setting or tea set, the store provides safe and reliable shipping.

SUSTENANCE

RISTORANTE/TRATTORIA

9 DA NOI
Via Fiesolana 40r
Tel. 24.29.17
Expensive; no credit cards accepted
Closed Sunday and Monday

A warm and friendly atmosphere pervades this restaurant, which undoubtedly serves the most creative cooking in Florence. The attentive, Swedish-born Sabrina offers complementary appetizers to customers at the six small tables as they wait for their first course. Her congenial husband Bruno is responsible for the imaginative, constantly changing menu. You might find, for example, shrimp-stuffed ravioli in sweet bell-pepper sauce, a delicate herb *risotto*, light crêpes stuffed with eggplant, warm pigeon salad, *salmone al curry* and *scampi al cognac*. Sabrina knowledgably helps you choose a fine wine. Leave room for a last round of pleasure—the best desserts in Florence, made on the premises and never overly sweet.

BOOKS

ENGLISH-LANGUAGE PAPERBACKS

10 PAPERBACK EXCHANGE
Via Fiesolana 31r
Tel. 24.78.154
Inexpensive; no credit cards accepted

This is the largest and most reasonably priced selection of English-language paperbacks in Florence. The Exchange will pay you for any used paperback books you'd like to unload, or will credit the amount toward any purchase from its wide selection of secondhand books on Florence and Italy as well as classics, children's books and current bestsellers. Although its prime concern is to supply you with interesting reading material during your Italian sojourn, the Paperback Exchange also sidelines as an unofficial community center for English-speaking tourists and permanent residents.

SUSTENANCE

RISTORANTE/TRATTORIA

11 IL CIBREO
Via dei Macci 118r
Tel. 67.73.94
Moderate to expensive; credit cards
    accepted
Closed Sunday and Monday

A charming, newly redecorated setting is the showcase for Tuscan cuisine as reinvented by the young Florentine Fabio Picchi and his wife Benedetta. There is no pasta selection for the first course, just an interesting mixture of the traditional and the creative. Begin your memorable meal with the excellent mushroom or pepper soup or the exceptionally fresh buffalo-milk mozzarella. The choice of seconds is large and difficult: light ricotta or vegetable *sformati* (crustless flans), tripe and chickpea salad (a regional specialty), paper-thin *carpaccio* with arugula sauce, and boned and stuffed sliced duck make up a menu simple enough for a pauper and delicious enough for a prince. This elegant *trattoria* offers a fine selection of red Chianti wines and an artistic display of delicious desserts.

SUSTENANCE

RISTORANTE/TRATTORIA

12 RELAIS LE JARDIN DELL'HOTEL
    REGENCY
Piazza Massimo d'Azeglio 5
Tel. 58.76.55
Expensive; credit cards accepted
Closed Sunday

If you're not blessed with the chance to stay in this elegant hotel, a dinner here can be an equally special event. Unlike most hotel restaurants in Italy, this paneled dining room, which opens onto a terrace overlooking a small garden, is worth the visit. There's fresh and delicate homemade pasta for starters—often the *ravioli maremma* (with olives and a meat sauce) or one with a shrimp sauce. The *tagliatelle Medici* is made with an unusually interesting sausage-and-cognac sauce. The carefully planned menus follow the seasons' whims, as do the excellent *risotto* dishes. Entrées include fresh fish and perfectly prepared meats, from filet mignon to pheasant and lamb. The small menu is accompanied by a sophisticated wine list and faultless service.

Life all'italiana *in a Santa Croce square.*

SUSTENANCE
RISTORANTE/TRATTORIA
Late-Night

13 CAFFÈ CONCERTO
Lungarno Cristoforo Colombo 7 (off map)
Tel. 67.73.77
Expensive; credit cards accepted
Closed Sunday; open till 2:00 A.M.

You won't be able to eat this well, this late, anywhere else in Florence. Even at a conventional hour, dinner here is a delightful and elegant affair in a spacious, cosmopolitan setting. There are some Tuscan standbys, but the real star is creative cuisine, with interesting meat and fish dishes that change every month, and careful attention to vegetables generally neglected in the regional cooking. Delicious *risotto* is made with asparagus or pumpkin squash, following the daily market's offerings. Fresh pastas may include *gnocchi* with a nut-flavored pesto sauce or salmon-filled

ravioli with a shrimp-butter sauce. You might find a delicious thyme-flavored rack of lamb or the quintessential Tuscan *bistecca alla fiorentina.* In summer, you can dine outside by the river if you don't mind the mosquitos.

SUSTENANCE
RISTORANTE/TRATTORIA
Taxi Away

14 LA CAPANNINA DI SANTE
Piazza Ravenna at Ponte de Verrazzano
 (off map)
Tel. 68.83.45
Expensive; credit cards accepted
Closed Sunday

It's worth the short cab ride to this "little shack" that serves the best fish in Florence. Situated beside the river, La Capannina offers you outdoor dining, with a menu that changes according to the daily fish market: tender shrimp and squid, octopus salad, clams, mussels and more. You can enjoy a sampling of the day's best by ordering the *antipasto al mare.* Pasta is served with lobster or salmon sauce, or try the *spaghetti di Sante* with a mixture of shellfish, or the *risotto nero*, a delicate rice dish made with the black ink of squid. This can be followed by elegantly baked or grilled fish; if you're inclined toward meat, it's best to go elsewhere. Almost all the seafood is fresh and from local waters; the few choices that are not will be brought to your attention, or noted as *surgelato* (frozen) on the menu. Sante Collesano, your charming Sicilian host, brings his culinary expertise and love for fish to a carnivorous city hungry for a change of pace.

Oltrarno

*M*ore than just a river separates the north side of the city (*Arno di quà,* or "over here") from the south-side Oltrarno area (*Arno di là,* or "over there"). In addition to being a residential neighborhood for both the working class and some of the oldest and wealthiest Florentine families, the Oltrarno has for centuries been home to the city's artisans. Only in the 14th century did the massive city walls of fortification expand to embrace this peripheral suburb as part of the city. But it has always remained distinctive in character, not unlike the Latin Quarters of the world. The rest of Florence looks upon it as a city within a city, and that's the way the residents of the Oltrarno like it.

The Germans spared the Ponte Vecchio, but they leveled the medieval towers and historic neighborhoods on either side of the bridge to block the arrival of the Allied forces. You'll notice that much of the commercial, store-lined Via Guicciardini and Borgo San Jacopo is post-World War II, and not particularly aesthetic, in architecture.

Shopping along the Via Guicciardini will lead you to the Palazzo Pitti, first made home to the Grand Dukes of Tuscany by Cosimo I, thereby making the Oltrarno the most fashionable address in Florence in the 16th century. A need to adorn the dukes' cavernous and rambling chambers and answer their extravagant whims gave rise to a network of workshops, wood-carvers, and silver- and goldsmiths who sprang up in the narrow back streets behind the Pitti and near the Santo Spirito area. Someone had to produce the intricately embroidered curtains, the table settings for hundreds, the mile-long murals and silk tapestries to cover the bare walls. The Medici and their patrician neighbors are now long gone, but artisans are still here chiseling and carving away, carrying on skills and crafts elsewhere lost with time. The Oltrarno is to silver, bronze and pewter what the *Arno di quà* is to gold.

The neighborhood around the Piazza Santo Spirito is the heart of the Oltrarno. The unfinished façade of Brunelleschi's 15th-century church shades a small and popular piazza lined with outdoor cafés and ice-cream bars. Each morning, a busy market occupies the piazza when farmers truck in their tomatoes, watermelons and bunches of flowers; in the

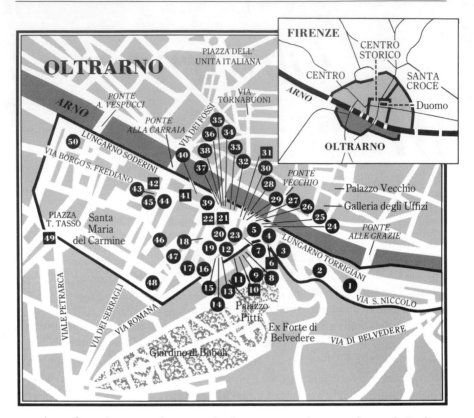

evening the piazza unfortunately becomes rather seedy and is best avoided.

The Via Maggio, from *majus* (wide), is still the Oltrarno's widest and most exclusive street, lined with somber palazzos of the grand-ducal period whose family crests hang over the entrance. It is Antiquities Row, though perhaps more a dealer's haunt than the Via dei Fossi area in the Centro. Nonetheless, discerning clients can find exquisite objects here.

Between the area's artisanal treasures and the exclusive antique stores, you can also find a growing range of boutiques for clothing and accessories.

BOOKS

ART

1 CENTRO DI
Piazza dei Mozzi 1
Tel. 21.32.12
Moderate; credit cards accepted

Centro di Documentazione Internazionale is one of the most serious art bookshops and publishers in Italy, although you'd never guess it from its humble location in a clean, whitewashed basement. The Center prides itself on the many fine catalogues it prints for major European art exhibitions, as well as on its exhaustive collection of books on art, architecture and cultural subjects. Almost half the works are in languages other than Italian; all are systematically grouped for easy browsing.

GIFTS

STATIONERY & ACCESSORIES

Marbleized Papers

2 IL TORCHIO
Via dei Bardi 17
Tel. 29.82.62
Moderate; no credit cards accepted

The name of this small, plain workshop translates as "The Printing Press." Every item for sale is covered with colorful marbleized papers. There are blank books of all sizes and coordinated desk sets that you can mix and match yourself from blotters, pencil and letter holders, and frames. The prices are so reasonable and the products so lovely, it's a great place to find dozens of little gifts that don't call for heavy expenditures.

HOME

TABLEWARE & ACCESSORIES

White Porcelain

3 LA PORCELLANA BIANCA
Via dei Bardi 53r
Tel. 21.18.93
Moderate; no credit cards accepted

You can roam about forever in this big, open space stocked with simple white porcelain objects for the kitchen and table. There's an extraordinary variety of plates, cups, coffeepots, pitchers, casseroles and terrines for pâté. Simple knife-rests are in the shape of animals, and rolling pins and mortar-and-pestle sets are made of marble. In keeping with the purity of form of the porcelain is the shop's own line of sleek, brass-handled stainless steel cookware.

LEATHERGOODS

GLOVES

4 MADOVA
Via Guicciardini 1r
Tel. 29.65.26
Moderate; no credit cards accepted
Open during lunch

Madova sells just gloves, but gloves of excellent quality from the supervised production of its own factory. They come in every type of leather, color and length, lined in cashmere, wool, silk or fur, in styles for men and women. Whether you buy just one pair or stock up for winters to come, Madova will ship your gloves home for free. After your first purchase, you can mail-order future requests from abroad at minimal airmail charges. If you want to bring back a pair of gloves as a gift, simply bring along a traced sketch of your friend's hand and Madova will take care of the rest. For problem hands too plump or too long, Madova will whip up custom orders.

JEWELRY

Cameos & Corals

5 QUAGLIA & FORTE

Via Guicciardini 12r
Tel. 29.45.34
Expensive; credit cards accepted

This is the best place in Florence and one of the finest north of Naples for delicate cameos, loose or set and mounted into gold or silver rings, necklaces or brooches. Only in the latter part of the 19th century did Naples and the nearby village of Torre del Greco become known for this precision art. It was then discovered that conch shells could be carved into cameos that reveal layers of colors like those found in onyx, quartz and agate. Torre del Greco became a

A museum-piece cameo carved by master craftsman Enzo Quaglia of the distinguished Quaglia & Forte firm. Naples-born, he was considered one of the greatest artists in his field.

major carving center, with only occasional outside competition from such distinguished firms as Florence's Quaglia & Forte. A magnificent cameo carved by the late nationally renowned master craftsman Enzo Quaglia is displayed in the window, testimony to a slowly disappearing art. A curious complement to the large cameo and coral collection is the store's contemporary-looking Etruscan-style jewelry in 18k gold. Quaglia & Forte has been licensed by various Italian museums to reproduce earrings, bracelets and rings whose designs go back well over 2000 years.

SUSTENANCE

GELATERIA

6 IL GIARDINO DELLE DELIZIE

Piazza Santa Felicità 3r
Tel. 29.53.33
Inexpensive; no credit cards accepted
Closed Monday

Despite its semi-hidden location in a small *piazzetta*, this veritable "Garden of Delights" has secured a faithful clientele of ice cream lovers. Specialties are the *gelato di macedonia*, whipped up from fresh melon, cherries, strawberries, pears and figs, and the richest and darkest chocolate ice cream in town.

The *gelateria*'s milk shakes, too, are worthy of serious recognition. Thick, frothy *frappés* are made with fresh fruit and fruit ice cream (instead of the conventional ice cubes and syrups). There are also slightly less dense variations called *frullati*, in which milk is substituted for the ice cream.

LEATHERGOODS
CLOTHING & ACCESSORIES
24-Hour Made-to-Measure

7 PARRI'S ⌂⌂⌂⌂
Via Guicciardini 12–18r
Tel. 28.28.29
Moderate; credit cards accepted
Closed 2:00–3:00 P.M. only

When time is of the essence for the rushed visitor, Parri's can supply quality custom-made leather clothing in just 24 hours, or sometimes even less. Ask to be shown the ready-to-wear, where you can pick your model from an extensive stock of men's and women's jackets, coats, trousers and skirts made of top-grade calfskin and antelope suede in a variety of colors. You can also have a stock item altered to your measurements. A standard of high-quality and courtesy for half a century, Parri's keeps its leather clothing in stock year-round.

Parri's has a handsome collection of crocodile evening bags. Their Bottega Veneta look-alikes cost considerably less than the real thing. Other bags, briefcases, wallets and small leather accessories fill the ground floor. Shipping to the States is a regular service, as are repair and alteration of garments at a later date. Ask for a ten-percent discount if you are paying with cash.

KNITTING YARNS
English-Language Knitting Instructions

8 FILATURA DI CROSA
Via Guicciardini 21r
Tel. 26.31.93
Moderate; credit cards accepted
Open during lunch

When Missoni began their knitwear revolution, Filatura di Crosa created their colorful, high-quality yarns. Filatura di Crosa continues to carry a Missoni "Malizia" line today, as well as the beautiful yarns it makes for the Valentino collection. Yarns come in pure virgin wool, mohair, silk, cotton, angora, alpaca and linen. Every season there's something new, as Filatura goes on experimenting with lighter, softer wools and even more imaginative color.

A highlight of this shop is its owner, Beatrice Galli, who offers charming service. She encourages a mail-order relationship with her overseas clients, sends out announcements of her new and forthcoming collections accompanied by yarn clippings, and will also mail the hard-to-come-by English-language booklets of knitting instructions distributed by Filatura di Crosa.

SHOES
MEN'S & WOMEN'S
Trendy

9 TIMO ⌂⌂⌂⌂
Via Guicciardini 41r
Tel. 29.21.06
Moderate; credit cards accepted
Open during lunch

Seasoned shoe-shoppers looking for up-to-the-minute shoe fashion at affordable prices will want to make a beeline for Timo's. This small store is well stocked with the best trendy footwear in Florence, with no compromise in quality. Commitment to quality also holds for the interesting though limited collection of leather handbags, briefcases, traveling bags, and even tennis and golf bags found here.

Handpicked articles of leather clothing from Milan's great names complete the picture.

Timo selects his shoe lines from all over Italy, and also designs styles which carry his own label. Handmade, classic men's loafers, at very reasonable prices, and large sizes for men and women are an added bonus.

SUSTENANCE

BAR-CAFFÈ

Pasticceria

10 PASTICCERIA MAIOLI
Via Guicciardini 43r
Tel. 21.47.01
Inexpensive; no credit cards accepted
Closed Tuesday

There's no lack of bars on the Via Guicciardini between the Ponte Vecchio and the Palazzo Pitti, but none of the others have the venerable charm of the Pasticceria Maioli. For over 50 years, delicious pastries have been prepared daily on the premises, including *bignoline* (small chocolate-covered creampuffs), butter cookies, fresh fruit tarts and the Florentine specialty *budino*—a pastry shell filled with a sweet rice pudding. There are three tables in the back where you can sit and rest your weary feet, and late-afternoon teatime is a pleasant pick-me-up.

GIFTS

DOLLS

11 A. MELOZZI
Via Guicciardini 35r
Tel. 21.60.84
Moderate; credit cards accepted
Open during lunch

Melozzi's selection of beautiful dolls is the largest in Florence and will make you want to buy one for every little girl you know. There are ceramic, porcelain and bisque dolls with historic costumes in all price ranges, as well as reproductions of antique dolls that make it hard to tell the difference. The famous Lenci doll is here (see Milan listing, page 168), issued in a limited edition of 999. It comes in a satin-lined box complete with a certificate of authenticity.

GIFTS

HOME ACCESSORIES

Top European Design

12 EMPORIUM
Via Guicciardini 122r
Tel. 21.26.46
Expensive; credit cards accepted
Open during lunch

Few can bypass the clever, attention-grabbing display windows of the Emporium. Owner Loli Baffetti scours all of Europe for items with an enduring sense of design and then exhibits

Loli Baffetti with Emporium's design objets.

them artistically as if at the Museum of Modern Art. There are slick table-top and office accessories, games and clocks, unusual serving pieces and costume jewelry. Italy is best represented by Alessi teapots, Memphis-style pens from Paraphernalia, and plexiglass sculptures from Tasca.

LEATHERGOODS

CLOTHING & ACCESSORIES

48-Hour Made-to-Measure

13 ANNA'S
Piazza Pitti 38r
Tel. 28.37.87
Moderate; credit cards accepted
Open during lunch

A stalwart medieval tower is home to an enormous selection of fine-quality leathergoods. On the ground floor, gleaming mahogany and glass cabinets display classic to contemporary leather handbags, briefcases, suitcases, and belts and wallets for both men and women, including the noted Tuscan label "The Bridge".

Most regular customers will breeze through such temptations on their way downstairs to more serious business. There they will find the largest selection in town of men's and women's leather clothing in supple skins and seasonal colors. Most of the clothing is made under the store's design specifications by small, specialized local factories. Light alterations can be done in just a few hours, and custom-made garments can be made up in 48 hours. It is advised, however, that you be sure the garment is completed in time for you to take it home with you, inasmuch as any problems with fit would be very hard to rectify from aboard.

Marbelized-paper items in Giannini's windows.

GIFTS

STATIONERY & ACCESSORIES

Marbleized Papers

14 GIULIO GIANNINI & FIGLIO
Piazza Pitti 37r
Tel. 21.26.21
Expensive; credit cards accepted
Open during lunch

Each of the five generations of the Giannini family has in some way improved and expanded their small paper-goods empire. Discerning visitors have long known that the only place to find such artistic stationery and marbleized-paper items was in Florence and, until recently, in this quaint shop alone. Desk accessories, frames, boxes, and blank notebooks of all sizes are covered in beautiful papers that are created with hand-mixed colors.

Giannini also carries handsome leather-bound and wood-covered books, some elaborately tooled and embossed in antique gold patterns, and does creative hand-bookbinding —a family tradition for well over a century—on commission only.

Ilio de Filippis at his work.

GIFTS

WORKSHOP/STUDIO

Semiprecious-Stone Inlay

15 PITTI MOSAICI

Piazza Pitti 16r
Tel. 28.27.21
Moderate; credit cards accepted
Open during lunch and Sunday

Young Ilio de Filippis is one of the most talented mosaic artisans around. His small, modern store offers many examples of this intricate and timeless art, all created by his hand or by his apprentices. Most popular as gift items, and less expensive because of their relative simplicity, are the innovative pieces of silver jewelry—pendants, necklaces, bracelets, earrings and brooches—that use semiprecious stones in varying mosaic patterns. More conventional are the small-scale mosaic "paintings" created by assembling semiprecious stones to depict people, flowers, landscapes and birds. You'll marvel at De Filippis' natural instinct for the hues, streaks, bands and spots found in each individual stone. No two are ever alike. In a workshop in the back, a young apprentice can be seen applying this tedious process.

GIFTS

HANDCRAFTED LEATHER DESK ACCESSORIES

16 TADDEI—CUOIO ARTISTICO FIORENTINO

Piazza Pitti 6r
Tel. 21.91.39
Moderate; credit cards accepted
Opens at 7 A.M.

Three generations of the Taddei family have carried on the Florentine art of handcrafting small leather gift items. Heavy tanned hides are worked and manipulated into boxes of all sizes and shapes, then buffed to a high gloss. The deep natural colors of the skin make these boxes and holders handsome desktop accessories for stationery, mail, cigarettes and cigars—or even jewelry cases. Desk sets and frames can make perfect gifts for the hard-to-please men in your life.

If jet lag has you up and around before the rest of the city wakes, get a jump on your souvenir buying at Taddei's, which opens bright and early at 7:00 A.M.

ANTIQUE JEWELRY

COLLECTIBLES

Art Deco

17 ANTICHITÀ IL MAGGIOLINO

Via Maggio 80r
Tel. 21.66.60
Expensive; no credit cards accepted

Il Maggiolino is well known among Florentine antique shops for its exquisite jewelry, tableware and precious little objects. The specialty is European and American art-deco earrings, brooches, pendants and necklaces set with diamonds, rubies and other gems. In addition, Il Maggiolino generally carries a wide selection of high-quality Italian, French and English silver: coffee and tea sets, cruets, tankards, cutlery and comb-and-brush sets.

What is on display is only an indication of what the salespeople will bring out from safekeeping, should your interest be piqued.

ANTIQUES

16th Century to Art Deco

18 GUIDO BARTOLOZZI & FIGLIO ANTIQUARI

Via Maggio 18r
Tel. 21.56.02
Expensive; no credit cards accepted

Each piece in Bartolozzi's extensive collection of primarily Italian antiques is of impeccable quality, be it early 16th century or stylized art deco. Room after room is appointed with fine furniture, paintings, mirrors, tapestries, sculpture and objets d'art. The Bartolozzi family has been in the antique business for over 100 years, and the fact that Signor Guido presently holds the prestigious position of president of the Antiquarians' Association of Florence unofficially guarantees the quality of his goods.

One of Guido Bartolozzi's choice treasures.

HOME

FURNITURE & ACCESSORIES

Wood-Carved Reproductions

19 BARTOLOZZI & MAIOLI

Via Maggio 13r
Tel. 29.86.33
Moderate; credit cards accepted
Open during lunch

Fiorenzo Bartolozzi is Italy's finest wood carver, although the term is far too mundane for the intricate artwork that leaves his busy workshop for New York, Jeddah or Monaco. His cluttered *bottega* is an interior designer's dream: everywhere are heavily carved chairs and columns, somber Madonnas, wooden frames dripping with fruit and garlands, bookends, candleholders, imitation Louis XVI commodes, imitation everything. A liquor cabinet in the shape of a life-size mummy decorated in gold leaf is an eye-opener. Seventy master artisans fill Signor Bartolozzi's orders for royalty and churches, deluxe hotels and private estates. Individual clients arrive with faded photographs of sentimental pieces they want duplicated, and Bartolozzi satisfies them. The shop's astonishing output has to be seen.

Bartolozzi's monumental work was their restoration of the historic Benedictine Abbey of Monte Cassino, which was destroyed by American bombers during World War II. One of the major restoration projects of the postwar period, involving hundreds of columns, statues, confessionals and pews, the job took 50 of Bartolozzi's top artisans over ten years to complete. For it, Fiorenzo Bartolozzi was awarded the title of Commendatore (Knight) by the Italian government.

HOME

FURNITURE

Neoclassical Reproductions

20 AMIDA

Via Maggio 13
Tel. 21.25.33
Moderate; no credit cards accepted

Marianna Gagliardi and Fiorenza Bartolozzi are two young Florentine women who have harnessed the creative energies of Florence's finest woodworkers to present a unique collection of furniture. Although many of their pieces are of neoclassical inspiration, Marianna and Fiorenza give them contemporary interpretations. Lemonwood and light-colored oak are fashioned into large, graceful urns or accommodating desks, simple in line. Elegant, stately campaign-style chairs of black-lacquered wood are upholstered in paisley or print silk. Half columns that stand flush to the wall are actually made of wood and not the cool, veined marble they imitate. Custom orders can be arranged, as Marianna and Fiorenza frequently work with professional decorators and designers.

Amida's inspirational wooden furniture.

SUSTENANCE

RISTORANTE/TRATTORIA

21 LE QUATTRO STAGIONI

Via Maggio 61r
Tel. 21.89.06
Moderate; credit cards accepted
Closed Sunday

Artistry and imagination flavor the menu of this fashionable restaurant frequented by neighborhood antique dealers and residents of the elegant Via Maggio. The *primo* should never be skipped here—the homemade *gnocchi* (dumpling-like pasta) are so light and the *risotto*, made with your choice of artichokes, asparagus or the black ink of squid, is too delicious. Nontraditional dishes such as swordfish and salmon often appear, and helpful waiters will steer you toward the reliably delicious boneless lamb stuffed with artichokes.

SUSTENANCE

BAR-CAFFÈ

22 CAFFÈ SANTA TRINITÀ

Corner of Via Santo Spirito and Via Maggio
Tel. 21.45.58
Inexpensive; no credit cards accepted
Closed Sunday

This convenient, modern and relaxed *bar-caffè* has small wooden tables that offer a welcome break from shopping. A leisurely cappuccino, a young Oltrarno crowd, a local newspaper and a fresh selection of morning pastries or afternoon *tramezzini* (sandwiches on sliced bread) make this a popular spot at any time of day.

The modern restrooms alone are worth noting.

HOME

KITCHEN & TABLE ACCESSORIES

Accent on Design

23 LA CASA ABITATA
Via dello Sprone 25r
Tel. 29.53.00
Moderate; credit cards accepted

This shop offers a wide assortment of sleek cooking utensils and unusual gadgets created for the state-of-the-art continental kitchen and table. Italian brands are well represented with Alessi and ICM stainless cookware, Guzzini plastics and Girmi black espresso makers that look like postmodern sculptures. While some of the other products featured are not Italian-made, all have been chosen with an Italian design sensibility. Owner Signora Loli Baffetti's eye for detail extends to the displays, with each item presented as a miniature work of modern design.

GIFTS

HAND-PAINTED ACCESSORIES

Fun & Whimsy

24 DODO
Via Barbadori 10r
Tel. 29.69.33
Moderate; credit cards accepted

This is the original location of the charming Dodo boutique, teeming with gift ideas for young girls: wooden hairpins, earrings and hangers, each hand-painted with whimsical cats, rabbits and pigs in hundreds of variations. Unlike the larger shop on Borgo SS. Apostoli in the Centro Storico, this small location does not carry clothes or furniture.

Kitchenware approaches art at La Casa Abitata.

FASHION

CHILDREN'S

25 BABAR
Borgo San Jacopo 5r
Tel. 21.97.11
Expensive; credit cards accepted

This sweet little boutique is all dressed up in small children's finery. It features smart, classic outfits, some handmade by the two young owners, both recent mothers. There are hand-embroidered overalls, velvet dresses with pretty smocking, hand-knit sweaters, and tops and bottoms trimmed with Naj Oleari fabric. Everything is in natural fibers.

FASHION

WOMEN'S

Made-to-Measure

26 LA LUNA E LE STELLE
Borgo San Jacopo 17r
Tel. 21.46.23
Moderate; credit cards accepted

Here's a chance to bring home a custom-made, Valentino-style dress at a fraction of what you'd pay in the Valentino boutique. Owner Anna Cei follows the fashion collections each year with a scrupulous eye and reinterprets them slightly, using only quality fabrics. All her production is done by a group of seamstresses at a nearby studio, and should you want a particular model made up, you'll need to wait just a few days or, at most, a week.

The window display is not always a good indication of the stock inside. Ask about *alta moda,* and Signora Cei will show you blouses, dresses, suits and coats that are often copies of current styles by Valentino, Laura Biagiotti, Enrico Coveri and Jean-Paul Gaultier—any of which can be made to measure.

FASHION

WOMEN'S & CHILDREN'S

Hand-Knit Sweaters

27 CINZIA
Borgo San Jacopo 22r
Tel. 29.80.78
Moderate; credit cards accepted

The Grevis were among the first to introduce the bulky Italian hand-knit sweater to America. Here in their own boutique is the full range of their beautiful women's and children's sweater collection, at very good prices. All sweaters are handmade with natural fibers—blends of fine wool, mohair, angora and, for summer, cottons—in colorful combinations and fantasy designs with a distinctive rustic look. Styles include turtlenecks, pullovers and cardigans. It's hard to leave with just one.

ANTIQUES

Italian Renaissance

28 LUZZETTI ANTICHITÀ
Borgo San Jacopo 28A
Tel. 21.12.32
Expensive; no credit cards accepted

An elegant, handsomely restored 12th-century palazzo is the perfect setting for this gallery of Italian Renaissance antiques. Rare furniture, paintings and statues from the 14th through the 16th century are joined by a superb collection of bronzes and ceramics from some of Italy's most prized medieval potteries, such as Deruta, Faenza and Castel Duranto. If Lorenzo il Magnifico were alive, he would thrill at the sight.

LEATHERGOODS

BAGS & ACCESSORIES

Sporty & Contemporary

29 GIACHI
Borgo San Jacopo 29A/r
Tel. 21.36.04
Moderate; credit cards accepted

Giachi's is a pretty little shop filled with the presence of its owner, Lorenza Giachi, who loves each bag she sells. She holds an exclusive in Florence for the Pitti line, which she supplements with other quality Italian lines such as Granelli and Coveri that are always a season or two ahead of other manufacturers. Big, roomy, casual bags are available in all kinds of specialty leather or in a very high-quality plasticized fabric trimmed in leather. Coordinated shoes, wallets and large tote bags respond to each season's demands.

HOME

SILVER

Restoration & Reproduction

30 PAOLO PAGLIAI, ARGENTIERE
Borgo San Jacopo 41r
Tel. 28.28.40
Moderate; no credit cards accepted

Restoring and repairing old silver pieces is Signor Pagliai's finest talent. He can produce an exact copy of any heirloom's missing piece, be it a teaspoon or a candlestick. In the back room you can glimpse a blazing blowtorch at work, while in the small front room Signor Pagliai receives his clients to discuss each challenge at hand. He also sells his own small production of silver objects, mostly picture frames decorated with classic, Renaissance or Victorian motifs.

SUSTENANCE

RISTORANTE/TRATTORIA

31 OSTERIA DEL CINGHIALE BIANCO
Borgo San Jacopo 43r
Tel. 21.57.06
Moderate; credit cards accepted
Closed Wednesday

As the wrought-iron wild boar above the entrance suggests, this king of game is the specialty here. It is best tried as a delicious sausage (antipasto) or, for more adventurous palates, as an entrée with *polenta*, a cornmeal side dish. The most interesting *primo* is the *strozzapreti*, small poached balls of spinach and ricotta cheese in melted butter that taste not unlike ravioli filling without the shell. Located on the ground floor of a 14th-century tower, the restaurant has a medieval ambiance.

Gone fishin' along the banks of the Arno.

FASHION

WOMEN'S

Blouses

32 PICCARDA MODA
Borgo San Jacopo 58r
Tel. 26.23.11
Moderate; credit cards accepted

This is the only Florentine store specializing in classic women's blouses. Simple, blouson, high-necked or with stock tie, these beautiful blouses are designed and produced by the shop's owner, Grazia Meacci. The fabric selection includes solid or print crepe de Chine and, for spring and summer, cotton and linen. Attention to detail, including hand-finishing and providing fabric-covered buttons, is Signora Meacci's signature. She was trained as a seamstress, and can make a blouse to order within a few days.

LAMPS & LIGHTING
Ultramodern

33 FLOS
Borgo San Jacopo 62r
Tel. 28.45.09
Moderate; credit cards accepted

This gallery is dedicated entirely to Flos' ultramodern lamps and fixtures. Chrome joins with transparent or colored plastics in standing lamps, table or desk lamps, sconces and office lighting. Pure in line, a Flos lamp can be a subtle accent in any room. Much of the merchandise is available in 110-volt adaptations for U.S. use, but be prepared to carry your purchase or arrange for your own shipping.

PINS & BROOCHES
Monomania

34 LO SPILLO
Borgo San Jacopo 72r
Tel. 29.31.26
Moderate; credit cards accepted

In Italian, *lo spillo* means "the pin," and this teensy shop is hardly much larger than one. However, scores of stickpins, lapel pins, brooches and decorative hatpins, together with some earrings and other small items, grace each shelf. Dating from the 1800s to the art-deco period, some of these pieces are timelessly contemporary in design, others nostalgically reminiscent.

PALAZZO STROZZI INTERNATIONAL ANTIQUES FAIR

Held every two years (in odd years only) in the massive Palazzo Strozzi, this prestigious international antiques fair has been drawing ever-increasing crowds since its inception in 1953. For three weeks, over 100 antique dealers converge from all over Italy, Europe and America to exhibit their prized pieces, which range from archeological findings to 20th-century items of the art-nouveau and art-deco periods. The palazzo is filled with a wealth of precious carpets, porcelain, drawings, paintings, silverware, sculpture, jewelry and furniture of every genre. A committee of experts inspect and approve each item offered for sale and provide their guarantee of authenticity. Purchasers may also visit a special lab on the premises equipped with the latest state-of-the-art technology.

The fair usually takes place from mid-September to mid-October (exact dates will be available from your concierge or the Tourism Office), from 10:00 A.M. to 8:30 P.M. on weekdays, and 9:30 A.M. to 11:00 P.M. on weekends.

ANTIQUES

FRAMES

35 MIRNA GABELLIERI, CORNICI ANTICHE

Borgo San Jacopo 80r
Tel. 29.21.64
Moderate; credit cards accepted
Open during lunch

Antique Italian picture frames from every period and in every style and size fill this charming shop. Customers who have a favorite painting in need of framing bring Signora Gabellieri a snapshot with the measurements, and she'll personally scout her sources for the appropriate frame. She selects with an eye for unusual designs and materials—gold-leaf decoration, carved wood (sometimes rosewood or precious ebony) or gilded bronze. The frames are so beautiful that many a customer buys them merely to encase wall mirrors.

COSTUME JEWELRY

36 ANGELA CAPUTI

Borgo San Jacopo 82r
Tel. 21.29.72
Moderate; credit cards accepted

Affectionately known as *Giuggiu* (gew-gew), Angela Caputi has been accessorizing Milan's major fashion lines for years with her wild and wonderful jewelry. Bold, chunky and imaginative, most of the pieces are made of light, brightly colored plexiglass, plastic or Galalith. In the summertime, there's also a sexy line of swimwear, most of which carries a distinctive Angela Caputi bauble at some strategic point.

A brand-new addition to the Caputi operation is the clothing bou-

Angela Caputi's bright, light plastic bijoux.

tique that it has opened next door. There's an obvious correlation between garment and accessory, but the real attraction remains the latter.

FOOD

DELICATESSEN

Perfect for Picnics

37 VERA

Piazza Frescobaldi 3r
Tel. 21.54.65
Moderate; no credit cards accepted

A gourmand's delight, Vera's is the city's best-stocked and most popular delicatessen store. In addition to stocks of olive oil, homemade breads, canned delicacies, fresh cheeses, hams, salamis and freshly roasted meats, Vera's is known for its hot and cold homemade, take-out foods, soups and cold salads. In the summer try the cold rice salad or *panzanella;* in the winter, the hearty *ribollita* soup. If you haven't yet orchestrated the perfect Tuscan picnic in the nearby Boboli Gardens, this is where to start. You can pick up fresh fruit for dessert just across the street.

A Biedermier triumph at Giorgio Albertosi.

ANTIQUES

Neoclassical

38 GIORGIO ALBERTOSI
Piazza Frescobaldi 1r
Tel. 21.36.36
Expensive; no credit cards accepted

Giorgio Albertosi is one of Italy's top antiquarians for the neoclassical period. His small, elegant store is filled with choice neoclassical antiques of both French and Italian origin. Furniture, miniature bronzes, ornate table-top clocks, paintings, elaborate frames and other exquisite objects, all in perfect condition, are gracefully displayed as if part of a fine private collection.

COSTUME JEWELRY

Unusual Collection

39 PARFUM BIJOUX
Piazza Frescobaldi 11r
Tel. 21.26.55
Moderate; credit cards accepted
Open during lunch

These striking bijoux are worth collecting and treasuring for years. They've received the same attention to detail and finishing as jewels commanding far superior prices, though most are far too big and bold ever to be mistaken for the real thing. An ex-model, the beautiful German-born owner is particularly trend conscious, choosing dramatic baubles often well ahead of their time. The collection includes dainty and feminine pieces as well as large ones. The pretty, brand-new boutique also offers a limited number of antique costume pieces.

ANTIQUES

Gothic to Renaissance

40 GALLERIA LUIGI BELLINI
Lungarno Soderini 3–5
Tel. 29.46.26
Expensive; no credit cards accepted
Open on Sunday by advance appointment

Owning the oldest and largest antique gallery in Italy is nothing to scoff at. The Bellini family have been antique collectors and dealers for well over two centuries. Their cavernous 18th-century Palazzo Soderini, which stands guard over the Arno River, is home to an enormous collection mainly of the Gothic and Renaissance periods (1200–1600). In 1953, Mario Bellini organized the first International Antiques' Fair. It now takes place in the Palazzo Strozzi, in odd years only (see box, page 126). Mario's son, Luigi, continues to operate the prestigious antique gallery and has recently opened a gallery of contemporary art on the ground floor.

RISTORANTE/TRATTORIA

41 ANGIOLINO
Via Santo Spirito 36r
Tel. 29.89.76
Moderate; no credit cards accepted
Closed Monday

A large, lively neighborhood *trattoria* where the good-natured waiters make even the newcomers feel right at home. Tuscan fare is simple and well prepared, with good pasta *al empolese* (with artichokes), grilled meats and the best *ribollita* in town. If you ask for a table in the back, you can keep watch on the open, bustling kitchen—less appealing in summer when you may want to avoid the extra heat.

BAR-CAFFÈ

Pasticceria

42 MARINO
Piazza Nazario Sauro 19r
Tel. 21.26.57
Inexpensive; no credit cards accepted
Closed Monday

This busy *pasticceria* (pastry shop)/ espresso bar has the freshest and most buttery *brioche* (croissants) in Florence. Since you'll definitely want to eat more than one, try those puffed up with light custard (*crema*) in chocolate, vanilla or marmalade. Dozens of delicious pastries, all made daily on the premises, vie for your favor. There are no tables, but join the Italians for a stand-up breakfast of rich espresso and savory *brioche*.

BRONZE ACCESSORIES

Restoration & Reproduction

43 BANCHI LAMBERTO, BRONZISTA
Via dei Serragli 10r
Tel. 29.46.94
Moderate; no credit cards accepted

Signor Banchi is a master bronze worker. His enthusiasm and skill are evident everywhere in this small, cluttered workshop. It is filled to the rafters with his bronze reproductions, many of them small and inexpensive enough to bring home with you, although you'll need some time and patience to unearth them. Choose from picture frames and candlesticks in art-deco, baroque and Empire styles, paperweights and desk ornaments in dozens of forms and sizes, door knockers, sconces, decorative plates and wall hangings. Larger pieces include clock cases, tabletops, table-lamp bases and just about everything imaginable that can be made in bronze. You can also ask Signor Banchi to repair broken pieces, restore damaged antiques or custom-make bronze trim for furniture or doors.

44 VINI E OLII
Via dei Serragli 29r
Tel. 29.87.08
Moderate; no credit cards accepted

In this modern, well-appointed specialty shop, owner Renzo Salsi will give you a rundown (in Italian) on the history of each of the translucent green olive oils and regional wines on display—or he will just leave you to browse. Tuscany's esteemed Villa Banfi offers a gift parcel of fine extra-virgin oil in pretty flasks. Signor Salsi will package your oil or wine purchases himself to ensure safe travel. If it happens to be a wintry Saturday afternoon, he will also invite you to an informal wine tasting in his store, enhanced by his wife's tasty *crostini*.

HOME

SILVER

45 GOZZINI E RESTELLI
Via dei Serragli 44r
Tel. 28.46.50
Moderate; no credit cards accepted

This small family-run silver store offers good-quality gift items at moder-

ate prices. Don't look for the elaborate or pretentious, just delicate little pillboxes, handsome silver frames in many sizes and, for your wine-loving friends, an ingenious vinometer: a device for measuring alcohol content and temperature, set in a graceful silver stand. All items are made on the premises.

JEWELRY

WORKSHOP/STUDIO

46 GIOIELLI DI ELISA GRANDIS & GIO CARBONE
Via Sant'Agostino 6r
Tel. 21.50.96
Moderate; credit cards accepted

This clean, modern workshop pro-

EXTRA-VIRGIN OLIVE OIL

There is nothing quite like Italian olive oil, and the Tuscan extra-virgin variety reigns supreme. It is taken from the very first, cold pressing of the olive and is never blended with other oils. A rich, deep green in color, surprisingly light in taste and very low in oleic acid (it may not contain more than 1 percent) it has a high nutritional value; scientists believe that it helps prevent heart disease.

A staple of the Italian diet for three millennia, *olio di oliva* is used liberally for dressing fresh salads and vegetables. Among the Tuscan oils, those produced in the Lucca, Chianti and Carmignano regions today qualify as the very finest. They are made on estates and labeled as such, much like fine wines. Quality producers of extra-virgin olive oil include Antinori, Capezzana, Villa Banfi and Badia Coltibuono. So cherished is the first pressing that a dishonest or questionable division of the dark green nectar by a Tuscan *contadino* has been known to create rifts within families.

duces handcrafted gold in two distinctly personal styles. Elisa Grandis is enamored of rich baroque ornamentation, studding her gold pieces with semiprecious feldspar, beryl, rubies, topaz and pearls. On the other hand, Gio Carbone, a master *cesellatore*, creates chiseled and gold-embossed designs that follow clean lines and forms. Each of them produces work whose quality and originality challenge that of the jewelry sold on the Ponte Vecchio, while maintaining more affordable prices.

Elisa and Gio have recently opened a goldsmith's school (Le Arti Orafe, Via dei Serragli 124, telephone 21.50.96) offering one- to six-month courses in gemology, gem-cutting, jewelry design, and stone inlay.

STATIONERY

Personalized Calling Cards

47 VAINIO
Via Mazzetta 22r
Tel. 21.39.65
Moderate; no credit cards accepted

Fine-quality personalized stationery and granite-textured calling cards in a wide range of pastel and bold-colored papers can be made up for you here in ten days. Minimum order for the latter is only 100 cards, so here's a chance to try out a fuchsia pink or sophisticated grey for a very small investment. Two graphic designers own this modern studio where they hand-operate a small press. If you won't be in Florence long enough, they'll ship to your home address abroad. They will also personalize for you their collection of silk-screen-printed stationery in modern, naif-style designs.

HOME

REPRODUCTIONS

Trompe-l'Oeil Specialists

48 FICALBI & BALLONI
Via delle Caldaie 25
Tel. 22.30.09
Moderate; credit cards accepted

Stefano Ficalbi and Maurizio Balloni are at your whim's command: in their studio, you can place custom orders for magnificent *trompe-l'oeil* neoclassical paintings, decorative panels or fake-marble columns. The two clever young Florentines welcome commissions to paint room-size murals for Arab sheiks, but they cater just as diligently to individuals who relish the idea of owning a small piece of classical art created for them alone.

Of particular interest are the panels of *trompe l'oeil* still lifes designed to cover cabinet doors, depicting shelves filled with hams, flasks of Chianti and wheels of cheese. While their inspiration comes mainly from old paintings, Stefano and Maurizio will include items chosen to reflect your own particular passions. No request is too outrageous. As an example, they'll point out a working pinball machine housed in a gilded faux-marble Louis XVI chest, which they made for themselves.

Trompe l'oeil *at Ficalbi & Balloni.*

SUSTENANCE

RISTORANTE/TRATTORIA

49 ALLA VECCHIA BETTOLA
Viale Ludovico Ariosto 32r
Tel. 22.41.58
Moderate; no credit cards accepted
Closed Sunday and Monday

This is a Florentine favorite, a lively *trattoria* with tiles, long communal tables, ceiling fans and old prints of Florence as it used to be when La Vecchia Bettola was a public house, as its name indicates. Simple and reliably fresh ingredients make for delicious home cooking. The crusty oven-baked bread and thick green olive oil will sustain you until your *primo piatto,* the homemade pasta of the day, arrives. A glimpse at your neighbor's starter will take some of the guessing out of ordering. Forever Tuscan, La Vecchia Bettola prides itself especially on good meats, whether the rabbit stuffed with ham and cheese or the veal and beefsteak on the grill.

HOME

SILVER

Handcrafted

50 G. BRANDIMARTE 🍶🍶🍶🍶
Via L. Bartolini 18
Tel. 21.87.91
Moderate; no credit cards accepted

Brandimarte is the most respected silversmith in Florence. Yet only a small, hand-scribbled sign ("G. Brandimarte Ingresso") marks the bustling workshop of this gifted, ofttimes flamboyant artist. Inside is a beehive of blowtorches, hammers and artisans working to fill orders from all over the world. The prototype is made by Brandimarte, and the production left to 50 workers whose personal variations on each theme are encouraged.

Brandimarte's credo is that silver is not for Sunday use alone. He takes everyday utensils and ennobles them in silver: frying pans, cheese graters, and wine bottles wrapped in silver instead of straw. Most coveted are the silver tulip-shaped goblets, which he has brought back into style. Like all his goblets, these come in water, wine and champagne-flute sizes. Nature is the driving inspiration behind his design, and various nut and fruit patterns decorate both the goblets and matching silver dining plates.

Many items can be purchased in considerably less expensive silver plate. Your initials can be chiseled into whatever piece you choose, which will also be stamped with Brandimarte's name and the date and weighed on a butcher's scale to determine the amount in silver.

Brandimarte's work is also available at a lovely gift shop owned by his daughter Giada, which specializes in contemporary silver (Tu, Via Santo Spirito 9, telephone 29.31.24).

SUSTENANCE

PIZZERIA

Late-Night

51 I TAROCCHI
Via dei Renai 12–14r (off map)
Tel. 21.78.50
Inexpensive; no credit cards accepted
Closed Monday

Carbohydrate fans will have a field day in this crowded and authentic *spaghetteria/pizzeria,* where the hearty and delicious pasta dishes for *primo* are followed by light and imaginative pizzas for *secondo*. Be assured that it is quite normal for Italians to follow one with the other, along with a good cold beer. The pizza variations go on forever, offering lots of generous toppings and good fun until the small hours.

SUSTENANCE
CREPERIA
Late-Night

52 IL RIFRULLO
Via San Niccolo 55r (off map)
Tel. 21.36.21
Moderate; no credit cards accepted
Closed Wednesday

Inside, there's the atmosphere of a turn-of-the-century bistro, with extra warmth in winter from a blazing hearth. Or, in summer, you can sip cocktails at candle-lit tables under the trees in the outdoor garden. This is a favorite for well-dressed and handsome youths—all of whom seem to own motorcycles, Sardinian tans and lots of free time. The popular discotèque Jackie O's is a stroll away, and carefree Florentines stop in the Rifrullo before and after to make sure they're not missing a trick. The Rifrullo is not what we would call a pub, but is a *birreria*, offering a host of imported beers and a delectable assortment of crêpes.

SUSTENANCE
GELATERIA

53 GELATERIA FRILLI
Via San Miniato 5r (off map)
Tel. 21.21.40
Inexpensive; no credit cards accepted
Closed Wednesday

A latticework of bridges.

For 35 years the Frilli family has run a plain and busy neighborhood bar and grocery store, with an area in the back for making ice cream. They produce a wonderful selection of ten fruit flavors, strictly limited to the fragrant fruits that are in season. Frilli is also known for its 18 *semifreddo* varieties made daily, including amaretto, *crème caramel*, and chocolate mousse.

SUSTENANCE
RISTORANTE/TRATTORIA
Taxi Away

54 OMERO
Via Pian dei Giullari 11r (off map)
Tel. 22.00.53
Moderate; no credit cards accepted
Closed Tuesday

Omero is a short cab ride and light-years away from the bustle of Florence. You enter through a country grocery store replete with hanging *prosciutti* and sausages, then pass into the large windowed dining area with commanding views of a Tuscan countryside, dotted with farmhouses. A fireplace blazes in winter. The food is classically Florentine, and what finer place to eat it than here? Spinach-ricotta *ravioli* in sage butter, soups and *panzanella* to start, then quality meats on the grill, including chicken, the house specialty.

INDEX TO STORES LISTED BY PRODUCT

The following index of stores in Florence is arranged by product category so that you can quickly find stores of particular interest to you. In each category, stores are grouped by neighborhood (CS = Centro Storico, PV = Ponte Vecchio, T = Via Tornabuoni, C = Centro, SC = Santa Croce, O = Oltrarno); the number following this designation is the store's location code on the neighborhood map and also represents the order in which the store is listed. Page numbers are provided for reference to the stores' descriptions in the text. An asterisk (*) means the store is usually open during lunch.

ANTIQUES
C-23 Fallani Best, p. 95
C-24 Paolo Romano
  Antichità, p. 95
C-28 Piero Betti Galleria,
  p. 97

O-18 Guido Bartolozzi &
  Figlio Antiquari, p. 121
O-28 Luzzetti Antichità, p. 124
*O-35 Mirna Gabellieri,
  Cornici Antiche, p. 127
O-38 Giorgio Albertosi, p. 128
O-40 Galleria Luigi Bellini,
  p. 128

ANTIQUE JEWELRY
PV-5 Melli, p. 84

O-17 Antichità il Maggiolino,
  p. 120
O-34 Lo Spillo, p. 126

BOOKS
CS-20 Libreria della Signoria,
  p. 50

T-10 Libreria Internazionale
  Seeber, p. 78

C-12 Alinari Photo/Bookstore,
  p. 91
C-21 BM Bookshop, p. 94
C-30 Franco Maria Ricci, p. 97

SC-5 Salimbeni, p. 109
SC-10 Paperback Exchange,
  p. 111

O-1 Centro Di, p. 115

CERAMICS
SC-1 Migliori, p. 108

SC-6 Al Tegame, p. 109
SC-8 Sbigoli Terrecotte,
  p. 110

COLLECTIBLES
C-46 Arte Cornici, p. 105

O-17 Antichità il Maggiolino,
  p. 120

COSTUME JEWELRY
CS-2 Bijoux Cascio, p. 43
CS-21 L'Oca Bianca, p. 51
CS-26 Mariella Innocenti,
  p. 52

O-36 Angela Caputi, p. 127
*O-39 Parfum Bijoux, p. 128

DEPARTMENT STORE
CS-55 Principe, p. 62

DISCOUNT STORE
C-37 Beltrami (discount
  outlet), p. 161

DOLLS
*O-11 A. Melozzi, p. 118

FABRICS, FASHION
CS-59 Casa dei Tessuti, p. 63

C-11 Naj Oleari, p. 91

FABRICS, FURNISHING
CS-15 DeAngelis, p. 48

C-17 Antico Setificio
  Fiorentino, p. 93
C-11 Naj Oleari, p. 91
C-20 Lisio Tessuti d'Arte,
  p. 94

FABRICS, TRIMMINGS
C-42 Passamaneria Toscana,
  p. 104

FASHION, ACCESSORIES
CS-37 Quercioli & Lucherini,
  p. 56

T-5 Ugolini, p. 77

C-14 Minetta, p. 92
C-36 Leonardo, p. 101

O-4 Madova, p. 115

FASHION, CHILDREN'S
CS-6 Cirri, p. 44
CS-9 Taf, p. 45
CS-41 Benetton 012, p. 57
CS-55 Principe, p. 62
CS-57 Prénatal, p. 63
CS-65 La Ragazzeria, p. 66

T-1 Baroni, p. 74

C-2 Pratesi, p. 87
*C-10 Enrico Coveri, p. 90

O-25 Babar, p. 123
O-27 Cinzia, p. 124

FASHION, DESIGNER
CS-62 Luisa Via Roma, p. 64

T-2 Ferragamo, p. 74
T-11 Gucci (men's & women's
  fashion), p. 78
T-13 Gucci (leather), p. 79

*C-10 Enrico Coveri, p. 90
C-39 Emilio Pucci, p. 102

*For additional designer
  boutiques, see directory
  on page 65.*

FASHION, JUNIORS'
CS-27 Benetton, p. 52
CS-28 Beltrami, Junior, p. 53

MILAN

Milano

*M*ilan is modern Italy. Impressionable first-time visitors consider it the least Italian of the peninsula's cities. So do the *milanesi* themselves, but when they're feeling expansive, they show a staunch provincialism they otherwise attribute to their compatriots of the South. While recognizing that politics remain traditionally entrenched in Rome, the *milanesi* hold their city to be the ultimate urban metropolis, the cradle of design, the runway of fashion, the promulgator of trends, the true industrial, economic and commercial capital of Italy.

Milan is, in fact, all these things and more. It is a city of 1000 faces— chaotic while practical, strong but discreet, given to fantasy yet down-to-earth. It has consistently exhibited exceptional courage in experimenting with the avant-garde, yet tempers its optimism with realism. While most of Italy struggles to keep alive its rich patrimony of culture, often infusing it with new interpretations, Milan creates new design without precedent. Businesslike and profoundly aware that Italy's most important raw material is its reservoir of creativity, Milan has grown rich and respected by tapping this vital resource.

Milan is not conventionally beautiful at first sight but, like a sophisticated and elegant lady, can be even more enticing for this very reason. It has money, a natural style and éclat. The *milanesi* exercise a chic wit, walk faster than the Romans and speak a less impetuous Italian. It's a city that boasts a hectic American work schedule, and one where ideas are born or adopted before being filtered through to the rest of Italy, Europe and the world.

Milan is loved by her two million *milanesi* and, although not part of the usual tourist itinerary, attracts international buyers and foreign businessmen by the hundreds of thousands. To procure a coveted seat at La Scala, to dine in one of the city's elitist restaurants or to glimpse a price tag in one of its sleek postmodern boutiques is to realize that Milan can be very expensive for visitors without expense accounts; few can afford to sample all its tantalizing wares. Milan is a magnet for high fashion, high design, high living and, for the most part, high prices—although it also offers abundant moderately priced merchandise.

It is not surprising that such fertile ground has drawn talents and energies from all parts. France's Philippe Starke, Germany's Richard Sapper and Austrian-born Ettore Sottsass came to Milan to help revolutionize the field of furniture and furnishings. Major fashion leaders such as Versace and Armani are Milanese by adoption. This migration of talented individuals to Italy's melting pot was already taking place over 500 years ago when one Tuscan-born youth, a certain Leonardo da Vinci, came to the big city to become ducal engineer and painter to Ludovico Sforza, called Il Moro. Centuries later came the renowned French writer Stendhal, who requested that his epitath read, "Henri Stendhal, Milanese," thus joining the ranks of those who have found fulfillment in what residents call the "moral capital" of Italy.

The antiquity of Milan, unlike that of most other Italian cities, is not easy to perceive. In this industrious and progessive metropolis, much of the old was sacrificed to make way for the new. Even more was obliterated by devastating World War II air raids. Milan was founded by the Gauls around the year 600 B.C. The early Romans made it the seat of their Western Empire. After marauding Goths and Huns came the Lombards, whose name the region still bears. Two great ruling clans, the all-powerful Viscontis and Sforzas, followed as the Dukes of Milan and, like the Medici of Florence, brought Milan into the Renaissance.

Other landlords included Napoleon, who made the city the capital of his Cisalpine Republic and later of the Kingdom of Italy. Years of Austrian domination left the Milanese with fair complexions, bread crumbs on their veal cutlets (here called *cotoletta milanese,* there called *wiener schnitzel*) and a liking for white wine. All of these influences have resulted in a unique open-mindedness and secessionist fervor in the way the Milanese approach design in everything from fashion to food.

The city's metamorphosis from rich agricultural town to industrial center to nucleus of artistic ingenuity is a remarkable phenonemon now being examined by philosophers, historians and economists. Always prosperous, Milan took about 50 years to cover the ground that England and France covered in nearly two centuries. Now the indisputable center of Italian fashion and design, it is both factory and showcase for "Made in Italy" products. Much has been said about its throbbing energy; it has been called a cultural locomotive and the European New York. Perhaps more than in any other Italian city, a successful economy has encouraged a diversified range of products.

The classy and understated strain in Milan's character is reflected in what has come to be internationally recognized as Milanese style. If the Milanese appear particularly style and status conscious, they are so with good taste. Though cognizant of their past, they are always looking for the new, and a nuance of the experimental is evident in everything from the layout of their subway to their gastronomy. The Milanese artisan is only a distant cousin to the Tuscan artisan of small, dusty *botteghe.* You will notice a ubiquitous sense of elegance, so don't go shopping for quaint local handicrafts. The Milanese artisan is at once artist and businessman, as aware of design aesthetic as he is concerned with advancement and modernity. The successful marriage of Milan's strong artisanal tradition with its developed industry is responsible for Italy's commercial comeback since World War II.

Milan has garnered recognition in many fields: La Scala has long been one of the leading opera houses in the world; the Pinacoteca di Brera museum houses one of the world's major art collections. For many decades, moreover, Milan has been prominent in the international banking and publishing worlds; it is also home to some of Europe's finest and most creative chefs.

The two sectors of industry that bring Milan its greatest worldwide acclaim, however, are fashion and design. Italian fashion really began in post-World War II Florence; it then moved to Rome in the 1960s and 1970s. But its subsequent shift to Milan was inevitable, for here the commercial and industrial interests of the country intersected. In addition to the atmosphere of unbridled creativity that the industry has brought to the city, it represents an important factor in national production and income.

Armani... Versace... Soprani... Missoni... Krizia... Trussardi... Moschino... the roll call of these global trend-setters goes on and on. Milan is the site of their ultramodern flagship boutiques, their sleek showrooms and often their factories. In a sense, today's designers have reached the same historical significance as the Dukes of Milan. Like their predecessors, they have eagerly taken on the role of patrons of the arts:

they have built theaters, designed costumes for the La Scala ballet troupe, sponsored and made possible restorations and cultural events, and established foundations. Under their aegis, they have created in Milan a prestigious mecca for design talents from around the world.

The dizzying profusion of such designers' stores offers the shopper a staggering choice of upscale possibilities. The range of moderately priced shops is equally wide. Such an array of boutiques makes shopping in Milan a natural citywide pastime. Milan is the test tube of Italy; trends originate here before sweeping down the peninsula and popping up on another continent a season later. If a trend takes hold—wild prints one year, postmodern décor another—it can soon monopolize the entire city, as a visual once-over of the city's boutique windows will confirm.

Milan is a big, open city. It boasts large department stores, wide streets, and a modern and clean subway for easy maneuvering. A bird's-eye view would give you a clear understanding of the three concentric ring roads laid out at different times in the city's past; they encircle the geographical center of the Piazza del Duomo and are essential to the plan of midtown Milan. The same bird's-eye view would reveal the many beautiful hidden courtyards that remain a secret to most visitors. A characteristic of the *meneghino* (native Milanese) architecture, these lush *cortili* and flowering gardens are tucked away behind the walls of imposing grey palazzos. Most remain inaccessible to the passerby, so if you're yearning for a shopping break in a cool, refreshing setting, go off to one of Milan's numerous large public parks.

For a more easily attained view of the lay of the land, pay a visit to the Duomo, the sanctum sanctorum dearest to the heart of every Milanese, which is second in size to Rome's St. Peter's. It's a mere 166 steps (or a modern elevator ride) to this citadel's roof for a peek at Milan through 96 gargoyles and 135 Gothic spires. You'll peer down at the Piazza del Duomo, meeting place for *tutta Milano* since the Middle Ages. Before you, stretching toward the La Scala opera house, is the Galleria Vittorio Emanuele, built in the late 1800s. It is the most magnificent of Milan's covered *gallerie,* covered pedestrian walkways lined with shops, boutiques and cafés that run perpendicular to wide avenues; they are as close an approximation as any Italian city offers to the modern American shopping mall.

The Duomo is the heart of our first neighborhood, the Duomo/ Vittorio Emanuele area. It is, logically, the most heavily visited, and makes for great "window walks" when shops close at the end of the day. Just north of here is the Montenapoleone/Spiga area, which exemplifies Italian

shopping at its most elegant. In search of space, boutiques and shops have spilled over into quaint side streets such as Via Sant'Andrea and Via Bigli. Brera lies beyond this area, a popular, recently regentrified neighborhood that snuggles between two major parks. Due west of the Duomo is the Magenta/Vercelli area, which takes its name from two handsome store-lined avenues, and south of the Duomo is Porta Ticinese. Each quarter has its own character and predilection for a particular kind of shopping, which is explained in the introductions to the individual neighborhoods.

Be sure to consult the specially prepared directories and guides for Milan: the Designer Boutique Directory, page 227; Shoe-Shopping Directory to Downtown Milan, page 232; A Guide to Italian Contemporary Design, page 189.

Shopping in Milan

STORE HOURS. The schedule for stores is generally 9:00 A.M. to 1:00 P.M. and 3:00 to 7:30 P.M. Many stores vary this by a half hour; numerous stores in the Duomo/Vittorio Emanuele and Montenapoleone areas close for only one hour at lunch, usually from 2:00 to 3:00 or from 1:30 to 2:30. Stores close all day Sunday and on Monday morning. Food shops stay open Monday mornings, but close on Monday afternoon.

Unlike other Italian cities that succumb to the summer heat, Milan does not change its store hours during the summer months, except that many stores take the option of closing Saturday afternoons. They also acquiesce in closing for part or all of the month of August.

In addition to the Italian national holidays (see page 11), all shops in Milan are closed on December 7, the day of its patron saint, St. Ambrose. Shopping won't come to a complete halt, however, for on December 7 the streets surrounding the medieval Basilica of Sant'Ambrogio come alive with a characteristic open-air market called "O Bej O Bej."

BANK HOURS. Milan banks are open from Monday through Friday, from 8:30 A.M. to 1:30 P.M. and from 3:00 to 4:00 P.M. or 2:45 to 3:45 P.M. All banks are closed on Saturday and Sunday. A number of American and foreign banks have representative branches in Milan. You can draw cash in lire against a Visa credit card at numerous branches of the Banca d'America e d'Italia; the most centrally located branch is at Via Manzoni 5

(telephone 8827). If you hold an American Express card, you can cash personal checks from your American bank at the American Express office at Via Brera 3 (telephone 85.571), Monday through Friday, 9:00 A.M. to 5:30 P.M. nonstop.

In addition to most banks, any exchange office (*cambio*) will change your foreign currency into Italian lire. A number of these offices are located in the Piazza del Duomo and Galleria Vittorio Emanuele area, and follow the customary store hours.

GETTING AROUND. *Subway.* There's something romantic about a city that still employs original trams dating back to the 1920s, but if you're more concerned with getting somewhere quickly and simply, follow the orange "MM" signs for the underground Metropolitana Milanese. Built rather late for a city as progressive as Milan, the subway system dates from the early 1960s and still looks fresh and grime-free. There is a red line and a green line, with a yellow line currently under construction, and large subway maps in each underground station or for sale at most newsstands outline its far-reaching routes. Tickets are sold at the newsstands at each subway stop, or can be bought from machines. A word about the subway's public bathrooms: they are usually unexpectedly clean and often welcomed finds.

Taxis. In Milan, unlike Florence and Rome, you can flag down a free taxi at any street corner, if you sight one. Most taxis are lined up at stands, which are often no more than a block

La Scala, the doyenne of opera houses.

or two away; these are usually located in large piazzas or along major avenues. The following are just a few of those in the neighborhoods we include in this chapter: Piazza del Duomo, Piazza Scala, Piazza Cinque Giornate (Duomo/Vittorio Emanuele), Largo San Babila (Montenapoleone), Largo Treves (Brera), Piazzale Baraca (Vercelli/Magenta), and Piazza XXIV Maggio (Porta Ticinese). In a pinch, you can always phone for a taxi, though you'll need to know some Italian or enlist an Italian-speaking friend (telephone 8585, 8388, 6767, or 5251).

SHOPPING ETIQUETTE.

Milan is perhaps the easiest of Italian cities for a foreigner to comprehend. The modern (and often English-speaking) Milanese are cordial, although not as immediately expansive as Italians you

may find in points farther south. The city boasts a number of large stores that are not unlike mini-department stores, and the sales help is generally more receptive to the American pastime of browsing than is true in other Italian cities. Much of this is due to the tidal waves of international buyers who converge on the many important trade fairs. They frequent the retail world to see what is new under the Milanese sun, enjoying the new blood of the young, entrepreneurial shop owners. The traditional custom of one-on-one service by skilled sales help still exists, however. You can usually tell by the relaxed atmosphere of the larger shops and the more formal air of specialty stores whether browsing is encouraged or frowned upon. Prices are inflexible, so this is not the town for bargaining, something the Milanese consider a Southern pastime. Credit cards are more widely accepted than elsewhere. Always ask if store owners will ship for you; the *milanesi* are both gracious and reliable.

SHIPPING SERVICES.

Italcargo is a reliable commercial shipper that has a New York City office [telephone (718) 656-3022]. Their Milan office is at Via Cassanese 214 in Segrate [telephone (21.39.9510)]. Italcargo will pick up your purchases directly at the store or at your hotel, and will ship by air or boat. If you want to save by sending by boat, Italcargo will consolidate your items with other shipments going to the same port, thus keeping prices down. They do not crate large items, however, although they (or the store) will recommend a reliable packing service.

Signor Renzo Zendron, director of the Milan office of Italcargo, speaks English and will help you with any arrangements. The firm also has conveniently located agents in Rome, Florence and Verona (outside Venice), who will coordinate all of your purchases throughout Italy.

INCIDENTALS. *Tourism office.* The EPT (Ente Provinciale di Turismo, or Milan Tourist Agency) has an office in Piazza del Duomo at Via Marconi 1 (8:45 A.M. to 12:30 P.M. and 1:30 to 6:00 P.M., closed Sunday). They have all information on hotels, reservations, tours, and museums. The Information Office (Ufficio Informazioni) can be found nearby, in the Galleria Vittorio Emanuele (8:00 A.M. to 11:00 P.M. daily; open Sundays in the summer). They have information and often have tickets for shows, concerts and cultural events taking place in Milan.

Milanesi, *the most un-Italian of the Italians.*

English-language films. For films shown in English, the best location is the Cinema Angelicum at Piazza Sant'Angelo 2 (telephone 65.92.748), Wednesday through Sunday. A number of other cinemas often run American films *in versione originale* (abbreviated "v.o.") with Italian subtitles (be forewarned that dubbing is otherwise widely found); these can be found in the newspaper or with the help of your hotel concierge.

Pharmacies. The pharmacy at the Stazione Centrale is open 24 hours. A number of pharmacies stay open from 9:00 P.M. to 8:30 A.M., including the Cooperativa Farmaceutica in Piazza del Duomo. Look in the newspaper *Corriere della Sera* for the list of pharmacies that take turns staying open on Sundays.

English-language publications. The bimonthly *Night & Day Milano* is distributed free by most hotels. It offers pertinent information about shopping, dining, happenings, current exhibitions and hotels. You'll find all of this, as well as an introduction to historical Milan, in the English *Tutta Milano,* available from EPT, the information office for tourists in Piazza del Duomo. *A Key to Milan,* a well-organized, detailed guidebook to the city, will tell you everything you ever wanted to know about Milan. It is available at most centrally located bookshops and some newsstands. *Milanbook* is a monthly magazine that lists what's new and what's happening in town. *Viva Milano,* a newspaper published in Italian (but easily decipherable) lists pizzerias, restaurants, night spots, and events, covering the contemporary scene in Milan.

Milan Specialties

DESIGN AND HOME FURNISHINGS

Design is the key to the character of Milan. The city thrives on a culture of modernism founded in the 1930s by a select group of Milanese and international architects; they nurtured a wave of design sensitivity that has affected every fiber of the Italian fabric. This, together with its burgeoning industrial productivity, has established Milan as a world-recognized design innovator. The same dynamic design seen in furniture, store and home décor, computer hardware and racing bicycles is reflected in everyday objects. It has left nothing untouched, it has overlooked no seemingly insignificant aspect of the Milanese milieu. The Compasso d'Oro, a prestigious biennial award for outstanding products of Italian design, originated in Milan in 1954; the Domus Academy, the first postgraduate design school in all of Italy, was founded here in 1983. Design talents have come from all corners of the world to work and live in this propitious atmosphere of experimentalism and high-energy creativity. If you are a lover of fine design, you can freely visit showrooms displaying such world-renowned names as Vico Magistretti, Achille Castiglioni and Ettore Sottsass. Most of them are concentrated near San Babila. (See A Guide to Italian Contemporary Design, page 189.)

FASHION

Milan is the indisputable seat of Italian fashion, a title that once belonged to Florence and, after that, Rome. The meteoric careers of Milan's premier fashion designers form a story that has been repeated at no other point in history. During the spring and fall "Fashion Week," new arrivals and established houses alike vie to orchestrate the most original and dynamic runway show, and buyers come from all continents to see what Milan heralds as next season's sensation. The presence of the highest-quality Italian fabric mills, the proximity of Como's deluxe silk industry, and the cultural dynamism that infuses the city all combine to cultivate one of the greatest success stories in international fashion. What is seen on these runways will later affect the colors and shapes dressing Europe, America and the Orient. It is a sophisticated, European look as well as one of avant-garde, forward derring-do. Whether traditional and updated or workday and relaxed weekend wear, Milanese fashion embraces all corners of the wardrobe. It includes accessories such as shoes and hats; the word "milliner" originated here. While the Milan look is aristocratic and refined, it is never showy. A large middle class supports the demand for up-to-the-minute fashion of moderate quality and price range, so the shopping possibilities are never one-dimensional. They can overwhelm the shopper who has limited time.

SHOES AND BAGS

The only problem you're likely to encounter while shopping for leather accessories in Italy is the enormous

Stores appear more like art galleries.

selection from which to choose. Milan, ever confident of its supremacy in the fashion industry, has a particularly alluring selection of shoe and handbag stores for all degrees of fashion consciousness and all budgets. You'll find a wide and bountiful cross section, from inexpensive and colorful stamped leathers to more precious and exotic skins at the most sophisticated designer level. These fine leathergoods are produced in Milan's periphery, where insuperable craftsmanship and artisan skills work hand-in-hand with advanced techniques and innovative designs. The creative stimulus of Milan's premier designers has taken this centuries-old art to new heights. Milan takes risks and thrives on novelty. You'll also find an unusually wide range of sizes and widths in the city's myriad shoe stores. Next season's *dernier cri* is found here

first, alongside the hand-sewn, classic models. For your one-shot whims or serious investment purchases, Milan's diversity in styles and prices is perhaps the greatest in Italy. (See Shoe-Shopping Directory to Downtown Milan, page 232.)

JEWELRY

As with its fashion, Milan's jewelry runs a glorious gamut of styles, while never violating the boundaries of good taste. What you might find in Florence in a few choice stores, you will find in Milan in sparkling abundance. Artisan skills are elevated to the very apogee of fashion by jewelers whose innovations show the influence of seasonal ready-to-wear collections. Jewelry designers are not afraid to make strong statements, nor are the self-assured Milanese women afraid to wear their creations every day, with jeans or formal wear. Jewelry is an intrinsic ingredient in Milan's status consciousness—one that is evident though never showy, bold but never brassy. Exquisitely made modern jewelry shares the common denominator of impeccable craftsmanship with more traditional pieces by established names like Del Vecchio and Buccellati. Demure, moneyed ladies from Milan's old families prefer the latter, while the more fashion-forward young women go with the latest materials, such as hematite and steel-and-gold combinations in new, sculptured forms.

The drama of Milan's gourmet food stores.

SALUMERIE

A gastronomic tour of Milan's best-known *salumerie* will show you that the city is as rich in epicurean offerings as in high fashion or jewelry. Deriving their name from *salumi,* salt-cured meats, these corner stores as rendered by the Milanese offer everything needed for a gourmet banquet, usually in a theatrical setting from another epoch. The *salumeria* has become a Milanese institution, as epitomized in the six-part, century-old Peck consortium in the Duomo area, said to attract as many visitors as the cathedral itself. Stop in any *salumeria* to look at the counters laden with cheeses, homemade pastas, salads, cold cuts, pâtés, truffled delicacies, and fresh pastries, and you will promise yourself never to eat out again. This is the ultimate takeout dream, whose sophistication and dramatic displays draw long lines of typically Milanese designer-clad clients.

BOOKSTORES

In a country that was a forerunner in manuscript illumination and then in printing, Milan heads the publishing field. Milanese publishers, long experts in color separations, still lead the world in the printing of art books. The innovator of the art catalog, Electa, is based in Milan and works with many prestigious foreign clients, such as New York City's Metropolitan Museum and Pompidou Center. Many national publishers who left an indelible mark on contemporary Italian literature and culture were educated in Milan, and paved the way for the then-nascent publishing sector. The country's largest book and periodical publishers are today based here, and most of them have their own state-of-the-art bookstores. Many acclaimed bookstores specialize in areas such as architecture and design; visiting international professionals and bibliophiles will find a wealth of high-quality artworks here. Even corner newsstands stock colorful, high-gloss magazines whose range of interests has grown far beyond their original sphere of fashion and business. Following a recent period of precarious transition, Milan's major publishing dynasties are once more on the upswing. It is not by chance that Milan is also home of the *Corriere della Sera,* Italy's most important daily newspaper.

Trade Fairs

More than one million visitors from around the world attend each year's Great April Fair, the largest of its kind.

Milan is an ideal city for trade fairs. This was already apparent in 1920 to a small group of merchants with a pioneer spirit who created the first Milan International Fair in a cluster of wooden shacks. It was so successful that it was moved in 1923 to its present site at the Milan Fairgrounds on Via Domodossola.

The Grande Fiera d'Aprile, as it is called today, is a gathering of minds and resources to showcase the spirit and quality of the "Made in Italy" label. Open to the public for two weeks each April, it is an enjoyable outing for Milanese families as well as professional and business people and an invaluable introduction for foreigners to the culture, technology and spirit of the Italian people. Today it is considered one of the most important trade fairs in Europe and the largest industrial and consumer-products exposition in the world.

Over 3000 Italian exhibitors from all industries participate, establishing contacts with visiting business representatives from around the globe. They exhibit the latest in products, services, and technology, from agricultural machinery and industrial computer systems to costume jewelry and equestrian sports accessories.

The growth of specialized markets, together with the unprecedented success of the Grand April Fair, has resulted in the spinoff of over 80 specialized annual fairs, with a total of 50,000 exhibitors. Unlike the Grande Fiera d'Aprile, most of these are open to the trade only. Some of the most important are:

Furniture (Salone del Mobile) & Lighting (Euroluce)—Third week of September.

Leather Bags & Luggage (MIPEL)—Third week in March; third week in October.

Men's Fashion, Designer (Collezioni) & Ready-to-Wear (Milanovendemoda Uomo)—Second and third weeks in January and second week in July.

Women's Fashion, Designer (Collezioni) & Ready-to-Wear (Milanovendemoda Donna,

Other specialized Milan fairs:

Antiques (Mostra dell'Antiquario)
Art (Biennale d'Arte Contemporanea)
Confectionery & Baked Goods (MIAD)
Costume Jewelry & Gifts (Chi Bi International)
Films & TV Films (MIFED)
Fine Jewelry (Gold Italia)
Home-Furnishing Textiles (STAR)
Housewares, Glass, China & Gifts (MACEF)
Knitwear (Anteprima-Ideamaglia, Esma-Eurotricot)
Sporting Goods & Accessories (MIAS)
Toys (Salone del Giocattolo)

MODIT)—Second week in March and first week in October.

Anyone interested in participating in the April Fair or any of these specialized fairs, either as an exhibitor or as a visitor, should contact the North American representative at (800) 524-2193 for more specific information.

A number of other fairs take place outside Milan.

COMO
Silks, Fabrics (Ideacomo)—First week in April, second week in October.

VICENZA
Gold & Silver Jewelry (Oreficeria & Argento)—Third week in January and second week in June.

FLORENCE
Men's Ready-to-Wear Fashion (Pitti Uomo)—Second week in January and first week in July.
Women's Ready-to-Wear Fashion (Pitti Trend)—Fourth week in February and third week in September.
Children's Ready-to-Wear (Pitti Bimbo)—Third week in January and second week in July.
Yarns & Fibers (Pitti Filati)—First week of February and second week of September.
Textiles (Prato Expo)—First week of April and fourth week of September.

BOLOGNA
Men's, Women's & Children's Footwear (MICAM)—Second week in March and first week in September.

For further information and specific dates on any of the above-listed special exhibits outside Milan, contact the Italian Trade Commission in New York City, (212) 980-1500; Los Angeles, (213) 879-0950; Chicago, (312) 670-4360; Atlanta, (404) 525-0660; or Houston, (713) 626-5531.

DISCOUNT STORES AND FACTORY OUTLETS

If you have a sense of adventure and don't need the security of doting sales help or the ambiance of a sleek boutique, try some of Milan's treasure hunts. A sense of fashion permeates the entire city, and most Milanese always manage to look like a million dollars. They check out the open-air markets and secondhand shops that are likely to stock special finds at low price tags. The Via San Gregorio, joining the train station with the Piazza della Repubblica, is a frequented strip of *engrosso,* or wholesale operations, of mostly junior fashions. They'll often sell to individual customers, cash only. But the real finds are the occasional factory outlet-style locations called *blocchisti,* such as those we list below; they sell last season's designer stock at discounts of sometimes up to 60 percent off

Continued next page

Continued from previous page
original retail prices. Savings can be major, but be prepared for a bargain-basement atmosphere, an amusing break from the red-carpet treatment of Via della Spiga.

Happy hunting!

GUCCI LIQUIDAZIONI
Via Corridoni 13
Tel. 78.47.21
Credit cards accepted
Open during lunch
Gucci items cost less than half their Italian retail price here, which is drastically less than you'd pay in the States. You're likely to find silk scarves, handbags, belts, small leathergoods and gift items on the ground floor. Upstairs is another floor of men's and women's sportswear and outerwear, shoes and boots. These are overproduction and end-of-season closeouts, not defective merchandise.

IL SALVAGENTE
Via Fratelli Bronzetti 16
Tel. 74.26.642
No credit cards accepted
This is the best-stocked closeout location in Milan for designerwear at 30- to 60-percent savings. You'll find Versace and Ferrè, Moschino and Biagiotti in abundance, but in fend-for-yourself order. Labels are usually left in clothing, but organization is at a minimum so come well rested and with a critical eye

for defective or used items among the new. The men's department is half the size of the women's; both can be found downstairs together with leather bags and shoes; children's is upstairs. These are samples, overruns, runway wardrobes and end-of-season closeouts. Try to shop here in the morning, when the store is less crowded. You'll also get first pick of the day's new arrivals. Before the annual August closing, there's a sale with reductions as great as 75 percent below the already discounted prices.

CENTRO DELLA SETA
Via Leopardi 26
Tel. 43.94.075
Credit cards accepted
If you can't make it to the silk-manufacturing town of Como, visit this Milan-based location for discounted buys of the prestigious Montero factory of deluxe silks. Beautiful scarves, ties, shawls, bolts of silk and some ready-to-wear with their own labels.

ARFLEX
Corso Lodi 102
Tel. 53.41.80
No credit cards accepted
This outlet offers floor samples, prototypes and end-of-series production from a noted furniture company, including a huge selection of sofas and chairs at substantial savings.

Outdoor Street and Flea Markets

If you plan to visit Florence as well as Milan, you may want to save your adventurous moments for the open-air *mercati* of that city. While Milan has a number of large, bustling outdoor markets, they are not as accessible or as accustomed to curious foreigners (no traveler's checks or credit cards accepted) as those in Florence. This could make them all the more inviting to the dauntless shopper, however. There are more flea markets and street markets selling used and antique items here than in other Italian cities. Regardless of their location, colorful Italian street markets will always hold a fascination for even the most timid of shoppers.

You'll have to appreciate something of the bargain-basement al fresco philosophy, where sharp elbows and patient rummaging through the mountains of goods can often result in some treasured finds, or at least provide an amusing break from Via Montenapoleone's sleek boutiques. If prices are not marked (and often even when they are), feel free to bargain, especially if you're buying more than one item from a particular stand and know a word or two of the language. Milanese store merchants may not be as receptive to bargaining as their compatriots in the south, but open-air markets bring merchants of another stripe—and they can only say no. Because this is Milan, you won't be surprised to find occasional articles of designer clothing and shoes; just in case, check them for defects even if you've been told they have none.

There are a number of small, rotating neighborhood markets that are quite charming and colorful when stumbled upon, but not necessarily worth the trip; one of the best is the Brera market, held in Piazza Mirabello on Monday and Thursday morning. "The early bird gets the worm" on any market day, but if you're just curious to experience the sights, sounds and smells of these authentic Milanese scenes, stroll through at your leisure—and, as always, watch your handbag.

FIERA SENIGALLIA
Via Calatafimi
(off Via Aurispa and Via Gian Galeazzo in the Porta Ticinese area)
All day Saturday
Peddlers and dealers converge here to unload records, books, bric-a-brac, antique clothing and linen, curiosities and antiques of questionable provenance. Stall-holders sell new or used clothing and lots of jeans, especially popular with teenagers looking for inexpensive finds. You may see an odd bicycle or tape player, probably of dubious origin. The Saturday markets here and at Papiniano will give you the biggest selection of goods.

MERCATO PAPINIANO
Viale Papiniano
(between Piazzale Cantore and Piazzale Aquileja in the Porta Ticinese area)
Tuesday morning and all day Saturday
Two hundred stands draw all of Milan here on weekends to check out the wide and ever-changing assortment of housewares, foodstuffs, flowers and clothes. You can find some good values in knitwear, jeans, costume jewelry, and cotton or woolen underwear.

MERCATO DELL' USATO
in Bollate's Piazza Carlo Marx
(in Bollate, outskirts of Milan; 10-minute
train ride from Ferrovie Nord)
Sunday from 9:00 A.M. to 6:00 P.M.

Those who love Paris for its "Marché aux Puces" (flea market) will find this an easy trip for a fun Sunday while retail Milan sleeps. This characteristic market has more second- and third-hand items than bona-fide antiques, but you might find good wrought-iron objects, unusual costume jewelry from the 1940s, or anything else under the sun.

ANTIQUES MARKET
Via Fiori Chiari, Piazza Formentini and
Via Madonnina (in the Brera area)
Third Saturday of every month;
dawn to dusk

Fifty antique dealers and collectors come from far and wide to hawk their goods. Interesting relics from the past include some good furniture, bric-a-brac, anything old and some things new.

MERCATONE DELL'ANTIQUARIATO DEI NAVIGLI (NAVIGLIO GRANDE MARKET)
Via Ripa Ticinese (which follows the Naviglio Grande Canal in the Porta Ticinese area)
Last Saturday of the month,
early morning to 7:00 P.M.

The Brera market is small and cozy compared to the 300 stands that appear for this monthly event. Visit it more as a curiosity than for serious buys, but it's an education just to see what turns up.

STAMP AND COIN MARKET
Via Armorari (behind Piazza Cordusio and
the Central Post Office in the Duomo area)
Sunday morning

This specialized market is for both true *appassionati* and curious strollers. Some of the collections that appear are considered rather impressive, and it is an interesting browse.

FLOWER MARKET
Piazzetta Reale (in the Duomo area)
Sunday morning

Not far from the above stamp and coin mart, this small *piazzetta* comes into brilliant bloom with a magnificent palette of fresh flowers and plants, from the exotic to the simple and beautiful.

SPECIAL FAIRS

O BEJ O BEJ
Piazza Sant'Ambrogio and surrounding
streets (in the Vercelli/Magenta area)
December 7, all day

If you're in town on the feast of Milan's beloved patron, St. Ambrose, you'll find that the only buying and selling going on in town is at this characteristic *meneghino* market. Its name (also written 'O Bei O Bei') comes from the old cry used by stall vendors to attract their customers. In addition to food stands and a lot of families with children, you'll find used and antique furniture and varied objects.

FESTA DEI NAVIGLI
Along the Navigli (canals) in the Porta
Ticinese area
First Sunday of June

Folkloric games and music highlight this colorful local festival, and although it's on a Sunday, you'll find the neighborhood's numerous antique and secondhand shops open for the day.

Milanese Cuisine

It is only fitting that a great urban center of such wealth and artistic sensibility has the means and taste to eat out often and in style. Lunch may more and more resemble the on-the-go sandwich or *panino* that the *milanesi* had previously regarded as an American weakness, but dinner remains a sacred ritual, whether at home or in one of the plethora of good restaurants that populate the city. It is both an epicurean art and an entertainment form.

Milan is the country's melting pot in a gastronomic as well as in a cultural sense, and has adapted many dishes from the countries lying just miles north of the city. Yet despite the tendency to mix and blend, there remains a distinct Milanese cuisine, one whose use of butter, cheese, milk and cream is what many foreigners generically identify as "Northern Italian" cooking. While some local specialties such as *risotto* and *cotoletta alla milanese* have crossed national borders and are today popular abroad, other more obscure dishes, such as *rostin negàa* or *cassoeula,* must be tracked down in Milan's typical *trattorie.*

The cuisine of Milan that most clearly reflects the city's role of trendsetter in contemporary Italian life, however, is *cucina nuova*—a personal, light and elegant approach to food that puts a new face on traditional dishes. It combines new and simple cooking techniques and ingredients with the tried and true, exploring unknown gastronomic horizons. Alongside the bastions of fine traditional dining, you'll find top-of-the-line restaurants such as Gualtiero Marchesi and La Scaletta, both trailblazing forces of this new wave. A growing number of inventive restaurants with excellent food and wines are springing up all over the city. Young, well-traveled entrepreneurial Milanese are replacing the older, family-run *trattorie* with their chic, handsomely decorated (and usually more expensive) new establishments.

Milan is said to have the freshest fish in all of Italy—fresher, they say, than on the coast. Landlocked yet considered the seafood capital, Milan can rely on the pick of the catch; packed in ice, it arrives daily at what is considered Italy's major fish market even before the island or coastal locals get a crack at it. Eating seafood, however, is never inexpensive.

If you've reached Milan by train or car, you will have seen the open stretches of rice paddies that make Italy Europe's No. 1 producer and one of the largest consumers of rice. *Risotto,* a delicious alternative to pasta, is a commonplace first-course choice made with a wide array of different ingredients. Most simple of these variations is the traditional *risotto alla milanese*, made with saffron broth and bright yellow in color. It is traditionally served with *ossobuco,* another Milanese favorite. Yet another staple in the local *meneghina* cuisine is Gorgonzola, *il re di formaggio,* "the king of cheese"; it takes its name from the small town just ten miles from Milan where it was originally produced. Made from cow's milk, it is pale and delicious. Its

continued on page 158

MILANESE CUISINE GLOSSARY

Milan's prominent position in the vanguard of trends is also evident at the table. The Milanese tendency to innovate makes dining a nouvelle experience, so finding the classic and traditional dishes we list below is not always easy. However, be the cuisine regional, imaginative or, as often happens, a combination of both, in Milan *si mangia bene.*

Primo Piatto (First Course)

Risotto–A short-grained, starchy rice dish sautéed, then cooked slowly with broth, forming a creamy sauce. Any number of ingredients can be added (vegetables, fish or seafood, meat, cheeses). Simplest is the *risotto alla milanese,* made with saffron threads and bone marrow, or the *risotto nero,* made with the black ink of squid.

Risotto al salto–Leftover risotto fried like a pancake.

Minestrone–Vegetable soup made with rice; served at room temperature in summer and hot in winter.

Secondo Piatto (Entrée)

Costoletta (also *cotoletta*) *alla milanese*–Breaded veal cutlet, cut very thin and sautéed in butter and served very crisp.

Asparagi alla bismarck–Boiled asparagus covered by a lightly fried egg and melted butter that creates a sauce for dipping your asparagus spears. Using the fingers is allowed.

Cassoeula–Typically a winter dish made up of many pork parts (ears, feet, ribs, skin and innards), cooked with cabbage, vegetables and wine. Often served with polenta, a cornmeal staple.

Ossobuco–Veal shin served with the bone, whose marrow is considered a delicacy. First lightly fried, then cooked with tomato pulp and wine before being sprinkled with *gremolata* (minced garlic, parsley and lemon peel). Usually served with *risotto alla milanese.*

Rostin negàa–Pork or veal pot-roasted in butter with herbs and wine.

Fritto misto alla milanese–Brains, liver, lung, marrow, and seasonal vegetables (mushrooms, artichokes, zucchini and zucchini flowers), all deep-fried.

Carpaccio–A Venetian creation adopted by the Milanese consisting of wafer-thin slices of raw lean beef, which can be served with various sauces or vegetable toppings. A new variation, *carpaccio di pesce,* or raw fish slices, will appeal to sushi lovers.

Formaggio (Cheese)

Gorgonzola–Strong, Roquefort-like cheese made from cow's milk. Its character often lends a distinctive note to sauces, or it can be enjoyed alone with a glass of *picolit,* a special wine from Friuli.

Dolce (Dessert)

Oss de mort–Literally, "bones to bite," almond or hazelnut cookies that are just as hard as bones.

Panettone–Now found year-round

throughout Italy and abroad, this egg-rich Milanese Christmas cake is made from yeasted dough and plenty of candied fruits and raisins. Dome-shaped and airy in texture, it can be filled with marmalade, ice cream or fresh whipped cream. The fresh-baked version tastes nothing like the boxed version found in profusion.

Panini

The *panino* (sandwich), the Milanese answer to a hot dog on the run, is considerably more nutritious and unquestionably more delicious. Follow the lunch crowds of businessmen who mark the site of a good *paninoteca. Alla piastra* means they'll make it up for you fresh on a roll (*panino*) or long French bread (*pane francese*). The following vocabulary will help you realize your desired combination.

Salumi generally refers to all sausages eaten cold. Other sandwich meats include:

Prosciutto–ham, whose favorite version is *crudo* (raw cured); air-dried and sliced paper-thin, it is considered a delicacy. The alternative is *cotto,* or boiled ham.

Bresaola–cured raw beef, mostly from the Lombardy region, sliced paper-thin.

Speck–smoked-cured raw ham.

Mortadella–a large, bologna-type cold cut made of pork meat laced with large bits of white pork fat.

Arista–cold roast pork usually flavored with rosemary.

Cotoletta–breaded veal cutlet, often used as a sandwich filler.

Cheeses are commonly added, and they're often lined up for your perusal and pointing. Fresh mozzarella, mild fontina or the typical Swiss Emmenthal is always on hand. *Caprino* and *stracchino* are creamy spreadable choices, both rather mild. If you expect tomatoes (*pomodori*) or any dressing, you'll have to ask for it: *maionese* (mayonnaise), *senape* (mustard), *salsa aurora* (russian dressing), or occasionally even ketchup.

Condiments will also spice up your creation, and there are *sottaceti* vegetables (pickled in vinegar) from which to pick: *funghi* (mushrooms), *carciofi* (artichokes) and *cipollini* (pearl onions). If you'd like to have your *panino* heated, ask to have it *riscaldato* (warmed up) or *tostato* (toasted on a grill), and enjoy!

continued from page 155
strong character and unmistakable scent are due to the thin veins of blue mold that often lead foreigners to compare it to the French Roquefort, although the latter is made from ewe's milk and, according to proud Italians, is not quite as good.

Milan is a working town, and many young career couples who eat out at the end of a long day would just as soon keep their meals easy and light. Pizzerias are a Milanese distinction, more abundant here than in Naples, their city of origin. The Milanese pizza, it is not surprising to note, adds flair, finesse and fantasy to its toppings in an atmosphere usually bright and upbeat. Together with the unpretentious *paninoteca* sandwich bars, where fresh, multiple-ingredient creations are made up at your request, pizzerias are champions of the fast-food lunch market in a quick-paced town.

But if it's evening, and you'd like to congratulate yourself on a productive day of shopping, seek out a fine restaurant and sit back with a local sparkling wine such as the superb Ca' del Bosco, Metodo Champenois or Franciacorta Pinot by Bellavista. Look for the quality reds Pinot Nero, Maurizio Zanella or Franciacorta Rosso, all smooth and dry, by Ca' del Bosco. While in Lombardy, don't miss the fine red wines from the neighboring Piemonte (Gaja and Ceretto) or the dry white wines from Friuli (Abbazia di Rosazzo, Livio Felluga, Schiopetto or Ronchi di Cialla); found in better restaurants, these are always an excellent choice.

Dinner is usually eightish. It is more commonplace and is recommended to reserve here than in other Italian cities, especially if a multitude of international buyers have converged on the city for one of its myriad trade shows.

Duomo/Vittorio Emanuele

*M*ilan life revolves around the Duomo. No other European city regards its cathedral with more affection. It is the most extravagant creation of religious Gothic architecture in the world, second in size only to St. Peter's in Rome. The Milanese will proudly point out the 135 lofty marble pinnacles, the 150 marvelous gargoyles and the 3500 pieces of pious sculpture that encrust this 14th-century monument inside and out.

It is a regal and stately piece of architecture surrounded by Milan's finest shopping. This is culminated by the Via Montenapoleone area, which we have treated as a neighborhood apart. Just north of the broad Piazza del Duomo at the entrance to the cavernous 19th-century Galleria Vittorio Emanuele II, old-time pensioners stand and argue for hours over national scandals and soccer scores. The four-story Galleria is Milan's largest and most elegant enclosed shopping arcade, referred to as the city's *salotto,* or living room. Its triumphal glass-and-iron cupola stands 160 feet over colorful mosaic pavements, and shelters locals and tourists alike from urban traffic and inclement weather. The Galleria's main artery, lined with boutiques, cafés, bookstores, banks, travel agencies and a large public telephone service, connects the Piazza del Duomo with the tradition-steeped Teatro alla Scala, the doyenne of opera houses.

When you walk east from the Duomo along the Corso Vittorio Emanuele II, you will come upon a number of smaller enclosed, shop-lined arcades. The handsome shops and boutiques of Vittorio Emanuele spill over into these *gallerie,* all built since World War II; the Caffè Moda Durini is a microcosm of 22 high-fashion boutiques a notch lower in price than those around the corner in the Via Montenapoleone area.

This wide strip of porticoed sidewalks is always alive, brightened by the window displays of its accessory and fashion shops, movie houses and bar-cafés. The Piazza San Babila, an example of how the whole city would have looked had Fascism realized its grand urban architectural plans in the 1930s, is better known today as the site of Burghy's, a major

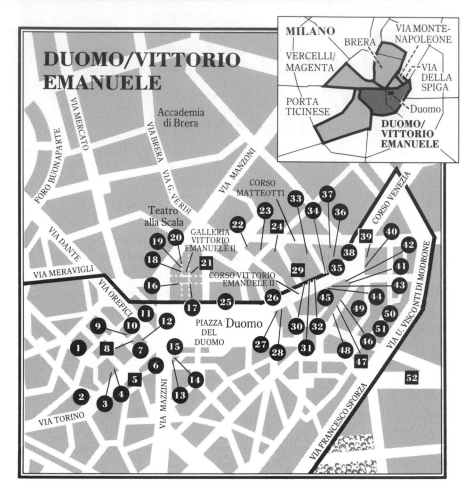

hamburger haven for Milan's fashion-clad youth.

A special gastronomic niche for shoppers lies just south of the Piazza del Duomo. The world-class Peck archipelago of gourmet food stores, together with premier greengrocers, wine shops, chic fish markets and old-fashioned pastry shops will impress you with just how important food is to the Milanese, as well as with the style in which it is presented. This Lucullan enclave nestled among such small streets as Victor Hugo, Speronari, Spadari and San Maurilio will let you discover a Milan different from the city whose windows blaze with designer gems.

Some shoppers may never leave this centralized area, seeing Milan as a one-dimensional city of style and class, impressive architecture and upscale stores. But here, too, are some of the country's most acclaimed restaurants and cafés, offering a little rest from a lot of shopping.

ANTIQUE JEWELRY

WATCHES

1 ERA L'ORA
Via del Bollo 3
Tel. 87.24.36
Moderate; no credit cards accepted

For years a passionate collector of antique timepieces, Massimo Baracca is renowned for his extraordinary selection. His specialty is high-quality antique wristwatches dating from 1900 to 1960, including the prestigious makes of Rolex, Patek Philippe, Jaeger Le Coultre and Vacheron Constantin. The boutique is redolent of the art-deco period, when many of his prized pieces were made. Every timepiece comes with a one-year guarantee, and Signor Baracca does repairs.

The spacious, enclosed four-story Galleria.

WINES

2 RONCHI
Via San Maurilio 7
Tel. 80.89.88
Moderate; no credit cards accepted

Maria Luisa Ronchi, great-granddaughter of the founder of this revered wine store, is no newcomer to the world of wines. Italy's first female sommelier in 1969, Maria Luisa today supplies her *enoteca* with over 600 labels of Italy's best vintages. Barolo, Barbaresco and Brunello (from 1937 to 1974) are the pearls. The selection of French wines is no less impressive, with over 150 Bordeaux and Sauternes and 120 Burgundies and Champagnes. To finish off, there are over 200 Italian *grappe*.

SPORTS GEAR

DANCE & EXERCISE WEAR

3 LA BOTTEGA DEL TUTU
Via Torino 48
Tel. 87.53.63
Moderate; credit cards accepted

The prima ballerinas of Milan would think of buying their ballet apparel and slippers nowhere else, and their autographed photos on the wall express their thanks. The Bottega's owners have been involved in costume design for the Scala, and pastel ballet costumes hang from the ceiling like petals. There are colorful cotton leotards that can be used for day or night and numerous dance, gym and exercise outfits and accessories. The stock is extensive, and although the name "Bottega" suggests simplicity, the décor is high-tech, with strobes and videos.

KNITTING YARNS

DESIGNER COLLECTION

4 CAGLIANI & CROCI
Via Torino 46
Tel. 80.00.96
Moderate; no credit cards accepted

A great find for the serious knitter, Cagliani & Croci stands proudly behind its original, early-1900s storefront. It is something like a supermarket of fine yarns, albeit a classy one, with endless skeins colorfully stocked from floor to ceiling. In the 80-year-old family-run shop, professionals will help you choose among wool, silk and cotton qualities, showing you the season's best from top Italian names such as Filpucci, Baruffa, Valentino, Trussardi, Coveri, Krizia and Filcrosci.

SUSTENANCE

RISTORANTE/TRATTORIA

5 LATTERIA UNIONE
Via dell'Unione 6
Tel. 87.44.01
Inexpensive; no credit cards accepted
Lunch only; closed Sunday

One of Milan's oldest *latterie,* or dairy stores, doubles as a good little vegetarian restaurant. It is open for lunch only, and is very popular with office workers in the Via Torino neighborhood, who love the packed-but-friendly atmosphere. It is best to come after 2:00 P.M., when the hubbub has settled—but before 3:00, when you'll find the daily dishes *finiti.* When you've secured one of the precious four tables pushed up against the wall, choose from a wide menu where any of the *casalinga* (homemade) selections are delicious:

chunky minestrones, fresh pastas, omelets and risottos with different vegetable combinations, soufflé-like *sformati* and stuffed vegetables. At other times, the Latteria returns to its role as neighborhood supplier of cheese, yogurt, butter, eggs, milk and cream.

LEATHERGOODS

BAGS & BELTS
Casual

6 FIORDIPELLE È
Via Speronari 8
Tel. 87.10.69
Moderate; credit cards accepted

Here is a tiny little shop that has nice artisanal work of its own production in big, natural-leather bags and tooled-leather belts with interesting buckles that are a great and timeless look for jeans. Imitation-silver earrings and jewelry are ethnic, bohemian and inexpensively priced.

FOOD, WINES & SUSTENANCE

Great Assortment of Delicacies

7 PECK (see addresses below)
Moderate; credit cards accepted

The islands of gastronomic delight that make up the Peck archipelago now number six. For food-loving tourists, pressing their noses to Peck's windows can be a Milan experience almost as memorable as viewing Leonardo da Vinci's "Last Supper." And there's a dizzying selection of windows to see, for Italy's most admired food emporium has expanded since first opening in Milan over 100 years ago, to include wine, cheese and other specialties.

Peck was founded in 1883 by Francesco Peck, a Czech *salumiere* from Prague who wanted to introduce Milan to his specialty of smoked meats. Today it is Italy's unrivaled gourmet delicatessen, and as much a *milanese* tradition as eating *panettone* at Christmastime. If this little niche of town is renowned as an epicurean heaven, the various Peck locations deserve much of the credit. There is poetic artistry in their displays and a guarantee of freshness, profusion and insuperable quality in their merchandise. This incomparable institution is today carried on by the four busy Stoppani brothers.

Each of the Peck stores is but a stone's throw from the others. Stop in any or all of them for a visual feast and great shopping. Unlike most food shops, they all take credit cards. With the exception of Il Ristorante, which is closed only on Sundays, all are closed Monday afternoons.

GASTRONOMIA PECK (Via Spadari 9, tel. 87.17.37). This is Peck's main shop, where you can find everything for a 5- or 50-course meal. Shelves groan under the enormous selection of platters of prepared foods and salads, fresh pastas, smoked and roasted meats, pâtés and preserved vegetables or fruits to go. Line up with Milan's housewives and maids waiting to be served by the good-humored, polka-dot-bow-tied employees.

BOTTEGA DEL MAIALE (Via Victor Hugo 3, tel. 80.53.528). Just across the street from the main store, Peck's "Pork Shop" offers every imaginable part of the pig, including snout, ears and feet. There is a proliferation of salamis, sausages and cold cuts from all over Italy; hams hanging from the ceiling are festooned with brightly colored bows.

Peck, Italy's most remarkable food emporium.

CASA DEL FORMAGGIO (Via Speronari 3, tel. 80.08.58). A heady concentration of over 350 cheeses represents every region in Italy, and ranges from its most sophisticated to its most provincial products. Many of these products cannot be found outside their native towns except at Peck's. There are cheeses made with nuts, olives and herbs; gourd-shaped provolone and *pugliese burrate* hang from the ceiling like ivory-colored grapes; 50 fresh cheeses arrive daily. The "House of Cheese" is especially noted for its high-quality *parmigiano reggiano*.

ROSTICCERIA (Via Cantù 3, tel. 86.93.017). The takeout rotisserie grill everyone wishes he had around the corner. Tender spit-roasted fowl and roasted meats are done to perfection with a number of fresh pastas or roasted vegetables to complete your takeout picnic in the park. There's standing room at a narrow counter along the wall for simple and savory samplings.

BOTTEGA DEL VINO (Via Victor Hugo 4, tel. 86.10.40). Avoid lunch hour here, when a wave of Milan's businessmen arrive for their gourmet fast-food break. Accompanying a stand-up sampling of Peck's delectables are over 200 fine wines that can be ordered by the glass, and as many as 500 are available by the bottle.

Food staged with drama and flair.

IL RISTORANTE (Via Victor Hugo 4, tel. 87.67.74). If you'd like to sample any or all of the above in modern and gracious surroundings and with excellent service, try the new Peck restaurant, located downstairs just below the Bottega del Vino. An extensive menu is made *espresso* (to order), and a changing selection offers creative cuisine such as salmon marinated in coriander and homemade tortellini in a light crab sauce. Your only complaint will be that the choice is far beyond human consumption.

SUSTENANCE

GELATERIA

8 PASSERINI
Via Victor Hugo 4
Tel. 80.06.63
Moderate; no credit cards accepted
Closed Wednesday

Blessed with a location in the heart of Milan's gastronomic niche, Passerini upholds its reputation as a *gelateria* par excellence. An array of creamy homemade flavors is displayed in an old-fashioned ice-cream parlor environment that hints of Passerini's nascent days in the early 1920s. You're welcome to sit and linger with one of the regulars' favorites: the rich *cioccolato gianduia* (chocolate hazelnut ice cream), or the best *granita al caffè* in town—a shaved-ice concoction soaked in rich coffee and piled high with fresh *panna* (whipped cream).

FOOD

CANDIES & SWEETS

9 GIOVANNI GALLI
Via Victor Hugo 2
Tel. 80.00.87
Moderate; no credit cards accepted

This charming little old-fashioned confectioner's shop is a fine spot for sampling the wealth of goodies that have brought fame to the Galli family for over a century. Galli is especially renowned for its rich *marrons glacés* (candied chestnuts), a traditional sweet invented not by the French (as they would have us believe), but by Catherine dei Medici for her ailing son. Enticingly displayed alongside are trays of delicate pralines, fresh tarts made daily with plump local fruit in season, and a delicious range of freshly baked pastries that are whisked from the back-room oven onto the worn marble counter. There are miniature sculpture-like *paste di mandorle* (marzipan confections), chocolate-dipped fruits, and rich chocolates filled with cognac or amaretto. Signor Galli takes special pride in his elaborate basket assortments and colorful arrays of candied fruits, exquisite gifts that he'll reliably send home for you or carefully wrap for traveling.

LEATHERGOODS

BAGS

Trendy

10 LA FURLA
Via Orefici 11
Tel. 80.53.944
Moderate; no credit cards accepted
Open during lunch

Furla, a Bologna-based bags and accessories company, is always the first to pick up on a trend if not create one. Attention-getting leather bags are rather avant-garde and always exciting, done up in good-quality leathers often stamped or colored in the demands of the season—and at noninvestment prices. The shop's modern and dramatic interior also highlights a nice collection of big belts and fashion jewelry to complete the Furla statement.

PIPES

11 SAVINELLI PIPE
Via Orefici 2
Tel. 87.66.60
Moderate to expensive; credit cards
    accepted

A 100-year tradition as Italy's most respected pipe shop makes Savinelli a must-see for pipe enthusiasts. Smokers come from all over the world for the selection of pipes, straight and classic or innovative and hand-worked, as well as for an aromatic selection of fine blended tobaccos. Savinelli carries its own handsome line of pipes, including the special handcrafted Autograph "designer collection" with mouthpieces boasting the initials of founder Achille Savinelli. You'll find other quality

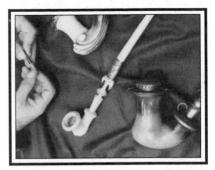

Curiosities from Savinelli's unique collection.

makes, from Italian to Nordic, and every accessory a pipe smoker could want or need. Curiosities such as the world's smallest pipe (the size of one's pinky) and the largest (carved out of a South African squash) are on display, as is a walking stick with a pipe concealed in its handle. If you can't make it to the store, Savinelli has a counter in the men's division of the Rinascente department store in the Piazza del Duomo.

FASHION

WOMEN'S

Career Dressing

12 RICCARDO PRISCO
Via Orefici (corner of Via Victor Hugo)
Tel. 87.80.32
Expensive; credit cards accepted

This is a miniature department store for career women that offers an entire well-coordinated wardrobe. It's one of the prettiest stores between the Piazza del Duomo and the Via Cordusio, with consistently attractive windows and three floors of dark-wood displays and well-merchandised selections. Riccardo Prisco offers his own collection of well-tailored separates, as well as hand-picked examples of other labels such as Moschino and

Anne Marie Beretta that are integrated with more traditional looks. There are interesting knits and coordinating accessories, most of them Italian-made. According to the season, you'll find everything from bathing suits to overcoats, always in distinguished taste.

LEATHERGOODS
GLOVES

13 AL GUANTO PERFETTO
Via Mazzini 18
Tel. 87.58.94
Moderate; credit cards accepted

This is the best glove store in Milan. In a recently redone, fresh and modern décor, you'll find an impressive selection of styles from the softest calfskins to the sporty pigskin that will last a lifetime. The newest in designer names are here, such as Valentino, Ungaro and Kensai. Hundreds of pairs of gloves are neatly stacked in open cubbyholes from floor to ceiling; they include colorful silk gloves in a range of lengths and fine wool and cashmere knit gloves.

GIFTS
FINE WRITING PENS

14 CASA DELLA PENNA
Via Dogana 3
Tel. 80.71.15
Moderate; credit cards accepted

A fine pen is the obligatory accoutrement for every successful individual, as well as the always perfect gift, and the Casa della Penna has one of the most interesting selections in town. You can choose from pens in gold and other prestigious metals from the houses of Pelikan (Italian), Mont Blanc, Shaeffer and Parker. For the most elegant writing, there are handsome pens with crystal and gold tips. There are colorful cartridges in purple, turquoise and brown inks to lighten serious writing. A number of beautiful 18th- and 19th-century fountain pens and inkwells are on hand, curious foils to modern plastic pen designs that are amusing or sleek, colorful or mat black. Casa della Penna is also reliable for delicate pen repairs.

FABRICS
FASHION & FURNISHINGS

15 GALTRUCCO
Piazza del Duomo 2
Tel. 87.62.56
Expensive; credit cards accepted

Galtrucco's artistic window displays of draped charmeuse silks and rich tweeds or camel's-hair wools will appeal to the tailor and seamstress in each of us. Since 1870, Galtrucco's reputation has been as Milan's biggest supplier of the finest yard goods.

In addition to stocking all the best Italian and European names, Galtrucco creates its own exclusive line of printed cottons, silks and wools. To give some indication of their range, at any given moment there may be as many as 70 different printed wool fabrics, each of which may come in five or six color variants. While the concentration is on fabrics for clothing, there is also a range of decorating fabrics. And in keeping with Galtrucco's superior taste is the ready-to-wear collection of men's and women's apparel from Italy's finest designers: Valentino, Missoni, Ermenegildo Zegna, Genny, Ginochietti, Byblos and Cerruti.

The Galleria honors King Vittorio Emanuele II.

This store has stood catty-corner to the Duomo since 1923, but a second Galtrucco location has recently opened at Via Montenapoleone 27 (telephone 70.29.78), dedicated entirely to men's ready-to-wear.

HOME
SILVER

16 BERNASCONI
Galleria Vittorio Emanuele 33–35
Tel. 87.23.34
Expensive; credit cards accepted

As one of the longest established silversmiths in the city, Bernasconi offers a huge selection of exquisite silver gifts that will please every taste. Table after table displays elegantly arranged place settings with every silver candlestick, salt-and-pepper set and tabletop object possible, from modern to antique in style. There are magnificent chandeliers, and lovely small frames, elegant clocks and ornate coffee and tea services. The immense range of possibilities is perhaps best appreciated when you're shopping for a special wedding present.

A second, smaller Bernasconi location is in the Vercelli/Magenta neighborhood at Via Magenta 22 (telephone 86.70.72).

SUSTENANCE
RISTORANTE/TRATTORIA

17 BIFFI GALLERIA
Galleria Vittorio Emanuele
Tel. 80.57.961
Moderate; credit cards accepted
Closed Sunday

A change of ownership and a refreshing facelift have brought Biffi back into the hearts of the Milanese people. Its super-centralized location in the Galleria has kept it a traditional point of rendezvous, one to which everyone is now returning with renewed enthusiasm. Of particular interest to hungry, non-Italian-speaking visitors is the inviting self-service area on the top floor, which offers a beautifully prepared buffet of cold and hot antipastos, pasta, salad, fish, seafood and meat entrées and homemade desserts. In addition, there is an elegant restaurant offering waiter service, fresh flowers and classic Milanese specialties. The ground floor is home of the well-known Biffi *bar-caffè*, a prestigious spot to meet for a "Slap," a Biffi invention that combines vodka, freshly squeezed grapefruit and pineapple juice with a splash of Blu curaçao. Small, linen-draped tables outside under the glass dome of the Galleria are ringside seats for the best, nonstop *passeggiata* show in town.

LEATHERGOODS
WOMEN'S

18 PRADA
Galleria Vittorio Emanuele 63–65
Tel. 87.69.79
Expensive; credit cards accepted

Prada, one of the oldest and most respected names in Milanese leather-goods, demands a detour for its unusual combination of ultramodern merchandise with a stately old-world décor. The elegance of marble, brass, mahogany, and crystal has remained unchanged since the shop first became a mecca for Milanese and European aristocracy, but the founder's great-granddaughter, Miuccia Bianchi Prada, has brought a new infusion of youthful freshness and creative energy. Prada is still a symbol of prestige and luxury (for example, look for their coveted alligator- and ostrich-skin loafers), but appeals now to a younger, more fashion-conscious clientele. These young customers enjoy the updated leather bags and shoes, while Prada continues its more traditional classic and conservative collection as well. The exquisite quality of the workmanship and the choice of sophisticated leathers are superlative for both.

A winding banistered staircase leads from a smallish upstairs room full of antique showcases to a spacious downstairs area whose famous murals are the first things to greet you. Done in the early 1900s by a well-known set painter for La Scala, they represent the grand old days of deluxe travel, when busy docks and bustling train stations were filled with the magnificent trousseau and steamer trunks for which Prada has always been noted. Prada's timeless travel pieces are today made in indestructible aluminum, handsome leather and industrial black nylon. Luxury travel games and cases are for the inveterate Grand Traveler, while beautifully made belts, gloves and agendas are for everyone. The refined shoe and handbag collection remains generally classic, but articles with Miuccia's touch create fashion trends upon their arrival each season; her quilted synthetic handbag with gold chains, for instance, became first a national, then an international rage.

A second Prada boutique with a striking contemporary décor has recently opened at Via della Spiga 1 (telephone 70.86.36).

DOLLS

19 LENCI
Galleria Vittorio Emanuele
Tel. 87.03.76
Expensive; credit cards accepted

Fashioned from felt and reminiscent of the 1920s, Lenci dolls are the aristocrats of the doll world. For almost 70 years, this Torino-based company has been producing dolls as luxurious art objects; a visit to their charming Milan store is obligatory for doll collectors as well as for little girls and for all the young at heart. Averaging two feet in height, these patent-protected dolls were the first to be produced in felt, and most of the original faces with endearing childlike expressions were first crafted by well-known Italian artists.

Today's creations are made from those same molds, and their exquisite and colorful outfits are made from the original patterns. Lenci took its name from the Latin motto "Ludus Est Nobis Constanter Industria," or "To play is our constant work." One glimpse and you'll understand why its dolls are even more sought after by doll enthusiasts than by precocious six-year-olds. For example, "Lavinia, the Boudoir Doll" is made of 1200 separate pieces that must be painstakingly cut, sewn and pieced to-

including both ancient and modern classics—yearly. Most of these have been translated from their original languages into Italian. The basement level offers the country's largest and most comprehensive display of Italian paperbacks from a number of publishers. General fiction, belles lettres, history, art and technical categories are a sampling. The ground floor features a comprehensive selection of guidebooks and books on Italian history and travel in English.

The world's most extravagant Gothic creation.

gether. Each of today's 60 different models (there have been 2700 in Lenci's history) is produced in a strictly limited edition of 999 and comes in an elegant, satin-lined box. A number corresponding to your certificate of authenticity is etched on the back of the neck of your little work of art.

BOOKS
ITALIAN & ENGLISH LANGUAGE

20 RIZZOLI
Galleria Vittorio Emanuele 79
Tel. 80.73.48
Moderate; credit cards accepted
Open during lunch

Founded in 1909, Rizzoli is one of the major forces in Italian publishing. As a press, printing and book empire, it has been a perennial challenger of Mondadori, offering 135 new hardcover titles and 100 paperbacks—

SUSTENANCE
RISTORANTE/TRATTORIA

21 SAVINI
Galleria Vittorio Emanuele
Tel. 80.58.343
Very expensive; credit cards accepted
Closed Sunday

If you care to impress cognoscenti of Milanese gastronomy, just mention that you've dined at Savini's in the Galleria, one of Italy's most illustrious restaurants. After a long period of decline, Savini has returned under new ownership to its former fame and glory. A regal air of the Grand Tour and continental elegance, together with the refined Italian and international menu, are its two inseparable attractions. At this bastion of tradition, old Milanese recipes are treated with reverence and artistry, but there are also other carefully chosen regional dishes, a variety of impeccably prepared fresh fish, and occasional bursts of fantasy in creation and presentation. A hushed ambiance, with crystal chandeliers, crimson salons, multilingual waiters and an impressive wine list, helps to produce a wonderful monument to "Vecchia Milano"—with prices to match.

LEATHERGOODS
LUGGAGE

22 PELLUX
Via Ragazzi del 99 (near Piazza San Fedele)
Tel. 86.41.04
Moderate to expensive; credit cards
    accepted

Pellux is your choice if you're looking
for the best assemblage of luggage in
every size, shape and quality under
one roof. Overnight and weekend
bags, large suitcases and steamer
trunks—rigid and canvas, durable
leather, indestructible metal and
ribbed synthetic—are displayed in
overwhelming profusion. Pellux' own
line of handmade classic leather suitcases is the most beautiful and
impressive; it includes handsome
briefcases and the timeless beauty-
and-cosmetic cases that are again in
fashion. There is also an assortment
of small leathergoods such as wallets
and shoes for men and women, but
the typical customer is the inveterate
traveler in quest of an attractive and
durable valise.

SPORTS GEAR
HUNTING & FISHING

23 RAVIZZA SPORT
Via Hoepli 3
Tel. 80.38.53
Moderate; credit cards accepted

Hunting and fishing enthusiasts will
have a field day in Milan's best-
equipped store for these two popular
sports. Ravizza's century-old expertise is obvious, with rifles and guns of
the finest makes lined up in endless
rows, as well as ammunition, and bait
for all kinds of prey. Handsome

The Galleria's imposing glass-and-iron cupola.

leather game bags and good-quality
hunting apparel complete this division. For fishermen, every rod, reel
and net ever manufactured seems to
be here, along with thigh-high boots
and an extensive arrangement of colorful tackle and feathered hooks. An
assortment of equipment and clothing for tennis, skiing and scuba diving is also available.

SUSTENANCE
RISTORANTE/TRATTORIA

24 CANOVIANO
Via Hoepli 6
Tel. 80.58.472
Expensive; credit cards accepted
Closed Saturday & Sunday

The unique and impressive neoclassical décor inspires a newly revised and
lauded menu. Canoviano excels both
with historical recipes from great
chefs of Milan's past and with its own
uninhibited creations in the nouvelle-
cuisine vein. For *primo*, try the delicate *minestra di zucca* (soup made
with pumpkin and bits of almonds) or
the homemade *agnolotti* pasta with a
duck and truffle filling. Also recommended are the unusual *risotto coi
fiori di zucca* (with zucchini blossoms) and the *gamberi con purea di*

crescione (shrimp with a light purée of watercress). Carnivores should make a special trip here for the exceptionally tender *agnello di latte* (baby lamb) or the *sella di coniglio* (saddle of rabbit) with aromatic herbs. The excellent house sorbet is an appropriate end to your meal at Canoviano, which is situated in the Hotel de la Ville.

FASHION

MEN'S, WOMEN'S & CHILDREN'S

Department Store

25 LA RINASCENTE 🛍🛍🛍🛍
Piazza del Duomo
Tel. 88.521
Moderate; credit cards accepted
Open during lunch

The Milanese are more comfortable with the idea and convenience of department-store shopping than most other Italians, and this is obvious in their six-floor extravaganza, Rinascente. It is the oldest and most prestigious department store in Milan, and its numerous offspring have livened up the central piazzas of Italian cities in recent years. In a modern and orderly layout, counters and departments provide every purchasable item in existence, from wallets to furs. The street level offers the usual assortment of international names in cosmetics and accessories' counters that carry scarves, hosiery and bags from a number of good European designers.

The other floors offer every kind of men's, women's and children's fashion, active sportswear and outerwear. Rinascente is slowly introducing some designer labels into its clothing merchandise, but its own attractive and well-made private label dominates the scene. There is the customary department-store range of selection—from bed to bath, from kitchenware to sports equipment—all represented here by good-quality Italian design. A top-floor cafeteria, Cento Guglie (open 12–2:30 P.M. only), is a welcome spot for a break if you've worked your way up; you'll find yourself at the same lofty level as the delicate white Gothic spires of Milan's Duomo, just feet away. Another curious detail about Rinascente is that it was destroyed by fire and, later, by World War II air raids; its name, first suggested by Gabriele D'Annunzio, means "Reborn."

FASHION

MEN'S & WOMEN'S ACCESSORIES

Hats

26 BORSALINO
Corso Vittorio Emanuele II, 5
Tel. 86.90.805
Moderate; credit cards accepted
Open during lunch

Europe's monarchs have been putting aside their crowns to don handsome Borsalino hats for well over a century. And where else could Mick Jagger get a special rose-colored hat made-to-measure? From the classic to the updated, Borsalino's hat-making industry has grown with the times to meet the ever-changing dictates of hat fashion while staunchly maintaining its reputation for quality. Today much of Borsalino's activity is in its custom business, which will service your every whim. Men wore hats less and less frequently in the years following World War II, but Harrison Ford's film interpretation of Indiana Jones has secured the hat's return to the wardrobe of many dapper young men. At this best-stocked Borsalino location you'll find the hallmark fur-felt hats—soft, waterproof, foldable and in various colors with varying brims. Less expensive renditions in wool-felt and cashmere blends are also available.

The original Borsalino location is on the corner of the Piazza della Scala in the Galleria Vittorio Emanuele at No. 92 (telephone 87.42.44), and a newer, smaller and trendier shop is in the Galleria Caffè-Moda Durini at No. 14 (telephone 70.67.39).

FASHION
WOMEN'S ACCESSORIES
Hosiery & Gloves

27 DE BERNARDI
Corso Vittorio Emanuele 4
Tel. 87.21.30
Moderate; credit cards accepted
Open during lunch

A quick stop here in Milan's best-stocked hosiery store will offer you all the finest Italian and French designer labels. Sales help will tirelessly pull out and show merchandise in an endless span of colorful patterns and textures from the myriad drawers that run to the ceiling. Professional and knowledgeable about size conversions, they'll show you every imaginable kind of hosiery (with designer labels such as Valentino, Ungaro, Pierre Mantoux and Dior), as well as garters, knee-high socks and anklets in opaques, laces and patterned cottons. Like most Italian hosiery stores, De Bernardi also carries a good selection of gloves in a range of colors and materials—leather, wool, knit and

lace. De Bernardi has a second location for more intimate apparel, the Corsetteria, located behind the Vittorio Emanuele store at Via Pattari 2 (telephone 87.60.14). There you'll find both traditional and contemporary stock in corselets and coordinated undergarments.

FOOD
PASTICCERIA

28 FRATELLI FRENI
Corso Vittorio Emanuele 4
Tel. 80.48.71
Moderate; no credit cards accepted
Open till midnight; closed Wednesday

Here's an authentic example of Sicily's inimitable art of marzipan confections, transplanted to this northern corner of Italy. Freni's colorful windows are filled with life-like cherries, salami, watermelon, cacti, miniature pears, mushrooms and bananas

Marzipan trompe-l'oeil *is Freni's specialty*

—all made from ultra-sweet Sicilian marzipan, whose recipe was brought to Milan by the Freni family upon their arrival in 1914. Freni has been famous ever since, producing this traditional Southern treat that was perfected by Sicilian nuns over two centuries ago and most probably introduced by the Arabs before then. Freni's marzipan artists are still predominantly Sicilian, and they sculpt and paint each "work of art" by hand with vegetable-based dyes. The marzipan is made from almond paste, together with watermelon, cherries and honey. There are also mounds of *torrone* (a kind of nougat), *cassata* ice cream, and chocolates. The Sicilians are world-renowned for their pastries, and Freni offers, among others, warm, fresh *sfogliatelle* filled with sweetened ricotta cheese.

SUSTENANCE

PIZZERIA

Late-Night

29 CHARLESTON

Piazza Liberty 8
Tel. 79.86.31
Inexpensive; credit cards accepted
Open till 1:00 A.M.; Closed Monday, and
    Saturday lunch

Disregard the un-Italian name and concentrate on some of the best pizza in town. Charleston's secret lies in its wood oven, the freshness and variety of its toppings, and its lively, upbeat crowd. There are many simple but recommended dishes other than pizza, including the vast layout of antipastos you will have reluctantly passed by at the entrance, the fresh pasta made in-house, and the quality-cut meats prepared in the same wood

oven as the pizzas; the *punta di vitello* (roast breast of veal) is not commonly found and is delicious here. The selection of wines and the fresh, homemade desserts also help to explain the success of this centralized *pizzeria*. The open, modern restaurant is enhanced by different levels, real damask tablecloths and impressive service, considering the very reasonable prices. You can also sit outside in a café extension.

LEATHERGOODS

BAGS & ACCESSORIES

Designer Names

30 DIANA DUE

Corso Vittorio Emanuele 15
Tel. 79.56.23
Moderate to expensive; credit cards
    accepted

If you can just never get enough of Italy's exciting accessories, Diana Due offers an excellent selection from the big names in designer handbags. Display windows are chock-full of bags, as is the tiny store. Your eye will invariably rivet on an outstanding item, be it a classic crocodile purse or an oversized, stamped-leather tote in a bold print. Diana Due holds the exclusive for the Ferrè bags, and also carries Valentino, Granello, Soprani and Donna Elissa in the fashion colors of the season. Coordinating wide belts and umbrellas serve as a pleasant postscript to the wealth of bags.

Another Diana Due shop, under the name Mali Parmi, is located behind the Via Vittorio Emanuele at Piazza Liberty 8 (telephone 70.23.80). Mali Parmi stocks less dressy and younger, sportier looks in coordinated bags, belts and gloves.

FASHION
WOMEN'S
Contemporary to Trendy

31 MAX MARA 🍶🍶🍶🍶
Corso Vittorio Emanuele
(corner of Galleria De Cristoforis)
Tel. 70.88.49
Moderate; credit cards accepted

If your time is limited, but you'd like to put together a coordinated, stylish wardrobe, go directly to Max Mara. It's a joy to browse through the spacious surroundings with striking visual displays and excellent sales help, and nowhere else will you find such excellent value in fabric, style and workmanship. There are reams of high-quality Italian fashions that are forward but never excessive. Max Mara's customers are career women with individual tastes that run from the timelessly classic to the chic contemporary, as well as the fun and avant-garde.

The Piazza del Duomo, Milan's veritable hub.

All of the stunning collections here are from Max Mara's own design and production, not yet widely exported. Everything has been grouped to facilitate your selection of separates and sweaters to mix or layer, casual or elegant dresses, tailored or boldly cut suits, and wonderful coats and raincoats. There is also an array of coordinated leather accessories, from belts to shoes. The Max Mara operation has recently been updated with the new input of Luigi, the dedicated and talented son of owner Achille Marimotti.

FASHION
CHILDREN'S & JUNIORS'
Trendy & Fun

32 LA RAGAZZERIA
Corso Vittorio Emanuele 13
Tel. 70.12.83
Moderate; credit cards accepted
Open during lunch

La Ragazzeria is a three-story mini-department store of trendy, fun and fashionable clothing just for 6- to 14-year-old boys and girls. Their own private label can be found in original T-shirts, jeans, warm-up suits and sweatshirts, and fun raingear that includes boots and umbrellas in every color. The surroundings are bright and modern, and everything is openly and cleverly displayed for easy and enjoyable browsing. Accessories like backpacks, plastic belts, printed socks, gloves and bags make great gifts. There is a nice assortment of sportswear for youngsters who want to imitate their older brothers or sisters.

Part of a 25-store chain, La Ragazzeria shares the same ownership as Prénatal, and you'll find other branches throughout Milan as well as in Florence and Venice.

LEATHERGOODS
BAGS & ACCESSORIES
Fun Fashion

33 EVE ⌂⌂⌂⌂
Via San Pietro all'Orto 9
Tel. 70.64.50
Moderate; credit cards accepted
Open during lunch

Eve is a paradise of colorful leather and vinyl bags—from handbags to travel bags, in solid bright colors, prints and plaids. Always up-to-the-season with new shapes and colorations, Eve employs various materials, including plasticized canvas, canvas trimmed with leather, and wearproof *cuoio* leather in lively colors. This is one of the larger Eve boutiques around town, with three levels of delightful merchandise that includes wallets, makeup bags, belts and some shoes. Young girls and young-minded women are Eve's faithful customers; she was the first to do "faux croc" bags of crocodile-stamped leathers in flashy colors. Smaller Eve boutiques are located off Corso Vittorio Emanuele in the Galleria Passerella at No. 1 (telephone 70.96.00) and in the Corso Vercelli/Magenta neighborhood at the corner of Piazza Tommaseo and Via Mascheroni (tel. 46.96.922).

LEATHERGOODS
LUGGAGE & TRAVEL ACCESSORIES

34 BOCCI
Corso Vittorio Emanuele 15
Tel. 79.08.39
Moderate; credit cards accepted

Every conceivable kind of traveling bag in a variety of sizes and forms can be found at Bocci (until recently called La Viaggeria). There are beauty cases and tote bags, weekend bags and steamer trunks. Makes from all over the world are grouped by size and material; this last runs the gamut from waterproof nylon to travel-resistant natural *cuoio*, which is used for beautiful handcrafted valises that will last for generations. Lightweight synthetics come quilted, smooth and in fun colors for the peripatetic youth. There is a type for every need, for the practical traveler and for the Grand Tourist more concerned with look. You'll also find matching umbrellas, portfolios, handbags and some small leathergoods, in the same diversity of materials. Bocci offers good value for your money, and a wide selection for a quick overview.

FASHION & SHOES
CHILDREN'S
Up-to-the-Minute Fashion

35 GUSELLA
Corso Vittorio Emanuele 37/B
Tel. 70.01.18
Moderate; credit cards accepted

After opening more than a dozen successful locations in Milan, Gusella has become something of a symbol for quality and contemporary fashion in children's shoes and apparel. A selection of clothes for children up to 16 years old can be found in Gusella's sister store in the nearby Galleria del Toro (telephone 79.01.33).

For more information, see listing for the location at Corso Vercelli 14 (page 275).

COMO,
CITY OF SILK

Silk, the most noble of fabrics, was discovered in the Orient over 23 centuries ago, and was introduced to Sicily by the Byzantines in the 10th century. It slowly moved north over the centuries until it settled in the Lombard city of Como, which today produces over 80 percent of all Italian silks; this represents one-third of world production. You'll join an illustrious roll call of customers such as Valentino, Luchino Visconti, the Pope and his cardinals when you come to Como to purchase from the widely acclaimed silk houses of Ratti, Stucchi, Canepa and Mantero. Their owners represent an unusual blend of the artisan, the industrial pioneer and the savvy businessman with the soul of a painter.

It's an easy and thoroughly enjoyable trip by train or car to this pretty lakeside city with ancient Roman walls, some 30 miles north of Milan. Of the 400 silk factories that are the backbone of the town, most are small and unobtrusive, hidden in the adjacent countryside around beautiful Lake Como. One could easily forget that Como is the teeming center of an elitist industry, if it were not for the air of quiet wealth and prestige that cloaks its homes and shops.

Como imports almost all of its raw silk from China, but it is the nonpareil Italian design sense and sophisticated printing and weaving of *seta*, or silk, that is responsible for the country's leap to world prominence. While the most advanced machinery available is used, luxury silk manufacture remains very much an artisanal handicraft, and continuous innovations in color and prints have even the most chauvinistic French couturiers eating out of Como's skilled hand. Many believe that Milan's *prêt-à-porter* designers would never have gained the success that has catapulted them to world recognition without the proximity of Como and its rich store of ideas.

All the leaders of fashion turn to Como twice a year for the Ideacomo fabric fair (held at the nearby Villa d'Este), where the fashion cycle begins. Here the *comaschi*, as the city's silk manufacturers call themselves, and top international designers together decide the colors, types and quantities of silks that will show up in collections more than a year later.

Como offers dozens of places to buy silk, many of which you'll come across when strolling through town. Some are direct outlets from nearby factories, others are small silk jobbers. Take a leisurely boat tour

An exquisite paisley-print silk from Ratti.

around the lake and stop in at any of the following before you head back to fast-paced Milan:

CENTRO DELLA SETA
Via Volta 64
Tel. (031) 27.98.61
Monday through Friday,
9:00 A.M.–12:30 P.M. and 3:30–7:00 P.M.;
and Saturday morning

Via Bellinzona 3
Tel. (031) 55.67.93
Monday through Saturday,
9:00 A.M.–12:30 P.M. and 3:00–7:00 P.M.,
closed Monday morning
Credit cards accepted
One of the largest mills, Mantero is a kingpin in *comasco* silk manufacturing. These factory outlets offer you exquisite Mantero yard goods and some ready-to-wear, scarves, shawls, ties and shirts at prices said to be two-thirds of Italian retail.

There is also a first-rate selection of men's cotton shirts.

RATTI
Via Cernobbi 17
Tel. (031) 23.32.62
Monday through Friday,
9:00 A.M.–noon and 2:00–6:00 P.M.
and Saturday morning;
closed Monday morning
No credit cards accepted
Como-born Antonio Ratti owns one of Italy's largest silk-printing companies and invites you onto its sumptuous grounds (on the road to the Villa d'Este) for a wide selection from his different collections. He prints for Europe's major houses; you'll see accessories from Valentino, Dior, Celine and Givenchy, as well as the highest-quality silks by the yard and some ready-to-wear, such as women's blouses and men's silk robes for the sultan you left behind. Paisley and geometric motifs are Ratti's most recognizable signatures.

SETERIE MORETTI
Via Garibaldi 69
Tel. (031) 27.30.49
Credit cards accepted
Monday through Saturday,
9:00 A.M.–12:30 P.M. and 2:30–7:00 P.M.
This shop is right in town near the main square. The rooms are filled with the same colorful and exquisite silks you would find in prestigious yard-goods stores such as Milan's Galtrucco or London's Liberty. Moretti retains the right to sell designer silks minus the signature or label for a fraction of the cost.

FASHION

MEN'S

Enormous Selection of Shirts

36 ZEBEDIA

Corso Vittorio Emanuele 37/B (in the
    Galleria del Toro)
Tel. 79.20.78
Moderate; credit cards accepted
Open during lunch

This shop sells men's shirts only, but
what an immeasurable stock! Zebedia
is small and simple, but its colorful
shirts dress a faithful clientele of
young men and women, for the fashion and color appeal are often unisex.
Whatever is trendy at the moment
can be found here, in various colorations and fabrics, including cottons,
linens, flannels, and seersuckers.
Much of the fashion is made exclusively for Zebedia. A whole shirt wardrobe is yours, from weekend play
shirts to some traditional work attire;
there are a number of formal evening
shirts as well.

FASHION

MEN'S

Made-to-Measure Shirts

37 PETRONIO

Corso Matteotti 20 (in the Galleria del Toro)
Tel. 79.20.84
Expensive; credit cards accepted

What a difference a tie makes, and
the variety and quality of Petronio's
selection can revolutionize the average wardrobe. Every coloration and
pattern imaginable shows up in luxurious silks, tweeds, knits, cottons and
linens. The dark wood-paneled walls
help to create an atmosphere of class
compatible with the executive Mila-

Only bus stops bring the milanesi *to a halt.*

nese businessmen who shop here.
There are tailor-made shirts to go
with your new purchase, and pajamas
for luxurious lounging. All of this
would have thrilled the Roman satiri-
cal writer Petronio (or Petronius), one
of Western man's first arbiters of elegance.

LEATHERGOODS

Luggage & Executive Accessories

38 VALEXTRA

Piazza San Babila 1
Tel. 70.50.24
Very expensive; credit cards accepted
Open during lunch

In a hushed and reserved atmosphere,
you'll find Milan's most traditionally
high-class leathergoods, from executive desk accessories to aristocratic
luggage. Despite Valextra's classic
hallmark, it has been important in
introducing new shapes in travel
pieces (such as the 24-Hour overnight

bag), and holds the coveted license for Armani leathergoods (including handbags, small leathergoods and agendas). This is a perfect spot to invest in that long-desired crocodile bag or other articles in elephant, ostrich or alligator; Valextra's choice of exotic skins is as infallible as the specialized craftsmanship employed. Handsome briefcases will last throughout a long career, and the rich-looking men's accessories, such as Valextra's patented rigid key-ring, make nice gifts for a special someone.

SUSTENANCE
BAR-CAFFÈ

39 DONINI
Galleria San Babila 4/B
Tel. 70.04.61
Moderate; credit cards accepted
Closed Sunday

To discover why real Milanese men drink pink cocktails, drop in at Donini's, known far and wide as the originator of a soothing (while potent) *aperitivo*. "Gin Rosa" is by now a staunch part of the Milanese tradition. Tasting strongly of gin, it hints of other flavors (the barman will vaguely divulge an *infuso di erbe*—infusion of herbs). Donini's is just as pleasant, however, for a late-afternoon tea in its *salon de thé* or a matinal cappuccino at an outdoor table. Settle in with a *panino* (sandwich) or an ice-cream sundae: you've got a front-row seat for the parade of fashion plates that passes back and forth along this gallery linking the Corso Vittorio Emanuele with the Montenapoleone shopping area. Donini's is popular with shop owners, tourists, design folk and business people from the nearby Stock Exchange.

FASHION
MEN'S
Classic

40 EDDY MONETTI
Piazza San Babila 4
Tel. 70.29.68
Expensive; credit cards accepted

Gentlemen shoppers who appreciate personalized service in a refined setting will enjoy a stopover here. Eddie Monetti offers everything in classic men's fashion from hats to shoes. A smaller women's area guarantees the same high quality in feminine apparel. Made-to-order suits are hand-tailored to perfection in three weeks.

FASHION
JUNIORS'
Sportswear

41 BENETTON
Galleria Passarella 2
Tel. 79.47.49
Moderate; credit cards accepted
Open during lunch

This is the larger of two Benetton stores in the Corso Vittorio Emanuele area, and one of over 4000 franchises in 56 countries. In record time, a clever and hefty advertising campaign has familiarized most of the civilized world with an unprecedented marketing strategy: fast-fashion. The four Veneto-based Benetton siblings, recently joined by a second generation, create simple knitwear that comes in dozens of colors, a key component in the Benetton philosophy. Each Benetton franchise varies slightly in merchandise, though generally the target is the trendy, upscale teenager. You'll find everything from shorts to dresses, from unisex sweaters to accessories— all meant to be mixed and matched, worn under or over, together or solo. Benetton keeps its finger on the pulse of its young market through ultra-advanced technology and production, often creating trends when not following them. Although still the world's leading consumer of wool, Benetton now also produces jeans and other cotton garments, and even uses an occasional synthetic or two.

FASHION

JUNIORS'

Humorous & Hip

42 FIORUCCI

Galleria Passarella 1
Tel. 70.80.33
Moderate; credit cards accepted
Open during lunch

The Fiorucci trend is alive and well at this spacious three-level flagship location. Fashion that is inexpensive, humorous and hip is displayed in a high-tech, loft-like area with piped-in music, graffiti murals by Keith Haring and young salespeople decked out in trendy costumes. Jeans, raingear, and down vests and jackets are the mildest of the otherwise attention-drawing clothes; all the colorful streetwear has Elio Fiorucci's amusing flair. Inexpensive accessories, avant-garde bijoux and gadgets make great gifts, and a children's division interprets the Fiorucci life style for small tykes. Upstairs there are records, tickets for concerts and video shows. The new Fiorucci operation Classic Nouveau two doors away (telephone 70.01.38) is less junior in atti-

Fiorucci—fun and ephemeral style.

tude, with fun 1940s and 1950s weekend sportswear *all'americana*.

FASHION

JUNIORS'

Sportswear

43 SISLEY

Galleria Passarella 2
Tel. 70.40.43
Moderate; credit cards accepted
Open during lunch

Sisley belongs to the Benetton family, but takes up where the Benetton store chain leaves off. Sisley offers a more mature look in casual and activewear, in a boutique-like setting. The genius of the four Benetton siblings is here in their color sense and in the profusion of knitwear, although Sisley's customer is somewhat older. Sisley also presents a wider choice for men, and an upgrade in yarn quality and finishing that explains a slight increase in prices compared to those of their friendly Benetton competitors.

BOOKS

44 MONDADORI
Corso Vittorio Emanuele 34
Tel. 70.58.32
Moderate; credit cards accepted
Open during lunch

Mondadori is Italy's biggest publisher and one of the most respected in Europe. Still controlled by the Mondadori family, it is responsible for some 650 new titles each year. Here are three floors of the company's best titles in Italian and English, along with those of other publishers. You'll see what's doing in Italian publishing today as you browse through sections dedicated to graphics, design, photography, fashion, travel and art.

FASHION

JUNIORS'
Sportswear

45 STEFANEL
Corso Vittorio Emanuele 28
Tel. 78.07.21
Moderate; credit cards accepted
Open during lunch

Circumvent the crowds of Milanese kids waiting around outside, probably on their way to or from one of the area's fast-food restaurants, and enter the spacious, bright interior that shows off high-tech fixtures and colorful, trendy fashion. This is the largest of Stefanel's Milan locations, and at first glance you may mistake it for another Benetton—which isn't far

BENETTON AND STEFANEL

The family-run dynasties of Benetton and Stefanel offer a young-minded clientele big wardrobes on small budgets. This practical everyday fashion has redefined the international sportswear industry.

Benetton now has close to 4000 boutiques in more than 50 countries. The family (designer Giuliana and her three brothers) rose quickly to fame thanks to a remarkably efficient organization. Their boutique franchises are stocked by Benetton's own ultra-modern factories with everything from mittens to coats, and pullovers to hats, in an endless range of colors and at prices more Fiat than Maserati. The Benetton empire includes the slightly more upscale Sisley division and 012, for infants to preteens.

Considerably less ubiquitous but just as popular, the Stefanel retail chain offers a fresh look created by the young and attractive Giovanna Stefanel. Giovanna designs in her family's restored villa in the Veneto, while her brothers tend to administration. They have come closer than any other rival in emulating the Benetton "fast food" clothing success.

from the owners' intent. The silhouette is similar, though Stefanel uses more novelty appliqués and prints, and offers more jeans and outerwear. You'll see hundreds of these stores throughout Italy and, more recently, in Europe and America.

BOOKS & MAGAZINES

From All Over the World

46 MARCO

Galleria Passarella 2
Tel. 79.58.66
Moderate; credit cards accepted
Open during lunch, and weekdays till
    10:30 P.M.

A veritable "supermarket of information," as its advertising proclaims, Marco is a new breed of book and magazine stand. It occupies a large, modern space and stocks hundreds of daily newspapers from all over the world as well as best-selling books (including children's), mainly in Italian and English. An impressively extensive glossy magazine section groups myriad titles by interest—design, travel, architecture, fashion, gourmet, politics, performing arts, and more. Always packed with browsers, Marco and similar prodigious collections have sprung from Milan's prominent role in the international publishing world.

PANINARI

While local professionals and visiting foreigners keep the city's myriad restaurants full and humming, the youth of Milan is under the spell of the "Great American Way." The quintessential fast-food symbol, the hamburger, sums it all up for a group called the *paninari* (sandwich eaters), and you'll usually find them hanging out—their favorite pastime—in hamburger joints.

   "Burghy's" in Piazza San Babila was the first McDonald-type restaurant in Milan, and it is worth a trip there to view the phenomenon in its natural element. Predominantly in their mid-teens, the *paninari* follow a rigid American-style dress code that resembles upscale preppy, and

if one (or one's parents) cannot afford the escalated prices of imported Timberland, Nike, or Van shoes, one has not yet arrived. American jeans are purposefully worn short to show off Burlington argyle socks. American rock music is the movement's anthem, and Levis, Ray-Ban sunglasses, sweatshirts with American logos, and L.L. Bean or Ralph Lauren weekend wear determine devotees' popularity with the kids on the block. In an innocent effort to adopt an individualized style of dress, Milan's *paninari* (and their followers throughout the peninsula) now wear an unofficial uniform.

SUSTENANCE

BAR/TAVOLA CALDA

47 BAR PRADA
Galleria Privata Strasburgo 3
Tel. 79.84.25
Inexpensive; no credit cards accepted
Closed Sunday

Conveniently located in the middle of
a bustling shopping area, Bar Prada
has welcoming tables both indoors
and outside in the Galleria. Local
business people eat here, in a
friendly, no-pressure atmosphere
where you can linger for hours over a
morning cappuccino or a simple
lunchtime pasta. The menu is light
and surprisingly good: crisp green
salads, fresh mozzarella cheese, *costoletta*, hot pastas, minestrone and *frit-
tata di verdura* (vegetable omelette).
Bar Prada will make up the sandwich
combination of your request, and grill
it if you like. If you're up and out for
an early start on a day of shopping,
the Bar Prada is a nice place for an
Italian breakfast or a mid-morning
snack featuring a tempting array of
fresh pastries and memorable coffee
with an ever-so-faint flavor of anisette.

SPORTS GEAR

BOATING EQUIPMENT

For Sailing Aficionados

48 SPINNAKER
Corso Europa 7
Tel. 70.84.26
Expensive; credit cards accepted

Spinnaker offers three floors of everything you ever wanted to buy related
to boating and sailing. You can begin
with rubber boats of varying sizes
and work up to windsurfing equip-

ment. Clothing and accessories appear in profusion, right down to the
badge for your captain's ego. Old
boat furniture has been refurbished
to lend a maritime air to your quarters, whether on your yacht or on
terra firma; there are bunks, desks,
tables and an odd steering wheel or
two. Italians are serious sea lovers,
and this shop does a smash business
with all those who have salt water in
their veins. Spinnaker will ship your
purchases home.

BOOKS

Art & Esoterica

49 FRANCO MARIA RICCI
Via Durini 19
Tel. 77.02
Expensive; credit cards accepted

Marchese Franco Maria Ricci brings
a new dimension to the Milanese publishing world. In a stunning black-
and-gold interior rumored to have
triggered the trend for postmodern
store design is a complete and exquisite collection of his small but expanding publishing empire. This is

Franco Maria Ricci's elegant postmodern shop.

FRANCO MARIA RICCI

The Milan flagship bookstore.

Franco Maria Ricci personifies the imagination and artistry of Milan. The most refined publisher of his time, he sells his exotic, handbound tomes as if they were works of art. Expensive and published in limited editions, these collectibles turn up in the world's most discriminating private libraries. The high-gloss monthlies *FMR,* an art review, and *KOS,* devoted to the history of medicine, have recently joined his elitist family of publications.

Respectfully called "the Exotic Aristocrat of Publishing," Ricci sells an elegance and quality that he recognizes as Italy's natural resources. He ferrets out texts and illustrations that are odd and arcane, often commissioning well-known contemporary authors and artists to enhance the stimulating and unexpected image of his books and magazines. His unpredictable catalogue of 150 titles includes works on Erté, medieval China, cannibals, lost Florence, Mao Tse-tung and Lewis Carroll. Most of the books are deluxe editions printed on quality Fa-

briano paper, illustrated with hand-tipped colorplates and protected by handbound black silk covers cloth branded with his distinctive gold Bodoni type. They are sold in more than a dozen FMR bookstores throughout Italy, whose sleek black-and-gold postmodern decor mirrors the FMR graphic image.

As a reformed playboy hailing from nearby Parma, Marchese Franco Maria Ricci gave up the idea of purchasing a new Ferrari with his family inheritance to buy instead two 150-year-old printing presses and the then-dormant 18th-century Bodoni type that he still uses exclusively in his extraordinary publications.

The odd and arcane, a favorite FMR theme.

his flagship store, a perfect setting for the elegant art books and magazines he produces in both Italian and English. Esoteric texts are printed in 18th-century Bodoni type on special Fabriano paper with rich color-plate illustrations and hand-bound with the black silk illustrated covers that have become his trademark. Ricci rediscovers lost themes and forgotten artists; he often couples arcane subjects with renowned modern authors: Italo Calvino discusses Tarot cards, Alberto Savinio muses on Isadora Duncan, and Jorge Luis Borges explores Dante. This mecca for bibliophiles also features tomes on the 16th-century artist Arcimboldo, India's maharajahs, and personalities from Casanova to fashion designers Valentino and Armani. You'll also find all past and current issues of Ricci's monthly magazine, *FMR*. No coffee table is complete without one of these black-and-gold-covered volumes. Elegant diaries and appointment books make fine gifts, too.

FASHION
MEN'S, WOMEN'S & CHILDREN'S

Designer Boutique

50 EMPORIO ARMANI
Via Durini 24
Tel. 70.90.30
Expensive; credit cards accepted
Open during lunch

The Armani look is here in its fabled silhouette, but at more accessible prices than the designer's high-fashion collection commands. This two-story shop sets the tone for the hundred or so spacious boutiques throughout Italy that constitute the Emporio Armani chain. The cavern-

ous, high-tech space is divided into separate men's and women's divisions, both stocked with well-tailored sportswear in handsome tweeds, wools, cotton and linens. The look is often unisex and more youthful and relaxed than Armani's most extreme styles. His input is unmistakable, though, in trench coats, jackets, jeans, shirts, blouses and coordinated accessories. There's a help-yourself atmosphere about the neatly stacked and displayed clothing, but don't expect budget prices from one of the world's greatest designers. Across the street at Via Durini 23 (telephone 79.03.06) is the Mani boutique for women who like simple career dressing. Mani, a separate sportswear division of the successful design house, is a bit more expensive and sophisticated than Emporio Armani, but less so than the Armani high-fashion ready-to-wear. If you'd like to start your children off in the right apparel, stop in at Giorgio Armani Bambini, Via Durini 27.

FASHION & HOME FURNISHINGS
CHILDREN'S

51 PISOLO
Via Cerva 18
Tel. 78.46.61
Expensive; no credit cards accepted

This store is for the adoring grandmother who spares no expense to create a make-believe atmosphere for her grandchild's nursery. *Pisolo* means "nap," and it is also the Italian translation for "Sleepy" of Walt Disney's Seven Dwarfs. Sleepy would be in heaven with these cute pajamas, infants' sheets and whimsical stuffed animals. There is also irresistible

Irresistible children's gifts at Pisolo.

handcrafted furniture, such as cradles, bassinets, and miniature chairs, as well as wooden toys hand-painted with balloons and rabbits. You'll also find everything imaginable for the newborn infant, including exquisite one-of-a-kind outfits.

SUSTENANCE

PASTICCERIA/TEAROOM

52 PASTICCERIA TAVEGGIA
Via Visconti di Mondrone 2
Tel. 79.12.57
Moderate; no credit cards accepted
Open 7:30 A.M. 9:00 P.M.; closed Monday

The Pasticceria Taveggia is fitted with *radica*-paneled walls and framed mirrors that hint of its golden 1930s days. One of the oldest tearooms in Milan, founded in 1910, Taveggia still offers its traditional sweet delicacies to a crowd of happy and handsome contemporary habitués. At the bar, attorneys discuss pending cases over some of Milan's best coffee, perhaps accompanied by *panettone* with raisins, before rushing off to the nearby Tribunale (courthouse). In the old-fashioned tearoom, the hot *brioche* (croissants) fresh from the oven make breakfast particularly alluring, especially on Sunday mornings when most of Milan is closed. Of equal renown is Taveggia's five-o'clock tea.

MUSIC
Music Lovers' Paradise

53 GALLINI (off map)
Via Conservatorio 17
Tel. 70.28.58
Moderate to expensive; credit cards accepted

Appropriately situated on the Via Conservatorio, Gallini is probably the only music store of its kind in the world. Accomplished pianist Annalisa Gallini (granddaughter of the store's founder Natale) and her maestro husband Giuliano offer a huge collection of everything that pertains to classical music, including exceptional out-of-print gems by lesser-known composers. On the main floor of the big, old-fashioned store are caricatures, portraits and prints of the world's great singers and composers, including an autographed sepia of Verdi. There are original and first-edition sheet music for serious collectors, antique libretti, and old and new books and magazines on music, predominantly in French and Italian. Rare finds include charming, yellowed *sonetti*—poster-like poetic proclamations which were written for favorite singers by enraptured fans or emotional poets, sometimes illustrated with a portrait of the artist and then posted about town. An adjacent room houses an outstanding collection of antique pianos (the instrument was, by the way, invented by the Italian Bartolomeo Cristofori) and *violini d'autore*, built for and used by known maestros. Signor Gallini's precious collection of 60 antique instruments, including the most impressive assemblage of Stradivarius string instruments in the world, has recently been bequeathed to the Instrument Museum at Milan's Castello Sforzesco.

STRADIVARI, THE VIOLIN MAN

Nestled in the southeastern corner of Lombardy and just over 60 miles from Milan is Cremona, "the City of Violins." A regular pilgrimage for professional musicians, it is also an interesting and enjoyable day trip for any lover of classical music. Cremona was the home of the greatest violinmaker, or *liutaio*, of all time, Antonio Stradivari, otherwise known as Antonius Stradivarius Cremonensis.

Stradivari created more than 1200 stringed instruments in a career that spanned 68 years, including violins, violas, cellos, mandolins, harps and guitars. More than 650 of these instruments have come down to us, and are scattered around the globe in the safekeeping of national museums or world-famous violinists.

Magical is the only word to use in describing the genius behind Stradivari's masterpieces. He used what was available to other violinmakers of his time: the same woods, the same range of varnishes. Mystical tales relate how he would seek out special woods or pick exotic herbs under a full moon to create a unique lacquer, but the true explanation for his unprecedented success lay in his keen intuition for the properties of wood and his perfected knowledge of carving. He also possessed an unusual vital energy. Any musician will attest that wood is a living material that absorbs and retransmits what is given

to it. One of Stradivari's secrets was to keep each semifinished instrument in his bedroom for one month before varnishing it; he believed he gave part of himself to each of his ultrasensitive creations. Their almost supernatural resonance is said to come from their *anima*, or soul.

Precious few are those who can afford an original Stradivarius today. But the violinmakers of Cremona remain a source of fierce local pride. Their sophisticated knowledge may not surpass the inimitable genius of Stradivari, but their prices are lower. Of the 50-odd maestros who work in *botteghe* scattered about town, almost all are graduates of and some are teachers at Cremona's International School of Violin Making. These artisans create some of the world's finest stringed instruments for an international roster of customers; they are usually willing to ship, and will do so carefully and reliably.

For further information on these modern-day *liutai*, stop by the office of the school's director, Professor Sergio Renzi. The school, which is located in Piazza Marconi, is open from 8:00 A.M. to 1:00 P.M.; Telephone (0372) 38.689. Professor Renzi does not speak English, but many members of his staff do. According to your budget and professional demands for custom-made or ready-made instruments, they will help direct you to the appropriate master artisans in town.

FASHION
MEN'S, WOMEN'S & CHILDREN'S
Department Store

54 COIN
Piazza Cinque Giornate (off map)
Tel. 78.25.83
Moderate; credit cards accepted

If the high prices and overly attentive service of Milan's many sleek boutiques stifle your urge for leisurely browsing, the Coin department store is a great place to spend an afternoon. Coin's own private label guarantees good value, and you can wander through six display floors to see what's dressing up Italy these days. There's ready-to-wear for children and executives in good Italian fabrics and fashion colors at moderate prices. An especially handsome selection of woolen sweaters and men's cotton shirts is worth seeking out, as is the assortment of useful accessories. Coin keeps up with the seasons and, apart from classic attire, offers some imaginative Milanese style. The shopper who fares best in a department-store ambiance with self-service and no pressure to buy will be happy to know that there are three other Coin locations, but this is the largest.

WINES

55 ENOTECA SOLCI
Via Morosini 19 (off map)
Tel. 54.52.720
Moderate; credit cards accepted

Each bottle here has its legend. There are wines from glorious and hard-to-find vintages, and homemade wines from Tuscan peasants. One variety is consumed in a small fishing village only on Christmas Eve; another is a limited collection's elixir from a small island off the coast of Sicily. This remarkable wine collection is assembled by Angelo Solci, one of Italy's finest wine consultants and connoisseurs. Over 1000 types of wines stock his *enoteca*, mostly Italian with some German and French and an odd Californian or two, as well as a complete selection of liqueurs and *grappe*. If you're a wine *appassionato* or would like a special gift for a friend who is, the taxi ride here is a breeze.

SUSTENANCE
RISTORANTE/TRATTORIA

56 L'AMI BERTON
Via Nullo 14 (off map)
Tel. 71.36.69
Expensive; credit cards accepted
Closed Sunday

Roberto Berton's Tuscan wife is in the kitchen, cleverly blending her inherited provincial traditions with creative innovations. An art-nouveau-style décor, low lighting and the exquisitely set tables form the backdrop for a dinner of simply but carefully prepared cuisine. The menu has a strong emphasis on fish, but there are many wonderful meat dishes as well. The delicate scallops sautéed with zucchini or shrimp with wild *porcini* mushrooms is an excellent starter. A specialty is *spaghetti mare e montagna* (sea and mountain), embellished with seafood and mushrooms. Dinner here is not complete without *bocconcini dai dai*, petit-four-sized cubes of coffee-flavored ice cream covered with chocolate. There is a great wine list.

A Guide to Italian Contemporary Design in Milan

At a time when the world moves towards sameness and mass-produced mediocrity, Italy pursues a limitless creative energy that has made design one of its major exports. New forms, new materials and new production methods are grounded in the history of Italy's artisans, allowing today's designers to give new meaning and appeal to the home furnishings and other objects that pervade our daily lives. Even to the nondiscriminating eye, something inimitably Italian can be detected in an eclectic array of cars, typewriters and furniture, as well as coffee machines and computers; they all possess an inherent and distinctive beauty, a quality that is recognized throughout the world as fine Italian design.

Zeus innovates in form, materials and production.

The collaborative partnership of creative designer with artisanal manufacturer has resulted in a sensitivity to quality materials and an astute attention to detail that secure Italy's place as a forerunner in international contemporary design, a distinction it has held since the days of the Renaissance. While satisfying functional needs, this new design now flirts with the poetic, and looks as comfortable in the museum as in the home.

Why Milan? Milan was already a center of industrial culture in the early 1900s, a position secured after World War II when Milan became Italy's industrial capital. The city's architectural and decorative arts milieu was fostered by a group of intellectuals intent on forging a new society out of the rubble of Fascism. By the mid-1960s, a design revolution was fomenting in Italy, nurtured by an important nucleus of prominent architects. Trailblazers like Gio Ponti, Marco Zanuso, Enzo Mari and Bruno Munari left their distinctive mark, and not on the urban landscape alone.

Colorful, bold, using new industrial materials such as plastics and linked to the world of fashion, Italian design moved into different dimensions. Whether for furniture, cookware or tabletop objects, the creative and avant-garde vision of modern-day designers is aided both by advanced technology as well as by the high traditional standards of the artisans who make these designs a reality. The resulting professional and personal camaraderie and "anything is possible" attitude are found nowhere else.

Occasional bursts of radical and avant-garde design all came to a head in the 1970s and 1980s. A quantum leap of aesthetic vitality was made in 1981, when Austrian-born Ettore Sottsass founded a collaborative group of architects and designers called Memphis/Milano. Memphis' hypercolorful furniture, fabrics and rugs followed function—but far more importantly, they followed fantasy. Sottsass believed that as designers their responsibility was to change, to surprise, to shock and to amuse. Creating products that ranged from seating to ceramics and glass, the Memphis group was called the most radical and unorthodox design trend of the decade.

It was also widely influential, however. It influenced design to be freer, more whimsical and more open, and to exalt color and pattern, relinquishing accepted molds of tradition and conformity. With wit and humor, Memphis' seemingly irreverent and unbridled imagination encouraged the evolution of already-established design studios and the birth of new ones. Luxury leathers and materials, always the hallmark of Italian furniture, were further explored along with the particular character and nuances of wood, stone, metal, plaster, plastics and finishes. Fine artisanal arts were retrieved from past centuries: intricate inlaid wood, handblown glass, engraved metals, lacquers and ceramics. In Memphis designs, the past met the future in a striking way.

Today's designers generally have their formal education in the field of architecture. It was not until 1983 that Domus, Italy's first postgraduate design school, opened in Milan. The locally held Triennale, a prestigious design exhibition that takes place every three years, has paled somewhat in the shadow of the yearly Salone del Mobile held at the Fiera di Milano (see Milan's Trade Fairs, p. 150). Quintessential recognition in the design field comes with the honor of the Compasso d'Oro, a highly coveted prize awarded every two years.

If you are a design professional or a design fan, Milan should be the ultimate destination on your European tour. As you visit Europe's most important showrooms and fine retail stores, you will come upon the names of Milan's premier designers time and again—a highly gifted Who's Who of Italian and international talents that have shaped the evolution of the "Made in Italy" style. Their versatile design sense graces all aspects of daily life from tabletop objects to skyscrapers.

While most design production takes place just outside the city in the area of Brianza, the sophisticated showrooms and headquarters of Italy's design magnates lie within a centralized area of downtown Milan. Hence collections can be seen in their entirety and in surroundings that highlight their distinctive qualities. All the locations listed below welcome the public, and many take credit cards. The limited few that do not sell retail are designated; even these will give you information regarding individual pieces, however, and tell you where they can be purchased locally or abroad. Showrooms often close Monday mornings and during lunch. Those that don't ship can steer you towards their own reliable sources, or you can consult the "Shipping Services" section (page 145).

FURNITURE

ARFLEX
Via Borgogna 2
Tel. 70.59.72
Montenapoleone area
No credit cards accepted

Founded in the 1950s with the launching of a series of sleek models designed by Marco Zanuso, Arflex is today a premier manufacturer of superior technical quality. It specializes in upholstered sofas and armchairs and also offers a number of coffee tables in both classic and modern design. Major contributors are Cini Boeri, Franco Albini and Burkhard Vogtherr.

GRUPPO INDUSTRIALE BUSNELLI
Galleria Strasburgo 3, at corner of Via Durini
Tel. 70.94.28
Duomo/Vittorio Emanuele area
No credit cards accepted

Busnelli specializes in sophisticated upholstered armchairs and sofas using natural leathers and exclusively designed fabrics. High esthetics and technical quality are obvious in pieces by Ugo La Pietra; fashion designer Nicola Trussardi; and Andrea and Marco Sironi, designers of *Azzurra I* and *Azzurra II*, Italy's sailboat entries in the 1984 and 1986 America's Cup yacht races.

CASSINA
Via Durini 18
Tel. 79.07.45
Duomo/Vittorio Emanuele area
Showroom only

This elegant, spacious showroom welcomes browsing, but will not sell. It is, however, a must for design lovers who want to see Cassina's timeless classics in sofas and armchairs, designed by such greats as Le Corbusier, Charles Rennie Mackintosh and Frank Lloyd

Inherent beauty from Poltrona Frau.

Wright. More recent works include those by Vico Magistretti, Paolo Deganello and Massimo Morozzi.

DE PADOVA
Corso Venezia 14
Tel. 70.29.25
Montenapoleone area
Credit cards accepted

Maddelena De Padova's taste is refined and respected; her showroom features simple-looking, well-made pieces designed by Italy's best. Contemporary sofas by Vico Magistretti, beautiful rugs and lamps, 1960s aluminum shelving by Dieter Rams, and an interesting Shaker-inspired collection that epitomizes 19th-century functionalism.

DILMOS
Piazza San Marco 1
Tel. 65.59.837
Brera area
Credit cards accepted

Here is a good two-floor representation of this century's best furniture design. You'll see Cappellini's neo-modern, brightly upholstered furniture, Zanotta's witty and clever designs, Philippe Starke's innovative line for Baleri's furniture, Poltranova's avant-garde and imaginative pieces, and a limited edition of Gufram's plastic rocks, cacti, and famous mouth-shaped sofa. (See also page 256.)

MARZOT & C.
Via Fiori Chiari 3
Tel. 87.18.28
Brera area
Checks accepted; no credit cards

In Marzot's assemblage of Italian avant-garde design, the prestigious Alias collection is the most prominent. The Forocolini brothers are designers themselves and commission work from such other figures as Mario Botta, whose novel furniture in industrial metals stands alongside that of Vico Magistretti and the famous spaghetti chair by Giandomenico Belotti, which you may have seen in New York's Museum of Modern Art. Original paintings and lithographs, featuring works by Man Ray, and lighting by Artemide and Technolumen complete the offerings in this stunning showroom. (See also page 249.)

MEMPHIS/MILANO
Via Manzoni 46
Tel. 79.89.55
Montenapoleone area
Credit cards accepted

Educational and fun, a visit here shows you Italy's best-known design phenomenon. An international consortium founded in 1981 by Ettore Sottsass, Jr., Memphis has broken ties with conformity by introducing hyperpatterned, bright-colored furniture, lighting, rugs, and glass and ceramic objects. Laminated plastics and radical shapes have brought fantasy and an innovative reinterpretation of suburban kitsch into vogue. In addition to Sottsass' signature, you'll find the unusual designs of Michael Graves, Andrea Branzi, George James Snowden, Michele De Lucchi, Matteo Thun and Marco Zanini, to name but a few.

POLTRONA FRAU
Via Manzoni 20
Tel. 79.68.65
Montenapoleone area
Credit cards accepted

Poltrona Frau creates both classic and sophisticated products, but is best known for traditional stuffed furniture upholstered in quality leather. Its timeless "919" leather armchair, first made in 1912, is still being successfully produced today. A more contemporary look is represented by F. A. Porsche's sleek, adjustable armchair, as well as the new Casanova line designed by Marco Zanuso, Mario Bellini, and Pierluigi Cerri.

SAPORITI
Via Montenapoleone 27/E
Tel. 70.91.09
Montenapoleone area
Credit cards accepted

Contemporary armchairs and sofas are upholstered in such luxury materials as Missoni-designed fabrics, butter-soft leathers, and exclusively patterned suedes. Coffee tables, dining tables, and cupboards are most interesting for their lacquered finishes and luxury materials. Saporiti is well represented worldwide, but you'll see the whole collection here, including the designs of Giovanni Offredi.

SIMON INTERNATIONAL
Via Durini 25
Tel. 79.63.22
Duomo/Vittorio Emanuele area
No credit cards accepted

Before Dino Gavina founded Knoll International, he promoted some of the world's first modern furniture under the name of Simon International. An eclectic and innovative collection of furniture, displayed in a minimalist showroom, includes classics such as the "hooved" coffee table designed expressly by Meret Oppenheim, tables by Carlo Scarpa, and the recently revived "Sanluca" armchair by Pier Giacomo Castiglioni.

TANZI
Via Fatebenefratelli 9
Tel. 65.26.92
Brera area
No credit cards accepted
This striking showroom displays the Driade collection of furniture designed by such talents as Enzo Mari, Achille Castiglioni, Massimo Morozzi, and Alessandro Mendini, as well as the complete Aleph Ubik collection of chairs and tables by Philippe Starke. The Tanzi brothers have another showroom at Corso Monforte 19 (tel. 65.26.92), but this one is more fun and reputed to have the latest and most innovative pieces of Driade's production. (See also page 256.)

Satisfying function and flirting with poetry.

ZEUS
Via Vigevano 8
Tel. 83.55.709
Porta Ticinese area
Credit cards accepted
Go through the gates and across the courtyard to find the Zeus gallery of original and often countercurrent design, fashion and applied arts. A studio of young international avant-garde designers provides lean, fundamental design in black metal chairs, tables and lamps. Zeus also hosts gallery exhibitions in all media from photography to sculpture. (See also page 291.)

OFFICE FURNITURE
B&B
Largo Corsia dei Servi 11
Tel. 70.55.31
Duomo/Vittorio Emanuele area
Showroom only
The comfortable and sophisticated furniture displayed here is not for sale. The largest producer of upholstered furniture in Italy, B&B is known for its advanced research and today supplies 80 percent of the world's furniture upholsterers with an exclusive polyurethane foam. Here in the company's office furniture division, you'll find pieces using natural and treated leathers, fine woods and exotic lacquers. Mainstays of B&B's design are Afra and Tobia Scarpa, Mario Bellini, and Richard Sapper. The firm's home furniture division is represented at Selvini, Via Manzoni 45 (tel. 65.07.22).

CASTELLI
Piazza Castello 19
Tel. 87.02.57
Near Brera area
No credit cards accepted
This beautiful showroom enhances

Castelli's modern and functional furniture, which sets the tone for today's office design. Their best-known product, also on display at the Museum of Modern Art, is the folding and stackable plexiglass chair "Plia," designed by Emilio Ambasz and Giancarlo Piretti. These two master designers are also noted for the classic "Vertebra," an extremely comfortable armchair that adapts to one's contours.

OLIVETTI
Largo Richini 6
Tel. 85.06.44.50
South of Duomo/Vittorio Emanuele area
For decades Italy's premier designer of modern office furniture, workspaces and environments, Olivetti excels in cabinets, desks, chairs, and mobile walls. This showroom sells to dealers only, and it does not carry Olivetti's information systems or data-processing equipment. The company originally specialized in typewriters and other office machines, but had already branched out in the 1930s by designing the first horizontal filing cabinet. Since the office furniture division was established in 1961, Olivetti has enlisted the collaboration of Ettore Sottsass, Michele De Lucchi, and Hans Von Klier—all world-class designers and winners of the prestigious Compasso d'Oro award.

LIGHTING
ARTEMIDE
Corso Monforte 19
Tel. 70.69.30
Duomo/Vittorio Emanuele area
No credit cards accepted
Since 1959 co-founders Ernesto Gismondi and Sergio Mazza have taken special pride in the advanced and enduring beauty found in their light-

The "Tizio" lamp, a classic from Artemide.

ing fixtures. A magnum opus is Richard Sapper's adjustable "Tizio" tabletop lamp; it keeps suitable company with other designs by Italy's best: Emilio Ambasz, Gae Aulenti, Vico Magistretti, Ettore Sottsass, Enzo Mari and the co-founders themselves. Ernesto Gismondi wears another hat, as the business-minded partner in Ettore Sottsass' Memphis consortium.

BLACKOUT
Via dell'Orso 7
Tel. 87.30.73
Brera area
Credit cards accepted
The newest ideas in illumination are here in one impressive showroom. Owner Alberto Baffiggi, formerly of Fontana Arte, has assembled the finest of exemplars: Fontana Arte, Artemide, O Luce, Quattrifolio, Leucos, Lumina, and Tranconi. There are

some 110-voltage models available, and other items can be converted and shipped. You'll find scores of desk and table lamps, wall and ceiling fixtures, and freestanding floor lamps.

FLOS
Corso Monforte 9
Tel. 70.16.41
Duomo/Vittorio Emanuele area
Credit cards accepted
Most of Flos' outstanding classic designs are from the hands of Achille Castiglioni, the "wizard of lights" (the first to introduce the use of halogen bulbs), and Tobia Scarpa. In this beautiful showroom designed by Castiglioni himself, you'll see the earliest models produced decades ago, which were so forward and well designed that they are still popularly sold today. Not far away is the important Arteluce showroom (Via Borgogna 5, tel. 78.16.60), also owned by Flos.

FONTANA ARTE
Via Montenapoleone 3
Tel. 79.10.89
Montenapoleone area
Credit cards accepted
An oasis of beautiful glass and crystal with a strong emphasis on lamps and lighting fixtures, Fontana Arte was founded in 1881 and took a quantum leap into modern design under the tutelage of Gio Ponti in 1931. He was followed by the glass master Piero Chiesa, and both their designs are still manufactured today. "Scintilla," lampshadeless fixtures designed by the brothers Achille and Pier Giacomo Castiglioni, are displayed with models by other prominent designers. Plate glass also shows up in the form of modern table consoles and furnishings.

QUATTRIFOLIO
Via S. Cecilia 2
Tel. 78.14.98
Duomo/Vittorio Emanuele area
No credit cards accepted
This is a reliable and favored resource on the illumination scene, a design house that does its own production of lamps, lighting fixtures, and bathroom accessories. Designs range from simple, sleek plastic fixtures to the clever and innovative.

VENINI
Via Montenapoleone 9
Tel. 70.05.39
Montenapoleone area
Credit cards accepted
Venini was begun in 1921 by Venetian Paolo Venini, who wanted to give a new image to glass art and illumination. It combines the products of master glass craftsmen with the modern design input of such noted names as Gio Ponti, Vico Magistretti, Cini Boeri, and Ludovico De Santillana. Venini's extensive range appeals to both avant-garde and traditional tastes.

TABLETOP ACCESSORIES
DANESE
Piazza San Fedele 2
Tel. 86.60.19
Duomo/Vittorio Emanuele area
Credit cards accepted
Street level offers an art gallery-like display, and downstairs is the Danese showroom of prestigious small objects for the home, including desktop and tabletop accessories. Since opening in 1957, Bruno Danese and Jacqueline Vodoz have manufactured functional objects with an innovative flair, designed by masters in their fields: Enzo Mari, Bruno Munari, Angelo Mangiarotti and Achille Cas-

tiglioni. Many of these industrial plastic, stainless steel, and more precious handcrafted objects in silver, porcelain, and marble can also be seen in the permanent collection of New York's Museum of Modern Art.

HIGH-TECH
Corso Porta Ticinese 77
Tel. 83.51.263
Porta Ticinese area
Credit cards accepted
Not a showroom, but an actual retail store of high-tech, high-design accessories for the home, with an especially extensive collection for the kitchen. (See also page 292.)

SABATTINI
Via della Spiga 2
Tel 79.84.49
Montenapoleone area
No credit cards accepted
This is the only place to see Lino Sabattini's entire collection of exquisite tabletop objects in extra-heavy silver alloy. An artist, a poet, and a professional manufacturer, Sabattini projects his sleek design sense in all his objects. You'll also find a few designs from other eminent sources, such as reproductions of Charles Rennie Mackintosh's timeless early 20th-century flatware and tabletop pieces, and the spiral-handled teapot and coffeemaker created by Neapolitan architect-scholar Filippo Alison.

HOUSEWARE MANUFACTURERS

Alessi. Alessi is Italy's largest manufacturer of kitchenware and is easily found in most *casalinghe* (houseware) stores large and small. Although its wares are mass-produced, Alessi's high-quality, recognizable design sense transforms its stainless-steel pots and pans into functional

Richard Sapper's "Bollitore" from Alessi.

works of art. The foresighted Alberto Alessi, grandson of the founder, is now at the helm of the family-run company. He has commissioned the successful collaboration of some of today's finest design names: Richard Sapper, Michael Graves, Aldo Rossi, Roberto Venturi, Achille Castiglioni, and Ettore Sottsass. Specializing in stainless steel, Alessi also features a number of more expensive designer series in silverplate under the name "Officina Alessi."

Brionvega. Primarily known for its radios and television sets of modern and sleek design, Brionvega can be found in any good electronics or radio-and-TV shop. Careful attention to detail, quality technology, and the important design collaboration of Marco Zanuso have been responsible for a number of design awards for this company, which is based in the northern Veneto region.

Guzzini. Guzzini is a 75-year-old family-run business known for their graceful and modern designs of clear acrylic tableware (tumblers, pitchers, ice buckets, serving platters) and bright-colored plastic accessories for the kitchen. The company started as makers of decorative objects of animal horn for the home and then turned their attention in the late 1930s to molding products from plastic as this new material was first being used.

Kartell. A world leader in colorful high-quality plastics for home furnishings since being founded in 1949, Kartell was one of the first to embody the successful combination of mass production using thermoplastic injection molding with creative design. Most objects are designed by Anna Ferrieri Castelli, wife of Kartell owner Guido Castelli, but Marco Zanuso and Vico Magistretti are frequent collaborators. Kartell manufactures chairs, tables, stacking storage bins, and numerous objects for the home which are now considered classics; they are simple, functional, comfortable and durable, and come in a variety of solid colors.

BOOKSTORES SPECIALIZING IN DESIGN PUBLICATIONS

Italy publishes a wide array of high-gloss, world top-class design and architectural magazines. Most renowned are *Domus* and *Casabella*, both founded in 1928 and still major harbingers of current and avant-garde trends. *Modo, Casa Vogue, Abitare, Gran Bazaar, Interni* and *Ad* are other equally beautiful contenders for the design throne. You can find these magazines for sale at most major news kiosks in downtown Milan, but the following bookstores specialize in design subjects and will have the widest collection.

L'ARCHIVOLTO
Via Marsala 2
Tel. 65.90.842
Brera area
Credit cards accepted
A small bookstore/gallery specializing in architecture, design, and cityplanning, L'Archivolto offers books, magazines and posters in all languages. An extensive mail-order catalogue that selects the most interesting titles on the current international market and a widely used database research operation are two of its unusual draws. Probably the only concentration of its kind in existence, L'Archivolto also has an antiquarian section featuring old magazines and rare or out-of-print books. (See also page 264.)

CENTRO DOMUS
Via Manzoni 37
Tel. 65.98.227
Montenapoleone area
This is the showplace for *Domus,* Italy's premier design publication. You'll find current and back issues, as well as a selection of other Italian and international magazines and books on design and architecture. Design and architecture exhibitions are also occasionally held here.

LIBRERIA SALTO
Via Visconte di Modrone 18
Tel. 70.10.32
Duomo/Vittorio Emanuele area
No credit cards accepted
Somewhat hidden, but well worth the search for design lovers, Salto has Milan's largest and most important selection of books on architecture, industrial and graphic design, applied arts and advertising. There are magazines covering these areas as well, including publications in a number of languages.

Via Montenapoleone

*N*owhere else will you find such an elegant showcase of "Made in Italy" products, nor such precious retail space as on Via Montenapoleone. Here you will understand why Milan is called "the Stylish Lady."

It is ironic that a number of religious orders once held sway on the Via Montenapoleone, living serenely behind the high walls of cloistered convents. The imperial Austrian rulers did away with most of them by the late 18th century. At that time, the prestigious Teatro alla Scala was under construction to the southwest and the elegant Public Gardens, where a new Royal Palace was to stand, were taking shape to the northeast. It was logical for Milan's aristocracy and upper middle class to settle between these two desirable poles. Many of the stately neoclassical buildings that you see today were built in the years following 1800.

A restrained and dignified neoclassical air still permeates the neighborhood. It has remained the focal point of the city's elite society. In the 1930s, attracted by this affluent and distinguished community, came the first sophisticated shops. Today they read like a Who's Who of high-

The entrance to this neighborhood monastery bespeaks wealth and dignity, past and present.

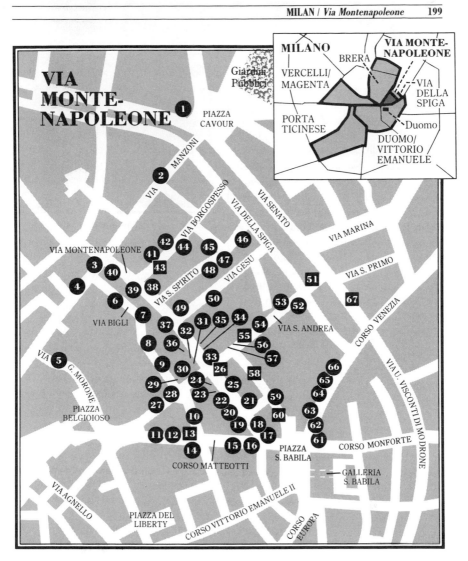

quality retail trade. Many of the high-fashion clothing boutiques that dominate the area are the flagship stores of Italy's star designers. In addition to such sartorial splendor, you'll find the headquarters of prestigious authorities on taste in fine jewelry, home furnishings, gift objects, antiques, hand-finished footwear, luxurious linens and exclusive furs. Nor are cafés, restaurants and gourmet food stores lacking.

This oasis from the chaotic hub of downtown Milan is not limited to Via Montenapoleone itself. In recent years, boutiques wanting to profit from the discreet profile of the neighborhood have spilled over into the narrow streets that branch off the primary artery.

JEWELRY

1 CARDI
Piazza Cavour 1
(entrance on Via Fatebenefratelli 23)
Tel. 65.92.495
Expensive; credit cards accepted

Cardi cleverly creates looks and styles inspired by Cartier, Bulgari or Faraone for much less than the price demanded by such top jewelry names. Here you'll find similar bold settings using different and less costly stones. Quality rubies, emeralds and diamonds are mixed with ersatz gems such as zirconium, quartz or other inexpensive materials. Cardi also devises ways of using less gold, such as substituting hollow for solid pieces. Most alluring is the chain department, where modern but classic designs are so numerous as to present a difficult choice. Cardi uses diamonds and precious stones, too, and will create pieces to your specifications.

JEWELRY

2 FIUMI
Via Manzoni 39
Tel. 65.99.074
Expensive to very expensive; credit cards
and personal checks accepted

For over 100 years the elegant Fiumi watches, prestigious accessories of simple design and superb quality, have been sold worldwide. Made in numbered-series and in such precious materials as gold, sapphire, onyx, ivory and tortoise, the Fiumi watch collection is as well known for its precision as for such details as its faceted jeweled stems and alligator bands. The collection, which now includes a modern model in gold and

Milan boasts a unique and dignified style.

steel, is the most complete here at the Fiumi flagship store. In this elegant, old-world shop with red brocade walls, you'll also find some other equally esteemed makes—Breguet, Piaget, Audemars, Piguet, Vacheron Constantin and others. Clocks old and new for the wall, desk or table are available, as is repairwork, which is done in Fiumi's workshop in the back.

ANTIQUE JEWELRY

TOP-NAME

Period Pieces & Collectibles

3 PENNISI
Via Manzoni 29
Tel. 86.22.32
Expensive; credit cards accepted

The elegant, old-style Pennisi is one of the best sources in Milan for fine antique jewelry. Owners Giovanni and Guido proudly display choice pieces from periods as early as the 1700s, with a concentration of 19th- and early-20th-century jewelry. The prized items include signed creations by European designers Van Cleef and Cartier, vintage watches from Piaget, Rolex and Movado, and Fabergé silver objets such as frames and letter openers. An impressive array of European art-deco pieces includes jewelry and cigarette cases. More exotic rarities include antique Oriental pieces intricately carved in ivory and jade, or you may be drawn to the elegant English antique silver tea or coffee services. Pennisi is adjacent to the Hotel Grand di Milano, a longtime favorite with visiting Milanophiles.

HOME
LINENS
Classic Luxury

4 FRETTE
Via Manzoni 11
Tel. 86.43.39
Expensive; credit cards accepted

For over 125 years, Frette has stocked the linen closets of Europe's aristocracy and draped the altars of St. Peter's. The firm originated in the nearby Lombardy town of Monza. Here in its most elegant Milan shop you will see the new Frette image, which joins its classic luxury linens for bed, bath and table with a fresh, updated approach. Cottons and silks in pastels and colorful patterns now appear side by side with traditional white linens. New details, such as lace decoration, are occasionally added even to traditional designs. There are beautiful sets of coordinated sheets, bed-covers, blankets and comforters, as well as terry-cloth bath towels and robes so that your color and theme will not be interrupted. One encounter with these linens and you'll understand why Frette was called upon to supply the original Orient Express and continues to drape the dining tables at the Quirinale and the beds of the luxurious Ciga hotel chain.

FASHION
WOMEN'S
Special Headwear & Romantic Attire

5 GIUSY BRESCIANI
Via G. Morone 4
Tel. 70.86.55
Expensive; credit cards accepted
Open during lunch

Step back into a romantic Middle European past in this exclusive, old-fashioned salon. A sitting area with inviting chairs, newspapers and chilled champagne helps while away time for those who wait to try on Giusy Bresciani's distinctive clothing. Her fashion is sporty and countrified yet classic—a Tyrolean look mixed with dreamy embroidery and lace. Unusual colors enliven her exclusively designed handmade sweaters and coordinated accessories, which are displayed on handsome antique furniture. Giusy Bresciani is particularly known for her artistic hats and flower arrangements. There are exquisite silk flowers arranged by hand for all tastes and occasions, as well as hairpieces and garlands for brides-to-be and exotic hair adornments with feathers for special evenings. These creations can be found in even greater profusion in her atelier next door at No. 8 (telephone 70.42.30; open 2:00–7:00 P.M. Monday to Friday).

ANTIQUES
Swords & Daggers

6 ALLE ANTICHE ARMI
Via Bigli 24
Tel. 79.23.18
Expensive; no credit cards accepted

A vast assortment of antique arms is Signor Colombo's pride. Each weapon has a story to tell, of famous duels and cavalry expeditions, of honor upheld and cowardice challenged. The illustrious collection includes muskets, inlaid swords, elaborate sheaths, gem-encrusted daggers and fancy sabers. A love of history and a penchant for fantasy are required for admission here.

GIFTS

DELUXE ARTICLES

7 I REGALI DI NELLA LONGARI 🏺🏺🏺🏺
Via Bigli 15
Tel. 78.20.66
Expensive; credit cards accepted

Nella Longari carefully selects an exciting array of gift items that are elegant, ultramodern and in unerring taste. Treat yourself to a visit here, to view high-style tabletop articles in silver, ebony, ivory and brass that are the exclusive, signed products of the skilled artisans and designers with whom Nella Longari collaborates.

Nella Longari's elegant, tasteful gifts.

There are sophisticated tea and coffee services, vases, picture frames and other decorative home accessories. Signora Longari was originally known for her consummate taste as an antique dealer; her high-society friends and clients were constantly asking her to find or create the perfect one-of-a-kind gift for the person who had everything. This two-floor emporium of gift novelties is the successful result.

The Nella Longari antique shop is located at Via Montenapoleone 23 (telephone 79.03.17) and features a singular collection of Italian furniture, sculpture, and paintings from the *alta epoca*—the 1400s and 1500s.

FASHION

MEN'S

Accessories & Furnishings

8 ETRO
Via Bigli 10
Tel. 79.52.03
Expensive; credit cards accepted

This is a store for the person who has everything and can afford the delightful luxuries of Etro's accessories. Etro's distinctive paisleys unfurl in rich, warm browns, greens, deep reds and oranges on cashmeres, silks, wools and cottons. Travel items such as bags, suitcases, briefcases, garment bags and trunks are made with Etro fabrics that have been plastic-coated and then finished with saddle leather. There are also jackets, robes, smoking jackets, shirts and pants, as well as a new line of fashion accessories such as ties, scarves and shawls. Meanwhile, if you'd like this same paisley to grace your home, you'll find a lovely Etro home furnishings

Deluxe paisley-printed extravagance at Etro.

boutique in the Brera neighborhood at Vicolo Fiori 17 (see page 254).

FASHION

CHILDREN'S

9 CALICO LION
Via Bigli 4
Tel. 78.18.05
Expensive; credit cards accepted

American owner and designer Holly Peltzer has created a fairy-tale land of pastels and whimsical prints for lucky newborns and young children up to eight years of age. In pure cottons, linens, silks and wools you'll find complete layette sets, exquisite baptismal gowns, delicately embroidered dresses, quilted buntings and jumpsuits, hand-knit sweater ensembles and myriad accessories such as tiny booties and tennis shoes. Coordinated linen for cribs or infants' beds and matching towels help create the ambiance of a dreamy nursery. There are antique toys, stuffed animals and flowered wallpaper whose theme is reflected in pillows and upholstery for bassinets, cribs and furniture. New grandmothers usually have a hard time not bringing home the entire store. The Calico Lion takes its name from the tale of a baby lion who was accidentally dropped by the stork into a meadow of wildflowers, which left their imprint upon him forever.

JEWELRY

TOP-NAME

10 POMELLATO
Via San Pietro all'Orto 17
Tel. 70.60.86
Expensive; credit cards accepted

Pomellato was one of the first to liberate jewelry from the constraints of traditionalism and infuse it with the spirit and fashion of the times. Bold chains and necklaces of distinctive links have an architectural approach; they seem like sculptured gold, often ornamented with diamonds or colored precious and semiprecious stones. Pomellato is highly design-conscious, yet classic enough to resist the tides of trends. The slick, post-modern style of the boutique is reflected in a new line of porcelain table settings with a gold-rimmed motif. There are also some exclusive leathergoods with attractive silver clasps for men and women. Dynamic and innovative, Pomellato's collection is crafted by master artisans.

Pomellato, design-conscious while classic.

FASHION
MEN'S SHIRTS
Made-to-Measure

11 TRUZZI ⌂⌂⌂⌂
Corso Matteotti 1
Tel. 70.05.68
Very expensive; no credit cards accepted

For generations this family-run *camiceria* has been the destination of the chic Milanese gentleman in quest of the ultimate shirt. Milan's oldest shirtmakers, the Ballini family has been hand-tailoring custom shirts fit for a king—or so Prince Charles, one of their satisfied customers, will attest—since 1890. The perfect shirt is Truzzi's forte, but ties, suits and pajamas are made to measure with the same century-old perfection in the quietly elegant shop. You can choose from bolts of quality fabrics in subdued, businesslike patterns, which are neatly stacked up on shelves before they're whisked to the workroom in the back. Every buttonhole is sewn by hand and every button attached by hand, while specialized collar- and cuff-makers do only that. First-time customers need to have one fitting and to order at least six shirts, which will be ready, depending upon the season, in two to four weeks. Once you've joined Truzzi's illustrious clientele, you may order your shirts by mail and have them sent to you.

HOME
PORCELAIN, CRYSTAL & SILVER

12 DOM
Corso Matteotti 3
Tel. 79.34.10
Expensive; credit cards accepted

Nunzio Amoroso's impeccable taste is evident in every item shown in Milan's best-stocked store for high-quality porcelain, crystal and silver. In a spacious environment with crystal chandeliers, you'll find table after table set with pieces from the finest international names, with different patterns tastefully mixed. Elegance is the only invariable in styles that run from the traditional to the modern. There are great luxury gifts: delicate porcelain rabbits, ebony salt and pepper shakers, salad tossers made from horn, and a range of silver frames. The Lalique collection is also exceptionally extensive. Signor Amoroso keeps your purchases on record for future replacements or additions, and will ship reliably and safely.

SUSTENANCE
BAR-CAFFÈ

13 SANT'AMBROEUS
Corso Matteotti 7
Tel. 70.05.40
Expensive; no credit cards accepted
Open 8:00 A.M.–7:30 P.M.; closed Sunday

Sant'Ambroeus' faithful clientele includes the elite of all nationalities. The bar is as popular for an *aperitivo* as for its renowned tea service and its morning breakfast of cappuccino and homemade *panettone* or croissants. Everything is served in a sophisticated Thirties-style ambiance. A salmon-colored tearoom is efficiently run by courteous waitresses in prim uniforms. Patrons may also sit in the outdoor area nibbling light, heavenly pastries and ice-cream dishes. Sweets and chocolates are lovingly packaged and wrapped in multicolored tulle for gift buying. And no important Milanese dinner party is complete without an elaborate ice-cream sculpture from St. Ambroeus' Signora Mimma. Try to top Gianni Versace's recent request: the Duomo, with its profusion of pinnacles, made up in edible perfection.

Stately architecture marks the tone.

CAPPUCCIO vs. CAPPUCCINO

If you draw disapproving looks when ordering a cappuccino, it is most likely after high noon. In Italy, this pillar of matinal ritual is taken early in the morning with a *cornetto* (croissant) or *brioche* pastry, then put to rest for the day. Made fresh with the same roasted beans and elaborate coffee machines used for the savory demitasse espresso, cappuccino is somewhat less heady (though still strong by foreign standards), and is topped with a frothy wallop of steamed milk (ask for *senza schiuma* if you prefer the hot milk without its foam). A sprinkling of powdered cocoa is optional; cinnamon topping is regarded as an Americanized affectation.

The etymology of the word is animatedly disputed by Italian coffee lovers. Most commonly heard is the explanation linked with the Church. Brown and white (the deep coffee color and the creamy milk) are the colors worn by the Capuchin religious order of monks and friars founded during the Middle Ages but now found only sparingly

throughout Italy. The humble and practical hood, or *cappuccio* (from *capo,* meaning head), was a recognizable element of their simple garb and became a kind of good-natured nickname. Today's coffee is called by the diminutive *cappuccino,* or frequently *cappuccio,* and is probably not at all what the monks imbibed to keep warm during those dreary medieval winters.

If espresso (referred to simply as *caffè*) is your choice, there are a number of variations on the theme of this national drink: *caffè macchiato* ("stained" with a dash of milk), *caffè lungo* (more watery), *caffè ristretto* (extra-strong), *caffè corretto* (with an added pick-me-up, usually of grappa, sambuca or Scotch), *caffè doppio* (a double dose), or *caffè con panna* (served with a topping of whipped cream). *Caffè Hag* (pronounced "ag") is a surprisingly savory brand of decaffeinated coffee that can also be ordered in all the varieties listed above.

LINGERIE
Boudoir Elegance

14 OFELIA
Corso Matteotti 10
Tel. 70.13.31
Expensive; credit cards accepted

This is a jewel of a lingerie shop. Sophisticated and elegant boudoir attire is sold in an intimate atmosphere with highly personalized service. Windows show off Ofelia's private collection of intimatewear: delicate bras, panties, garters, camisoles, teddies and corselets. There are also nightgowns, kimonos and robes, all of Ofelia's own production. Most are done up in luxurious silks, satins and lightweight wools with hand embroidery and airy lace trim. This is an excellent place to get fitted for a custom-made bra or corselet, or to pick up an exquisite trousseau for yourself or a thoughtful gift for someone special. The shop is tiny, and fitting rooms are upstairs. It takes its name from its owner, Ofelia Lasnaud, who is as chic and elegant as her special collection.

HOME
Rubber Monomania

15 MORONI GOMMA
Corso Matteotti 14
Tel. 31.66.41
Moderate; credit cards accepted

Everything that can feasibly be made up in rubber (*gomma*) can be found at Moroni. Set amidst the fancy giftware and lingerie stores of an elegant shopping street, Moroni is an unpretentious, seriously stocked hardware store that can keep a curious cus-tomer captive for hours. There is everything from hoses to gardening gloves to shower curtains to rafts. Especially popular is the selection of foul-weather gear, such as slickers, ponchos and galoshes. High rubber boots are on hand for fishing and boating. The store is popular with the Milanese, who don't seem to mind that there's no self-service.

TOYS
Enormous Selection

16 MASTRO GEPPETTO
Corso Matteotti 14
Tel. 79.12.12
Expensive; credit cards accepted

With a vast array of games and dolls from all over the world, Mastro Geppetto is "the" toy store of Milan. On the first floor you'll find Bugatti, Alfa Romeo and Rolls Royce model cars made by such Italian firms as Burago, Rivarossi, Italeri and Pocher. Little and big boys alike go for the one-of-a-kind antique model cars and trains and toy soldiers, though they often settle for their less expensive modern copies. Little girls head for the third floor and its profusion of dolls. There are, among many, felt Anili dolls from Turin in colorful provincial costumes and Migliorati's *appena nato* dolls, which look just like wrinkled newborn infants. The second floor is a happy meeting ground for both boys and girls, with all makes of rocking toys, bikes and a horse-drawn carriage on wheels. Mastro Geppetto was the name of the carpenter who created Pinocchio, so it is not surprising to find an exceptionally large assortment of hand-carved and painted wooden Pinocchio dolls here, from the tiny to four-foot-tall models.

MUSIC

Recordings, Instruments, Sheet Music

17 RICORDI
Via Montenapoleone 2
Tel. 70.19.82
Moderate; credit cards accepted

For generations, Milan has danced
and sung to the music published by
Ricordi. The company's flagship
store here is one of the oldest and
best-stocked sources for recordings of
jazz, classical and pop music in the
city. The bright and modern two-floor
store houses instruments such as guitars, drums and keyboards on the
ground level, while upstairs are located high-fidelity records, cassettes,
compact discs and videos. In addition, Ricordi is the respected publisher of scholarly books on music
and art, also available here.

FASHION

WOMEN'S

Designer Flagship Boutique

18 MILA SCHÖN
Via Montenapoleone 2
Tel. 70.18.03
Very expensive; credit cards accepted

"La Mila" is a member of the Old
Guard of Italian couture. The imposing size of her quarters on Via Montenapoleone suggests something of
her worldwide success since she first
took scissors in hand in 1958. Wealthy
Italian women justify her high prices
by the timeless quality of her classic
fashion and the durability of her excellent workmanship and rich fabrics.
The look of Mila Schön is effortlessly
elegant and classic but never somber;
one of her identifiable specialties is

Arcaded shopping galleries are an urban plus.

the double-facing of most garments, a
deluxe way of hand-finishing that
does away with linings. The first story
of this neoclassical palazzo houses
her boutique of women's ready-to-
wear dresses, suits, separates and
sweaters, while upstairs is her elegant
made-to-measure *haute couture*, available by appointment only. Mila Schön
has also put her signature on fine
accessories such as linens, perfume,
eyewear and porcelain, some of which
can be found in this flagship store.
And a few doors away at Via Montenapoleone 6 (telephone 70.13.33) is a
small but select assortment of her
menswear, emphasizing classic ties
and sweaters.

JEWELRY

Diamond Specialist

19 PEDERANZI
Via Montenapoleone 1
Tel. 70.17.28
Expensive; credit cards accepted

Diamonds are forever the specialty at Pederanzi, suppliers of fine engagement rings to Milan's high society. The two Pederanzi brothers were the first jewelers in Italy to fashion diamonds in the shape of a heart, an extremely difficult procedure that few others have managed to imitate successfully. Those special heart-shaped diamonds, along with cabochons and pavés, used in earrings, necklaces and rings, continue to draw discriminating customers to this tiny but elegant store. Also appealing are the other top-quality precious stones, usually on the large side, set in Pederanzi's classic yet modern style.

FASHION
WOMEN'S
Ready-to-Wear & Made-to-Measure

20 PIROVANO
Via Montenapoleone 1 (ready-to-wear); tel. 70.24.73
Via Montenapoleone 8 (couture); tel. 70.25.71
Expensive; credit cards accepted

Owner of one of the oldest and best-known couture establishments in Milan, Signora Pirovano specializes in classic, structured and tailored shapes for day, with far more fantasy in her celebrated eveningwear. The latter is known for its liberal application of sequins, feathers and metallic inlays. But it was Pirovano's beautiful leather handbags and accessories that first attracted a clientele of aristocratic Milanese ladies before World War II. Using luxury skins such as crocodile, alligator and ostrich, her handmade bags, like her fashion, are made for both day and evening. Coordinated shawls, belts, jewelry and bi-

joux complete the offering. All of Signora Pirovano's ready-to-wear clothes and accessories can be found in her boutique at Via Montenapoleone 1. Her special eveningwear can be made to order at her atelier, located at No. 8. Each year, Signora Pirovano shows two collections of these extravagant gowns with hand-stitched pearls, which are worn to galas, receptions and outlandish affairs by her most fashionable customers.

JEWELRY
TOP-NAME

21 MARIO BUCCELLATI
Via Montenapoleone 4
Tel. 70.21.53
Expensive; credit cards accepted

The imaginative artistry and extraordinary craftsmanship of Buccellati's jewelry has never been successfully replicated by others. Today the Buccellati family continues to interpret the world-famous, intricately worked designs originated by Mario Buccel-

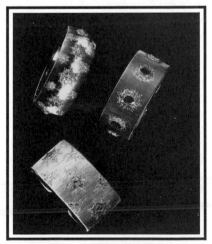

Detailed, engraved gold of Buccellati fame.

lati in the 1920s, along with more modern designs by the firm's specially trained artisans. Feather-light necklaces and bracelets that look like Venetian lace made in gold or silver are decorated with delicate *bullino* engraving, a Renaissance technique for which Buccellati is famous. The style, which has come to be known simply as "Buccellati gold," incorporates diamonds, precious stones and pearls, but the detailed, engraved setting always holds center stage. Buccellati's fame was reconfirmed when he became the preferred jeweler of Gabriele D'Annunzio, one of Italy's premier poets, who described Buccellati's creations as "the maximum exaltation of beauty, a homage to the beauty of the receiver."

Buccellati is also renowned for its hand-hammered sterling silver tabletop objects, which are timeless in their appeal. This jeweled legacy is today run by the four Buccellati sons.

JEWELRY

22 TRABUCCO
Via Montenapoleone 5
Tel. 79.28.56
Expensive; credit cards accepted

Trabucco is one of the most fashion-conscious of high-style jewelry designers. Large, colorful, geometric-shaped semiprecious stones are set in gold to create exceptional pieces. Unusual stones such as fire opal (orange in color), as well as amethyst, topaz and aquamarine, are used in ornate designs, often with a generous smattering of pavé diamonds. The size of each dazzling piece is as bold as the color combination is unusual. Price tags are as sleek as the store's high-tech setting.

JEWELRY
TOP-NAME

23 FARAONE
Via Montenapoleone 7/A
Tel. 54.56.256
Expensive; credit cards accepted

Six bejeweled windowcases on Montenapoleone give a hint of the precious finds that await beyond the elegant pink marble door. New owner Cesare Settepassi fuses his own flawless, classic designs with Faraone's modern fantasy, using lots of precious and semiprecious stones. Milan's high society shops here for status fashion jewelry studded with rubies, diamonds, and sapphires in multiple shades, together with less expensive Brazilian stones. An interesting innovation is joining steel and gold in bold, heavy-linked necklaces and bracelets that are at once sporty and chic. On the second floor, Faraone keeps a remarkable collection of antique English silver services as well as contemporary pieces of their own production. Settepassi is of famous Florentine lineage; his family have been jewelers to royalty and distinguished goldsmiths since the Renaissance (see page 76).

FASHION
MEN'S

Ultraclassic

24 LARUSMIANI
Via Montenapoleone (corner of
     Via P. Verri, 7)
Tel. 70.69.57
Expensive; credit cards accepted

Larusmiani is the last word in refined haberdashery for the gentleman with ultraclassic tastes; it makes few concessions to passing trends. Frequented by well-heeled Milanese who find it young and casual but also classic and elegant, this is one of four Larusmiani locations. It offers superb cashmere sweaters, handsome suits, tweed jackets and raincoats, and such accessories as shirts, ties and belts. Everything in the two stories of dark wood-paneled rooms is identified by the Larusmiani private label. The firm will also custom-make suits from a wide range of deluxe fabrics.

The other three locations are at Galleria Vittorio Emanuele 15 (telephone 87.50.85), Via Manzoni 43 (telephone 65.96.361) and, the largest, Corso Vittorio Emanuele 5 (telephone 87.48.65).

LINGERIE

INFANTWEAR

Luxurious & Classic

25 ARS ROSA
Via Montenapoleone 8
Tel. 79.38.22
Expensive; credit cards accepted

The dream of every Milanese woman is to spend a night in the classic luxury nightwear of Ars Rosa. To call these delicate items of silk, satin and lace "precious" would seem a grand understatement. Exquisite hand embroidery embellishes camisoles, nightshirts, robes and peignoir sets that will romanticize your life. Few can resist the delicate sets of pastel lace undergarments—scant panties and matching bras. And when the weather turns colder, Ars Rosa makes a stylish concession to practicality with smocked robes in soft flannels and warm Viyella. There are also tiny

outfits for princely babies in pastels and whites with intricate decoration. It is best if you enter with something specific in mind and the inclination to buy; browsing is limited.

SUSTENANCE

PASTICCERIA/TEAROOM

26 COVA
Via Montenapoleone 8
Tel. 70.05.78 or 79.31.87
Moderate to expensive; no credit cards
   accepted
Closed Sunday

Traditionally considered one of Milan's best *caffè/pasticcerie*, Cova is a perfect place for tea, complete with pink-lace-covered tables set with delicate porcelain, polished silver and fresh flowers. But it's also popular for morning breaks, afternoon *aperitivi,* and as a general meeting ground for the habitués of this swank quarter. Professional waiters with tails and good manners have waited on generations of VIPs who have come to nibble on exquisite tea sandwiches with truffle, tuna or salmon spread; baby pizzas on *vol-au-vent* crust; profoundly rich *sacher torte*; and fresh plum cakes. This same luxury is lavished upon armies of tiny sweets and exquisite chocolates, which make lovely gifts (favored by the Aga Khan): arranged on porcelain dishes or silver trays, they come wrapped in elegant tissue and brocade ribbon. If you try the local specialty *panettone* anywhere, you must try it here, for it was Cova's own invention back in the early years following the *pasticceria*'s 1817 opening.

ERMENEGILDO ZEGNA

A young Ermenegildo Zegna set up shop at a time when well-heeled Continental gentlemen would think of wearing nothing but a suit made of British flannel or tweed. He began his own weaving business in 1910 with three looms in his Alpine hometown of Trivero. His goal was to achieve and surpass the traditional excellence of English fabrics. Because of his vision and entrepreneurial daring, his contemporaries considered him a dreamer and a madman.

Today Zegna's two sons and five grandchildren head a fashion and textile dynasty of outstanding quality. To the superiority of English woven fabrics, Zegna added a distinctive Italian flair for colors and color combinations. Two years after his death in 1966, his sons Aldo and Angelo decided to enter the ready-to-wear clothing sector. As Aldo would often say, they took up where the upper-class men's tailor left off. Modern, dynamic men who demand lasting elegance in their wardrobe gladly pay four-digit price tags for a Zegna suit. The look in Zegna silhouettes is tailored, neat and well-defined, never controversial or over-designed.

Every Zegna garment is made exclusively from Zegna textiles, whose superior quality is still the most important aspect of the family's dynasty, although fabric sales now constitute only 30 percent of their business. Since the Zegnas begin

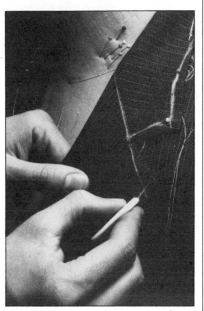

Zegna takes up where a man's tailor leaves off.

with the raw product, they exercise total control over each garment from start to finish. Members of the family go personally to the Australian outback to choose merino fleece, to Mongolia for cashmere, to Peru for alpaca and to South Africa for mohair.

With the success of their deluxe ready-to-wear in the upscale men's market, Zegna has gone on to design an extensive range of men's accessories. Loyal customers like the Aga Khan and King Juan Carlos of Spain can now be royally accoutred from head to toe in Zegna's total look.

FASHION

MEN'S

Impeccable Tailoring

27 ERMENEGILDO ZEGNA ▯▯▯▯
Via Pietro Verri 3
Tel. 79.55.21
Expensive; credit cards accepted
Open during lunch

The Zegna name has become synonymous with superlative fabrics and impeccable tailoring. The modern two-floor store offers the discriminating male shopper everything from shoes to tuxedos (called a *smoking* in Italian), all manufactured by the Zegna family with prestigious Zegna fabrics. On the first floor you'll find accessories, casual sportswear, and activewear, while on the second floor is a wide selection of handsome Zegna suits, outerwear, and formalwear. Other than a similar boutique in Paris, this is the only store that carries solely Zegna products, and the only place where you can have an authentic Zegna suit tailor-made; such custom orders take approximately three weeks.

LINENS & LINGERIE

INFANTWEAR

Embroidery

28 PRATESI
Via Pietro Verri (corner of Via Bigli)
Tel. 79.45.11
Expensive; credit cards accepted

Perfect workmanship and luxury are but two qualities of this renowned Tuscan name in linens. The guard at the door hints at the high cost of Pratesi's merchandise, which you may

Pratesi linens for the discerning home.

be able to afford only in small quantities. This location carries the full line of lingerie and loungewear for men, women and babies. A second, smaller location nearby at Via Montenapoleone 21 (telephone 70.97.91) carries household linens only.

See Florence listing (page 87).

JEWELRY

WATCHES & WATCHBANDS

29 PISA
Via Pietro Verri (corner of Via
    Montenapoleone 9)
Tel. 79.19.98
Expensive; credit cards accepted
Open during lunch

If you're attached to the old timepiece you have, but would like to give it a lift with a new band, Pisa's specialty is a wide range of tasteful and colorful bands in leather and exotic skins to fit every possible make of watch. Gone are the days when Cartier made the only bands to fit Cartier watches, and Piaget catered to Piaget models alone. Pisa now has watchbands that fit perfectly and will update them all. If you're ready to buy a brand new watch, you won't find any bargains at Pisa, just the finest and most extensive watch collection in Milan.

FASHION

MEN'S

Young, Up-to-Date & Sporty

30 VERRI UOMO

Via Pietro Verri
Tel. 79.28.17
Expensive; credit cards accepted
Open during lunch

Demanding dressers who want the
novelty of the avant-garde without the
flash and with no compromise in
quality are happy at Verri Uomo. Unconstructed jackets and constructed
suits in exceptional fabrics, plus
beautiful Jacquard sweaters, offer diversity and new possibilities each season. There are also supple leather
and shearling jackets and coats. The
tendency is toward a relaxed and updated *classico nuovo* style, elegant
but *sportivo*. A complete range of
belts, ties, shirts and scarves helps
personalize and tie together the Verri
Uomo look—personified by the handsome, English-speaking salesmen.
Verri Uomo's success is due to its
stylish design and quality-controlled
private production.

CUTLERY

Enormous Selection

31 G. LORENZI

Via Montenapoleone 9
Tel. 79.05.93
Expensive; credit cards accepted

One of the world's finest and best-
stocked cutlery stores, Lorenzi carries
every kind of knife ever made. Of
course, there is the popular Swiss
army knife with 100 blades (Lorenzi
has an even larger knife with 200
blades in his private collection), as

well as a delicate truffle slicer, oyster
huskers, coordinated tray and knife
sets for fresh salmon, scissors and
manicure sets with crocodile-covered
cases, and over 100 varieties of razors
and shaving equipment. Lorenzi's offerings are not limited to knives.
Other selections include over 2000
varieties of pipes, a portable mini-
espresso coffee machine for the individual always on the go, and a gourmet's caviar spoon made from bone.
The list goes on forever. Founder
Giovanni Lorenzi sharpened his first
blade in Milan in 1919 and set up
shop on this celebrated street in 1929.

HOME

GLASSWARE & LIGHTING

Contemporary Design

32 VENINI

Via Montenapoleone 9
Tel. 70.05.39
Expensive; credit cards accepted

If you won't be going on to Venice, go
see Venini's exquisite glass collection
here. A comfortably large space offers
some fine contemporary design,
along with traditional glassware and
lighting.
    See Venice listing (page 457).

JEWELRY

33 MARTIGNETTI

Via Montenapoleone 10
Tel. 70.15.09
Expensive; credit cards accepted

The finest pearls and corals from the
sea can be found at Martignetti's. In
this traditional old shop, you'll find a
wide selection of loose real, cultured

FURS

Italian furriers combine the distinctive creative genius of their fashion designers with sophisticated techniques to produce the most beautiful and desirable furs in the world. Increased sales to savvy foreign buyers are due in large part to the guarantee of outstanding workmanship and high-fashion styling. Eighty-five percent of the skins used are imported from abroad; the influential Italian brokers are able to buy excellent skins because they have first pick of the international options market. Their purchases are then meticulously treated in Italian *concerie,* or tanneries, by master craftsmen.

The classic and traditional can be found alongside the highly fashionable whose unique and unusual silhouettes bow to the dictates of seasonal ready-to-wear. The only invariable is the technical know-how, both new and centuries old, that shows off each skin's potential for supple, lightweight beauty. The artisan *pellicciaio,* or furrier, still works with painstaking attention to detail that has become a lost art in most modern-day fur production outside of Italy. Deluxe linings are made of Como silks or of fine, supple leathers that allow reversibility, and furs are dyed in a palette of rich colors. Look for a certificate marked A.I.P. (Associazione Italiana Pellicceria), the Italian division of a worldwide organization promising professional expertise.

The period between January and May is the best time to buy both made-to-measure and ready-to-wear furs. Christmas is over and prices will probably be reduced, even at the most prestigious furriers. From late spring onward, the new collections for the following winter start to arrive. You'll want to familiarize yourself with each store's policy of shipping if it's too warm to wear your new treasure home.

LUXURY FURS

CARLO TIVIOLI
Via Santo Spirito 26
Tel. 70.14.90
No credit cards accepted
This Torino-based fashion-fur genius creates custom-made, exclusive, extravagant furs using the most precious and costly skins on the market. His technical acumen enables him to produce feather-light creations despite the bulk of precious furs such as mink, sable, bukhara and lynx. A palette of natural and unusual colors is another distinctive hallmark of his status furs.

FENDI
Via Sant'Andrea 16
Tel. 79.16.17
Credit cards accepted
Rome's celebrated Fendi sisters create Italy's most innovative fur fashion. Having collaborated with Karl Lagerfeld for more than 20 years,

they have wrapped the world's most fashion-conscious women in fantasy furs with flair and originality.

VERY EXPENSIVE

TABAK
Via Bigli 4
Tel. 79.50.17
Credit cards accepted
Although a relative newcomer to the fur scene, Tabak has landed a faithful young and fashionable clientele with the help of a clever and aggressive advertising campaign. It offers high quality with a bit more youthful kick than its competitors.

GIULIANA TESO
Via Gesù 9
Tel. 79.81.24
Credit cards accepted
Beautifully detailed workmanship enhances the innovative styling of furs that are sometimes sporty, sometimes luxuriously dressy. Giuliana makes personal pilgrimmages to Russia's fur auctions to guarantee the highest-quality pelts.

MELEGARI E COSTA
Via Montenapoleone 7A/5
Tel. 79.47.85
Credit cards accepted
Vying with Fendi's fantasy are these masterpieces of fur high fashion. A specialty is mink and fox in a highly exotic array of the season's richest colors, worked in extravagant and original styles for both custom-made or ready-to-wear. The display window is a work of art in itself and worth the detour.

DELLERA
Via San Damiano 4
Tel. 79.61.51
No credit cards accepted
The Milanese Dellera family has stood behind their furry collections for over 100 years, following their production from start to finish. Their large shop holds an ample selection and a rainbow of fashion colors that are favorites with Milan's fur-draped ladies.

CORRADO IRIONÈ
Via Santo Spirito 7
Tel. 79.56.30
Credit cards accepted
One hundred years of Irione family experience result in ever-changing innovation and an excellence of technique that is even protected by a patent. Known for the extreme lightness and softness of his creations, Irionè limits production of both made-to-measure and ready-to-wear to ensure their quality.

MODERATE

LEVI
Piazza Santa Maria Beltrade 2
Tel. 80.92.76
Credit cards accepted
Just off Via Torino is this fur emporium of ready-to-wear coats and jackets of good-quality skins. It offers a wide selection of models, mostly in a simple and classic vein, with few flights of fantasy and relatively low prices.

and freshwater pearls of the highest quality. They can be individually handpicked, strung or woven according to your preference—or taken elsewhere, should you want a more elaborate clasp (Martignetti's selection leans toward simple elegance). Pearls can also be fashioned into earrings and rings, and there is a large selection of pearl bracelets. Exquisitely carved cameos and corals, including the hard-to-find, quasi-transparent *peau d'ange* (angel-skin), are sold loose or set in delicate brooches and rings. Martignetti is also known for its collection of stones (turquoises, opals, lapis lazuli, and jade in many colors), often imaginatively combined in *colliers*, large cocktail rings, and pendants.

FOOD

SALUMAIO

Gourmet Emporium

34 IL SALUMAIO DI MONTENAPOLEONE ⌂⌂⌂⌂
Via Montenapoleone 12
Tel. 70.11.23
Expensive; no credit cards accepted

The reputation-conscious Milanese will tell you that there is only one *salumaio* worth note, and that is the unique Il Salumaio on Via Montenapoleone. It sells not only salami by the dozens, but everything needed for a five-course gourmet banquet. Its windows, artistically displaying the season's freshest delicacies, are but a modest indication of the feast for the senses within. Shelves and counters are laden with homemade pastas, vegetable and rice salads, and pies, including *torta di formaggio* (a kind of pie layered with a combination of

cheese, nuts, herbs, salmon, etc.), one of many store specialties. Deep barrels of pickles and jars of olives and artichoke hearts line the walls, while from the ceiling hang cured and smoked meats and fresh game when in season. Myriad pâtés compete with layered *bavaresi* vegetable molds, and there are over 200 delicious cheeses, Italian and imported. In the center is an island of creamy desserts, cookies, tortes and cakes, all made daily. The wonderful *torta di pane* and *latte alla milanese* are some of the best local specialties in town. Il Salumaio seems not at all out of place in this swank neighborhood.

JEWELERY

WATCHES & CLOCKS

Fashion in Timepieces

35 LORENZ
Via Montenapoleone 12
Tel. 79.42.32
Moderate; credit cards accepted

In a street as ultraelegant as Montenapoleone, the Lorenz watch shop is a pleasant surprise. Its watches are interesting for their design and technol-

Lorenz offers the latest timepiece fashion.

Award-winning desktop steel clock at Lorenz.

ogy, but moderate in price. There are snappy modern timepieces as well as traditionally elegant designs. The quintessence of the latter is the "Montenapoleone" model that celebrates the shop's recent fiftieth anniversary. Technomaniacs will be drawn to the original "Asymetrique," which hugs the side of your wrist so you can steal a glance during a boring business lunch or while speeding down the highway. All Lorenz watches embody the philosophy of absolute reliability, high-class finishings, and an average price. These qualities were already evident in such early models as Richard Sapper's "Static" (still in production), a cylindrical steel table clock that won Lorenz the prestigious "Compasso d'Oro" design award in 1960. The shop is run by the offspring of Tullio Bolletta, an expert watchmaker who, just after World War II, took out a patent in Switzerland for a watch mechanism of his own invention, and then concentrated on the look of his timepieces. This concern for style is still evident in the shop.

(Lorenz is not to be confused with the Lorenzi shop of a million blades just across the street.)

FASHION

CHILDREN'S

Sportswear

36 BENETTON 012
Via Montenapoleone 15
Tel. 70.18.34
Moderate; credit cards accepted

From the genial marketing of the Benetton dynasty comes this bright and fun store for young fashion plates. Though not as ubiquitous as the Benetton chain for teenagers and up, this division of moderately priced fashionable sportswear for infants to 12-year-olds has many hundreds of shops wordwide. Here young Benettonites are introduced to the pleasures of creating a coordinated wardrobe at an early age. The Benetton philosophy of basic styles in a rainbow of color variations, together with quality knits and natural fibers, guarantees this division the same success as the rest of the family's remarkable operation. Many of 012's colors and shapes are similar to what Benetton offers for older siblings or parents, but a generally childlike feeling permeates the collection.

FASHION

WOMEN'S

Feminine Individualized Dressing

37 ALBERTA FERRETTI
Via Montenapoleone 21/A
Tel. 70.90.95
Expensive; credit cards accepted

The last few seasons have seen Alberta Ferretti closely followed as a new, influential talent in Italian fashion. Ferretti thrives on impact, and a visit to her gallery-like boutique is obligatory for fashion pioneers. Displayed in a sparsely furnished space with exposed cement walls, the fashion is contemporary, yet surprisingly feminine in appeal and line. It is a fashion of many faces, at once sporty and elegant. Ferretti designs for the young, modern, very feminine woman who can self-assuredly carry off original fabrics and high-tech detailing: shiny lycras and knits are mixed with dramatic lacings, zippers and snaps. The boutique is not overly warm or welcoming; it is for the brave and curious. As you enter the store, you pass through a large area punctuated by constantly running videos of Alberta's most recent fashion shows; a sales assistant will meet you there and escort you back into the boutique.

SPORTS GEAR

MEN'S, WOMEN'S & CHILDREN'S ACTIVE SPORTSWEAR

Top European Designers

38 DOLOMITI CENTRO MODASPORT
Via Montenapoleone 22 and 26
Tel. 70.13.26 and 70.02.96
Expensive; credit cards accepted
Open during lunch

Children's sports clothing is in the smaller of these two shops, located at No. 26, with adults' a few doors away at No. 22. The latter offers two full floors crammed with colorful sportswear from Italy's and Europe's leading designer houses. Men's and women's sporting fashion from Ellesse, Ermenegildo Zegna, Fila, Valentino, Daniel Hechter, and Moncler will turn heads on any tennis court, ski trail, or golf course. There's a huge range of style and color in ski pants, parkas and jumpsuits, sweaters,

après-ski wear and shearling coats. In the second-floor women's department, your eye will most probably rest on fun items like polka-dotted, fringed sneakers or pastel-colored fake-fur ski parkas for the unconventional champion.

A Dolomiti store selling equipment is located at Piazza del Duomo 17 (corner of Via Mercanti, telephone 86.90.750). There you'll find a large assortment of sports equipment.

FASHION

MEN'S

Elegant Tailored Apparel

39 GALTRUCCO
Via Montenapoleone 27
Tel. 70.29.78
Expensive; credit cards accepted

These refined and elegant surroundings, designed by the noted architect Piero Pinto, reflect the men's fashion offered in the shop. The marvelous yardgoods you may have seen at the Galtrucco store in Piazza del Duomo are made here into a beautiful private-label collection of suits and sportswear. The selection of ready-to-wear comprises irresistible cashmere jackets and overcoats, as well as flannel trousers by Zanella, suits by Ermenegildo Zegna, and a wide assortment of beautiful knitwear and Jacquard sweaters, including a fashionable representation from Claude Montana. A made-to-measure tuxedo from Galtrucco is the most coveted example of sartorial splendor; they'll ship as well as send future mail orders once they have your measurements. But if you can't wait the necessary month, you can choose from equally elegant formalwear from Brioni and

The nearby La Scala, a mecca for music lovers.

D'Avenza on the second floor. You can bring it all home in a set of Galtrucco's own distinctive, masculine-looking luggage.

JEWELERY

SILVER & GIFTWARE

40 DAL VECCHIO

Via Montenapoleone 29
Tel. 70.87.40
Expensive; credit cards accepted

Special requests for silver pieces, be they home furnishings, objets, or jewelry whims, can be made up to your specifications by Dal Vecchio's master silversmiths. In the store, traditional 18th- and 19th-century silver objects are juxtaposed with handsome modern silver pieces made in Dal Vecchio's own workshops. The silver collection is more than equaled by the gold and steel jewelry designed by Antonio Fallaci, alternating the two distinctive metals in modern classic chains and bracelets. Other gold designs use a heavy chain link in settings that are traditional but updated, punctuated by a colorful use of stones. If you can't afford a real racing car for your friend the racing fan, bring home a miniature gold Ferrari or Maserati key ring. Other unique gift ideas are the gold cigar cutter, magnifying glass, and pocket knife.

HOME

GLASSWARE

41 VETRERIE DI EMPOLI

Via Borgospesso 5
Tel. 70.87.91
Moderate; no credit cards accepted

The celebrated mouth-blown glass collection from Empoli is here in its entirety, from precious crystal glasses to lamps, vases, and tabletop articles made by Tuscan artisans. Glassware comes in a number of colorful choices and is generally heavier, more rustic and less ornate in design than some of its more sophisticated Venetian rivals. Prices are reasonable, considering the decorous address. Three large rooms have everything casually and compactly displayed on open tables that facilitate browsing. Lamps and glass fruits and vegetables are bestsellers, while hovering above it all are beautiful 18th-century frescoes from the school of Tiepolo.

FASHION

WOMEN'S

Bridal Gowns

42 WANDA ROVEDA

Via Borgospesso 15
Tel. 79.42.12
Very expensive; credit cards accepted

Wanda Roveda is a name on the lips and in the dreams of every well-heeled bride-to-be. The large store is all class and elegance; its superb bridal gowns transform every bride into a princess. Dresses are made to order from samples available for you to see and try on, and a handful can be purchased ready-made. Each dress is exquisite, starting with the simple and stately and culminating with elaborate models that are studies in hand embroidery, pearls, beads, intricate lace insets and trains deserving of Gothic cathedrals. The living-room-like setting has a focal chandelier, overstuffed sofas and chairs, and silver coffee and tea services that offer respite from the never-ending prenuptial preparations. Wanda guarantees you a very special gown for a very special day; if not your wedding day, it may be for a debut or a society bash.

SUSTENANCE
RISTORANTE/TRATTORIA

43 BICE
Via Borgospesso 12
Tel. 70.25.72
Expensive; credit cards accepted
Closed Monday

Bice is always packed with smart-looking customers who are busy chatting, eating and being seen in what is, by now, a Milanese institution. Half a generation has seen little change in the traditional Tuscan cuisine served here (see glossary on page 39), despite Milan's tendency for gastronomic innovation. The elegance here derives from the crowd and the genuine peasant fare, such as *ribollita*, pasta and *fagioli*, and ultra-tender Florentine steaks from the grill. Some unmistakable departures from the average Tuscan menu are the variety of fresh fish and the token *risotto* and *carpaccio*. The wine selection is good, with some vintage gems, and the service is efficient and pleasant, especially if you're dining with Gianni Versace or Giorgio Armani, two of the many prominent habitués.

GIFTS
Radica Monomania

44 GIULIA SCHMID
Via Borgospesso 22
Tel. 79.02.51
Expensive; credit cards accepted
Open during lunch

Traditionally known as "pipe wood" or brierwood, *radica* is used here to make everything under the sun. A rich burnished brown in color, it appears together with silver or leather on tasteful gifts for smokers such as cigar cases, lighters, humidors and tobacco boxes. Non-smokers will revel in *radica* canes, clocks, playing cards, frames, calculators and other desk accessories, razors, *radica*-handled umbrellas, and even a *radica* radio. Unusual luggage is made with polished *radica* and trimmed with leather, and you'll be surprised to see *radica* faces on men's and women's watches. You'll realize that nothing has been spared when you happen upon a luxurious cashmere sweater with *radica* buttons or silk scarves in a *trompe-l'oeil radica* print.

FASHION
ACCESSORIES
Eyeglass Frames

45 L'OCCHIALAIO
Via Luigi Rossari 5
Tel. 70.08.38
Expensive; no credit cards accepted

The *ne plus ultra* of eyewear design in a city that lets no accessory escape the dictates of high fashion, this small store has an enormous assortment of exclusive eyeglasses of its own production. They are available as frames for prescription lenses or as nonprescription sunglasses, ranging from fantasy to more reserved models for every kind of face, in such precious materials as ivory, tortoise, mother-of-pearl, gold and silver. The most unusual frames are plastic in unusual shapes and color combinations. L'Occhialaio also carries a number of designer lines such as Mikki and Jean Patou. An impressive selection of merchandise that embraces the bizarre and the tasteful draws a similarly varied clientele.

Architectural detail is a Milanese gem.

ANTIQUES

15th-to-18th-Century Majolica Ceramics

46 FLORENCE TACCANI

Via Santo Spirito 24
Tel. 78.12.48
Expensive; no credit cards accepted

Florence Taccani is considered an expert in majolica ceramics, as will be apparent from a look at her rare collection. Majolica is believed to have its roots in Islamic and later Hispano-Moresque ceramics; the term comes from the Spanish island of Majorca, from which Italy first imported much of its tin-glazed ware. The craft flourished in Italy in the 15th century, when rich, stylized geometric motifs embellished earthenware jars, plates, figurines and numerous other objects. Signora Taccani's collection is representative of the 15th to 18th centuries, with an emphasis on the latter; most of her pieces are Italian, although there are a good number of French and Spanish entries. In addition to these exquisite hand-painted finds, Signora Taccani shows some beautiful furniture of the same period, as well as some equally fine paintings and objets d'art.

ANTIQUES

15th-to-16th Century

47 PAOLO CANELLI

Via Santo Spirito 14
Tel. 70.21.24
Expensive; no credit cards accepted

In a city of highly professional, specialized antique dealers and collectors, Paolo Canelli is reputed to be one of the most successful. A tasteful selection of *alta epoca* furniture (15th and 16th centuries) is displayed in high style in a setting deserving of such prized pieces. Complementing the furniture collection, made up predominantly of chairs and tables, are 16th-century Flemish tapestries, 17th-century portraits and still lifes, and a number of sculptures and objets d'art.

FASHION

WOMEN'S

One-of-a-Kind Look

48 GULP

Via Santo Spirito 14
Tel. 79.49.03
Expensive; credit cards accepted

If you want to be a walking sensation, you'll find the appropriate fashion at Gulp—original, unusual and, more often than not, just a little bizarre. Gabriella Gulp will dress you for afternoon or evening, in ready-to-wear or made-to-order, and will guarantee you a one-of-a-kind look. Clothes in stamped leather, and knitwear decorated with feathers, sequins and appliqués encourage the sense of fantasy evoked by the store's eclectic display of antiques, including a vintage jukebox. Cocktail dresses are glitzy and attention-grabbing—perfect for the woman who wants to make sure she's seen. As if the clothes weren't enough, there are also accessories in interesting leathers with typical Gulp adornments. A new Gulp shop at Via della Spiga 44 (telephone 70.48.18) offers this same fantasy for a younger clientele.

SHOES
MEN'S
Hand-Made Classics

49 RONCHI
Via Gesù (corner of Montenapoleone 18)
Tel. 70.62.70
Expensive; credit cards accepted

In a city that abounds with high-fashion footwear boutiques, Ronchi is one of the oldest and finest sources for beautiful, hand-sewn classic men's shoes. Half a century's worth of wooden lasts represents the feet of the famous and discerning Milanese who have taken advantage of Ronchi's fastidious attention and detailed craftsmanship. Once your foot has joined the privileged roster, you can order shoes by mail according to your specifications (since your foot will be spoiled for life). The five-week waiting period can be avoided if you buy directly from Ronchi's ready-to-wear collection.

FASHION
WOMEN'S
Fashion as Art & Function

50 NANNI STRADA 𝄀𝄀𝄀𝄀
Via Gesù 4
Tel. 79.97.08
Moderate to expensive; credit cards accepted
Open during lunch

Nanni Strada is an award-winning fashion innovator, in a city lauded for its design impetus. Enter into this stark new space that serves as store/showroom/design studio, and you'll sense Nanni Strada's formula. Her geometric, one-size garments are art and design objects, far transcending the boundaries of fashion doomed to die with the season. Nanni treats fabrics the way artists approach other media. Her traveling clothes maxi-

From Nanni Strada's trailblazing studio.

mize linen's "crumplability"; they are industrially treated to be permanently wrinkled. Hung and lit like a work of art, each of these Torchon pieces is flanked by a large photograph to show how it will wrap the body in tidy pleats; surprisingly, these clothes are very wearable. Other outfits are made of linens lacquered to highlight the natural brightness of the fabric, giving it a lustrous glaze. Who knows where Nanni's passion and spirit will bring fabric next in her pursuit to defeat the tailored dress. Winner of the Compasso d'Oro award for outstanding design, she is a zealous trail-blazer whose design philosophy blends Oriental sensibility with Western style.

SUSTENANCE

RISTORANTE/TRATTORIA

51 ST. ANDREW'S

Via Sant'Andrea 23
Tel. 79.31.32
Expensive; credit cards accepted
Closed Sunday

In the middle of this opulent shopping neighborhood is the relatively new St. Andrew's restaurant, whose only Britannic elements are its name and its club-like English décor. Blinis with Beluga caviar, *foie gras* served on a bed of crisp spinach, and very good beef Wellington are among the menu's few non-Italian choices. Everything is excellently prepared, however, from the favorite *tagliolini al limone* (in a light lemon sauce) to the *risotto con grancevola* (with crabmeat) and the quintessentially Milanese veal cutlet, here called *l'orecchio d'elefante* (elephant's ear). The wine *cantina* contains some major *crus* from both Italy and France.

FASHION

WOMEN'S

Flagship Designer Boutique

52 LUCIANO SOPRANI

Via Sant'Andrea 14
Tel. 79.83.27
Expensive; credit cards accepted

This ultramodern shop is a relative newcomer to the scene, although for years Soprani has been lauded for his elegant women's collection and, more recently, for his men's fashion. The sleek and modern lines of the boutique complement the fluidity of line for which his clothes are known. Clean shapes and an updated tailored look are set off by unusual combinations of interesting fabrics. Soprani's use of color and detail is understated and effective. The breadth of his creations can be seen here, from daytime separates and dresses to glittery eveningwear, from coats to accessories (bags, belts, shoes and eyewear). Soprani is the design talent behind the Basile label, and he has also worked with Gucci, Chloe and Pims. Here you will find his women's fashion only; his men's fashion is available at Kashimaya at Via della Spiga 19 (telephone 78.14.69).

FASHION

MEN'S

Sleek & Sporty

53 BARBA'S

Via Sant'Andrea 21
Tel. 70.14.26
Expensive; credit cards accepted

For fashion-conscious men, Barba's handsome separates, suits, sportswear, and bomber jackets and other outerwear in soft kidskin are a natural. This large store has a sleek modern look, and so do the clothes, which are favored by Milan's upscale professionals. Both are classic and *sportivo*; the store's blond-wood and black-lacquer décor is discreet enough to keep the spotlight on fashion. There's an excellent selection of accessories, and personalized attention for the asking. Clever displays show off the private label of owner Italo Araldi, who seeks to offer his discriminating customers a chance to dress somewhere between the elegant and the sporty. For the man who likes his clothes made to measure, Barba's offers the highest-quality cut without intimidating custom prices.

JEWELRY

Conversational Pieces

54 LO SCARABEO D'ORO
Via Sant'Andrea 3
Tel. 70.05.47
Expensive; credit cards accepted

Fashion is high and prices, while not low, are moderate for the unusual and handsome jewelry created by Lo Scarabeo d'Oro. The look is on the sporty side: bold-linked necklaces that mix steel with gold and studded with cubic zircons, replicas of Roman coins, or authentic Chinese coins. Most of these pieces are made in limited editions. Innovative ingredients such as steel and zircon, in addition to titanium, iron, hematite, tortoiseshell, and various semiprecious stones, keep the design fresh and prices reasonable. A school of hand-carved fish in multiple hues of agate charm a heavy gold chain and hematite beads set off a heart-shaped

silver medallion. A number of decorative gift items, such as tortoise frames and crystal-and-silver bar sets, also grace this beautiful shop set in a picturesque courtyard.

SUSTENANCE

RISTORANTE/TRATTORIA

55 BARETTO
Via Sant'Andrea 3
Tel. 78.12.55
Moderate; credit cards accepted
Closed Sunday

Quietly tucked away among the shops in this lovely corner of the city is Baretto, a small wood-paneled restaurant with the atmosphere of a men's club, where you'll have to vie for one of the 30 coveted seats. Once your table is secured, start your meal with the exceptional *tortellini con salsa di peperone dolce* (with a sweet bell-pepper sauce) or risotto with eggplant, prosciutto and mozzarella cheese. If kidneys are your pleasure,

Milan rivals Rome for seat of national power.

try the delicious *rognoncino trifolato* (sliced, floured and lightly fried in butter and oil), or sample the *salmone con salsa di gamberi* (fresh salmon with shrimp sauce). Also enjoy the very good wine list. This is a favorite haunt of the neighborhood's fashion professionals, particularly for lunch or cocktails. Baretto's American Bar is a pleasant place to sit and sip while watching some of the city's most stylish earthlings.

ANTIQUES

18th- to 19th-Century

56 DOMENICO PIVA
Via Sant'Andrea 8/A
Tel. 70.06.78
Expensive; no credit cards accepted

One-of-a-kind collector's items fill the three floors of this elegant shop dedicated to traditional Italian antiques. Young Domenico Piva specializes in furniture dating from 1750 to 1850, mainly from the northern regions of Lombardy and the Veneto. His tasteful offerings also include Renaissance bronzes, Italian majolica and European porcelain, 18th-century silver, and 17th- and 18th-century paintings. A serious and passionate Milanese clientele has confirmed Domenico Piva's position among the leaders in his field.

FASHION

WOMEN'S

Forward Fashion Specialist

57 MARISA
Via Sant'Andrea 1
Tel. 79.92.25
Expensive; credit cards accepted

The owner, Marisa Lombardi, picks and chooses from every season's wealth of collections to provide her faithful clientele with her edited version of fashion's best. Marisa's favorites are Enrica Massei, Moschino, Armani, Guido Pellegrini and, from non-Italian sources, Muriel Grateau, Jil Sander, Issey Miyaki and Norma Kamali. Beautiful handmade sweaters produced exclusively for Marisa are a store specialty, and the clean, modern interior depends upon them and other clothing merchandise for décor. Top looks join together to create eye-catching windows that always draw a crowd. A second Marisa location on Via Cino del Duca near Via Durini (telephone 79.10.54) offers more casual and slightly less expensive fashion.

SUSTENANCE

RISTORANTE/TRATTORIA

58 BAGUTTA
Via Bagutta 14–16
Tel. 70.27.67
Moderate; credit cards accepted
Closed Sunday

In this comfortable *trattoria*, which in its earliest days thrived as a meeting place for artists and writers, Italy's first literary prize originated. The Bagutta today continues to be both the home of a prestigious award and a famous restaurant, a combination that attracts a host of journalists, publishers, artists, actors and models. Founded in 1926 by Tuscan-born Alberto Pepori, the restaurant still has a menu featuring Tuscan dishes (see glossary for Tuscan cuisine on page 39) under the guidance of Alberto's sons. Another highlight of dining here is the magnificent self-service antipasto display, so elaborate and extensive that you may never make it to the first course. There is beautiful outdoor seating in the shade of an enormous tree, although inside you can feast both your palate and your eyes, since Bagutta's walls are covered with murals, panels, pictures and caricatures of and by famous artists.

GIFTS

STATIONERY & ACCESSORIES

Marbleized Papers & Books

59 ALBRIZZI
Via Bagutta 8
Tel. 70.12.18
Moderate; no credit cards accepted

Elegant windows display the artistically bound books, agendas and diaries that are Albrizzi's pride. A waft of serenity greets you as you enter to the sound of opera music and the sight of beautiful papers inspired by the ancient art of bookbinding. *Carta varese*, *galuchat* paper from the 1920s, and myriad marbleized variations are used to cover collectibles and gift items: photograph albums, address, guest and recipe books, travel diaries, frames, boxes and blank notebooks. The Albrizzi family began this artisanal tradition back in the

Milan is Italy's gateway to Northern Europe.

1700s, and Alba Albrizzi is still binding away together with a longtime friend, Adalberto Cremonese, who resigned from the hectic world of public relations to take up his passion on a full-time basis.

SUSTENANCE

PIZZERIA

60 PAPER MOON
Via Bagutta 1
Tel. 79.22.97
Moderate; credit cards accepted
Closed Sunday

The Paper Moon is a study of the Milanese character. Spacious, attractive and elegant, it serves delicious and light meals both for those on the go and for those more inclined to leisure, and is frequented by a happy and handsome crowd of regulars. The pizzas are especially popular and good; try the *quattro stagioni* (four seasons) topped with grilled vegetables, or the version with *porcini* mushrooms. The *bomba* is a kind of puffed-up *calzone* with a prosciutto filling. The light-crusted pizzas can be your meal, or can be preceded by a delicious *primo* course of pasta, such as the *tagliolini ai porcini* (flat noodles with a *porcini* mushroom sauce) or *spaghetti alla tarantina* (with mussels). You can also enjoy a nice house wine and a good selection of desserts.

FASHION

MEN'S

Contemporary & Casual

61 NEGLIA
Corso Venezia 2
Tel. 79.52.31
Moderate to expensive; credit cards accepted

DESIGNER BOUTIQUE DIRECTORY

The following designer boutiques in Milan are listed in alphabetical order by last name. All are located in the Montenapoleone neighborhood except where indicated in italics. All take credit cards and follow store hours.

Giorgio Armani (Men's & Women's)
Via Sant'Andrea 9
Tel. 79.27.57

Laura Biagiotti (Women's)
Via Borgospesso 19
Tel. 79.96.59

Enrico Coveri (Men's & Women's)
Via San Pietro all'Orto (corner of
   Via Matteotti)
Tel. 70.16.24

Fendi (Furs & Accessories)
Via Sant'Andrea 16
Tel. 79.16.17

Fendi (Women's)
Via della Spiga 11
Tel. 79.95.44; *Spiga*

Salvatore Ferragamo (Men's)
Via Montenapoleone 20/5
Tel. 70.66.60

Salvatore Ferragamo (Women's)
Via Montenapoleone 3
Tel. 70.00.54

Gianfranco Ferrè (Women's)
Via della Spiga 11
Tel. 79.48.64; *Spiga*

Gianfranco Ferrè (Men's)
Via Sant'Andrea 10/A
Tel. 70.03.85

Gucci (Men's & Women's)
Via Montenapoleone 2
Tel. 79.99.55

Gucci (Leathergoods)
Via Montenapoleone 5
Tel. 54.56.621

Krizia (Women's)
Via della Spiga 23
Tel. 70.84.29; *Spiga*

Missoni (Men's & Women's)
Via Montenapoleone 1
Tel. 79.09.06

Mila Schön (Women's)
Via Montenapoleone 2
Tel. 70.18.03

Luciano Soprani (Women's)
Via Sant'Andrea 14
Tel. 79.83.27

Trussardi (Men's & Women's)
Via Sant'Andrea 5
Tel. 79.03.80

Valentino (Women's)
Via Santo Spirito 3
Tel. 70.64.78

Mario Valentino (Men's & Women's)
Corso Matteotti 10
Tel. 78.16.59

Gianni Versace (Men's)
Via Pietro Verri (corner of Via
   Montenapoleone)
Tel. 79.02.81

Gianni Versace (Women's)
Via della Spiga 4
Tel. 70.54.51; *Spiga*

You'll find here the quality merchandise of Milan's serious, better clothing stores, but in a friendly and relaxed atmosphere where browsing and self-service are encouraged. Young, managerial Milanese are at home in the modern décor of two well-stocked floors of fashionable menswear. There are contemporary and updated suits by St. Andrews, Ermenegildo Zegna, Cerruti and Brioni; sweaters by les Copains, Burberry raincoats, shirts and ties by top designers, and a range of accessories. There's a more *sportivo* look for the informal life-styler. If you'd like a tailor-made suit, you might consider the multimillionaire look in the finest of cashmere blends, attractive to very few budgets. It's the only hint of sartorial snobbery in the place.

JEWELRY

Gold Supermarket

62 IL VENDORO
Corso Venezia 2
Tel. 79.41.07
Inexpensive to moderate; credit cards
    accepted

Big, no-frills and always bustling, Il Vendoro has the air of a gold market where you can find everything and anything in gold at reasonable prices. There are endless arrays of lightweight chains of every link and length, earrings, rings and bracelets—all in 18K gold, and some set with moderate-priced stones such as cubic zirconium (synthetic diamonds). Designs run from classic to modern, and while the quality is not outstanding, it is commensurate with the prices. There are also good-value silver objects that make nice gifts, such as frames for wall or desktop.

LINGERIE

63 SORELLE NEGRI
Piazza San Babila 5
Tel. 70.17.86
Moderate to expensive; credit cards accepted

An attractive and diversified selection of intimatewear can be found at Sorelle Negri. The small shop's delicate items evoke other times; they range from black lacy corsets and garters to proper, grandmother-type nightgowns decorated with lace insets or hand embroidery. The surroundings are as intimate as the apparel, and most articles will have to be taken out for you from behind mirrored doors or from lacquered cabinet drawers. Excellent sales assistance will help with the fitting of bras, panties and loungewear from Dior and Valentino, as well as from Sorelle Negri's own private production, which is original, tasteful and highly exclusive. Luxurious silk and satin robes and charmeuse teddies are joined in springtime by fashionable swimwear from La Perla.

LEATHERGOODS

BAGS

Large Assortment of Styles

64 ALLA PELLE
Corso Venezia 5 and 9
Tel. 79.117 and 70.52.47, respectively
Moderate; credit cards accepted

Few shoppers leave Italy without having purchased at least one handbag, and Alla Pelle is the perfect destination for an overview of what's available and currently fashionable in the handbag world. A reliable and impressive selection of quality bags has been the reason behind Alla Pelle's growth into a four-store chain. At No. 9 you'll find an assortment of casual and slightly less expensive bags in the season's colors. Next door, at No. 5, is a wider range of styles, from the same trendy look to the classic and refined. All kinds of treated and stamped leathers come in a rainbow of shades, and there's a nice selection of ultra-expensive crocodile as well. Alla Pelle does a commendable job of editing the market's seasonal offerings, supplemented by a number of models from their own production. Everything is organized into color groups and look, and the help is accommodating and willing to let you "just look around." There's a good selection of large, fashionable belts and shoes in the back, but shoppers usually never make it back that far.

A third Alla Pelle location is at Via Durini 27 (telephone 79.38.67).

FASHION

MEN'S & WOMEN'S

Avant-Garde

65 KOMLAN

Corso Venezia 11
Tel. 70.02.71
Moderate to expensive; credit cards
    accepted
Open during lunch

Fashion cognoscenti run here to what once was a family-run fruit and vegetable stand (since 1772) and is now the forward, high-fashion Komlan boutique. Always crowded and popular with a young, fashion-minded clientele, Komlan is as known for its rock-star and entertainment patronage as for its unusual fashion. Owner Alberto Sedini and his in-house de-

signer Giorgio Louis Fory are behind the novel selection of exclusively designed, often unisex clothes. Milan's best T-shirts are here, some in a fine, shiny cotton that read *"classico con twist,"* Komlan's slogan. There's everything from weekend wear to the trendy, sexy eveningwear, and everything is made in the fabrics, prints, and silhouettes of the moment. Interesting accessories, including original belts and buckles, pull the Komlan look together. Komlan is adjacent to an interesting 15th-century rococo seminary, a pecular foil to this converted vegetable-stand now turned fashion front-runner.

SPORTS GEAR

ACTIVE SPORTSWEAR & EQUIPMENT

66 BRIGATTI

Corso Venezia 15
Tel. 70.55.52
Expensive; credit cards accepted

Serious sports shoppers and country squires should not miss a trip to Milan's principal and best-stocked sporting goods store. An entire three-floor palazzo stocks *tutto per tutti gli sports* ("everything for every sport"), as their modest insignia reads, from curling to tennis and golf, from croquet to squash, from baseball umpires' masks to every kind of skiing equipment imaginable. But be forewarned that there are no price tags and no self-service. In the old-world dark wood-paneled surroundings with wall-to-wall displays, Brigatti has catered to the Milanese carriage trade for a century; none of their well-heeled clients have ever gone home empty-handed. In addition to top-of-the-line equipment from Europe's finest houses, there is an extensive selection of active sportswear and of the clothing one must have for weekends at the lodge or country club. For men and women, there are British-style tweed and loden jackets, wool meltons in every color and cut conceivable, Tyrolean-type fashions, and an enormous selection of ski and après-ski wear.

There is a second, though much smaller, Brigatti location at Galleria Vittorio Emanuele 67 (telephone 87.05.273).

SUSTENANCE

RISTORANTE/TRATTORIA

67 ALFIO

Via Senato 31
Tel. 70.06.33
Moderate; credit cards accepted
Closed Saturday, and Sunday lunch

Tuscan-born Alfio Bocciardi is a kingpin in Milan's world of gastronomy, and has recently opened a number of Alfio restaurants in Japan as well. This institution has been here for over 30 years, and the small rooms in crimson velvet with damask tablecloths bear testimony to an extensive menu and refined clientele. There are a number of Tuscan favorites on the menu; but surprisingly, Alfio's specialty is that un-Tuscan ingredient, fish. You might begin with the delicious pasta and risotto dishes made with seafood, such as *spaghetti con polpa di granchio* (with crabmeat) or *alle vongole* (with clams). For your entrée, fresh fish from today's catch will be brought to your table upon request, so that you'll know the size of the fish about to be grilled. Alfio's Tuscan predeliction for quality-cut meats prepared on the grill balances out the menu's choice.

The last word in cookware from Alessi.

HOME

Cookware & Restaurant Supply

68 EUGENIO MEDAGLIANI

Via L. Razza 8 (off map)
Tel. 65.51.745
Moderate; no credit cards accepted

A household name to the great chefs of Italy, Eugenio Medagliani supplies the country's premier restaurants and gourmands with kitchen cookware. He is particularly known for his extensive selection of high-quality cooking utensils and copper cookware. You'll find everything here in a series of rooms in a large warehouse space, neatly stocked on shelves according to size and series. English-speaking help is on hand, and the accommodating management will gladly ship, making it easy for you to buy anything from the tiniest saucepans to cauldron-sized pots. The dazzling range of utensils is appealing to the professional chef, the mother of many, or the aspiring weekend gourmet. Whether you're cooking for yourself or the Sixth Fleet, Medagliani has an astounding selection at reasonable prices.

SUSTENANCE

RISTORANTE/TRATTORIA

Taxi Away

69 GUALTIERO MARCHESI

Via Bonvesin de la Riva 9 (off map)
Tel. 74.12.46
Very expensive; credit cards accepted
Closed Sunday, and Monday lunch

Gualtiero Marchesi is Italy's only restaurant to have garnered three well-
deserved stars from Michelin's rigidly
demanding judges. The owner, who
has been called a high priest of *nuova
cucina* and a gastronomic architect
for having redefined the landscape of
Italy's cuisine, has become something of a national celebrity. Talented, bold, farsighted, and a clever
businessman, Marchesi creates the
avant-garde, often by taking recipes
lost over the generations and execut-
ing them with his own personal, contemporary genius. Marchesi is continuously evolving, however, and the only
way to experience his remarkable relationship with food is to partake in
the gastronomic rite at his restaurant.
You may order à la carte from a
general menu or request one of the
special menus—a vegetarian menu, a
pasta menu, or one offering more
traditional dishes (always prepared in
his unique fashion). Adventurous palates will thrill at his daring combination of ingredients—lobster with bell-
pepper purée; cold spaghetti with
caviar; risotto with peas and frogs'
legs; lasagna with scallops, scampi,
and cucumbers; roast pigeon with
lobster; or mullet and scallops with a
meat sauce. It all works. It is all
astonishing, and if you imbibe liberally from the outstanding wine cellar,
so will your check be. To avoid that

surprise, come for lunch or after the
theater for the attractive *piatto unico*
(one-course meal); five tastes of either
fish or meat dishes are served with a
glass of nice wine, all for a third the
price of a more elaborate dinner.

SUSTENANCE

RISTORANTE/TRATTORIA

Taxi Away

70 CALAJUNCO

Via Stoppani 5 (off map)
Tel. 20.46.003
Expensive; credit cards accepted
Closed Sunday

A quick cab ride will seem to bring
you to the sea, for Calajunco is meant
to evoke the flavor, in many ways, of
the Lipari Islands off Sicily and their
cuisine. This small and *simpatico* restaurant, whose name comes from a
picturesque street on the island of
Panarea, offers fresh fish prepared
with expertise and delivered with a
smile. Try the appetizers or the
lunchtime *piatto unico* (one-course
meal) for a simplified version of Calajunco's kitchen. You'll find the tradition of the South married with the
creativity that is a Milanese trait.
Fish are often poached in a paper
cartoccio or prepared with just the
right light sauce. *Salsiccia di mare
grigliata* (a seafood "sausage" made
with mixed fish), *ostriche fritte* (delicately fried oysters), or *involtini di
pescespada* (rolled fillets of swordfish
on the grill) are offered, along with
more traditionally prepared possibilities such as the ever-popular *spigola*
(sea bass). Begin with a uniquely savory *patè di peperoni* (made with
sweet peppers) and finish with a
homemade miniature *cannoli*.

Shoe-Shopping Directory to Downtown Milan

Milan's image as a slick and technically advanced trailblazer is also discernible in its wide range of fine footwear. The industrial areas of Vigevano and Parabiago a few kilometers outside the city are crowded with well over 1000 specialized firms that supply most of Italy and much of the world with beautifully designed and crafted shoes for men, women and children. The companies' artisanal character remains as strong and as renowned as when local practitioners of the shoemaker's art were first organized into the prestigious guilds of the Middle Ages. Today's shoemakers successfully marry tradition with the future, and Milanese shops offer a selection of their "Made in Italy" wares as diverse in look as in price range.

Because such a staggering concentration of shoe stores is found in the Duomo/Vittorio Emanuele and Montenapoleone areas, we list them all here, alphabetized by last names, to help you grasp the possibilities at a glance.

ALBANESE & MAURI
Via Montenapoleone 26
Tel. 70.60.27
Some fun, and lots of glitz in high-fashion shoes and leatherwear for men and women. Specialties are precious skins and patchwork detailing. Moderate to expensive.

ALDROVANDI
Via Montenapoleone 27
Tel. 78.42.56
High-quality handmade shoes. Men's

are classic, while women's start with the sporty but go all out with elaborate and decorative interpretations. There is a second location at Corso Vittorio Emanuele 15 (tel. 79.59.62). Expensive.

ALEXANDER-NICOLETTE
Via Montenapoleone 19
Tel. 70.18.86
Luxury, exceptionally well-made classic shoes for men's and women's mature tastes. Expensive.

BELTRAMI
Via Montenapoleone 16
Tel. 70.29.75
Men's and women's shoes in styles from the very classic to the very original. You'll also find excellent leatherwear, bags, and bijoux. A second location is at Piazza San Babila 16 (tel. 70.05.46). Expensive.

CARRANO
Via Sant'Andrea 21
Tel. 70.94.95
Colorful, trendy and fashionable women's shoes and more classic,

Luxury footwear, an international trend-setter.

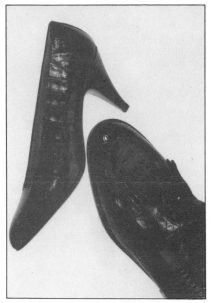

Classics like these sustain Italy's fame.

handsome men's shoes. Beautiful accessories and leatherwear. Another store is located at Via Solferino 11 (tel. 86.77.33) in the Brera area (see page 261). You can also find discounts at Via Rasori 4 (tel. 43.90.588) in the Vercelli/Magenta area (see page 273). Moderate to expensive.

FRANCO COLLI
Via Sant'Andrea 12
Tel. 70.08.32
Contemporary, casual shoes and handbags of unusual, high-fashion design are displayed in a spacious and elegant showroom. Models range from sporty to elegant, with the most advanced looks in styles and materials. For women only. Moderate.

TANINO CRISCI
Via Montenapoleone 3
Tel. 79.12.64
This classic line for both men and women features extra-fine quality in workmanship and hides. Expensive.

DIEGO DELLA VALLE
Via della Spiga 22
Tel. 70.24.23
One of the most up-to-date shoe designers displays his fashion-forward creations for both men and women in a slick, minimalist setting. Known for the comfortable fit of his shoes, Diego designs for Italy's great fashion houses. Expensive.

DIVARESE
Via Montenapoleone 12
Tel. 79.02.80
This shoe manufacturer was recently purchased by the Benetton family. Sleek modern looks and fun casual-wear complement the Benetton look for a young, collegiate customer. The most notable of many Divarese locations. Others include the nearby store at Corso Vittorio Emanuele 9 (tel. 70.87.74). Moderate.

VALERIANO FERRARIO
Via Montenapoleone 6
Tel. 79.09.28
A vast assortment of hand-made, updated classics in footwear and leathergoods for men and women. Expensive.

FERRAGAMO
Via Montenapoleone 3
Tel. 70.00.54
Elegant shoes for both men and women combine high fashion with optimal fit. A beautiful range of accessories, especially in women's bags. Expensive.

LARIO 1898
Via Montenapoleone 21
Tel. 70.26.41
Shoes, boots and bags for men and women where the classic joins with fantasy, usually in a sporty, casual look. Moderate to expensive.

LINEA LIDIA
Via San Pietro all'Orto 17
Tel. 79.16.60
Conversation-piece women's shoes that make the outfit. Interesting leather treatments and bold innovations team with quality materials and workmanship for very fashion-forward footwear. Expensive.

LUCA
Via Montenapoleone 27/E
Tel. 79.11.15
Frescoed walls help to provide a refined atmosphere for a collection of men's and women's young, contemporary shoes and handbags. Styles range from the classic to the updated. Other locations include Corso Vercelli 11 (tel. 46.44.63) in the Vercelli/Magenta neighborhood (see page 274). Moderate.

BRUNO MAGLI
Corso Vittorio Emanuele, corner of San Paolo
Tel. 86.56.95
Long known for his classic, dressy patent pumps and his casual everyday wear for men and women, Magli claims both comfort and fashion appeal. There are two other Magli shops in the center at Via Manzoni 14 (tel. 78.12.64) and Via Orefici, corner of Via Cantù (tel. 80.53.719). Moderate to expensive.

Every season new trends are launched.

The result of artistic ability.

NICA
Via della Spiga 42
Tel. 70.68.35
Seasonal musts for women in the latest looks and colors, together with more conservative models. There is also a good selection of contemporary women's and men's footwear and leatherwear at a second Nica location, Galleria Passerella 1/2 (tel. 70.04.43). Moderate.

CESARE PACIOTTI
Via Sant'Andrea 8
Tel. 70.11.64
Updated classics and elegant handmade shoes for the man with taste, as well as a recent line of casual shoes for women. Both are well priced for shoes designed for high-fashion labels. Moderate to expensive.

PANCA
Corso Vittorio Emanuele 15
(corner of Via San Pietro all'Orto)
Tel. 79.36.73
Men's and women's classic shoes are interpreted in the season's favorite leathers and colors, never overly detailed and always reliably good value. A second location can be found at

Creative novelty calls for exotic skins.

Corso Porta Ticinese 103 (tel. 83.21.363) in the Porta Ticinese area (see page 292). Inexpensive.

GUIDO PASQUALI
Via Sant'Andrea 1
Tel. 70.16.45
Unusual hides and high fashion in collections often designed for the major fashion houses. Pasquali is famous for his boots. His men's shoes are available at another location, Via Gesù 6 (tel. 78.35.508). Moderate to expensive.

POLLINI
Corso Vittorio Emanuele 30
Tel. 79.49.12
Fun, imaginative and trendy footwear for women and men in the latest materials and colors. There are also well-made handbags. Moderate to expensive.

Imagination and craftsmanship are inseparable.

PRADA
Via della Spiga 1
Tel. 70.86.36
Styles here are somewhat more fashion-forward than at Prada's flagship location in the Galleria Vittorio Emanuele (see page 167), but you'll find the same exquisite quality in men's and women's footwear and small leathergoods. Expensive.

RONCHI
Via Montenapoleone 18 (corner of Via Gesù)
Tel. 70.62.70
Expert craftsmanship in men's custom-made and ready-to-wear footwear. One of the oldest sources for classic, high-quality and hand-sewn shoes. There are also old-fashioned but fine women's slippers. (See also page 222.) Expensive.

FRATELLI ROSSETTI
Via Montenapoleone 1
Tel. 79.16.50
Classic, high-quality men's shoes, and beautiful updated classics and sandals for women. Deluxe leathers and a rather dressy look. Expensive.

FAUSTO SANTINI
Via Montenapoleone 1
Tel. 70.19.58
Colorful and up-to-the-moment trendy footwear for men and women that can add an original twist to classic dressing. Big color ranges are divided by style. Moderate.

SEBASTIAN
Via Borgospesso 18
Tel. 78.05.32
Here women can help design their own shoes in every possible material or color. The results, whether sensible walking shoes or detailed evening attire, will fit like gloves. There is a two-week wait for custom-made shoes, but they can be shipped. Expensive.

VALENTINA
Via San Pietro all'Orto 17
Tel. 78.25.20
Young, spirited shoes for young-at-heart women. The shop is owned by the prestigious house of Carrano, but prices are lower here for updated classics in fashionable leathers and colors. Moderate. Another store is located at Corso Magenta 27 (tel. 87.11.93) in the Vercelli/Magenta area (see page 277).

EL VAQUERO
Via San Pietro all'Orto 3
  (corner of Corso Vittorio Emanuele)
Tel. 79.56.94
A unique interpretation of the Western look blends the ethnic with fantasy in men's and women's shoes and boots. Interesting and colorful hides will bring you attention back home on the range. Moderate to expensive.

Italian boots, the ever-coveted accessory.

Via della Spiga

V ia della Spiga is an integral part of the Via Montenapoleone enclave, but we have isolated it to underline its importance to the Milan shopping scene and its allure for the curious visitor. Via della Spiga takes the established character of Via Montenapoleone and brings it to a new and youthful generation, featuring the finest of the finest, the *crème de la crème*.

Except for an occasional errant taxi, Via della Spiga is closed to automobile traffic. Until relatively recently, it was a quiet neighborhood street of artisans and antique shops. Today its five flagstone-paved blocks are lined with potted camelia trees, birches and azalea bushes, and sleek glass storefronts reveal the high-tech interiors and elegant merchandise of fashion luminaries, renowned antique dealers and exclusive jewelry designers. Gio Moretti, whose spacious high-fashion boutiques are a Spiga landmark, was a pioneer in proposing Via della Spiga as an alternative to Via Montenapoleone.

Typical of the Via della Spiga ambiance are sleek glass storefronts, each a showcase.

One of the most elegant streets in the world, it is out of the spending league of most shoppers. But a stroll along this flawless and serene byway is a must, with the cacophony of the Corso Venezia seemingly miles away. The street is a polished microcosm of what is happening in Milan and in Italy, displaying the latest and best of the nation's creativity. We have not included Beneggi, Milan's most famous coiffeur for dogs; it's definitely worth a peek.

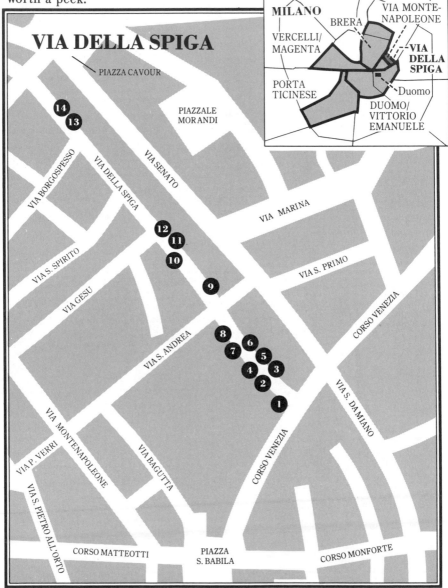

JEWELRY

1 RONDINA
Via della Spiga 1
Tel. 70.58.10
Expensive; credit cards accepted

Milan's elite love bold jewelry with colorful semiprecious stones, and they find it in this pink-marble neoclassical boutique. Daniela Rondina follows each season's ready-to-wear color trends and plans her collection accordingly. A look reminiscent of the 1930s and 40s is created with quartz, rock crystal, hematite, onyx and other stones set in 18k gold or less expensive metals such as steel, silver or vermeil (18k-gold-plated silver). Rondina also offers the collection of designer Ferruccio Fiorentini, created for her exclusively using imaginative combinations of gold and steel.

FASHION
WOMEN'S

Contemporary & Trendy

2 CROTTINI
Via della Spiga 3
Tel. 70.26.77
Expensive; credit cards accepted

If you have high-fashion tastes, or would like to develop them, Crottini's *au courant* salesgirls will help you put together a look drawing from a wealth of seasonal offerings. It's a small shop big in the dernier cri shown on Milan's most eminent runways, from Moschino's and Romeo Gigli's striking silhouettes for evening to Byblos' casual sportswear. Crottini edits each season's best to facilitate a precise selection of either humorous or sophisticated fashion for the young and

forward-looking customer. A second, slightly larger Crottini location can be found at Galleria Passarella 2 (telephone 70.10.94).

FASHION
MEN'S, WOMEN'S & CHILDREN'S

High-Fashion Collections

3 GIO MORETTI 🛍🛍🛍🛍
Via della Spiga 4 (women's); tel. 70.91.86
Via della Spiga 6 (men's); tel. 70.21.72
Via della Spiga 9 (children's); tel. 78.00.89
Expensive; credit cards accepted
Open during lunch

The quintessential status symbol is Gio Moretti's speckled, multicolored shopping bag, proof that one has shopped where it counts. The women's boutique at No. 4 is a sleek and elegant marble environment that showcases fashion's most important talents: Complice (designed by Claude Montana), Claude Montana, Gianfranco Ferrè, Albini, Byblos, Genny (designed by Gianni Versace), Soprani and Callaghan (designed by Romeo Gigli). Non-Italian *griffes* include Yoghi Yashimoto, Azzedine Alaïa and Sonia Rykiel, among others. Gio Moretti is known for a fine selection of leather outerwear, especially that designed by Montana, as well as for coats in rich, warm fabrics. Sleek, minimal displays are accented with the accessories available to make the look complete.

Gio Moretti has now joined the ranks of men's retailers with her smaller shop next door at No. 6. The look of her artfully presented men's fashion is British with dash; there is also a sprinkling of more avant-garde, less serious items. And for chic children who will wear nothing less than the designer labels favored by their parents, there's Gio Moretti Baby. The fine design sense of Valentino, Cacherel, Enrico Coveri, les Copains and Giorgio Armani is evident in beautiful sweaters and solid or print woolen bottoms for winter, followed up by bright and lively summertime prints. All are in choice fabrics and colors, and there are quality accessories to match. Such a prestigious wardrobe will dress that special child from age 2 to 16.

LEATHERGOODS

Luxury Fashion

4 BOTTEGA VENETA
Via della Spiga 5
Tel. 79.16.51
Expensive; credit cards accepted

Bottega Veneta will always be most famous for its buttery-soft woven-leather bags in rich fashion colors. There is also a wide selection of luggage, shoes, slippers, and small leathergoods and accessories.

See Venice listing (page 469).

JEWELRY

TOP-NAME

5 BULGARI
Via della Spiga 6
Tel. 70.54.06
Very expensive; credit cards accepted

The Bulgari dynasty opened its sixth elegant store, and Milan's first, in September, 1986. Curved ceilings and Roman columns that separate the salons barely soften a bank-vault look.

For further information on some of the world's most exquisite jewelry, see Rome listing (page 355).

FASHION

WOMEN'S

High-Fashion

6 COSE
Via della Spiga 8
Tel. 79.07.03
Expensive; credit cards accepted

A study in minimalist décor, *Cose* (Things) is another mecca for high-fashion trendies. Exposed brick walls result in a somewhat cold ambiance, but Cose relies upon its attractive mix of the season's best to warm things up. Until Milan's darling, Romeo Gigli, decides to follow the pattern of the stars and open his own boutique, this is his Milan showcase store. His romantic and unconstructed looks are joined by the designs of French favor-

A microcosm of the nation's latest creativity.

ites Claude Montana and Azzedine Alaïa. Imaginative accessories such as architect Sine Carvana's zigzag briefcase make browsing here an education in design.

COSTUME JEWELRY

Fun, Fantasy Accessories

7 SHARRA PAGANO
Via della Spiga 7
Tel. 70.91.01
Moderate; credit cards accepted

This costume jewelry is always up-to-the-second, perhaps because Sharra Pagano helps determine the direction for fashion bijoux each season. Sharra Pagano, *nome d'arte* of young Lino Raggio, carries his fantasy throughout an inspiring costume jewelry collection of gold-electroplated metals with experimental finishings, such as *patine* (burnished or oxidized effects) paired with fake gemstones, plastics and other novelties ad infinitum. There is also a small selection of pieces in vermeil (18k-gold-plated silver) accented by turquoise, ivory and semiprecious Brazilian stones. Bold and conversational, imaginative and fun, the boutique has a million temptations, which also include marvelous belts and evening bags.

LEATHERGOODS

BAGS & ACCESSORIES

Best High-Fashion Handbag Collection

8 COLOMBO
Via della Spiga 9
Tel. 70.01.84
Expensive; credit cards accepted

At your disposition are two floors of what many connoisseurs believe to be the best handbag collection in Milan. In addition to a range of high-quality conventional leather in myriad colors, there are exotic skins from ostrich to crocodile, all in the highest-quality production from top fashion names or from the Colombo private label. Upstairs you'll find an array of stylish luggage, from overnight and weekend bags to beauty cases. A smaller Colombo shop is found off Piazza Cavour at Via Turati 7 (telephone 65.97.607). Both are part of the high-design empire of Gio Moretti, a name synonymous with Via della Spiga.

FASHION

WOMEN'S

Chic & Sporty

9 FRANCESCA FERRARIO
Via della Spiga 20
Tel. 78.24.75
Expensive; credit cards accepted
Open during lunch

Francesca Ferrario uses an eagle eye to edit and mix contemporary collections: Timmi, Alberta Ferretti, Claudio LaViola and England's Betty Jackson all help Francesca realize her fashion viewpoint. Clothes are sportswear-oriented but chic, relaxed yet urban *alla milanese*. A highlight of shopping here is the superb choice of accessories created by Francesca herself—great oversized handbags and clutches, soft leather totes, belts with original buckles, shawls, gloves, fedoras and berets. Track lighting, minimal display and an aura of sleekness form a backdrop for Francesca's sophisticated city look.

FASHION

WOMEN'S

Sophisticated, Sleek Sportswear

10 ERREUNO
Via della Spiga 15
Tel. 79.55.75
Expensive; credit cards accepted
Open during lunch

Those who love Giorgio Armani but prefer his style a little less severe and a little less expensive come to Erreuno for his lower-priced collection. Career women will feel comfortable in a wardrobe of stylish jackets and separates with that distinctive Armani sensibility and quasi-masculine fabrics. Armani's subtle mix of colors and prints and his impeccable tailoring make this excellent investment wear. Compared to the impressive glass frontage of neighboring stores, it is easy to breeze by Erreuno's smaller windows, but inside you'll find a sophisticated shop with rose-marble floors and friendly sales assistance.

ANTIQUES

TOP-NAME

11 ALBERTO SUBERT
Via della Spiga 22
Tel. 79.95.94
Very expensive; no credit cards accepted

Alberto Subert's name and fame are reflected in the ultra-deluxe setting of his antique store. He offers perhaps the most important selection of inlaid furniture from Lombardy's school of Maggiolini (one of Italy's most renowned intarsia artisans), as well as antique scientific instruments such as astrolabes and ivory sextants for wayfaring collectors. Furniture dates from early 18th century to neoclassical, with precious objects, paintings, statues, bronzes, fine porcelain and majolica all dating from the same periods. Subert also carries charming · 17th-century miniature paintings on semiprecious stones, called *paesini.*

FASHION

WOMEN'S

Classic & Feminine

12 ADRIANA MODE
Via della Spiga 22
Tel. 70.84.58
Expensive; credit cards accepted

This store's exclusive fashion is designed by Adriana's daughter, Daniela Gerini. The style is classic but highly feminine and uses an excellent selection of fine fabrics. Whether your life style is demanding or casual, you'll find the fashion easy to wear, with separates that can be mixed and matched with imagination. Known for her exquisite window displays, which are among the most avidly watched in town (but which unfortunately include no prices), Adriana has been drawing demanding fashion shoppers to Via della Spiga for 20 years.

ANTIQUES

TOP-NAME

13 MAURO BRUCOLI
Via della Spiga 42
Tel. 79.37.67
Very expensive; no credit cards accepted

This large, elegant store is for serious

antique collectors only, though everyone is welcome to come in for a browse. Young Mauro Brucoli is credited with being the first to "rediscover" the furniture of the 1800s, particularly in the Directoire, Biedermeier and Charles X styles. Brucoli's large and expensive pieces come predominantly from the northern Italian regions of the Veneto and Lombardy. There are also paintings, smaller objects and important silver pieces from the same period as well as from the early 1900s. Exquisite jewelry once owned by Austro-Hungarian nobility is especially worth a peek.

HOME

TABLETOP ACCESSORIES

Italian Country Style

14 L'UTILE E IL DILETTEVOLE

Via della Spiga 46
Tel. 70.84.20
Expensive; credit cards accepted

The ultimate stroll past Spiga's temptations.

"The Useful and the Delightful" is just what you'll find in this airy, bleached-wood showroom set in a pleasant courtyard off Via della Spiga. In a romantic and charming atmosphere that exemplifies the Italian country style, there's a casual though coordinated clutter of credenzas made from pine and cypress, small cane easy chairs and old English rattan chaises, complemented by delicately embroidered drapes and exclusive hand-hooked rugs. Stylized displays of new and antique linens for the bed and table join antique quilts and lace-trimmed cotton and linen clothing such as aprons, blouses and nightshirts. Also arranged for delightful country living are tables set with silverware, glassware, ceramics and dried flowers on tablecloths of provincial or Liberty-type fabrics.

Brera

*F*or most shoppers, old or young, adventurous or cautious, Brera is the city's most enjoyable neighborhood. It is this very "neighborhood" quality that gives it a quaint and charming air, with narrow cobblestone streets lined with shops, cafés and restaurants and often closed to traffic. Comparable to New York City's Greenwich Village or Soho, it is a working-class quarter that has now been gentrified.

Brera was once a hub of intellectual and artistic activity and was known as the Montmartre of Milan in the 1920s. Some of its bohemian character has been sacrificed in the recent trendy, upwardly mobile make-over, but this is an advantage for shoppers; you can now spend untold hours strolling along back streets and winding pedestrian walkways, happening upon a succession of sophisticated boutiques and up-to-the-minute eating spots.

While here you will want to visit the 18th-century Accademia di Brera (Art Academy) and the nearby Pinacoteca, a colossal treasury of paintings. Brera is also home to the *Corriere della Sera*, the country's leading newspaper. In the small streets surrounding these important centers, you'll find some of Milan's more interesting art galleries, artisan ateliers,

An authentic neighborhood atmosphere lingers in Brera's store-lined back streets.

*The world-renowned
Palazzo e Pinacoteca
di Brera, rich in the
works of North
Italian artists.*

curiosity shops and antique stores.

Much of the old Brera character remains intact. Some places have stayed locked in time, such as the Enoteca Cotti wine shop, the family-run Novara herb store, the Bar Giamaica and the Trattoria Rovello. And many new enterprises have painstakingly preserved their original décor, such as the Drogheria Solferino clothing boutique, set in an old pharmacy, and Naj Oleari's English-bakery-turned-gift shop. Everywhere the old tolerates and complements the new.

The main shopping street is Via Brera, which leads into Via Solferino. Off these, you'll find smaller streets, sometimes for pedestrians only, such as the Vie Fiori Chiari, Fiori Oscuri and Madonnina. At the end of Via Madonnina, peek into the charming church of Santa Maria del Carmine, and stop for a *caffè* in the small *piazzetta* in front where a daily fruit and vegetable *mercato* takes place (see Outdoor Street Markets, page 153). Stroll along the Corso Garibaldi, only now becoming fashionable. You'll understand something of Brera before its metamorphosis as you browse

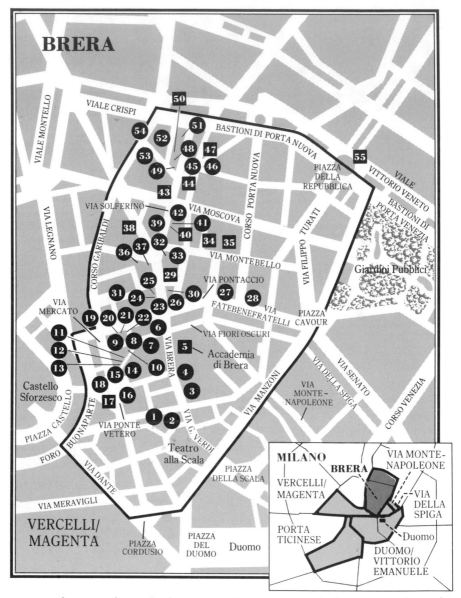

among the street's many less expensive stores, including a number of vintage- and used-clothing shops.

Brera has kept its reputation as Milan's center for nightlife. Jazz and piano bars stay open late, as do many bar-cafès and restaurants. Nestled between Milan's two major parks, the Sempione and the Public Gardens, Brera is much like a village; the nearby Duomo seems light-years away.

GARDENING

PLANTS & GIFTS

Botanical Heaven

1 CENTRO BOTANICO
Via dell'Orso 16
Tel. 87.33.15
Moderate; credit cards accepted
Open during lunch; closed Monday

This oasis of tranquility was born from the passion for nature of the Naj Oleari brothers (see below). A small, unobtrusive sign at No. 16 announces that this is the place, and you'll pass through a courtyard and small garden where every potted plant is neatly tagged with its botanical origin. The heady aroma of the Centro's exotic blend of potpourris and fragrances leads you to the delightful second-floor shop (first floor Italian style). There you'll find the brothers' own line of organic toiletries made from the scents of nature (honeysuckle, tuberose, mint, moss, and fern); there are natural essences and oils, soaps and sachets in ribbon-tied handkerchiefs made of the fabrics that are the brothers' predominant interest. These handsomely packaged articles make wonderful gifts. Also featured are an enormous selection of indoor-outdoor gardening books in English and Italian, posters and garden-theme stationery items. Frescoed rooms offer seeds, bulbs, gardening supplies and utensils, while an enclosed porch serves as a miniature working greenhouse for potted plants, including bonsai and cacti. Naj Oleari's serious and aesthetic approach to gardening will move the most indifferent of urbanites.

HOME

LAMPS & LIGHTING

2 BLACKOUT
Via dell'Orso 7
Tel. 87.30.73
Moderate; credit cards accepted

The newest ideas in illumination from Italy's major houses are assembled in one bright and impressive showroom. Owner Alberto Baffiggi, formerly of Fontana Arte, has overlooked nothing: there are scores of table and desk lamps, freestanding floor lamps, and ceiling and wall fixtures. They represent the finest from Fontana Arte, Artemide, O Luce, Quattrifolio, Leucos, Lumina and Tranconi, among others. Some of the products are available in 110-voltage models; many of those for European current can be wired for American use in three weeks and reliably shipped to you.

GIFTS

FABRICS, ACCESSORIES & CLOTHING

3 NAJ OLEARI
Via Brera 8
Tel. 80.06.33
Expensive; credit cards accepted
Closed 1:30–2:30 P.M. only

The young and innovative Naj Oleari brothers.

If you happen to come here the week before school opens or during the Christmas holidays, be ready to line up with the Italians anxiously waiting to purchase the most famous and fashionable of all the store's offerings: the *cartella postino*, a plasticized schoolbag with handle and shoulder strap. The young Naj Oleari (pronounced NAY OLAY-ARI) brothers are renown for their whimsically designed fabrics for home and fashion. Their products have become status symbols in Italy for the young and young at heart. The main and original Naj Oleari store at No. 8 (one of the many) is housed in what was once an English bakery, and it still has a charming country air.

You'll be joining their passionate following when you browse through the hundreds of deck chairs, bags, suitcases, notebooks, picture frames, umbrellas, quilts, lamps, place mats and more, created from Naj Oleari's gaily patterned 100-percent cotton fabrics. Under the same vaulted ceiling, Naj Oleari offers infinite yards of these cottons for your own use. There are 750 designs, hand-drawn by artists—simple or crowded, reserved or, more commonly, naïf. The most familiar motifs feature floating candles, eyeglasses, airplanes, clouds, and palm trees on a brightly colored background. They are available in chintz, quilted and plastic-laminated versions. Downstairs, there is a fun though limited selection of adults' and children's clothes and whimsical sneakers.

Across the street at No. 5, you'll find irresistible items for your baby, including coordinated pillows, blankets, crib accessories, traveling bags, and toys, as well as matching clothing for mother and child.

The whole enterprise is a family industry originated by Riccardo Naj Oleari in 1916, and constantly developing imaginative new products. Among the newest Naj Oleari creations is the Centro Botanico line of scents (see above). Charmingly packaged essences, soaps and potpourri sachets smell of basil, *petit grain* (distilled from the twigs and leaves of the orange tree, not the blossom), and moss, as well as the more conventional flowers. The store is designed to let you smell, touch, and browse to your heart's content.

GIFTS & COLLECTIBLES
"Galleria" of Kitsch

4 PIERO FORNASETTI
Via Brera 16
Tel. 80.50.321
Expensive; no credit cards accepted

This compact, eclectic store/art gallery is for the *appassionato* of curious objets d'art. Fornasetti first acquired international fame in the 1950s for his unique style that belongs somewhere between the avant-garde and the indefinable. The Fornasetti stamp is recognizable here in a concentrated collection of his work that includes eccentric enamel furniture, *trompe*

Piero Fornasetti's fame, out of the 1950s.

l'oeil objects, hand-painted bicycles and Venetian blinds, decorative wall plates, demitasse cups, and slightly risqué ceramic anatomical parts. Styles range from op art to postmodern, with repeated motifs of Roman architecture, oversize newsprint type and gold-leaf highlights. Fornasetti was, in fact, the inspiration for many of today's young postmodern artists; a recent resurgence of interest in his creations has made them collector's items.

If you're a serious collector of kitsch or a gift giver with a sense of humor, don't miss this store.

SUSTENANCE

BAR-CAFFÈ

5 BAR GIAMAICA
Via Brera 26
Tel. 87.67.23
Moderate; no credit cards accepted
Closed Sunday

When Brera was like a small Montmartre, this was the watering hole for intellectuals, painters and highbrow poets. The place still has something of that aura, although it is far less bohemian and more stylish in its clientele nowadays. A small open-air garden and terrace invite you for an *aperitivo* or a light lunch: there are good *panini* (sandwiches) and salads, such as shrimp with arugula, and delicious soups and pastas of the day.

ANTIQUES

ART DECO

6 ROBERTA E BASTA
Via Fiori Chiari 2
Tel. 86.15.93
Expensive; credit cards accepted

You'll never see a more valuable selection of art-deco treasures or one displayed in such a spectacular space. Important Italian and French pieces from 1920 to 1940 include credenzas, sofas, armchairs, tables, screens and objets, each unique and all in excellent condition. Vying for your attention is the setting: the black-tiled floor, gold columns and dramatic lighting. A second location owned by the same dealer, Roberta Tavaglini, is at Galleria Strasburgo near the Duomo (telephone 79.58.70). There you'll find mostly objects signed by Tiffany, Gio Ponti and Venini. Both locations are favorites with collectors and fashion professionals.

HOME

FURNITURE & LIGHTING

7 MARZOT & C.
Via Fiori Chiari 3
Tel. 87.18.28
Expensive; no credit cards accepted; checks
    accepted

Lovers of leading design in Italian avant-garde furniture should schedule a visit to Marzot's stunning showroom. Most striking and predominant is the prestigious collection of Alias. You'll also find Mario Botta's renowned all-metal chairs and his other furniture in novel industrial materials, which have secured him an honorable position in the hierarchy of designers. There are pieces by Vico Magistretti and Giandomenico Belotti, whose famous handmade spaghetti chair is in the permanent collection of New York's Museum of Modern Art. Original paintings and lithographs by Man Ray, Gianfranco Pardi and Emilio Tadini are also for sale.

ANTIQUES

FRAMES

8 FRANCO SABATELLI
Via Fiori Chiari 5
Tel. 80.52.688
Expensive; no credit cards accepted

Franco Sabatelli's fame for frames draws clients from all corners of the world, many of them with snapshots and measurements of a unique painting that demands a unique frame. They're assured of finding it in this concentration of antique Italian frames from small to enormous, dating from the 16th to the 19th centuries. These elaborate, hand-carved, gold-leaf-covered works of art won't fit in your suitcase, but Signor Sabatelli will carefully package and ship, so browse about for what that special painting back home deserves. This is no small, dark artisan's *bottega*; in a well-lit, high-ceilinged space, frames are neatly hung along the walls or stacked according to design and style. The stately Signor Sabatelli, in suit and tie, represents some of Milan's most sophisticated artisans, and doubles as the resident craftsman; his bench in the back is the site of skilled frame restoration.

Franco Sabatelli and his collection of frames.

ANTIQUES & COLLECTIBLES

ITALIAN DECO

9 DECOMANIA
Via Fiori Chiari 7
Tel. 80.80.27
Expensive; no credit cards accepted

Decomania is an exquisitely cared-for little shop that is rightly regarded as the best in Milan for art-deco objects. It specializes in Liberty and art-deco furniture and objects designed by Italians, which have a cleaner look than the more commonly recognized French deco. A clientele of collectors regularly snatches up Decomania's remarkable finds; on any given day, you might find a table designed by the renowned, multi-talented Gio Ponti or a selection of beautiful Venini glass from Murano, circa 1925 to 1940. Most pieces, in fact, are signed and can be considered collector's items as well as objects that lend beauty to interior furnishing. Decomania is frequented by appreciative American customers and very capable of shipping prized acquisitions home.

FASHION

MEN'S

Updated Classics

10 CASHMERE, COTTON & SILK
Via Madonnina 19
Tel. 80.57.426
Expensive; credit cards accepted

The luxurious fabrics that give this store its name are what you'll find here, used in the kind of sophisticated, classic fashions that dressed Milan's gentry long before chasing ephemeral seasonal trends became a national pastime. Most of this new shop's collection is the private label of Bardelli, long known as a refined outfitter, whose original store still prospers on Via Magenta. Here he offers his fashion acumen to a younger clientele. A subtle assortment of cashmere sweaters, scarves and socks invites your caressing touch, as do beautiful ties and scarves in quality silks. There are also suits, jackets, pants, raincoats and coats in the finest Italian and English wools, cashmeres and tweeds, and a large selection of shirts in quality cottons.

JEWELRY

WORKSHOP/STUDIO

Chic, One-of-a-Kind Pieces

11 BALDAN 🍶🍶🍶🍶

Via Fiori Chiari 14
Tel. 80.87.14
Expensive; credit cards accepted

Exotic, chic, bold and highly original, the jewelry of this upcoming star, Maria Grazia Baldan, is a guaranteed conversation stopper. She combines modern artistry with precious and sometimes antique pieces. You might find anything from imperial jade and old Chinese coral and coins brought back from trips to the Far East, to decorative enamel and semiprecious stones. These timeless materials are mounted in gold or silver and worked into very imaginative, one-of-a-kind pieces. Maria Grazia works with real natural pearls that are artificially colored (pink, green, blue); she can also rework an old strand of your own pearls into an individualistic necklace according to your request. She'll do the same with an old coin, a family heirloom, or a sentimental piece that you'd like transformed by her artistic

touch. Everything is handmade in her workshop, located at the back of this dramatic 18th-century palazzo.

COSMETICS

PRODUCTS & TREATMENTS

Beauty Make-Overs

12 MAKEUPSTUDIO

Via Madonnina 13–15
Tel. 87.68.18
Moderate; credit cards accepted
Open during lunch

Cover girls flock to this headquarters of Diego della Palma, Milan's most renowned makeup artist. A one-hour makeup session with one of the Makeupstudio's English-speaking specialists can have you looking glamorous as well, and once you've seen the results you'll want to bring home some of Della Palma's nicely packaged, quality cosmetic products. The studio is an important point of reference in a fashion-conscious city, where even those who aren't models look as if they should be. Success has encouraged the studio to expand to a new beauty center on Via Agnello near the Duomo (soon to open).

COSTUME JEWELRY

Bold Ornaments

13 ANGELA CAPUTI

Via Madonnina 11
Tel. 80.73.84
Moderate; credit cards accepted

Known for her sense of fantasy in costume jewelry and a recent collection of coordinated swimwear, Angela Caputi has her home base in Florence.

See Florence listing (page 127).

FASHION

WOMEN'S

Romantic & Sophisticated

14 LUISA BECCARIA
Via Madonnina 10
Tel. 80.63.69
Expensive; credit cards accepted

This romantic and sophisticated collection of clothes is designed by Luisa Beccaria, a young Milanese-born former classics teacher. Her attractive modern boutique is an interesting foil for the feminine but tailored dresses of high-quality fabrics made in her own workshop. There's good value in their distinctive style—a ladylike, almost prim expression with an offbeat twist of sophistication. They are for the working woman who often needs to wear such daytime dresses to evening cocktail occasions. Browsing is limited; selections will be shown to you by a helpful salesperson.

COLLECTIBLES

Bizarre Curiosities

15 L'ORO DEI FARLOCCHI
Via Madonnina 5
Tel. 85.05.89
Moderate to expensive; no credit cards
   accepted

The bizarre, the curious and the unusual fill this small shop of collectibles with the air of an offbeat art gallery. It's a great place for novel gift ideas and fun browsing. You might find giant optician's glasses, signs from Victorian stores, an old wooden carousel horse or a statue of a squaw with a cigar in hand; in fact, most of the pieces tend to be on the large side. Antiques dealer Maurizio Epi-

fani offers eccentric and "kitsch" conversation pieces that often border on the folkloric and are bound to please shoppers with esoteric taste.

LEATHERGOODS

Contemporary Bags

16 MAC BORSE
Via Ponte Vetero 22
Tel. 80.79.47
Moderate; credit cards accepted

This neighborhood shop offers an appealing array of today's styles from leading labels as well as from several small but equally quality-conscious artisan suppliers. There are belts, luggage and some briefcases as well as a limited but reliable collection of casual bags. Mac Borse is just far enough from the chic hub of Brera to register a reasonable drop in prices. The result is a welcome combination of good taste and good value.

SUSTENANCE

GELATERIA

17 GELATERIA TOLDO
Via Ponte Vetero 11
Tel. 87.25.17
Inexpensive; no credit cards accepted
Closed Sunday

You'll know you're here when you see the line of regulars waiting outside for the best homemade ice cream in the neighborhood. There are no frills and nothing chic about Toldo's, just high-quality natural ingredients for the discriminating Milanese palate. The shop has two glass counters—one with fresh fruit flavors that change with the local harvest, the other with creamy *semifreddi*, which have a light, mousse-like consistency.

Characteristic wrought-iron terraces.

From this second counter, favorites include crême caramel, *tiramisu*, *amaretto* and chocolate chip.

FASHION

MEN'S & WOMEN'S

Made-to-Measure

18 G. SCALFI 🍾🍾🍾🍾
Via Mercato 3
Tel. 87.47.46
Moderate; credit cards accepted

If you'd like to try the expert tailoring for which Italy is world-famous, but can't afford to patronize the exclusive outfitters who clothe European monarchs, G. Scalfi is a fine choice. You can choose from a rich selection of Italian and English fabrics, including cashmeres, linens and silks from Como, under the guidance of a helpful and pleasant English-speaking staff. Women can select from a number of prototype suits in classic or updated styles and then be measured for any needed modifications. Men require a more precise initial fitting and will be measured from head to toe. Most garments can be made up in less than five days, including a second suggested, though not obligatory, fitting. Everyone should own at least one beautifully cut Italian suit, and if you're not around to pick it up, Scalfi will have it shipped home in time for your fashionable return to the office.

GIFTS

HAND-PAINTED ACCESSORIES

For Fun & Whimsy

19 DODO
Corso Garibaldi 55
Tel. 80.58.269
Moderate; no credit cards accepted

A small shop of gift ideas that are pure fantasy, Dodo will enchant child and adult alike.
See Florence listing (page 47).

HERB SHOP

Homeopathic & Natural Beauty Products

20 ERBORISTERIA NOVARA & SERAFINO
Via Pontaccio 19
Tel. 87.05.47
Moderate; no credit cards accepted

If your interest lies in the organic approach to health and beauty problems, keep an eye out for this *erboristeria*'s dimly lit window filled with old pharmaceutical bottles. Dr. Alessandro Novara's vegetable- and mineral-based panaceas are widely used to treat maladies ranging from indigestion to respiratory ailments. Considered among the best at the art of healing with herbs, Dr. Novara, helped by his English-speaking son, will patiently listen to your complaints before prescribing one of his natural remedies handed down from his great-grandmother. Century-old formulas are used in pomades to treat skin irritations, lotions to prevent baldness, and a shelfful of *tisane* (herbal-tea infusions) kept in old-fashioned wooden cabinets. If your only concern is cosmetic, choose from natural face and body creams, colognes and extracts in every possible fragrance, hennas, shampoos and lovely perfumed soaps.

COLLECTIBLES

21 RODOLFO II

Via Pontaccio 17
Tel. 80.06.36
Moderate; credit cards accepted

Anna Rabolini's shop is an ideal place for finding unusual gifts. She specializes in objects that are precious for their craftsmanship rather than their materials; this keeps prices reasonable for some choice finds. The period covered is approximately 1870 to 1950, decades when craftsmen would still dedicate time and skill to what was intrinsically only semiprecious. You'll find splendid brooches, necklaces and earrings studded with rhinestones and marcasite, curious boxes in celluloid and Galalith, dressing-table sets in Xylonite, as well as rare ceramics and proto-rationalist 1920s lamps. If you're looking for something in particular, ask the multilingual Signora Rabolini; she hasn't the space to display all her treasures. You might happen upon the store during one of the special exhibitions it holds once or twice a year; some

Rodolfo II, an ideal stop for unusual gifts.

recent themes were early plastics, fine costume jewelry and hand-painted greeting cards.

FABRICS

FURNISHINGS

Paisley Heaven

22 ETRO

Vicolo Fiori 17 (corner of Via Pontaccio)
Tel. 80.77.68
Expensive; credit cards accepted

Even if you're not intending to redecorate, you should peek into the singular Etro showcase, which epitomizes luxury and Old Milanese elegance. The name Etro has become synonymous with the richly colored paisleys that adorn aristocratic Italian homes. These tapestry-like prints with Oriental overtones come in cottons, brocades and jacquards. They are used for pillows, silk comforters, wall coverings, curtains, runners and towels, as well as to upholster furniture. Together with his wife Roberta, Gemmo Etro has always been an obsessive collector; the firm, begun in 1969, was a natural result. The original antiques and paintings so important to the store's luxurious ambiance are among their passions.

Downstairs, you'll find a collection of luxurious leather-trimmed luggage, wine coolers and ice buckets made in a plasticized Etro fabric. There are also agendas, wallets, silk ties, woolen shawls and scarves in that Etro motif. An even wider collection of elite men's gift items can be found in the Etro accessories shop at Via Bigli 10 (see page 202).

LEATHERGOODS

BAGS & ACCESSORIES

High-Fashion Selection

23 LUCIA
Via Solferino (corner Via Pontaccio)
Tel. 86.77.08
Moderate to expensive; credit cards
    accepted

Lucia's is the best place in Brera if you're planning to buy an important high-fashion handbag and like the idea of finding a good selection under one roof. Sales help will show you bags from some of the finest Italian manufacturers, such as Granello, Pitti and Mabiani, embodying the most up-to-date trends in colors, leathers and shapes. Styles range from the casual to the dressy; there's a nice selection of coordinated small leathergoods as well.

SHOES

WOMEN'S

Casual

24 SPELTA
Via Solferino (corner Via Pontaccio)
Tel. 80.52.592
Moderate; no credit cards accepted

Known for their comfortable fit, Spelta's women's casual leather shoes are made in the workshop at the back of the store, which will also fill custom orders. Colorful summer sandals are a big favorite, but wintertime boots and shoes come in an array of equally up-to-date colors and leathers. Almost everything is flat or with a low, low heel. Prices are also low, and the workmanship is dependable.

FASHION

MEN & WOMEN'S

Contemporary Sportswear

25 DROGHERIA SOLFERINO
Via Solferino 1 (corner Via Pontaccio)
Tel. 87.87.40
Moderate; credit cards accepted

The Drogheria Solferino's black-and-white 1930s insignia recalls its days as a neighborhood *drogheria e profumeria*. The shop's old-world decor, with original ceiling fans, silver-plated cash registers and heavy wooden cabinets, is worth a visit in itself. It also sets off the contemporary high-quality fashion now sold here. The young owners' keen sense for sophisticated yet casual separates draws a youthful and professional clientele. French and English as well as Italian manufacturers offer creative high-quality knitwear in wools and wool blends, linens and cottons, all under the boutique's own private label. The salespeople are friendly and helpful if you'd like some pointers on putting it all together; alterations are gratis.

Around the corner at Via Pontaccio 2 is a new Drogheria that offers high-quality lounging and intimate wear for women only.

HOME

FURNITURE

Avant-Garde 20th-Century Design

26 DILMOS

Piazza San Marco 1
(entrance on Via Solferino)
Tel. 65.59.837
Expensive; credit cards accepted

An impressive assemblage of this century's furniture design can be found at Dilmos. The ground-floor display is but a sampling of the selection downstairs of styles from various houses. You'll find Cappellini's modern, brightly upholstered furniture; Zanotta's witty and clever designs; chairs, sofas and lamps from Baleri (who founded Alias), including an innovative line from French architect Philippe Starke; Zabro's hand-crafted wood furniture; Poltranova's avant-garde and imaginative pieces; Gufram's famous plastic rocks and cacti, as well as its eye-catching red sofa in the shape of a giant pair of lips. Dilmos hasn't enough display space for much of its extensive stock, so the items you see are only a representation of each manufacturer's collection; ask to see the catalogue.

FASHION

MEN'S TAILOR

Made-to-Measure

27 A. CARACENI

Via Fatebenefratelli 16
Tel. 65.51.972
Expensive; no credit cards accepted
Closed Saturday

Both generations of the Caraceni family have been considered the best tailors in town. With amiable son Mario now at the helm, you'll be measured and fitted with the same sartorial expertise that has pleased such illustrious clients as the Agnellis and Baron Von Thyssen. The results can be guaranteed: impeccable suits, eternal for their elegance, style and luxury fabrics. A Caraceni specialty is evening tails. As in most made-to-measure ateliers, orders require two fittings. Bank on Caraceni being in demand, with a two- or three-month wait as part of the deal. Should you not be around to pick up your purchase, the shop can arrange for shipping abroad. You may never buy off the rack again.

HOME

FURNITURE

Modern Design

28 TANZI

Via Fatebenefratelli 9
Tel. 65.26.92
Expensive; no credit cards accepted

This spacious and sophisticated setting is home to the furniture manufactured by the four young Tanzi brothers as well as the production of Driade, a hallmark of Italian design. A complete range of furniture from the latter includes sofas and beds designed by celebrated architects such as Ettore Sottsass and Paolo Deganello, and armchairs designed by Achille Castiglioni, Alessandro Mendini and Massimo Morozzi. Driade has gone international with the beautiful Aleph Ubik collection of tables and chairs by the popular French star Philippe Starke.

Brera, recently regentrified and cosmopolitan.

RISTORANTE/TRATTORIA

29 LA NAZIONALE
Via Ancona 3 (Piazza San Marco)
Tel. 65.72.059
Inexpensive; no credit cards accepted
Closed Sunday, and Saturday lunch

This is as much a meeting as an eating place. The limited lunch menu grows in variety for evening fare when a lively crowd of professionals and students from Brera's Accademia Museum gathers to enjoy the brasserie setting. Crêpes, salads and *carpaccio* are good, fast and informal. If you hope to mingle with Milan's young and attractive, this is a perfect start.

LATE-NIGHT MILAN

No other city in Italy stays awake as late as Milan. Romans may eat much later, but go to bed much earlier. There's another world out there in Milan for after-dinner entertainment, be it strolling along the elegantly windowed shopping streets or taking in some jazz.

Night wanderers will find three large quarters of the city that offer interesting diversions: the Duomo or *centro*, Brera, and the Navigli. If your idea of a pleasant evening is some nocturnal window shopping to prep you for the morrow's spree, try a stroll in the Duomo area. Follow the arcaded Corso Vittorio Emanuele from the Duomo east to San Babila or the nearby Via Montenapoleone and its pleasant segues.

If you'd like something more musical and gregarious, the Greenwich Village-like atmosphere of Brera and the Navigli ("canals") area is your answer. Both abound in small, colorful locales full of young people and music that offer a glimpse into after-hours Milan.

In Brera, a number of nighttime spots can be found along the Via Madoninna and the Fiori Oscuri area. In the Navigli neighborhood, start at the Darsena basin and wander along the characteristic streets bordering the two main canals, the Naviglio Grande and Naviglio Pavese. You'll hear strains of jazz and reggae and find pleasant outdoor verandas and turn-of-the-century *gelaterie*.

HOME
ACCESSORIES
Accent on Design

30 PENELOPI 3
Via Solferino 12
Tel. 65.99.640
Moderate; credit cards accepted

A spacious setting shows off Penelopi's striking collection of fun and modern housewares, gifts and toys. Good design and color are the only invariables in an array of MAS ceramics, Alessi teapots, a rainbow of espresso coffeepots, desk accessories, postmodern clocks, kitchen gadgets, toys for adults and children, and small wooden sculptures of animals and birds, a store specialty. There are house linens in fresh provincial prints and a number of colorful hand-woven rugs and hammocks.

FASHION
WOMEN'S
Tailored, Classic Maternity Collection

31 NICOL CARAMEL
Piazza San Simpliciano 7
Tel 80.78.80
Expensive; credit cards accepted

Leave it to Milan to dress expectant mothers with the same attention to style and quality that it gives to those with less obvious waistlines. Nicoletta Neri has launched a whole prêt-à-*maman* collection for everyday wear, travel and evening. The look is classic and tailored (except around the waist), and uses fashionable choices of color and fine fabrics that keep abreast of the fashion world. These garments are not mass-produced, and

the detailed workmanship is a delightful surprise in an area long neglected. There are even bathing suits and bermudas for those expecting during the hot summer months.

HOME
LINENS
Contemporary

32 MIRABELLO
Via Montebello (corner Via S. Marco)
Tel. 65.59.785
Moderate to expensive; credit cards
    accepted

This charming bed-and-bath boutique sets trends in home design for both country and city dwellers. Myriad cotton prints in bright floral or

Not all is food and fashion.

geometric designs cover coordinated sheets, down-filled quilts, pillows and towels. Mirabello's selection is always enormous, and when it isn't following fashion, it's creating it with its own production. There are deluxe cashmere and silk paisley bed throws from nearby Como, and beautiful mohair bedspreads in every color imaginable. Lined, fluffy terry-cloth robes and fun sleeping bags in solid colors and prints complete the collection. Quality customwork is available for your special requests. Two doors away is a second Mirabello shop with the same fine designs in upholstery and curtain fabrics. Another, smaller shop, Lo Sbadiglio (The Yawn), is located downtown at Corso Monforte 7 (telephone 79.32.97).

HOME

SILVER

Hand-Crafted

33 ARGENTERIA DABBENE
Largo Treves 2 (corner Via Montebello)
Tel. 65.98.890
Moderate to expensive; credit cards
    accepted

Founded over 100 years ago, this well-known silver shop produces some of Milan's last true artisanal work. A modern, well-lit space offers a large selection in both modern and classic designs. An occasional antique is mixed in among Roberto Dabbene's hand-signed pieces. There are silver photo frames, ice buckets, serving platters, cigarette cases, tea and coffee services and some jewelry. A charming gift for the traveling executive is a silver cover for his or her calculator or a toothbrush with a silver handle.

SUSTENANCE

BAR-CAFFÈ

Late-Night

34 CAFFÈ MILANO
Via San Fermo 1 (at Piazza Mirabello)
Tel. 65.59.300
Moderate; no credit cards accepted
Closed Sunday

This *caffè* is as much a command post for people watchers as a casual eating spot. A light and interesting menu is available. Five choices are offered for each first course; they change frequently, but are always fresh, simple and inclined toward the elegant. Once frequented by artists, and now by a *caffè* high society, the Milano is nicest late at night, when in warm weather the tables are moved out into the small piazza; you can eat there until 1:00 A.M.

SUSTENANCE

RISTORANTE/TRATTORIA

35 IL VERDI
Piazza Mirabello 5
Tel. 65.14.12
Moderate; credit cards accepted
Closed Sunday, and Saturday lunch

Il Verdi has a clean, modern décor and is frequented by an elegant crowd. You can't reserve, so be ready to wait during rush hours. Apart from its centralized location, an attraction here is the list of over 50 imaginative meal-sized combination salads that allow you to eat well, but "light." In fact, it was Il Verdi's owner, Corrado Buonacasa, who introduced Milan to the now wildly popular "maxi-salad." His most recent novelties are *piatti unici* (one-course meals) that are deli-

In Brera, a neighborhood air still persists.

cious, filling, and perfect for lunch: *riso pilaf alla valenziana* (a kind of mini-paella) or grilled *gamberoni* (shrimp) with rice pilaf. Homemade pasta is treated as an art, and sauces are light and inventive. There are also interesting risottos, a great steak tartare and excellent local cheeses. Although eating light is Il Verdi's rule of thumb, don't overlook the delicious chestnut mousse with whipped cream.

FASHION
WOMEN'S

Imaginative Knits

36 SILVI SÍ
Via Palermo 5
Tel. 80.24.35
Moderate; no credit cards accepted
Closed 1:00–2:00 P.M., except by
appointment

For years, Silvi Sí has been selling her original, hand-finished sweaters and coordinates to Italy's and America's finest specialty stores, and her Milan showroom and workspace offer a first-hand look and advantageous prices. Known for her ladylike knits, Silvi Sí can create the basic but is most imaginative when it comes to elaborating with the pailettes, pearls and appliqués that are responsible for her distinctive and feminine look. Her showroom (in a residential building on the second floor) is filled with her creations in angora, mohair, pure wools and silk. There is excellent value here at her close-to-wholesale showroom prices.

GIFTS
STATIONERY & ACCESSORIES

Marbleized Papergoods

37 LEGATORIA ARTISTICA
Via Palermo 5
Tel. 86.11.13
Moderate; no credit cards accepted

One of the few ateliers in Milan to use the ancient technique of paper printing called *ebrû* (or marbleization), the Legatoria uses the colorful results to cover and create a breadth of objects and gifts, including pencils, photo or wedding albums, and jewelry boxes in myriad sizes. If you approach the shop from Via Solferino, you'll see the open window of the *bottega* in back. In addition to making decorative objects, the Legatoria (book-bindery) is known for its fine work in rebinding and restoring old books on special commission; the artisans rarely mind if you look in to watch them work.

SUSTENANCE

RISTORANTE/TRATTORIA

38 SARPINELLO
Via Statuto 16–18
Tel. 65.52.219
Expensive; credit cards accepted
Closed Sunday, and Saturday lunch

You'll sense the comfort of home upon entering a cozy sitting room of chintz-covered armchairs and attractive art. The same concern for a gracious setting is reflected in the fine linens and china and the relaxed ambiance of Sarpinello's dining room, where the food is as refined and delicious as it is asthetically beautiful. Pierre Clauwarct, the young Belgian chef, who was raised and trained in Florence, excels in his imaginative combination of ingredients. Everything is equally delicious, and varies daily according to the market's vicissitudes. For starters, you might find fresh pasta in thyme sauce or ravioli stuffed with bean purée in a tomato and basil sauce. Fresh fish is steamed, poached or broiled, and usually appears on the menu alongside delicious veal, beef and lamb dishes. Pierre triumphs with desserts such as the *pavone* (peacock), an exquisite combination of homemade sherbets, and the lemon mousse. The wine list is also good.

SHOES

WOMEN'S

High-Fashion Footwear

39 CARRANO
Via Solferino 11
Tel. 86.77.33
Expensive; credit cards accepted

Carrano has recently relocated its Vittorio Emanuele shoe store in the newly fashionable area of Brera. The sporty, dressy and evening footwear and coordinated bags found here are all in reliably good taste.

See Shoe-Shopping Guide to Milan (page 232).

SUSTENANCE

RISTORANTE/TRATTORIA

40 L'ALTRO CALAFURIA
Via Solferino 12
Tel. 65.59.627
Moderate; credit cards accepted
Closed Tuesday

This is a *simpatico* spot that draws a steady crowd of regulars from the fashion and art worlds, who often come especially for the delicious *cotoletta milanese*. Super-thin and crisp, this regional specialty is large enough for two and can be ordered just that way, adorned with chopped basil, arugula and tomato. The light-crusted pizza provides serious competition, although it is often eaten here as a first and not a second course; it runs the gamut from simple (*napoletana* with tomato sauce and mozzarella) to exotic. If you like the pungent local Gorgonzola cheese, you can have your pizza smothered with it. This is also a good place to try the homemade pastas or such local specialties as *riso al salto*, *rognone* (kidneys) or fresh fish. Affable owner Doriano strolls about the art-filled room greeting guests and keeping the ambiance *allegro*. He has good reason to smile; he has recently opened six other locations around town called Pizza Calafuria.

GIFTS

AVANT-GARDE FUN

41 CONTROBUFFET
Via Solferino 14
Tel. 65.54.934
Moderate; credit cards accepted

Pop art and kitsch curios are Controbuffet's attractions. Wittily designed everyday objects (such as ceramic teapots and cups that stand on little feet with shoes) are the store's hallmark. Transparent plastic raincoats, totes and ties from Avant de Dormir contain colored rainwater, sand, fake fish and pasta. Three-dimensional tabletop puzzles, hand-painted gesso replicas of Milan and other cities, come in their own traveling box for the visitor who wants to bring back a little bit of Italy. There's also whimsy in the collection of clocks, Aquilone ceramic figurines, home accessories, small furniture and pipes. Anyone with a sense of humor will surely find something to bring home—and maybe even put to use.

COLLECTIBLES

Conversational Curios

42 LO SCARABATTOLO
Via Solferino 14
Tel. 65.90.253
Moderate to expensive; no credit cards
    accepted

Scarabattolo means glass cabinet or showcase, and the name fits this tiny, specialized curiosity shop. A refined though crowded display offers one-of-a-kind period objects and peculiar conversation pieces. For the collector who appreciates 18th- and 19th-century scientific instruments and sports-related articles, there are binoculars, antique golf clubs, ship models, walking sticks with hidden flasks in the handle, decoys and pipes, to name but a few. There are also some objects in crocodile from the 1930s and an interesting selection of antique jewelry for him and her.

SUSTENANCE

BAR-CAFFÈ-TRATTORIA

43 LA PIAZZETTA
Via Solferino 25
Tel. 65.90.176
Moderate; no credit cards accepted
Closed Sunday

This is the best spot in Brera for a leisurely breakfast or mid-matinal respite. Bring your fresh croissant and steaming cappuccino to a table and linger with your friends—or your newspaper—in this big, open bistro-type *bar-caffè*. La Piazzetta also plays the role of *trattoria* with a menu based on simple and authentic Milanese home cooking. Amid palm trees, pretty brass fixtures and lace-trimmed curtains, enjoy a quick and casual lunch or a more leisurely dinner in the evening. The menu is small but very good, including all of the fresh pastas made by Antonetta, the chef.

SUSTENANCE

RISTORANTE/TRATTORIA

44 IL SOLFERINO
Via Castelfidardo 2
Tel. 65.99.886
Expensive; no credit cards accepted
Closed Sunday, and Saturday lunch

Charm and bonhomie at the popular Solferino.

Reservations are a must for an elegant and romantic evening of Milanese cuisine at Il Solferino, part of the charming Locanda Solferino inn. The atmosphere is friendly but proper and the guests casual but fashionable, mostly members of the design community. Fresh linen and flowers grace the table for excellent starters, such as hot antipasto or the house pâté. The menu includes fresh pasta and some authentic Milanese dishes, including the famous *cotoletta milanese* and *rostin negàa*. *Tartufi* (truffles) are also a specialty when in season and flavor a number of dishes; highly recommended are the *gingilli* (small ravioli stuffed with ricotta and truffles).

Around the corner you'll find the Via San Marco entrance to the popular Take-Away, which shares the talented gourmet kitchen that serves Il Solferino. It is not take-away at all, but more like a buffet self-service where you can enjoy an inexpensive light dinner of fresh grilled vegetables or delicious pasta, as well as some great people-watching at one of Milan's few sidewalk cafés.

WINES

45 ENOTECA COTTI
Via Solferino 42
Tel. 65.55.736
Moderate; no credit cards accepted

The Enoteca Cotti ranks among the best wine stores in all of Milan, boasting a very well-stocked cellar. Popular since the day it opened in 1952, this informal *enoteca* owes much of its success to the knowledgeable and always available Signor Luigi Cotti. The counter area is a friendly place—you're bound to exchange "chin-chin's" and banter with any of the regulars—and a quick or lingering visit here will fortify you for your wanderings. The monthly wine tastings are an event; check to see if one is scheduled during your stay.

COLLECTIBLES & CURIOSITIES
Art Nouveau to Art Deco

46 LA TENDA GIALLA
Via Castelfidardo 2
Tel. 65.29.81
Moderate to expensive
Open during lunch

A *tenda gialla* (yellow canopy) will confirm your arrival at this charming antique and curiosity shop. Small and crowded but quaint, La Tenda Gialla specializes in collectibles from 1900 to 1940, with an emphasis on fine jewelry and art-deco glassware. You might find Sheffield silver, Bakelite lamps, Lalique glass, framed prints and tabletop clocks. Some interesting Alessi tea services from the 1950s sit alongside old crocodile suitcases in perfect condition. Prettily decorated with antique lace curtains, lamps, posters and vitrines in which merchandise is displayed, the shop has a friendly atmosphere that is inviting to browsers. The owners will ship purchases abroad.

SUSTENANCE
RISTORANTE/TRATTORIA
Pizzeria

47 BEBEL'S
Via San Marco 38
Tel. 65.71.658
Moderate; credit cards accepted
Closed Wednesday

Locals say the pizza made here in the wood-burning brick oven in front is outstanding. Gracious host Sergio Bebel will see that your other gastronomic wishes are fulfilled as well. A glance at the buffet table, beautifully arranged with, among other things, fresh pasta made in-house, will probably convince you to order *pappardelle alla Bebel's*, made with *speck* (smoked ham), cream, parmesan cheese and saffron. You'll also see live lobsters on ice, which will be served grilled or used in a delicious spaghetti dish. Rare *ovoli* and *porcini* mushrooms are a delight when in season, as is fresh game. A fondue-like *fonduta* made with fontina cheese is rich with the taste of truffles. Fresh combination salads can be made to your request, to accompany a number of fresh grilled fish or meat entrées. A good wine list includes the special Grignolino d'Asti from Piedmont.

SUSTENANCE
RISTORANTE/TRATTORIA

48 LA BRICIOLA
Via Solferino 25
Tel. 65.51.012
Moderate; credit cards accepted
Closed Sunday and Monday

A fun place for people-watching, La Briciola is especially popular when the activity in the lively café pours outdoors with the first hint of warm weather. Indoors, a Parisian bistro-like décor with ceiling fans, wrought-iron chairs and tables is the backdrop for young regulars from the world of fashion and advertising. While you wait for your first course, a complimentary *tris* of salami, small meatballs and local bread is offered. The specialty of the light menu is *carpaccio* prepared in 35 different ways, but *grancevola* (crab) vinaigrette and *zuppa di cipolla* (onion soup) are also favorites.

BOOKS
DESIGN & ARCHITECTURE

49 L'ARCHIVOLTO
Via Marsala 2
Tel. 65.90.842
Moderate; credit cards accepted

This small specialized bookstore/gallery is a must for enthusiasts of architecture, design and city planning. There are books, magazines and posters in Italian and foreign languages, with a high percentage in English. An interesting section of old magazines, rare books and out-of-print books offers antique architectural drawings and prints and old postcards. L'Archivolto also publishes an extensive mail-order catalogue that selects the most interesting titles on the current international market. In addition, it has developed a research operation for architects, students and public administrators that utilizes a highly specialized data bank hooked up with a worldwide service. Probably the only concentration of its kind now in existence, L'Archivolto is worth seeing, especially during exhibitions in the gallery division.

SUSTENANCE

RISTORANTE/TRATTORIA

50 GIALLO
Via Milazzo 6
Tel. 65.71.581
Moderate; credit cards accepted
Dinner only; closed Sunday

The designer Rocco Barocco, they say, is an habitué. So is everyone else from the fashion world, or so it would seem. A sister restaurant to La Briciola (see page 264), Giallo also has a fun atmosphere. Upper-floor seating offers even better people-watching and also a glimpse into the open kitchen. *Pizzettine* (tiny pizzas) are good antipastos, but save room for one of the delicious risottos (for example, *riso dello Zar* with salmon and caviar) or the *carpaccio* specialties. If it's on the menu, try the *cotoletta alla parigina*, a tender, breaded veal cutlet covered with melted cheese. A charming touch is the jars of fresh homemade *biscotti* (cookies) brought to your table with an after-dinner *caffè*.

From daisies to garlic at a corner stand.

COLLECTIBLES

20th-Century Avant-Garde

51 GALLERIA MICHEL LEO
Via Solferino 35
Tel. 65.98.333
Moderate to expensive; credit cards
accepted

Just a bit north of the Brera action, but well worth the detour for deco enthusiasts, is the fascinating Galleria Michel Leo. Anything from 1900 on is welcome here. One particular specialty is a selection of the popular Bakelite and Galalith plastics; jewelry, eyeglasses, small lamps and tabletop accessories are attractive collectibles. French Lalique glass is displayed alongside industrial household objects such as radios from 1920 to 1950 and chrome appliances from the 1950s. Among the latter, you'll find toasters, blenders, juicers, coffeepots and food grinders which have never been used, most of them still in their original boxes. Each category is carefully displayed in curio cabinets or on tables.

LEATHERGOODS
BAGS & ACCESSORIES
Workshop/Studio

52 EMILIO BOFFI
Via Milazzo 6
Tel. 65.92.113
Expensive; no credit cards accepted
Closed Saturday

Emilio Boffi is a young designer who supplies his handcrafted leathergoods to some of Milan's better retail stores. By coming to the source, you can find a far more extensive selection at a considerable savings. In Emilio's workshop, you can watch his cutters and sewers busy working thick *cuoio* (natural cowhide). The workmanship is good, the stitching bold, the look simple and casual, often highlighted with a piece of simple brass hardware. The *cuoio* takes well to vegetable dyes, and the rainbow selection of colors is surprising; if you're looking for a particular shade, he'll dye it for you.

In addition to big shoulder bags, there are portfolios, backpacks, weekend travel cases in the shape of doctors' bags, as well as other luggage pieces, oversized belts, wallets, agendas and diaries. The atmosphere is simple and friendly, and salespeople will help you with ideas for custommaking to your specifications. To reach Boffi, you pass through the courtyard of a residential building; just follow the heady smell of leather hides.

GIFTS
Fun Stationery & School Accessories

53 LA CARTOLERIA
Corso Garibaldi (corner of Via Marsala)
Tel. 65.70.672
Moderate; credit cards accepted

La Cartoleria (the stationery store) is one of Milan's oldest. The ambiance is traditional, with old-fashioned dark wooden shelves; the shop's private Creare line of bright modern papergoods is a fun contrast. Papers with coordinated themes such as fashion prints or plaids cover notebooks in all sizes, folders, pen and pencil cases, and backpacks. A pen collection may begin with the inexpensive and playful and finish with serious and handsome name brands. La Cartoleria is a charming place to browse for last-minute gift ideas.

New meaning for paper goods at La Cartoleria.

GALLERY

GALLERY

Architectural Drawings & Avant-Garde
Furniture

54 ANTONIA JANNONE
Corso Garibaldi 125
Tel. 65.57.930
Expensive; credit cards accepted
Open 3:30–7:30 P.M. only, or by
    appointment

Fine dining at Ciga Palace's Casanova Grill.

The secret is out: Antonia Jannone's specialized collection of architectural drawings and prints has been discovered by prominent galleries and institutions such as New York's Museum of Modern Art. If you come directly here, you may happen upon magnificent antique or contemporary collectibles before they're snatched up by her regular cognoscenti clients. In addition to architectural themes and set designs, there are watercolors and oils by international architects, some dating back to the 17th century. In an adjacent space, Signora Jannone exclusively showcases young designers with limited productions of avant-garde furniture, carpets and glassware. Recognized award winners, they represent the design force of tomorrow.

SUSTENANCE

RISTORANTE/TRATTORIA

55 CASANOVA GRILL DELL'HOTEL
    PALACE
Piazza della Repubblica 20
Tel. 65.08.03
Expensive to very expensive; credit cards
    accepted
Closed Saturday

Hardly a grill despite its name, the Casanova is a dignified dining experience to be saved for that special evening. The skilled and doting service, the refined classical décor in pastel shades, the impressive wine list and the elegant presentation of an outstanding Mediterranean-inspired menu are all as seductive as Casanova himself. You can choose from an imaginative range of risottos or light pastas, although the traditional onion soup and the more novel shrimp soup with coriander are equally exquisite. This alternation between the old and new is the beauty of the impeccably prepared menu, with dishes ranging from traditional *pasta e fagioli* to *pappardelle* noodles with fish, prosciutto with saffron sauce, or the vegetable-stuffed swordfish *carpaccio*. It will be difficult to go wrong at the Casanova, and the English-speaking waiters take the guesswork out of the evening. The refreshing homemade *sorbetto* and the sweet concoctions from the dessert cart offer final triumphant confirmation that one can eat very well indeed in a grand hotel. A second Ciga location, the regal Principe e Savoia Hotel, is just steps across the Piazza della Repubblica.

BICYCLES

Bicycles are very much a part of the Italian scene. You may see them ridden by professional teams making training runs on country highways, housewives with bulbous shopping bags hanging from the handlebars, artisans with gilded wooden frames slung over their shoulders, or *contadini* (farmers) with melons tucked under their arms. Racing champions and practical pedalers alike are strongly committed to bicycling, and together have fostered a lively national bicycle industry. For the past decade, well over two million bicycles have been manufactured each year, most of them in Lombardy and other northern regions. Whether your interest lies in touring, racing or the simple pleasure of owning an Italian two-wheeler, Milan offers you the widest selection and the highest quality.

The unmistakable design of Italy's virtuoso bikes is born from an innate aesthetic awareness, while their aerodynamics and functional value are the result of both artisan workmanship and high technology. The cycling champions of the Giro d'Italia, held each May, are national heroes, and foreign cognoscenti have come to understand that the mystique of Italian craftsmanship is based on sophisticated science. Foreigners who buy directly from Italian sources have found that their pedal purchases cost approximately two-thirds the American market price, that major Italian firms often export only their more expensive models, and that some don't export at all.

If you're looking for a good, reliable, well-proportioned city bike, you'll find that Bianchi, Bottecchia, Dei, Doniselli, Legnano and Taurus all produce some splendidly classic models. Legnano also has a similar line in brighter, high-tech versions. Manufacturers that excel in lighter bikes for touring and precision models for racing are Legnano, Bianchi, Rossin, Colnago and Olmo. Garelli Torpado has a heavy-duty bike with thickish, non-skid tires, as does Olmo, which is also favored for its city bike and mountain bike— the former with 18 gear changes, the latter with 36. Unquestionably the king of mountain bikes, however, is the Rossin model. In the long run, you might just let the style or feel of the bicycle be the deciding factor in your choice.

Prices vary according to the quality of the frame and parts. Bikes made only with Campagnolo components are the best. In general, you should aways ask if the frame (*telaio*) is handmade (*artigianale*). Expect a bike with a handmade frame to be more expensive but still reasonably priced by American standards. You'll want to check out the parts, especially the gearshift (*cambio*) and brakes (*freni*), and whether replacements are available in the States. Many shops will ship your bike for you by air freight. It costs almost twice as much to ship it assembled as unassembled. You can also take your bike with you on the plane at no cost if it is dismantled, boxed (or packed in a specially designed airline bag) and checked in as a piece of luggage. Most stores have salespeople who are bikers themselves, and there's usually someone who speaks English.

CINELLI GRAN CICLISMO
Via Folli 45
Tel. 21.51.643 or 21.58.616
Credit cards accepted
Although considered Milan's best-stocked bike store, this is worth the trip to the outlying district of Lambrate only if you are a serious enthusiast. Many of the regulars are professional bikers, who understand that the rather high prices here are reasonable for the handmade and factory-made merchandise and the knowledgeable service. Next door at No. 43 is a boutique for accessories and clothing.

LEGNANO
Via Barona 33
Tel. 81.64.41
No credit cards accepted
This shop is also far enough removed from downtown Milan to discourage the trip, unless you are particularly interested in any of Legnano's prestigious and high-quality models.

NART & ABBIATI
Corso di Porta Ticinese 53
Tel. 83.53.678
Credit cards accepted
A fairly large shop that stocks most

of the best makes, this is one of the 20-store Bianchi operation and offers moderate prices and a wide selection.

ROSSIGNOLI
Corso Garibaldi 71
Tel. 80.49.60
No credit cards
This shop carries its own quality brand of bicycles, and specializes in racing models. You'll also find every conceivable part and accessory, and a good stock of clothing.

SGANZERLA
Via Maiocchi 9
Tel. 27.81.32
No credit cards accepted
It's a short cab ride away to this old family firm that offers real quality. Among other makes, you'll find the whole Olmo line here, including their city and mountain bikes.

Milan also has some of the most skilled artisan bicycle workshops to be found anywhere. For made-to-measure racing bikes, the wait is often six weeks, depending upon the model, and these small traditional shops rarely accept credit cards. The following artisan bike-builders are considered the very best:
ROSSIN POGLIAGHI, Via Cesarino 11
Tel. 95.01.497
MARNATI, Via Delfico 26, Tel. 31.82.632
GUERCIOTTI, Corso Buenos Aires 55
Tel. 20.04.24
FRESCHI, Piazza Gramsci 10
Tel. 34.93.468
If you're content to rent a bike by the day, hour or even month, stop by Vittorio Comizzoli, Via Washington 60 (Tel. 49.84.694).

Vercelli/Magenta

*T*he Vercelli/Magenta district, found directly west of the city center and not far from the Duomo, is one of Milan's most desirable residential neighborhoods. This stately area with wide tree-lined streets wears its elegance with self-assured grace. The refined standard of the proud upper-middle-class community is reflected in the numerous boutiques and cafés; if you come here to shop, you'll do so with less frenzy and with a more authentic feel for the true upscale Milan life style.

In 1860, Porta Baracca, the old city gate, was renamed "Magenta" to commemorate a small Lombard town where a battle took place against the Austro-Hungarians. The gate was later demolished, as was much of old Milan, to make way for the then-new residential district that today still carries its name. Corso Magenta lies east of Piazzale Baracca, where the gate once stood, while Corso Vercelli stretches west. The latter has a larger concentration of shops than Corso Magenta, including a number of neighborhood branches of important stores such as Coin, Casa Croff, Bassetti and Frette linens.

The chief attractions of Corso Magenta are its tourist sites. Halfway down the street is the impressive 15th-century Dominican church of Santa Maria delle Grazie. The apse of the church was designed by the high Renaissance architect Bramante, but it is Leonardo da Vinci's world-

August palazzos and broad tree-lined streets wear their old-world elegance well.

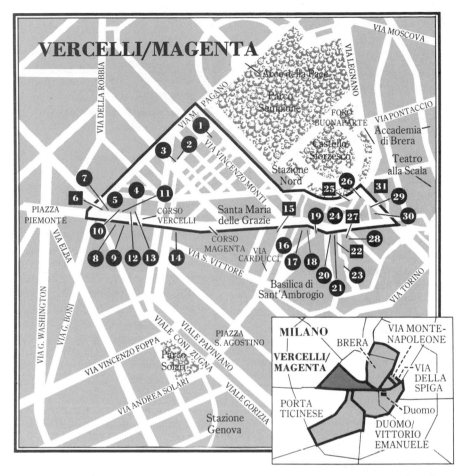

famous, recently restored "Last Supper," found in what used to be the monastery rectory, that is its undisputable gem. Nearby in the Piazza Sant'Ambrogio is the basilica founded in the 4th century by Saint Ambrose, Bishop of Milan and today its beloved patron saint. You are also in the vicinity of Milan's 15th-century Castello Sforzesco and its large public garden, the Parco Sempione, a beautiful spot for a picnic.

Although you may visit the area on your tourist itinerary, the Vercelli/Magenta stores are handsome enough to lure you here for shopping alone. There are varied possibilities, especially for shoes, accessories, household linens and high-quality classic fashion. You'll also find a healthy smattering of renowned cafés and some of Milan's best restaurants.

It's easy to imagine this Milanese quarter at the turn of the century—refined and endowed with a wealth of handsome buildings.

RIDING GEAR

Made-to-Measure Boots & Accessories

1 STIVALERIA SAVOIA DI BALLINI
Via Petrarca 7 (corner of Via V. Monti)
Tel. 46.34.24
Expensive; credit cards accepted

One of Milan's most fascinating leathergoods stores since 1870, Stivaleria Savoia specializes in men's and women's made-to-measure riding and polo boots and a variety of other footwear for men only: from golf shoes, loafers and walking shoes to elegant formalwear. There are a number of ready-made models, and a handsome selection of saddles, riding crops, stirrups, reins and other equestrian accessories. Signor Ballini, descendant of master leatherworkers, uses the softest of high-quality skins and materials. It takes about a month to make a pair of shoes by hand, but for shoes that fit like a glove as these do, people would wait a lifetime. The shop will reliably ship if need be.

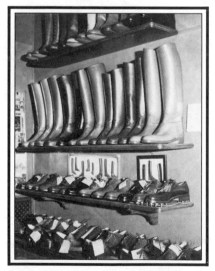

Stivaleria Savoia's made-to-measure treasures.

FASHION

WOMEN'S & CHILDREN'S

Classic Milanese Chic

2 PUPI SOLARI 🏠🏠🏠🏠
Piazza Tommaseo (corner of Via
    Mascheroni 12)
Tel. 46.33.25
Expensive; credit cards accepted
Open during lunch

Pupi Solari's flawless taste in fashion is the last word for well-to-do Milanese women. Start with the décor of her celebrated specialty store: soft floral carpeting and wallpaper, high pastel-painted ceilings, and a quiet corner to sip tea while taking a break. Pupi's intuitive eye for color determines her choice from the collections of Romeo Gigli, Alberto Asperi, Enrica Massei and others, which she then blends with her own distinguished label. The result: a look that is chic, simple, intelligent and unique, from her fine cashmere topcoats down to hand-picked shoes and bags. Pupi also makes exquisite little cashmere sweaters and coats for infants and children of all sizes. There is precious sportswear, but much of the children's clothing is on the fancy side, perfect for that party dress or Sunday outfit. A well-heeled Milanese mother would not think of shopping elsewhere.

LEATHERGOODS

BAGS & ACCESSORIES

Contemporary

3 EVE
Via Mascheroni 12
Tel. 46.96.922
Moderate; credit cards accepted

Just around the corner from Pupi Solari is this location for Eve's great collection of fashion handbags in contemporary shapes and colorful leathers. There are also belts, luggage, briefcases, and some shoes.

See listing for Eve's larger location in the Duomo/Vittorio Emanuele neighborhood (page 175).

SHOES
MEN'S & WOMEN'S
Bargain Discounts

4 BAZAAR CARRANO
Via Rasori 4
Tel. 43.90.588
Inexpensive; no credit cards accepted

A prestigious designer of high-fashion shoes, Carrano sells his precious leftovers at exceptionally low prices in this small and unassuming shop. There's a sprinkling of other designer names, but most of the shoes available are last season's advances from Carrano. If you've breezed by his elegant boutique on the Via Sant'Andrea, you'll realize just how much you're saving. The shop is not big on service, but most customers don't seem to mind.

LEATHERGOODS
BAGS & ACCESSORIES
Mainly Pigskin

5 LA CASA DEL CINGHIALE
Via M. Pagano 69A
Tel. 49.84.597
Moderate; credit cards accepted

If you love pigskin, the "House of Pigskin" stocks an impressive collection of leathergoods made of this exotic-looking skin in styles that are classic to contemporary, at remarkably low prices. Known for its durability, *cinghiale* works best with rigid shapes; you'll find the schoolbag shape (*cartella*), as well as solidly constructed shoulder bags and briefcases. There's also a range of smaller leathergoods for men and women—desk accessories, agendas, address books, wallets and traveling accessories. Most articles come in the natural *cinghiale* color or in burgundy, navy, dark green and black. A wide range of luggage comes in more conventional skins, as well as in nylon and synthetics.

SUSTENANCE
BAR-CAFFÈ

6 TORREFAZIONE VERCELLI
Via Cherubini 2 (corner Corso Vercelli)
No telephone
Inexpensive; no credit cards accepted
Closed Sundays

Just inhale deeply, and you'll absorb a day's quota of caffeine. *Torrefazione* means that fresh coffee beans are continuously being roasted and ground on the premises, and you'll taste the difference in freshness when you step up to the bar for a savory sampling. Big burlap sacks loaded with beans could keep coffee connoisseurs happy, and awake, for life. If the sight of them doesn't draw you inside, the aroma of fresh coffee will. Neighborhood cognoscenti will take their coffee nowhere else.

FASHION

MEN'S, WOMEN'S & CHILDREN'S

Department Store

7 COIN

Corso Vercelli 8
Tel. 43.21.60
Moderate; credit cards accepted

A smallish, neighborhood-sized branch of the popular Coin department stores, but one well stocked with moderately priced fashion and accessories.

See listing in the Duomo/Vittorio Emanuele neighborhood (page 188).

HOME

LINENS

Contemporary Colors

8 BASSETTI

Corso Vercelli 25 (inside gallery)
Tel. 43.96.518
Moderate; credit cards accepted

Bassetti is a 200-year-old tradition in Lombard industry, and although you'll see a number of the company's attractive boutiques for dining, bed and bath linens about town, this is one of the largest and best stocked. You'll find a wide selection of coordinating bed-linen and bath-towel sets in everything from pastels to prints, as well as the latest fashion colors in high-quality cottons. A special Bassetti technique prints contrasting but compatible prints on reverse sides of sheets, in small floral or geometric patterns. Scalloped or decoratively trimmed edges and its high-quality workmanship have made Bassetti one of Italy's major names in household linens.

SHOES

MEN'S & WOMEN'S

Young & Contemporary

9 LUCA

Largo Settimio Severo (corner of Corso
    Vercelli)
Tel. 46.44.63
Moderate; credit cards accepted

This is one of five young and contemporary Luca shoe stores in Milan, offering a wide range of styles from the classic to the updated at affordable prices.

For Luca's main location, see Shoe-Shopping Directory to Downtown Milan (page 232).

FASHION

MEN'S, WOMEN'S & CHILDREN'S

Tailored Fashion for the Family

10 GEMELLI

Corso Vercelli 16
Tel. 49.00.57 (men's); 43.34.04 (women's);
    46.46.89 (shoes)
Expensive; credit cards accepted

A large, handsome palazzo houses the three elegant boutiques of Sergio Gemelli, which are by now an institution in Milanese shopping. Face the large arched entranceway: on your left is the women's boutique, on your right is the men's, and in the rear is the shoe store. Across the street is the new children's boutique.

Women will find a streamlined selection from each of Italy's finest houses, including Basile, Erreuno, Complice, Genny, les Copains and Cadette, plus a number of exclusive Gemelli designs known for their fantasy knits and fine tailoring. Excellent coordinating accessories are attractively

Imposing residential façades.

displayed with the clothing. The spacious rooms of the men's boutique display sweaters and casual apparel, suits and coats from Valentino, Cerrutti, St. Andrews and others. The shoe store is smaller, but the selection is just as refined. The children's store completes the picture, allowing Gemelli to offer quality shopping for the whole family, with service to match.

Across the street and farther on, at No. 5, you'll find a smaller, simpler Gemelli boutique where you can find discounts on the season's leftovers at more affordable prices.

FASHION

CHILREN'S SHOES & CLOTHING

11 GUSELLA
Corso Vercelli 14
Tel. 48.14.144
Moderate; credit cards accepted

After opening more than a dozen successful locations in Milan, Gusella has become something of a symbol for fashion and quality in children's shoes and clothing. If you—or your child—are tired of the same old sneakers, you'll both swoon at the selection of top-name labels in a wide range of styles: classic Mary Janes, espadrilles, Topsiders, sneakers, patent-leather party shoes, whimsical bedroom slippers, boots and just about everything grown-ups and teens wear, but in lilliputian size. (There are some sturdy, no-nonsense shoes that seem indestructible, and orthopedic shoes are also available—with consultation—for problem feet.) The clothing to go with it all is extremely fashionable but very wearable—a wide selection of sporty to dressy looks for children up to 16 years of age.

Another Gusella clothing store is in the Galleria del Toro (telephone 79.01.33). Nearby it is a Gusella location for shoes only, at Corso Vittorio Emanuele 37/B (telephone 70.01.18).

HOME

TABLEWARE & ACCESSORIES

Contemporary Design

12 CASA CROFF
Corso Vercelli 10
Tel. 46.33.73
Moderate; credit cards accepted

For years Casa Croff has been known for its contemporary design at affordable prices. In a spacious, one-floor department-store layout, you'll find household furnishings and accessories from A to Z: casual furniture, colorful bed and bath linens, hardware and plastic accessories, kitchen containers and gadgets, china, glassware and flatware. All merchandise is made exclusively for Croff and has a sleekly modern look. Popular with youthful customers setting up house, the shop offers good quality and easy browsing. There are Casa Croff stores in Florence, Venice and Rome and three others in Milan, of which the location near the Piazza del Duomo at Piazza Diaz 2 (telephone 86.27.45) is the largest.

PERFUME & COSMETICS

Extensive Collection

13 ROSABIANCA
Corso Vercelli 8
Tel. 43.95.696
Moderate; credit cards accepted

If you're curious to see and smell what's happening in Europe's market of cosmetics and scents, Rosabianca offers one of Milan's biggest and best-displayed selections. There are knowledgeable sales help, mirrors, tester counters and every hue of eye shadow imaginable. Try out the perfumes recently introduced by Milan's top fashion designers Armani, Missoni and Versace. New arrivals are joined by timeless standbys such as Chanel, Guerlain, Van Cleef & Arpels, and scores of others. Advertising boards promise to make you cover-girl material. Phone 46.32.64 for a beauty-treatment appointment.

SUSTENANCE

PASTICCERIA/TEAROOM

14 BIFFI
Corso Magenta 87
Tel. 43.95.702
Moderate; no credit cards accepted
Closed Sunday

Traditional *pasticceria* and renowned tearoom, Biffi is an institution for a late-afternoon tea with the well-coiffed matrons of Milan. Crystal chandeliers hanging from high ceilings, pink napkins and proper waiters make this a lovely resting spot for a pick-me-up cappuccino as well. Everything is made on the premises, and Biffi is known for the freshness and quality of its sweets, especially its light *panettone*, the local traditional sweet bread found most easily around Christmas time. It makes for one of the best breakfasts in town.

SUSTENANCE

BAR-CAFFÈ

15 BAR MAGENTA
Via Carducci 13 (corner of Corso Magenta)
Tel. 80.53.808
Inexpensive; no credit cards accepted
Closed Monday

A turn-of-the-century, history-evoking locale, the Bar Magenta seems never to have known an empty day. You can have a simple lunch outdoors, but inside it's just as informal and inviting—a dark interior lit by hanging stained-glass lamps and furnished with heavy wooden tables on wrought-iron bases. *Panini* (sandwiches) are made to order, which guarantees their freshness, and you can choose from a big selection of meats and cheeses with such trimmings as olive-oil-marinated mushrooms, artichokes and eggplant. The Bar Magenta also serves as a *birreria*, with a long list of imported beers on tap and bottled. Open till late and always lively, it even has a working jukebox.

FASHION

WOMEN'S

Classic

16 ELLA

Via Terraggio 28
Tel. 86.71.115
Expensive; no credit cards accepted

In the shadow of Sant'Ambrogio is this small boutique for women whose professions and tastes demand discreet, high-quality dress. A faithful following of Milanese career women find a reliable selection of suits and separates picked from this season's offerings. Ella's best sellers are her shirts, attractively tailored in crisp cottons and rich silks, with subtle details that make them young and fresh but classic enough to fit that refined business image. There's a nice range of sweaters from which to choose as well and, in winter, beautiful shearling coats.

LEATHERGOODS

BAGS & ACCESSORIES

Casual

17 FIGUS

Corso Magenta 31
Tel. 80.74.85
Moderate; credit cards accepted

In this small, rustic atelier you'll find a good-sized collection of handmade leather bags in natural untanned leather. This is the durable *cuoio* that can be dyed in myriad hues and lasts forever; here it has been crafted into fine handbags distinguished by their bright colors, interesting trims and unusual shapes. There are also great belts with original buckles, as well as a number of larger doctor-style bags, backpacks and knapsacks and a selection of summer totes made of plasticized canvas.

SHOES

WOMEN'S

Young, Spirited Shoe Fashion

18 VALENTINA

Corso Magenta 27
Tel. 87.11.93
Moderate; no credit cards accepted
Open during lunch

You'll get a lot of the fashion consciousness and quality of the prestigious Carrano house at more moderate prices here. Updated classics like ballerina shoes and medium-heeled pumps are made in a wide range of colors and leathers, making them spirited accessories for the young customer at a good value. Each of the three Valentina shoe boutiques in town is small and modern, with every available model, color and size displayed to facilitate self-service. Incidentally all the shops are owned by Carrano.

The two other Valentina locations are at Via San Pietro all'Orto 17 (telephone 78.25.20) in the Duomo/Vittorio Emanuele neighborhood, and at Corso Europa 18 (telephone 79.90.31).

FASHION

MEN'S & WOMEN'S

Tailored Chic

19 BARDELLI 🛍🛍🛍🛍

Corso Magenta 13
Tel. 80.68.43
Expensive; credit cards accepted
Open during lunch

An entire palazzo is dedicated to serving the young Milanese managers and bankers who have a taste for traditional British and Italian fashion. Men and women are guaranteed impeccable quality in fabrics and workmanship; here they can find everything from ultra-soft cashmere sweaters to British raincoats, from elegant shoes to undergarments. The hushed and understated atmosphere is not very conducive to browsing and can be uncomfortable for the customer without the inclination or budget to pay what the wealthy Milanese do. In a recent attempt to add a fresh breath of fashion, Bardelli has brought in such famous names as Ralph Lauren, les Copains, Basile and Bogie. This is also an excellent place for the custom fitting of an elegant tuxedo or suit.

WINES

20 PROVERA
Corso Magenta 7
Tel. 80.50.522
Moderate; no credit cards accepted

Three generations of a wine-loving family have run this fine old *enoteca* since 1927. You can buy by the glass

Provera carries on a spirited tradition.

from a restricted though impressive variety of wines; by the bottle there is no end to the selection. Special attention is given to Italian wines, particularly from the northern regions of Piemonte, Friuli, the Veneto and the Alto Adige. It's a pleasant place to engage in your own personal *degustazione,* with the help of the knowledgeable Signor Pietro Provera or his wife Aurelia. No food is served, but there are some tables where you can relax and enjoy the traditional surroundings.

JEWELRY

21 FALLIVA PANIZZA
Corso Magenta 5
Tel. 80.48.29
Expensive; no credit cards accepted
Closed Monday

Patronized for generations by Milan's discriminating jewelry devotees, Panizza maintains a reputation for high-quality, artistic production in a refined and unusual style. Handworked gold is fashioned into classic shapes with enough of a Panizza twist to make them individualized and modern. Uncommon semiprecious stones are used in elegant settings at prices that are moderate for such imaginative pieces. Customers enjoy the charming environment of the early 1900s, with dark wooden fixtures and stained-glass windows.

SUSTENANCE

RISTORANTE/TRATTORIA

22 LA BRISA
Via Brisa 15
Tel. 87.20.01
Moderate; credit cards accepted
Closed Saturday, and Sunday lunch

It's best to reserve, especially if the weather is warm and La Brisa has opened its delightful garden and veranda for spacious dining. The menu is traditional and genuine (and it changes every day), but expect the chef's very inventive imagination to lighten the evening. There is good risotto in the wintertime, and a cold rice salad with *rucola* (arugula) in the summertime. Try the unusual *carpaccio di pesce spada* (swordfish), seasoned with oil, lemon and herbs; the *riso all'indiana* (rice with curry and greens); the *rognoncino* (kidneys) with curry or any of the delicious vegetarian entrées. A good wine list is available, and delicious desserts are made on the premises of this charming restaurant, located on a quiet street off the busy Corso Magenta.

COSTUME JEWELRY

High-Fashion Fantasy Bijoux

23 PELLINI BIJOUX 🛍🛍🛍🛍
Via Morigi 9
Tel. 86.90.178
Moderate; credit cards accepted

See for yourself this 18th-century treasure chest of a store, especially if you're one to thrill at ingenious, bold and spirited bijoux. The young and striking Donatella Pellini is a forerunner of each season's look in accessories; her bauble or bejeweled bangle often accents the runway collections of Europe's finest *prêt-à-porter* fashion. Her jewels hover between the avant-garde and the ethnic; she works with pearls and rhinestones as well as interesting plastics and metals. Most popular are her earrings and matching bracelets in bold dimensions, which can transform a simple dress

Pellini Bijoux, always a forerunner.

into a statement on style. In addition to her own conversational bijoux, Donatella offers a collection of art-deco pieces, hatpins from the turn of the century, jewels from the 1930s and from the Victorian period, and other *trouvailles* that her discerning eye has fallen upon in her travels. She has recently added some gift items of her own design—lovely glassware, frames, gloves and boxes.

PERFUMES & COSMETICS

Original Empire-Style Interior

24 VECCHIA MILANO
Via San Giovanni sul Muro 8
Tel. 87.36.51
Moderate; no credit cards accepted

Even if you're not in need of a new lipstick, find any excuse to stop by and take a peek at the frescoed ceilings of the city's most elegant *profumeria*. You'll experience Milan shopping as it was over 100 years ago. Vecchia Milano is furnished in its original 19th-century Empire style, with dark wood, glass-fronted cabinets and fine marble-topped counters trimmed with classical motifs in gilt bronze. Today the shop carries a distinguished line of mostly European cosmetics and perfumes.

SUSTENANCE

RISTORANTE/TRATTORIA

25 LE QUATTRO MORI
Via San Giovanni sul Muro 2
Tel. 87.06.17
Expensive; credit cards accepted
Closed Sunday, and Saturday lunch

As noteworthy as the menu is the
décor: a marvelous and expansive garden in the summertime and a warm
and welcoming dining room when the
weather turns cool, with antique
bread bins and winepress. To name
just two suggestions, try the *risotto
con grancevola* (spider crab) or the
trenette al curry (flat noodles with
curry). Fresh seafood plays an important role in the second-course offerings, such as the *moscardini fritti*
(small squid, fried) and the *orata al
cartoccio* (sea bream garnished with
herbs and baked in a foil envelope).
Of the many excellent meats, you
might sample the *lombatina alla car-
ciofara* (veal loin with artichokes).
The *cantina* and homemade desserts
here are impressive.

BOOKS

English-Language

26 AMERICAN BOOKSTORE
Via Camperino 16 (at Largo Cairoli)
Moderate; credit cards accepted
Open during lunch

Adriano Lavino couldn't be born
American, but at least he could open
an American bookshop—and make a
grand success of it. Exceptionally
well-stocked in both fiction and nonfiction paperbacks as well as in illustrated nonfiction hardcovers, the
American Bookstore will keep you
supplied during your trip with guidebooks and best sellers galore. The
staff expects you to browse and allay
any pangs of nostalgia for things
American—a delightful way to spend
a free hour when the rest of the city is
closed for lunch. If you're more hurried, rely upon the accommodating
young sales assistants, who can find
you anything in their stock on a certain subject, even if you can't remember the title. In the back room is the
owner's hobby and specialty, a collection of English-language antique
books also for sale.

SUSTENANCE

BAR-CAFFÈ

Traditional Pasticceria

27 MARCHESI
Via Santa Maria alla Porta 11/A
Tel. 87.67.30
Moderate; no credit cards accepted
Closed Monday; open during lunch

There's no seating area, but that
hasn't stopped the Milanese from fre-
quenting this old-world *pasticceria*
for generations. Exquisite chocolates,
pralines, chocolate-covered nuts and

Marchesi is a daily rite for many milanesi.

creams are displayed on silver trays lined with doilies, while fresh plum cakes, Venetian pastries and buttery croissants are snatched up by Milanese sipping a coffee at the bar during the rite of between-meal breaks. Pink-and-white-uniformed ladies will help you with your choice of sweet gifts: *marrons glacés* decorated with tiny candied violets, or other elegantly packaged goodies. If you're there at Christmas time, try the Marchesi specialty, *panettone* (Milan's favorite holiday treat) filled with fresh Chantilly cream.

ANTIQUES

Neoclassical & Marble

28 GIAN CARLO RICCO

Via Santa Maria alla Porta 11
Tel. 87.59.56
Very expensive; credit cards accepted

Gian Carlo Ricco is de rigueur *for neoclassical.*

There is no finer nor more extensive collection of neoclassical antiques in Milan than at Gian Carlo Ricco's. It's hard to match such a prodigious selection from the late-18th- and early-19th-century Empire, Charles X, Directoire and Biedermeier styles. Every piece is choice, some are in rich blond wood, and all have distinctive gilt-bronze trim. In addition to the furniture, there are objects in the same style, such as candelabra and clocks, as well as a number of handsome Pre-Raphaelite paintings. Just next door is the sister shop, L'Obelisco, which specializes in marble for the home from the 15th century to the Neoclassical period. In optimal condition and beautifully displayed as if in a garden of marble are busts, benches, statues, columns, capitals, fountains and fireplace mantels. Shipping can be arranged.

TOYS

Educational & Great Design

29 LA CITTÀ DEL SOLE 🛢🛢🛢🛢

Via Dante 13
Tel. 80.60.68
Moderate; credit cards accepted

From a country in love with its precious *bambini* comes a toy store par excellence that will enthrall both the adult shopper and the child recipient. La Città del Sole is a great place to find "intelligent toys" of top design requiring skill and dexterity. Imported toys from all over Europe brighten the large and modern store, and years of success as the city's prime supplier of diversions and games have recently encouraged the company to introduce its own Il Leccio line of wooden puzzles and toys.

The store was founded 15 years ago by Carlo Basso, a Harvard-educated father of twins who wanted solid toys with a lot of play value. Dottore Basso's eye for design is evident in many of the toys; there are also two series of children's books, by Bruno Munari and Enzo Mari, produced by Danese —nice introductions to Milanese design as interpreted for the youngster. Sleek red-and-green wooden yo-yos slip easily into the corners of your suitcase; or bring home Italy's famous monuments for the young architect, miniature paper cutouts of Florence's Duomo or Pisa's Leaning Tower. "Italia" is a memory game, where you score points Pinocchio by Pinocchio and gondola by gondola. Another branch of La Città del Sole is appropriately located nearby at Via dei Meravigli 7 ("Street of Marvels"); it specializes in *giochi per adulti* (games for adults).

FASHION

CHILDREN'S

30 PRÉNATAL
Via Dante 7
Tel. 80.25.35
Moderate; credit cards accepted

The Prénatal chain comprises 100 delightful stores throughout Italy offering fashion for children up to eight years of age and for expectant mothers. The Prénatal focus is on children's clothes—a wide selection of active clothing and coordinated accessories for little fashion plates. In a big, high-tech space, the outfits arc displayed hanging against the walls for easy browsing and self-service. The merchandise often reflects the colors and looks of the moment in adult fashion, for tykes who want to dress like their parents. There are miniature sweaters, jeans and overalls in every color, as well as party dresses and outerwear. Adorable hats, umbrellas, socks, gloves and belts—along with just about everything else in the store—make great gifts at moderate prices. There's a special nursery line for the first months of baby's life, with matching sets of stretchies, towels, sheets, bibs, socks and booties.

You'll also find Prénatal shops in Florence, Venice and Rome.

SUSTENANCE

RISTORANTE/TRATTORIA

31 ROVELLO
Via Rovello 18
Tel. 86.43.96
Moderate; credit cards accepted
Closed Sunday, and Saturday lunch

Directly across the street from the *trattoria* Al Piccolo Teatro, this small and charming restaurant has recently come under the expert and enthusiastic management of a new, young owner. There is an excellent array of *antipasti*, but don't miss the pâté or the homemade pastas such as ravioli with *zafferano* (saffron) or *salmone* (salmon), and gnocchi with a delicate basil-based shrimp sauce. Also recommended are the meats and fish on the grill with herbs or wild mushrooms, and the delicious desserts such as streudels, mousses and sorbets, all made on the premises. There can never be too many cooks in the kitchen, as Rovello's three expert chefs will affirm. Choose from an excellent wine list, and if they're on the menu, don't miss the owner's homemade *cioccolatini* (after-dinner chocolates).

SUSTENANCE

RISTORANTE/TRATTORIA

Taxi Away

32 AIMO E NADIA

Via Montecuccoli 6 (off map)
Tel 41.68.86
Expensive; credit cards accepted
Closed Sunday

Nadia is today considered one of Italy's finest cooks, and her husband Aimo one of its most daring restaurateurs. Who else would open a modest *trattoria* in the nondescript periphery of Milan and expect anyone to come? Yet the utterly authentic, pure Italian cuisine rediscovered and interpreted by this talented couple draws a savvy Milanese crowd time and again. Most vegetables are grown in the small garden behind the *trattoria*. The clever use of these, the knowledgeable addition of fresh herbs and the savory presence of extra-virgin olive oil hint of Aimo and Nadia's Tuscan roots. While the menu changes every day, certain favorites often remain: a warm pâté made of *fegati di coniglio* (rabbit livers), scampi, or *fiori di zucca* (zucchini blossoms); hot ricotta cheese with bitter *rucola;* a gently spicy spaghetti dish with onion and hot pepper; and a delicious *risotto con tartufo e fior di zucca* (with truffles and pumpkin blossoms). For entrées, there is fresh fish prepared in a number of imaginative ways, such as *rombo con carciofi* (turbot with artichokes) and *dentice* (bream) or *pesce spada* (swordfish) with black olives. Aimo's unerring taste holds for his wine selection as well, and the exceptional desserts are another of Nadia's passions.

SUSTENANCE

RISTORANTE/TRATTORIA

Taxi Away

33 FRANCA, PAOLA E LELE

Viale Certosa 235 (off map)
Tel. 30.52.38
Moderate; no credit cards accepted
Closed Saturday, Sunday and Monday

While Lele relentlessly roams northern Italy in quest of special, hard-to-find ingredients, mamma Franca and wife Paola are in the kitchen whipping up some of Milan's most creative food. This tiny and genial *trattoria* seats a mere 30, many of them from the discovery-happy fashion world (it is not far from the site of Milan's International Trade Fair). But Franca has been here for over half a century, making her own delicious salamis, cold cuts and pâtés from her small farm in the south. From there come most of her fresh herbs and vegetables as well. Soups are recommended, especially the leek, *fior de zucca* (pumpkin blossom), lentil or chunky minestrone. Small gnocchi are prepared with a light cream *porcini* sauce or with *carciofi* (artichokes), and the homemade lasagna has a distinct chicory flavor. But save room for the daily-changing entrées such as *vitello con peperoni* (veal with peppers), *anitra con mirtilli* (duck with a light blueberry sauce), or tender *manzo con cipolle* (steak with onions). For such wonders in such a delightful setting, it's necessary to book in advance.

Porta Ticinese

*O*nly in recent years has Porta Ticinese offered an alternative to shopping in downtown Milan. Neighborhood color survives comfortably alongside the avant-garde, and a subtle anti-establishment tone is tempered by a talented design energy that grows ever more evident. Like Brera, the Porta Ticinese area was (and largely still is) a *quartiere popolare* (working-class area), now on its way to being regentrified. The curious blend of these components gives a special character to this neighborhood.

If you take the Via Torino beyond Largo Carrobbio, you will find yourself at the Corso di Porta Ticinese. Here is one of the precious few vestiges of ancient Milan: a row of sixteen Roman columns dating back to the 2nd century A.D. The quarter has today become a meeting spot for the young bohemians of Milan, a peculiar juxtaposition of antiquity with avant-gardism. The Corso di Porta Ticinese that stretches beyond this point is experiencing a renewed popularity. Not slick, but full of atmosphere, this pleasant area is where it's happening for young artisanal studios. Parallel to the Corso di Porta Ticinese is the Corso Genova, where the trendy fashion store Biffi draws an interested crowd.

Interest these days is focused on the area south of the Porta Ticinese itself (the gate for which the street is named and whose location is sometimes noted on maps as the Piazzale 24 Maggio). Here the Corso di Porta Ticinese becomes the Corso San Gottardo. West of this busy and lively street is the Navigli, or canal area. Considered the *periferia* (outskirts) in Milan's recent past, this part of the city has a more open and

Footbridges, eclectic shopping and quiet canals keep Porta Ticinese a neighborhood apart.

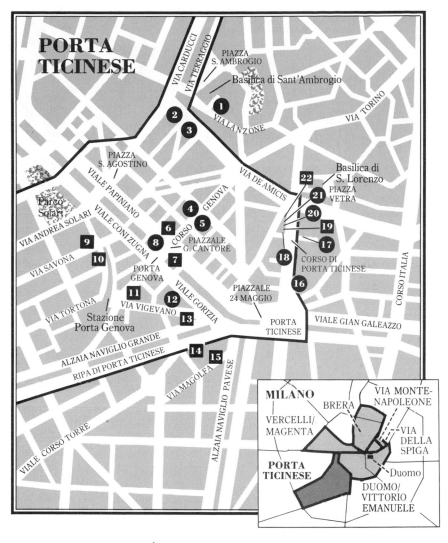

uncrowded layout. Footbridges link quays lined with small boutiques, secondhand shops and workshops, where a new generation of crafts-people and avant-garde designers are luring a young and savvy crowd. A number of important outdoor markets take place in the canal area (see page 153).

The Navigli nightlife is giving favored Brera some serious competition. There are intimate wine bars, inn-like taverns and beer houses, refined *trattorie* and restaurants; and *gelaterie* and bar-cafés often keep their tables out until the wee hours if the evening is warm. Jazz and piano bars make music a natural component of the evening's enjoyment.

WORKSHOP/STUDIO

1 PILGIO
Via Lanzone 23
Tel. 80.69.64
Moderate; credit cards accepted

Those who love the daring and extravagant in jewelry design should visit the young and talented Antonio Piluso. Each piece is artistic while unusual, primitive while modern, and always in good taste. Traditional materials like gold and silver join with plexiglass, elephant skin, feathers, copper, bronze and precious and semiprecious stones to create one-of-a-kind necklaces, bracelets, earrings and pins. Antonio often works with his customers to create unique pieces, and will rework any materials you bring him, such as loose stones or old gold pieces in disuse. The shop looks like someone's living room, and you can peep into Antonio's workshops, which is located just beyond the back door.

WOMEN'S

With a '50s Twist

2 BIANCA E BLU
Via de Amicis 53
Tel. 83.61.139
Expensive; credit cards accepted

For afficionados of fun fashion, Bianca e Blu is a must-see. Monica Bolzoni designs her original and feminine fashion using "conversational" antique fabrics and silhouettes from the 1940s and 50s. Set in a postmodern shop, the look is surprisingly contemporary; it is for the woman

Must-see fun fashion at Bianca e Blu.

who wants to create her own personal style. Monica also offers all the necessary accoutrements—matching hats, gloves, belts and scarves. Monica's hats, together with her one-of-a-kind romantic fashions, have long been featured in European fashion magazines. You can even buy a hatbox in a matching fabric to store your accessory. Monica, who used to work for Fiorucci in the States, was impressed by the American style of mixing vintage with new clothing.

Monica Bolzoni has helped to set the tone of this residential street that continues to draw new and young designers. A few doors down the street, you'll find her smaller shop featuring a less expensive line of modern jersey knit separates and markdowns.

MEN'S & WOMEN'S

Casual & Trendy

3 FRANCO FIORENTINO
Via de Amicis 51
Tel. 83.54.992
Moderate; credit cards accepted

Just next door to the popular Bianca e Blu, Franco Fiorentino offers a contemporary shoe collection that is as comfortable as it is fashionable. Some models are trendy, most are casual, and all are of good quality considering their reasonable prices. The season's colors and leathers are repeated in a number of matching casual handbags. The store is modern and inviting, with attractive window displays.

FASHION

MEN'S & WOMEN'S

Trendy, Top-Name International Fashion

4 BIFFI ▯▯▯▯
Corso Genova 6
Tel. 83.97.182
Expensive; credit cards accepted

One of the best-merchandised stores for men's and women's trendy, high fashion in all of Milan, Biffi is well worth the trip across town. Biffi's private-label creations keep up with fashion's vicissitudes, and you'll also find famous names like Azzedine Alaïa, Norma Kamali, Byblos, Gaban, Yamamoto, and Ivan e Martrie for women and Guido Pellegrini, Paul Smith, Allegri and C.P. Company for men. It's all well displayed in a big, slick, high-tech space that is conducive to browsing and self-service, although the sales help is friendly and professional. Fashion is individualized and unusual, but wearable and cleverly accessorized with hats, belts and scarves.

There's a much smaller outlet for Biffi's fashion near Piazza Repubblica that favors women's clothing. It is conveniently located near some of Milan's best hotels at Via Fabio Filzi 45 (telephone 66.86.700).

FOOD

SPECIALTY SHOP

Mushrooms & Truffles

5 FUNGHI E TARTUFI
Corso Genova 25
Tel. 83.91.327
Expensive; credit cards accepted
Closed Monday afternoon

Called simply "Mushrooms and Truffles," this small store carries these treasures gathered from all over Italy. Appreciative customers come from all parts to buy the precious *bianco d'Alba* (white truffles) that appear fresh and much awaited each September to January. *Nero di Norcia* (black truffles) from Umbria can be found all year round, and there are always pickled truffles and delicious truffle pâtés and spreads. As if these bulbous nuggets weren't ambrosia enough, there are all kinds of fresh mushrooms, from the humblest to the big, expensive *porcini,* which also come dried and packaged. There's usually a big rush at Christmastime when *tartufi,* literally worth their weight in gold, are a prized gift for gourmet friends.

Delicacies from Funghi e Tartufi.

TRUFFLES AND PORCINI MUSHROOMS

The two favorite ingredients in the Italian kitchen are probably *tartufi* (truffles) and *porcini* mushrooms. When the large wild mushrooms are in season, you will find them in most restaurants, while the costly truffle usually shows up only in more select establishments. Both can be brought back (packaged only, never fresh), as the ultimate gift for gourmet friends.

According to myth and folklore, truffles were the result of lightning striking a tree or the ground. Pliny described them as "miracles of nature." In actuality, the precious *tartufo* is a parasitical fungus that grows four to eight inches below ground among roots of oak, poplar, chestnut, hazelnut, willow and walnut trees. Black truffles, *tuber melanosporum,* are found from December through May, mostly in Piemonte and Umbria. They can be served cooked and are not considered in the same league as the rarer *tuber magnatum,* the white truffle, which is found from late September through January in northern and central Italy. The best white truffles in the country come from Piemonte and are eaten raw, sliced paper-thin on an *affettatartufi* or "mandolin,"

a special truffle slicer.

Scientists claim that the distinctive truffle perfume resembles the smell of pigs in rut. Exploiting lovesick pigs is the technique used by the French, while Italian truffle hunters, who find pigs hard to control, have selectively bred dogs for the job. With a professionally trained hound, a *trifulao* can dig up to two kilos in an evening and sell them for prices approaching that of gold. Italy's most famous truffle fair is held at Alba, in the northern region of Piemonte, every October.

The other object of the Italians' affection, the *boletus edulis* mushroom, is called *porcino,* or pig, probably because of its size. Late in August, huge baskets of these mushrooms start arriving in the open-air markets for a brief two-month period. Their mild, wild taste is pronounced when they are grilled whole, quickly fried, or used to flavor a risotto or pasta sauce. Recipes for *porcini* go back to the time of imperial Rome. Although native to most of Europe, they are still particularly loved by Italian epicures, who find them as substantial as steaks and often order them as a second course or entrée.

SUSTENANCE

GELATERIA

6 POZZI

Piazzale Generale Cantore 4
Tel. 83.99.830
Inexpensive; no credit cards accepted
Closed Monday; open till 1:00 A.M.

Big open terraces and pleasant pergolas for a *gelato* break are de rigueur for leisurely strollers in the Navigli area. Pozzi's tradition goes well back into the 19th century, when *gelato* was a novelty, a period that still colors its décor. Experience the rite of choosing from over 30 flavors of homemade ice cream, then sit for a bit or stroll on. There are all the delicious regulars, as well as unusual flavors such as *tè* (tea), *pompelmo* (grapefruit) and *liquirizia* (licorice). A delicious alternative to your after-dinner coffee or drink is the *gelato affogato* ("drowned" ice cream, smothered in coffee or liquor). A dozen *semifreddi* (whipped consistency) flavors appear in little pastries, and if diet has no meaning for you, try the artistic *coppe* (sundaes) with fresh fruit and liqueurs.

SUSTENANCE

RISTORANTE/TRATTORIA

7 AL PORTO

Piazzale Generale Cantore
Tel. 83.21.481
Moderate; no credit cards accepted
Closed Sunday, and Monday lunch

There's no more appropriate place for a wonderful seafood meal than in this old canal tollhouse, fitted with fishing nets, ropes and other authentic marine paraphernalia. Neptune controls the market's daily offerings, but you'll find all kinds of fresh fish prepared simply and superbly. Among chef Anna Buonamici's fine creations are a number of risotto and spaghetti dishes served with fish and seafood, such as *scampi alla livornese* (shrimps in a tomato sauce) and *seppie con carciofi* (cuttlefish with artichokes). There are delicious fish pâté, stuffed squid, and shellfish soups. Life moves out onto the terrace in the warm weather, where dinner finished off with a homemade *tiramisu* can approach perfection. There's a nice selection of Italian white wines.

FASHION

MEN'S, WOMEN'S & CHILDREN'S

Department Store

8 COIN

Piazzale Generale Cantore
(entrance on Corso Cristoforo Colombo)
Tel. 83.24.385
Moderate; credit cards accepted

This five-story branch is often less crowded than Milan's three other Coin department stores, and offers the same varied shopping for moderate-priced clothes, with full department-store features.

For more information, see listing for the largest Coin store in the Duomo/Vittorio Emannuele neighborhood (page 188).

SUSTENANCE

RISTORANTE/TRATTORIA

9 AURORA

Via Savona 23
Tel. 83.54.978
Moderate; credit cards accepted
Closed Monday

This delightful turn-of-the-century Liberty dining room will make Via Savona seem gloomy by comparison. The menu is a mixture of French and Piedmontese with a dash of imagination. Both the hot and cold appetizers could pass as a whole meal, as could the excellent cheese fondue. Try the sausage served with melted cheese or any of the truffle-accented dishes when in season. A traditional *piemontese* specialty is the *batsoa* (breaded pig's feet). The selection of roast and boiled meats is also typical of the region. There are fine Piedmont wines and very fine desserts.

SUSTENANCE

RISTORANTE/TRATTORIA

10 OSTERIA DEI BINARI
Via Tortona 1
Tel. 83.99.428
Expensive; credit cards accepted
Dinner only; closed Sunday

In a stereotyped quarter of Old Milan near the railway station (*binari* means tracks) is this wonderful little restaurant that has become a classic for its long popularity. It has a nice *osteria* (country inn) feeling, romantic in winter when a large fireplace warms the cozy rooms and a joy in summer with outdoor dining in the vine-covered garden. Emphasis is on dishes from the Lombardy area, with Piedmont and Liguria represented as well. Try any of the light mousses of fish or cheese; the *fegato d'oca* (goose liver) with pears, Calvados or apple vinegar, the *sella di coniglio* (saddle of rabbit) with thyme; or the excellent *anitra brasata all'arancia* (braised duck with orange). A favorite fall dish is a veal interpretation of *carpaccio;* here it is lightly cooked and topped with a healthy helping of arugula and tomatoes. A handsome red-and-chrome slicing machine is an eye-catcher; so is Gianfranco Ferrè, a frequent diner. Bocce ball courts near the garden add a neighborhood air.

SUSTENANCE

RISTORANTE/TRATTORIA

11 LA SCALETTA
Piazzale Stazione Genova 3
Tel. 83.50.290
Very expensive; credit cards accepted
Closed Sunday and Monday

Pina Bellini is in love with her work as one of Italy's finest chefs; so is her amiable son Aldo with his work as sommelier and host. This is why you'll need to reserve days in advance to eat in this small (seating about 30), refined and welcoming *ristorante* in a working-class area of Milan. "La Pina" is a genius, and her imagination appears in such creations as *baccalà* (raw cod) marinated in chives;

A hint of other times in today's new scene.

snail pâté; risotto with wild mushrooms and blueberries; ravioli made with asparagus and white truffles; ground veal in cabbage leaves; saddle of rabbit, and sliced foie gras with watercress. All are beautiful to the eye and remarkable to the palate. There are exquisite desserts and homemade ice creams (try the one made with cinnamon) and an excellent wine cellar. The experience is more than worth the high prices. Be careful not to miss the entrance; there's no sign, just a gate as reference point.

DESIGN GALLERY
FURNITURE, FASHION & ART

12 ZEUS
Via Vigevano 8
Tel. 83.73.257
Moderate to expensive; credit cards
    accepted
Open during lunch

Zeus is a dynamic team of many talents sharing a similar point of view on design, fashion and applied arts. The fashion boutique of dark, avant-garde clothing is directly on the street, but to get to the design studio, Zeus' most interesting division, go through the gates and across the courtyard. A gallery setting offsets the clever mélange of original and often countercurrent design. Furniture and lamps are no-frills, almost skeletal in shape. Sleek chairs and tables offer proof that such individuality need not belong to a signature showroom. The Zeus Gallery also hosts exhibits of young international avant-garde designers and artists in all media from photography to sculpture. Opening evenings are social and fun and open to design enthusiasts

(call or write for the schedule). Zeus prides itself on this direct connection with the public, a finger on the pulse of what's happening in design.

SUSTENANCE
RISTORANTE/TRATTORIA

13 POSTO DI CONVERSAZIONE
Alzaia Naviglio Grande 6
Tel. 83.26.646
Moderate; no credit cards accepted
Dinner only; closed Monday

As conducive to conversation as its name promises, this is a pretty, wooden-beamed restaurant along the canal. It has earned its reputation for fine cuisine with a menu that begins with hot or cold appetizers and risotto or *crespelle* (crêpes) as a first course. Steak fillets come with a number of interesting cream sauces: *paprika dolce* (sweet paprika), *fichi secchi* (dried figs) and *ginepro* (juniper). *Carpaccio* also comes with a number of inventive sauces, and an unusual, barely cooked *doppio carpaccio* (double-decker) comes stuffed with *gamberetti* (shrimp), *noci e finocchi* (nuts and fennel) or mozzarella and *rucola.* Lettuce lovers will adore the big salads that contain everything from apples to the omnipresent *carpaccio.* Nice wines.

SUSTENANCE
RISTORANTE/TRATTORIA

14 SADLER—OSTERIA DI PORTA CICCA
Ripa di Porta Ticinese 51
Tel. 83.24.451
Expensive; credit cards accepted
Closed Sunday

A savvy young Naviglio crowd frequents this new and suddenly fashionable restaurant opened by chef Claudio Sadler and his wife Vittoria. Accolades go to their devotion to detail, from the low lighting and sleek grey-and-pink modern interior to the presentation of the carefully prepared food. Homemade pastas are both traditional and novel, such as a *maccheroni di pane*, made with bread and sauced with clams. There are fresh sturgeon, steamed salmon and smoked fish served with zucchini, and an unusual duck dish with fresh dates. A helpful *degustazione* menu lets you sample much of this, accompanied by a number of knowledgeably selected wines. The opulent chocolate-coffee dessert rivals the homemade *sorbetto di fragola* (strawberry sorbet).

SUSTENANCE

RISTORANTE/TRATTORIA

15 LA MAGOLFA
Via Magolfa 15
Tel. 83.21.696
Moderate; no credit cards accepted
Dinner only; closed Sunday

Time seems to have stopped in this characteristic Old Milan *trattoria*. An outside veranda extends over a small canal, and downtown Milan seems light-years away. The menu consists of traditional Milanese specialties. Recommended are the *risotto al peperone* (with sweet bell peppers) and the veal *involtini* (thin slices rolled, then lightly braised in butter and oil). What really counts is the ambiance, though; if you're lucky the guitar and harmonica will appear, and everyone will join in with old favorites and a romantic ballad or two.

SHOES

WOMEN'S

Fun & Casual

16 PANCA
Corso di Porta Ticinese 103
Tel. 83.21.361
Inexpensive; credit cards accepted

Fun and fashionable footwear from Panca is inexpensive and hard to resist. If you like flats, this is a great place to buy a season's worth.

For other locations, see Shoe-Shopping Directory to Milan (page 232).

HOME

HOUSEWARES & TABLETOP ACCESSORIES

Design Conscious

17 HIGH-TECH 🥛🥛🥛🥛
Corso di Porta Ticinese 77
Tel. 83.51.263
Moderate; credit cards accepted

You'll find high-tech everything for the house, from kitchen utensils to sleek bedroom furniture. High-Tech is actually two adjacent stores: one is a very clean, black showroom that features functional objects from around the world, including many that are in the permanent collection of New York's Museum of Modern Art. Each piece, from a razor to a desk set, is recognized for its design sensibility. There also is a small selection of furniture and stainless-steel kitchen units. The adjacent housewares store is lined in steel shelving with the latest housewares for the kitchen, chosen for High-Tech with the collaboration of professional chefs. There are a polychromatic assortment of espresso makers in every color and size,

French copper cookware, chef's knives with red-and-green plastic handles from Sanelli, modern porcelain from Richard-Ginori, and stainless steel from Alessi and others. Many of the products have been exported, but are available here at a savings.

GIFTS
HAND-PAINTED KIDS' ACCESSORIES

18 PREM LEGNODIPINTO
Corso di Porta Ticinese 76
Tel. 83.72.934
Moderate; credit cards accepted

This tiny shop is awash with bright, hand-painted wooden accessories in bold primary colors. Rows and rows of tiny earrings and coordinated hair clips come in the shape of polka-dotted bow ties, ice-cream cones, sea horses and flowers. Prem's whimsical, carefully painted artwork is as popular with pre-teens as with spirited women who have decided to remain young, at least at heart. There are also wooden piggy banks, clock cases, frames, decorative clowns, and buckles with colored elastic belts—all signed by the young artist, "Prem," who also operates this charming shop. Success has spawned three new shops in other areas of the city.

Hand-painted whimsy at Prem Legnodipinto.

SUSTENANCE
RISTORANTE/TRATTORIA
Late-Night

19 OSTERIA DELL'OPERETTA
Corso di Porta Ticinese 70
Tel. 83.75.120
Moderate; credit cards accepted
Closed Sunday

This is where Porta Ticinese nightlife got its start just a decade ago. With a small, popular bar set in postmodern surroundings, this *osteria* offers its loyal habitués the chance to stop in for a drink, or to stay for a delicious meal of *verdure ripiene* (stuffed vegetables) or fresh *tagliatelline* with a delicate pesto or cream-of-mushroom sauce. The menu changes weekly, but you'll always find crêpes, risotto, salads and *carpaccio*. On a number of evenings with live jazz music, you can come just for an Irish coffee, hot chocolate or cognac, and linger until the house closes at 2:00 A.M.

LEATHERGOODS
BAGS & ACCESSORIES
Handmade, Casual Fashion

20 LO GNOMO
Corso di Porta Ticinese 70
Tel. 83.75.163
Inexpensive; credit cards accepted

Who wouldn't appreciate these very good prices for fashionable casual bags? There are original artisan designs in large, easy bags made of natural untanned leather (*cuoio*) dyed in many bold fashion colors. Bright canvas is also used, sometimes plasticized and sometimes with prints. It's a plain, rustic shop that comes alive with its imaginative display of bags, totes, knapsacks, schoolbags, belts and sandals, all made on the premises by young artisans—not by busy little gnomes, as the name of the shop implies.

GIFTS

FABRICS & ACCESSORIES

21 NAJ OLEARI
Corso di Porta Ticinese 58
Tel. 83.99.857
Expensive; credit cards accepted

This was the first of many delightful and colorful Naj Oleari stores to open in Milan. It was considered a rather audacious strategy when the neighborhood was still transitional.

This is a small-scale version of the Naj Oleari wonderland you'll find at the Brera location (see page 247).

SUSTENANCE

GELATERIA

22 GELATERIA ECOLOGICA
Corso di Porta Ticinese 40
Tel. 83.51.872
Inexpensive; no credit cards accepted
Open 7 days a week from March to October

A pilgrimage here is obligatory for the true ice-cream lover. The name says it all: no preservatives, all-natural flavors, strictly fresh fruits, and not an artificial color to be seen. The

The nearby 12th-century Basilica Sant'Ambrogio.

gelateria draws a loyal crowd with its reputation for authentic-tasting, out-of-the-ordinary flavors such as chestnut, date, rhubarb, yogurt, honey and sesame (said to have been around since Homer), wheat germ, green apple, and whatever else is in season at the time. There's no sign outside and no seating inside, but you can stop in until midnight.

INDEX TO STORES
LISTED BY PRODUCT

The following index of stores in Milan is arranged by product category so that you can quickly find stores of particular interest to you. In each category, stores are grouped by neighborhood (DVE = Duomo/Vittorio Emanuele, M = Via Montenapoleone, S = Via della Spiga, B = Brera, VM = Vercelli/Magenta, PT = Porta Ticinese); the number following this designation is the store's location code on the neighborhood map and also represents the order in which the store is listed. Page numbers are provided for reference to the stores' decriptions in the text. An asterisk (*) means the store is usually open during lunch.

ROME

Roma

*E*ternal Rome is one of the few cities in the Western world that can boast two and a half millennia of history and artistic development. For shoppers, Rome's special beauty lies in the fact that shopping and culture are delightfully inextricable.

Rome offers big-city and small-town shopping at once. There's a sense of colorful conviviality in the hustle and bustle of Via del Corso and other major arteries, but in the small, winding *vicoli* where open *botteghe* pour out onto the cobblestones, the silence is broken only by the steady hammer of woodworkers' tools. This dichotomous character is evident as well in the curious compatibility of the ancient with the modern, the monumental with the mundane, genius with disorder. Rome gives the impression of a very busy city of leisurely citizens, whose raucous, chaotic activity magically ends when the sacred siesta hour arrives. The flow of Roman life creates a remarkable stage set—an age-old comparison that is inevitable in Rome, where the love of display is inborn.

"*Italia meridionale*," or Southern Italy, begins in Rome. A day in Milan, to the north, would bring the contrast into sharp focus for the innocent foreigner who thinks there is only one Italy. Although capital of the government, the Church, and the television and film industries, Rome is a city strangled by bureaucratic complications and does not pretend to offer Milanese efficiency. Romans consider the Milanese too obsessed with punctuality, money and hard work. In fact, the expression "*Roma, non basta una vita*" ("One lifetime is not enough for Rome") may well have been coined to describe the long periods of insufferable waiting between plausible promises and actual delivery—a complaint probably as old as Rome itself. The ubiquitous city seal of Rome with the initials "S.P.Q.R.," for *Senatus Populusque Romanus* (The Senate and People of Rome), has long been interpreted by the Milanese as *Sono Pigri Questi Romani* ("These Romans are lazy"). Life moves to a different rhythm in Rome, and you'll do best to sit back, relax, enjoy the leisurely tempo and, as an inspired St. Ambrose advised St. Augustine some 1500 years ago, do as the Romans do.

You'll embrace most of the city's other Southern tendencies far more readily—the vivacious street life, the outdoor dining, the amusingly staged diatribes, the earthy open-air market scenes and the warm-hearted openness of the local *civis Romanus* who regards his citizenship as a priceless privilege. When a store owner offers you a spirited soliloquy, hoping you'll buy two, you may remember that one of the most important areas of ancient Roman education was oratory. As long as you're not driving in it, you may also marvel at the hopelessly snarled traffic jams and the dauntless Fiat drivers who race about with the valor of quick-witted gladiators. Everything and nothing has changed over the millennia.

Since remote, almost mythical ancient times, Rome has been a major shopping mecca. The Forum, identified with the city's legendary founding by Romulus in 753 B.C., was the nucleus of daily life and the shopping center of the ancient world. Visitors to today's Rome will constantly happen upon traces of a magnificent history that boggle their 20th-century imaginations but leave most Romans proudly unfazed. A sleek contemporary design store may be housed in a Renaissance palazzo built with stones plundered from the Colosseum. Young goldsmiths use precious ancient Roman coins as pendants; artisans covered with marble dust re-create the timeless perfection of Ionic capitals to meet the demand from today's postmodern decorators. Rome offers a fascinating amalgam of styles, a bewildering collage wherein lies its fascination.

Under the very streets you stroll slumber the remains of a vanished world, stratum upon stratum of ancient stones, bones and artifacts, barely touched by the archeologist's spade, that lead backwards through the centuries to the dawn of history. The historical stratification continues vertically, above ground as well. In picturesque disorder, you'll see medieval buildings leaning against Renaissance palazzos; built for worldly cardinals and flourishing merchant families, their façades incorporate classic Roman columns and their foundations rest upon imperial ruins.

Much of the architecture you see today is a testament to zealous papal power, when a second city grew out of the ancient ruins to surpass

A sweeping view of the Castel Sant'Angelo, which holds sway over Rome's Tiber River.

the splendor of its classical past. Rome's heritage would always be two-fold, from its dual role as the seat first of the Roman emperors, then of the Popes.

The 15th century was Rome's Golden Age, when the Popes, recently back from Avignon after the Great Schism, were patrons of the arts on a grand scale, like the wealthy Medici of Florence. Neither group had particularly spiritual motives. The Popes attracted and supported artists, artisans, architects and scholars to beautify and culturally enrich a city that was indeed proving eternal. Their 17th-century successors gave birth to the baroque movement; personalities like Gianlorenzo Bernini, architect and sculptor known for his splendid statuary and elaborate fountains, best symbolize the spirit of that age.

Then, as now, the city acted as an alluring magnet for streams of pious and commercial pilgrims from every corner of the globe. Such religious tourism has always been Rome's thriving industry; it was a city of small businesses and skilled artisans who offered services and souvenirs to those who came for the Church's periodic jubilees, to procure a guarantee of salvation.

Some of Rome's most important streets and bridges were first straightened, widened and embellished to impress the multitudes of wide-eyed pilgrims on their way to the Vatican, herding them along in the right direction, lest they get lost or sidetracked in the warren of winding medieval alleyways. The contemporary shopper's peregrinations are not very different from those of the pilgrims who passed this way before. For close to 2000 years, visitors have strolled down the busy Via del Corso (last extension of the ancient Via Flaminia and one of the many roads that led to Rome), contributed to the babel of foreign tongues, made the obligatory visit to St. Peter's, did a little souvenir shopping, and took a welcome break for sore feet in a local tavern.

Walking has always been the best way to navigate Rome. Unlike most Italian cities, Rome has no self-contained historical center, or *centro storico*—except the city itself. Traveling on a sweltering Roman bus isn't the party it's cracked up to be, and stalwart explorers can reach any likely destination in town, with the possible exception of the Vatican, on foot. An occasional visitor, in fact, never makes it to the Vatican at all, but no one misses the Piazza di Spagna. This is the heart of town, where the sidewalks and streets have been given back to the pedestrians, whose traffic can at times be as congested as that on wheels. It is the first port of call for shoppers, an integral part of the Roman experience.

Rome's couture salons and most of its deluxe shops can be found here, lining narrow, straight streets that create a grid at the foot of the monumental triple staircase. Romans and visitors alike stroll up one street and down the next, past sophisticated windows displaying Italy's finest design in everything from fashion to home furnishings. These large, spacious and expensive boutiques are air-conditioned oases that invite you in off the street for a leisurely respite. Shoppers who appreciate convenience love the concentration of shops, the handsome displays, the sales help accustomed to foreign languages and needs, and the diversity of merchandise within a few square cobblestoned blocks.

The adventurer will love the vastly different atmosphere of less pretentious, more authentic neighborhoods like those of Campo dei Fiori and Piazza Navona. Their strategic location, in a bend of the gently curving Tiber River just this side of the Vatican, led early pilgrims and tourists to lodge there, establishing the area as the city's first commercial hub and spawning small clusters of artisan communities. The artisans are still there, supporting a flourishing antiques trade or working on their own. Their expertise in handcrafted goods gives a unique quality to *"lo shopping"* in these neighborhoods.

Your predominant impression of the Romans will be their prodigious talent for pleasure. Whether in a small family-run shop or at the daily *mercato* in Campo dei Fiori, you'll experience their special *gioia di vivere*, first nurtured by the incorrigible hedonists who were their imperial ancestors. It is infectious, and if you fall into the spirit of it, you'll echo Stendhal's words, "I realize every day that my heart is Italian." Never feel victimized by the errant taxi driver who charges you one supplement too

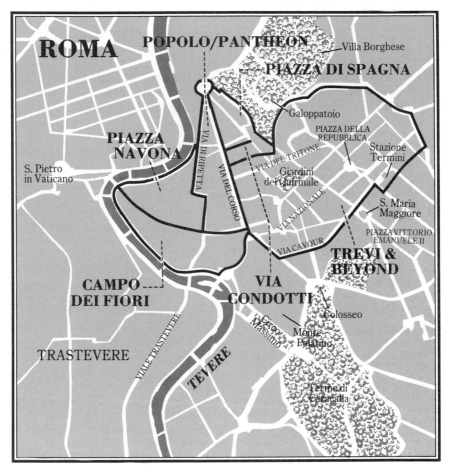

many; a hundred other Romans will redeem him by opening their hearts and their city to you.

Between sprees, draw up a seat and dawdle at a *caffè* that invites you, "*Siste, viator*" ("Stop, traveler"). You will enjoy street theater of award-winning caliber. People-watching, particularly women-watching, is the favorite national pastime, rivaled only by soccer and good eating, and cafés abound with well-dressed masters of the art. No one seems seriously preoccupied by the city's abiding economic plight or its legendary crushing debts. This is a city whose daily chronicle of minor events is revealed in high comedy and high drama, staged against a backdrop of historic and artistic splendor.

Be sure to consult the Designer Boutique Directory to Rome on page 348 for a complete listing of designer boutique addresses.

Shopping in Rome

STORE HOURS. With the October to June winter schedule in effect, most shops are open between 9:00 A.M. and 1:00 P.M. and from 3:30 to 7:30 P.M. They are closed all day Sunday and Monday morning.

From June through September, Rome's hottest months, morning hours stay the same, but the afternoon siesta is slightly extended to a 4:00 or even a 4:30 opening, and the evening closing is at 7:30 or 8:00 P.M. Roman shopkeepers rarely stay open during lunch in the summer months—it's just too hot! Shops are closed Saturday afternoons and all day Sunday, but open Monday morning.

Food shops are usually open from 8:30 A.M. to 1:30 P.M. and from 5:00 to 7:30 P.M.; they close Thursday afternoons in winter only.

In addition to the Italian national holidays (see page 11), many shops close on April 21 for Rome's birthday. Flickering Roman candles (large candles with many wicks) lining the sweeping Michelangelo-designed staircase and roof of the Capitoline Hill create a memorable sight.

BANK HOURS. All banks are open Monday through Friday from 8:30 A.M. to 1:30 P.M., and some reopen briefly from 2:45 to 3:45 P.M. One of the few exceptions, the Banca Nazionale del Lavoro (Via Veneto 11, telephone 47.50.421) is open 8:30 A.M. to 6:00 P.M., Monday through Saturday. Another exception, conveniently located in the Piazza di Spagna, is the American Service Bank at Piazza Mignanelli 15, open 8:30 A.M. to 6:30 P.M. Monday through Saturday. The centrally located American Express office (Piazza di Spagna 38, telephone 67.64.1) is open Saturday morning as well, from 9:00 A.M. to 12:30 P.M.; its weekday nonstop schedule from 9:00 A.M. to 5:30 P.M. always comes in handy. If you're a cardholding member, you can also cash personal checks from your American bank. A number of affiliated Italian banks will give you Italian currency against your Visa account, including many branches of the Banca d'America e d'Italia. One of the most centrally located is at Largo Tritone 161 (telephone 67.181). The central Banca del Fucino (Via Tomacelli 106, telephone 67.93.237) offers the same service, as does the Banca Nazionale Agricoltura (Via del Corso 518, telephone 67.83.657, and Piazza della Rotonda 1—in front of the Pantheon—telephone 65.41.268). There are a number of exchange bureaus (*cambi*) around town. The one at the Stazione Termini (central train station) is open till 9:00 P.M. weekdays and Saturday and until 2:00 P.M. on Sunday and holidays. Be prepared for a long wait.

GETTING AROUND. Despite its sprawling image, you can easily explore Rome's interesting sites and shops on foot. This is a blessing, as one look at the honking, snarled traffic jams will confirm. A subway system, La Metropolitana, runs below ground in an attempt to avoid what has become a severe municipal problem; geared mainly toward suburbanites working in the city, it is still in its

Dauntless artisan delivers his newest creation.

infancy, since every ten feet of digging yields another set of ancient ruins. The subway cars can get unpleasantly hot in the summertime and, with the exception of the Linea A connecting the Vatican (Ottaviano station) with the Piazza di Spagna, it's not a particularly convenient manner of getting from one shopping neighborhood to another. Buses are best avoided during rush hours, when professional pickpockets are at their busiest. The ancient adage, *"Noli me tangere, cives Romanus sum"* ("Do not touch me, I am a Roman citizen"), does not seem to apply to tourists.

You can hail a yellow taxi anywhere in Rome, and taxi stands are spread throughout the city. Most principal piazzas (except those closed to traffic) have taxi ranks, such as Piazzas Barberini, Venezia, San Silvestro, and Piazza di Spagna. You'll pay for distance as well as time, and meters are not always adjusted to reflect frequent rate increases. Also expect to pay supplements for evenings, Sundays and holidays, luggage and trips to the airport. A 24-hour radio taxi service can be reached at 49.94, 38.75, or 35.70.

Only the most intrepid and experienced motorists should consider renting a moped from Scooter-A-Long at Via Cavour 302 (telephone 67.80.206) or the Barberini Agency at Via della Purificazione 66 (telephone 46.54.85), or a bicycle from R. Collati at Via del Pellegrino 82 (telephone 65.41.084) or "I Bike Rome." With the latter, all you need to do is call 65.43.394 from 10:00 A.M. to 7:00 P.M., and bikes will be delivered to your hotel the following morning, a pleasant way to spend a traffic-calm Sunday. You can soar above it all and see the Eternal City by helicopter, a novel approach. The trip lasts about 20 minutes, and the helicopter holds up to five people (call CSA Compania one day in advance, Monday through Friday, at 81.23.017 or 81.23.754).

SHOPPING ETIQUETTE.
Southern Italy begins in Rome; most important for the shopper, this means that everything will take twice as long. You can't fight it, so decide upon your arrival to join the Romans in their slower-paced life style. Once you've seen northern Milan, you will understand something of the dichotomy in the nation's character and geography. Not all Romans are as punctual and trustworthy as they would have you believe. They are, however, generous, sympathetic, histrionic, enterprising, witty, and resourceful. The international stream of pilgrims and tourists to Rome is as

old as the Via Flaminia that brought them here, and a little universal gesticulating dissolves all language barriers. Unbridled bargaining attempts will fare best in the open-air markets where they're meant to be exercised; you'll have a better chance for a *sconto* with multiple purchases or by asking to round off the price. There's no need to tell you that bargaining is considered rather gauche in Rome's swanker boutiques, and even in small family-run shops, which uphold a sense of pride and tradition.

SHIPPING SERVICES.

If possible, you'll do best if you hold off until Florence to consolidate your shipments with Fracassi, the reliable agency listed on page 29. But you can send small packages (up to two kilos) yourself from Rome's central Post Office in Piazza San Silvestro (telephone 67.71), which is open weekdays from 8:15 A.M. to 8:00 P.M. nonstop and on Saturday from 8:15 A.M. to noon. For larger packages, you'll have to go to the Centro Pacchi branch located at Piazza dei Caprettari, near Piazza Sant'Eustachio, open from 8:15 A.M. to 3:30 P.M., Monday through Friday, and from 8:15 A.M. to noon on Saturday.

INCIDENTALS.

English-language films. Still the capital of Italian film, Rome boasts over 200 movie theaters. But only rarely do American and British movies escape professional dubbing; check the English-language periodicals listed on the facing page for films shown in English with Italian subtitles ("v.o." for *versione originale*). The small Pasquino theater in Trastevere (Vicolo del Piede 15, telephone 58.03.622) is an old, creaky moviehouse that is devoted solely to

British and American productions (showings from 4 to 11 P.M.; closed Wednesday). There is no air-conditioning (although on hot summer nights the roof opens) and movies are a few seasons behind their American releases (the most recent selections appear on weekends). The Pasquino is really for those expatriates lucky enough to live in Rome; one can run into every English-speaking person in town there.

Tourism office. The EPT (Ente Provinciale di Turismo, or Rome Tourist Agency) has an office at Via Parigi 11 (telephone 46.18.51) and a Tourists' Assistance Center at Via Parigi 5 (telephone 46.37.48). They have all information on hotels, reservations, tours, and museums. There are other branches at Fiumincino Airport and at Stazione Termini, the central railroad station.

One-hour photo service. If you're leaving tomorrow and can't wait to have your film developed back home, QSS offers a convenient one-hour service; it is centrally located near the Fontana di Trevi at Via Poli 43 (telephone 67.92.335). Or, while you're having a *gelato* in the magnificent Piazza Navona, you can drop off your film for the same one-hour developing service at Corso Vittorio Emanuele II, No. 227 (telephone 65.69.658).

Pharmacies. Drugstores (called *farmacie*) follow regular store hours. For those with American or British products and an English-speaking assistant, try Evans-Coran at Piazza di Spagna 63 (telephone 67.90.626); Geo. Baker & Co., opposite the Grand Hotel at Via Vittorio Emanuele Orlando (telephone 46.04.08); or Tucci at Via Veneto 129 (telephone 49.34.47). A dozen or so pharmacies stay open all night, alternating shifts; ask your hotel for the one nearest you. Some that regularly stay open all night are DeLuca, Via Cavour (telephone 46.00.19); Internazionale, Piazza Barberini 49 (telephone 46.29.96); and Piram, Via Nazionale 228 (telephone 46.07.54).

English-language publications. The *International Daily News* and *The Daily American* are both published in Rome, giving international and local news; they can be found early every morning from Tuesday to Sunday. The Sunday edition of the English-language *Rome International Courier* is found at convenient newsstands. *A Guest in Rome* and *This Week in Rome,* weekly magazines published in both English and Italian, provide a listing of all shops and restaurants, English-language movie schedules, cultural events and entertainment. They are sold at most kiosks in tourist areas and may be available at your hotel. A number of kiosks stay open until 9:00 P.M. Two kiosks on the Via Veneto and the one in Piazza Navona are open until midnight.

MADE-TO-MEASURE SHIRTS

Rome is the perfect destination for indulging in some made-to-measure luxury. A number of the fine artisan shirt makers here are considered the very best in Italy, a country where sartorial perfection is pursued with prodigious ardor. Most shops are quietly elegant, with bolts of fine domestic and imported shirt fabrics stacked to the ceiling.

A first fitting will often take a week, and a minimum shirt order is usually required from a first-time customer. Your order will be ready in three to four weeks and can be shipped abroad on request. Successive orders can be filled much more quickly and, since your personal pattern will be on file, will not require your presence. Shirt makers' policies vary on minimum orders.

The Italian made-to-order shirt is one of life's niceties and, for many exigent dressers, necessities. Most welcome is the customer's opportunity to express his individual style in the selection of fabrics. Less obvious, except to the lucky wearer, are the subtle nuances of fit and proportion. The shirt takes on what seems to be a personal relationship with the owner, who may never have known such comfort before.

Expect to pay accordingly for custom-ordered shirts. If you are a relatively standard fit, you may want to try the Italian ready-made shirts first; many offer much of the same tailoring expertise and such details as premium fabrics, hand-fitted collars and hand-sewn buttonholes. Italian monograms are usually discreetly placed below the left breast pocket unless you specifically request otherwise.

Roman Specialties

ENGRAVINGS

Original prints depicting Roman monuments, flora and fauna, and other interesting subjects make attractive souvenirs that travel easily. Some are hand-colored, some already mounted and framed.

Artists have always come to Rome to paint and sketch its ancient ruins. Engravers painstakingly reproduced these (and their own) images on metal plates. Considered an art in itself, metal engraving blossomed during the 17th and. 18th centuries together with Rome's publishing trade, and was soon one of the capital's most flourishing businesses. Giambattista Piranesi, an 18th-century Venetian who fell in love with Rome's splendors, became Italy's most renowned and prolific etcher, hoping to leave behind him something for posterity. He left no Roman monument unetched, producing more than 1000 engravings, including his famous "*Vedute di Roma,*" or "Views of Rome," on 135 copper plates. If you're interested in rare, first-edition prints made under the supervision of Piranesi or any other great etcher, prices can be very high and you'll need an educated eye to tell a good copy from an original. (The numerous Piranesi copies touched up by later printmakers drop in price and often in quality.) Prints done in volume by anonymous engravers still flood the unpretentious shops around the Pantheon, however, and are usually inexpensive. There is also an enjoyable open-air print market in the Piazza Fontanella Borghese; 20 stall keepers are there year-round, except on Sunday, from 10:00 A.M. to 4:00 P.M.

HIGH-CLASS FASHION

For classic and conservative fashion with an emphasis on elegance, Rome may be Italy's best shopping destination. For a variety of sartorial tastes, the spectrum here is limited by comparison with Florence and Milan. In lower-priced shops, you'll notice a Roman tendency toward showy products and mediocre quality, in contrast to the reserved and tasteful ready-to-wear that can reliably be found at higher prices. Rome is a favorite destination for demanding style observers, who gladly pay a premium for made-to-measure men's suits or shirts that are skillfully cut, stitched, shaped and fitted by expert individual artisans. The same artisanal finesse is found in the exquisite collections of the great couture houses for women. Rome, like Paris, is the birthplace of a coterie of the world's most illustrious names in *alta moda,* or *haute couture.* Forecasters may look to Milan for prophecies of ephemeral fads, but no one can ignore the worldwide trends set by Valentino's new colorations or skirt lengths. Pin-drop-silent couture ateliers are clustered around the Piazza di Spagna and along the prestigious Via Gregoriana. Sophisticated and pricey ready-to-wear finery can also be found in the Piazza di Spagna neighborhood and along the Via Condotti. Whether because it is the seat of the country's government and the headquarters of its television and cinema industries, or because it was the original arbiter of taste, Rome continues to be the undisputed center of artistic and theatrical high fashion.

ANTIQUES

Florence was the home of the Renaissance, but Rome found its glory in the 1600s to 1700s, when the ornate baroque taste was born and flourished there. Then excavations at nearby Pompeii in the mid-18th century revived an interest in ancient Rome and Greece in the form of the neoclassical movement. Today, together with precious classical artifacts, the baroque and neoclassical styles continue to be most characteristic of Rome's antiques, but other genres can be found.

The dealers who operate the high-quality antique stores along Via del Babuino and Via Margutta are as serious about their specialties as art history professors and prefer equally serious shoppers. A more strollable street is the Renaissance jewel, the Via Giulia, where younger dealers with sophisticated tastes operate small, stylish galleries. Even more renowned is the Via dei Coronari, where outdoor antique fairs are held every May and October. Prices here tend to be rather inflated, however, for antiques that are mostly English or French anyway. For reproductions and bric-a-brac, explore the narrow side streets around Piazza Navona and the Campo dei Fiori neighborhood, which are filled with artisan restorers and woodworkers; and don't miss the Sunday Porta Portese flea market (see Outdoor Markets, page 310). It is not surprising in a city with

Timeless adornment recreated today.

such ancient roots that Romans have a special appreciation for antiquities.

JEWELRY

Attractive and unusual fine jewelry can be found at all price levels in Rome. From the simple, small and affordable to the large, luxurious and lavish, jewelry is the timeless adornment for Roman women whose look is just this side of flashy. After all, you're in the cradle of national television, a city still called Hollywood-on-the-Tiber. Rome is the home base for Bulgari and other eminent jewelry names, whose shops can be found in the distinguished Via Condotti and Piazza di Spagna neighborhoods. Less mainstream, but with no compromise in quality, are the independent goldsmiths, whose small *botteghe* offer one-of-a-kind, imaginative creations. After millennia of success, jewelry is still often styled after ancient Roman, Etruscan, and Greek inspirations—frequently incorporating an authentic coin or small archeological artifact.

Rome's Outdoor Markets

Few of Rome's outdoor markets cater to a heavy tourist crowd, adding to their colorful authenticity. This is life Roman style and is worth any front row seat at the opera. Bargaining is the rule. You may be taken less seriously once tagged as a tourist, but stick to your guns, especially if you're buying a particularly expensive item, or more than one. If you're interested in buying, remember that the early bird finds the choicest worms. If you're going for the living theater of these *mercati romani,* don't forget to watch the sellers as well as their merchandise; go fairly early anyway, because the market may close early on a particularly slow or hot day. Some great last-minute bargains can also be negotiated with vendors who'd rather not pack up and haul home what you offer to take off their hands.

MERCATO SANNIO
Via Sannio at Porta San Giovanni
Monday through Friday, 8:00 A.M.–1:00 P.M.
Saturday, 8:00 A.M.–7:00 P.M.

You may be in this neighborhood to visit San Giovanni in Laterano (St. John Lateran), the city's cathedral and one of the four major basilicas of Rome. If not, as a shopping enthusiast you'll want to stop by anyway at the bustling outdoor market that takes place every day but Sunday (the day many of these vendors reserve for the Mercato di Porta Portese); the stalls begin at the Piazzale Appio and unfold along the wide Via Sannio. Take an American Army-Navy surplus store, introduce the exotic flavor of a Middle Eastern souk and saturate it with the staged theatrics of Italian *brio,* and you'll have a pretty good picture of this lively bazaar. The highlights here are new and secondhand jeans and other clothing that is practical and fun but not fancy. Students and eagle-eyed grandmothers are familiar with label-less copies of faddish fashions and don't expect investment quality—or prices. Look for medium-quality knitwear and leatherwear, shoes, beads and baubles, and a number of miscellaneous booths.

MERCATO DI PORTA PORTESE
between the Tiber and Viale Trastevere,
from Ponte Sublicio to Ponte Testaccio
Sundays, 7:00 A.M.–1:00 P.M.

On Sunday, all roads lead to Porta Portese. So dress down, carry your cash safely (in a hidden money belt or pouch, not in a pocketbook), and go early to enjoy the best show in town. While the rest of Rome is shut down, here a local circus of approximately 1000 flea-market vendors is busy hawking everything from ballet slippers to binoculars, from refrigerators to kittens, with an emphasis on medium-quality clothing. Watch out for fake instant antiques, "genuine" Etruscan artifacts, defective items and overpriced junk. There are endless good buys, however, especially if you enjoy haggling; these include Abruzzese bedspreads, silk ties, antique linens, and mountains of household goods. A mile-long stretch becomes twice that when you segue into narrow alleyways and side streets, joining the estimated 100,000 people who attend what is considered the biggest open-air trading center in the Western world. An entire section is given over to automotive parts; you can probably buy back your missing hubcaps there. Adding to the exotic hodgepodge, you'll see gypsies, wandering minstrels and ambulatory peddlers. You probably won't see the professional pickpockets, so be very, very careful.

MERCATO CAMPO DEI FIORI
Piazza Campo dei Fiori
Monday through Saturday, dawn to 2:00 P.M.

Campo dei Fiori is the biggest and best of Rome's many fish, vegetable and fruit markets. A handful of tourists blend with *trattoria* chefs, robust housewives, wizened grandmothers and prim palazzo servants who scrutinize, argue, survey, haggle, then proudly return home with the market's best pickings, only to return again the following morning. On a blanket of crushed ice, makeshift stalls display tangles of octopus and squid, heaps of dried and salted *baccalà* (cod), tiny clams, mussels and oysters. A patchwork of sun-bleached canvas awnings is spread over every square inch of the piazza, where luscious displays of fruits, vegetables, cheeses and flowers are offered. You'll stroll past mammoth *porcini* mushrooms, glossy purple eggplants, bouquets of deep-purple *asparagi*, pyramids of Rome's distinctive *carciofi* (artichokes), the delicate zucchini blossoms, and a dozen varieties of olives that bob in giant vats. The brooding, hooded statue of philosopher Giordano Bruno presides above it all, reminding us that piazza life wasn't always this joyous: in 1600 he was burned here at the stake for supporting the Copernican system.

MERCATO VITTORIO
Piazza Vittorio Emanuele II
Monday through Saturday,
7:00 A.M.–2:00 P.M.

A few blocks from the Termini train station and stretching all the way around this huge green piazza is Rome's most entertaining open-air supermarket. Start on the north side, where food stalls are located, and loop your way past specialized booths selling only lemons, calves' livers, slabs of fresh tuna, and live crabs, to name but a few. Here you'll find Rome's best poultry and game vendors; a stroll past their crowing stalls is almost like a day in the country. Some less fortunate specimens get plucked by stall holders between customers. You may be more drawn to the south side of the square and its endless booths of shoes, medium-quality clothing, leathergoods, costume jewelry and novelty souvenirs. Don't forget to bargain.

MERCATO DEI FIORI
Via Trionfale 47–49 (at Via Paolo Sarpi)
Tuesday, 10:00 A.M.–1:00 P.M.

Rome's only flower market is held just far enough outside the city's *centro* to be rather inconvenient—unless you're a flower lover who will consider this paradise an obligatory destination. In an enclosed two-story building, an enormous wholesale market takes place daily for the city's florists; the gates open to the public only on Tuesday mornings. You'll be taken by the ground floor with its array of small and giant house plants. But you'll swoon at the colorful show of flowers on the second floor.

TRASTEVERE

For evening dining and warm-weather strolls, Romans and foreigners alike flock to the popular Trastevere quarter, much as Parisians seek out the colorful Quartier Latin. No other area of Rome preserves its character as strongly as Trastevere, found, as its name implies, "across the Tiber"—a boundary that is more than just physical. After remaining locked in time for centuries, the neighborhood is slowly becoming gentrified, with chic rents to match its new image. The old comfortably accompanies the new in the maze of narrow, cobblestoned streets and unpretentious *piazzette* (small squares) where, even if you're not treasure hunting, you'll stumble upon interesting new shops and small boutiques.

The picturesque Piazza Santa Maria Trastevere.

The gentrification is bemoaned by the Trasteverini, who claim (incorrectly) to be the only true descendants of ancient classical stock. They encourage the survival of their dialect (still generally unintelligible to "foreigners" living across the river), the result of their isolation and the one-time presence of polyglot Oriental commercial communities, especially Jews. Until recently, you'd hear old-timers boast of never having strayed far enough to visit the Piazza di Spagna. They stage their own summertime festival, "Noiantri" (meaning "We the Others" in their dialect), in the last two weeks of July, with a mixture of religious and profane fanfare. The wide and relatively modern Viale Trastevere is festooned with lights, and food and souvenir stands spill out onto the side streets. Similar dancing, music, wine drinking, and fireworks in Trastevere were described by Ovid 1900 years ago.

Sunday morning's remarkable Porta Portese flea market draws many tourists and a sea of locals to this side of town (see Rome's Outdoor Markets, page 310). Trastevere also offers extensive opportunities for characteristic dining and for nightlife; even Romans consider a trip here a fun night out. In pleasant weather, you'll find many outdoor *trattorie* in the small piazzas where you can gaze at real-life medieval backdrops between courses. Many advertise guitar strumming, gypsy singing, and guaranteed conviviality. Stores often stay open late for this reason.

Shoppers should stroll down the narrow Via Lungaretta, lined with leather, silver and artisanal workshops, ice-cream bars and eating places. Meander down alleyways, poke your head in dusty shops, but save your buying energies for Il Centro d'Arte e dell'Artigianato Tradizionale (the Center for Traditional Arts and Crafts).

IL CENTRO D'ARTE E DELL'ARTI-GIANATO TRADIZIONALE
Via della Pelliccia 30
Tel. 58.16.614.
Moderate; credit cards accepted
Open during lunch and until 10:00 P.M.
Beautifully displayed in a recently restored 18th-century carriage

Original and authentic regional craftwork.

house is a wide selection of traditional handicrafts from the far recesses of the Italian peninsula. Most of Italy's regions are represented in authentic and original styles handmade by professional artisans and ferreted out by the center's two enthusiastic young owners, Clotilde Sambuco and Maria De Santis. Many of the objects are rarely found outside their home towns, and the Centro is a special opportunity for the culturally inclined shopper to see them all in a gracious, relaxed setting. It is not unlike a museum where everything is for sale.

The ceramic section is extensive (the owners will carefully pack and ship), with pottery from all the major Italian kilns. From Signora De Santis' native Puglia come hand-painted ceramic *fischietti,* whistles in the shape of birds or animals, and blue *puttini*-patterned wine pitchers, decorative platters and complete services. Green sponge-flecked pottery and terra-cotta casseroles hail from Umbria. There are beautiful hand-painted *acquasantiere* (holy-water fonts) to grace your walls and a selection of Sardinian basketry that truly raises basket-weaving to an art form. From Sicily come *santoni* (hand-carved and painted wooden saints) and characteristic ceramic dolls. From the Dolomite region, a family of five daughters supplies hand-woven tablecloths and bedspreads in delicate pastel linen/cotton blends. The list goes on forever, as interesting to the merely curious as to the visitor who is intent on buying.

Roman Cuisine

It is no secret that Romans love to eat. Theirs is a poor man's cuisine, although one relished as if it were the food of kings. More than anywhere else, dining here is a way of life, a major social occasion, so don't plan on rushing through an al fresco dinner when it's far more pleasant—and expected—to sit back, enjoy the conviviality, and take in the show.

Little now remains of the lavish, sumptuous banquets of the imperial Romans, the original epicureans. Today's local cooking is a mirror of the Roman character. It is simple, colorful, hearty and unpretentious. Italians eat according to the seasons, and the home-grown vegetables and fresh greens from the verdant surrounding countryside, such as the indigenous curly *puntarelle,* flood the daily outdoor markets. Omnipresent pasta is often made from wheat and water

The ubiquitous Senatus Populusque Romanus.

instead of the usual egg-based dough. *Alla carbonara* and *all'amatriciana* sauces are the regional specialties, and Thursday is the traditional gnocchi day. Since gnocchi are made fresh that morning, it's best to order them for lunch; you'll need the rest of the day to walk them off, and they're usually so good they don't last until dinner. Friday, when the Catholic world traditionally abstained from meat, is still fish day. Romans love fresh Mediterranean seafood, despite its high cost, and usually eat it cooked simply on the grill.

When you choose your second course, you may benefit from the resourcefulness of poor Romans of the past. Entrails and sweetbreads were once leftovers in the larders of the nobility and the Vatican, and were gladly relegated to the masses. Such specialties as pigs' trotters, brains, tripe, and oxtail are now considered rich men's delicacies, although they are usually not as popular with squeamish foreigners. The first Romans were shepherds, not greatly unlike those who still populate the hills of Latium; their simple diet dominates the regional cuisine, with its *abbacchio* (young milk lamb) and *capretto* (kid) prepared in a number of ways and found in most authentic Roman *trattorie.* An enormous variety of the full-flavored *pecorino* (sheep's-milk cheese) is joined by a singular ricotta and by plump mozzarella balls made from the milk of the water buffalo that graze south of Rome.

The history of the Jewish ghetto has left its imprint on Roman cuisine. Its hallmark is the *carciofo alla*

Every street boasts a touch of the mythical.

giudia, a small, spineless artichoke flattened like a flower, then fried. Strips of salted cod (*baccalà*) and mozzarella-stuffed zucchini blossoms, also deep-fried, have been passed down over the centuries as well. In general, salt is often used generously, especially on green salads that come to your table already dressed; a polite request for *senza sale* will hold the sodium. Romans are not particularly known for baked desserts, and delicious sun-ripened fruit in season is the usual finale. They are known, however, for their ice cream, so save yourself for the ancient Roman tradition of an after-dinner *passeggiata* and a creamy *gelato* in the Pantheon or Piazza Navona area.

Since the days of Pliny, Roman wines have been nectar to the gods. As with food, Romans consume wine copiously, ordering the red or white house *sfuso* wine in quarter-, half-, or full-liter carafes. The light white wines are best; these come from the Alban Hills southeast of Rome, also known as Frascati or Castelli Romani. Look for the refined labels of Paola di Mauro (white, red, or "golden" Colle Picchioni, or rich red Vigna del Vassallo) and Boncompagni-Ludovesi (red and white Fiorano, or Semillon, a white dessert wine). You may decide to go light on the wine during lunch—it tends to induce sleep and not shopping. An informal alternative is a memorable gourmet picnic bought at any neighborhood deli-like *gastronomia,* or a stop at one of the many *pizzerie rustiche.*

It is hard not to eat well in Rome's 5000 restaurants, many of which move outdoors from April to October. Expect a crowd if you arrive at the peak hours of 1:00 to 1:30 for lunch or 9:00 to 9:30 for dinner; if you show up too early, however, you'll miss half the fun. Leave your shopping bags at the hotel and take a quick nap before dinner, or *cena,* the all-important event of any Roman's day. Perhaps the Eternal City stays eternally young because, as the Romans say, *alla tavola, non si invecchia.* "At table, you never grow old").

A grotto effect graces a palazzo facade.

ROMAN CUISINE GLOSSARY

Antipasto (Appetizer)
Bruschetta–Garlic bread brushed with olive oil—simple peasant fare.

Primo Piatto (First Course)
Pasta:
Gnocchi–Dumplings made from potatoes (*di patate*) or semolina flour (the latter are usually baked in the oven with butter and grated cheese *alla romana*).
Rigatoni con pagliata–Diced milk-fed veal intestines stewed in a tasty tomato-based sauce.

A range of different pastas served in the following ways are Roman specialties:
All'amatriciana–A tomato-based sauce with bacon, onion and chili pepper and sharp *pecorino* cheese.
Alla carbonara–Tossed with beaten eggs, *pecorino* cheese and diced bacon; said to be named after a coal miner because of the abundant use of black pepper.
Alla checca–In an uncooked, summertime sauce made with fresh tomato and herbs.
Alla puttanesca–The reference to women of ill repute comes from the prominent use of chili pepper, together with tomato, black olives and garlic.
All'arrabbiata–In an "angry" (spicy) tomato sauce made with chili pepper and garlic.

Zuppa (Soup):
Stracciatella–A light egg-drop soup.
Pasta e ceci–A hearty pasta-and-chick-pea soup.
Zuppa di telline–Soup of tiny clams.

Secondo Piatto (Entrée)
Carne (Meat):
Abbacchio–Milk-fed baby lamb roasted (*al forno*), braised in a sauce of herbs, onions and white wine (*alla cacciatore*), or prepared as small "finger-burning" (*scottadito*) lamb chops on the grill.

Bottling some of Rome's eternal springs.

Life moves outdoors when spring moves in.

Coda alla vacinara–Oxtail stewed in a rich tomato sauce with cooked celery.

Porchetta–Tender suckling pig roasted with herbs.

Saltimbocca alla romana–Thin slices of veal that "jump in the mouth" because they are so tasty, covered with sage and prosciutto and cooked in white wine.

Pollo alla romana–Chicken stewed with yellow and red sweet bell peppers.

Pollo al diavolo–Chickens split open and cooked on the grill flattened under the weight of bricks.

Fritto misto–A mixed selection of deep-fried meats, sweetbreads (*animelle*) and seasonal vegetables.

Pesce (Fish):

Filetti di baccalà–Strips of salted cod deep-fried or in a tomato sauce.

Arzilla–Skate, a favorite local Mediterranean fish, usually poached in broth.

Ciriole–Small, tender eels from the Tiber, traditionally prepared with peas.

Contorno (Vegetable)

Carciofi alla romana–Small artichokes sautéed with olive oil, garlic and mint.

Carciofi alla giudia–Jewish-style artichokes, deep-fried and squashed to resemble a flower, served with anchovy-garlic sauce.

Fagioli con le cotiche–White haricot beans slowly stewed with thick slices of pork rind.

Fave con guanciale–Fresh fava beans cooked with bacon.

Peperonata–Stewed red and yellow bell peppers.

Verdure saltate–Fresh greens, first boiled, then sautéed in olive oil with garlic; also called *in padella.*

Puntarelle–A curly chicory-like salad green in a pungent anchovy dressing.

Rughetta–A leafy wild green with a bitter taste that becomes more pronounced the farther south you venture.

SPECIAL SHOPPING STREETS

For Romans, shopping, like eating, is a way of life. The peripatetic army of well-dressed locals engaged in the ritualistic *passeggiata is* doing serious window shopping, studying the *ultimo grido, dernier cri,* or latest trend in color, length and fabrication. The lively open-air markets are filled with savvy Roman housewives who put in a daily visit not just for the supplies, but for the social banter as well.

Italy is a country of specialists, where one goes to a *profumeria* for perfume, an *ortolano* for produce, a *latteria* for dairy products, and a *tabaccaio* for cigarettes—and salt, due to a peculiar state law. At the market there is a mushroom lady,

Shop stocked with woven straw and wicker items.

a tripe vendor, a cheese monger and a florist. Streets still recall the guilds and artisans whose shops were found there until not long ago: Via dei Cappellari (hat makers), Via dei Cestari (basket weavers), Via dei Giubbonari (jerkin makers), Via dei Chiavari (locksmiths). Modern Rome, more than the other cities covered in this book, still adheres to this historical tradition of keeping similar shops grouped together, though usually with no relationship to historic street names.

High-Class Shopping–Via Condotti, Via Borgognona and Via Bocca di Leone
Art Galleries and Studios–Via Margutta
Antiques–Via del Babuîno, Via Giulia, Via dei Coronari
Food Shops–Via della Croce
Inexpensive Shoes–Small streets around the Fontana di Trevi
Leather Apparel & Leathergoods–Via Due Macelli and Via Francesco Crispi (near the Largo del Tritone)
Artisan Workshops–Via dell'Orso
Fabrics–Via del Tritone
Notions & Trimmings–Via Campo Marzio
Woven Straw Articles & Wicker Furniture–Via dei Sediari and Via del Teatro Valle
Religious Supplies–Via della Conciliazione (St. Peter's) and Via dei Cestari
Medium-Quality Fashion (generally at low prices)–Via Nazionale, Via del Corso, Via Cola di Rienzo, Via del Tritone and Via Giubbonari
Couture Ateliers–Via Gregoriana

Piazza di Spagna

*H*ere is Rome's world-class nucleus for shoppers and visitors alike, conveniently and esthetically concentrated in the pedestrian-only area that unfolds at the foot of the monumental Spanish Steps. An international crowd comes here for Rome's finest view from atop the steps, as well as some of the world's most stunning window-shopping below. This is home for Rome's big-name designers and ultra-smart shopping.

The Piazza di Spagna neighborhood is bordered on the east by the piazza itself, and on the west by the busy mile-long stretch of Via del Corso, so called because the Romans used to hold wild horse races (*corsi*) from the Piazza del Popolo to the Piazza Venezia. The only race now is among teen-age Roman fashion slaves who snatch up the season's newest arrivals from the Corso's inexpensive clothing boutiques. These shops usually offer a good indication of the trends of the moment, and can provide fun and inexpensive gifts for family and friends, although quality is uneven. Once you leave behind the flashy strip and turn toward the Spanish steps, you enter a crisscrossed grid of cobbled streets lined with expensive boutiques where the merchandise is noticeably more tasteful and elite.

Stately palazzos conjure up images of privileged aristocrats living within. This is no longer considered a residential neighborhood, however; the street level of these courtly homes was converted into shops and boutiques way back in the 17th century, and the Piazza di Spagna area gradually assumed an important commercial role as a center for foreign

A moment's respite at the Spanish Steps, located amidst Rome's chicquest shopping enclave.

visitors, while the Campo dei Fiori area declined. During Napoleon's reign particularly, French merchants established themselves in this up-and-coming quarter.

It is ironic that the steps are called Spanish, since they were designed and built by an Italian in 1723, were paid for by the French government, were affectionately adopted by the transient British community, and are today haunted by Americans. The Italians call them the Scalinata della Trinità dei Monti, referring to the baroque church that sits atop the 137 steps; the name more familiar to English-speaking visitors refers to the nearby palazzo which has housed the Spanish Embassy to the Vatican since 1622. Eighteenth- and nineteenth-century British adventurers were lured to sunny Rome for its supposedly salubrious climate (you'll beg to differ on a hot summer afternoon) and a desire to rediscover classicism. All northern European Grand Tourists were indiscriminately tagged "the British," and many of them settled in the then-less-expensive Piazza di Spagna neighborhood, which became known as *"il ghetto degli inglesi."* One respectful note in the colorful hubbub of the Spanish Steps is the small plaque commemorating the house where, in 1821, a young and romantic Keats spent the last three months of his life in the company of Shelley.

Keats, Shelley, Byron, Dickens, Goethe, the Brownings, and Liszt were but a smattering of the expatriates who came to bask in inspiration offered them by the Eternal City. Artists settled in the quiet streets around the Via Margutta, nowadays still lined with artists' studios and galleries; outdoor art shows held here in June and October offer a peaceful respite from the Via Condotti crowds. Peek into No. 88, a workshop where Cremona-trained craftsmen spend hundreds of painstaking hours in handmaking a single stringed instrument for one of the world's virtuosos. It's a charming stroll along the parallel Via del Babuino, home to long-established antique shops harmoniously juxtaposed with modern stores selling contemporary Italian design and home furnishings.

Don't miss the boutique-lined Via delle Carrozze, named after the handsome horse-drawn carriages that arrived from points north and were left here to be serviced and parked. Just as characteristic is the Via della Croce, known for its variety of small food stores and clothing boutiques. It offers a charming "real people" foil to the grandeur of the Via Condotti, such a singular address in this ne plus ultra shopping neighborhood that we have treated it separately (see Via Condotti, page 349).

Parallel to the Via Condotti, Via Frattina and Via Borgognona also stretch from the Piazza di Spagna towards the Via del Corso. Together

with their network of narrow side streets such as Via Bocca di Leone and Via del Gambero, they constitute the core of smart shopping in this area. And just atop the steps, in an appropriately lofty position along the prestigious Via Gregoriana and Via Sistina, are located Rome's hushed *alta moda* ateliers, where you can be fitted with that once-in-a-lifetime ball gown. Twice a year, Rome's great couturiers parade their magnificent collections down the Spanish Steps in one of Italy's most dazzling spectacles. Every bit as entertaining is the daily *passeggiata* that crowds these elegant runway-streets early every evening, when stylish Romans join with insatiable window-shopping tourists to see and be seen.

A baroque church presides over the 137 steps.

FASHION

MEN'S

Contemporary Sportswear

1 PIATELLI
Via San Silvestro 17
Tel. 67.93.452
Expensive; credit cards accepted

Four generations of the Piatelli family have clothed the Roman carriage trade, and Bruno Piatelli has successfully carried this tradition into a modern era. Executives of all ages who like to dress in comfortable quality sportswear of an almost British sensibility can find the Piatelli private label around the world, or at three Roman Piatelli locations. There's a handsome array of sweaters, pants and accessories, and shirts and suits can be made to measure or purchased ready-made in the finest of fabrics. Perhaps most appealing are Piatelli's cotton shirts, made in quality fabrics and in a classic cut. The customer

who appreciates fine finishing will note such touches as handsewn buttonholes and the silver buttons engraved "PP" on Piatelli jeans. This attention to detail and guarantee of uncompromising quality make Piatelli a household word with the celebrated denizens of Rome's theater and cinema world. The other Piatelli locations are at Via Convertite, 19 (telephone 67.92.450), for men and Via Condotti, 20/A (telephone 67.91.352), for women. Both shops offer more traditional attire.

SHOES

MEN'S & WOMEN'S

Comfort with Fashion Appeal

2 BRUNO MAGLI
Via del Gambero 1
Tel. 67.93.802
Moderate; credit cards accepted

From this world-renowned Bologna-based shoe designer comes fashionable footwear that is both elegant and sensible, from dressy pumps to casual everyday shoes for men as well as women. Noted for his superlative combination of comfort and stylish appeal, Bruno Magli also boasts excellent workmanship that guarantees the longevity of his shoes. His season's colors are also reflected in his ladies' handbags, and there's a small but good selection of leather apparel.

LINGERIE & DANCEWEAR

3 LET'S DANCE
Via della Mercede 40
Tel. 67.93.509
Moderate; credit cards accepted

The name of this modern shop

doesn't prepare you for the youthful, sexy lingerie that it offers in addition to its colorful leotards, ballet slippers, and dancewear. Lacy bras and corselets and fashion-oriented nightwear come from a number of small and moderately priced Italian companies. There's also an array of cotton gloves in all lengths and hues. Swimwear is for the young and shapely, and a nice selection of hosiery includes designer names such as Valentino, Gerbe, Christian Dior and Yves Saint Laurent. Before you enter the store, take a look at its display windows; they're jazzy and colorful and an authentic indication of the kind of merchandise you'll find inside.

FASHION
CHILDREN'S

4 LAVORI ARTIGIANALI FEMMINILI 🏠🏠🏠🏠
Via Capo le Case 6
Tel. 67.92.992
Expensive; credit cards accepted

A look at this handmade infantwear may unleash in you a wave of tender poetry. Once upon a time, the de Lellis family specialized in traditional layette sets (magnificent crib and basinette covers in embroidered organza are still a specialty), but they have expanded to include ready-to-wear fashion for children from birth to seven years old. Everything is done completely by hand and in grand style. New styles may inspire some ephemeral trends and colorations, but the image is generally rooted in classic tradition. Exquisite ceremonial and baptismal outfits and party dresses featuring piqué collars with scalloped edges, fabric-covered but-

tons, delicate embroidery across shirred bodices, and tiny cuffs and matching piping will tug at your heartstrings. Whether for dressy or casual clothes, expect nothing less than the best in fabrics—quality cotton, velvet, lace, silk and Viyella will spoil young customers. To keep them spoiled, Lavori Artigianali Femminili creates made-to-measure garments for children over seven in the back workroom.

HOME
KITCHENGEAR
Copperware

5 SELVI REGINA
Via Francesco Crispi 33
Tel. 67.91.164
Moderate; no credit cards accepted

The same family of artisanal coppersmiths have been at this location since 1902. Most of the practical and simply designed articles you'll find here seem not to have changed much since then in style or quality. In this small shop housed in a palazzo dating back to the 18th century is a copper collection of everything from pots to cookie cutters. Shelves are stocked with copper mugs, teapots, casseroles and skillets with sturdy iron handles, and all types of dessert molds.

Selvi's Regina's and practical copperware.

There's easy and pleasant browsing in this small, cluttered shop, where everything you see is handcrafted by a number of small independent artisanal sources, and is sold by the kilo.

FURS

6 GIANCARLO RIPÀ
Via Gregoriana 5/A
Tel. 67.84.025
Very expensive; credit cards accepted

Giancarlo Ripà's mastery of furs creates special effects that make them veritable works of art. The exceptional lightness of his furs and his advanced techniques result from an innovative system of cutting and design. A special preference for mink evolved into a remarkable fabric-like weave of three different types of mink skins that continues to be his trademark. Always changing, Ripà is lauded as having revolutionized fur fashion. He creates a fantasy *alta moda* line of exclusive furs for the self-assured woman who dares, as well as an updated line realized in a larger choice of materials.

FASHION

ACCESSORIES

Designer Eyeglass Frames

7 OTTICA BILECI
Via Due Macelli 83
Tel. 67.84.683
Expensive; credit cards accepted

Even confirmed contact-lens wearers will sway to the eyeglass fashion of Italy's most celebrated designers. Emilio Pucci, Nicola Trussardi, Valentino, Gianni Versace, Missoni, and Fendi all take time from their cloth-ing collections to design the latest in eyewear style. Non-Italian contributors include Ted Lapidus, Yves Saint Laurent, Nina Ricci, Porsche, and Zeiss. Relying upon the professional service for which Bileci is known throughout Rome, you can have any of these frames made up with your prescription in one or two days, or you may simply want to have a pair made up as sunglasses. Bileci also creates a number of its own designs, including unusual styles in polished wood or real tortoiseshell.

FASHION

CHILDREN'S

8 CALICO LION
Via della Vite 80
Tel. 67.84.626
Expensive; credit cards accepted

This enchanting little shop offers one of the best collections of infants' fashion for style, quality, and comfort. Clothes for children from birth to 4 years old are displayed in a small shop decorated with flowered wallpaper and pretty pink cupboards. This is an excellent source for adorable handknit sweaters and children's furnishings with a coordinated theme. See also Milan listing (page 203).

BOOKS

ENGLISH-LANGUAGE

9 ANGLO-AMERICAN BOOK COMPANY
Via della Vite 57
Tel. 67.95.222
Moderate; credit cards accepted

For more than three decades, the slightly cramped quarters of this refined book-lovers' den have offered an up-to-the-minute selection of titles from many British and American publishers. Both hardcovers and paperbacks can be found on floor-to-ceiling shelves categorized among fiction and special interests, and there are, of course, a large number of books on Italy—cuisine, architecture, history, culture and travel, with a natural emphasis on Rome. If you'll be in Rome for a while, you can place special orders and subscribe to any foreign publication here.

LEATHERGOODS

BAGS & LUGGAGE

Natural Hides

10 LE BAGAGE

Via della Vite 44–45
Tel. 67.94.597
Moderate; credit cards accepted

Leather-lovers will want one of everything in this handsome store specializing in natural *cuoio* hides. Soft, burnished leathers are used to create beautiful bags of every kind for both men and women. Trim, everyday styles follow the season's shapes, while big, oversized styles have a constant fashion appeal. You'll find large totes, backpacks, overnight and weekend bags, tennis, golf and duffel bags, as well as a range of luggage pieces that can be purchased individually. There's a particularly nice selection of rugged-looking men's shoulder bags and a number of styles trimmed in crocodile for an upscale look. In addition to its own collection, Le Bagage carries the Granello and Barbara brands, and it also offers some small leather accessories, including belts and wallets.

Everything in natural cuoio *hides at Le Bagage.*

FASHION

JUNIORS'

Contemporary Sportswear

11 BENETTON

Via del Corso 172
Tel. 67.97.470
Moderate; credit cards accepted
Open during lunch

Yet another Benetton boutique, this one is particularly convenient and browser-friendly. For more information, see Milan listing (page 179).

FASHION & SHOES

MEN'S & WOMEN'S

Designer Boutique

12 MARIO VALENTINO

Via Frattina 84
Tel. 67.91.246
Expensive; credit cards accepted

Not to be confused with Valentino the fashion designer, Mario Valentino is known for his ready-to-wear leather, coordinated shoes, and small leather-goods, all to be found in this beautiful setting. Although he was born in Naples to a clever and imaginative shoemaker, Mario Valentino's home base can be considered Rome, where his two-story beige marble location is the largest of all his stores. Fashionable, classy while sexy, and beautifully tailored, Mario Valentino's creations use the most supple of high-quality leathers in interesting styles, colors, and treatments. Unlike most Italian retail stores, Mario Valentino tries to stock his winter collection as early as July and his spring/summer collection in January.

HOME
CHINA, SILVER & GLASS

13 FORNARI
Via Frattina 71
Tel. 67.92.524
Expensive; credit cards accepted

All discriminating Romans put their trust and wedding lists in the expert hands of Fornari. This is Rome's foremost store for contemporary Italian silver, with an enormous selection of stylish table settings that can keep the undecided in a quandary. Makes offered include Milan's important Sabattini (see page 196). During its 80 years of experience, Fornari has expanded to two brightly lit floors of beautifully displayed crystal, china, silver, stainless steel, and household goods. There are endless gift ideas for the house that has everything, such as oversized ceramic platters textured in faux granite or marble colorations, or a sleek oil and vinegar set trimmed in silver.

LINGERIE
COLORFUL COLLECTION

14 VANITÀ
Via Frattina 70
Tel. 67.91.743
Moderate; credit cards accepted

Concentrated within the radius of just a few blocks, you'll find a large number of sexy and inviting lingerie stores. At Vanità, a visual magnet is the extensive choice of colorful bras and matching panties of the shop's own production. Pick a lacy top from their range of 20 fashion colors—peacock blue, fuchsia, olive green and so on—and match it with a bottom in any of various bikini styles. There are also garter belts to complete your coordinated set, and peignoirs, teddies, corselets and babydolls in a variety of colors, in both silks and cottons. Choose from a full line of La Perla, Italy's doyenne of lingerie, and Christian Dior. Summertime brings a racy selection of swimwear.

Nearby are the following lingerie shops, most of which carry interesting swimwear as the warm weather approaches: Brighenti, Via Frattina 7–8 (telephone 67.91.484); Tusseda, Via Frattina 25 (telephone 67.93.576); Simona, Via del Corso 83 (telephone 67.90.077); and Tina, Via Bocca di Leone 9 (telephone 67.84.076).

COSTUME JEWELRY

15 CASTELLI
Via Frattina 54
Tel. 67.90.339
Moderate; credit cards accepted

There are a number of Castelli beauty salon/*profumeria* locations around town, this one in particular known for its delightful array of glittering accessories. Its display cases hold a large selection of classic costume jewelry, much of it from French houses such as Nina Ricci, Christian Dior, and Givenchy, along with Castelli's own line of large, pavé-diamond-studded pieces. Also from the shop's own production are decorative pillboxes and powder cases, perfume atomizers, and glamorous gold-mesh evening bags. For "him," there are handsome brass shaving sets.

FASHION
JUNIORS'

Sportswear

16 BENETTON
Via Frattina 45
Tel. 67.90.364
Moderate; credit cards accepted
Open during lunch

Part of the Benetton empire, this particular franchise also offers children's clothes upstairs. A more complete collection of Benetton's fashion-plate clothes for kids can be found just down the street at Via Frattina 1 (telephone 67.84.698). See the Milan listing (page 179).

GIFTS
CERAMICS & HANDICRAFTS

17 MYRICAE 🛍🛍🛍🛍
Via Frattina 36
Tel. 67.95.335
Moderate; credit cards accepted

First you should know that *myricae* is Latin for "little gracious things," and this store is brimming with them. Colorful, hand-painted ceramics represent all of Italy's regions and styles;

Hand-painted ceramics from all parts of Italy.

many items are made exclusively for Myricae. Two floors are precariously stocked with decorative terra cotta from Sardinia, Renaissance designs from Deruta, bright, solid-colored services from Vietri, the distinctive blue-and-yellow Innocenti reproductions from Tuscany, and the collectible De Simone naif designs from Palermo. Serving platters come in all sizes and shapes, glasses and jars are hand-painted with flowers and fruit, and there are charming, typically Roman lampshades made of ceramic and hand-decorated. A second location, at Piazza del Parlamento 39 (telephone 67.81.541), is called 2 Myricae.

FASHION
MEN'S

Designer Collections

18 A. SERMONETA 🛍🛍🛍🛍
Via Frattina 34/A
Tel. 67.94.555
Expensive; credit cards accepted

Sermoneta's well-clad salespeople pose.

Rome's leading boutique for sophisticated men's fashion, Sermoneta offers the best from Europe's most influential designers. The young, professional salesmen will help you coordinate a look with Versace sportswear, Claude Montana leather outerwear, creations by J.C. de Castelbajac for Iceberg, Gian Marco Venturi, or Byblos, along with such fashion accessories as Cesare Paciotti's handsome classic loafers. In a modern, well-laid-out two-story space, you can enjoy top-to-toe shopping. Sermoneta also allows you to get a jump on the season, stocking its winter collections as early as mid-July and summerwear in mid-January—a rare concession to the shopping habits of its non-Italian customers. Owner Angelo Sermoneta also orchestrates a sister store for women's fashion, Eleanora, nearby at Via Borgognona 5/B (page 333).

FASHION
JUNIORS'
Contemporary

19 STEFANEL
Via Frattina 31
Tel. 67.92.667
Moderate; credit cards accepted
Open during lunch

An ambitious competitor of the colorful Benetton knitwear dynasty, this chain of young, trendy sportswear shops is almost as ubiquitous and just as popular. See the Milan listing (page 181).

FASHION
WOMEN'S
Contemporary/Trendy

20 MAX MARA
Via Frattina 28
Tel. 67.93.638
Expensive; credit cards accepted

If time constraints should force you to choose just one clothing store, then go directly to Max Mara, where you'll find reams of high-quality Italian fashion in a great number of styles and variations. Whether your taste is timelessly classic, chic contemporary, or borderline avant-garde, Max Mara is reliable for its value in fabric, style and workmanship. The different collections displayed here all come from Max Mara's own design and production, most of them not yet widely exported. Everything is well grouped to facilitate your selection: separates and sweaters to mix or layer; casual or elegant dresses; tailored or boldly cut suits, coats, and raincoats. An array of coordinated leather accessories, from broad belts to shoes, also runs the gamut from the casually sporty to the sophisticated. The most up-to-date collection is presented at the new Max Mara on Via Condotti 47; (telephone 67.87.946).

At Elsy, Via del Corso 106 (telephone 67.92.275), Max Mara shoppers will find two more floors in a family-run environment; Griffe, a few doors down at Via del Corso 89–90 (telephone 67.85.771), carries the younger and sportier Penny Black collection, one of Max Mara's labels.

FASHION

WOMEN'S

Designer Collections

21 LIONELLO AJÒ
Via Borgognona 35
Tel. 67.82.660
Expensive; credit cards accepted

This is a very small, modern boutique where a variety of Europe's finest and latest fashion can be found under one roof. With a skillful eye and a keen fashion sensibility, Lionello Ajò handpicks a limited selection of stylish garments from the avant-garde side of high fashion's most noted designers, including such French and Italian masters as Franco Moschino, Angelo Tarlazzi, Sonia Rykiel, Jean-Paul Gaultier, Anne Marie Beretta and Junko Koshino. The articles are meant for easy mixing and matching.

SHOES

MEN'S & WOMEN'S

22 FRATELLI ROSSETTI
Via Borgognona 5/A
Tel. 67.82.676
Expensive; credit cards accepted

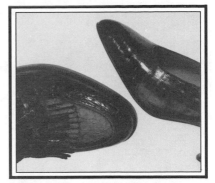

Beautiful crafstmanship from Rossetti.

Most of Fratelli Rossetti's creativity is expressed in their beautiful updated classic pumps and sandals for women. Both the men's and women's collections boast excellent craftsmanship, comfort, style, and deluxe leathers. The look is often dressy; you may recognize it from the brothers' ambitious advertising campaign and in their string of classy boutiques around the world. Women's heels are on the low side, a preference of Renzo and Renato Rossetti, who founded the company 30 years ago; they'll follow the dictates of fashion, but feel that high heels can disturb the spine.

BOOKS

ART & ESOTERICA

23 FRANCO MARIA RICCI
Via Borgognona 4/D
Tel. 67.93.466
Expensive; credit cards accepted

With his exquisite tomes on esoteric subjects, Franco Maria Ricci has added a new dimension to the Italian publishing scene. Books with beautiful color plates and rich handmade papers are displayed in an appropriately luxurious setting. See the Milan listing (page 183).

Deluxe pelts arrive at Fendi's fur salon.

WOMEN'S

Designer Flagship

24 FENDI

Via Borgognona 36
Tel. 67.97.641
Expensive; credit cards accepted

Many now call it Fendi Street, so inundated is it with the world-famous double-F logo. The five Fendi sisters are from Rome, and this series of elitist boutiques offers the world's most extensive selection of Fendi fashion. Tourists wear a path to the No. 36 Via Borgognona location, the largest and most popular of the Fendi boutiques. Stocked mainly with ultra-status accessories in plastic-coated fabric or stamped leather, this luxurious mini-department store seems to sport the famed "F" everywhere. Besides the coveted handbags and initialed luggage, there are many small items such as address books, wallets and keycases, which are accessible enough in price to make great gifts. The Fendi production never seems to age, although seasonal innovations keep it fresh and young. There's less congestion next door at No. 39, where the exquisite Fendi furs are shown in a spacious two-story atelier. Adjacent, also at No. 39, you'll find ready-to-wear, and No. 4/E, once the only Fendi shop in town, is now the showcase for their popular shoe collection.

MEN'S & WOMEN'S

Designer Flagship

25 LAURA BIAGIOTTI

Via Borgognona 43–44
Tel. 67.91.205
Expensive; credit cards accepted

In a modern, airy environment that reflects her fashions, Laura Biagiotti showcases her consistently romantic women's collection. Her early experience working for the great couturiers of Rome, the city she loves best, developed the sensibility still felt in her women's ready-to-wear creations. Since her première in 1972, Biagiotti has always favored soft silhouettes and colors, and when the rest of the fashion world falls victim to the new color of the season, she continues to show a selection of winter whites. When done up in the luxurious cashmere knits for which she is famous, they are the utmost in feminine appeal. She also surprises with original colors and fabrics. You can easily mix and match her sportswear separates with her outerwear and licensed accessories, also on display here. There is also a Biagiotti men's collection, perhaps most notable for its cashmere sweaters.

THE FENDI SISTERS

In 1925, Adele and Edoardo Fendi opened a small workshop in Rome specializing in leathergoods and simple furs. Adele would eventually tell her daughters Paola, Anna, Franca, Carla and Alda that they were like five fingers on one hand and worked best together. They worked so well, in fact, that they went on to build an empire of furs, leathergoods, and ready-to-wear that is today one of the most exclusive and successful fashion enterprises in the world.

If Italy's fur industry is renowned for its innovative artisanal treatment and imaginative design, the Fendi sisters are largely responsi-

The queenpins of the Fendi dynasty: (above) Franca, Carla and Alda; (below) Anna and Paola.

ble. At a time when the well-heeled wore matronly minks in deep natural colors, the Fendis experimented with dyeing furs rich, unheard-of hues like emerald green and apricot. They brought high fashion to fur. They promoted lesser-known "poor" skins like squirrel and weasel and combined sable with possum, mink with mole. They revolutionized the very feel of fur, making it supple and ultra-light. They have collaborated since 1965 with Paris designer Karl Lagerfeld, who also created their double-F status logo. Their first couture fur collection was presented in 1966 to instant success and was followed in 1969 by a *prêt-à-porter* collection, which offered comparable Fendi fantasy for more accessible prices.

The sisters' expertise in fur extended naturally to leather, which they printed, tested, tinted and tanned. Customers who could only fantasize about owning a Fendi fur could now snatch up soft, pouchy Fendi bags and coordinated wallets, agendas, luggage, shoes and other treasures. The prestige "F" soon graced a classic canvas and plastic-treated material as well. To complete the Fendi look, the sisters—now joined by four husbands and 11 offspring—introduced a ready-to-wear collection in 1977. The latest additions to this ever-evolving dynasty are the less-expensive "Fendissime" collections introduced by third-generation members.

LAURA BIAGIOTTI

In the American fashion market she is known as the "Queen of Cashmere," and where else should an attractively feminine contemporary monarch live and work but in a romantic 15th-century castle just minutes outside Rome? If it all sounds like a fairy tale, the comparison is not far off: the genteel character, steadily increasing success, and unique home surroundings of Roman-born Laura Biagiotti make an idyllic combination.

Laura Biagiotti began her fashion career in 1972 with the launching of her first *prêt-à-porter* women's collection, geared, as her work still is, toward the working woman. She creates high-quality, easy-to-wear clothing that dresses active women in a romantic and feminine way. Her passion has always been cashmere, particularly white; she invented for it an updated image by using it in elegant everyday knitwear for women.

Roman-born Laura Biagiotti, "Queen of Cashmere."

Only in Italy has ready-to-wear reached such heights of luxury, and Laura Biagiotti has done much to make this a reality. As with many top-name designers, her creativity flourishes in the use of fabrics; each Biagiotti garment is partially finished by hand. Much of her inspiration comes from her home, a frescoed castle (one of the four towers dates to the 11th century) that she has restored with magnificent taste. She gave up her early study of archeology to pursue her interest in design, so it is no surprise that she considers fashion a cultural phenomenon and aims to create pieces that outlast the trends of the moment.

Twelve boutiques around the world carry the Laura Biagiotti name. Her bastion is the newly remodeled Rome location on the elite Via Borgognona, where shoppers can find her entire range of ready-to-wear and articles from the 26 licenses that complement it, including scarves, perfume, hosiery, leathergoods, and bathing suits.

SHOES
MEN'S & WOMEN'S

26 DIEGO DELLA VALLE
Via Borgognona 45–46
No telephone
Expensive; credit cards accepted
Open during lunch

This is one of Italy's most up-to-date shoe designers of an avant-garde, fashion-forward look. Young, ambitious, and a true international trendsetter in footwear, Diego della Valle dedicates most of his attention to his women's line, which, though not always ultra-feminine, is always ultra-fashionable. His men's collection is limited by comparison, but both lines are known for their comfortable fit, quality workmanship, unusual skins and hardware, and a heavy-soled, sporty look that he was the first to use. Young Diego designs for Italy's and Europe's greatest fashion houses; he is in the middle of a strategic plan of expansion that will have his outlets opening throughout Italy, Europe, and abroad.

SHOES
MEN'S & WOMEN'S

27 ANDREA CARRANO
Via Borgognona 2/A–B
Tel. 67.91.580
Expensive; credit cards accepted

Andrea Carrano creates colorful, stylish women's shoes and handsome, more classic men's footwear. A 40-year veteran of the world of high-fashion shoes, Carrano has always provided excellent quality. Men's shoes are well tailored, with lots of personal touches and subtle seasonal details. Fantasy is most evident in the women's collection, where updated classics approach the trendy; pumps and ballet slippers have a Carrano twist and come in a rainbow of fashion colors. There's also a line of beautiful accessories and leatherwear.

FASHION
WOMEN'S
Designer Collections

28 ELEANORA 🛍🛍🛍🛍
Via Borgognona 5/B
Tel. 67.91.220
Expensive; credit cards accepted

Attentive, professional service here will help you coordinate sophisticated knitwear from Italy's and France's top names. Eleanora boasts one of the area's most in-depth collections; well-displayed separates include sweaters, jackets, pants and shirts. Mix and match from the latest designs of Rocco Barocco, Claude Montana, Luciano Soprani, Azzedine Alaïa, J.C. de Castelbajac for Iceberg, Complice, and Gianfranco Ferrè's Mondrian line. A counterpart of Sermoneta, the nearby men's fashion boutique, Eleanora also offers the latest seasonal collections far sooner than the local competition.

LEATHERGOODS
GLOVES
Big Fashion Assortment

29 MEROLA
Via del Corso 143
Tel. 67.91.961
Moderate; credit cards accepted

The calling card will tell you that the Merola family has been producing

"Luxury gloves since 1885." Here one finds the best selection of high-quality gloves in all of Rome, with as wide a variety for men as for women. In addition to the classic colors, you'll find such shades as pearl gray, olive green, bottle green and mauve. All the "musts" in buying fine gloves are here: straight seams and tiny, even stitches, seams sewn on the inside, and perfect, uniform color. Gloves lined in silk cashmere, rabbit or wool are patiently pulled out of the highly polished *radica*-wood drawers that line the walls by the amiable Alberto Merola or his assistants. Women will be especially happy with the endless unusual details like bows, pleats, buttons, fur cuffs and, for evening, rhinestone-studded black suede gloves. Men also will find dressy gloves, as well as every style conceivable for sports (boating, driving, golf, riding) and sturdy cotton gloves for gardening.

FASHION

MEN'S

Accessories

30 RADICONCINI
Via del Corso 139
Tel. 67.91.807
Moderate; credit cards accepted

One of the few old-fashioned gentlemen's shops left on the bustling Via del Corso, Radiconcini proudly represents a 200-year-old Roman tradition in men's haberdashery and accessories. This is a small treasure trove of cashmere sweaters in traditional colors, fine silk ties in handsome prints, woolen socks in classic patterns, walking sticks, and dapper hats of Panama and Borsalino style. Radicon-

cini's is like a leap back into the good old days, when shopping meant being attended by knowledgeable, gracious sales help in a refined Anglo-Roman ambiance.

FASHION

WOMEN'S

Designer Flagship Boutique

31 VALENTINO
Via Bocca di Leone 15
Tel. 67.95.862
Very expensive; credit cards accepted

To see the collection that keeps the international fashion scene on tenterhooks from one season to the next, visit the sleek showcase of Rome's own Valentino. Sexy and sophisticated while young and fresh, Valentino's *prêt-à-porter* clothes are carefully grouped here into three rooms for daywear, eveningwear, and suits. Valentino's utterly feminine collections will affect future fashion trends for seasons to come. If a classic Valentino accessory is all you can permit yourself, you'll find his handbags, umbrellas, evening shoes and silk scarves at more accessible prices. The much-awaited July 1 sale offers spring and summer pieces at a 40-percent reduction and any of his previous winter remnants at 60-percent off until the new collection arrives. Fall and winter merchandise goes on sale in mid-January.

One of the world's undisputed fashion greats, Roman-born Valentino is best known for his *alta moda*. Not meant for the timid of soul or bank account, it can be found in his atelier at Via Gregoriana 24, just a few blocks away (telephone 67.20.11).

VALENTINO

Garavani Valentino is a mythic figure, a synonym for exquisite Italian fashion. His is one of the most photographed faces in the international fashion industry, with the serene, serious look of an impeccably groomed Italian aristocrat.

Wealthy women who want to stand out in any crowd flock to the embassy-like Valentino atelier at the top of the Spanish Steps. *Haute couture* was Valentino's first introduction to fashion and, while today he also designs elegant men's and women's ready-to-wear and supervises 90 licensing divisions, it remains his passion, his chance to follow his fantasies to create opulent eveningwear.

When he was 17, his supportive northern Italian family sent him to the then-capital of fashion, Paris. Valentino compares his apprenticeship to those of the great Renaissance masters, who began in their maestro's *bottega* before striking out on their own. During his years of technical training and practice, first with Jean Dessès and then with Guy La Roche, Valentino was already developing an image of ultrafeminine chic and rich fabrications that turned the heads of Paris' *grandes dames.*

When he returned to Rome and opened his Maison de Couture in 1959, his success was almost immediate and astounding. His earliest supporters were Farah Diba, Jacqueline De Ribes, Audrey Hepburn and Jacqueline Kennedy; the first prominent Italian personality to embrace the Valentino look was Sophia Loren. Valentino was soon known the world over and played a vital role in drawing international attention to Rome as the new capital of *alta moda.*

Valentino began offering ready-to-wear fashion in the early 1970s. He became famous for his smart suits and for the "Valentino red" featured in every collection. His simple 'V' had become an intensely coveted status insignia by the time he opened his first boutique in Rome in 1969. He now has well over 100 boutiques and selling locations around the globe; his licensing divisions produce such varied items as bags, foulards, intimatewear, children's fashion and bathroom tiles, and he has also designed the uniforms of the Italian Olympic athletes. He recently celebrated a resounding 25th anniversary in the fashion world. His elaborate outdoor fashion shows in the small Piazza Mignanelli (near the Piazza di Spagna) reflect his other great love, for the theater. Only the privileged attend. But everyone who sees his creations senses his aspiration to blend fashion with culture and to make every woman feel as beautiful as possible.

The high priest of Italian fashion.

FASHION

MEN'S

Designer Flagship Boutique

32 VALENTINO UOMO
Via Mario dei Fiori 22
(corner of Via Condotti)
Tel. 67.83.656
Expensive; credit cards accepted

Roman designer Valentino showcases his men's fashion and accessories in a classic and understated ambiance which, though smaller than his women's flagship boutique, befits his prestigious image. Sweaters, suits and sportswear guarantee you that Continental look, and every bridegroom aspires to a perfectly tailored Valentino tuxedo. A handsome array of accessories offers less imposing price tags, and you can find nice gifts such as travel manicure sets or fine belts. Bring it all home in Valentino's distinctive rigid luggage, made in durable black leather trimmed in red.

HERB SHOP

33 BOTTEGA DI LUNGAVITA
ERBORISTERIA
Via Mario dei Fiori 24/A
Tel. 67.91.454
Moderate; no credit cards

This exquisite little "long-life" herb shop is as popular for its quality products as for its central location. The English-speaking salespeople will share their expertise in treatments for all types of maladies, including dermatological problems, bloodshot eyes, sore throats, gout and hair loss, as well as just general pampering. Products, beautifully packaged and daintily displayed on old wooden shelves, include fragrant herbal shampoos; bath or shower gels and oils made with rose, verbena, and magnolia extract; and delicate floral-scented soaps. There are also toilet waters, creams and moisturizers, suntanning coconut oil, and a line of natural cosmetics. Infusion or *tisane* (teas), feature a rare white blend obtained by sacrificing 24 kilos of leaves for every 100 grams of white tea produced.

SHOES

MEN'S, WOMEN'S & CHILDREN'S

34 RAPHAEL SALATO
Piazza di Spagna 34
Tel. 67.95.646
Expensive; credit cards accepted

Rome's acclaimed shoe designer has three different locations, of which this is the most convenient. Raphael Salato's fashion footwear is reliably sexy and elegant, with occasional digressions into fantasy and novelty. Excellent skins, embroidered leather, and attention to detail characterize both the everyday and dressy footwear in Salato's women's division where the high heel is a relatively constant feature. The children's collection tends toward the updated classic and colorful, with Mary Jane-like styles for her and two-tone oxfords for him. For men, Salato carries the prestigious handmade A. Testoni shoes from Bologna, as well as classic loafers and dress shoes with an occasional touch of novelty such as ostrich or crocodile. The largest single collection of Raphael Salato shoes for men and women can be found at Via Veneto 149 (telephone 49.35.07), with another not far away at Via Veneto 104 (telephone 48.46.77) for women and children only.

Pride prevails over the generations at Petochi.

SUSTENANCE

RISTORANTE/TRATTORIA

35 HASSLER VILLA MEDICI
Piazza Trinità dei Monti 6
Tel. 67.82.651
Expensive; credit cards accepted
Open 7 days a week

A magical vista looking down the Spanish Steps toward Via Condotti and the Eternal City beyond makes dinner here into an indelible lifetime memory. This panorama is meant to eclipse the food, but with a recent change of chef, the intercontinental and Italian cuisine has notably improved. On a glassed-in and air-conditioned terrace, impeccable multilingual service and exquisite sunsets set the tone for such house specialties as delicate veal medallions with snails and a regional *abbacchio al forno,* served Fridays only. Make your choice quickly and concentrate on the priceless skyline: you'll recognize the outlines of Castel Sant'Angelo, the Ghetto's synagogue, the Pantheon, and the Quirinale Palace. Marlene Dietrich and Charlie Chaplin succumbed to this same Roman spell, and the guest list here remains illustrious. Don't expect to get Audrey Hepburn's table unless she's with you.

JEWELRY

36 PETOCHI
Piazza di Spagna 23
Tel. 67.90.635
Expensive; credit cards accepted

For 100 years aristocratic Romans have come here to buy their wedding bands and classic gifts bearing Petochi's hallmarks: reliable good taste together with excellent craftsmanship. The charming Signor Petochi presides with his young American wife over the handsome, second-floor shop, when he is not overhead in his workshop of 20 skilled jewelers. Like the generations before him, he prides himself on supervising the handfinishing of everything produced by his craftsmen. A series of historic monuments, fountains, and piazzas intricately interpreted in silver make perfect though costly souvenirs for the Romophile. There is also a beautiful selection of antique and modern silver tea services, and Petochi's silversmiths will duplicate or replace any piece you may be missing to complete your own set. Also on display is the private family collection of miniature mosaics, mostly from the 18th-century Vatican school.

A throwback to the age of The Grand Tour.

SUSTENANCE
TEAROOM

37 BABINGTON'S TEAROOM
Piazza di Spagna 23
Tel. 67.86.027
Expensive; credit cards accepted
Closed Thursday

In 1896, two British maiden ladies met in Rome and set up a cozy tearoom for transient expatriates in town during their Grand Tour days. Immediately successful, it took its name from Anne Marie Babington and has long been an exclusive society gathering place that still serves delicious traditional specialties following Miss Babington's 19th-century cookbook. In this refreshing and quiet dark-paneled refuge, you can enjoy tea for two replete with silver service and fresh scones, not to mention Welsh rarebit, chicken supreme, curries, the ever-favorite plum cake, or an American breakfast of scrambled eggs and bacon, pancakes and waffles. Half the fun is checking out the handsome crowd of TV stars and imperious Roman ladies who look as if they've just come from an exhausting fitting at Valentino's.

LEATHERGOODS
BAGS & ACCESSORIES

38 BOTTEGA VENETA
Salita San Sebastianello 16
Tel. 67.82.535
Expensive; credit cards accepted

Updated woven leather is Bottega Veneta's most popular look in soft, pouchy bags and tasteful, coordinating accessories. For more on this noted Veneto-based firm, see the Venice listing (page 469).

BOOKS
ART & ART HISTORY

39 LIBRERIA INTERNAZIONALE BOCCA
Via delle Carrozze 50
Tel. 67.90.988
Moderate; credit cards accepted

Bibliophiles love to linger about this historic bookstore, possibly elbow-to-elbow with such regulars as Marcello Mastroianni and Federico Fellini. Current owner and art historian Giorgio Torselli, himself an author, is responsible for the impressive collection of titles and illustrated books on art and art history. Housed in a seignorial 17th-century palazzo, the Bocca offers books in English and French as well as Italian and includes the topics of theater, film, and interior design. There is also a small archive of antique books in rare bindings. Since its opening in 1860, many customers have made a visit to this refined *libreria* a must; prior to that, it was the charming Caffè degli Inglesi, popular with noble youths passing through on their Grand Tour.

ANTIQUE JEWELRY

40 SIRAGUSA
Via delle Carrozze 64
Tel. 67.97.085
Expensive; credit cards accepted
Closed Saturday

Sicily's Siragusa (Syracuse) was a major outpost of Magna Graecia for 400 years until the Romans took over in 300 B.C.; its name is appropriate to this store, with its aura of classic antiquity and archeological discovery. Like a little museum, Siragusa specializes in ancient, precious one-of-a-kind pieces set into handcrafted chains and settings that enhance their timeless beauty and their value. Coins date back as far as the 4th century B.C., and there are ancient beads excavated in Asia Minor. A steady clientele comes from all corners of the world to purchase these original pieces, which, if you can afford them, are quintessential souvenirs of the Eternal City.

FASHION

MEN'S

Shirts & Furnishings

41 IL PORTONE
Via delle Carrozze 69 and 73
Tel. 67.97.807
Moderate; credit cards accepted

Il Portone offers a fantastic selection of all-cotton shirts made in every color and every width stripe. Good-quality fabrics and workmanship with an eye on fashion trends make these shirts a great buy and a perfect gift. In five days, for a nominal fee, the shop will personalize your purchase with a monogram (the Italian style is to wear initials below the left breast pocket). Il Portone will also make to measure or do alterations. Its shop next door at No. 73 is for men's intimatewear. Short- and long-sleeved kimono-style robes are made from the same shirting fabric or from terry-cloth lined with cotton prints. There are also classic men's pajamas and nightshirts in paisley and madras cottons that women snatch up to belt and wear as dresses. Matching slippers come in their own travel case. A big selection of boxer shorts in bright and witty prints, bathing suits, socks and scarves complete the stock.

FASHION

WOMEN'S

High-Fashion Made-to-Measure Swimwear

42 MARISA PADOVAN
Via delle Carrozze 81
Tel. 67.93.946
Expensive; credit cards accepted

An international clientele has discovered Marisa Padovan's answer to the less-than-perfect body: custom-made bathing suits. In a small, attractive shop run by Signora Padovan and her three daughters, you can pick Lycras and other suitable fabrics in prints and fashionable solids. The Padovans have been leaders in high-fashion swimwear design, predominantly the one-piece type, for 20 years. Their specialized seamstresses, who work all year round, will make up your summertime creation in a month and ship it home for you. There are also a number of ready-made styles, including shoulder-padded, pearl-studded models that can pass for eveningwear body suits. Matching coverups and beach robes complete the look.

An arresting façade on the Via Gregoriana.

LEATHERGOODS
BAGS & ACCESSORIES

43 ARMANDO RIODA
Via Belsiana 90
Tel. 67.84.435
Moderate; credit cards accepted
Open during lunch

Two flights of poorly lit stairs bring you to the workshop of Armando Rioda. If you have an appreciative eye for beautifully handcrafted leathergoods of a structured, classical line and don't mind the no-frills shop, you'll find good quality and accommodating service here. Everything, from Signor Rioda's famous suitcases and overnight bags to his handbags, briefcases, wallets and belts, is handmade with the finest leathers and finished with care. Since first opening shop right after the war, Signor Rioda has been known for his quality handwork. He sells to a number of upscale shops, but by coming here, you can see his collection in its entirety and can save close to 40 percent. You can also have any special requests custom-made in a short time.

FASHION
CHILDREN'S
Sportswear

44 PRÉNATAL
Via della Croce 48–49
Tel. 67.93.932
Moderate; credit cards accepted

Fun and fashionable active clothing and accessories for children up to eight years of age. See the Milan listing (page 282) for more information. There is a second Prénatal Rome location at Via Nazionale 45 (telephone 46.14.03).

Nearby at Via Frattina 138 is the four-story La Cicogna, or "the Stork" (telephone 67.91.912). One of a chain of nine Roman stores, it has a large selection of maternity clothes and apparel for newborns to 14-year-olds, in a modern, self-service setting.

FASHION
ACCESSORIES
Women's Hosiery

45 CALZA & CALZE
Via della Croce 78
Tel. 67.84.281
Moderate; no credit cards

A small, crowded shop overflowing with women's stockings and bright tights, Calza & Calze doesn't miss a color, stripe, or pattern. This is a family-run shop that began by selling notions and has grown to be the best-stocked hosiery stop around. Refreshingly, the family still seems to be involved for the mere pleasure of it; even when the store is crowded, which is almost always, you can rely upon their patience, expertise, and tolerance of your linguistic limitations.

PARTYGOODS & NOVELTIES

46 VERTECCHI 🛍🛍🛍🛍
Via della Croce 38 and 70
Tel. 67.90.100, 67.83.110
Moderate; credit cards accepted

This is Rome's, and possibly all of Italy's, largest stationery store, although to call it anything less than a design center would be misleading. At No. 70, you'll find everything from colorful school supplies, designer school bags and artists' materials to a large stock of pens, including both inexpensive novelty items and sleek Mont Blanc and Valentino models. There are notebooks, bright-colored writing papers, desk sets and all kinds of accessories for the upbeat office. Across the street at No. 38 is Vertecchi's *Fantasia della Carta* ("paper fantasy"). Here are the newest Italian ideas for picnic and party

An imposing element of the Roman legacy.

things in bright prints and patterns: initialed and fun-patterned napkins and paper plates and gaily colored plasticware, including glasses, ice buckets, trays, and thermos bottles. There are greeting cards, wrapping papers and a vast array of candles in all colors, shapes, and sizes. Upstairs is an imaginative assortment of *bonbonnière*—hand-wrapped candies that are traditional wedding table favors. After an entertaining browse through both these locations, you'll understand why Romans ask, "But have you tried Vertecchi's?"

BAR-CAFFÈ

47 FRATELLI D'ANGELI
Via della Croce 30
Tel. 67.82.556
Moderate; no credit cards accepted
Closed Sunday

D'Angeli's is a big, bustling *bar caffè* in the heart of the shopping district, where you can enjoy a mid-morning snack or an informal lunch. When you enter the well-stocked *gastronomia,* you are greeted by extensive pastry counters on the left, where everything is fresh, tempting, and made on the premises. During lunch hours, if you can't find a table in the restaurant area on the right, you can choose from a wide variety of *tramezzino* sandwiches and snacks at the stand-up bar. You can have a light lunch of salad, pasta, soup, or simple grilled meat without the obligation of multiple courses. You can also have anything wrapped up to take out (*da portare via*) and picnic in the nearby Villa Borghese gardens.

WINES

48 ANTICA BOTTIGLIERIA PLACIDI
Via della Croce 76
Tel. 67.90.896
Inexpensive; no credit cards accepted
Closed Sunday

Stroll down one of the few streets in this sleek area to have retained its old neighborhood color, and stop in here for a dose of local character and a glass of good wine. Opened in 1860 much as you see it today, the Bottiglieria is one of the few remaining classic Roman oil and wine shops. Large wooden doors lead into a long room with shelves of bottled wines on the right and a long counter on the left. A bulletin board next to the cash register tells you which wines are available by the glass. Most of the bottles of white and bubbly wines are still cooled in a large marble tub filled with running water from an open tap. An interesting cross section of boutique owners and area old-timers argue over Sunday's soccer scores and hide away from the summer heat.

SUSTENANCE

RISTORANTE/TRATTORIA

49 OTELLO
Via della Croce 81
Tel. 67.91.178
Moderate; no credit cards accepted
Closed Sunday

Set back from the street just enough to be often overlooked by newcomers, Otello is nevertheless one of the area's most popular eating spots with Romans and tourists alike. Friendly waiters recite in countless languages an extensive menu of local and tradi-tional favorites that varies with the season. The art-covered walls remind guests of the proximity of the artistic Via Margutta community; and the small, charming courtyard is worth the wait in good weather.

HOME

LINENS

50 IL BIANCO DI ELLEPI
Via della Croce 4
Tel. 67.96.835
Expensive; credit cards accepted
Open during lunch

Italy's best lines of quality linens for the home are all represented here. Shelves are stocked to the ceiling with pure cotton sheets and coordinating bedspreads in a complete range of colors and print designs from Missoni and other houses. There are also rainbows of towels, with terry-cloth bathrobes to match, and woven, tapestry-like bedspreads in muted earth tones. Tablecloths in a range of pretty pastels can be made to order.

FASHION

WOMEN'S

51 ROMANI
Via del Babuino 94
Tel. 67.92.323
Expensive; credit cards accepted

This small specialty store is popular with well-heeled Roman ladies. Romani's offers a sophisticated combination of high-fashion clothing and quality leathergoods under one roof. On the first floor are expensive daytime handbags in fine leathers, elegant and classic models simply ornamented with a decorative clasp or an unexpected twist. Upstairs are all the clothes to go with them: knitwear, dressy looks, and a good sampling from such top Italian labels as Moschino and Calla.

FURS

52 RAMPONE
Via del Babuino 98
Tel. 67.84.231
Expensive; credit cards accepted

The Rampone family's 80 years and three generations of experience in the fur market have paved the way to this new and elegant salon. Styles are classic with a sharp eye on fashion, and nothing but the highest-quality skins are used here—Canadian and Russian sable, American mink, Scandinavian fox and Russian squirrel. The creative dynamism of third-generation Anna Rampone is seen in a new line that is sportier, though created with the same artisanal methods for which the family is renowned. Only 400 coats are produced each year, guaranteeing rigid quality control.

ANTIQUE JEWELRY

ART NOUVEAU & ART DECO

53 BONCAMPAGNI STURNI
Via Maria dei Fiori 59/B
Tel. 67.83.847
Expensive; credit cards accepted

This is a superb showcase of jewelry and collectibles from the end of the 1800s through the early 20th century—the period popularly known as art nouveau and art deco. Unusual French and Italian pieces include clips, earrings, brooches, and bracelets. From the same period comes a very handsome collection of original

Unusual piece at Buoncampagni Sturni.

men's and women's watches by Rolex, Vacheron, and Patek Philippe. Many of the lovely objects decorating the store are also for sale, including vases, statuettes, and silver dressing-table articles.

SHOES

MEN'S & WOMEN'S

54 GUIDO PASQUALI
Via Bocca di Leone 5
Tel. 67.95.023
Expensive; credit cards accepted

In this tiny modern boutique you'll find products of the excellent craftsmanship that has established Guido Pasquali as one of Italy's most fashionable shoe designers over the last decade. Unusual hides and a sense of high style have made him popular as a private designer to Milan's major fashion houses. The industry often looks to him for future trends, especially in boot design.

FASHION
WOMEN'S ACCESSORIES
Fun Hosiery

55 BRUSCOLI
Via del Corso 113
Tel. 67.95.715
Moderate; credit cards accepted

Street-level windows will entice you downstairs, where novel hosiery with great fashion appeal comes in florals, paisleys, laces and abstract art. There are some solids and woolens, but the choice of classic items is limited— young and trendy is the order of the day. You'll find designer names like Christian Dior and Yves Saint Laurent along with lesser-known makes. Although hosiery is Bruscoli's specialty, there's also an amusing selection of gloves, socks, swimwear and lingerie, as well as colorful leotards and dance outfits.

ANTIQUES
17TH-to-19TH CENTURY ITALIAN

56 W. APOLLONI
Via del Babuino 133–134
Tel. 67.92.429
Expensive; no credit cards accepted

On this street lined with serious antique dealers, W. Apolloni is one of the most respected. For two generations it has catered to a clientele of museums and professional collectors, but any art lover is welcome in the gallery-like shop with dark-burgundy velvet walls. Here each 17th- to 19th-century Italian antique is treated as a masterpiece, be it a large piece of furniture such as an armoire, table or cabinet, a rare silver piece, or an old master drawing. For a selection of

sculpture and marble pieces of the same period and quality, visit the nearby Galleria Antiquaria Tuena located at Via Margutta 53/B (telephone 67.95.116), housed in a palazzo behind wrought-iron gates.

GIFTS
FABRICS & ACCESSORIES

57 NAJ OLEARI
Via di San Giacomo 25/A
Tel. 67.80.045
Expensive; credit cards accepted

The colorful printed cottons of the young Naj Oleari brothers cover everything from umbrellas to teddy bears, from desk diaries to lampshades. One of dozens of locations throughout Italy and selected international cities, this is a great source for fun, status gifts for children and adults alike. See the Milan listing (page 247).

FASHION
MEN'S, WOMEN'S & CHILDREN'S
Designer Boutique

58 EMPORIO ARMANI
Via del Babuino 140
Tel. 67.88.454
Expensive; credit cards accepted

The fabled Armani silhouette is here in a relatively new ready-to-wear division from one of Milan's greatest design names. Priced considerably lower than his high fashion, the collection here is almost as large as in the Milan flagship store, with a great selection for children 4 to 13 years old. You'll also be able to choose from all the handsome Armani accessories. See the Milan listing (page 185).

FASHION

MEN'S & WOMEN'S

Designer Discounts

59 IL DISCOUNT DELL'ALTA MODA
Via Gesù e Maria 16/A
No telephone
Moderate; no credit cards accepted

This is the only closeout store of its kind in Rome, but since it is new and not yet widely known, shopping here can be a pleasure. As in all designer-discount operations, the selection available on any given day can vary greatly; count on an impressive range of high-design labels from Italy and France, such as Jean-Paul Gaultier, Giorgio Armani, Claude Montana, and Erreuno, at approximately 50 percent off the regular European retail prices. This is not defective merchandise but overproduction and cancellations. Clothes are not grouped according to designer, although labels are left in the garments. They are often a bit late in arriving for the season—a small price to pay for these discounts. Fashion is mostly daytime and sportswear, but women can occasionally find evening dresses. Dressing rooms are available. A limited supply of accessories usually includes shoes, ties and handbags from leading designers.

ANTIQUES

TABLETOP SILVER

60 IL GRANMERCATO ANTIQUARIO BABUINO
Via del Babuino 150
Tel. 67.85.903
Moderate; credit cards accepted

The Great Babuino Antiques Market offers two open floors of easy browsing for those who enjoy antiques-hunting without a stifling museum setting. Roam through a tidy display that seems like an estate's inventory; each piece is carefully marked with price and date. Emphasis is on antique English silver, with numerous items of jewelry, tabletop accessories and frames. For gift-shopping without major expenditure, look at the decorative silver napkin rings and pillboxes, or pick up an antique pipe or fishing reel if you have the appropriate someone in mind. A wonderful selection of turn-of-the-century walking sticks is also usually on hand.

BOOKS

ENGLISH-LANGUAGE

61 THE LION BOOKSHOP
Via del Babuino 181
Tel. 36.05.837
Moderate; credit cards accepted
Open during lunch

A frequent life-saver for all English-speaking visitors to Rome, the well-stocked Lion Bookshop is conveniently located and is browser-friendly. This British-owned institution boasts large quarters that are divided into well-displayed sections of guidebooks, phrase books, maps, and very handy "menu masters" for helping you through any gastronomic excursion. There are books on Italian architecture, art and archaeology and a large stock of British and American fiction paperbacks, including the complete range of Penguins. Since its one-time rival Economy Book Center has recently left the Piazza di Spagna for larger quarters near the train station, the Lion is now the largest bookstore of its kind in this tourist-populated downtown area. It has long played the role of unofficial home base for the city's English-speaking community.

SUSTENANCE

RISTORANTE/TRATTORIA

62 MARGUTTA VEGETARIANO
Via Margutta 119
Tel. 67.86.033
Moderate; credit cards accepted
Closed Sunday

After a rash of rich food and marathon shopping, you might enjoy a wholesome light lunch in a serene spot that houses Rome's best vegetarian restaurant. When you have studied the chalkboard menu of innovative dishes that is changed daily according to the availability of fresh ingredients, you won't be surprised to learn that one of the owners once owned a nearby macrobiotic store. Choose from chunky minestrone or lentil soup, wholewheat pastas, interesting mixed salads, *frittate* (omelets) or soufflés, vegetables *alla parmigiana,* or delicious zucchini blossoms stuffed with ricotta and fried in a light tempura batter. There are baskets of crusty whole wheat *filone* bread—but don't expect any butter or sugar. The only alchohol is an excellent white kosher wine from the Jewish community in Pitigliano in southern Tuscany and a surprisingly good biological beer imported from France. You'll enjoy the gracious, simple and open setting.

The attractive Osteria Margutta.

HOME

LAMPS & LIGHTING

63 ARTEMIDE
Via Margutta 107
Tel. 67.84.917
Expensive; credit cards accepted

Designed by some of Italy's most noted names, Artemide's advanced and enduring lighting fixtures can be found here in all their sleek and stylish beauty. See the Milan listing (page 192).

SUSTENANCE

RISTORANTE/TRATTORIA

64 OSTERIA MARGUTTA
Via Margutta 82
Tel. 67.98.190
Moderate; credit cards accepted
Closed Sunday

Here's a favorite old-fashioned *osteria* with a very inviting art-nouveau stained-glass front and deep-toned wood paneling inside. True to the owners' claim, the cooking is genuine and simple: home-cooked Roman dishes such as oxtail soup (see glossary), *pasta e ceci* soup, or grilled slabs of the delicious nutty-flavored *scamorza* cheese made from buffalo milk. There's a range of uncompromisingly regional possibilities, with an occasional twist of the unexpected, such as *risotto al curry* or Hungarian goulash. Waiters are pleasant and unhurried and will wheel over an enticing desert cart at the end of the meal.

GIFTS

SICILIAN CERAMICS

65 GALLERIA DUN
Via Margutta 47/A
Tel. 36.14.091
Moderate; credit cards accepted

If you can't make it to Sicily, Sicily will come to you by means of this large open gallery hosting Rome's best collection of Sicilian crafts, particularly ceramics. The bright and vivid colors of the Mediterranean decorate a wide range of ceramicware here, from bowls, mugs, and urns to tiles for the kitchen and bath. The gallery promotes a number of contemporary Sicilian artists, each from a different area such as Erice, Sciacca, Caltagirone, and Santo Stefano di Camastia. The most famous is Giovanni De Simone from Palermo, who has brought this ancient art to a new and vibrant level of development. Trained in Faenza and compared to Chagall and Picasso, De Simone explores the roots of his island's folklore and legend to create tile paintings in the warm, distinctive colors of Sicily. The store's owners will gladly ship.

SUSTENANCE

RISTORANTE/TRATTORIA

Taxi-Away

66 LE JARDIN
Lord Byron Hotel
Via Giuseppe de Notaris 5 (off map)
Tel. 36.09.541
Expensive to very expensive; credit cards
     accepted
Closed Sunday

With a reputation independent of the small Hotel Lord Byron in which it is located, Le Jardin is one of Rome's prime restaurants for distinguished French cuisine. In peaceful and gracious surroundings that simulate a garden's delight, guests rely upon the knowledge of *maître-sommelier* Antonio Ciminelli and the creative fancy of renowned head chef Antonio Sciullo. Light and inventive dishes are artfully prepared and simply presented. You might begin with delicate herb risotto flecked with borage, sage, rosemary, mint and basil, or ravioli with a light shrimp sauce. Always-changing entrées may include grilled veal chops with rasberry vinegar or lettuce-wrapped *rombo* (brill or turbot) that is stuffed with salmon mousse. Exquisite little cookies are made fresh daily, as is the rich ice cream. There's a wonderful selection of wines, fine regional Italian and French. It is no wonder that the Lord Byron Hotel, together with its Florentine counterpart the Hotel Regency, is a rare Italian member of the prestigious Relais et Châteaux chain.

DESIGNER BOUTIQUE DIRECTORY

The following designer boutiques in Rome are listed in alphabetical order by last name. They are all located in the Piazza di Spagna neighborhood. All take credit cards and follow store hours.

Giorgio Armani (Women's)
Via del Babuino 102
Tel. 67.93.777

Basile (Men's & Women's)
Via Mario dei Fiori 29
Tel. 67.89.244

Laura Biagiotti (Men's & Women's)
Via Borgognona 43–44
Tel. 67.91.205

Fendi (Women's)
Via Borgognona 36
Tel. 67.97.641

Salvatore Ferragamo (Women's)
Via Condotti 73–74
Tel. 67.98.402

Salvatore Ferragamo (Men's)
Via Condotti 66
Tel. 67.81.1130

Gianfranco Ferrè (Men's)
Via Borgognona 6
Tel. 67.97.445

Gianfranco Ferrè (Women's)
Via Borgognona 42B
Tel. 67.80.256

Gucci (Ready-to-Wear & Shoes)
Via Condotti 77
Tel. 67.96.147

Gucci (Leathergoods & Accessories)
Via Condotti 8
Tel. 67.89.340

Missoni Uomo (Men's)
Piazza di Spagna 78
Tel. 67.92.555

Trussardi (Men's & Women's)
Via Bocca di Leone 27
Tel. 67.80.280

Valentino (Women's)
Via Bocca di Leone 15
Tel. 67.95.862

Valentino Uomo (Men's)
Via Mario dei Fiori 22
Tel. 67.83.656

Mario Valentino (Men's & Women's)
Via Frattina 84
Tel. 67.91.246

Gianni Versace (Women's)
Via Bocca di Leone 26
Tel. 67.80.521

Gianni Versace (Men's)
Via Borgognona 29
Tel. 67.95.292

Via Condotti

Via Condotti plays center stage to shoppers in Rome. Because of its legacy, its world-class character and its big-name stores, we have treated it as an area independent of the Piazza di Spagna neighborhood that surrounds it. More eyes peruse the Via Condotti's elegant windows than

Mercifully closed to traffic, the elegant Via Condotti is set off by a spectacular backdrop.

Celebrated stores like Bulgari set the tone.

are raised to the Sistine Chapel ceiling; few historical monuments vie for your attention here, leaving you free to self-indulge. This is superlative shopping, especially for the lucky few who can afford to buy Bulgari trinkets or to have their names written in diamonds, a Capuano specialty.

Some say that this celebrated street was named after the subterranean conduits (*condotti*) built by Pope Gregory XIII in the late 16th century that brought fresh water from the Acqua Vergine aqueduct to feed Rome's myriad fountains and ancient public baths. Others insist that the name refers to an artery of another kind: the via was once a conduit for the steady stream of pilgrims making their way from the Vatican to the Trinità dei Monti, the church at the top of the Spanish Steps.

Many of the rather austere palazzos that line the street were built in the 18th century by aristocratic European families who came to visit on the last leg of the Grand Tour and never left. Fashionable English milords and men of letters such as Tennyson and Thackeray lived here at the smartest of Rome's addresses. This was one of their first ports of call, especially once the Caffè Greco opened its doors in the mid-18th century. The social tide flowed uphill only after 1870 with the building of the glamorous Via Veneto. The Via Condotti continues to draw tourists and crowned heads like a magnet with its aggregation of elegant and famous stores as well as its historical and aesthetic character. A point of interest can be found at No. 68; slip into the beautiful courtyard to see the seat of the Sovereign Military Order of Malta, first founded as the Knights of St. John in 1113. The only Crusaders on the *via* today are those on their way to Bulgari's.

Onetime religious, now commercial, this hallowed path is still well-trodden. Modern-day pilgrims are the shoppers who come from all corners of the world to marvel at this "Made in Italy" showcase.

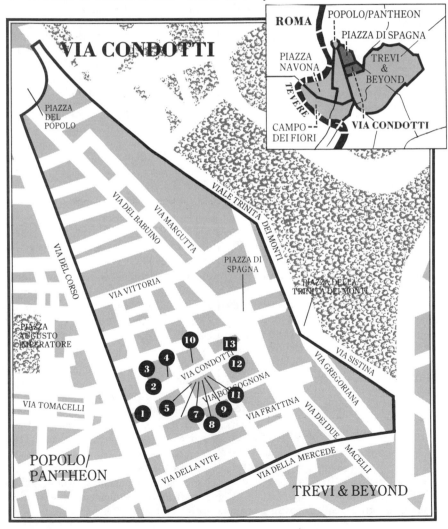

LEATHERGOODS

BAGS & ACCESSORIES

Fashion Collection

1 DESMO
Via Condotti 34
Tel. 67.91.122
Expensive; credit cards accepted

Desmo stands out for its bag selections in exotic skins, such as ostrich and crocodile, stamped leathers and bright fashion colors. See Florence listing (page 76).

FASHION

MEN'S

Made-to-Measure Classic Elegance

2 BATTISTONI ⌂⌂⌂⌂
Via Condotti 61/A
Tel. 67.86.241
Expensive; credit cards accepted

For decades considered to be Rome's most fashionable tailor, Battistoni has made fine custom shirts and suits for the Duke of Windsor, Gianni Agnelli, Gore Vidal, Leonard Bernstein, and film stars and royalty from around the world. The exquisite shop featuring dark wood, Persian carpets, and framed antique prints is located off a quiet courtyard and is covered with a blue-and-gold awning. Choose from close to 2000 different quality shirting fabrics in classic prints and stripes of every width and color, or order a custom-made suit from a remarkable selection of styles and materials. Service is crisply efficient and highly professional. Begun by Guglielmo Battistoni in the years after World War II, the firm later opened a ladies' boutique a few doors down at Via Condotti 57. Silk dressing gowns,

Society's most fashionable tailor.

British scents and toiletries, cashmere sweaters, and scarves and ties designed by famous artists such as Renato Guttuso are part of the refined world of Battistoni.

JEWELRY

3 CAPUANO
Via Condotti 61
Tel. 67.95.996
Expensive; credit cards accepted

The affable Signor Peppino Capuano will tell you that jewelry must be a manifestation of joy, showing you photographs of happy-looking customers Brigitte Bardot and Ursula Andress. His classic look with important colorful gems has been keeping customers happy for years, the last 26 spent in the elegant palazzo he shares with the renowned Battistoni tailor's atelier. Meticulously set diamonds on wide cuff bracelets spell out "Darling" or "Sweetheart," and whatever name you desire can be specially ordered. The same attention to detail is given to less precious stones. Their hundred years of tradition began when the three Capuano brothers relocated from Naples, where skilled craftsmen still produce the family's collections.

ANTIQUE JEWELRY

TOP-NAME

4 CARLO ELEUTERI
Via Condotti 69
Tel. 67.81.078
Expensive; credit cards accepted

Pricey collectors' pieces of predominantly art-deco jewelry are Eleuteri's specialty. In his very small, elite shop with tiny windows showcasing his exquisite finds, you'll see important original pieces that date from the 1920s through the 1940s. This is for serious buyers, who will appreciate the unique signed objets by that period's most noted designers. There is also an impressive selection of wrist and pocket watches, and table clocks.

JEWELRY

TOP-NAME

5 FEDERICO BUCCELLATI
Via Condotti 31
Tel. 67.90.329
Expensive; credit cards accepted

An offshoot of Milan's Mario Buccellati, and carrying the same exquisite, highly worked jewelry, this elegant store appointed with crystal chandeliers and radiating old-world grace has been here for 60 years. See the Milan listing (page 208).

SHOES

MEN'S & WOMEN'S

Handmade & Made-to-Measure

6 BARRILA 🛍🛍🛍🛍
Via Condotti 29
Tel 67.93.916
Moderate; credit cards accepted

Savvy Romans shop here for carefully crafted handmade shoes whose guaranteed comfort does not diminish their fashion flair. The enterprise is run by a family of seven cousins, children of two industrious Sicilian brothers who set up shop almost 20 years ago. Their footwear is based on classic styles that, while not trendy, does reflect seasonal trends and colors. The real draw here is the shoes' fit and high-quality workmanship. Barrila has its own small factory of 20 craftsmen, who can produce only 50 to 60 pairs a day. A number of widths are available, and alterations or other modifications can be made on ready-made pairs, or you can special-order made-to-measure shoes within 2 to 3 weeks, an option especially popular with large-sized customers. A second Barrila location at Via del Babuino 33 (telephone 67.83.830) features a slightly younger, more up-to-the-minute line.

FASHION

CHILDREN'S

Designer Names

7 ESMERALDA
Via Condotti 23
Tel. 67.97.806
Expensive; credit cards accepted

If you're looking for investment clothing for children 1 to 14 years old, don't be misled by the second-floor location of this small shop. You'll find exquisitely made fashion by small artisan companies such as I Pinci Palloni as well as by such major names as Gianfranco Ferrè, Rocco Barocco, Blu Marine and Enrico Coveri. One of the finest children's collections in Italy comes from Sermonetta, which is well represented here. La Perla's charming beachwear for young girls is also featured. Beautiful fabrics, fine finishing, and a range of design from sporty practicality to grown-up elegance more than compensate for the undistinguished ambiance.

FABRICS

FASHION

Couture Silks

8 POLIDORI
Via Condotti 21/A
Tel. 67.84.842
Expensive; credit cards accepted

If you have the talent to do justice to the ultimate in yard goods, visit Polidori's women's location for its special collection of classic printed silks. Every season leading couturiers Valentino, Yves Saint Laurent, Renato Balestra, and Jean Patou leave their imprint on high-quality Italian and French silks meant to be made up into their exquisite fashion designs. Bolt after bolt of these extraordinary silks are available for sale here. Polidori first opened shop in 1950 at Via Borgognona 4/A; that original location is still an elite resource for both men's and women's fabrics. Another Polidori offers sophisticated fabrics for men only at Via Condotti 84, with a refined men's tailor shop nearby at Via Condotti 61/A.

SHOES

MEN'S & WOMEN'S

9 BELTRAMI
Via Condotti 19
Tel. 67.91.330
Expensive; credit cards accepted

This spacious, modern shop houses the whole collection of the Florence-based leathergoods company. Unusual combinations and treatments of quality leathers and skins in shoes, accessories, and clothing are Beltrami's trademark. See the Florence listing (page 53).

FASHION

WOMEN'S

Eveningwear

10 MARISELAINE
Via Condotti 70
Tel. 67.95.817
Expensive; credit cards accepted

Rome offers truly an abundance of eveningwear boutiques, but Mariselaine is particularly favored by young debutantes looking for that special ball gown. Elegant evening fashion with a subtle bent toward sexiness can be purchased ready-to-wear or made-to-measure; exquisite wedding gowns are also created to order.

The look is somewhat more mature and sophisticated at the nearby Eli Colaj, at Via del Babuino 65 (telephone 67.88.993). Silks and voiles appear in simple evening silhouettes that hint of a late 19th-century inspiration. The refined, rather mysterious woman is a regular customer here and also appreciates Signora Colaj's talent for designing unique wedding gowns. And for the more flamboyant nighttime fashion at which Rome excels, you'll want to visit the For You Boutique at Via Frattina 60 (telephone 67.96.238).

HOME

DESIGNER ACCESSORIES

11 VALENTINO PIÙ
Via Condotti 13
Tel. 67.95.207
Expensive; credit cards accepted

A dreamy street-level display window draws you up an elegant staircase to this second-floor home-furnishings store of Rome's own Valentino. Here a sophisticated international clientele can fill their homes with furniture and objets d'art showing the distinctive Valentino flair. Dining tables beautifully laid with hand-painted china; coffee tables in lacquered wood, bamboo and rattan; colonial cane chairs and tables of various sizes; lamps, photo frames, and decorative boxes are all delightfully exhibited. One room is dedicated to Valentino's signed, distinctively colored fabrics: silks, linens and cottons, many of which have been used on chairs, sofas, beds and cushions displayed to trigger your imagination.

JEWELRY

TOP-NAME

12 BULGARI
Via Condotti 10
Tel. 67.93.876
Very expensive; credit cards accepted

As befits its celebrated clientele, the Bulgari jewelry store is palatial. This is the gem of Via Condotti, and if you intend to buy some of the world's finest jewelry, let any or all of the three liveried doormen usher you in. You may want to spend nothing at all, but just admire a floor-to-ceiling glass case of exquisite antique silver that

Bulgari—open, sleek, palatial.

stands testimony to Bulgari's liaison with the past. Three brothers and two cousins work under the direction of Signor Paolo Bulgari, the grandson of Sotirio Bulgari, an immigrant silver- and goldsmith from northern Greece who set up a far more modest stand at this same location in 1905. The identifiable Bulgari look features beautiful settings of big, colorful gems and elaborate, glittering creations of diamonds, rubies, and emeralds. The Bulgari's most-copied design is a Renaissance setting of large precious stones high on their mounts. They were also the first to use ancient Roman coins set in bold necklaces. Men's cuff links decorated with miniature mosaics are exquisite oddities. Although the Bulgaris remain closely linked with a classic design tradition, a new line of sleek watches, pens and 18k gold lighters emphasizes their prominence in the contemporary market as well.

SUSTENANCE

BAR/CAFFÈ

13 CAFFÈ GRECO
Via Condotti 86
Tel. 67.82.554
Expensive; no credit cards accepted
Closed Sunday

This is one of Rome's most celebrated cafès, praised in the memoirs of its illustrious habitués: Casanova, Liszt, Keats, Shelley, Berlioz, Stendhal and Goethe. Opened in 1760 by a Greek-descended Roman (hence its name), it has preserved its early-18th-century character. In the long narrow back rooms, local dowagers still come for their ritual tea, seated at tiny marble tables alongside the shopping-bag-laden tourists. Waiters in white tie and tails serve dainty pastries and politely trimmed chicken sandwiches for those who make it through the crowd at the front bar. For everyone it's a quiet respite from the crowds of the Via Condotti.

BULGARI

Romans love to recount how the young Sotirio Bulgari courageously escaped in 1884 from his small home town in Greece and the growing oppression of the Ottoman Empire. He was from the region of Epirus, known since antiquity for its skilled silversmiths, and brought the ancient art with him to Rome via Naples. In the ensuing 100 years Sotirio Bulgari and his children built a glittering empire on precious stones, high design and flawless workmanship.

Much as today's young artisans throng the Piazza di Spagna area, Sotirio had his humble beginning in the Piazza Trinità dei Monti. Far superior in quality to the tawdry crafts one finds nowadays displayed along the Spanish Steps, his unique and carefully crafted silver buckles were eventually successful enough to enable him to move down to the Via Condotti, thereby moving up in the world. The year was 1905, the Via Condotti had only a hint of its current glamour, and his *bottega* was a modest but always busy place.

Sotirio's two young sons Giorgio and Constantino took up the golden torch with a passion and a design sense instilled by their father, though tempered by changing times. Following World War II, they modernized the unpretentious family shop, eventually transforming it into the temple-like gem it is today.

Grandson Paolo Bulgari presides over what is now an appropriately splendid showcase for the inimitable collections of Bulgari jewels, as prestigious for those who wear them as for those who give them as the ultimate gift. Large, colorful stones in High Renaissance-like settings are the hallmarks of the universally recognized Bulgari look, although the designs have diversified and developed fashionably modern spin-offs while never relinquishing the family's scrupulous guarantee of quality. One admirer, Andy Warhol, once called Bulgari Rome's most important museum of contempo rary art.

Piazza Navona

*T*he magnificent Piazza Navona is an open-air baroque gallery and an essential Roman experience for a memorable after-dinner ice cream. Most visitors fall prey to its time-worn spell that lures you back the next morning, its provocative charm that follows you through winding streets and cobblestoned alleyways. Here you can truly explore Rome's historical wealth even as you discover one-of-a-kind artisan shops where centuries-old crafts still flourish. You'll find yourself with one foot in the past, one in the present.

It is not immediately obvious to the first-time visitor that this can be a good shopping neighborhood. But if you want to buy artisan-crafted or antique souvenirs such as brassware, old prints, handknit sweaters, and fine and costume jewelry, then scout out some of the entries we've listed.

With the Vatican nearby, the Piazza Navona area blossomed as a prosperous commercial center.

Most tourists come to the Piazza Navona for the living theater of its unrivaled nocturnal *gelato* ritual. There is no other stage quite like this one, and no thespians as natural as those who nonchalantly stroll back and forth, decked out in their Sunday best, dodging the resident fire-eaters, palm readers, caricature artists, children on bicycles, and errant gigolos. Most guidebooks add drug peddlers to this list, but if there are any, they are unobtrusive and easily lost in the motley crowd of foreigners and students, actresses and pensioners. It goes without saying, however, that nowhere in Rome, or the world, is it particularly safe for the unfamiliar visitor in the *piccole ore,* or wee hours.

You won't need to see the elliptical-shaped "square" deserted to appreciate its serene architectural beauty. You'll feel yourself riveted to the piazza's centerpiece, Bernini's extraordinary baroque fountain representing four of the world's great rivers. But don't forget that this was once the site of the Circus Agonalis, the stadium built by the Emperor Domitian in A.D. 86. Tiers of stone bleachers that seated 30,000 raucous spectators were used until the 15th century, when a number of the buildings you see today replaced them. This was the arena for athletic games, the place where Rome watched Christian gladiators meet their death. If you're unlucky enough to experience the stifling heat of a Roman August, you'll understand why in the 17th to 19th centuries cardinals and princes had the piazza flooded for water pageants, an innocent vestige of the more bellicose mock sea battles staged by their ancient ancestors.

This once-prosperous bourgeois quarter is an extension of the Campo dei Fiori area in character, separated from it by the Fiat-jammed Corso Vittorio Emanuele II and embraced by a half loop of the Tiber River to the north and northwest. Because of its proximity to the Vatican, the Piazza Navona neighborhood also blossomed as a center for merchants, artisans, and tourists. You will find a new wave of these artisans today: proud young craftsmen who have fused innovation and creativity with an innate Roman respect for history.

Conveniently for the shopper, and following in the footsteps of tradition, most of these young artisans can be found clustered along the charming Via dell'Orso and its narrow perpendicular offshoots—Vicoli della Palomba, del Cancello, and dei Soldati. Ambitious and mutually supportive, the craftsmen have formed an association named for the Via dell'Orso, where a yearly outdoor exhibition is held every September and October. There are dancing and artisan demonstrations, as well as general merry-making; although you'll have to compete with the vociferous regulars, try to secure a coveted table at the lively Trattoria dell'Orso.

More established, more expensive, and in some respects less vibrant is the beautiful Via dei Coronari and its community of elegant antique stores. It attracts the sophisticated antique hunters with ample bank accounts, but even enthusiasts with thin pockets will enjoy the window shopping. Once the most important access to the Vatican, this elegant lane was literally cut out of the medieval clutter of twisting and congested byways during the Renaissance; it was named after the shops selling devotional objects to the stream of pilgrims on their way to redemption just across the Tiber (*coronari* means "Rosary Makers"). Now it remains a significant commercial and residential street, exuding the romance of centuries past. Workshops on the nearby Via dei Soldati (named after the

PIAZZA NAVONA CHRISTMAS FAIR

The Piazza Navona, one of Italy's most beautiful squares, becomes the site of an annual Christmas Fair beginning in mid-December and culminating on January 5, the eve of the Epiphany, or Feast of the Three Kings (in Italy "La Befana").

The elongated horseshoe-shaped piazza is filled with stalls, colorful lights, strolling families and small children crazed by the nearness of the holidays. The entire piazza becomes a giant Christmas market, with temporary booths selling toys and stuffed animals, handicrafts, Christmas decorations and sweets. The latter are an experience in themselves, with extensive selections that feature what appear to be large lumps of coal; these are actually candy, given as a gift to children who seem to need the warning.

Especially interesting are the components necessary to create your own *presepio*, or crèche. Miniature to mammoth in size, these Nativity scenes were once hand-crafted and artistically painted and came almost exclusively from Naples. Today, many of them are mass-produced, but still offer you much more than the average manger and Magi selection. You can pick from crumbling ruins, elaborate inns, little fountains, and troupes of angels heard on high. The ubiquitous bagpipe-playing shepherd dressed in sheepskin jerkin and crisscrossed leather leggings is a centuries-old figure; he is one of the *zampognari* who still come down from the upland plains to play their bagpipes on Rome's street corners, much like our Santas ringing their bells.

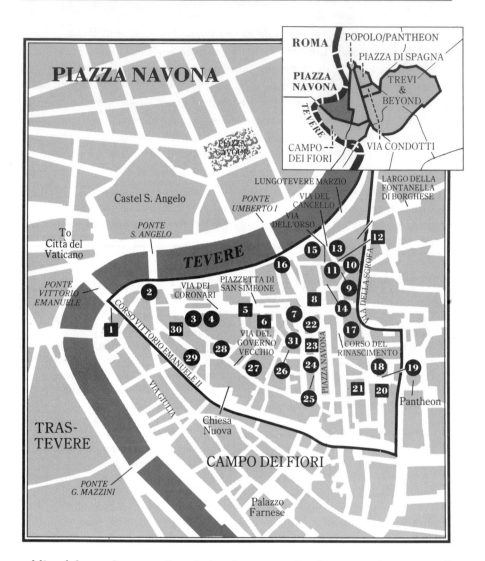

soldiers' barracks once found there) restore the furniture that you will probably soon see in one of Via dei Coronari's elaborate window displays. For over thirty years the Via dei Coronari has become a major attraction during the last two weeks of May and again in October, when an important antiques fair is held.

Don't miss a visit to this neighborhood, whether to witness the parade of evening strollers, the piazza's famous *tartufo* ice cream, the artisans or the antiques. Any Roman will tell you that when you are in the Piazza Navona, you are in the heart of Italy.

BAR/CAFFÈ

1 BIANCANEVE
Piazza Pasquale Paoli 1
Tel. 65.40.227
Moderate; no credit cards accepted
Closed Monday

Most mornings the soft, buttery crois-sants here are still warm from the oven in the back. You can sip your frothy cappuccino at an outside table with a regal view of the Castel Sant'Angelo and the Tiber before you. Every evening, things take a turn for the social, when the bar's special *mela stregata* ("bewitched apple") becomes Rome's after-dinner sweet. A thin chocolate covering in the shape of an apple encloses layers of chocolate and vanilla ice cream and is topped with fresh whipped cream. "Biancaneve," the bar's name, means "Snow White."

ENGRAVINGS & PRINTS

2 ROBERTO BOCCALINI
Via del Banco di Santo Spirito 61
(at Piazza Ponte Sant'Angelo)
Tel. 65.65.944
Inexpensive to expensive; credit cards accepted

Owner Roberto Boccalini and his prized prints.

Both the serious collector and the casual browser will enjoy hours spent here, leafing through piles of original engravings and lithographs of every subject imaginable. The prized works of some veritable *maestri* can be found, such as Giovanni Battista Piranesi, Giuseppe Vasi, and Bartolo-meo Pinelli, who was known as the painter of Trastevere life. Almost everything available dates from the 15th to the 18th century, with framed and unframed decorative prints of birds, botanical and musical themes, historical fashion, landscapes and maps, to name but a few. Views of Rome and its fountains, piazzas, and bridges show just how little it has changed. There is also a collection of antique watercolors which, together with every print in the store, come with a certificate of authenticity stat-ing the work's year or epoch, the artist, and its technique.

COLLECTIBLES

CAR MODELS

3 99 ARTE CLUB
Via dei Coronari 22
Tel. 65.43.853
Moderate; no credit cards accepted

On seeing Gianni Mizzoni's awe-inspiring collection, you'd think he had been collecting car and train models for a lifetime, not for just 15 years. His small shop seems like an attic, housing his hundreds of makes of antique model cars, trains, planes, boats and fire trucks. They date from the 1920s to today, and many are in their original boxes. If you've always yearned for an antique Ferrari, Bu-gatti or Alfa, this is your big chance to pick up a miniature rendition; Ger-many's prestigious Bing cars are also yours for the asking. A handmade 18k-gold-plated miniature train sporting three freight cars and a tidy price tag will guarantee the success of any little or big boy's Christmas morning. Signor Mizzoni also has contemporary reproductions of old car models. Keep an eye out for the tiny window in the downstairs doorway, or you'll miss the whole show.

HOME

TABLEWARE & ACCESSORIES

Porcelain

4 LA PORCELLANA 55
Via dei Coronari 55/A
Tel. 65.40.053
Moderate; credit cards accepted

Keep your elbows tucked in and walk lightly through this charming shop stocked from floor to ceiling with white porcelain. Owner Griselda Lagostena imports the simple and clean-looking porcelain from all parts of the world and displays it in neatly stacked rows on wooden-topped tables, giving the shop a country air. The collection includes everything from plates and cups to pitchers and tureens. In addition, white marble from Carrara is used for mortars and pestles and cutting boards, and an occasional piece

A natural setting for Rome's living theater.

of black porcelain shows up, in a teapot, for example. Handmade horn utensils make other interesting gifts that are easy to pack—salad servers, cheese slicers, and wine bottle openers. The porcelain travels better than you would think, and Griselda will arrange for shipping.

SUSTENANCE

RISTORANTE/TRATTORIA

5 OSTERIA DELL'ANTIQUARIO
Piazzetta di San Simeone 27
Tel. 65.96.94
Moderate; no credit cards accepted
Closed Sunday

Dinner is enjoyable in this small, cozy dining room, but the real pleasure, when weather permits, is to sit at an outside table in the charming Piazzetta di San Simeone. Emilio and Anna offer home-style Roman cooking at its best, which is not to downplay their refined and at times *nouvelle* inclinations. Their menu is limited, with a number of unvarying masterpieces and a handful of delicious daily specials, including a fresh pasta and one or more of the following: *fiori di zucchini fritti, stufatino con il sedano* (a hearty beef stew with celery), *culatello* (the heart of Parma ham), *abbacchio* (spring lamb), and *polpettine* (meatballs), a savory favorite with the regulars. For dessert, wild strawberries and raspberries seem to be available even when not in season, and there is an exceptional chocolate mousse. The owner makes his own after-dinner *digestivo* (liqueur), which caps off a good-sized wine selection. The *osteria* takes its name from the antique dealers of Via dei Coronari, just a minute's walk away, many of whom are faithful customers.

SUSTENANCE

RISTORANTE/TRATTORIA

6 PINO E DINO
Piazza di Montevecchio 22
Tel. 65.61.319
Expensive; credit cards accepted

Reservations are essential at this tiny tavern in one of Rome's little-known ivy-covered piazzas. The owners are two debonair young men, Pino from southern Taranto and Dino from Venice, and their imaginative menu (recited to you in the language of your choice) covers all the provinces in between. Fresh flowers and fine china set the tone for elegant dining. Begin with the excellent *orecchietti* ("little ears") *con broccoli, fusilli con melanzane* (with eggplant), or *risotto con castagne e tartufi* (with chestnut and truffles). Any of the entrées is recommended, from game (a specialty when in season) to veal with a light salmon mousse. Desserts are first class, with some provincial in their simplicity, others sophisticated, such as the chocolate and walnut pie.

ENGRAVINGS & PRINTS

7 CASCIANELLI
Largo Febo 14
Tel. 65.42.806
Moderate; credit cards accepted

Cascianelli places special emphasis on historical prints, heraldry, and papal paraphernalia. It also runs a small but interesting publishing operation, reviving out-of-print historical works, guidebooks to Rome, and old titles on heraldry. Among its publications is an unusual small volume: *Stemmi Pontifici,* an illustrated record of the papal coats-of-arms from 1300 to 1925.

SUSTENANCE

RISTORANTE/TRATTORIA

8 LA MAIELLA
Piazza di Sant'Apollinare 45–46
Tel. 65.64.174
Moderate; credit cards accepted
Closed Sunday

There's always a crush for the outdoor tables, while the large, cave-like inside dining room remains empty at La Maiella, one of Rome's favorite establishments. The specialties here are fresh grilled fish and prime meats simply cooked with a rustic Abruzzese approach. *Capretto scottadito* (grilled baby goat), *lattonzolo al forno* (roast suckling pig), *agnello* (lamb), and the famous *frittura mista* (every kind of seafood, lightly fried) are all recommended. When in season, *tartufi* (truffles) and *porcini* (wild mushrooms) are perfectly prepared, as is the *spaghetti all'amatriciana* (with fresh tomato, bacon, and onions). Desserts are made on the premises and, like the rest of the menu, change with the daily market's provisions. Owners Antonio and Dante are your gracious hosts.

GIFTS

PUPPETS & MARIONETTES

9 MONDO ANTICO 🗓🗓🗓🗓
Via dei Pianellari 17
Tel. 65.61.261
Moderate; no credit cards accepted
Open afternoons only

You won't know where to look first in this tiny shop cluttered with the work of the multi-talented Saro Lo Turco. Charming miniature theater sets are made from 18th- and 19th-century

One-dimensional marionettes at Mondo Antico.

engravings that are painstakingly hand-colored, then cut out and set up three-dimensionally in glass-fronted boxes. Also on display are cardboard *Images d'Epinal*—flat, handpainted marionettes—as well as puppets created by Signor Lo Turco and his assistants Armando and Paola representing such traditional stock Italian theatrical characters as Harlequin and Pulcinella. Most imposing are the large Sicilian puppets dressed in full armor hanging from the ceiling. The shop is open only in the afternoon, as Signor Lo Turco spends his mornings doing *trompe-l'oeil* work in private homes.

HOME

BRASS FURNITURE & ACCESSORIES

Workshop/Studio

10 VITTORIO PUNIELLO
Via dell'Orso 42
Tel. 65.64.133
Moderate; no credit cards accepted

Vittorio Puniello can make any brass object your heart desires in just a day to two weeks, with the top-of-the-line craftsmanship for which he is known. There's a whole *bottega* full of his work to give you some ideas: table bases (minus the glass tops), elegant lamps, planters, fireplace tools and screens, wall sconces, and headboards. Although his pieces are generally modern in design, with sleek, geometric shapes, custom work is done according to your preference. You'll need to arrange your own shipping, but most large items can be dismantled to facilitate the procedure.

Just down the street at No. 26 is Sergio Sansovini, another store specializing in brass. Sansovini's has a somewhat larger assortment, but an appraising eye will tell you that the workmanship is better at Vittorio's.

JEWELRY

WORKSHOP/STUDIO

11 FERIOZZI—ORAFO
Via dell'Orso 64–65
Tel. 65.44.039
Expensive; no credit cards accepted

Franco Feriozzi is an award-winning goldsmith who creates aristocratic yet affordable jewelry. Franco's creations are original, while drawing inspiration from the baroque designs of the 1800s. Only precious stones are used, tastefully and intricately set in gold or silver. With the exception of a few pieces from his stock, his work is available only on a commission basis. Earrings, necklaces, chains, and cuff links—everything is handmade and can be altered to your specifications, usually in two to four months. Franco, who embraces the Roman tradition of goldsmiths who held themselves to be true artists, was awarded the prestigious "La Ruota d'Oro" in 1986. The shop's exterior of dark, polished wood hints at other times.

RISTORANTE/TRATTORIA

12 L'ORSO '80
Via dell'Orso 33
Tel. 65.64.904
Moderate; credit cards accepted
Closed Monday

You'll barely be seated before your waiter brings you fresh, warm bread baked in the restaurant's red-brick ovens and a sampling of tasty appetizers. But save room for the fresh pasta dishes such as *tagliolini con porcini* (with wild mushrooms) or spaghetti with fresh fish or seafood. There are excellent meat entrées; try the Chateaubriand or the *abbacchio scottadito* (grilled baby lamb) or the expertly prepared quality-cut steaks. Fresh fish changes daily and is grilled just right. Two large rooms are always crowded with neighborhood artisans and an increasingly sophisticated crowd. Service is fast and courteous. Don't miss the simple desserts made by the owner's wife or the growing, intelligent selection of wines.

JEWELRY

WORKSHOP/STUDIO

13 MASSIMO MARIA MELIS—ORAFO
Via del Cancello 19
Tel. 65.69.188
Moderate; credit cards accepted

Unique handcrafted jewelry marries antiquity with a modern creativity. Massimo Maria Melis ferrets out authentic Etruscan, Roman, and Greek artifacts and sets them in gold, using his own interpretation of ancient techniques and styles. The archeological finds that are an integral element

ment of his exquisite jewelry can be anything from gold coins to small engraved stones or Roman glass beads. Massimo's experience in set design explains his window display of jewelry set in the sands of time. As you enter the small, polished-wood shop you'll be facing Massimo, who usually sits entranced behind his workbench.

HOME

LAMPS & LIGHTING

14 ALBERTO MARTINANGELI
Vicolo della Palomba 2–3
No telephone
Moderate; no credit cards accepted

Alberto Martinangeli brings his expertise in stage lighting into the home, producing lamps of striking theatricality. His wooden bases (some with attractive inlaid motifs) support shades made of silk batik or *ebrû* (marbleized paper). They come as table or desk lamps, standing lamps or wall fixtures, or they can be specially interpreted according to a customer's needs. Alberto's talent for theatrical set design and special effects is apparent in his beautifully executed illuminated panels, marbleized columns, and stylized fake doors and windows.

HOME

LAMPS & TABLETOP ACCESSORIES

15 AVIGNONESE
Via dell'Orso 73
No telephone
Moderate; credit cards accepted

Avignonese is the clean, modern showcase for Attilio Amato's collection of beautiful table and floor lamps. If Milanese design is too sleek and traditional Venetian lighting too ornate for you, Amato's work will win accolades for its striking combination of classical lines from southern Italy and from Renaissance Florence with a modern artisan's eye. His ingenious choice of materials includes terra cotta, faux marble, and porcelain, sometimes combined with travertine or wood. Fruit baskets, urns, columns, obelisks, and bookends made from the same materials lie scattered amid the lamps and resting on the Indian dhurrie or French dalmac carpets, which are also for sale. Another Avignonese is located near the Piazza di Spagna at Via Margutta 16 (telephone 36.14.004).

BOOKS
International Cinema & Theater

16 IL LEUTO
Via di Monte Brianzo 86
Tel. 65.69.269
Moderate; no credit cards accepted

Il Leuto is a haunt for serious cinema and theater devotees. This small, crowded bookshop was one of director Lee Strasberg's favorite destinations when passing through. It is the only bookstore in the country to stock all titles published in Italy on theater, cinema and ballet, as well as a large selection of English, American, and French publications. There are postcards, posters, playbills, and a large photographic archive, along with performing arts magazines in many languages. Il Leuto (the historical word for "lute," the instrument that was used to accompany Renaissance performances) does a large mail-order business both in Italy and abroad.

Ai Monasteri, stocked with historic panaceas.

GIFTS
Made by Monks

17 AI MONASTERI 🏠🏠🏠🏠
Corso del Rinascimento 72
Tel. 65.42.783
Moderate; no credit cards accepted

Medieval abbeys and convents across Italy are the sources for the astounding collection of liquors, natural remedies, organic beauty treatments, and honeys found at Ai Monasteri (literally "to the monasteries"). More than 20 monasteries are represented; Trappist monks vie with the Franciscans and Carmelites in the concoction of centuries-old recipes for everything from herbal tea infusions to digestive and medicinal liquors. The latter is an important element of Ai Monasteri's stock, with over 100 kinds of liquors from which to choose. The anise-based Flixir Imperiale is reputed to soothe toothaches, while Extract Eucalyptus will treat respiratory problems; many brews are purchased simply for the pleasure of imbibing. A large selection of wines is available, most of them certified by the local diocese as suitable for Mass wine. The entire rear wall of the dark-wood-paneled shop is stocked with honeys made from every blossom conceivable, from sweet-pea to sunflower. The store's line of beauty supplements is a modern addition, a collaboration between owner Aldo Nardi and his son Umberto and the many monasteries with which their family has collaborated for generations. There are toothpastes made from sage, facial masks made from tomatoes and carrots, and bath oils made from peaches, orchids, and azaleas. There's even a special hyssop shampoo for your dog.

Baroque fantasy at Diego Percossi Papi.

JEWELRY

WORKSHOP/STUDIO

18 DIEGO PERCOSSI PAPI ⬠⬠⬠⬠
Via di Sant'Eustachio 16
Tel. 65.41.466
Moderate; no credit cards accepted

The distinctive gem-studded elaborations sparkling from Diego Percossi Papi's ground-floor window will give you some indication of the baroque fantasy that is his specialty, an unusual blending of self-taught artistry and the design inspiration of the 18th century. Diego works only on commission, so most of these pieces and those inside his shop are waiting for their lucky owners to pick them up. Each piece is made in collaboration with its owner-to-be, with Diego sketching it out on paper and placing his precious or semiprecious stones (or those the customer brings to be set) on top to complete the design. Using a unique silver and copper alloy along with a rare cloisonné or enamel technique, to keep costs moderate and originality high, Diego treats his customers with unfailing charm, precision and care, whether he is discussing a pair of simple earrings for a student or an exclusive, ornate piece for socialite Marta Marzotta. Diego's creations tour the world and are sold in choice locations from New York to Monte Carlo, so it's no wonder he'll sometimes need up to three months to finish your order. A sentimentalist at heart, however, he'll always try to accommodate birthdays and weddings.

HOME

FURNISHING FABRICS

19 ACHROMATICHIC
Piazza di Sant'Eustachio 47
Tel. 65.45.215
Expensive; no credit cards accepted

Young Laura Raggi conducts one of Rome's finest sources for interior-decorating fabrics. Her small store stocks a remarkably wide supply, not just from Italy but also from London (chintzes) and Paris (Canova and Frey). Laura keeps abreast of fashion trends, while holding a special respect for such timeless classics as Venetian brocades, Fortuny creations, and Etro paisleys. Among her special interests are artisanal fabrics; many of those she sells are hand-printed on pure linen by special order. Coordinated wallcovers, carpeting, and fabrics range from silks to velvets; some are modern, but many are reproductions of antique patterns. It is not surprising that the American Ambassador had Laura furnish the Embassy and his private residence. Laura will ship to your home.

SUSTENANCE
BAR/CAFFÈ

20 BAR SANT'EUSTACHIO
Piazza di Sant'Eustachio 82
Tel. 65.61.309
Moderate; no credit cards accepted
Closed Monday

Behind the Senate and near the Pantheon, this bar is renowned for the best espresso in town. The reason has puzzled Romans since the bar opened to immediate success in 1938, but it may have to do with the fresh beans that are roasted on the premises. Discriminating coffee lovers are drawn from all over Rome by the aromatic odor to jostle at the standup bar with senators and pensioners. Things stay lively until *dopo cena,* when a new stream of local citizenry drifts by after dining in nearby *trattorie* or restaurants. Other specialties at this austerely decorated sanctorum are coffee parfait and *granita di caffè;* good fresh croissants are available at breakfast.

SUSTENANCE
RISTORANTE/TRATTORIA

21 PAPA GIOVANNI
Via dei Sediari 4
Tel. 65.65.308
Expensive; no credit cards accepted
Closed Sunday

Genial owner Renato Sentuti prides himself on having brought nouvelle cuisine to Italy. First established by his wine-merchant father, Giovanni (hence the restaurant's name), as a much humbler neighborhood *trattoria,* Papa Giovanni is a colorful, bohemian setting with wall-to-wall wine bottles to remind you that its wine selection is one of the best in Rome. There are some tasty traditional Roman dishes such as *pasta e ceci, trippa alla romana,* and *vermicelli cacio e pepe* (with pepper and grated pungent *pecorino* and *romano* cheeses). If you won't make it to Milan this time around, try the *carpaccio* (paper-thin slices of raw beef) here. Interesting fish entrées include the Roman-style cod, *baccalà,* and the *polpettone di spigola* ("meatballs" made of sea bass). The toasted *pizza bianca* is served with *mascarpone* cheese instead of butter. To cap it all off, there are light sorbets and ice creams made on the premises. Reservations are a must.

TOYS
DOLLS & STUFFED ANIMALS

22 AL SOGNO
Piazza Navona 53
Tel. 65.64.198
Moderate; credit cards accepted
Open during lunch

Al Sogno's collection of stuffed animals in sizes from tiny to titanic is as popular with parents as with their children. The second-floor menagerie pairs white elephants with bobtail sheepdogs and peacocks with leopards, cats, pandas or rabbits, all in lifelike poses. Most of these *pelouche* are made in the Veneto region by the old Italian firm Jockline. If the creature that captures your heart is bigger then you are, you can have it shipped home or air-freighted at a reasonable rate. Al Sogno also carries the collectible felt Lenci dolls (see the Milan listing, page 168) and a wide selection of toys and games on the ground floor.

Living art, the Piazza Navona.

SUSTENANCE

BAR/CAFFÈ

Gelateria

23 TRE SCALINI
Piazza Navona 28
Tel. 65.61.234
Moderate; no credit cards accepted
Open 7 A.M.–2:30 A.M.; closed Wednesday

The Tre Scalini is an institution both for its justly celebrated *tartufo* and for the ringside seats from which patrons can observe the piazza life on a summer's night. Contemplate Bernini's splendid fountains in the center of one of Europe's most beautiful and animated squares, but do so only in the company of a rich *tartufo* (truffle), a chocolate-covered ice-cream ball with a whole cherry that comes buried under a mound of fresh whipped cream. You can try one of the rainbow of fresh ice-cream flavors and sundaes as well. Even though these are the most coveted tables in town, the waiters will never rush you.

ENGRAVINGS & PRINTS

24 NARDECCHIA
Piazza Navona 25
Tel. 65.69.318
Moderate; credit cards accepted

Signor Nardecchia is one of Rome's most illustrious antiquarian print dealers; there's little you won't find in his comfortable and well-stocked store. His encyclopedic knowledge of this field is matched by a selection that begins with curious prints and crescendoes to masterpiece engravings. Browse through details from famous or forgotten maps, romantic 18th-century birds and flowers, and views of Rome from other centuries. Established some 30 years ago, Signor Nardecchia's store is a meeting ground for collectors, would-be buyers, and friends who drop in for a *caffè* or to discuss life in general.

JEWELRY

CORALS & CAMEOS

25 GIOVANNI APA

Piazza Navona 27
Tel. 65.65.609
Expensive; credit cards accepted

Don't compromise on the quality or quantity of selection if you're considering a cameo investment: go right to the family that invented the art. It was master artisan Giovanni Apa who, in the 1850s, first carved cameos on conch shells at a time when they were carved only on gems or hard stones. Giovanni set up a factory, establishing Naples and nearby Torre del Greco as the center of cameo production. This Rome location is still run by the Apa family and carries the finest in cameo production from their own factory. Its two rooms exuding old-world elegance are full of lovely cameo brooches, rings, earrings, and necklaces. There is also an impressive array of coral jewelry in all sizes and prices, from simple everyday items to more elaborate pieces, as well as an extensive collection of unset coral in pure white and pinks.

HOME

FURNITURE & ACCESSORIES

Marble Mosaic

26 ZANON

Via Santa Maria dell'Anima 18
(corner of Via Sant'Agnese in Agone)
Tel. 687.50.40
Expensive; credit cards accepted

Giovanni Zanon's store is all about marble—tables, chairs, mantlepieces, lamps, and other artistic items that pair rich, multicolored marbles with

At Zanon, intricate inlaid-marble work.

wood, brass, and glass. Zanon knows all the extraordinary potential of this hard and precious stone, and he works wonders in combining ancient marble motifs with bold designs of today. Zanon's specialty is inlaid mosaic found in the tabletops masterfully made with geometric-patterned marble. Their harmonious diversity of colors and the austere beauty of the marbles used is a throwback to an ancient Roman art called *tarsia*. The same kind of inlay is often used as decorative trim for lamps, coffee tables, and chairs. Signor Zanon spent more than 30 years as an antiquarian, an art restorer, and a collector of Imperial Roman marbles before undertaking his modern interpretations.

FASHION

WOMEN'S

Hand-knit Sweaters

27 MORGANA

Via del Governo Vecchio 27
Tel. 68.79.995
Moderate; credit cards accepted
Open during lunch (summer)

If you've always heard such wonderful

Morgana and her hand-knit designs.

things about hand-knit Italian sweaters, then a visit to Morgana's small charming shop will confirm that this specialty is still alive in highly original form. Here are some of the most imaginative folkloric designs made in Italy—fairy tales interpreted in yarn, as her card calls them. Intricate patterns create autumn landscapes replete with chestnut trees and grapevines; others are abstract designs in bright and sophisticated colors—the latter being the influence of Maga Morgana's artistic son, Marco. Each sweater is unique; only pure wool or cotton is used, and colors are dyed by hand with vegetable dyes, to ensure the muted and soft hues. You can wear Maga's sweaters for a lifetime, and compliments will never cease.

GIFTS

PLASTER MODELS

28 LORENZO SALEMI
Via di Monte Giordano 26
Tel. 65.47.866
Inexpensive; no credit cards accepted

This is not your average gift shop. Lorenzo Salemi is one of Rome's best plaster casters, creating molds for ar-

chitecture and restoration studios. Here, in his garage-like workshop, you'll find an array of unusual Roman objects that make great gifts. A miniature Doric or Corinthian *capitello,* or column capital, makes the ultimate postmodern paperweight or desk ornament. Tiny sarcophagi serve as amusing jewelry or cigarette holders. For the architecture enthusiast, why not bring home the façade of St. Peter's, or at least a faithful 11-by-14-inch replica that would honor any wall? Busts of Roman patriarchs may be a little cumbersome to pack, but are truly quintessential souvenirs.

COSTUME JEWELRY

29 NOVITÀ DUE
Corso Vittorio Emanuele 273
Tel. 68.79.784
Inexpensive; no credit cards accepted

Bijoux fans will feast on five large windows glittering with enough fun and chunky costume jewelry to supply all of Rome for life. You'll have to hunt (but that's half the fun) through enormous collections of clip and pierced earrings, bracelets, necklaces and pins made with imitation gems in all sizes and shapes. Imitation pearls and rhinestones, fake turquoise, and plastic coral fill out this treasure chest. Do-it-yourselfers will have a field day at Novità Due's sister establishment around the corner, which sells mostly raw materials (Via Sora 17, telephone 65.68.685).

If you prefer more serious, and expensive, costume jewelry, just a few doors away, at Corso Vittorio Emanuele 211, is Bigi, a small shop that specializes in high-fashion bijoux. They carry, to name just two, Sharra Pagano and Ugo Correani.

Annual artisanal street fair on Via dell'Orso.

RISTORANTE/TRATTORIA

30 NEL REGNO DI RE FERDINANDO
Via dei Banchi Nuovi 8
Tel. 65.41.167
Moderate; credit cards accepted
Open for dinner only; closed Sunday

This is far more convenient than driving to Naples or Palermo for dinner, and equally authentic. In what once housed an old stable, Neapolitan-Sicilian cuisine (delicious, but not light) is prepared with gusto and expertise. Fresh seafood is the specialty, such as fish poached in *acqua pazza* (crazy water, actually a light tomato broth) or *lo sfizzietto del re* ("the king's whim," linguine with a spicy tomato-shellfish sauce). *Pizzella napoletana* is a small fried pizza, and although you probably won't make it this far, try the *torta caprese* dessert, a luscious chocolate-almond cake. There's a good wine selection from the Campania region, including white Biancolella from the island of Ischia.

Popolo/Pantheon

The area surrounding the spacious 19th-century Piazza del Popolo was sometimes referred to as the Foreigners' Quarter. What could be more appropriate than to start a morning of shopping with a frothy cappuccino in one of the square's two renowned outdoor cafés? Many foreigners took up residence in this neighborhood, part of an endless stream of pilgrims who arrived from the north on the Via Flaminia, heading for the Vatican. Merchants and artisans appeared to accommodate their needs, and in this triangular neighborhood whose base incorporates the area around the Pantheon, you will still find a delightful mixture of artisan shops and moderately priced commercial stores.

Among the following listings, the age-old tradition of family-run enterprises holds fast, with each proud store owner touting his specialty—candles, toys, belts, antique prints or decorative boxes. Valiant shoppers who stray from the well-trodden Via del Corso, the neighborhood's eastern boundary, will enjoy meandering through narrow side streets, exploring

Brio, outdoor cafés and Rome's many fountains for those who venture off the beaten track.

old-fashioned herb shops, bookstores, cabinetmakers' *botteghe,* fashion boutiques, and colorful morning street markets. A favorite is the Mercato di Stampe, a small outdoor market specializing in old prints that is held every morning in Piazza Borghese. As the sophisticated Via Condotti continues on toward the Tiber, it turns into the less expensive Via Tomacelli, known for its varied shoe stores. Near the site of Italy's stately Parliament building, between Piazza Colonna and Piazza Montecitorio, small men's stores and old-world haberdashers become more elegant, offering a blend of British style and Italian workmanship. Antique hunters will enjoy browsing the fashionable antique shops around Via Fontanella Borghese. The whole area around the Pantheon and the Campo Marzio offers good-quality shopping in moderately priced family-run stores that cater as much to their loyal local customers as to tourists.

This historic quarter shares the flavor of the bordering Piazza Navona area. Its focal point is the somber Pantheon, originally built by Consul Marcus Agrippa (a contemporary of Antony and Cleopatra) more than two millennia ago. Hadrian's remarkable reconstruction, which you see today, is only a century younger and is the best-preserved of all ancient monuments in Rome; some consider it the single most perfect building in the world. Here you'll almost believe that the city truly is eternal. In the first century B.C., this warren of winding cobblestoned streets was an open plain, the Campo Marzio (Campus Martius), used for military excercises and athletic recreation. It was soon covered with magnificent public buildings—circuses, baths, and theaters, as well as Agrippa's beloved Pantheon. By the Middle Ages, the population of Rome was concentrated in this district, and except for the disappearance of a large and bustling fish market, it has not changed drastically.

One curious vestige of that period is "Religious Row,"the long and narrow Via dei Cestari. The Pantheon had been built as a pantheistic temple (hence its name) but was consecrated as a church in the seventh century A.D. This encouraged the arrival of religious supply shops catering to the Roman Catholic hierarchy and to pious pilgrims, many of whom found lodging in this neighborhood. The shops are still here, offering liturgical articles for archbishops and altar boys alike; elaborate hand-embroidered silk chasubles, crimson cardinals' stocks, and handcrafted gold reliquaries. You may not be in the market for ecclesiastical high fashion, but the window shopping is fascinating.

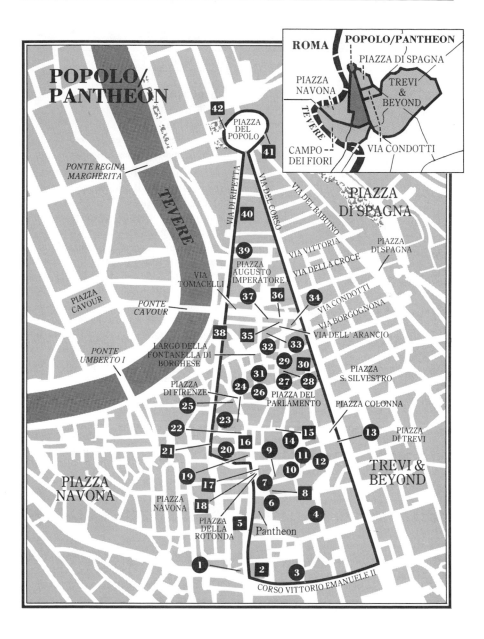

POPOLO/
PANTHEON

PONTE REGINA
MARGHERITA

TEVERE

PONTE
CAVOUR

PIAZZA
CAVOUR

PONTE
UMBERTO I

PIAZZA
NAVONA

PIAZZA
DEL
POPOLO

VIA DI RIPETTA

VIA DEL CORSO

VIA DEL BABUINO

PIAZZA
DI SPAGNA

PIAZZA
DI SPAGNA

VIA VITTORIA

VIA DELLA CROCE

VIA
TOMACELLI

PIAZZA
AUGUSTO
IMPERATORE

VIA CONDOTTI

VIA BORGOGNONA

VIA DELL' ARANCIO

LARGO DELLA
FONTANELLA DI
BORGHESE

PIAZZA
S. SILVESTRO

PIAZZA
DI FIRENZE

PIAZZA DEL
PARLAMENTO

PIAZZA COLONNA

PIAZZA
DI TREVI

TREVI &
BEYOND

PIAZZA
NAVONA

PIAZZA
NAVONA

PIAZZA
DELLA
ROTONDA

Pantheon

CORSO VITTORIO EMANUELE II

ROMA

POPOLO/PANTHEON

PIAZZA DI SPAGNA

PIAZZA
NAVONA

TREVI
&
BEYOND

TEVERE

CAMPO
DEI FIORI

VIA CONDOTTI

HOME

CANDLES

Monomania

1 CERERIA PISONI
Corso Vittorio Emanuele 127–129
Tel. 65.43.531
Moderate; no credit cards accepted

Candlemakers to the Pope since 1803 and still considered Rome's most important candle manufacturer, Pisoni has slowly expanded his wax kingdom to encompass everything from tiny birthday-sized candles to enormous torches and mammoth Paschal candles. The windows of this small, homey shop display a grab bag of corner-store products, but Pisoni's true specialty is the hand-dipped candles made in his own factory. Hand dipping ensures better and slower burning. The popular *torcie a vento*, found nowhere else, are windproof saucer-shaped candles that have thick wicks for breezy roof terraces. Decorative, tapered, spiraled, two-toned and even rose-shaped candles line the shelves; gently scented candles effuse aromas of roses, lavender, pear, honey and sandalwood. You can also see the elaborate, award-winning hand-painted creations commissioned by parishes as gifts to the Pope, a tradition that goes back to the Middle Ages, when wax was a precious commodity for the light its candles produced. Pisoni will create candles to order of any length, in any quantity; a box of 45 wax chips represents the color possibilities. Candle accessories such as snuffers, wind guards, and holders complete their stock.

SUSTENANCE

BAR/CAFFÈ

2 PASCUCCI
Via di Torre Argentina 20
Tel. 56.48.16
Inexpensive; no credit cards accepted
7 A.M. to midnight; closed Monday

This is the best bar in town specializing in fresh-fruit milkshakes *(frullati)* at the lowest possible prices. It's the quality, not the bargain rates, that keeps Romans coming from miles around to crowd this small, standup bar till midnight. You'll find the freshest of whatever fruit is in season, blended with milk and sugar (if you find that the fruit's natural sweetness is enough, ask for it *senza zucchero,* without sugar). Fruits whipped and blended with ice cubes and a splash of lemon instead of milk *(senza latte)* are a less fattening alternative. Kiwi, banana, apricot, peach, pear, coconut, cherry, nut and other flavors can be combined with a little pointing. If you're just as happy with an iced tea or coffee, it's especially good at Pascucci and is made without sugar, contrary to Italian custom.

FABRICS

FASHION

Huge Selection

3 BISES
Via del Gesù 93
Tel. 67.80.941
Moderate; credit cards accepted

A rambling, four-story 17th-century palazzo houses Rome's widest assortment of fashion and home-furnishing materials. An old, established name in retail-fabric shopping, Bises attracts a Roman clientele which has been coming here for almost half a century to choose from bolt after bolt of medium- to high-quality yard goods in wools, tweeds, cottons, jerseys, linens, silks, velvets, and more. You'll find prints and solids, designer and other fabrics for men and women, as well as tablecloths, knitting yarns, and a variety of handsome ready-to-wear clothing. The place has something of a bargain basement atmosphere, despite its lofty, frescoed ceilings and the prestigious Bises name.

LEATHERGOODS

WORKSHOP/STUDIO

Bags & Accessories

4 BOTTEGA ARTIGIANA

Via di Sant'Ignazio 38
Tel. 67.95.119
Expensive; credit cards accepted

A select clientele snatches up a limited production of beautiful hand-sewn bags and small leathergoods. In this tiny shop, the young Ferretti husband-and-wife team is proud to be among the last to use the traditional two-needle sewing technique: the *cucitura a sellaio,* or saddler's stitch. This means that each item takes painstaking hours to be completed, time rarely lavished in these days of mass production. There are classic, Hermès-like ladies' handbags dyed in fashion colors, as well as carefully made briefcases, polished-leather tabletop boxes, rigid luggage, and trunks of varying size. All models are simple and classic and crafted with a scrupulous attention to detail.

SUSTENANCE

RISTORANTE/TRATTORIA

5 SANTA CHIARA ARCHIMEDE

Via di Santa Chiara 31
Tel. 68.75.216
Moderate; credit cards accepted
Closed Sunday

A window displaying a fresh arrangement of fruit and vegetables is your invitation to this comfortable old trattoria, home to a savvy crowd of local habitués. Outdoor dining overlooking Bernini's elephant obelisk in a tiny square behind the Pantheon is a ritual for those in quest of reliably delicious Roman cooking. A favorite dish is the *fritto vegetariano,* a lightly fried assortment of mozzarella, shoestring zucchini, stuffed zucchini blossoms, artichokes, and whatever else the marketplace offers that morning. Consider having it as an entrée, though you'll have to skip the first course of homemade pasta if you want to make it through dessert. Flattened, crisp *carciofi alla giudia* look like pressed flowers, and remind you that you are around the corner from the Jewish ghetto. The homemade dessert specialties here include a creamy *tiramisu* and cheesecake.

ENGRAVINGS & DRAWINGS

6 CASALI

Piazza del Pantheon 81/A
Tel. 67.83.515
Moderate; credit cards accepted

The original Casali began almost a century ago as an antiquarian-book dealer and acquired an expertise still recognized today. One of two Casali locations, this more accessible shop is crowded with 16th- to 19th-century drawings and engravings on Roman subjects, as well as very detailed local *vedute* or scenes from other European cities. Also represented are decorative fruits, birds, and flowers, and just about anything can be tracked down on request for you by the accommodating third-generation Casali family in three or four days. Charming sketches by "unknowns" are quite inexpensive, while precious Piranesi originals can attract museum prices. The other Casali shop is a little off the beaten track at Piazza Firenze 30/A (telephone 67.80.259); it specializes in *vedute,* landscapes, hunting scenes and maritime battles. At both locations, framing is optional.

PERFUME & COSMETICS

International Brands

7 PROFUMERIA DE PAOLA
Piazza della Rotonda 70/A
Tel. 67.98.384
Moderate; no credit cards accepted

There are three De Paola stores in town, but this is the most convenient for Pantheon visitors. Small but well stocked with all the best European and American brands of cosmetics and perfumes, De Paola is run by an efficient bilingual staff. You'll find Lancôme, Christian Dior, Chanel, Clinique, Estée Lauder, and a host of others, as well as the new Italian designer perfumes. Another De Paola shop, near the Piazza di Spagna at Via della Croce 23 (telephone 67.89.607), is larger and takes credit cards.

SUSTENANCE

BAR/CAFFÈ

8 LA TAZZA D'ORO
Via degli Orfani 84
Tel. 67.89.792
Inexpensive; no credit cards accepted
Closed Sunday

Any survey ranks the Tazza d'Oro as one of Rome's best cups of coffee. The bar's specialty is a secret blend of coffee taken from the huge burlap sacks of freshly roasted beans that line the standup area. Neighborhood regulars like to think that the Tazza d'Oro first set up shop here in order to make its brew with the local Acqua Vergine, considered the best of Roman waters. Apparently everyone here drinks espresso with sugar, which is how you'll get yours unless you ask for it *senza zucchero*. Even for Italy, it is unusual that this purist bar sells only coffee and coffee-flavored *granita,* a refreshing, full-flavored pick-me-up made with shaved ice and topped with fresh whipped cream (if you'd like it without, ask for *senza panna*). Freshly roasted and ground coffee packed in airtight foil bags makes a great gift, but be sure you wrap the bags in plastic or their potent aroma will permeate the entire contents of your suitcase.

LEATHERGOODS

BAGS & BRIEFCASES

Huge Selection

9 FABRIS
Via degli Orfani 87
Tel. 67.95.603
Moderate; credit cards accepted

A stock of more than 1,000 attractive moderately priced bags has drawn shoppers to Fabris for more than 30 years. The wide selection is only partially repesented in the large store windows, so you'll need to step inside to understand the endless possibilities. Not unlike a mini-department store dedicated to bags alone, Fabris offers everything from classic to trendy, from evening to casual, from briefcases to sturdy luggage. Three rooms are filled to the brim with handbags organized according to color, while a fourth is filled with leather attaché cases. Yet another room offers a generous array of luggage—handsome leather suitcases, but also the indestructible synthetics now favored by the Italians, from such names as Samsonite, Valaguzza, and Fila (for sturdy nylon bags). A second, smaller, Fabris location is just blocks away at Via Colonna Antonina 29 (telephone 67.95.861).

FASHION

MEN'S

Avant-Garde

10 DEGLI EFFETTI
Piazza Capranica 79
Tel. 67.91.650
Expensive; credit cards accepted

Rome's most avant-garde boutique for men's fashion is worth a visit just for the "effects" that its name promises. In a minimalist setting of milky travertine marble, coffered ceilings, and synthesizer music, the collections of Europe's most forward fashion creators are hung like works of art; among the artists are Jean-Paul Gaultier, Anne Marie Beretta, Adolfo Dominguez, Piero Panchetti, Thierry

Mugler, and Marithe & François Giribaud. Degli Effetti is also an exception to the rule by stocking winter fashion in July (and, conversely, summer fashion in March).

FASHION

WOMEN'S

Contemporary Sportswear

11 PAOLO PAGLIUCA
Via Colonna Antonina 36
No telephone
Moderate; credit cards accepted

Here you'll find a professionally selected collection of ready-to-wear sportswear in classic good taste. The small, inviting boutique is run by two young women who treat their customers well; they are attentive and knowledgeable but are never over-solicitous, encouraging you to browse if you're more interested in looking than in buying. Together they have a clever eye for picking interesting separates among top Italian sportswear names such as Krizia Poi, Oaks (Gianfranco Ferrè), Spazio (Soprani), Calla, and Biagiotti and Moschino jeans. Their selections can be coordinated into a number of looks and complemented by stylish Pitti and Granello bags and belts.

The Pantheon, a gem of classical Rome.

PIPES

12 CARMIGNANI
Via Colonna Antonina 41
Tel. 67.80.413
Expensive; credit cards accepted

Around the corner from the Italian Parliament lies Rome's oldest and most elegant tobacco shop. Opened in 1892 by Gianni Carmignani's Tuscan grandfather, this shop has been stocked by three generations of Carmignanis with smoking articles of the highest quality. If you're interested in buying a pipe, you'll find Rome's largest selection here. Among the names represented are the handmade Castello and Baldo. There are beautiful wooden cigar boxes made of *radica di tuya* and complete lines of smoking accessories, many of them designed by Carmignani himself. Pipe repairs are lovingly performed even years after your purchase.

FASHION
CHILDREN'S & JUNIORS
Sportswear

13 BENETTON AND BENETTON 012
Piazza Colonna 350
Tel. 67.95.214
Moderate; credit cards accepted
Open during lunch

This centralized Benetton clothing boutique that combines junior and children's fashion is fun for one-stop shopping. Benetton's modern stores are known for their easy, fashion-conscious style, their wide palette of colorations, and their dime-a-dozen accessibility. See the Milan listings (page 179 and 217).

Three generations of impeccable shirt-making.

FASHION
MEN'S
Made-to-Measure Shirts

14 CALEFFI
Via Colonna Antonina 53
    (in Piazza di Montecitorio)
Tel. 67.93.773
Moderate; credit cards accepted

In the first years of this century, Caleffi was already building an international clientele and an impeccable reputation as a shirtmaker. Three generations later, the family is still producing some of Italy's finest custom-made shirts from quality solid and striped cottons. On the second floor of the shop you'll find ready-to-wear suits made with the same attention to tailoring in regular and extra-large sizes (up to European size 60, American size 44). Pick from their enormous selection of Italian and English summer- and winter-weight fabrics. The alterations take a day or two and, as with your custom-made shirts, can be shipped if necessary. Caleffi's own handsome cotton pajamas and silk ties mix with English makes, all lovely gifts for the appreciative man.

SUSTENANCE

GELATERIA

15 GIOLITTI
Via Uffici del Vicario 40
Tel. 67.94.206
Moderate; no credit cards accepted
Open 7:00 A.M. to 2:00 A.M.; closed Monday

All roads lead to Giolitti, Rome's richest and most popular ice-cream experience. Run by the same family for four generations, this always-crowded *gelateria* near the Pantheon has become something of a legacy. Dozens of flavors are produced continuously during the day according to demand, with only two gallons of any variety made at one time. Ice cream appears bright and early, but most morning patrons gravitate to the gleaming brass counters laden with fresh pastries. A *tavola calda* (literally, hot table) serves lunch until 2:00, then is replaced by a full range of 57 ice-cream flavors, up from the morning's select 15. No syrups or preservatives are used in their making, and the hazelnut, banana, coconut and lemon flavorings come from their original sources. Fresh fruit in season is blended in by the bushelful, and the use of ricotta, "After Eight" mints, and champagne as ingredients is unique to Giolitti. Roman-watching is at its best here.

SUSTENANCE

GELATERIA

16 GELATERIA DELLA PALMA
Via della Maddalena 20–23
Tel. 65.40.752
Moderate; no credit cards accepted
Closed Wednesday

A relative newcomer to Rome's ice-cream scene, Gelateria della Palma is proud to offer 100 different flavors to dazzled tourists and locals alike. In a spacious, white-marble interior, two long counters boast every conceivable flavor from rich chocolate to exotic papaya and kiwi. A number of desserts are also translated into ice-cream flavors, such as trifle, *crème caramel, tiramisu,* and *marron glacé;* there is also a wide selection of *semifreddi,* mousse-like semi-frozen creams. True to its name, the *gelateria* boasts a solitary palm tree with an encircling bench that offers seating for some of the usually young and lively crowd. In the back is a piano bar/tearoom, where you can linger late at night over drinks or lavish sundaes.

SUSTENANCE

RISTORANTE/TRATTORIA

17 DA FORTUNATO AL PANTHEON
Via del Pantheon 55
Tel. 67.92.788
Moderate; credit cards accepted
Closed Sunday

Comfortably located between the Senate and the House, Fortunato's is a popular spot for Roman-style power lunches, though no one seems to be checking watches. White-jacketed, bow-tied waiters serve the simple, well-prepared Roman cuisine here. *Funghi* (mushrooms), when in season, are excellent, as is the fresh fish flown in daily and displayed on ice as you enter the *trattoria.* Carnivores can choose from a range of quality meats, especially steak tartare, grilled baby lamb chops, and thick, juicy *bistecca alla fiorentina* from Tuscany. In summer there's a good pasta *alla checca* made with uncooked tomato sauce and also the rice-stuffed tomatoes (*pomodori al riso*). Delicious home-made desserts feature the classic *torta di ricotta* (cheesecake).

SUSTENANCE

RISTORANTE/TRATTORIA

18 LA ROSETTA

Via della Rosetta 9
Tel. 65.61.002
Expensive; credit cards accepted
Closed Sunday, and Monday lunch

It was Carmelo Riccioli who first brought fame to this fish restaurant; although he has recently gone on to open the new and immediately suc-cessful Il Veliero (see Campo dei Fiori neighborhood, page 398), he has left La Rosetta in the capable hands of his son Ettore. Even without Carmelo, you'll have to reserve at this lively *trattoria* hung with fishing nets, for it is touted to offer the freshest seafood in town. The Riccioli family hails from Sicily, which supplies their daily provision of fish and their traditional skill in its preparation. Risotto and *al dente* pastas are coupled with the day's arrivals in such first-course dishes as the spaghetti *ricci di mare* (made with sea urchin) or *all'aragosta* (with a lobster-like sea crayfish). For a memorable entrée, try any of the fresh fish—perfectly grilled, roasted, or fried. Service is attentive; deep green olive oil graces each table, and there is excellent homemade Sicilian ice cream.

The young and innovative owners of Art'È.

GIFTS

Design with a Sense of Humor

19 ART'È

Piazza Rondanini 32
Tel. 65.48.995
Moderate; credit cards accepted

Here's a delightful gift shop full of originality, wit and modern technol-ogy. Young owners Marino Giusa and Corrado Barone, both Roman archi-tects, have designed most of the items offered here. Best sellers are their unusual lighting pieces, particularly the four-foot-high transparent acrylic Manhattan skyscraper. Other lights come in the shape of compasses, bows and arrows, balloons, columns, and even tennis shoes. Less cumbersome gifts to carry home are hand-painted objects made with synthetic resin and keen imagination: bathroom tooth-brush holders, soap dishes, whimsical frames and clocks. Packed and ready for shipping is Rome's perfect sou-venir—a miniature three-dimensional tabletop plaster replica of the city. This re-creation of the Eternal City was commissioned as part of a decora-tive series of international cities. The result is an exquisite pastel puzzle of the talented designers' home town.

HERB SHOP

20 ANTICA ERBORISTERIA
CENTAUREA
Via del Pozzo delle Cornacchie 26
Tel. 65.30.741
Moderate; no credit cards accepted

Dating back to 1740, the Antica Erboristeria is Rome's oldest and most renowned herb shop, not unlike Florence's famous Farmacia di Santa Maria Novella (see *Erboristeria*, page 100). Panacea-seeking Romans and curious tourists alike come here to pick from the array of herbs and spices, tea-like mallow infusions, pomades, tinctures, and natural potions. Its old pale-green cupboards and drawers and ceramic apothecary jars have preserved this charming shop's original appearance, and the diverse centuries-old treatments prescribed for simple maladies have not changed much either. The resident herbalist, Myriam Sergio, speaks a little English. The only recent addition to the store is a French line of natural beauty products that includes facial masks and creams and the popular *cure capillaire*, which claims to stop hair loss. Most curious visitors stop in for a peek and buy some of the aromatic herbal teas and lavender or potpourri sachets that make appealing gifts.

SUSTENANCE

DELICATESSEN

21 VOLPETTI ALLA SCROFA
Via della Scrofa 31–32
Tel. 65.61.940
Moderate; no credit cards accepted
Open 8:00 A.M. to 9:00 P.M.; closed Sunday

Delicatessen is hardly the proper word to describe this neighborhood institution and gourmet's delight. Open during lunch and until late, Volpetti offers fast food Roman style; you'll have to eat it at a standup counter, but the choice of food for an unfussy meal or a delicious snack makes it worthwhile. There's a generous assortment of local cold cuts, and in the cheese department there are a number of international cheeses for nostalgic expatriates as well as Italian varieties. You can also create the perfect picnic to go (tell them it's *"da portare via"*), choosing from stuffed peppers, tomatoes, and zucchini, a variety of cold salads, roast meats and chicken, and hot dishes that change with the seasons.

LEATHERGOODS

WORKSHOP/STUDIO

Bags, Shoes & Accessories

22 LEONI—ARTIGIANATO DEL CUOIO
Piazza delle Coppelle 65
Tel. 52.73.456
Moderate; no credit cards accepted

The young and accommodating Leoni couple produce sturdy and well-made leathergoods from belts to hand-sewn walking shoes. An eye-catcher is the popular handbag made of a heavy, tapestry-like fabric and trimmed with *cuoio* (natural leather hide). Shoulder bags, backpacks, doctors' bags with brass fittings, and small luggage pieces are part of an imaginative array. The tapestry look in both floral and geometric prints is also used for smaller leathergoods such as makeup cases and belts. A limited but handsome selection of handcrafted shoes for men features classic loafers and

Leoni combines tapestry with sturdy leather.

oxfords, as well as boating shoes. There are also a few simple sandals for men and women.

GIFTS

BOXES

23 LABORATORIO SCATOLE
Via della Stelletta 27
Tel. 65.42.053
Moderate; no credit cards accepted

Need a decorative cardboard box of a particular size, shape or color? For more than 40 years, Silvana Palaferri has been making attractive hatboxes, shoe boxes, jewelry boxes, boxes for presents and storage boxes for well-organized neatniks. Boxes fit within boxes, and come in square, oblong, round, and rectangular forms. You can choose from stock, or have anything custom-made from a choice of patterns and colors. Or do as the Vatican does and order in white only.

FASHION

EXPERT CLOTHES REPAIR

24 EMILIA SERMONETTA
Via della Stelletta 28
Tel. 65.61.618
Moderate; no credit cards accepted

The Italian royal family, Mussolini, the future Pope Pius XII, ministers, senators, and noblemen have all availed themselves of Emilia Sermonetta precious services: she is Rome's best and, by now, most famous invisible mender. Thanks to mentions on radio and television, she has become something of a celebrity for her ability to repair what seems irreparable, but she is as charming and cheerful as ever. Some foreigners wait until their next trip to Rome and bring Emilia suitcases full of their damaged clothing. Her prices vary according to the work and time required.

SPORTS GEAR

ACTIVE SPORTSWEAR & EQUIPMENT

Camping Goods

25 MARCHETTI SPORT
Piazza di Firenze 25
Tel. 68.79.098
Moderate; credit cards accepted

Thirty years of servicing Rome's athletes have given Marchetti a deserved reputation for fine camping and sports equipment. Also called La Bottega del Campeggiatore, this well-stocked store carries a vast selection of tents, sleeping bags, and cookware from all the best European names. You'll also find skis and skiwear, soccer clothing and balls, sports bags and shoes, tennis equipment and attire, and mountain-climbing, jogging, and gymnastics gear. Quality Italian brand names such as Fila, Ellesse, Piumini Ski, and Invicta Trekking will have you in fashionable shape for the Great Outdoors.

FASHION

MEN'S & WOMEN'S

Made-to-Measure Shirts

26 CAMICERIA PIERO ALBERTELLI
Via dei Prefetti 11
Tel. 67.84.138
Expensive; credit cards accepted

Rapidly becoming known as one of Rome's finest haberdashers, Piero Albertelli offers an excellent selection of fabrics for custom-made shirts that will be ready (and shipped) in three weeks. Signor Albertelli's forte, however, is men's nightwear: long, elegant nightshirts in the styles of centuries past, classic pajamas, and boxer shorts. In addition to his own terry-lined cotton robes and splendid dressing gowns in cashmere silk, linen, or light wool, there are a number of men's accessories by Etro, such as distinctive cotton paisley kimonos with silk lining and matching slippers. Signor Albertelli first acquired his reputation as a theatrical costume designer, and his original studio is still across the street. This small *camiceria* is a recent adjunct, as is a limited but attractive selection of women's blouses and dresses.

KNITTING YARNS

27 CANGURO
Via di Campo Marzio 45
Tel. 67.95.439
Inexpensive; credit cards accepted

Canguro's stock could keep you knitting for decades, so extensive is the selection of fine yarns made up in the firm's own factory in the northern

Canguro's wall-to-wall stock of fine yarns.

province of Biella. Available here at factory prices is an endless array of cottons, cashmeres, Scotland wool, angora, alpaca, linen, metallics, lurex, and so on, in every color imaginable. Canguro has more than two dozen stores throughout Italy; this location doubles as distribution center for half of them, all here in Rome. In the back is a warehouse with even more yarn, should stock from the front area not suffice. You can't miss this place: bulky, colorful skeins hang outside.

ANTIQUE JEWELRY & SILVER

28 MANASSE
Via di Campo Marzio 44
Tel. 67.80.853
Expensive; credit cards accepted
Closed Saturday

Serious collectors of antique jewelry and silver will all find their way to Manasse, a respected Roman enterprise for three generations. The shop guarantees the authenticity and originality of its prized objects, which date from the 17th century through the 1930s. In addition to an impressive collection of antique English, Russian, and Italian silver, highlights include remarkably detailed objects made of ''micro-mosaics'' from the important school of Augusto Castellani. Another specialty of this small, old-world shop is its collection of Jewish objects, such as engraved silver menorahs and sabbath wine goblets from Prussia and Russia. Depending upon your luck and timing, you might also find an early 18th-century bracelet carved in pale coral, delicate cameos made from semiprecious stones or conch shells, opera glasses, Russian icons, and elaborate cigarette boxes.

HOME
HOUSEWARES

29 VITTORIO BAGAGLI
Via di Campo Marzio 42
Tel. 67.90.693
Moderate; credit cards accepted

Started in 1855 as a cork and wine-bottle concern, this old-fashioned, friendly shop today stocks a large selection of Italian kitchen- and housewares, from everyday gadgets to elegant dining accessories. A favorite with both locals and tourists is the La Pavoni espresso coffeemaker, conveniently available in both the American 110v and the European 220v versions. La Pavoni, considered a leader in its field, began by making large, steaming espresso machines for neighborhood bars and *trattorie,* then turned to the production of these attractive, smaller machines. They can be purchased in brass, copper, stainless steel and gold-plate; and the deluxe model can make up to 16 cups. Vittorio Bagagli will ship them home for you. He also. offers the stainless steel Alessi collection, sleek wooden salad bowls, cheese boards, and giant pepper mills. The store carries Richard-Ginori china (see the Florence listing, page 71), as well as the hand-painted ceramic platters made in Bassano del Grappa.

SUSTENANCE
PASTICCERIA

30 EUROPEO
Piazza di San Lorenzo in Lucina 33
Tel. 67.86.251
Moderate; no credit cards accepted
Closed Monday

This tiny bar is known for its Sicilian specialties—creamy, rich pastries as authentic as anything you'll find in Catania. Sit until 11:00 P.M. at any of the tables inside or out in the small piazza; here you can also enjoy homemade *gelato,* which many people claim was invented by Sicilians, or *cassata siciliana.* This delicious house specialty consists of a slice of chocolate, vanilla and strawberry ice cream mixed with almonds and candied fruit. Another favorite here is the ice-cream-and-fruit-filled tangerine, especially appreciated on a taxing summer's day. Edible *trompe-l'oeil* sweets made of marzipan are painstakingly sculpted and hand-painted to look like green olives, cherries, and chestnuts; the *monte bianco,* resembling a ball of twine, is actually made of chestnut paste and filled with *panna* (whipped cream).

ART GALLERY
19TH- & 20TH-CENTURY ITALIAN DRAWINGS

31 GALLERIA CARLO VIRGILIO
Via della Lupa 9
Tel. 67.83.914
Expensive; no credit cards accepted

This is a small, serious art gallery that displays original Italian art from 1740 to 1940. The passion for collecting European drawings was launched in the 1800s by young milords passing through Rome on their Grand Tour and snatching up artistic souvenirs with a connoisseur's eye. You can find similar valuable mementoes in this gallery's noteworthy collection of drawings in ink and watercolor. A recent exhibition, for example, featured sketches of Italian theater and opera set designs and was accompanied by an attractive color catalogue. Such shows and sales are often mounted in conjunction with prestigious New York City galleries.

FASHION

MEN'S

Made-to-Measure Shirts

32 AMEDEO MICOCCI
Largo della Fontanella di Borghese 69
Tel. 67.80.587
Moderate to expensive; credit cards accepted

On their way to La Caccia, Italy's most exclusive club, Roman aristocrats drop in next door to have their shirts made by Amedeo Micocci. Amedeo learned the art of shirtmaking from his mother, who started back in 1932; he opened this small shop ten years ago. Bolts of fine cotton, linen, and silk are there for you to choose from. Classic styles that will please both men and women can be ready in ten days. There's also a generous array of top-brand ready-to-wear men's sweaters, pants, and suits.

LEATHERGOODS

BELTS ONLY

Made-to-Measure

33 CINTURE MODA
Via Monte d'Oro 18–19
Tel. 68.76.198
Moderate; credit cards accepted

This is one of Rome's most specialized makers of fashion belts. You can pick from a limited number of ready-made models, but the real attraction here is the possibility of having just about anything custom-made to your measurements. There are hundreds of colors to choose from in top-grade calfskin, suedes, pigskin, and other leathers. There are also a number of fashion fabrics on hand, or bring your own fabric if you want a new belt to match a particular outfit. Cinture Moda's look is mainly classic. You can pick from a number of solid or nickel-plated brass buckles, and the staff will give expert advice on what style will best compliment your outfit and figure. They will also do modifications on belts that you bring in. The emphasis is on women's belts, although men's can be made up upon request; both can be ready in three to four days.

JEWELRY

34 DELETTRÉ 🔔🔔🔔🔔
Via della Fontanella di Borghese 39–40
Tel. 68.76.498
Expensive; credit cards accepted

In a small jewel box of a store decorated with period art-deco fixtures, one of Rome's most stylish couples designs highly fashion-oriented jewelry. She is the beautiful Silvia Venturini, daughter of one of the five famous Fendi sisters; he is Bernard Delettré, a sophisticated French-born Brazilian gemologist. Together they design modern pieces vaguely nostalgic of the deco period, made from the Brazilian stones Bernard loves and understands. Their designs are large, bold and unique, using stones that range from priceless diamonds to

Priceless statuary survives modern-day Rome.

sculpted rock crystal, set in both gold and steel. Invisible settings where gem-stones seem to float in place are a Delettré specialty; there is also a striking selection of men's jewelry. Upstairs is an exquisite display of deco tabletop objects and jewelry, which are also for sale. The Delettré logo of a crescent moon and five stars was designed by Karl Lagerfeld, hinting at the star-studded roster of friends and customers who eagerly snatch up these high-fashion creations.

SUSTENANCE
RISTORANTE/TRATTORIA

35 DA SETTIMIO ALL'ARANCIO
Via dell'Arancio 50
Tel. 68.76.119
Moderate; credit cards accepted
Closed Sunday

Students, journalists, and aristocrats all resist divulging this special neighborhood find, a friendly *trattoria* that's reliably good, always busy, and known by few tourists. Da Settimio's lure is its unpretentious Roman-style cooking, well prepared and using fresh ingredients. If you go on a Friday, you'll find fresh fish for reason-

able prices as well as an excellent *risotto alla pescatore* (a paella-like rice-and-seafood dish). Daily-changing pastas (look for the *fusilli alla melanzana*—with eggplant) are always delicious, and entrées include roast and grilled meats and vegetables.

SUSTENANCE
BAR/CAFFÈ

36 BAR ANTILLE
Via Tomacelli 13
Tel. 68.76.150
Moderate; no credit cards accepted
Closed Sunday

This conveniently located bar is frequented by a steady stream of neighborhood residents and shop owners. Mid-morning coffee breaks are a ritual, with the different coffee blends roasted on the premises and also sold by the *etto* (100 grams). Excellent fresh pastries are made in the back—warm, buttery croissants *(cornetti)* and fruit-filled danish-type rolls. Mounds of them disappear by late morning, to be replaced by freshly made sandwiches: *tramezzini* (on sliced white bread) and *panini* (on rolls or French bread); they'll also heat up the small pizzas for you. Light and fresh *frullati* (milkshakes) are made with whatever fruits are in season, and fresh vegetable juices are prepared while you wait. There's a counter of homemade ice cream, too, in a dozen irresistible flavors. A drawback no one but shopping-weary tourists seems to mind is the lack of tables. Antille is large and friendly, with telephones and restrooms a plus.

PERFUME & COSMETICS
Big Selection of Hair Accessories & Combs

37 RIGHI
Via Tomacelli 22
Tel. 68.76.256
Moderate to expensive; credit cards accepted

Righi's outstanding display of decorative hair ornaments will attract you. There is also a small *profumeria* section, but the real attraction is the assortment of faux tortoiseshell and plastic hair combs decorated with beads, bijoux, pearls, fabrics, bows, flowers, and what not. Headbands, barrettes, and clips are imaginative gifts that are easy to carry home for little girls or sophisticated friends.

SUSTENANCE
RISTORANTE/TRATTORIA

38 PORTO DI RIPETTA
Via di Ripetta 250
Tel. 36.12.376
Expensive; credit cards accepted
Closed Sunday

Maria Romani, who operates this small, elegant and centralized restaurant has become known especially for her imaginative presentation of fish. Begin with a soup of *fagiolini con sepioline* (green beans and cuttlefish) or ravioli stuffed with ricotta and *gamberetti* (small shrimp). Try the unusually delicious *gamberoni con salsa cipolla e champagne* (large prawns in a light onion-and-champagne sauce), or *rombo* (brill or turbot) filet with *porcini* mushrooms. Carnivores can feast on quality-cut steaks on the grill or *faraona* (roast pheasant). A special afternoon menu limits the choice but not quality of a memorable lunch, for half the cost of dinner; ask for the *colazione del professionista* (professional's lunch), which will restore any wilted professional shopper.

SPORTS GEAR
Nautical Everything

39 DENTICE
Piazza Augusto Imperatore 18–21
Tel. 36.06.050
Moderate to expensive; credit cards accepted

Boating and fishing enthusiasts will enjoy a stop at the large and well-stocked Dentice. Everything for the high and low seas, from scuba-diving equipment to antique boat fixtures, can be found here. All of Italy's and Europe's top brand names are represented, and all water-related equipment is available—water skis, fishing rods, reels and nets, bait, sailboat and motorboat gear, wet suits, and even anchors. Infinitely easier to carry home is the selection of maritime fashion from the ultra-practical to the stylish. This is perhaps Rome's best selection of active sportswear, with heavy sweaters in waterproof wool, windbreakers and heavy jackets, deck shoes and boots, raingear, and linens for your yacht.

SUSTENANCE
BREAD-&-CHEESE SHOP

40 PANEFORMAGGIO
Via di Ripetta 7/A–8/A
Tel. 36.10.271
Inexpensive; no credit cards accepted
Closed Thursday afternoon

This smart bread-and-cheese shop doubles as a popular gourmet snack bar during lunch hours. Pull up a stool and join a well-dressed crowd at the marble-topped counter or take your order to one of the small tables. Choose from a vast assortment of sandwiches and freshly baked quiches and pies. Try the special *caprino* (goat) cheese wrapped in smoked salmon with a glass of wine, a fruit juice, or even a milkshake. Afterwards, take a look at the retail area featuring all-natural, homemade breads studded with olives, nuts, tomatoes, spinach, rosemary, carrots, and bran. For a snack that will sustain you till dinner time, buy a bunch of long, light *grissini* (breadsticks)—either plain or flavored with natural onion, rosemary, or tomato.

SUSTENANCE

BAR/CAFFÈ

41 CANOVA

Piazza del Popolo 16
Tel. 36.12.231
Moderate; credit cards accepted
Closed Monday

As much a part of this famous piazza as its rival Rosati across the way, the Canova offers a wide choice of facilities to a regular clientele of well-heeled businessmen as well as for international tourists. You can dawdle outdoors, choosing between the warm sunshine and welcomed shade, or relax in a quiet walled-in garden or in the indoor cocktail lounge. The *tavola calda* (hot counter) offers a good quick meal of fresh vegetables, pastas, and roast meats. If you'd rather be served the full menu with waiter service, take a table in the dining room. There's also an area with fresh and tempting pastries, a tobacco shop, and a well-stocked gift shop with regional and local preserves, boxed candies, chocolates, wines and champagnes that could solve the dilemma of any last-minute Sunday shopping. Canova's is popular and open until 11:30 P.M. for a piazza-watching nightcap.

SUSTENANCE

BAR/CAFFÈ

42 ROSATI

Piazza del Popolo 5/A
Tel. 36.05.859
Moderate; no credit cards accepted
Closed Tuesday

One of Rome's most attractive caffès, Rosati has kept its original décor, an early art-deco pink-and-white stuccoed interior that competes with outdoor tables for preferred seating. A traditional clientele of journalists, actors, and politicians has favored Rosati's as a meeting place since its opening in 1922. A longtime favorite of Fellini's, here you can often see the famous director at a small pink outdoor table sipping one of Rosati's superb cocktails. The most frequented hour is sixish, for a fashionable *aperitivo* appointment after a day at the Forum. Over the years Rosati has maintained its first-class service, as well as the excellence of its liqueur-filled chocolates, homemade jellies, and lemon *granita*. It can't be beaten for a fresh croissant and a frothy cappuccino in the early-morning sun.

Campo dei Fiori

Although not a major shopping area, Campo dei Fiori is perhaps the most picturesque and intriguing neighborhood in Rome. A handful of curious tourists visit it to experience the daily produce and flower market that has kept the Piazza Campo dei Fiori bustling since 1869. This colorful *mercato all'aperto* is considered, if not the most beautiful, surely the most fascinating open-air market of its kind (see Outdoor Street Markets, page 310). Adventurous visitors who come here to mix leisurely shopping with cultural browsing will find themselves immersed in the sights, smells, and joyful cacophony of Roman daily life without the frills. This spontaneous local character is the district's principal draw, more important than any of the offbeat shops, restaurants, and *trattorie* that we have listed below.

Tucked between the Tiber River and the heavily trafficked Corso Vittorio Emanuele, the neighborhood is made up of a warren of narrow back streets surrounding its nucleus, the lopsided Piazza Campo dei Fiori. Vendors work half in, half out of their small shops, and artisans' *botteghe* still cluster together according to their centuries-old specialties, often on streets named for the medieval craft guilds originally located there.

The Mercato Campo dei Fiori, one of the most colorful and authentic spectacles of its kind.

Plan a morning itinerary, when you can wander through the market-place, then stroll along the Via dei Banchi Vecchi, named after the old stalls that once lined it, and the Via dei Cappellari, the street of the hat makers; peruse the bric-a-brac shops on the Via Monserrato and the dusty pawnshops of the Via Monte di Pietà. The Via dei Pettinari, named for the wool combers who once lived there, today offers a number of antique-jewelry stores; the Via dei Giubbonari, the street of the jerkin makers, still features inexpensive clothing stores. If you lived in Renaissance Rome and needed to buy a crossbow, you would come to Via dei Balestrari; today you'll find *erboristerie,* dressmakers, and an old-fashioned wine store. Itinerant thrift shops, peddlers, and wooden carts clog the narrow streets much as they did centuries ago.

Still called the "field of flowers," the district was just that until the 12th century, when the mighty Orsini family began to urbanize the landscape. By the 15th century, stately palazzos built by Rome's powerful families gave it fashionable status. Although it is now predominantly a working-class area, its Renaissance glory is still evident in the sophisti-cated Via Giulia and the elegantly somber Piazza Farnese (site of today's French Embassy); they lend an air of prestige to many of the area's stores.

The Via Giulia is worth searching out. In a network of short twisting medieval streets, it unwinds parallel to the Tiber like some Renaissance beauty. It is named after Pope Julius II, who was responsible for the building of this more accessible and impressive route to the Vatican. The artery is a marvel of 16th-century city planning. Along its arrow-straight 1000-yard length, a series of small expensive antique stores housed in patrician palazzos invite serious collectors and dealers. A petition to close this handsome street to traffic is currently under consideration; it already is one of Rome's most recommended evening *passeggiate.*

Not big for its shopping but of great historical interest, the nearby Jewish Ghetto is still home to one of Europe's oldest Jewish communities. In the 16th century, as in Venice's Ghetto, Jews were obliged to live and conduct their businesses within confining walls and gates that were locked at sunset. Various pontiffs changed the restrictions, and Napoleon ended them. Today the boundaries no longer exist, and the Ghetto has taken on a different air. Romans shop here for wholesale trimmings and notions, inexpensive clothing, and miscellaneous bargains, including Leone Limen-tani's famous well-stocked warehouse of discounted china and housewares. Ghetto dining spots have become local landmarks, featuring traditional Jewish specialties that long ago became part of the regional cuisine. The

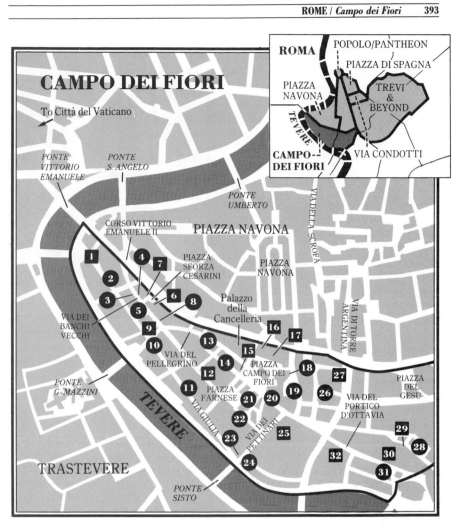

only synagogue that remains is an imposing, relatively recent addition, its dome a prominent feature of Rome's skyline. The Ghetto, the Renaissance palazzos, and the medieval shopping streets blend together to form the fabric of this lively but unhurried neighborhood.

RISTORANTE/TRATTORIA

1 TAVERNA GIULIA
Vicolo dell'Oro 23
Tel. 65.69.768
Expensive; credit cards accepted
Closed Sunday

The best pesto sauce south of Genoa is especially delicious here. The basil-based sauce is so aromatic and the gnocchi are so plump that once you step into this characteristic 15th-century palazzo with beamed ceilings and white stucco walls, you'll imagine ordering nothing else. But there is stiff competition among the Ligurian fare available: the oversized tortellini called *panzerotti* are dressed with an irresistible creamy walnut sauce *(sugo di noci)*; the *bistecca al basilico* is a tender cut of steak coated with basil; and the *stinco di vitello al forno* is a roasted young leg of veal served in its gravy. All are house specialties, together with the fresh fish favored by the Genovese. There is a good wine list and an interesting crowd.

HOME

FURNITURE & LIGHTING

2 FONTANA ARTE
Via Giulia 96
Tel. 65.64.148
Expensive; credit cards accepted

On the ground floor of this Roman palazzo-apartment house are the striking display windows of Fontana Arte, a stunning showroom of designer lamps and glass furniture. See Milan listing (page 193).

Natural and delicious at l'Albero del Pane.

FOOD

NATURAL PRODUCTS

3 L'ALBERO DEL PANE
Via dei Banchi Vecchi 39
Tel. 65.65.016
Inexpensive; no credit cards accepted
Open during lunch

If you're curious to see what's happening in the world of natural foods in Italy or interested in buying some beautifully packaged gourmet health foods for friends and family back home, stop by "The Bread Tree." Four young people run this delightful natural-foods cooperative, an interesting antithesis to the customary heavy though delicious Roman cuisine. Everything is without chemicals or preservatives, relatively recent additions to the Mediterranean diet. From Italy's provinces come cold-pressed olive oils, honeys and marmalades, and sun-dried tomatoes, eggplants, and mushrooms preserved in fine olive oil.

If you've decided to set up house in Rome, you'll want to keep in mind the selection of whole-grain pastas and macrobiotic foods. L'Albero del Pane also acts as an informal center for natural-food followers, dispersing information about yoga, meditation centers, and environmentalist happenings. And to take out, there are fresh vegetable pies *(torte di verdura)* and whole-wheat pizza with sprouts.

KNITTING YARNS

4 LE VIE DELLA LANA
Via dei Banchi Vecchi 116
Tel. 65.30.005
Moderate; no credit cards accepted

Despite its unpretentious location, this charming neighborhood yarn shop has a big selection of high-quality and designer yarns at reasonable prices. There are more than 70 kinds, including angora, alpaca, cashmere, and mohair, over 30 different blends of cotton and selections of silk and lurex, all in vast arrays of color. Every season the new creations of Valentino, Fendi, Roberta di Camerino, and Crosa di Biela restock the store's large, open bins; you can look and touch and create your future knitwear masterpiece in your mind's eye. This successful operation is a cooperative effort of four friends who decided to invest their own work in exchange for partnership. Their own beautiful hand-knit creations are on display and, fortunately, for sale: modern and sophisticated models are juxtaposed with bulky, oversized geometric-design pullovers, all personal interpretations of what is happening in this season's fashion knitwear.

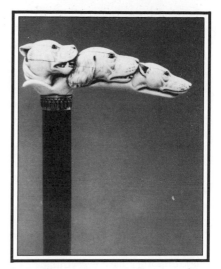

La Gazza Ladra, for men who have everything.

COLLECTIBLES
WALKING STICKS

Monomania

5 LA GAZZA LADRA
Via dei Banchi Vecchi 29
Tel. 65.41.689
Moderate to expensive; credit cards
    accepted

The walking stick is the star attraction at La Gazza Ladra (The Thieving Magpie). Young Maurizio De Simone, a passionate collector himself, opened this telephone-booth-sized shop to keep up his habit, and stocks it with a fascinating collection of antique walking sticks. Most date from the 1800s, when they were the ultimate accessory for fashionable men and women, although their story originates with the Egyptian pharoahs, who considered such staffs a token of power. Maurizio's 19th-century specimens (mostly English and French) often reflect the style and profession of their original owners—a carved ivory handle in the shape of a serpent and skull belonged to a pharmacist, while an ebony head with markings indicated the owner's interest in phrenology. Ladies' walking sticks may be in silver with decorative art-nouveau motifs or Sèvres porcelain embellishments; one has the owner's painted portrait still delicately intact. The well-known walking sticks of mystery and surprise are here, with innocent-looking handles that unscrew to reveal everything from pens to pipes to guns. Don't be misled by the size of this shop; Maurizio sells over 1000 of his prized accessories every year. They are the perfect gift for friends who think they have everything.

SUSTENANCE

RISTORANTE/TRATTORIA

6 POLESE
Piazza Sforza Cesarini 40
Tel. 65.61.709
Moderate; no credit cards accepted
Closed Tuesday

If your weary body would rather be in bed when most of Rome is just sitting down to a late dinner, Polese offers good, unpretentious regional cooking that is served as early as 6:00 P.M. It is always crowded with regulars and tourists alike. Try for a table outside under the trees when the weather is good, and sample any of the fine pasta dishes, many of which are Genovese with Roman inflections, such as *trenette al pesto* or *linguine al gorgonzola. Scamorza* cheese is grilled to perfection, and there are tomatoes stuffed with cold rice salad in summer. Try the *cuscinetti*, delicious little cushions of veal stuffed with ham and mozzarella. There are tasty vegetables, including *porcini* mushrooms

when in season, and seasonal fresh-fruit desserts such as poached pears or peaches in wine.

SUSTENANCE

BAR/CAFFÈ

Pasticceria

7 LA BELLA NAPOLI
Corso Vittorio Emanuele 246–248
Tel. 65.70.48
Inexpensive; no credit cards accepted
Closed Wednesday

This *pasticceria*'s name—"Beautiful Naples"—indicates how proud its owners feel about their regional pastries—as well they should. Rome's large Neapolitan community confirms that this is the best *pasticceria napolitana* in town. Amidst all the sweet temptations shine the bakery's two superb specialties: the cream- or chocolate-filled *sfogliatelle* (something like the French *mille feuilles*), and the *cassata* ice cream. Try one of the excellent coffees at the long standup bar, or, if the weather is pleasant, hope for a free table outside.

COLLECTIBLES

20TH-CENTURY MURANO GLASS

8 VITRUM
Via dei Banchi Vecchi 140
Tel. 65.61.040
Expensive; credit cards accepted

Glass collections such as this are hard to come by outside Venice. The small, uncluttered shop displays its prized Murano glassware dating from 1900 to the 1950s, together with catalogs and books that explain their identity and value. There's an eclectic variety of shapes, sizes, styles, and colors of vases, glasses, and serving bowls. A number of these pieces are signed by such important designers as Venini, Flavio Poli, Cenedese, Barovier e Toso, Nason e Moretti, Seguso, and Cappellini. Much less expensive is a colorful collection of contemporary necklaces, earrings, and bracelets made from remnants of old glass by the store's owner, Benedetta Igliori, an enthusiastic glass connoisseur.

SUSTENANCE

RISTORANTE/TRATTORIA

9 IL DRAPPO
Vicolo del Malpasso 9
Tel. 68.77.365
Moderate; credit cards accepted
Closed Sunday, and Monday lunch

If you've eaten one too many Roman specialties in garlic-festooned *trattorie,* here's a charming restaurant that offers the savory and interesting cuisine of nearby Sardinia. Brother-and-sister team Paolo and Valentina Tolu use traditional ingredients that are sent weekly from their native island to create rich and authentic recipes, some with their own refinements. One interesting antipasto is *carta di musica* (sheet music), a wafer-thin bread used by Sardinian shepherds, topped with diced tomato and pepper, parsley, and olive oil. *Malloreddu* pasta is made from durum wheat, served in a delicious saffron-tomato sauce; and *spaghetti con granchi* is a delicious mixture of pasta and crabmeat. *Abbacchio all'umido* is a roasted shank of young lamb basted with a bitter aperitif wine and served with onions and mushrooms. A carefully selected *cantina* of Sardinian wines complements the cuisine.

Neoclassical expertise at La Chimera.

ANTIQUES

NEOCLASSIC & "NEO-DECO"

10 LA CHIMERA
Via Giulia 122
Tel. 65.48.344
Expensive; no credit cards accepted

The lovely Paola Cipriani is known for her good taste and expertise in the world of antiquities. Her beautiful antiques gallery on this hallowed street of dealers' stores displays her lifelong passion for furniture and paintings of the Neoclassic period, which she believes to be the most beautiful. A collector since childhood, Signora Cipriani has recently singled out the small collection of lovely neo-deco room-dividers/screens and tables by Barbara Mastroianni, daughter of the actor Marcello.

Architectural detail of the lovely Via Giulia.

ANTIQUES
ITALIAN COUNTRY FURNITURE

11 ANTIQUARIATO VALLIGIANO
Via Giulia 193
Tel. 65.69.505
Expensive; no credit cards accepted

Valligiano is the only antique shop in Rome to carry this genre of handsome country furniture from the Piedmont region of the 1800s to 1900s. Simple in line, solid, rustic and seemingly indestructible pieces are made of pine, chestnut, or walnut and often sport charming, hand-carved details or motifs on their corners or panels. There's usually a collection of chests, bookcases, armoires, and cupboards that would add a quaint, old-world air to an American country kitchen or vacation home.

SUSTENANCE
RISTORANTE/TRATTORIA

12 IL VELIERO DA CARMELO
Via Monserrato 32
Tel. 65.42.636
Expensive; credit cards accepted
Closed Monday

Carmelo Riccioli, the ex-owner of the famous La Rosetta restaurant (see Popolo/Pantheon neighborhood, page 382), has brought his expertise in the preparation of fresh fish to this new location with instant success. One of the finest chefs specializing in seafood in all of Italy, Carmelo is now exploring both the classic and the nouvelle, with a number of very un-Roman marinated fish offerings. Those with more traditional palates will appreciate the perfectly grilled, fried, or roasted fish that arrives daily from Sicily, Carmelo's *terra madre*. Fresh seafood antipastos are simply dressed with oil and lemon, and a number of delicious pasta *primi* are predictably made with fish and seafood. A wonderfully exotic mix of fresh fruit offers a light and grand finale. In a city not known for fine fish, you may find the prices high; try the early Sunday lunch (brunch is still a novelty here), which has a more accessible fixed price.

JEWELRY
WORKSHOP/STUDIO

13 SIMONA ERSANILLI—ORAFO
Via del Pellegrino 132
Tel. 65.61.183
Moderate; credit cards accepted

Charming young Simona Ersanilli, a goldsmith with exceptional taste and skill, creates exquisite, unique pieces by hand in clean geometric or naturalistic shapes. In gold or silver settings she uses all kinds of stones for their color and texture—lapis lazuli, topaz, amethyst, coral, and pearls. Simona is inspired by antique forms, but the only thing her modern, wearable jewelry has in common with those remote sources is its richness

Simona Ersanilli's simple, striking settings.

and beauty. Necklaces that become brooches offer you flexibility, and Simona will also work with you to design your own very personalized creation.

FASHION
NOTIONS

14 ERMANNO & RITA
Via dei Cappellari 61–62
Tel. 65.40.654
Inexpensive; no credit cards accepted

The milliners are gone from this "Street of the Hat Makers," but Ermanno & Rita is still here, a no-nonsense store with a complete stock of notions and ornaments. An inexhaustible supply of special buttons from the 1920s to 1930s (Italian style) is a special attraction. Big, chunky buttons in plastics and metals come in many colors and shapes; some have been made up into sweater guards to jog your imagination as to their possible uses. There are antique and new trims and borders, pearls and rhinestones, and a whole treasure chest for browsers. Shoulder pads in various forms and colors hang from the ceiling.

SUSTENANCE
RISTORANTE/TRATTORIA

15 LA CARBONARA
Campo dei Fiori 23
Tel. 65.64.783
Moderate; credit cards accepted
Closed Tuesday

There's no more characteristic piazza in which to dine. When winter moves you indoors, you'll find a number of oak-paneled rooms and a fine view of the site of the bustling morning market from the upstairs windows. There's a host of delicious first courses to pick from, such as fettuccine with salmon; but as the restaurant's name suggests, *pasta alla carbonara* is the specialty. Here it is made with short, tubular *rigatoni* in a rich, peppery sauce of egg, cheese, and *pancetta* (bacon). *Fritto misto* is another must-try—a delicious sampling of deep-fried mozzarella and whatever vegetables are in season, such as artichokes or zucchini blossoms. Many Roman habitués return regularly for the fried brains *(cervello fritto)* or the baby lamb grilled to perfection and surrounded by crisp roast potatoes. You may prefer to try a simply grilled fresh fish, if you're planning to make it to the exquisite meringue dessert.

From the mercato *to La Carbonara's kitchen.*

PIZZA RUSTICA

Slices to Go

16 PIZZERIA PANADORA
Via dei Baullari 140
Tel. 65.40.665
Inexpensive; no credit cards accepted
Closed Monday

For delicious and healthy fast food *alla romana,* try a snack at Pizzeria Panadora. Recently opened by a friendly young Roman couple, the Panadora currently offers 20 different and imaginative variations on the pizza theme and is working its way up to 35. Those already perfected are all the regulars, plus such less likely ingredients as potatoes, figs, tuna, eggplant, and zucchini. Pizza is sliced, then weighed and sold by the *etto* (100 grams). It's not meant to replace dinner, but one hearty slice will tide you over without ruining your appetite. The modern yellow-tiled décor with a touch of high tech has already helped to attract a young crowd that lingers until 11:00 P.M. every night.

BREADS & PIZZA RUSTICA

17 IL FORNAIO
Via dei Baullari 5–7
Tel. 65.43.947
Inexpensive; no credit cards accepted
Closed Thursday afternoon

When your get-up-and-go is on the wane, stop by Rome's most aromatic corner for a delicious takeout treat. Few bakeries are as extensively supplied as this new but popular neighborhood *forno,* where everything is baked fresh on the premises each day.

A slice of thick, warm pizza prepared *bianca* (plain, brushed with olive oil) or with *cipolle* (onions) or zucchini, is a delicious pick-me-up. There are dozens of different breads if you're contemplating a picnic on the steps of a nearby church or on the rim of a neighborhood fountain. Rustic specialties are made with grapes *(pane con uva),* walnuts *(noce),* bran *(crusca)* or sesame. Mouth-watering cookies include *brutti ma buoni* ("ugly but good") and small tarts made with sweetened ricotta, *mandorle* (almonds), or fresh fruit in season. The bakery is particularly pretty, with an old-fashioned light-wood décor, and all the breads are conveniently labeled.

SCALES

18 MISDARIS
Via dei Chiavari 73–74
Tel. 65.61.327
Moderate; no credit cards accepted

This tiny, cluttered shop offers an idea for the perfect kitchen gift—a

Dozens of breads fresh from Il Fornaio.

big brass hanging fruit and vegetable scale like those that add so much character to Roman markets. There are two sizes, either of which makes an attractive fixture in any kitchen, as a plant holder if not for practical use. Myriad other scales for bathrooms, doctors' offices, jewelers' workshops, and butcher shops are displayed in ordered chaos. Your eye might fall on a large, old-style marble-and-wood table scale with brass weights and two brass weighing dishes, another choice gift for a deserving kitchen.

POSTER GALLERY

19 GOUACHES
Via dei Chiavari 75
Tel. 65.61.322
Moderate; credit cards accepted

Gouaches is the gallery for anyone with an eye for avant-garde, counter-culture art. Dozens of colorful contemporary posters line the walls of this small modern space, representing all the latest trends in Italian, French, and Dutch art. There are also a number of posters from art gallery exhibits throughout Europe. Fun, innovative post cards and musical greeting cards from European sources are a colorful break from the garden variety; included is a whole section of offbeat views of Rome.

FASHION

WOMEN'S

Contemporary

20 LOLLY POPS
Via dei Giubbonari 76–77
Tel. 65.64.574
  Moderate to expensive; credit cards
    accepted

Amid a plethora of cheap neighborhood shops appear the elegant windows of Lolly Pops. The unexpected location is one reason for the reasonable prices—up to 20 percent lower than in competitive stores with higher overhead—for contemporary fashion such as Max Mara, Enrico Coveri, and Leonia. The personable atmosphere of this small, two-level shop makes for pleasant browsing. You'll find everything from separates to eveningwear, with accessories and bathing suits not overlooked. Among Lolly Pops' regular customers are the wives of the American and French ambassadors.

HOME

TILES

21 GALERIE FARNESE 🍶🍶🍶🍶
Piazza Farnese 50
Tel. 65.41.842
Expensive; credit cards accepted

The beautiful ceramic tiles of Mario Di Donato's Galerie Farnese are the most prestigious in Italy. After decades of researching and collecting authentic designs and techniques from monasteries, castles, and country villas, Di Donato now faithfully reproduces an art that had disappeared over the centuries. He also applies his expertise to a recently opened division which is evolving new colors for terra-cotta tiles and for glazed tiles of modern design, using special kilns based on 16th-century models. More and more frequently, tiles take a leading role in interior design. Italy's top architectural design studios have used Galerie Farnese's artistic tiles in the French Embassy, the home of Carlo Ponti and Sophia Loren, Franco Zefferelli's

Positano villa, and Laura Biagiotti's country retreat, as well as in sheiks' pavilions from Jeddah to Qatar.

HOME
HAND-PAINTED TILES & STATUARY

22 SERGIO DE BENEDETTI
Vicolo dei Venti 5
Tel. 65.60.810
Moderate; no credit cards accepted

In the white-powder-dusted workshop of Sergio De Benedetti is a forest of statues and busts large and small, birdbaths, balustrades, columns and column capitals, pedestals, fountains, and friezes. All have been collected by Signor De Benedetti, skillfully restored to life, and are here offered for sale. Newly arrived armless putti and cracked statuary not yet attended to lie about in various degrees of disrepair. Most impressive is a collection of antique hand-painted tiles, many of them from 17th- to 19th-century Naples. Each tile is marked with the

Enjoyable browsing at Sergio De Benedetti.

number of matching pieces (from dozens to hundreds) in stock downstairs; it can be slipped into an ingenious kaleidoscope-like contraption to let you see the effect of placing many coordinating tiles together. Signor De Benedetti is an important source for architects and home owners restoring old villas. It is not surprising to learn that he was once a successful businessman, who gave all that up to pursue more creative goals.

HOME
BRASS ACCESSORIES

23 HANDLES
Via dei Pettinari 53
Tel. 65.43.119
Moderate; credit cards accepted

Whether you're looking for the perfect doorknob or just for ideas, immerse yourself in this remarkable collection of decorative hardware. There are door handles and knobs in every style, most of them made of brass, others of plastic, lacquered or gold-plated metal, fake tortoise, and Chinese lacquer. You'll be able to study the historical vicissitudes of door ornaments from the classic Louis XVI to the contemporary sleek, in every material from porcelain to steel. If you've decided to bring home a massive carved wooden Italian portal and haven't a thing to go with it, you'll find a series of huge door pulls from which to choose. Apart from the wall display of these items, there are also such lovely brass paraphernalia as fireplace accessories and towel racks and other bathroom fixtures, but the name of the store says it all. If the impressive selection gives you ideas about reknobbing your whole neighborhood, Handles will ship.

FASHION

CHILDREN'S

Handmade

24 IL PALLONCINO ROSSO 🍼🍼🍼🍼
Via dei Pettinari 50
Tel. 65.64.213
Moderate; credit cards accepted

Buoyant and spirited, the imaginative children's clothing at Il Palloncino Rosso (The Red Balloon) is the colorful creation of an ex-costume designer for Italian TV and films. When she started making children's clothes for her own baby, they were an immediate smash; the opening of this small shop was a logical eventuality. She emphasizes bright-patterned natural fabrics: patchwork, seersucker, calico, Liberty and Naj Oleari prints are all made up into casual activewear for real kids—never too grownup or too restrictive. Designed for children from birth to ten years of age, Il Palloncino's clothes are all handmade and include a number of attractive wool and cotton hand-knit sweaters. Everything shows an unmistakable flair for color combinations and fashion sense.

SUSTENANCE

RISTORANTE/TRATTORIA

25 IL PIANETA TERRA
Via dell'Arco del Monte 94–95
Tel. 65.69.893
Expensive; credit cards accepted
Open for dinner only; closed Monday

The cuisine at "The Planet Earth" is unique. Presented in an elegant upstairs setting, the menu created by the young couple Patrizia (Sicilian) and Roberto (Tuscan) evokes de-

International design at Spazio Sette.

lighted reactions from Roman regulars bored with the predictability of their regional dishes. First courses, for example, might include ravioli filled with *coniglio tartufato* (rabbit in a pigeon and truffle sauce). Spaghetti is made with a sauce of smoked swordfish, sole with a light shrimp sauce, and prawns done in butter and thyme. Such descriptions are useless, however, as the menu changes constantly with chef Roberto's inexhaustible imagination. White-gloved waiters provide drama by whisking away covers to reveal Roberto's latest creations; but the biggest surprise is the gigantic portions—just when nouvelle cuisine had programmed us for the minuscule. Their wine list is superb.

HOME

TABLEWARE & ACCESSORIES

International Modern Design

26 SPAZIO SETTE
Via dei Barbieri 7
Tel. 65.47.139
Expensive; credit cards accepted

Palazzo Cavallerini, with its superb 17th-century painted ceiling and grand contemporary marble staircase, is the appropriate setting for Spazio Sette, Rome's premier home-furnishings store. The best in Italian and international design is artistically displayed in a mélange of furniture, kitchenware, glass, china and terra-cotta objects, aprons, leather and canvas shopping bags, modern lamps, and even stationery. Established names blend effortlessly with talented newcomers, and the overall effect is a new and fresh look at high design for the modern home. The amiable owners, Beatrice and Nino Borzi, are often around to offer customers a friendly, professional opinion, and they will also ship your purchases.

SUSTENANCE
BAR/CAFFÈ

Pasticceria

27 BERNASCONI
Largo di Torre Argentina 1
Tel. 65.48.141
Moderate; no credit cards accepted
Closed Monday

This is Rome's oldest and one of its busiest *pasticcerie,* which has baked well over 100 years' worth of award-winning pastries. Its unanimous favorite since 1868 has been the *bigne,* a cream-puff-like shell filled with fresh whipped cream and *zabaione.* Bernasconi's ice cream is nothing to overlook, either. Everyone using the convenient phone center downstairs (where you can call long distance or intercontinental and pay at the end of the call) usually buys some on the way down or on the way up.

HOME
MODERN FURNITURE CLASSICS

28 ALIVAR 🏠🏠🏠🏠
Piazza di Campitelli 2
Tel. 67.99.891
Moderate; no credit cards accepted

You wouldn't expect that this modern showroom on the ground floor of a beautiful 16th-century palazzo might offer discount bargains. Yet Alivar's classic furniture masterpieces cost at least 50 percent less than the big Milan showrooms would charge. Alivar faithfully reproduces designs by such furniture greats as Mies Van der Rohe, Le Corbusier, Eileen Gray, and Marcel Breuer, as well as lesser-known Bauhaus students. Many of these pieces, which date chiefly from the 1920s, have been out of production for half a century; others never made it to production at all. Leather sofas, club chairs, and other clean-lined objects are scrupulously replicated by a talented young American and Italian duo, Vincent Masucci and Nilo Checchi. Their conviction that such design beauty should not be limited to a few wealthy owners, together with their small, specialized factory and low overhead, is the secret behind their marvelous prices.

SUSTENANCE
RISTORANTE/TRATTORIA

29 VECCHIA ROMA
Piazza di Campitelli 18
Tel. 65.64.604
Moderate; no credit cards accepted
Closed Wednesday

Many restaurants move their tables outdoors in the warm weather, but perhaps none has a setting as pretty as this piazza, which boasts a charming baroque church and three handsome palazzos. The menu changes with the season, and the two hosts, brothers Giuseppe and Tonino, promise a different specialty every day of the year. Unless you can't resist the large assortment of seafood appetizers, move on to broad *pappardelle* noodles with shellfish, *porcini* mushrooms and fresh tomatoes. Lamb (*agnello*) and goat (*capretto*) are specialties, and there is veal braised with artichokes and perfectly grilled fresh fish. Superb wine list.

FOOD

JEWISH BAKERY

30 IL FORNO DEL GHETTO
Via del Portico d'Ottavia 119
No telephone
Inexpensive; no credit cards accepted
Closed Saturday

This cave-like, dimly lit bakery is reason enough for a trip to the Ghetto. Its secret is rumored to be ancient Jewish recipes, and fortunately the selection is limited or you'd be compelled to try them all. The *torte di ricotta* is the all-time favorite, a cheese-filled sweet that comes in three varieties—plain, with chocolate, or with sour cherries (*visciole*). It is soft, creamy, not too sweet, and sold by the *etto* (100 grams) so that, despite the temptation, you don't have to buy the whole thing. *Teccie* is the other pastry vying for favor, filled with raisins and candied fruit. There are a number of other goodies, including delicious macaroons, but you probably won't have room after the above-named openers.

HOME

HOUSEWARES & TABLEWARE
Hugh Selection at Discount Prices

31 LEONE LIMENTANI
Via del Portico d'Ottavia 47
Tel. 65.40.686
Moderate to expensive; no credit cards accepted

Every self-respecting Roman, from a dowager *contessa* to a newlywed professional, buys housewares at Limentani. Prices are about 20 percent off local retail listings for an enormous selection of European names. Browsing through a thousand square yards of precariously stacked china and scattered boxes of silver is a treat if you don't mind dust and disorder. Here's just a sampling of the wares: Richard-Ginori, Villeroy & Boch, Rosenthal, Limoges, and Royal Worcester porcelain; Waterford, Orrefors, Kosta Boda, Sèvres, and Reidel crystal; IVV glassware; Alessi and Sambonet stainless steel; and a wide range of flatware, pans and skillets, coffeepots, and other everyday items. Limentani will sell the single plate to complete your set, and will arrange for shipping when you buy much more. The story behind this Ghetto landmark begins in the 16th century with an edict from Pope Paul IV requiring that Jews do business only in salvage; when a Limentani of the time responded by starting to deal in rags and bits and pieces, a major enterprise was born.

RISTORANTE/TRATTORIA

32 AL POMPIERE
Via Santa Maria dei Calderari 38
Tel. 65.68.377
Moderate; no credit cards accepted
Closed Sunday

When you dine in this large, vener-
ably worn upstairs room with heavy
beamed ceilings, you'll think you're
in the grand salon of a pivate palazzo.
For reasons lost in time, the charming
restaurant is named after an unknown
fireman. Because it's located in the
Ghetto, it offers the local Jewish cuisine (see Roman Cuisine, page 314).
The *carciofi alla giudia* (Jewish-style
artichoke) is flattened, then fried, and
arrives at your table looking like a
pressed flower; the *fiori fritti* (lightly
fried zucchini blossoms) are also a
favorite when in season. The house
specialties are the *paste fatte a casa*
(homemade pastas), which change
daily, the *abbacchio* (baby lamb), and

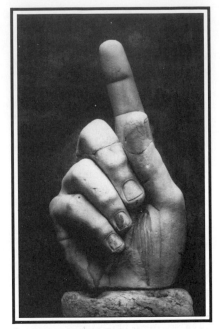

Rome's every niche offers a suggestion.

the *baccalà* (dried cod). For dessert,
the tart made from sweetened ricotta
cheese and the *zuppa inglese* (trifle)
are suggested when available.

Trevi & Beyond

T his is the hinterland of Rome's central shopping frontier, an area not commonly associated with must-buy experiences and perhaps more enjoyable to the indefatigable tourist for that reason. There is no concentration of noteworthy stores in any particular section of the amoeba-shaped Trevi & Beyond neighborhood; yet some of the entries listed are special enough to elicit a visit.

The busy Via del Corso appears again here, with its hordes of young shoppers who clog the sidewalks, window-shopping the moderately priced shoe and clothing stores at all hours of the day. The grandiose white marble monument to King Vittorio Emanuele II at the avenue's end was nicknamed the "Wedding Cake" by the Allied troops in World War II; it took 26 years to build and is either loved or loathed by the Romans. The wide boulevards of the nearby Via Nazionale and Via del Tritone are like the Via del Corso in feeling—interesting, middle-class shopping strips with large and small temptations.

Rare is the tourist who misses a visit to the Fontana di Trevi to view this powerful flight of 18th-century high-baroque fantasy—and to toss a coin at Neptune's feet for a guarantee that the visitor will return to Rome. Taken from *tre vie*, the name refers to the three narrow streets that converge here. The theatrical fountain seems overbearing for so small a space. It is most spectacular when you happen upon its floodlit majesty in the evening, with the enjoyable sensation of personal discovery. But if you want to take advantage of the "shoe country" surrounding it, you'll have to schedule your visit to coincide with store hours. Although much of the merchandise can be passed over, some good buys are to be had.

South of the Trevi area, north of the Colosseum and straddling the Via Cavour artery, is the old Monti neighborhood, or *rione*. This is one of the most genuinely Roman districts left more or less intact, where a centuries-old vocation of art and craftsmanship lives on in worn, working-class side streets and their dusty *botteghe*. You won't run into too many tourists on the narrow byways named degli Zingari, Boschetto, Madonna dei Monti, and Urbana.

In radical contrast is the imperial Via Veneto, immortalized by Fellini

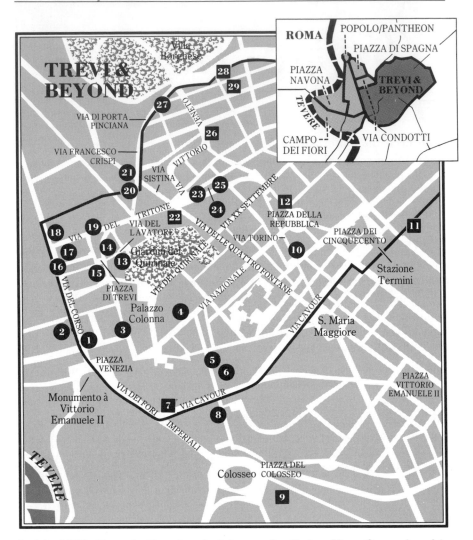

in his 1959 film of glittering indolence, *La Dolce Vita.* Once the chic gathering place for international movie stars, aristocrats, flashy gigolos and *paparazzi*, the Via Veneto today is peopled by foreigners who sit in pleasant outdoor cafés patiently awaiting the return of this flamboyant spectacle. Meanwhile, its expensive, elegant hotels remain a draw, and many of its smart shops and boutiques (especially a proliferation of shoe stores) continue to do well, offering tranquil browsing and high price tags. Gracefully unwinding downhill, the broad, tree-lined Via Veneto comes to a natural stop at the Piazza Bernini, an appropriate homage to the man whose genius transformed Rome's celebrated fountains into glorious art.

SHOES
MEN'S & WOMEN'S

1 PERONI
Via del Corso 283/A
Tel. 67.94.855
Moderate; credit cards accepted

This is the most accessible of the three very popular Peroni shoe store branches in Rome. In its simple décor you'll find a big selection of men's and women's shoes, ranging from sporty to dressy, that are consistently above average in quality, considering their fairly moderate prices.

LEATHERGOODS
BELTS ONLY

Bargains

2 FELLINI
Via del Corso 340
Tel. 67.85.800
Inexpensive; credit cards accepted

You might never find such a selection of belts anywhere else, for hundreds of belts in over 500 styles hang from the walls. The price is right and the self-service setup lets you try on to your waist's content. You can belt your entire wardrobe, and those of your friends as well, with good-value leather belts in all the colors that are currently in vogue as well as some that are not. Styles lean toward the bold and wide, with interesting buckles; the men's selection is far more limited, mostly of a classic or cowboy inclination. In the 1950s, the young Loren and Lollobrigida did their fair share of belt cinching, helping to make these fashion accessories an integral component of any stylish wardrobe; Italy has been churning them

out ever since. Fellini's lies a bit beyond the Via del Corso's thickest concentration of shops and stores, within sight of the imposing Piazza Venezia.

FOOD
CHOCOLATES

3 MORIONDO & GARIGLIO
Via della Pilotta 2
Tel. 67.86.662
Moderate; no credit cards accepted

For as long as Rome can remember, *marrons glacés* and fine chocolates have kept sweet-toothed nobility and common gentry alike coming to Moriondo & Gariglio. Owner Marcello Proietti, diligently following venerable original recipes, personally glazes the chestnuts and decorates chocolates with candied violets. After the shop's 120 years of sweet success, its previous owner was about to close it down when young Proietti, who had worked there since he was ten years old, took on the legacy. He changed the location to the palazzo of Prince Colonna, a loyal customer who offered the space rather than risk the loss of his favorite sweets. The fruits of young Proietti's labor come from the same tradition that made regular customers of such literary gourmands as Gabriele D'Annunzio and the Roman dialect poet Trilussa, who had dedicated poems to the store. Try the real hen's eggs filled with chocolate, an Easter specialty, or the celebrated *marrons glacés* regularly ordered by the President of the Republic for his guests at the Quirinale Palace. You can have your order sent to your hotel or shipped home.

FASHION
MEN'S
Contemporary & Trendy

4 AREA
Via Nazionale 239–240
Tel. 48.44.212
Moderate; credit cards accepted

The seemingly effortless success of the casually thrown-together look can be found here in all its carefully chosen components. The attractive young sales assistants will help you pull it all together with the up-to-the-second young men's fashion of Area's private label. Good-quality fabrics and knits in the season's favored colors are used in jackets, trousers, shirts and sweaters, with the necessary accessories for the finishing touch. A large assortment of fun sneakers echo the colors of the store's stained-glass ceiling.

FASHION
MEN'S & WOMEN'S
Dance Costumes

5 DANZA NON SOLO
Via del Boschetto 34
Tel. 47.56.215
Moderate; no credit cards accepted

For the prima ballerina in each of us, Lia d'Inzillo creates Italy's largest selection of ready-made classic ballet and dance costumes. All are made by hand and executed with fine attention to detail. Signora d'Inzillo will throw open her armoires to show you clouds of colorful tulle, chiffon, satin and organza bodices decorated with beads, sequins, lace and feathers. Much sought after in the entertainment world, Signora d'Inzillo's spe-

cialized atelier also does custom work. If your fashion tastes border on the theatrical, or if you need a standout masquerade ensemble, you can have an heirloom fantasy dress made here to your specifications. If your tastes and needs are tamer, browse amid the more conventional selection of leotards and tights in every hue.

HOME
TABLEWARE & ACCESSORIES
Handmade Terra Cottas

6 TERRECOTTE SUBURA
Via degli Zingari 43
Tel. 47.58.279
Moderate; no credit cards accepted

Kitchenware lovers will be delighted at the special terra-cotta cookware designed and produced by Antonio Scutiero here on the "Street of the Gypsies." As practical for the stove as it is esthetic for the table, it is inspired by traditional peasant terra cotta. Large and small pieces are specifically designed for the preparation of certain dishes: the "Cinzia" model for cauliflower has a special basket for herbs to eliminate its cooking odor; "Titina" serves as a double boiler, and "Ricciolina" is perfect for

Artisan Antonio Scutiero at Terrecotte Subura.

risottos. The properties of terra cotta are optimal for many types of cooking, letting the steam breathe rather than condense (ideal for stews and artichokes), while slowly and evenly conducting thermal heat throughout (something needed for risotto). All the solid, fire-glazed earthenware is of Antonio's own design, and his lead-free glazes keep to earthy tones. If you have a particular request, he'll work with you on special order.

SUSTENANCE

ENOTECA (WINE BAR)

7 ENOTECA CAVOUR
Via Cavour 313
Tel. 67.85.496
Moderate; no credit cards accepted
Closed Sunday

In an unusual setup, this lively *enoteca* sells its wines and spirits till 1:00 P.M., then reopens at 5:30 as a homey, comfortable neighborhood wine bar where you can choose between snacking on generous appetizers or enjoying a full meal. Its wine selection is one of the city's best, and whether you're standing at the bar or seated, the patient, knowledgeable barman and waiters will help you with your choice. A sampling of cold cuts includes prosciutto made from *cinghiale,* or wild boar, salamis, and delicious regional cheeses such as the fresh *mozzarella di bufola* from the Naples area. There are eight different pâtés, a number of imaginative salads, and smoked salmon or trout. The atmosphere here is pleasant, with wooden booths and a mixture of chic and working-class customers. The Cavour stays open until 11:00 P.M. for a glass of cold champagne and a dessert of fresh wild berries and cream.

HANDICRAFTS

TEXTILE ART & CLOTHING

8 LA BREBIS NOIRE
Via del Cardello 14
Tel. 48.69.70
Moderate; no credit cards accepted

One of the most charming streets in one of Rome's oldest neighborhoods is the entrancing setting for this light, spacious gallery of woven art. Everything here is hand-loomed by young fabric artist Florence Quellien. Her striking creations in wool and mohair, in rich gem or earthy colors, are versatile enough to use as wall hangings or as bedspreads. Double-woven for warmth, her fabrics are also fashioned into one-of-a-kind sweaters, jackets and coats, simple in line and finished off with big, striking buttons and sculptural closings. And original woven silks are offered for summer months.

SUSTENANCE

RISTORANTE/TRATTORIA

9 AI TRE SCALINI
Via SS. Quattro 30
Tel. 73.26.95
Very expensive; credit cards accepted
Closed Monday, Saturday lunch, and
    Sunday dinner

Also called "Rosanna e Matteo" after its owners, and not to be confused with the famous *gelateria* in Piazza Navona of the same name, the Tre Scalini is one of Rome's most exalted restaurants. Rosanna, once an oil engineer stationed in Saudi Arabia, rules the kitchen. According to what her perfectionist husband Matteo procures at the local food market, the menu changes its creative offerings daily. You might find scampi or *mazzancolle* (large prawns) in a *ginepro* (juniper berry) sauce, steamed *spigola* (sea bass) stuffed with shrimp and sage, *anitra agli agrumi* (an ancient recipe of duck in a light apple-and-citrus sauce), or *rognoncino* (kidney) in an unusual champagne sauce. Desserts here are delicious, but the wine list is Matteo's pride and joy, an excellent selection of well-known domestic and French wines as well as his own discriminating discoveries.

BOOKS

ENGLISH-LANGUAGE

New & Used Paperbacks

10 ECONOMY BOOK & VIDEO CENTER

Via Torino 136
Tel. 47.46.877
Moderate; credit cards accepted

For two decades a meeting place for Rome's English-speaking community, this American-run book center has recently left its Piazza di Spagna location to triple its space. The largest shop of its kind in Italy, it offers a complete range of history and guidebooks on Rome and Italy. There's also a vast selection of new and used softcover editions of fiction, nonfiction, children's books, science fiction, best sellers and mysteries. The center will buy your used paperbacks for cash or credit toward other purchases. A novelty in Italy, it also rents English-language videos for those who have set up house in Rome: feature films, musicals, documentaries, drama, ballet, cartoons, how-to and more.

SUSTENANCE

RISTORANTE/TRATTORIA

11 GEMMA E MAURIZIO

Via Marghera 39
Tel. 49.12.30
Moderate; no credit cards accepted
Closed Saturday and Sunday dinner

The Termini station area does not abound in good restaurants, making this a special find for those waiting for a connecting train or an imminent departure. Gemma, amiable and talented wife of Maurizio, interprets the traditionally heavy Roman cuisine as a light and imaginative one. The spot is now frequented by a sophisticated crowd that doesn't mind the trip. The exquisite *tagliatelle ai funghi* (flat noodles with mushrooms), *alla carbonara* (with egg, diced bacon, and onion), and *alla matriciana* (in spicy red tomato sauce with olives and onions) are favorite starters. Suggested entrées are the tender *punta di vitello* (roast brisket or breast of veal), the delicious *trippa* (tripe), and *polpettone* (a large meatball that resembles a gourmet meatloaf). The desserts are not outstanding, but the house wine is particularly good.

SUSTENANCE

BAR/CAFFÈ

12 LE GRAND BAR

Grand Hotel
Via Vittorio Emanuele Orlando 3
         (near Piazza della Repubblica)
Tel. 47.09
Expensive; credit cards accepted
Open 7 days a week, 10:00 A.M. to 1:00 A.M.

While virtually everyone has his own opinion when asked what *is* the world's best bar, no one denies that the Grand Hotel's bar is one of the prime contenders. The hotel, as part of the luxury Ciga chain, has played host to some of the world's most celebrated personalities since its opening in 1894 by Charles Ritz. Illustrious VIPs still populate the bar, a classic and graceful spot where mixed cocktails, the traditional request, are prepared by the charming barman Mauro Lotti. Ask for his special "Vodka Imperial" served from a frosted pitcher packed with fresh fruit, or a "Rosy" made with *crème de framboise,* fresh grapefruit juice, and Aperol (an orange-flavored *aperitivo* popular for its low alcohol content). Linger in this grand drinking establishment and you'll understand how *dolce la vita* can be.

A proud Alberto Menasci and friend.

COSTUME JEWELRY

Avant-Garde Taste

13 I GIOIELLI DEL DRAGO
Via del Lavatore 28
Tel. 67.86.347
Expensive; credit cards accepted
Open during lunch

Costume jewelry here runs a colorful gamut from extraordinary to outlandish. Artistic concoctions—the kind that transform a simple dress into a sensational ensemble—fill this unpredictable store, where the specialty is unusual costume pieces. English-speaking owner Victoria Schileo will show you the whole assemblage, ranging from American Wendy Gill's avant-garde ornaments to exotic Afghanistan collectibles. The store windows often feature the show-stopping work of Carlo Zini, whose "investment" costume jewelry is an alternative to precious stones and metals.

TOYS

WOODEN PLAYTHINGS

14 ALBERTO & MARINA MENASCI
Via del Lavatore 87
Tel. 67.81.981
Moderate; credit cards accepted

A life-sized wooden Pinocchio halts you in your tracks, warning you not to pass by this small, charming shop without witnessing the delights inside. Pinocchios of all sizes keep company with other hand-painted wooden playthings. There are small rocking horses, animals from Noah's ark, colorful coat hangers, clever games and puzzles, Christmas tree ornaments, music boxes and miniature dollhouse furniture. The Menascis have kept their shop stocked with whimsy for over 45 years, and Signor Menasci continues to visit every corner of Italy to ferret out and acquire the work of the most talented artisans who work in wood.

SPORTS GEAR

ACTIVE SPORTSWEAR & EQUIPMENT

15 GIUSTI

Piazza di Trevi 91
Tel. 67.90.726
Moderate; credit cards accepted

Sports lovers itching for a spree will have a field day at Giusti's. The store has an outstanding reputation for its quality clothing and equipment suited to every sport: tennis, skiing, horseback riding, biking, trekking, golf, scuba diving, and more. Four floors of what once was a private home now hold an athlete's treasure, with each room devoted to different sports. Italy is well represented with Fila, Ellesse, Sergio Tacchini, and Invicta, but all major European and American lines worth note are here. Sales help is both knowledgeable and pleasant.

FASHION

MEN'S, WOMEN'S & CHILDREN'S

Department Store

16 LA RINASCENTE

Piazza Colonna
Tel. 67.97.691
Moderate; credit cards accepted
Open during lunch

The first floor is the most interesting here, with a nice perfume and cosmetics area and some designer bijoux and accessories. The impressive Milan flagship for this famous nationwide department store chain is much larger and more contemporary in its fashion selection, but you'll still enjoy the air-conditioned, help-yourself atmosphere here. See the Milan listing (page 171).

BOOKS

ITALIAN & ENGLISH-LANGUAGE

17 LIBRERIA INTERNAZIONALE RIZZOLI

Largo Chigi 15
Tel. 67.96.641
Moderate; credit cards accepted

Especially good for its selection of art and cultural titles, Rizzoli is one of Italy's most prestigious bookstore chains, and this is its largest location. On its spacious ground-level and basement floors, there is a good selection of books in English, including paperbacks and guidebooks. See the Milan listing (page 169).

FASHION

ACCESSORIES

Watches

18 OROLOGI SAVONA

Largo Chigi 7
Tel. 67.89.983
Moderate; credit cards accepted
Open during lunch

If you're in the market for a watch, you'll be drawn to the colorful windows brimming with the latest imaginative timepiece fashions for the young and the young-thinking. Savona's selection comes predominantly from the popular lines of Lorenz, Hip Hop, and Swatch, as well as the slightly more serious Seiko. If you're still too attached to your old faithful to replace it, then take a look at the fun and decorative wall clocks that are perfect for the kids' room.

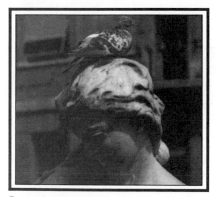

Rest stop with a bird's-eye view.

FABRICS

FASHION

19 GALTRUCCO
Via del Tritone 18–23
Tel. 67.89.022
Moderate; credit cards accepted

The Milanese fabric store has a sizable representation here, with two spacious floors of medium- to top-quality fashion fabrics, the majority of which come from their own mills. See the Milan listing (page 166).

The Galtrucco clothing store is just a few steps away at Piazza San Claudio 166 (telephone 67.97.534). The selection of men's suits is the attraction, almost all of them handmade from Galtrucco's quality fabrics by Brioni's famous tailors (see page 416). The same superlative combination of fabric and workmanship is available in Galtrucco's made-to-measure clothing. Other Italian labels carried are the prestigious Zegna and Missoni. Women's clothing is more fashion-oriented, offering names like Byblos, Claude Montana, Fendi Jeans, Miss V, Galitzine *prêt-à-porter*, and Ginochietti sweaters. Service is courteous, and the ambiance relaxed.

FASHION

WOMEN'S

Hand-Loomed Mohair Suits

20 ANNA LA MARRA ▢▢▢▢
Via Francesco Crispi 93
Tel. 67.90.827
Moderate; no credit cards accepted

Stop by, if only to look through a pile of Signora La Marra's irresistible hand-loomed stoles in mixtures of beautiful colors that could accessorize your wardrobe for life. For almost 30 years the ebullient Anna La Marra has been loom-weaving her warm mohair creations in rich and vibrant color combinations. Her exceptional fabric is also used to create Chanel-type suits that are completely finished by hand. Pick from a small ready-to-wear collection or have her custom-make a suit with your choice of trim; the finished product will be shipped in about a month. The small shop, furnished with Signora La Marra's worn loom, has the air of a seamstress' atelier.

LINGERIE

Classic & Hand-Embroidered

21 TOMASSINI
Via Sistina 119
Tel. 46.19.09
Expensive; credit cards accepted

You'll risk losing your reserve in this sumptuous boudoir shop. Tomassini is filled with the exquisite production of owner Luisa Romagnoli, who offers elegant attire for evenings spent lolling around the house, presumably in the company of someone special. Pure silk nightgowns and matching peignoirs come in soft colors like cream and peach and are elaborated with satin ribbons, lace or hand embroidery. Tomassini's style is delicate and simple, be it a lovely camisole or a more practical slip with hand-finished seams and embroidered trim. There are crisp cotton batistes in summertime, along with a sampling of Christian Dior designs.

SUSTENANCE

PIZZERIA

22 GIOIA MIA

Via degli Avignonesi 34
Tel. 46.27.84
Moderate; no credit cards accepted
Closed Wednesday

In a warm and polite family-run atmosphere, join a regular crowd who come for traditional Roman cooking of the kind Mama would make. For a light and easy lunch, most customers will swear by Gioia Mia's wood-oven-baked pizza or *calzone,* which is renowned for its delicious taste and variety of fresh ingredients. This is not to say you should skip the fine, down-home starters, most of which are regional specialties: try the oven-roasted *crostini* sandwiches or the garlic-brushed bread *bruschetta.* This may be as close as you come to being a guest at a Roman family's dinner table. There's no fish on the menu, but the main-course *abbacchietto*

Three coins in Rome's most famous fountain.

(baby lamb) is excellent whether done *al forno* (roasted) or *scottadite* (grilled). The homemade strudel should be kept in mind for later.

FASHION

MEN'S & WOMEN'S

Classic & Made-to-Measure

23 BRIONI

Via Barberini 79
Tel. 48.45.17
Expensive; credit cards accepted

Time was when this famous Roman tailor wielded a monopoly on made-to-measure suits for Europe's well-heeled clients of gentle birth. Brioni is still the last word in custom work, but also successfully went the ready-to-wear route some 35 years ago. The ready-made collection is just as classic and as impeccably detailed; you'll recognize Brioni's perfectionism and quality control. Custom tailoring continues to be this elegant store's main attraction, however. Each garment takes at least 18 hours of labor, not counting the time that it must rest between adjustments, as Signor Savini-Brioni would remind you that wool is a living material which needs to adjust and breathe. Your suit will be pressed no less than 184 times during a two-month period, the time you'll need to wait for it to be finished.

SHOES

MEN'S, WOMEN'S & CHILDREN'S

Designer Stock at Discount

24 NICKOL

Via Barberini 3/A
Tel. 48.38.21
Moderate; credit cards accepted

Not all the merchandise at this shop is discounted; you'll have to browse through the appropriate racks of Rafael Salato and Andrea Pfister (for women) and Fratelli Rossetti, Yacht, and A. Testoni (for men). Depending upon the season and your luck, you'll find boots, sandals and shoes from last season or even last year. But some of the choices here are so trendy—and others so classic—that no one would ever know. Prices can be 25 percent off local retail price. You'll be particularly happy if you're a size 36 (women's American size 5-6) and able to slip into the usually large selection of samples. Styles for women are generally dressy, with heels for day or evening, while men's shoes are more classic and traditional. Service is patient and helpful, more concerned with pleasing the customer than with selling the stock.

LINENS & LINGERIE

Great Toweling & Terry Robes

25 CESARI
Via Barberini 1
Tel. 46.30.35
Expensive; credit cards accepted

If you're not interested in a set of monogrammed sheets for your yacht, come by anyway to revel in Rome's most impressive collection of linens and towels. The ground floor has an entire room dedicated to robes— fluffy, luxurious terry robes in all weights and colors for him and her. Also on the ground floor are Cesari's pastel bed-and-bath linens, which have outfitted some of the world's most patrician trousseaux, as well as an enormous selection of kitchen and dining linens, including tablecloths,

place mats, towels and aprons. Downstairs are home-furnishing fabrics, comforters and blankets, while upstairs is a whole floor of exquisite ladies' lingerie, featuring Cesari's own deluxe nightgown and peignoir sets and delicate undergarments from the special LaPerla label, Italy's most stylish, high-quality name in lingerie.

Another retail location that has brought fame to Luigi Cesari is his elegant home-furnishings store at Via del Babuino 16 (telephone 67.97.061).

SUSTENANCE

RISTORANTE/TRATTORIA

26 LA CUPOLA
Via Veneto 125
Tel. 47.08
Expensive; credit cards accepted
Open 7 days a week

The elegant Excelsior hotel and its deluxe restaurant have been extolled for decades. One of the city's few fine hotel restaurants, La Cupola is decorated in French Empire style and glitters with white and gold. Here you can choose from a medley of expertly prepared regional and nouvelle cuisine specialties. Featured among renowned chef Vittorio Saccone's light pasta dishes are homemade fettucine with salmon and fresh tomato, and linguine with a lemon-and-bacon sauce. For the main course, a typical Roman-style chicken with pepper vies with top-quality beef and fresh fish delivered daily. The service is impeccable, the waiters multilingual, and the napery and smallest details perfect. Famous in his own right is the convivial maître d' hôtel, Edmondo dell'Orco, who has been here a lifetime.

GIFTS

Handmade Dolls & Folkloric Items

27 PORTA PINCIANA
Via di Porta Pinciana 6
Tel. 47.40.603
Moderate; credit cards accepted

The Porta Pinciana is a great spot to pick up authentic handmade gifts from various Italian provinces at extremely good prices. There are lovely fabric dolls, felt Pinocchios and stuffed animals, and folkloric costumes for both children and adults. Especially appealing gifts are all-wool, hand-knitted crib blankets in soft colors and interesting patterns. From the Abruzzi and Umbria come hand-loomed, green-and-red Christmas tree rugs, as well as woven round and rectangular tablecloths and king-size bedspreads that are true finds for the quality of the handwork. This eclectic shop is run by two gracious and accommodating English-speaking sisters, Rena and Carla Matrona, who love showing their inventory and will ship as well. Their store is on an upper floor of a residential building in what was apparently once a private home.

SUSTENANCE

RISTORANTE/TRATTORIA

28 GIRARROSTO TOSCANO
Via Campania 29
Tel. 49.37.59
Expensive; no credit cards accepted
Closed Wednesday

This well-frequented *trattoria* will be best appreciated if you're not visiting Florence to experience Tuscan cuisine on its home turf. Be ready for hearty, American-sized portions that unabashed locals order until 1:00 A.M. As its name implies, roast meats from a spit are the restaurant's specialty; you can sample top-quality beef and veal and exceptional *bistecca alla fiorentina.* A glance at the Florence food glossary (page 39) will familiarize you with the choice of appetizers and pastas. Although few diners can accommodate the desserts, it is a shame to miss the fresh fruit tarts when in season. There is also an especially good selection of Tuscan wines.

SUSTENANCE

RISTORANTE/TRATTORIA

29 ANDREA
Via Sardegna 26
Tel. 49.37.07
Expensive; credit cards accepted
Closed Sunday

Furnished with a modern elegance that bespeaks its proximity to the Via Veneto, Andrea is a small *trattoria* highly regarded by demanding regulars. Freshness is the prime concern of its owner, who brings home the finest of rustic, simple ingredients (artichokes, truffles, mozzarella cheese, olive oil) as well as the exotic and imported (caviar, salmon). Exceptional dishes here include *tonnarelli al foie gras* (a pasta-liver combination), *tagliolini con gamberi e broccoletti* (pasta with shrimp and broccoli), and *zuppa di carciofi e vongole* (artichoke-and-clam soup). The menu follows the whims of the season, as do the delicious desserts made on the premises. The wine selection is good.

INDEX TO STORES
LISTED BY PRODUCTS

The following index of stores in Rome is arranged by product category so that you can quickly find stores of particular interest to you. In each category, stores are grouped by neighborhood (PS = Piazza di Spagna, C = Via Condotti, PN = Piazza Navona, PP = Popolo/Pantheon, CF = Campo dei Fiori, TB = Trevi & Beyond); the number following this designation is the store's location code on the neighborhood map and also represents the order in which the store is listed. Page numbers are provided for reference to the stores' descriptions in the text. An asterisk (*) means the store is usually open during lunch.

VENICE
Venezia

*T*here it is, the Venice of your dreams—every cliché you ever heard it would be, and yet nothing you could ever have imagined or put into words without experiencing it for yourself. If Venice didn't exist, surely it would have been created by Shakespeare or one of the Romantic poets. Mysteriously beautiful, it can awe, dazzle, confuse, disorient and even overwhelm. But if you relax and approach it with a spirit of discovery and adventure, you will be better able to enjoy the city's intriguing allure.

Venice has always been a showcase accustomed to tourists, be they Crusaders on their way to vanquish the infidels, pilgrims en route to the Holy Land, or contemporary travelers armed with map and comfortable walking shoes who have come to see and shop. Foreigners have always been an important part of the scene—turbaned ambassadors from exotic lands where Venice had holdings; dealers in silks, antique manuscripts, spices, teas, aromatic coffee, gold, precious gems and slaves; small communities of Greek, Dalmatian, Jewish, Slavic and Turkish merchants. Shopping in this treasure box is a centuries-old attraction.

Yet few visitors come to Venice exclusively to shop. Few visitors, in fact, allot Venice much more than the time needed to do the triangular Piazza San Marco/Rialto/Accademia foray. No one expects the profusion of small shops of exotic wares, nor the runway of ultramodern boutiques of famous designers. Since space is at a premium, stores are small, and many divide their merchandise among several locations—sometimes across town from each other, sometimes across the street. Those who have visited the souks and bazaars of points farther east will sense something intangibly similar in the labyrinth of narrow *calli* always crowded with people and shops.

Venice remains a city of dauntless individualism, a city apart. The Orient began in Venice, a city half Eastern and half Western that was independent of both. Nothing about Venice was or is ordinary. It was a pioneer city, a supreme naval power, a mercantile empire distrusted and envied by everyone. Outsiders have always marveled at this city built on an archipelago and supported by a petrified forest of wooden piles beneath the surface of its waters. Today even Italians visit Venice as if it were a wondrous foreign city.

Much of the dazzling booty that came back from the Crusades and the sacking of Constantinople embellished the city and enriched the coffers of Venetian merchants, renowned for their cleverness in commerce. Byzantine traces remain in the city's architecture, haphazard city planning, folklore, cuisine and ambiance. Today's shopper will find similar Oriental themes in the luxuriant fabric patterns, glass designs, antiques, curio objects and jewelry that fill Venice's stores. A sense of faded Eastern beauty has become second nature to the Venetians; they are no longer aware, as are we newcomers with a Western eye, of the lingering Oriental influence in their passion for elaborate pageants, ceremony and fantasy, or in their love for opulent colors, fabrics, carpets and porcelains.

A city whose "streets are filled with water," Venice is exotic, romantic and mysterious.

You'll hear mention of Doges, the Golden Book, "la Repubblica Serena," silk and spice trade routes, Marco Polo, St. Mark's body spirited away from the Moslems, faraway Cathay, and the fearsome Council of Ten. But in its time the glorious "Dominante" had also been reduced to a city of famous courtesans, unbridled Carnivals and wild gambling casinos that drew curious visitors from all over the Continent. If it all seems as surreal as Venice on a foggy night, it is because the history of Venice is startlingly unlike that of any other place.

Founded as a refuge from the marauding Huns and Goths in A.D. 451, the island community banded together in 697 to elect its first Doge, or duke (from *dux,* meaning "leader"). Eleven hundred years later to the day, in 1797, the last of Venice's 120 Doges handed over his power—or what was left of it—to young Napoleon. Between these two events, Venice had reached its zenith as the Serene Republic, queen of a formidable overseas dominion, mistress of trade routes in Persia, India, Turkestan and Arabia. Venice became rich by collecting the precious spices and products of the East and selling them for a tidy profit throughout Europe. Its policy was to be on the side of no one and to have the best navy in Europe.

Pride in their "Stato da Mar" and profit were inextricably linked. The Venetian sea lords were, above all else, expert moneymakers. A 15th-century Pope wrote that they were slaves to the "sordid occupations of trade." He may have been referring to Venice's not-so-religious involvement in the Crusades, which was monitored by an eagle eye for a quick economic return. Venetians were also the first to organize pilgrimages to the Holy Land on an exclusively commercial basis. There was no doubt that their vocation was—and, though softened over time, still is—strictly commerce.

The city today is alive with commerce—handsome modern clothing boutiques, sleekly designed home furnishings, enterprising glass and lace studios, fine shoe stores, mask makers, and inspired artisans and their apprentices. Despite this contact with the present-day world, the city still seems unreal, as if a magnificent and never-ending stage set.

Venice is a city to be savored, explored casually and idly with the "*far niente*" attitude prescribed by Italians. Dawdling and flexibility are *de rigueur.* A slower pace is demanded in this amphibious city whose "streets are filled with water," where the only wheels you'll see are on a tourist's luggage. Many well-intentioned guidebooks suggest that you throw away your map and get lost. We suggest holding onto your map (the city's layout is not beyond human comprehension) and bringing it to the top of the campanile in the Piazza San Marco. From there you will see Venice in all her glory, and gain some understanding of the location of her different neighborhoods.

This is not to say that you must tread only the beaten paths. While a large number of the stores and restaurants listed on the following pages are located around the Piazza San Marco area or the busy Mercerie that runs from San Marco to the Rialto Bridge, many more lie just a block beyond, around a corner, across the next canal, or in more residential neighborhoods. Popular commercial strips such as the Mercerie or Frezzeria are best seen or shopped in while at their emptiest during the early morning hours, and then save your afternoons to wander in less-trafficked areas. Losing yourself in Venice is half the beauty of the experience. Once you disengage yourself from your compatriots, you will understand the joy of finding yourself alone in a Venice that is yours. You can spend days in the neighborhoods of San Polo or Dorsoduro and never hear a word of English.

The city is comparable in size to New York City's Central Park; there is no place in town you cannot reach by foot. Mark Twain's opinion that Venice was a city for cripples and of no use to anyone with legs makes one wonder just how little he saw if he never got out of his gondola. Henry James' comparison of the city to a "magnificent treadmill," though unromantic, is more appropriate. It is an easy and fascinating city for walking, each step of the way offering a surprise, a curious detail or local invention, a hidden shop, a pretty bridge (there are over 400 of them), a narrow street that ends in a dark canal, or a sun-bathed *campo* with a family-run *trattoria* and an outdoor *caffè*. That hidden shop you've stumbled upon most likely offers a precious something that one can find only in Venice, and should not be put on tomorrow's schedule for a return visit, once you've "thought it over"; a word to the wise shopper in Venice is to buy it *now* if you like it, for you may never find that store again. The well-intentioned shopper who arrives in Venice with a list will never enjoy the city. This chapter, designed to eliminate much of the frustration, works best when applied with a Venetian philosophy of going with the tide.

Venetians are used to lost visitors meandering about in their labyrinthine city. Yellow signs scattered across town ceaselessly point you in the direction of San Marco, the Rialto, or the Stazione, and the citizens are kind and accommodating about pointing the way to other sights, although their directions, which usually consist of "*sempre diritto*" (straight ahead) or "*giù il ponte*" (beyond the bridge), may be only marginally helpful.

Venetians are insular in temperament, as are most islanders. Given the span of the Venetian Republic, they have only recently become Italian citizens—comparable, as Goethe said, only to themselves. Venice has always been alone, a minority that developed and encouraged its own manners, dialect and customs. The Venetians still hold firmly to the local way ("*alla veneziana*") as the only right, if not the only, way. They are reserved, courteous, somewhat aloof and rather patronizing toward those unlucky enough to have been born anywhere else. They are enduringly proud descendants of an empire that ran the gamut from splendor to decrepitude, and there is an element of melancholia in both the city and its residents.

A glow of narcissism also colors their character, like that of their city, which marvels at its own reflection in its myriad canals. The Venetians' self-esteem comes from centuries of firm conviction, but minus strut and swagger. Every Venetian is a connoisseur, with a strong predilection for the local product, particularly that which he is trying to sell to you. The merchant of Venice is forever the sharp, hardheaded businessman, though with finesse—making bargaining a herculean challenge for the determined buyer. His prime concern is making the sale, however; he may be more accommodating about accepting various forms of payment or shipping your purchases than is his Milanese or Florentine counterpart.

The Venetians are a handsome and serious people. For all of the fantasy that their city evokes, its men and women today prefer a surprisingly conservative fashion for everyday wear. Attention to fashion is deeply rooted in their history. As early as the 13th century—and again in the 17th and 18th centuries, when Venice slipped from power to decadence and licentious luxury—everyday dress (men's and clerical attire included) got so far out of hand that strict sumptuary laws unsuccessfully tried to govern the lengths of hems, the opulence of fabrics and the quantity of gold, gems, and strands of pearls to be worn in public. It is not surprising that 16th-century Venice, capital of frivolity and sartorial splendor, was also the cradle of lacemaking.

Venice's artistic fashion sense today is tempered by practicality. Women wear comfortable low heels or flats. Warm sweaters and other woolen garments ward off the damp and protect against harsh winter conditions. Men gravitate to a serious British look, but the touch of cashmere or a silk ascot in the evening hint of less somber inclinations. Indeed, for evening and Carnival wear, anything goes—if designed and worn with good taste.

For all its fantasy, Venice has the air of a small town, and subtle dress codes are more carefully observed here than in a more metropolitan city. This small-town atmosphere prevails largely because the city has been

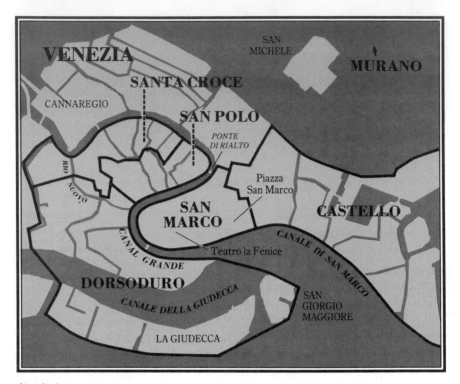

divided into six *sestieri,* or wards, since 1171. The largest and most easily recognizable *sestiere* is San Marco. This is the "downtown" neighborhood, which has the highest concentration of stores and restaurants. Everything south of San Marco, including the island of Giudecca, is Dorsoduro. Castello, to the east of San Marco, is the largest of the *sestieri;* it includes the celebrated Arsenale shipyards, upon which the wealth and might of the Serenissima once depended. We have incorporated Santa Croce, the residential area around the train station, into its neighboring San Polo area. The residential Cannaregio neighborhood, of interest to visitors mainly because it contains Marco Polo's home and the site of Europe's original Jewish ghetto, is treated as an appendage of San Marco.

   Wherever you wander, you're bound to stumble upon products of Venice's new wave of creativity and design. Founded upon centuries of skill and refinement of technique, a sophisticated experimentalism is keeping alive Venice's role as arbiter of culture and the arts. You'll see diversification and clever imagination in textile, glass and fashion design and begin to understand something of the immortality of Venice.

Be sure to consult the Designer Boutique Directory to Venice on page 448 for a complete listing of designer boutique addresses.

Shopping in Venice

STORE HOURS. The Venetians' historic inclination towards trade and commerce results in an unusually long "high season" (March through November), during which store hours are generally 9:00 A.M. to 12:30 P.M. and 4:00 to 7:30 P.M., Monday through Saturday. There are frequent exceptions, however; many stores open or close half an hour earlier than is standard. Winter hours are 9:00 A.M. to 1:00 P.M. and 3:30 to 7:00 P.M., and most stores close on Monday morning. Food stores are generally closed on Wednesday afternoon, although in high season there may be exceptions.

A number of stores, usually those along the well-trodden tourist tracks, stay open during lunchtime and for part of Sunday during the high season. This has been noted where applicable; see also the separate listing (page 429).

Summer is hot and crowded, the only compensation being that, unlike merchants in other Italian cities, the practical Venetians do not close down in August when tourism is highest. September and October here are the nicest months, however; beautiful fall merchandise is just coming into the stores, the weather is pleasant, and a number of annual festivals and cultural events are going on.

In addition to all the national holidays (see page 11), November 21 is a special Venetian holiday, Festa della Salute, which originated as a time of thanksgiving for having been saved from the plague. Most stores close that day, but a handful remain open. Stores usually take their annual break during and after the

Each window, a natural showcase.

Christmas holidays, sometimes for a month or more, but are always open for the Carnival season.

BANK HOURS. Banks in Venice are open Monday through Friday, from 8:30 A.M. to 1:30 P.M.; some reopen from 2:45 to 3:35 P.M. You can draw cash in Italian lire against your Visa card at the Banca d'America e d'Italia at Calle Larga XXII Marzo 2217 (telephone 70.07.66), open only in the mornings.

Cambi (exchange bureaus) follow store hours, and so are open in the afternoons, as well as Saturdays. A convenient *cambio* at the American Express Travel Service, Salizzada San Moisè 1471 (telephone 52.00.844), follows a special nonstop summer schedule: 8:00 A.M. to 8:00 P.M., Monday through Saturday. American Express cardholders can cash their personal checks there from American banks.

GETTING AROUND. If you wanted, you could walk from one end of Venice to the other in an hour. If you are tired or in a hurry, a very efficient water system costs little and runs regularly. You can get a good public transportation map at the train station, from your hotel, or from the Ufficio Informazioni at Piazza San Marco 71/C.

The *vaporetti,* or waterbuses, which service the main canals, are numbered and marked with their points of destination so that you don't go east when you intend to go west. If you're coming from the station, you'll be charged for each large suitcase you bring aboard. Line 5, *il circolare,* is everyone's favorite as an inexpensive sight-seeing orientation; for two and a half hours it travels the magnificent periphery of Venice and passes through the Arsenale shipyards, which were closed to the public for centuries to guard naval secrets.

Water taxis (*taxi acquei*) can be called from anywhere in the city (telephone 52.22.303 or 32.326). Their rates are high but regulated, and if there are more than one of you with luggage or shopping bags, it may be worth your while. Be aware of supplements for nighttime travel, baggage and telephone orders. You may save by going to a water-taxi stand (*stazione motoscafi*), such as those at the train station, Piazzale Roma, Rialto, San Marco, the Lido and the airport.

If you're not going far, but are loaded down with purchases or luggage, you can engage a porter (*portabagaglio*) for a fixed price per one or two pieces between any two points within Venice. (Each additional piece costs extra.) You can call or walk to a dozen porters' stands, including those at the train station (telephone 71.52.72), San Marco (70.05.45), Calle Vallaresso (52.24.904), the Rialto (70.53.08) as well as the Accademia (52.24.891).

The Grand Canal is two and a quarter miles long, yet only three bridges cross it. Reaching those bridges can mean making tiresome detours unless you know about the *traghetti* or gondola ferries, inexpensive public gondolas which make short, direct crossings: Santa Maria del Giglio (in the San Marco neighborhood) to the Salute (on Dorsoduro); San Samuele (near the Palazzo Grassi) to Ca' Rezzonico (Dorsoduro); San Tomà (in San Polo) to Sant' Angelo (San Marco); Palazzo Dona (near San Silvestro) to Palazzo Grimani (San Marco); the Pescheria market (San Polo) to Palazzo Segredo (near Ca' D'Oro, Cannaregio); Ca' Pesaro (Santa Croce) and Palazzo Brandolin (San Polo) to Palazzo Grissoni-Grimani della Vida (Cannaregio); San Marcuola (Cannaregio) to Fondaco dei Turchi (Santa Croce).

ADDRESSES. Even the Venetians get confused. There may appear to be different addresses for the same store: for example, Frezzeria 4463 and San Marco 4463. The former is the specific street address, the latter the official mailing address. The postal number sequence used for San Marco, for instance, begins with No. 1 (the Doge's Palace) and ends with no. 5612 near the Rialto. It follows no logical order, wrapping around corners and making the circuit of *campi,* or squares.

If you ask directions, *campi* are often used as points of reference. Where helpful, we have also included the name of the nearest *campo* in parentheses after an address; small *calli* (streets) do not always appear on maps, but *campi* always do. To add to the general confusion, street names are commonly repeated from one neighborhood to another; if you set off for Calle dell'Olio, for example, be sure that you have the right *sestiere* in mind.

SHOPPING ETIQUETTE. Venetian merchants do not encourage the pleasant banter and bargaining that is a rite of shopping in Italy's southern cities. However, there is the possibility of getting a *sconto,* or discount, if you're going to be spending a substantial amount and paying with cash or traveler's checks, and if it is a slow period or off-season. There is no harm in a genteel attempt; Venetians are ultimately concerned with not losing the customer. For this reason, they are also generally willing to ship and to accept personal checks and even mail orders upon occasion.

SHIPPING. It is easier to find merchants in Venice who will ship your

THE WINGED LION, SYMBOL OF THE CITY

Winged lions adorn columns and clock towers, piazzas, tombs, banners—and the bottom of your coffee cup.

The winged lion is the patron beast of Venice, inseparable from his master St. Mark, Venice's patron saint. The legend goes, in fact, that the winged lion is St. Mark himself; the saint supposedly asked God if he might ascend into heaven to discover the secret of thunder and lightning, a phenomenon that intrigued him greatly. God granted his wish, and then repented that he had divulged a divine secret. He turned St. Mark into a lion, so that he might never talk, yet gave him wings so that he might return to earth, where his roar would sound like thunder itself.

The lion became to Venice what the dragon was to China. He proudly rode the bow of the war galleons and certified all state documents. Some local patrician families had live lions brought in from exotic ports, keeping them as pets in their gardens. Lions graced thrones, crests and thresholds, the way they today grace postcards, T-shirts and key chains. There are 75 lions on the Porta della Carta alone, the main entrance to the Doge's Palace. But the most imperial is the agate-eyed, winged lion on his column in the Piazzetta del Molo. He was part of the booty from the pagan East, perhaps a chimera or other mythological creature who was given wings and an open book tucked neatly under his paw upon arriving in his new position as saint's companion.

purchases than in other cities. If you need a shipping agent, however, Intersped s.r.l. is the city's most reliable. It is located at Calle Ragusei 3478 in the Dorsoduro sector (telephone 52.24.888). Efficient, English-speaking Signor Balarin will insure your package, ship it by air or sea, and even pick it up at the store or at your hotel. Hours are 8:00 A.M. to 12:00 P.M. and 2:00 to 6:00 P.M., Monday through Friday.

Some deluxe hotels offer the courtesy of packing and shipping your purchases, for there are no wrapping services in Venice as in other Italian cities. If your package is small and light, you might buy a padded envelope at a stationery store (*cartoleria*) and send it off yourself from the central post office near the Rialto at Fondaco dei Tedeschi (telephone 89.317). It is open Monday through Friday, 8:00 A.M. to 4:00 P.M. and Saturday, 8:00 A.M. to 1:00 P.M. A smaller post-office branch is located near Piazza San Marco at Calle dell'Ascensione.

INCIDENTALS. *English-language Newspapers.* A small weekly tourist magazine called *Un Ospite a Venezia/ A Guest in Venice* is distributed free by hotels. It gives all pertinent details regarding hours, addresses, current events, and water transportation and rates. The monthly publication *Marco Polo,* sold at newsstands, has articles in Italian, but the information about cultural events is in English as well.

Pharmacies. A 24-hour emergency shift is rotated among Venice's many pharmacies. The weekly *Un Ospite a Venezia/A Guest in Venice* or your hotel concierge will tell you who has the 24-hour duty for the period you're in town. Or, if your Italian is

good enough, call 30.573 for a recording.

Spelling. As if things weren't strange enough, you'll often come upon discrepancies in the spelling of a street (Salizada vs. Salizzada), a *campo* (San Zulian vs. San Gulian), or a neighborhood (Canareggio vs. Cannaregio). You'll initially think one version is a mistake, but the truth is that there are no generally accepted spellings for proper names that are indigenous to Venice. The local dialect, once waning, is being revived, and Venetians are resisting any attempts to impose official Italian spellings. "Calle del Lovo" continues to alternate with "Calle dell'Ovo," and "Marzaria" with "Merceria." It is all part of the colorful Byzantine experience that only Venice can provide.

Telephones. Almost all telephone numbers in the center of Venice now have the new prefix 52. This changeover may not be reflected in all telephone numbers listed in this section. If you get a recording, it will tell you to hang up and redial with the 52 prefix, followed by the old number.

Tourism Information. For tourist information about the city and province of Venice, go to the EPT located in Piazza San Marco 71/C (telephone 52.26.356), at the train station (telephone 71.50.16) or in Piazzale Roma (telephone 52.27.402).

For specific information on cultural events, exhibitions, the annual International Film Festival, the Carnival or the Biennale Art Show go to the Assesorato al Turismo, Ca' Giustinian (Calle del Ridotto 1364), just a minute from Piazza San Marco (telephone 70.99.55).

Venice Mart. An annual crafts exhibition takes place every autumn, usually in September. For approximately two weeks, over 60 Venetian artisans pool their finest work in lace, embroidery, silver, jewelry, wrought iron, masks and other minor arts. Appropriately set in one of the *scuole* (historic seats of guilds or fraterni- ties), the show offers a fascinating look at traditional and contemporary local craftsmanship. For more information, contact the Associazione Artigiani Venezia, 888 Dorsoduro, 30123 Venezia (telephone 52.207.88).

CALLI, CAMPI E CANALI

If you were beginning to familiarize yourself with a map vocabulary from other Italian cities, put it aside for the moment and look at the following terms unique to this city built on water:

ca'   The home of the Doge is a palazzo. A less imposing palace is often called a *ca'*, which is Venetian for *casa*, or house.

calle   Elsewhere called a *via* or *strada*, a *calle* is one of the more than 3000 narrow and meandering little streets in Venice.

campo   A large, open space, often in front of a church, from which it takes its name. The *campo* was a field where horses and cows grazed before it was paved over. *Campielli* are small *campi*.

canale   There are just three: the Canale Grande, or Canalazzo, and the Cannaregio and Giudecca Canals. Everything else is a *rio*.

fondamenta   Refers to the foundations of the houses lining a quay. Usually a wide promenade.

piazza   There is only one piazza, the Piazza San Marco. Two smaller *piazzettas* flank its sides, the Piazzetta dei Leoncini and the Piazzetta del Molo. Everything else is a *campo*.

piscina   A small pond or basin of water filled in.

ramo   A branch of a *calle*, often used interchangeably with *calle* in street addresses.

rio   There are 160 *rii* that empty into the Canale Grande.

rio terrà   A filled-in canal now used as a street.

riva   A waterside promenade.

ruga   From the French word *rue*, this means a street flanked with shops.

salizzada   A paved street, from the word *salizo*, for flint. It was once so rare that the name distinguished it from the majority of dirt-packed streets.

sottoportego   An archway or covered street.

Venetian Specialties

MASKS

With the recent revival of Venice's Carnival (see page 500) came a renewed interest in masks. The most popular and traditional is the dog-faced mask called the *larva,* worn by both men and women, together with a full-length cape, a three-cornered hat and a black lace capelet or veil; this was the *bauta* costume, the Venetian uniform.

Masks were worn whenever anonymity and caprice were desired. There was a time when women could not enter the theater without wearing a mask and every young girl's trousseau contained at least one. The Doges denounced it, the Popes condemned it, but nothing dampened the Venetian penchant for masquerading. Today's artisans re-create the traditional *larva* and the dainty black oval *moreta* masks in papier-mâché (*carta pesca*). The characters from the 16th-century Commedia dell'Arte have also been revived—Pulcinella, Arlecchino (Harlequin), and Pantalone. You'll also find primitive and modern masks that are decorated with plumes and sequins all of which make perfect wall ornaments or Carnival costumes.

Masks have experienced a renewed popularity.

A "taxi stand" for local gondolas.

SHOES

Shoes are among Venice's best buys. Great quantities of them are made in the nearby Brenta valley, in small, specialized shoe factories whose proliferation is due to the Venetians' dependence on their feet to get around; champion urban walkers, they consume more shoes per capita than residents of any other European city. The city's wide selection of shoe boutiques ranges from the traditional and classic to the very elegant and unique. Prices for designer shoes are considerably lower than in the United States and often less expensive here than in other Italian cities. During the last centuries of the Venetian Republic, the city's importance changed from commercial to cultural leadership, and Venetian dress and manners affected the attire of much of Europe. One peculiarity was the extraordinarily elevated platform shoe invented to keep a lady's delicate foot out of the mud of unpaved *calli* and the water of flooded *campi*. The greatest height ever recorded was 20 inches; the teetering wearer had to be supported by two *cicisbei* (menservants).

PAPER

A hint of the Orient is evident in the decorative papergoods of Venice. You'll find objects covered with marbleized paper in Florentine workshops, too, but the Venetians claim that they were the first to "import" the paper from Turkey, probably during the time of the Crusades; hence its name of Turkish origin, *ebrû,* meaning "marble." It is handmade by a time-consuming procedure using natural vegetable and plant dyes dribbled on a bed of water; the swirl effect results from raking or combing these colors before they are absorbed onto a sheet of paper.

Many of the shops selling these decorative papergoods (used to cover books, frames, desk blotters, pencils and countless other gift items) are called *legatorie,* or bookbinders. Unfortunately, many of them no longer bind, although Venice was a printing capital of 15th- to 17th-century Europe, with more working presses than Milan, Florence and Rome put together. Its publishing importance underlined its role as a cultural crossroads having a free circulation of uncensored ideas.

GLASS

Venice—or, more specifically, the island of Murano—recently celebrated its 1000th year of glassmaking, thanks to a 19th-century revival and a post-World War II rebirth of interest that has kept this elegant art alive and flourishing.

Don't be misled by the hordes of silly glass animals that inundate the city today; these cheap, volume-made trinkets are a setback to the integrity

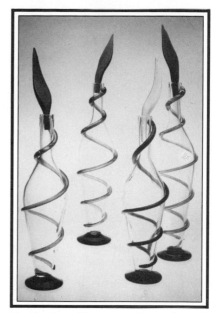

A millennium of fine glassmaking survives today.

of the Murano glassmaking industry. With a patient eye you'll seek out the high-quality glassware still being produced today—meticulous reproductions of elaborate classic designs that once appointed Europe's noble banquet tables, as well as modern interpretations of this ancient art for which Venice once fiercely held a worldwide monopoly. The top names, such as Salviati, Venini and Moretti, have their flagship stores in Venice, although all production continues to come from their furnaces on Murano. A side trip to Murano is pleasant and interesting. The extraordinary glass museum especially is a must for glass enthusiasts and collectors, and some major houses such as Barovier & Toso sell only from their Murano location.

FABRICS AND TEXTILES

Sumptuous textiles have been syn-

High-quality classic reproductions.

onomous with Venice since long before Marco Polo first traveled the silk route to Cathay in the late 13th century. Exotic Oriental fabrics arriving at the city's docks first enriched the wardrobes of its noble families. Then the Chinese art of sericulture was introduced to Italy because of its temperate climate, and Venice's silk production soon rivaled that of the East. Some of the most beautiful finery in the world is still made here—rich damasks, printed velvets, silks, brocades, taffetas, satins and linens, in reproductions of classic patterns as well as fresh modern designs.

LACE

The intricate hand production of fine lace has just recently experienced a revival after practically dying out in the mid-19th century. Although prices are high, they only partially compensate the local women whose hours, days and months of tedious, eye-taxing labor produce exquisite works of art. During the 15th and

16th centuries, Venice produced the finest lace in all of Europe; Spain's Philip II ordered Mary Tudor's bridal trousseau from Burano, and Louis XIV of France ordered a lace collar for his coronation to be made from white hair, for nowhere else was the thread or the workmanship delicate enough. Venetian pattern books circulated throughout noble Europe. Soon Venetian bobbin lace and needlepoint lace came to be widely imitated and took on the generic meaning of a style of lace, not of the place in which it was produced. Venetian supremacy in the field declined with the Republic, and France, whose initial lacework was nothing but a good imitation of the Venetian art, became the leading authority and producer.

A trip to the lace-making island of Burano (see box, page 000) is an easy and interesting excursion.

Age-old crafts surface in contemporary design.

THE GONDOLA

Do not brush it off as too touristy an indulgence. It is the quintessential Venetian experience and a memory so cherished that it cannot be too expensive. Venice was meant to be admired from the water, and the Venice seen from a gondola is a special one whose rippling, distorted reflections are sliced through by your silently gliding vessel.

The gondola, a peculiar though elegant boat, is rowed "in the Venetian manner" (standing in the stern with one foot ahead, using the single oar as a pole) and exists nowhere else in the world; it is the only boat known to be built asymmetrically. Made from seven different kinds of wood, the flat-bottomed gondola is 36 feet long and 5 feet wide (on one side 12 inches off the axis), and weighs 1300 pounds. It is made entirely by hand of 280 separate pieces of wood.

In the 17th century, more than 15,000 gondolas jammed the canals of Venice, each one more pompous and gaudy than the next. Just as restrictive sumptuary laws severely limited pretentious dress, the "Superintendents of Pomp" intervened to decree that all such display must cease and a sober, unembellished black gondola be substituted. Until 1800, there were still some 10,000 gondolas. Today, a mere 350 or so continue to slip through back canals, flirting with corners and imminent collisions that never take place; the industry is limited almost exclusively to tourism and is so close to extinction that the City Council has been taking measures to secure its future.

Today's *gondolieri* are independent operators with a powerful union. Their coveted licenses and skills have been passed down over the centuries from master to apprentice and from father to son. When the four-month tourist season is over, however, they turn to part-time fishing and odd jobs. Their rates are governed by the municipality; a consensus from one or two of them will confirm the current price of a 50-minute ride for a party up to and including five people. (You can also check with the Tourist Office.) If you want to make friends with your gondolier, don't ask him to sing. Candlelit enclaves of gondolas accompanied by a professional singer drift down the Grand Canal on summer evenings; ask any gondolier about the logistics.

For independent rides, you can merely show up at any of the following *stazioni gondole* (gondola stands): Bacino Orseolo, Calle Vallaresso, Hotel Danieli, Ferrovia (San Simon Piccolo), Isola Tronchetto, Piazzale Roma, Santa Maria del Giglio, San Marco, Santa Sofia (Cannaregio), San Tomà, Trinità (Campo San Moisè) and the Rialto. Expect to pay about 30 percent more after 9:00 P.M., when a nighttime supplement is in effect.

Open-Air Markets in Venice

THE RIALTO MARKETS

Although there are a number of outdoor vegetable and fish markets in some of the small *campi,* Venetians refer to the historic Rialto market as if no other existed. To Europeans of the Middle Ages and the Renaissance, the Rialto was not unlike Wall Street, the principal channel of money between East and West and the power center of the Serene Republic. As Shakespeare's Shylock asked, "What's new on the Rialto?" was a question on everyone's tongue.

The old commercial meeting place along the quay, where mighty fleets once deposited their cargo of exotic coffee, spices and dyes, and silks and slaves, is today a lively and popular food market crowded with Venetian housewives and restaurant chefs, singing vendors, and travelers curious to see local color. Not much is left to stimulate your sense of history except the few small cargo boats that unload the day's arrivals.

THE ERBERIA
8:00 A.M. to 1:00 P.M.,
Monday through Saturday.

Offerings at the *erberia* (vegetable market) depend upon the season. Occupying a large open *campo* near the Church of San Giacomino and the adjoining streets, it is no longer limited to greens but sells anything that cannot be bought at the nearby fish market: magnificent wheels of parmigiano and gourds of provolone cheeses, wines from the Venetian hinterlands, rigid hares and plucked chickens. The market vendors are a cheerful lot, prone to badinage, dramatic price haggling and an occasional aria. Their stalls are loaded with succulent peaches, garlands of onions and garlic, fennel, red Treviso lettuce, mountains of artichokes, Sicilian blood oranges and deep red strawberries.

THE PESCHERIA
8:00 A.M. to 1:00 P.M.,
Tuesday through Saturday.

The incomparable fish market, *pescheria,* is the true spectacle. The Venetians insist it's the best and freshest in Europe, and you'll see sea creatures you never knew existed—all caught in Adriatic waters. There are *gamberi, gamberoni* and *gamberetti* (varieties of shrimp, prawns and lobster), soft-shelled crabs, wriggling live eels, and octopus still ejecting their ink. Squid and cuttlefish stretch their tangle of tentacles, sea turtles flat on their backs wave their flippers, and sea bass, red mullet, John Dory fish, and sea bream, lying on biers of damp green fronds, stare at you with beady eyes.

From the pescheria's *sampling of aquatic life.*

Venetian Cuisine

Venice is not generally thought of as one of the great food cities of the world. Yet in few other places will you find such a wide variety of fresh, light, simply prepared fish and shell-fish. Why eat meat, Venetians will ask you, when you can eat this morning's catch from these sparkling Adriatic waters? Moreover, seafood here is usually eaten in idyllic settings on an open terrace or along a moonlit canal.

Rice is a staple of Venice's simple though sophisticated cuisine; the *risotto* cooked with seafood is a delicious and commonplace alternative to pasta as a first course. Pasta is not as important as in most other regions, although here it is especially good when mixed with fish or shellfish such as clams (*vongole*), mussels (*cozze* or *peoci*), or cuttlefish (*seppie*) cooked in their own purplish-black ink. The *zuppa di pesce,* the Venetian bouillabaisse, is a specialty that, although listed as a first course, is filling enough to be a main dish.

While fish is abundant, it is not cheap, so keep an eye on menu prices. And don't expect fresh fish in the restaurants on Sunday and Monday when the *pescheria,* Venice's imcomparable fish market, is closed. Among meats, veal is popular, but calves' liver served with onions (*fegato alla veneziana*) is the local specialty. Polenta (cornmeal) is often served like potatoes—roasted, grilled or fried.

Most of the Veneto's wines come from the area around Verona or from Conegliano-Valdobbiadene, where Nino Franco and Pino Zardetto produce good dry to semi-sweet spar-

kling wines (Prosecco and Cartizze). The dry, straw-colored Soave of Anselmi and Pieropan and the deep ruby-red Amarone of Masi and Quintarelli are among the best in the Veneto. Nearby Friuli produces some of Italy's finest white wines, such as Tocai, Pinot Bianco and Pinot Grigio, as well as rich reds like Merlot, Cabernet and Refosco. Abbazia di Rosazzo, Livio Felluga, Ronco di Cialla, Borgo Conventi and Jermann are among the top wineries in the area.

If you've just arrived from Rome or Florence, you will invariably sense that something is missing: the *gelateria.* The Venetian sweet tooth is satisfied instead by a proliferation of *pasticcerie* (pastry shops). Influenced by its former Austrian domination and by the old Jewish ghetto in Cannaregio, they serve strudels and *sachertortes,* fruit-studded sweets and macaroon-like cookies in myriad variations. Another typically Venetian institution is the popular *enoteca,* or wine bar, and its *cicchetti* (snacks). Venetians stop by for their *ombra* (literally "shadow," here meaning glass of red wine) at any hour of the day and nibble a toothpick-speared *cicchetto* or two while discussing what's new on the Rialto. It's a refreshing tradition, which visitors can adapt for a light and casual lunch.

Venice turns in early, as you will probably want to do after having invariably walked so much. Restaurants, especially those not catering to tourists, often take their last orders as early as 9:30 or 10:00 P.M.. Those that stay open until midnight are given a special "Late-Night" notation.

VENETIAN CUISINE GLOSSARY

Antipasto (Appetizer)

Insalata di mare–Shrimp, squid and/or mollusks in an oil-and-vinegar marinade.

Antipasto misto di mare–A selection of seafood appetizers.

Primo Piatto (First Course)

Risi e bisi–A springtime soupy risotto with fresh baby peas.

Risotto con cozze (or *peoci*)–A rice dish made with mussels.

Risotto in nero–Rice and cuttlefish cooked with its own black ink.

Bigoli in salsa–Homemade spaghetti made with whole-wheat flour and seasoned with anchovies or a duck ragout.

Pasta e fagioli–A popular vegetable soup with pasta and beans.

Spaghetti alle vongole–Spaghetti with clam sauce.

Zuppa di pesce–Also called *broeto* or *brodetto.* Venetian bouillabaisse or fish stew.

Secondo Piatto (Entrée)
Pesce (Fish):

Grigliata mista di pesce–A grilled assortment of the seasonal catch: shrimp, scampi, octopus, soft-shelled crabs, scallops and sardines.

Sanpiero or San Pietro–John Dory fish.

Bisato, anguilla alla veneziana– Eel cooked with onion, vinegar, garlic and bay leaves.

Coda di rospo–Angler or monkfish, which has a white, flaky flesh.

Branzino–Sea bass.

Calamaretti–Small baby squid.

Granseola–The local Adriatic spider crab, served boiled and dressed with oil or lemon and considered finer than lobster.

Baccalà mantecato alla veneziana–Salt codfish, puréed with olive oil, garlic and parsley.

Cape sante–Scallops.

Fritto misto–Assorted deep-fried fish.

Sarde in saor–Fresh sardines marinated in onion, vinegar, raisins and pine nuts, and sautéed.

Moleche–Soft-shelled crab sprinkled with flour and fried.

Carne (Meat):

Fegato alla veneziana–Calves' liver sautéed with onions.

Torresani–Tiny pigeons served roasted or grilled on a spit.

Contorno (Vegetable)

Polenta–Cornmeal, boiled and then either baked, sautéed, deep-fried or grilled, or served plain like mashed potatoes.

Formaggio (Cheese)

Asiago–A rather dry, sharp cheese from the Venetian mainland.

Dolce (Dessert)

Zaleti–Small, oval raisin cornmeal cookies.

Baicoli–Thin, slightly sweet biscuits, dry and crumbly.

Tiramisu–Rich dessert of layered espresso-soaked ladyfinger cake in a *mascarpone*/triple cream.

San Marco

San Marco is the commercial and tourist center of Venice, beyond which the majority of visiting day-trippers never venture. There is, in fact, enough here to amaze and amuse even the most seasoned traveler. All the world comes to visit Venice, or so it would seem in the elegant Piazza San Marco, the "drawing room of Europe," where crowds of tourists now vie with the pigeons for control. Looming above them all you'll see the Basilica of San Marco, an Eastern beauty that is one of the most mysterious and magical of churches. If there weren't so many surprises beyond this piazza to enthrall you, it would almost be enough to visit the basilica's magnificent mosaics and the adjacent quarters of the Republic's legendary Doges—and call it a day.

San Marco is not just the piazza but an entire *sestiere*, or neighborhood, that can change drastically just a *calle*, bridge and *rio* away from its central square. Everyone invariably winds up on the Mercerie (literally Haberdashers' Street), the busy main shopping street that connects the Piazza San Marco with the Rialto Bridge. The Mercerie originates under the Torre dell'Orologio (Clock Tower), where two bronze Moors strike the hour. This street together with Calle Larga San Marco, which branches off from it just north of the Clock Tower, offers hundreds of shops that range

Everything revolves around San Marco, the heart—and most congested neighborhood—of Venice.

Basilica of San Marco, an Eastern gem and one of the world's most magical churches.

from the ultra-refined to those better avoided. If you leave the Piazza San Marco from the west instead, you'll find yourself on the Calle dell'Ascensione and then the Salizzada San Moisè and the Calle Larga XXII Marzo. An extensive range of designer boutiques and modern stores makes this an enjoyable runway for browsing on your way to the Accademia museum.

San Marco's *campi* add a quality all their own to this *sestiere*. In Campo San Fantin is the world-renowned Teatro La Fenice, said to have the most handsome interior of any opera house in the world. Its artistic flavor spills over into the surrounding shops, restaurants and wine bars. The Palazzo Grassi, recently purchased by Fiat's Agnelli Foundation and renovated by Italy's acclaimed architect Gae Aulenti, has drawn new attention to the nearby Salizzada San Samuele and Campo Santo Stefano. The palazzo, open until 10:00 P.M., is the perfect setting for major artistic exhibitions and has encouraged a burgeoning of artisanal activity in the area. Another hub of independent artisans can be found in the charming Campo San Maurizio.

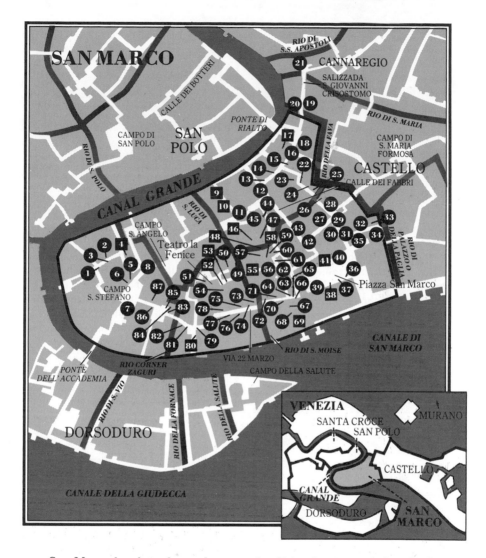

San Marco has long been the seat of politics, business and trade. It is a wealthy quarter of elegant palazzi, deluxe hotels, and famous bars and restaurants. Prices are higher than elsewhere, but nowhere else is there such a concentration of diverse shops and boutiques. San Marco also offers you hidden corners and untrafficked alleyways where you can still glimpse a Venice that has remained unchanged over the centuries.

Since the neighboring *sestiere* of Cannaregio is predominantly a non-tourist area, those few entries worth the jaunt have been included in this section.

GIFTS
Wood Trompe-l'Oeil Objects

1 LIVIO DE MARCHI
Salizzada San Samuele 3157/A
Tel. 52.85.694
Expensive; credit cards accepted

What Livio de Marchi does with wood is a highly unusual form of *trompe l'oeil*. He sculpts everyday objects out of light-colored wood, with such accuracy that you'd swear these life-size replicas were the real thing. You can almost feel the worn-out leather of his beat-up cowboy boot, the soft drapery of his cloth-covered table, the bruise spots on his bunch of bananas and the wind-swept mane of his lean, rearing horse. The objects are amusing conversation pieces. If you visit Signor de Marchi's shop, you can watch him intently at work in the sawdust-covered backroom.

GALLERY
COLLECTIBLES
Unusual Finds

2 ROBERTO PEDRINA
Salizzada San Samuele 3357
Tel. 52.29.656
Expensive; credit cards accepted
Closed mornings during summer

After scoring a resounding success with his first shop, L'Ixa (see facing page), young Roberto Pedrina has opened this new gallery that showcases his taste for unusual objects, art and furniture. The only common denominator of this sophisticated collection is that every piece has been handpicked by Roberto. He continually scours Paris and Rome for 20th-century finds, and also commissions

At Roberto Pedrina's, a cache of objets d'art.

work from local artisans and artists. For example, Venetian Principessa Esmeralda (daughter of Count Volpi di Misurata, the celebrated founder of the Biennale Art Show, the International Film Festival and the Ciga Hotel chain), has created some three-dimensional tabletop paper sculptures on sale here. Roberto's partner in L'Ixa, architect Alessandro Alessandra, designs the "marble" *trompe l'oeil* paintings on wood and has them crafted by an expert woodcutter whose *bottega* is next door. For the gallery's only sign, look to the pavement, where you'll see Roberto Pedrina's name written in gold.

GIFTS
STATIONERY & ACCESSORIES
Marbleized Papers

3 ALBERTO VALESE 🏠🏠🏠🏠
Salizzada San Samuele 3135
Tel. 70.09.21
Moderate; credit cards accepted

This young Venetian craftsman makes some of the loveliest, inventive marbleized paper and gift items around. He operates two shops, and here at his San Samuele location you can watch him re-create the ancient method of decorative printing in the

Marbleized-paper items from Alberto Valese.

Turkish style of *ebrû*, or marbleizing. Painstaking precision is evident in each of his paper-covered gifts—books, boxes, desk sets, diaries and frames. Alberto also prints on fabric, producing exquisite silk crepe-de-Chine scarves, stoles and pillows. Always experimenting and developing his self-taught artistry, he even applies his marbleizing process to wooden candlesticks, to pedestal-like Corinthian *capitelli*, or column capitals made of plaster, and to copies of Roman statue fragments (life-size feet, fists and busts)—all great postmodern accessories for your home or office.

   Alberto, who is very accommodating, will fabricate an article in a special blend of colors upon request. His second shop, also in the San Marco neighborhood, goes by the name Ebrû (see page 463).

SUSTENANCE

RISTORANTE/TRATTORIA

4 AL BACARETO
Calle Crosera 3447 (corner of Salizzada
   San Samuele)
Tel. 89.336
Moderate; credit cards accepted

This rustic neighborhood *trattoria* is a home away from home for many of the artisans and residents of the Sa-

lizzada San Samuele area. Try to get one of the few tables outside, and order from the Venetian specialties on your menu. Inside, the atmosphere is welcoming, with a wooden-beamed ceiling, fresh flowers and a host of regular patrons. All the traditional dishes of the Laguna are here, from *bigoli in salsa* (whole-wheat spaghetti with anchovy and onion sauce) to *fegato alla veneziana* (sautéed liver with onions).

SUSTENANCE

BAR-CAFFÈ/GELATERIA

5 PAOLIN
Campo Santo Stefano 2962/A
Tel. 25.576
Inexpensive; no credit cards accepted
Closed Friday

Here's the best ice cream in Venice. An unpretentious neighborhood bar, Paolin's is Venice's oldest and best-loved *gelateria*. There are only 12 flavors, including a very nutty-tasting pistachio and the coffee-est of coffee. The quality is creamy, the variety of sundaes interesting and the people-watching great at the outdoor tables in the expansive Campo Santo Stefano. In the summertime, you can stroll by for a late-night *gelato* till midnight; the rest of the year, Paolin closes at 9:00 P.M.

COLLECTIBLES

GLASS

One-of-a-Kind Signed Collectors' Pieces

6 L'IXA
Campo Santo Stefano 2958/A
Tel. 29.656
Expensive; credit cards accepted
Closed summer mornings

Serenely nestled between the Hotel San Stefano and Paolin's Caffè, this tiny shop has a rarefied collection of carefully selected objects of enduring design. Its collection is always changing, but you'll find anything from elaborate mirrors to hand-painted porcelain plates, pieces from prior Biennales (from 1890 to 1960), decorative urns, bronze-cast statues and lamps. If you're an art-deco enthusiast, this store has great one-of-a-kind signed pieces of Murano glass from the 1920s and 30s and a number of other exquisite deco objects. An international clientele follows the consistent design sensibility of owner Roberto Pedrina, who keeps his mind on investment value. See also his second shop, Roberto Pedrina, (page 444).

FASHION
WOMEN'S

Fantasy Looks

7 FIORELLA
Campo Santo Stefano 2806
Tel. 53.10.636
Expensive; credit cards accepted

Fiorella's dresses are so close to fantasy that one might mistake them for Carnival costumes—which wouldn't disappoint Fiorella Mancini at all. Using Bevilacqua's precious brocades and Fortuny-like hand-stamped velvets (see page 476), Fiorella creates exotic clothes with slits and transparent laces that can let a woman play hide-and-seek with reality. Although prices are considerably lower than they would be in deluxe specialty stores outside Italy, you might prefer to buy one of her tamer, and less expensive, numbers. Fiorella is a prominent figure in the yearly Vene-

tian Carnival, and it wouldn't be quite the same without the fantastic balls, organized "happenings" and outlandish masks for which she is famous. Made with feathers, sequins, lace and a lot of imagination, the masks are also available at her boutique. With typical humor, she has recently added kitsch souvenirs such as plexiglass gondolas, in a parody of Venice's ubiquitous cheap trinkets.

GIFTS
CERAMICS

Huge Assortment of Regional Styles

8 RIGATTIERI
Calle dei Frati 3532
Tel. 31.081
Moderate; credit cards accepted
Open during lunch and Sunday

Three stores make up Rigattieri, each chockablock with colorful ceramics. Inside there's a beautiful assortment of huge white serving platters that are handmade and reasonably priced

A colorful ceramic assortment from Rigattieri.

as well as an array of hand-painted plates, vases, bowls, and fruit- and vegetable-shaped tureens that hail chiefly from the Bassano del Grappa area in the Veneto region. If you've admired the lovely Garofano Colori ceramics from Imola at Tiffany's in New York or at the Christian Dior boutique in Paris, you'll find an enormous selection here at much lower prices. You can reorder by mail if you break a piece or wish to expand your place settings. There's also some porcelain, pewter, brass and silver.

SUSTENANCE

ENOTECA (WINE BAR)

9 AL VOLTO

Calle Cavalli 4081
Tel. 28.945
Inexpensive to moderate; no credit cards
   accepted
Closed Sunday

Join the Venetians in their habit of sipping an *ombra* at the finest *enoteca* in the area. It's the best place in town to educate your palate, with over 2000 different types of wine from all over the world and 70 foreign beers. Known to the Venetians as "the prince of sommeliers," owner Giancarlo Carbon is a modest, affable man who will discuss wine with anyone who shows a spark of interest, and will proudly display his 1790 bottle of port, the oldest in Italy. In addition to rare and costly wines, he offers the best from current and more affordable vintages. Al Volto is a delightful place for a snack: there are Hungarian meatballs, homemade liver pâté, cheese, small pizzas and *tramezzini* sandwiches. The bar follows the same basic schedule as Venice's stores, although it stays open until 9:00 P.M.

SUSTENANCE

ENOTECA (WINE BAR)

10 LEON BIANCO

Salizzada San Luca 4153
Tel. 52.21.180
Inexpensive; no credit cards accepted
Closed Sunday

In the busy, crowded Campo San Luca is Venice's best *tramezzini* sandwich bar. Choose from dozens of combination fillings like *prosciutto e funghi* (ham and mushrooms), *gamberetti e uovo* (shrimp and egg) and *tonno e uovo* (tuna and egg) or from heartier made-to-order sandwiches on French bread: roast beef, roast pork, chicken, and mozzarella with tomatoes. Armed with a toothpick, you can help yourself to *cicchetti* (hors d'oeuvres) of potato, rice or cheese croquettes or of grilled *calamari* that can become a light meal.

BOOKS

ART

International Selection

11 FANTONI LIBRI ARTE

Salizzada San Luca 4119
Tel. 52.20.700
Moderate; credit cards accepted

Fantoni's has the best selection in Venice of big illustrated art books and works on architecture, design, ceramics, textiles and jewelry. Titles from Italian, English, American, French and Japanese publishers are included, with an accent on the most recent output of Italy's Electa, highly respected in the field. Fantoni also publishes books, and features a particularly beautiful volume (sold in a limited, numbered edition) of reproductions of Venetian views as depicted by the 18th-century Venetian masters Canaletto, Visentini and Brustolon.

LEATHERGOODS

BAGS

Top Names

12 BUSSOLA 🛍🛍🛍🛍
Calle dei Fabbri 4608
Tel. 29.846
Expensive; credit cards accepted
Open during lunch

This is one-stop shopping, just across from the famous Goldoni Theater, for the woman determined to find the perfect handbag without much ado. The store's large and prestigious selection of handbags includes the most famous names in leathergoods: Valentino, Missoni, Versace, Giorgio Armani, Nazareno Gabrielli, Enrico Coveri and Krizia, not to mention Céline and other fine French lines. Every size, shape and color is here in myriad renditions.

DESIGNER BOUTIQUE DIRECTORY

The following designer boutiques in Venice are listed in alphabetical order by last name. They are all located in the San Marco neighborhood. All take credit cards and follow store hours.

Laura Biagiotti (Women's)
Calle del Teatro 4600/A
Tel. 52.23.709

Enrico Coveri (Men's & Women's)
Frezzeria 1135/A

Fendi (Women's)
Salizzada San Moisè 1474
Tel. 70.57.33

Gianfranco Ferrè (Men's & Women's)
Calle Larga San Marco 287
Tel. 52.25.147

Gucci (Leathergoods)
Merceria dell'Orologio 258
Tel. 29.119

Krizia (Women's)
Calle delle Ostreghe 2359
Tel. 52.32.162

Missoni (Men's & Women's)
Calle Vallaresso 1312/B
Tel. 70.57.33

Trussardi (Men's & Women's)
Via Spadaria 695
Tel. 52.85.757

Valentino (Women's)
Salizzada San Moisè 1473
Tel. 70.57.33

Mario Valentino (Men's & Women's)
Calle dell'Ascensione 1255
Tel. 52.31.333

Gianni Versace (Women's)
Frezzeria 1722
Tel. 52.36.369

FIORELLA

Born by mistake in Ferrara, Fiorella Mancini is perhaps more Venetian at heart than most of those born and raised in Venice. She is loved by many, disliked by some, and known by everyone. Fiorella is a noted fashion designer whose creations are sold in Cortina and New York as well as in her Venice boutique. But it is her role as "performer" that has made her Venice's most controversial personality. She combines respect for the past with desire to shock an apathetic public. Since Carnival was revived in 1980, Fiorella has become its unofficial Queen, promoting cultural events and hosting elaborate masked balls featuring her own highly original masks.

Fiorella blends the traditional and the shocking.

Fiorella also stages frequent "happenings" to dramatize contemporary problems. She once created a realistic 30-foot rat that traveled Venice's canals on a barge littered with refuse—a powerful statement on unsanitary conditions in the city.

For a recent Carnival, Fiorella organized the world's top 25 fashion designers, dubbed the "Doges of Fashion," to create something inspired by the magic of the occasion. The startling results, which included a black bridal dress by Versace, were exhibited on wooden statues of 25 important Doges with female bodies.

Fiorella's blend of the traditional and the shocking is evident in her own fashion design. It is an unpredictable collection of whatever fires her fancy at the moment—18th-century theatrical costumes or renovated outfits from the 1920s, embellished with antique Venetian fabrics, brocades and damasks from Bevilacqua, lace, sequins and imagination. Her creations make every day Carnival for the woman who thrives on drama. Her clothing is produced exclusively for her, as are her striking masks, which are made in numbered limited editions. Behind them all is her artisanal spirit: she experiments with vegetable dyes and hand-printing of fabrics, not unlike the celebrated Fortuny from whom she takes much of her inspiration.

Venetians look forward to Fiorella's next spectacular statements. She has focused attention on the city's physical and cultural decadence, while loving the limelight her activities have brought her.

FASHION

MEN'S & WOMEN'S

Contemporary & Trendy Sportswear

13 ARBOR BOUTIQUES

Calle dell'Ovo 4759
Tel. 27.697
Expensive; credit cards accepted
Open during lunch and Sunday

Arbor is Venice's only retailer selling the upbeat collection of Byblos for both men and women. For women there are also selections from Max Mara and Florence-based Enrico Coveri. Men will find an even more extensive range of apparel from Basile and Henry Cottons and a wonderful assortment of high-fashion ties. Arbor is a particularly good source for contemporary Italian knitwear. The clientele is very young and geared to up-to-the-minute styles.

A second Arbor is located on the Lido at Gran Viale 10 (telephone 76.10.32).

FASHION

WOMEN'S

One-of-a-Kind Hats

14 MARZATO

Calle dell'Ovo 4813
Tel. 26.454
Moderate; no credit cards accepted

If you are looking for an authentic and truly traditional Carnival hat, you must buy it here. For many generations, Marzato has produced beautiful hats, and its traditional *tricorno*, or three-cornered model, made of the finest woolen felt is a basic ingredient in the centuries-old *bauta*, or Carnival costume. The *tricorno* hat comes

Serious Carnival millinery at Marzato.

in a variety of colors, and is worn at Carnival time by both men and women with a long veil of lace and a lace-trimmed *larva* mask. You'll find cheaper versions of the tricornered hat elsewhere, but if you're like the Venetians, you'll consider your Carnival attire serious fashion and go for the best. The other eleven months of the year Marzato returns to its role as a millinery institution offering high-quality and exclusive finds. A creative mother-daughter team dreams up every kind of hat imaginable, as well as combs with sweeping feathers and jewels to decorate your hair.

LEATHERGOODS
BAGS & ACCESSORIES
Big Selection

15 MARFORIO
Merceria Due Aprile 5033
Tel. 25.734
Moderate; credit cards accepted
Open during lunch

Look for the antique glass lighting fixtures in the form of colorful umbrellas at the entrance of this mini-department store for leather accessories. This old, family-run store stocks three floors with well-made and well-priced handbags in every color for every taste in all quality leathers. Bags are practical and classic in style with occasional traces of updated design. If you're set on a bag of a particular color, be specific and you'll be shown to the appropriate room, as all merchandise is grouped according to color. There's also a large assortment of luggage, small leather goods, briefcases, and the umbrellas foretold by those entrance fixtures.

FASHION
MEN'S & WOMEN'S
Design Collections

16 VOLPE
Campo San Bartolomeo 5257
Tel. 52.22.524
Expensive; credit cards accepted
Open during lunch and Sunday

On a little square near the Rialto Bridge is the largest of the elegant Volpe boutiques—this one catering to men's and women's high fashion. A second Volpe location at Frezzeria 1286 carries a slightly more classic selection of men's fashion only. A convenient third location in the San Polo neighborhood (see page 501) offers men's casual sportswear in a contemporary vein.

At any of the three Volpe boutiques, you'll find a good assortment of renowned designer labels such as Giorgio Armani, Valentino, Genny, Enrico Coveri and Gianmarco Venturi.

SUSTENANCE
RISTORANTE/TRATTORIA

17 AL GRASPO DE UA
Calle dei Bombaseri 5094
Tel. 52.23.647
Expensive; credit cards accepted
Closed Monday and Tuesday

You'll be torn between trying to decipher the Venetian sayings on the overhead beams and ogling the fresh seafood appetizers on the groaning table from which you can choose your order. The ambiance and the proximity to the Rialto make this *trattoria* look touristy, but the food is very good, as any discerning Venetian will tell you. With some exceptions, the cuisine is Venetian. Try the light *gnocchetti sardi al gorgonzola* (in a pungent cheese sauce), the *vermicelli con datteri di mare* (with sea mussels), or the delicate linguine with squid in ink. For your main course, choose from fresh fish fried or grilled, delicious lobster fritters or *branzino al cartoccio,*—sea bass baked and served in oiled parchment paper. All desserts and pastries are homemade. A colorful 100-year tradition makes the venerable Graspo de Ua (Bunch of Grapes) part of Venice's culinary "who's who."

Little has changed since Marco Polo's time.

BOOKS

Venetian Themes

18 FILIPPI EDITORE VENEZIA
Calle della Bissa 5458
Tel. 52.36.916
Moderate; no credit cards accepted

An enthusiast of all things Venetian, Franco Filippi is the third-generation publisher of a series of books on topics related to the Serenissima. Most books are in Italian, but many are illustrated and show secret, hidden angles of Venice and its history. The limited edition of Zompini's *Le Arti che Vanno per Via nella Città* is a beautiful collection of engravings depicting everyday life in the streets (and canals) of 18th-century Venice. There are books on the city for children, an elaborately detailed four-foot-long poster of Venice, and art-quality black-and-white photographic postcards and prints, at very reasonable prices. Franco Filippi speaks only Italian, but if you are serious about studying anything Venetian, his shop is the perfect point of departure.

A second location nearby at Calle del Paradiso 5762 is run by his father, Luciano Filippi, who specializes in rare antique volumes.

FASHION
MEN'S, WOMEN'S & CHILDREN'S
Department Store

19 COIN
Salizzada San Giovanni Crisostomo 5788
(Cannaregio)
Tel. 52.27.192
Moderate; credit cards accepted

Recently remodeled by the prestigious Piero Pinto architectural firm, this handsome 15th-century building is the home base for the Venetian department-store chain. A welcome change from the city's plethora of small boutiques, Coin offers four floors of enjoyable browsing and easy shopping. You'll find clothing for a total look from head to toe, as well as an extensive perfume and cosmetics section. The Coin private label promotes young, stylish fashion that can be both classic and up to the minute. The shop also carries a limited number of other designers. The largest of Italy's 30 Coin locations is in Milan. For further information, see Milan listing (page 188).

GIFTS
ARTISANAL COLLECTION

20 ROSE DOUCE
Salizzada San Giovanni Crisostomo
5782 (Cannaregio)
Tel. 27.232
Moderate to expensive; credit cards
accepted
Open during lunch and Sunday

Amid all the stores selling garish souvenirs and Murano trinkets, this tasteful gift shop prompts a sigh of relief. Due to the fragility of most pieces, you are welcome to browse but not to touch the many beautiful items displayed on the shelves: Carlo Moretti's artistic glassware; exquisite collector's masks with primitive expressions, crafted in leather and sometimes trimmed in fur; beautiful glass paperweights and ashtrays made of gray, granite-like ceramic. A line of Tuscan ceramics has been designed by and exclusively produced for Rose Douce: tiny three-dimensional strawberries cover everything from demitasse cups to oil and vinegar sets. There is a contemporary feeling to these Italian products, although not the sleek high design of tomorrow.

FASHION
CHILDREN'S
Designer Collection

21 LES ENFANTS
Calle Dolfin 5674 (near Campiello
   R. Selvatico) (Cannaregio)
Tel. 38.272
Expensive; credit cards accepted

This children's boutique is irresistible for grandmas and mothers with a fashion bent. Les Enfants is the best high fashion boutique for *bambini* in Venice, as you will surmise from its windows' array of outfits. Let Valentino or Enrico Coveri dress your precious child for only a little less than what you might pay for your own wardrobe. Adorable accessories and shoes are available to complete the look. The shop is just past the Coin department store, and somewhat off the beaten tourist trail.

Touches of Byzantium color the city.

SHOES
MEN'S & WOMEN'S
Trendy Casual to High-Fashion Elegance

22 RENÉ
Merceria San Salvador 4983
Tel. 29.766
Moderate to expensive; credit cards
   accepted

Hollywood actresses and international socialites order René's standout evening shoes sight unseen. High-heeled, gem-studded, elegant and inventive, each of Venetian René Caovilla's master-crafted shoes is produced in a numbered, limited quantity, as if a collectible work of art. His distinctive footwear has accessorized the elegant runway collections of Valentino, Ungaro and Yves Saint Laurent. In his boutique you will also find high-quality casual shoes and boots from other local shoe manufacturers for both men and women. Mixed skins of reptile and stamped suedes, for example, are expertly crafted in the small factories in nearby Brenta.

JEWELRY

Primitive

23 PAOLO SCARPA
Merceria San Salvador 4850
Tel. 86.881
Expensive; credit cards accepted
Closed from November through February

The most unusual and extensive collection of glass beads ("Venetian pearls") is but one of many star attractions here. This small gallery resembles a pirate's cache of exotic primitive jewelry collected from all over the world by the peripatetic owner. African and American Indian beads are strung together and combined with Tibetan turquoise or mother of pearl from the Phillipines. Big silver and ivory bracelets and unusual earrings are among the other beautiful pieces. The store is closed from November through February while the owner is off scouring the world in quest of new acquisitions.

FASHION

MEN'S & WOMEN'S

Designer Collections

24 AL DUCA D'AOSTA
Merceria San Salvador
  4922 (women's; Tel. 70.40.79)
  4946 (men's; Tel. 52.20.733)
Expensive; credit cards accepted
Open during lunch

Al Duca d'Aosta is the Veneto's finest haberdashery. The men's shop is just across the Merceria from the women's store, and both nurture a passion for the latest high-quality Italian fashion. The men's shop has an equally good representation of England's best menswear. You'll find Burberry suits there (Duca d'Aosta has the exclusive right to sell Burberry coats in Venice), together with clothing and accessories from Pellegrini, Ferrè, les Copains, Church and Longhi. Women can achieve that distinctive Duca d'Aosta style by mixing labels from Pellegrini, Ferrè, Moschino, Soprani, Prada, Ferragamo and Timmi. Both men and women can effortlessly put together an entire wardrobe, while leisurely shopping in spacious settings that hold a range of fine apparel: daytime sportswear, coats and rainwear, dresses, suits and eveningwear—each displayed in its own area. The smartly coordinated windows will give you but a glimpse of the many offerings inside. Service is professional, and the staff very helpful.

LEATHERGOODS

BAGS & ACCESSORIES

High-Fashion Styles

25 GRANO
Merceria San Salvador 4928
Tel. 22.272
Moderate; credit cards accepted
Open during lunch

This relatively new shop has a wonderful assortment of well-made leather handbags, briefcases, wallets and portfolios. Grano stands behind the excellent detailing and good value of its merchandise, all of which carries the store's own label. Bags run the gamut from soft and pouchy to constructed and classic. There is a wide range of high-fashion colors as well as natural leather hues, and if you're looking for accessories in exotic skins such as crocodile or ostrich, this is a good source.

LEATHERGOODS

SHOES, CLOTHING & ACCESSORIES

Top-Name

26 LA BAUTA

Merceria San Zulian 729
Tel. 52.23.838
Expensive; credit cards accepted
Open during lunch and Sunday

Most Venetians will unhesitatingly tell you that La Bauta is the best shop in Venice for leathergoods. Wood-paneled walls and rich leather seats are conducive to spending some time—and money—browsing through the handsome leather sportswear for men and women. There's a heavy emphasis on shoes, and the finest Italian lines are carried—Ferragamo, Prada, Diego della Valle and Guido Pasquali. A nice selection of bags by Granello and Pitti are on hand. Leather lovers with generous budgets will have a field day here.

FASHION

JUNIORS'

27 BENETTON

Merceria San Zulian 712
Tel. 70.55.96
Moderate; credit cards accepted
Open during lunch

Benettons seem to be a dime a dozen in this tourist-trafficked area, but this is one of the best-stocked and most spacious.

See Benetton (page 179).

You can also check out their competition a few shops further on at Stefanel (San Zulian 702-3), another chain of moderately priced jeans and colorful knitwear.

Wooden puzzles, like paintings, at Signor Blum.

GIFTS

HAND-PAINTED WOOD PUZZLES

Unusual Venetian Souvenirs

28 SIGNOR BLUM

Campiello San Zulian 602/A
Tel. 71.04.36
Moderate; credit cards accepted
Open during lunch

Named after a children's book character, Signor Blum is the delightful creation of a group of young local artisans (see Dorsoduro, page 492, for workshop listing) who work exclusively in wood. The walls of the modern shop are lined with wooden puzzles, painted in rich, muted colors, which are made to hang like miniature paintings. Most beautiful are those that depict Venice as seen by Venetians, not your average touristy interpretation; they capture the city's dreamlike quality and are far more interesting mementos than yellowed snapshots.

Piazza San Marco, the center of town.

FASHION

WOMEN'S

Contemporary/Trendy

29 MAX MARA
Merceria dell'Orologio 268
Tel. 26.688
Moderate; credit cards accepted
Open during lunch

Smaller than the Max Maras of other Italian cities, but still filled with great fashion and quality.
See Florence listing (page 63).

FASHION

MEN'S

Classic

30 NINO FABRIS
Merceria dell'Orologio 223–26
Tel. 25.608
Expensive; credit cards accepted
Open during lunch and Sunday

Serious shopping under excellent guidance is a pleasure in this elegant salon. The look is traditional and features some of the best English fashion houses and fabrics. But the complete collections of Ermenegildo Zegna and Nino Cerruti are available

as well. You may either choose ready-made suits or have outfits custom-made. If you prefer the latter, allow 40 days for completion, or have your purchase sent home. Signor Nino Fabris will personally supervise the mixing and matching of English and Italian fabrics and designs to produce an ensemble with elegance and dash.

FASHION

MEN'S

Designer Collections

31 ÉLITE
Calle Larga San Marco 284
Tel. 52.30.145
Expensive; credit cards accepted
Open during lunch and Sunday

As the name indicates, only the elite need apply. High-class tailoring and fine ready-to-wear fill the large store, which features friendly yet professional service. Exceptionally well-finished tuxedos can be made to order in two weeks (and shipped if necessary), or can be purchased ready-made, complete with top hat and carved walking cane. Luxurious silk pajamas, cashmere sweaters and handmade *capretta* (kidskin) shoes are also available.

SHOES

MEN'S & WOMEN'S

Casual & Trendy

32 MACRI
Calle Larga San Marco 420
Tel. 29.956
Moderate; credit cards accepted
Open during lunch

Macri is known throughout Venice for original footwear that keeps ahead of fashion trends. Its Veneto-produced private label is found in richly detailed fantasy shoes featuring interesting contrasts of colors and skins and a whimsical use of ornaments. Shoes range from the very dressy to the casual and sporty.

Stylish men's and women's jackets are made from shearling and fine leathers in both natural and dyed high-fashion colors. Exquisite jackets for women from Florence's Roberto Cavalli combine stamped and hand-painted leathers.

GIFTS

DECORATIVE ACCESSORIES

Venetian Handicrafts

33 VENEZIARTIGIANA
Calle Larga San Marco 412
Tel. 52.35.032
Moderate; credit cards accepted
Open during lunch

Under one roof you'll find an interesting overview of all the specialties for which Venice is known—glass, lace, linens, jewelry, silver and paper products. Founded by Contessa Anna Maria Foscari, herself an artist, Veneziar-

All things Venetian at Veneziartigiana.

tigiana is a consortium of 59 local artisans who are keeping alive traditional crafts, at times using innovative methods. Their prices are moderately low. The setting is the beautiful old Al Redentor pharmacy, with original fixtures and wooden cabinets still intact.

BOOKS

GENERAL & RELIGIOUS

English-Language

34 LIBRERIA PIO X (STUDIUM VENEZIANO)
Calle di Canonica 337
Tel. 52.22.382
Moderate; credit cards accepted
Open during lunch

If you're on your way to visit Pauly's glass emporium (see page 481), you'll find yourself near the Ponte della Canonica and this *studium* well stocked with English-language books. Liberia Pio's concentration is religious, but there is also an extensive selection of books on Venetian art, history, architecture and literature, together with an appealing group of children's books. Everything is laid out for delightful browsing, giving you a chance to familiarize yourself with the ever-fascinating story of the Laguna.

HOME

GLASS

Contemporary Design

35 VENINI
Piazzetta dei Leoncini 314
Tel. 52.24.045
Expensive; credit cards accepted
Open during lunch and Sunday

Venini's simple, artistic glassware.

This is the only retail outlet in Venice for this Murano-based glassware company recognized for its innovative combination of color, design and function. Simple, contemporary, generally heavy handblown glass is displayed in diverse forms: vases, lamps, decorative objects, tableware and architectural lighting. The designs of Laura de Santillana and Gio Ponti are featured. The prices are considerably cheaper than in the United States, and Venini will reliably ship.

LINENS & LINGERIE
Venetian Hand Embroidery

36 TREVISAN
Piazza San Marco 45
Tel. 29.640
Moderate; credit cards accepted
Open during lunch and Sunday

Trevisan and Martinuzzi (see below) are the two recommended stops for lace and embroidery shopping in the tourist-inundated Piazza San Marco. Trevisan carries outstanding buys on beautiful tablecloths of all sizes and shapes (round, oval, rectangular), elaborately decorated in the Venetian style of needlepoint and hand embroidery. Prices are more than reasonable

for the hours of tedious labor that go into the creation of these future heirlooms. A number of tablecloths are antique, and new ones come in soft pastels as well as the traditional white and ivory. Trevisan has no sheets, but there are exquisite decorative pillowcases in different sizes and hundreds of beautiful initialed handkerchiefs for presents. Some of the store's merchandise comes from the Orient, but the sales help will point out which are which, and explain the difference in price. Due to the small size of the shop, precious little is on view, so ask to be shown what you want to see. The Trevisan shop next door at No. 42 carries embroidered children's and infants' clothing.

LINENS, LINGERIE, & CHILDREN'S WEAR
Venetian Hand Stitching

37 MARTINUZZI
Piazza San Marco 67A
Tel. 25.068
Moderate; credit cards accepted
Open during lunch and Sunday

This is a reputable, well-stocked shop selling lace and embroidery; much of it handwork from Burano. Martinuzzi is an especially good choice for infants' and children's clothes— bonnets and booties, Communion and christening gowns, and tiny pillowcases. The embroidered table linens and blouses are very pretty, and the delicate lace handkerchiefs make lovely gifts. The styles are classic and tasteful, the workmanship beautiful, and the prices far lower than for Florentine embroidery. Folding lace fans, some with lovely handpainted scenes, might prove useful on a midsummer day's jaunt aboard a very crowded *vaporetto.*

SUSTENANCE
BAR-CAFFÈ

38 CAFFÈ FLORIAN
Piazza San Marco 56–59
Tel. 85.338
Expensive; no credit cards accepted
Closed Wednesday

Undoubtedly the most Venetian and arguably the most beautiful of all cafés, the Florian has been spreading its tables out onto the Piazza San Marco since 1720. You can sit outside with a cappuccino as Venetians have done for centuries, since coffee was first introduced here through trade with Turkey. An old-world orchestra plays tunes not necessarily Italian, and no one will hurry you away from your delightful command post. Inside, a number of small rooms with marble-covered tables and velvet banquettes were renovated and frescoed in 1858 to evoke the elaborate style of the 1700s. At the bar in the back, Roberto prepares his hot-weather specialty, a blended version of the local Bellini.

Following Napoleon's departure in 1814, an Austrian occupation settled upon Venice for 70 harsh years.

Caffè Florian, a local institution since 1720.

During that period, Venetians patronized the Florian, while Austrians took to the Caffè Quadri directly across the square (see page 460). The Venetians have not forgotten the association more than a century later.

JEWELRY
Top-Name

39 S. NARDI
Piazza San Marco 68–71
Tel. 25.733
Expensive; credit cards accepted

Nardi takes its inspiration from 17th-century methods of jewelry making, and much of its work looks antique in design. Its unconventional specialty is jewelry that depicts the famous Moor of Venice. The face is usually carved out of ebony or amber, and the gold setting is studded with precious and semiprecious stones, recalling the Eastern opulence that once colored Venetian life. Other original Nardi designs include a set of three flower-shaped, gem-studded rings that can be worn separately or fit together as a bouquet, and their delicate gold charms of Venice's monuments—the Lion of St. Mark, the Clock Tower, the Rialto Bridge, and a slender gondola. If you're looking for coral, pieces of the pale and precious "angelskin" coral are delicately carved and set in gold.

Nardi also specializes in decorative objects made of malachite, tiger's eye and lapis lazuli, to name a few precious substances. In Nardi's new postmodern shop at Piazza San Marco 71, you can order custom-made furniture inlaid with these materials.

JEWELRY
Top-Name

40 MISSIAGLIA
Piazza San Marco 125
Tel. 52.24.464
Expensive; credit cards accepted

Many of Venice's master silversmiths and other craftsmen have been working exclusively for the Missiaglia family for 150 years. Everything in this understated jewelry store is worked entirely by hand, using the same techniques as in the past. Missiaglia's designs are classic and elegant and feature precious stones of the highest quality. One of Missiaglia's better-known creations is the set of silver salt and pepper shakers in the shape of long-stemmed artichokes resting horizontally—a gift that well-heeled customers can't resist.

SUSTENANCE
BAR-CAFFÈ

41 CAFFÈ QUADRI
Piazza San Marco 120–124
Tel. 22.105
Expensive; no credit cards accepted
Closed Monday

With your back to the magnificent Basilica of San Marco, you'll see the Caffè Quadri at the far end of the piazza on your right. Its outdoor orchestra vies with those of the square's other cafés, although rumor asserts that the Quadri's quartet is the only one to entertain personal requests from guests. Oscar Wilde, Noel Coward and Cole Porter all took their afternoon *aperitivi* here. It's also the perfect spot to bask in the early-morning sun with a frothy cappuc-

Caffè Quadri's outdoor musical quartet.

cino and a fresh *brioche,* even though patriotic Venetians may prefer Caffè Florian (see page 459).

FABRICS
FURNISHINGS

Antique Patterns

42 LORENZO RUBELLI
Campo San Gallo 1089–91
Tel. 52.36.110
Expensive; credit cards accepted

Rubelli is one of the last great Venetian textile merchants and one of Europe's finest houses for upholstery fabrics. It has decorated the chairs at La Scala, the home of Guy de Rothschild, Khashoggi's yacht *Nabila* and the private train of King Victor Emanuel. In recent years, Rubelli has created fresh modern patterns on silk, cotton and linen, while continuing to produce the striped, damask and marbleized antique prints that are still in great demand. It is one of the few sources in Venice, and in the world, that still makes luxurious *soprarizzo* (cut velvet) by hand on 15th-century wooden looms. While most of Rubelli's other textiles are now made on sophisticated electric looms, all are worthy of a Doge's home.

MEN'S & WOMEN'S

Designer Boutique

43 EMPORIO ARMANI
Calle dei Fabbri 989
Tel. 52.37.808
Expensive; credit cards accepted
Open during lunch

From the design board of Milan's premier arbiter of high fashion comes this chain of modern boutiques offering the Armani look somewhat toned down in choice of fabrics and price.

See Milan listing (page 185).

MEN'S & WOMEN'S

Designer Collections

44 ELYSÉE
Calle Goldoni 4485/A
Tel. 52.36.948
Expensive; credit cards accepted
Open during lunch and Sunday

This is the first of the two sleek Elysée boutiques, which have Venice's exclusive representation of Giorgio Armani. Armani's ready-to-wear collection for men and women is complemented by a superb selection of fashion shoes by such stars as Maud Frizon, Mario Valentino, and Linea Lidia, as well as by Armani himself.

The larger, more recent Elysée 2 boutique is just a bridge away, at Frezzeria 1693 (telephone 52.23.020). There you'll find even more Giorgio Armani fashion, this time for women only, including the less expensive Mani line, together with Valentino's Miss V collection and selections from Kensai.

WORKSHOP/STUDIO

Contemporary Designs

45 STUDIO LABORATORIO ORAFO STEFANIA FESCINA
Calle dei Fuseri 4458
Tel. 70.78.82
Moderate; no credit cards accepted

The only display of Stefania's artistry is in her window, for inside there is just room for her worktable, a small receiving space, and lots of books on jewelry making. Young Stefania creates expressive, modern gold jewelry highly original in design. Her work has simple geometric lines and unusual mixtures of precious and semi-precious stones, some uncut and unpolished, some engraved. Pieces can be adapted to the wearer, for she also does excellent customwork.

RISTORANTE/TRATTORIA

46 ZORZI
Calle dei Fuseri 4359
Tel. 25.350
Inexpensive; no credit cards accepted
Open only for lunch until 3:00; closed
    Sunday

To the innocent, this is a neighborhood *latteria,* a bar selling dairy products and a sandwich or two. But an unobtrusive stairway in the back leads you to a charming upstairs dining area that is a special find for vegetarians, light eaters, or those on slim budgets. Daily specials are on display for easy pointing, and friendly waiters do not pressure you to consume a conventional three- or four-course meal. You can mix and

Seeing Venice as it was meant to be seen.

match hot and cold pasta dishes with crisp, delicious salads or boiled or grilled vegetables either served with olive oil or baked in simple casseroles. Specials often include tomatoes, zucchini or peppers stuffed with rice and seasoned with herbs. There is also a good selection of cheeses. Zorzi is a bright and tranquil place for lunch, quite well-appointed when one considers the low prices.

SHOES

MEN'S & WOMEN'S

Made-to-Measure High Fashion

47 CALLEGHER ROLLY SEGALIN
Calle dei Fuseri 4365
Tel. 22.115
Expensive; credit cards accepted

In Venetian dialect, *callegher* means shoemaker, and that is what Rolly Segalin is par excellence. Rolly is known as the *haute couture* or *alta moda* shoemaker of Venice, as his father was before him. Shoes here are made to measure, and you may choose your own models and leathers. If you're staying two weeks or longer in Venice, you can pick them up; if not, you can have them sent home. When Rolly has made a wooden foot form for you, you may order by mail, sending a sketch or clipping of a favorite design from a magazine. Boots are his specialty, and a pair of ostrich-leather riding boots is displayed for your inspiration. Even if you choose something less extravagant, be prepared to pay handsomely for Rolly's craft.

SUSTENANCE

RISTORANTE/TRATTORIA

Late-Night

48 DA IVO
Ramo dei Fuseri 1809
Tel. 52.85.004
Expensive; credit cards accepted
Closed Sunday

Meat lovers who grow weak at the thought of juicy steaks—rarely found in this city—take heart. Ivo, who hails from Tuscany, has married the best of his own cuisine with the finest of the Venetian. Situated beside the pretty Rio dei Fuseri, this fashionable restaurant offers a number of Florentine favorites, including such quality grilled meats as *lombatina di vitello* (thick veal chop) and the culinary glory, *bistecca alla fiorentina* (prime steak). If fish is still your choice, try the *sogliola allo champagne* (sole in a champagne sauce). Venetian classics are also available. Ivo personally greets all his guests and keeps his kitchen open until an unusual 11:30 P.M. for late dining.

FASHION

WOMEN'S

Sophisticated and Contemporary

49 ARABA FENICE
Calle del Frutarol 1862
Tel. 29.906
Moderate; credit cards accepted

Loris Chia, the young proprietor of this tiny shop, is also the designer; and if his style complements yours, you can make an excellent investment in your wardrobe here. His simple, elegant separates and dresses in solid-color jerseys can readily be mixed and matched, dressed up or dressed down. Easy draping and belting define these comfortable clothes, which you can wear from work into evening. Loris has an excellent eye for fit and detailing, but his passion is for unusual, sophisticated color combinations. His quality wool knits for winter are followed by light cotton knits for summer wear.

MUSIC

WORKSHOP/STUDIO

Handmade String Instruments

50 ANTONIO GALLINA DA MONTE
Calle del Frutarol 1864
No telephone
Moderate; no credit cards accepted

Master artisan Antonio Gallina makes stringed instruments by hand, as he has done for some of the world's most famous virtuosi. The only musical-instrument maker of his kind in Venice, he will gladly create a violin or *contrabasso* for you in 40 days. It is a rare treat for musicians or music lovers to watch him at work, and to peruse the memorabilia and apprecia-

tive letters from great artists that crowd his walls. Appropriately, his small atelier is just in front of the famous La Fenice Theater.

GIFTS

STATIONERY & ACCESSORIES

Marbleized Papers

51 EBRÛ
Calle della Fenice 1920
Tel. 86.302
Moderate; credit cards accepted

See the listing for Ebrû's sister shop (page 444).

SUSTENANCE

RISTORANTE/TRATTORIA

52 ANTICO MARTINI
Campo San Fantin 1983
Tel. 52.24.121
Expensive; credit cards accepted
Closed Tuesday, and Wednesday lunch

Save this spot for a grand occasion or your last night in town; a dinner at Antico Martini's makes a perfect Venetian evening. The restaurant has one of the very few Continental menus in town, but there are also

Antico Martini, snuggled into a back calle.

many Italian and regional specialties, elegantly prepared and especially delicious when enjoyed on the open-air terrace. The local *San Daniele prosciutto* (with figs) is a perfect light appetizer. The pastas are exquisite—try the *cannelloni dogaresse* (with a tasty meat filling)—as is the seafood risotto. The fish is the freshest in town and never overcooked, so order any of the day's arrivals with confidence: grilled scampi or *orata in vino bianco* (bream in a white wine sauce), for example. The Antico Martini has been around since the early 18th century, even longer than the La Fenice Theater just across the lovely Campo San Fantin. Be sure to reserve a table in advance.

SUSTENANCE

ENOTECA (WINE BAR)

Late-Night

53 VINO VINO
Calle delle Veste 2007/A
Tel. 52.24.121
Moderate; credit cards accepted
Closed Tuesday

The enterprising owners of the nearby Antico Martini have just opened this fashionable wine bar. Vino Vino opens at 10:00 A.M., so the locals can allay that first emptiness with an uplifting nectar. All products of the noble grape are available by the glass or bottle—wine, *grappa*, champagne, *spumante*, Armagnac and cognac. At the bar, or at any of the eight marble-topped tables, a Venetian snack of *cicchetti* (hors d'oeuvres) can even pass for a light lunch or dinner: tomatoes stuffed with fish or rice; croquettes made with fish, rice or meat; stuffed olives;

Balconies overlook Venice's web of canals.

marinated anchovies; or sardines in *saor* (a marinade of vinegar, pine nuts, raisins and onions). The bar closes after lunch at 2:30 and reopens from 5:00 P.M. until 1:00 A.M., catching the chic after-theater crowd from La Fenice.

FASHION

WOMEN'S

Designer Collections

54 ELISABETTA ALLA FENICE
Calle dietro della Chiesa 1996
(Campo San Fantin)
Tel. 29.315
Expensive; credit cards accepted

Sonia Rykiel, Claude Montana, Muriel Grateau, Azzedine Alaïa and Thierry Mugler are all sold at prices comparable to those in Paris and, on occasion, a bit lower. Elisabetta also carries all the greats from Italy, but what's most interesting is her own production of feminine, tasteful and at times trendy high fashion. She executes everything elegantly, with hand-sewn zippers and buttonholes and hand-stitched seams and hems. There's a separate entrance for a selection of men's and women's shoes from such designers as Diego della Valle, Guido Pasquali and Maud Frizon.

SUSTENANCE

RISTORANTE/TRATTORIA

Late-Night

55 LA COLOMBA
Piscina di Frezzeria 1665
Tel. 52.21.175
Expensive; credit cards accepted
Closed Tuesday

Many art lovers come here as much for the impressive collection of fine Italian modern art as for the vast selection of authentic Venetian and

M.'s dramatic display.

classic Italian fare. Fish predictably dominates the menu: you can find a wide range of fresh possibilities, grilled, baked or fried. An unusual and delicious house specialty is the giant *scampi al curry* with rice pilaf. Your choice of meats is equally extensive, not a common occurrence in Venice. La Colomba enjoys a pretty setting with outdoor tables on a quiet street, and you can order from the kitchen until a late (by Venetian standards) 11:15 P.M.

ANTIQUES & COLLECTIBLES

Exotic Accessories & Jewelry

56 M. (ANTICHITA ⌂⌂⌂⌂ E OGGETTI D'ARTE)
Calle di Frezzeria 1651
Tel. 35.666
Expensive; credit cards accepted

Lovers of the exotic and theatrical must see this antique shop/gallery that is an homage to Venice. Here East meets West in treasures that once flooded the Venetian marketplace from the Orient: luxurious silks and brocades, hand-printed cottons and velvets, and dresses fit for a palazzo ball. The precious fabrics are often draped over the enormous wooden horse (modeled after those atop the Basilica of San Marco) that is the store's hallmark. Exquisite antique jewelry and the standout modern jewelry of Diego Percossi-Papi (see Rome listing, page 367), curious objets d'art, ornate mirrors and myriad decorative home accessories all crowd this eccentric store. Dark niches, heavily brocaded curtains and upholstered walls heighten the aura of sumptuousness and mystery.

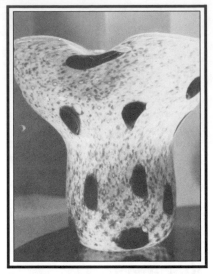

Franca Petroli creates unusual glassware.

HOME

GLASS

Artistic Collectors' Pieces

57 LE COSE ⌂⌂⌂⌂
DI FRANCA PETROLI

Frezzeria 1799
Tel. 52.87.116
Expensive; credit cards accepted
Open during lunch and Sunday

Architect and glass designer Franca
Petroli creates some of Venice's most
imaginative glassware, as you'll see
from her colorful window display. Unusual lamps, bowls, vases, and even a
glass car, chess set and table are
molded to her specifications. Some
objects are hand-painted. Her designs
may ask collectors' prices, but you'll
be guaranteed that each is one of a
kind. Attention-drawing and conver-
sation-evoking, Franca's pieces require the right home. She oversees
the glass blowing, and everything is
signed by her and her glass *maestro.*

SUSTENANCE

RISTORANTE/TRATTORIA

58 DA NICO

Frezzeria 1702
Tel. 52.21.543
Moderate; credit cards accepted
Closed Monday

It is both surprising and convenient
to find such a good restaurant on the
touristy Frezzeria. Its chef, Donato
Iezzi, got his experience at Venice's
supreme Cipriani and Harry's Bar. At
Nico's, he creates some delicious
dishes with the light influence of
nuova cucina, emphasizing fresh vegetables in season and the daily fish
arrivals determined by the tides. The
insalata di sedano e polpi (octopus
and celery salad) antipasto is recommended, as are a number of delicious
pastas, including *spaghetti al granchio* (with crab meat) and *tagliatelle
alla boscaiola* (with wild mushrooms,
bacon and tomatoes). For the main
course, Adriatic sole *alla mugnaia*
(with wine and butter sauce) is joined
by chicken breasts, sautéed calf's kidneys and veal scallops. The newly
decorated *trattoria* is a pleasant, unhurried spot with good service.

MASKS & COSTUMES

Extravagant Styles

59 IL PRATO

Frezzeria 1770
Tel. 70.33.75
Expensive; credit cards accepted
Open during lunch and Sunday

Two enormous windows displaying
dramatic and bizarre masks stop
passersby in their tracks. The two
young Venetian artisans who orga-

nized this emporium of Carnival accessories take special pride in the objects created exclusively for them by local craftsmen. There are masks designed to cover the entire head: a copy of the elaborate swan mask from the film *Amadeus,* and a unicorn mask with gleaming golden horn and real horsehair. Masks are trimmed with gold-dipped chains, metallicized lace and real Swarovski crystals. Hats are decorated with fantastical feathers and veils. Extravagant period costumes have real silk petticoats, handmade lace trim, Murano-glass buttons and luxurious antique fabrics.

LINGERIE

Seductively Stylish

60 JADE MARTINE

Frezzeria 1762
Tel. 31.978
Moderate; credit cards accepted
Open during lunch and Sunday

Lingerie from Italy and France that is feminine, luxurious, and just a little naughty fills this modern boutique. Beautiful silk, satin and cotton undergarments and hosiery come in soft pastels or unusual prints. Satin Cinderella slippers match inviting gowns and peignoirs in a wide range of colors. Seductive bustiers and bras are shown by expert friendly sales assistants, who will help you with a professional fit. Much of the merchandise carries the Jade Martine private label; it can be found in selective specialty stores outside Italy for far higher prices. In early spring, sleek swimwear appears with designer labels such as La Perla, Missoni, Valentino and Mani. Male shoppers in quest of an extra-special gift are warmly welcomed.

FASHION

MEN'S & WOMEN'S

Designer Collections

61 LA COUPOLE

Frezzeria 1674
Tel. 70.60.63
Expensive; credit cards accepted
Open during lunch and Sunday

This is the larger location of a well-known two-store operation; both stores carry many high-fashion lines. Top original fashion comes in a few French labels (Kenzo, Claude Montana, Anne Marie Beretta) and many Italian ones: Erreuno, Enrico Coveri, Luciano Soprani, Valentino Boutique, Loretta di Lorenzo (for women), Gianmarco Venturi (for men) and Rocco Barocco. There are bold and interesting accessories to complement such sartorial splendor. The boutique at Calle Larga XXII Marzo 2366 carries styles that are sportier and more casual, but not any less expensive.

FASHION

WOMEN'S

Sophisticated Silk Blouses

62 PIER

Frezzeria 1189
Tel. 52.31.990
Moderate; credit cards accepted

There's a sense of Venetian chic in Pier's blouses, most of which are of the store's own production. Their high-quality silk separates are made in attractive florals, plaids and geometrics as well as solid-colored jacquards and crepes de Chine. Pier's focus is on the blouses, which have updated collar and sleeve treatments.

They can be combined with selections from a separate line of more conservative skirts and pants for a stylish, coordinated look.

FASHION
CHILDREN'S

63 BENETTON 012
Frezzeria 1489
Tel. 52.24.762
Moderate; credit cards accepted
Open during lunch and Sunday

This Benetton store for children is actually a part of the adjacent one for juniors.
See Milan listing (page 217).

LEATHERGOODS
BAGS, CLOTHING & ACCESSORIES

64 VOGINI ⌂⌂⌂⌂
Calle II dell'Ascensione 1291, 1292 and 1301
Tel. 52.22.573
Expensive; credit cards accepted
Open during lunch and Sunday

There are three Vogini stores, all within a few steps of each other, and together they offer Venice's largest collection of fine leather. Most recognizable are the Bottega Veneta look-alike handbags. (See Bottega Veneta listing, page 469.) There is speculation as to who originated this deluxe woven-leather line. Regardless, the prices for these supposed impersonators can at times be less than half those of the real thing, with only a minimal compromise in leather quality. Vogini has an enormous selection of buttery-soft handbags, small leathergoods, suitcases, shoes and leather apparel. Venice's oldest leathergoods shop, founded more than 100 years ago, Vogini has long been known also for its genuine crocodile-skin items; if you're ready to pay a tidy sum, you can travel in the epitome of style with a four-piece luggage set made of this luxurious material. You might want to choose instead from the colorful Mandarina Duck line of synthetic luggage and handbags, for which Vogini holds the exclusive in the city of Venice. Venice's own Roberta di Camerino's classic velvet purses can be found here as well.

ANTIQUE JEWELRY
Top-Name

65 A. CODOGNATO
Calle II dell'Ascensione 1295
Tel. 25.042
Expensive; credit cards accepted

As one of Italy's most respected dealers in antique jewelry, Attilio Codognato carries on the family enterprise that was started in 1866 by his grandfather, Venice's crown jeweler. The store invites international connoisseurs who recognize the insuperable caliber of Codognato's precious pieces, as did the Duke of Windsor, Coco Chanel and Luchino Visconti.

A 1920s aviation pin at A. Codognato.

Codognato has spent a lifetime scouting out exquisite antique jewelry and objects such as cameos, coffee sets, urns, cases, swords, goblets and icons. The most recent jewelry in his old-fashioned, velvet-walled shop dates from the 1950s.

SHOES

MEN'S & WOMEN'S

Comfort with Fashion Appeal

66 BRUNO MAGLI
Calle II dell'Ascensione 1302
(corner Calle Vallaresso)
Tel. 27.210
Moderate; credit cards accepted

Venice boasts the widest selection of the high-quality footwear from this Bologna-based shoe designer. Bruno Magli's designs run from the elegant to the sensible, from dressy patent pumps to casual everyday shoes for both men and women. He has become known worldwide for his superlative combination of comfort and fashion appeal, and his excellent workmanship guarantees the longevity of his shoes. The same colors are picked up in ladies' handbags, and there's a small but good selection of leather apparel.

Another, smaller Bruno Magli shop is located nearby at Frezzeria 1583 (telephone 23.472).

FASHION

MEN'S & WOMEN'S

Made-to-Measure Shirts & Blouses

67 CAMICERIA SAN MARCO
Calle Vallaresso 1340
Tel. 52.21.432
Expensive; credit cards accepted

Shirts are an art at Camiceria San Marco, but Signor Erranti also creates pajamas, dressing gowns, and other clothing for men and women. You may choose from among dozens of bolts of fine Italian cottons, silks and linens and have your custom-made shirts ready in 24 hours, complete with monograms. Men's and women's suits may take three days or longer. If you must leave town before your purchase is finished, it can be sent home gift-wrapped and duty-free. Peggy Guggenheim, Ernest Hemingway and undisclosed royal personages have loyally upheld Signor Erranti's 30-year tradition in tailoring.

LEATHERGOODS

BAGS & ACCESSORIES

68 BOTTEGA VENETA
Calle Vallaresso 1337
Tel. 28.489
Expensive; credit cards accepted

This Vicenza-based firm continues to offer some of the most beautifully made leather accessories around. Updated woven leather is Bottega's most popular look, occasionally combined with snakeskin and other materials, and presented in rich colors that change from season to season. Soft, pouchy bags are the most commonly found items, coordinated with tasteful shoes, wallets, luggage, belts and travel accessories. This is a small and not particularly welcoming shop. Minimal display of the merchandise discourages browsing, and you'll have to direct your requests to the sales help. But the superb quality of the leather-goods and the prices (compared to those in America) may make it worth your while.

SUSTENANCE

BAR-CAFFÈ & RISTORANTE/TRATTORIA

69 HARRY'S BAR

Calle Vallaresso 1323
Tel. 85.331/36.797
Expensive; credit cards accepted
Closed Monday

What is an afternoon in Venice without a Bellini at Harry's? You don't have to be one of their seasoned habitués to enjoy the legendary experience of this fashionable bar-cum-restaurant that was frequented by Hemingway and his entourage. When you see the modest, understated décor of the downstairs bar, you may wonder what all the fuss is about. But the ambiance is relaxed and perfect for people-watching; Harry's has been a watering hole for the world's "who's who" for over half a century. The summertime drink that originated here before traveling the world over is the Bellini. It is made of fresh peach juice and a white Prosecco wine and named after the famous 15th-century Venetian painters, brothers Giovanni and Gentile. The bar is open from 10:30 A.M. to 11:00 P.M. Upstairs Harry's moonlights as a very fine, very elegant and very expensive restaurant. Faithful clients enjoy the atmosphere of a private club, with dependably excellent food and impeccable service. From your pale-yellow, linen-draped table, you'll look out over the illuminated island of San Giorgio Maggiore. Harry's menu is a refined mix of the traditional and the inventive, notably the beef *carpaccio* (raw with a light mayonnaise-based sauce), named after a Venetian Renaissance painter. As a first course, try the fish soup (a saffron-rich broth with large chunks of fish), the *risotto primavera* made with fresh seasonal vegetables, or the fish ravioli. As entrées, the liver, veal, steaks and fresh fish specialties are delicious, but save room for the desserts—a highlight of dinner at Harry's, especially the bittersweet chocolate cake and the meringue with fluffy whipped cream. You can order until 11:00 P.M. (highly unusual for these parts). If you can afford it, you should eat at Harry's at least once in your life.

ENGRAVINGS & PRINTS

Venetian Scenes

70 OSVALDO BÖHM

Salizzada San Moisè 1349–50
Tel. 52.22.255
Moderate; credit cards accepted
Open during lunch

More than 30,000 negatives comprise the priceless photographic archives of Osvaldo Böhm. Founded in 1910, the firm has been enhancing its collection since first acquiring the entire archives of a mid-19th-century local photographer, Carlo Naya. The ar-

Museum-deserving artwork at Osvaldo Böhm.

L'Isola—a gallery of fine Venetian glass.

chive today documents the art and architecture of Venice since the Byzantine period, as well as the daily life of the city during the 1800s. In addition to making reproductions of these photographs available for sale in prints and books, Böhm has collector's items such as original etchings by Canaletto, old maps of Venice, and beautiful reproductions of engravings depicting Venetian scenes.

SHOES

MEN'S & WOMEN'S

71 FRATELLI ROSSETTI

Salizzada San Moisè 1477
Tel. 52.20.819
Expensive; credit cards accepted
Open during lunch and Sunday

Milan's Rossetti family has two equally beautiful and spacious Venice locations. The other is near the Rialto at Salizzada San Salvador 4800.

HOME

GLASS

Contemporary Design

72 L'ISOLA 🕭🕭🕭🕭

Campo San Moisè 1468
Tel. 52.31.973
Expensive; credit cards accepted
Open during lunch and Sunday

If you don't make it to Murano, this modern and elegant store/gallery is the best showcase in town for contemporary Murano glass. It is the perfect setting for the artistic glassware designed by the Carlo Moretti firm and highlighted here. Moretti's simple, clean and lightweight design appears in bowls, vases, wine carafes, goblets for wine and champagne, and the well-known octagonal glasses rimmed with a simple gold band. Modern, dark-wood display cases exhibit these glass *capolavori* (masterpieces) in function and style, with prices clearly labeled.

ANTIQUES

OLD MASTER PAINTINGS & DRAWINGS

Venetian School

73 PIETRO SCARPA

Calle Larga XXII Marzo 2089
Tel. 27.199
Expensive; no credit cards accepted

It's hard to believe that some of Venice's most important artworks are sold from this tiny gallery. But Pietro Scarpa is well known as a specialized dealer in master drawings and paintings, above all those of the Venetian school dating back to the Renaissance, and his miniscule store commands the respect of a museum. Personal checks accepted.

BOOKS
GENERAL
English-Language

74 LIBRERIA INTERNAZIONALE SAN GIORGIO
Calle Large XXII Marzo 2087
Tel. 38.451
Moderate; credit cards accepted
Open during lunch

The service is exceptionally helpful in this well-known, conveniently located Venetian bookstore. Your main interest will probably be in the wide selection of English-language books on Venice. A number of other Italian cities and regions are also well represented, however. You'll find books on travel, art, architecture and history, along with a small selection of paperback literature. In addition, there are some appealing and unusual postcards and posters from Venetian museums and the archives of local photographers.

ANTIQUE JEWELRY
TOP-NAME
Signed Art-Deco Pieces

75 HERRIZ
Calle Larga XXII Marzo 2381
Tel. 70.42.76
Expensive; credit cards accepted

Erminio Rizzoli has been on the scent of priceless gems most of his life, seeking out estate sales, aristocratic auctions and chance opportunities. A wholesaler until two years ago, he now sells his priceless finds directly to the public from this small and exclusive boutique. There are choice signed pieces of the 1930-to-1960 period from Tiffany, Cartier, Van Cleef & Arpels and Fabergé. Since he participated in a Fortuny Museum exhibition of art-deco jewelry, praise has been lavished on Signor Rizzoli's talent for ferreting out what many believe to be the most beautiful jewelry in the world.

SHOES
MEN'S & WOMEN'S
High-Fashion Styles

76 LA FENICE
Calle Larga XXII Marzo 2255
Tel. 52.31.273
Expensive; credit cards accepted
Open during lunch

La Fenice is top-of-the-line in Venice for shoes. Its calling card is an exclusive representation of the forward shoe collection of Maud Frizon, produced in nearby Veneto factories. This is one of Frizon's largest selections in all of Italy. The ultrafashionable shoe boutique also carries collections from Stéphane Kelian designed by Claude Montana, as well as from Jean-Paul Gaultier, Lario

Two of Venice's 400-odd bridges.

1898, Valentino, and Guido Pasquali. There is an equally stylish assortment of dressy handbags for women, many of which cost far more than a pair of shoes. Especially high-priced are the crocodile bags from Italy's refined Donna Elissa line, which come in a number of rich colors and shapes.

FASHION

MEN'S & WOMEN'S

Designer Collections

77 DRAGANCZUK
Calle Larga XXII Marzo 2288
Tel. 70.82.80
Expensive; credit cards accepted
Open during lunch

A good selection of creative fashion for men and women is shown in a Venetian-style postmodern décor. The designer roll call includes, among others, Ungaro, Valentino, Complice and les Copains. If you spot a garment from any of these houses in a fashion magazine early enough in the season, you can write to Signora Draganczuk and she will mail-order it to you, as a courtesy the store has been offering its regular American customers for years.

LINGERIE & CHILDREN'S WEAR

Hand Embroidery

78 MARICLA
Calle Larga XXII Marzo 2401
Tel. 32.202
Expensive; credit cards accepted

The refined lady will find a profusion of elegant lingerie at Maricla. Silky satins, charmeuses and fine cottons are made up into simple, pretty gowns, pure white or soft pastel in color, with delicate lace inserts and lovely hand-embroidered highlights. There's also a collection of charming, exquisitely detailed clothing for infants (bibs, bonnets, tops) and children (slips, blouses, blazers, smocked dresses). All can be personally monogrammed by Maricla, who will even include little crowns for aspiring princes and princesses.

FASHION

WOMEN'S

Great Sweaters

79 BARBARA
Campo Santa Maria del Giglio 2463
Tel. 70.58.20
Expensive; credit cards accepted

This tiny shop is most noteworthy for its selection of Umberto Ginochietti sweaters. Ginochietti is known for his handsome and well-made apparel, but it is his sweaters that are truly extraordinary. A Ginochietti sweater is a piece of art, timelessly worn season after season. Made with various yarns that play with colors and patterns, it is for the romantic and young in spirit. Barbara also carries updated classic skirts and trousers that go well with these very special tops.

SUSTENANCE

RISTORANTE/TRATTORIA

80 CLUB DEL DOGE DELL' HOTEL GRITTI
Campo Santa Maria del Giglio 2467
Tel. 26.044
Very expensive; credit cards accepted
Open seven days a week

Banquet befitting a Doge at the Gritti Hotel.

If you're not lucky enough to be a guest in one of the world's most distinguished and luxurious hotels, you must at least come to the Gritti Palace for a drink or dinner. Few things are more romantic than to dine on the lovely open-air terrace directly on the Canale della Giudecca and then to linger sipping a mellow Amaretto. You'll appreciate the sophisticated professionalism of the Gritti's waiters, and (if it's cool weather) the décor of the intimate indoor dining rooms appointed with an exceptional collection of antiques. The restaurant features classical Italian cuisine enriched with regional and local specialties. The homemade pasta, quality-cut meats, perfectly fresh fried or grilled fish, delicate shrimp (the best in Venice) with herbs and vegetables, and the house special, filet of sole *alla dogaressa* (with a light shrimp sauce), are all equally delicious. The wine list is superb and the desserts astonishing.

ANTIQUES & OBJETS D'ART

Byzantine to Renaissance

81 BEPPE PATITUCCI
Campiello della Feltrina 2511/B
Tel. 36.393
Expensive; no credit cards accepted

Every piece in Beppe Patitucci's antique collection is unique and arresting, and comes with a fascinating story as recounted by Beppe himself. In his small shop you're likely to find everything from religious art, old engravings, and antique lace and velvet to musical instruments, ivory boxes, and masks. Many of the objects figured in Venetian history, from the Byzantine period to the Renaissance. When Signor Patitucci is around, you'll be amused by his euphoric personality and his super-superlatives: everything in his store is *bellissimissimissimo*. He is an independent merchant who does not always adhere strictly to his purportedly regular store hours.

GIFTS

STATIONERY & ACCESSORIES

Hand-Decorated and Stamped Papers

82 LEGATORIA PIAZZESI
Campiello della Feltrina 2511
Tel. 52.21.202
Moderate; no credit cards accepted

Legatoria means bookbindery in Italian, and this small store originated as such in 1905. Today, it is the city's oldest and best-known source of beautifully patterned, hand-printed papers. They are used to cover books, picture frames, paperweights, carnival masks and kaleidoscopes, to name a few objects. There is also a large and impressive collection of antique woodblocks. Some blocks date from the 15th century, when they were widely used to create *carta varese,* a unique form of stamped paper named after the city of Varese, near Milan, whence this art came. The Legatoria is the only place that still produces hand-printed paper in this way. A precious few of the small carved woodblocks are for sale as objets d'art.

ENGRAVINGS & PRINTS

Contemporary Venetian Engravings

83 BAC ART STUDIO
Campo San Maurizio 2663
Tel. 52.28.171
Moderate; credit cards accepted
Open during lunch

The BAC Art Studio provides a living link with the 18th century, when Venice's artistry in engraving was at its finest. The inviting art gallery/boutique exhibits original designs in fabrics and posters, along with numbered, limited-edition prints and lithographs. All engravings come from the local Cadore Art Workshop (see San Polo listing, page 501) and are exclusively available through the BAC

A moment's respite between shops.

Art Studio or from the workshop itself. The master engraver of the studio is young Paolo Baruffaldi, whose engravings depicting dreamlike visions of Venice and Carnival are also available as prints on small notepapers and postcards.

FABRICS

FURNISHINGS

Fortuny Patterns

84 V. TROIS
Campo San Maurizio 2666
Tel. 22.905
Expensive; no credit cards accepted

Mariano Fortuny died in 1949 (see page 476), but he left the legacy of his exquisitely printed fabrics in the hands of the quintessentially efficient Contessa Elsie McNeill Lee Gozzi. Keeper of the Fortuny secrets, she alone knows how to make these radiant prints, whose rich nuances of color and shading give them the same allure as the silks and brocades that first made Fortuny famous. Today, because of the prohibitive price of silk and velvet, the Fortuny patterns are printed only onto cottons.

   Some vintage pieces of the luxurious original velvets are still available, however, and make exquisite framings. No one knows who will carry on when the elderly Contessa Gozzi dies, and this lends a note of urgency to the purchase of these most exalted of yard goods. Personal and traveler's checks are accepted.

MARIANO FORTUNY

Fortuny saw himself as a Renaissance man. A visit to his home, the 15th-century Palazzo Orfei (later called the Palazzo Fortuny, now the Museo Fortuny), will overwhelm you with the diversity of talents displayed; there are etchings, tempera and oil paintings, advanced techniques in photography, set designs and lighting arrangements for the theater and home, but most of all, Fortuny's exquisite textile designs and the timeless dress designs that were born from them.

Mariano Fortuny y Madrazo was born in Spain in 1871, but spent most of his life in Venice. His creations represent a marriage of cultures and sensibilities; he was inspired by the Venetian school of painters and the Italian Renaissance and classical Greece, but also by Islamic, African and even pre-Columbian patterns. He did his own printing, tediously and diligently, onto lengths of rich silk and velvet, creating sumptous designs that simulated gilded brocades and luxurious woven fabrics. Jealously guarding the secrets of his complex dyes, he first printed in the privacy of his home, then in his factory on the island of Giudecca, which is still operating today.

Elenora Duse, Sarah Bernhardt and Isadora Duncan became Fortuny fans. They confidently wore the fashion that he created as anti-fashion, draping women with something that allowed them to move. He invented and patented a device for pleating silk. His Greek-inspired Delphos dress made from this pleated silk never changed in design over 50 years; it is still worn by women today and echoed by fashion designers time and again. It is stored by being rolled up into a ball, then placed in a tiny box to preserve its pleats. He died in 1949, taking to his grave the secret of how to use this patent, as he took with him the formulas for many of his extravagant dyes.

Today, a mere fraction of Fortuny's 5000 designs are kept in production by American-born Countess Elsie McNeill Lee Gozzi, the loyal business associate in whose efficient hands he left the operation. Cottons and linens are often used to keep the prices, still very high, less opulent than the silks and velvets once exclusively used. Like Fortuny, she zealously protects the secrets behind the dyeing and printing of these unique fabrics. She has made no arrangements for a successor, and Venetians feel that when she dies, so will the legacy.

Museo di Palazzo Fortuny
Campo San Benedetto 3780
(San Marco neighborhood)
Daily 9:00 A.M.–7:00 P.M. except Monday.

Norelene's owners—as lovely as their fabrics.

FABRICS

FURNISHINGS & FASHION

Hand-Printed Velvets

85 NORELENE 🏠🏠🏠🏠
Campo San Maurizio 2606
Tel. 52.37.605
Expensive; credit cards accepted

With the centuries of rich textile tradition in Venice, it is not surprising to find the artistry of Norelene's deluxe, hand-stamped velvets. Drawing inspiration from Byzantine mosaics and floor pavings, Helene and Nora handprint fabrics with simple geometric patterns in subtle colors whose blends and contrasts produce shimmering three-dimensional effects. Printed on velvets, silks and cottons, their designs have been exhibited around the world. They are also made up into elegant shawls, short mandarin-collared evening jackets and long, kimono-style robes. Lengths of fabric are sold to be hung or framed as art, perhaps their most appropriate destiny.

JEWELRY

WORKSHOP/STUDIO

Unusual Contemporary Designs

86 FRANCO DE CAL
Campo San Maurizio 2604
Tel. 70.60.15
Moderate; no credit cards accepted
Open during lunch

This *campo* is a cache of talented artisans. Take, for instance, Franco de Cal and his wife, who produce unusual gold jewelry by commission in their tiny atelier. His specialty is using perfectly cut precious stones in an intarsia style—an ancient method of arranging inlaid gems (opals, turquoise and pearls) to form a geometric pattern. Pieces are occasionally available in the studio, but generally you'll have to count on special orders, which take about a month or longer to fill. His wife's jewelry is best represented in her large gold cuffs and necklaces inlaid with precious or semiprecious stones.

GIFTS

STATIONERY & ACCESSORIES

Marbleized Papers

87 IL PAPIRO
Calle del Piovan 2764
Tel. 52.23.055
Moderate; credit cards accepted
Open during lunch and Sunday

The largest of all of the Florence-based Il Papiro stores is located here in Venice.

See Florence listing (page 69).

THE BIENNALE AND VENICE'S CONTEMPORARY ART GALLERIES

The Biennale (held in even years only, from June to October) has secured Venice's importance in the world of art. Originated by Venetian Count Volpi di Misurata and now approaching its 100th anniversary, it has become the world's largest modern art show. The Biennale represents hundreds of professional artists in all media from over 50 countries, who exhibit in 30 permanent pavilions in and around the Giardini Pubblici (Public Gardens).

A flurry of contemporary art galleries has resulted from Venice's position as an international art center. The following are a few of the best; all relatively close to each other, they could easily be seen in one afternoon.

AL TRAGHETTO
(Campo Santa Maria del Giglio 2460
Telephone 52.21.188)
A small space for major Venetian artists, the young and promising as well as contemporary masters such as Vedova and Guidi.

IL CAPRICORNO
(Calle Dietro della Chiesa 1994,
near Chiesa San Fantin
Telephone 70.69.20)
Venice's most important gallery for international contemporary art, the elegant Capricorno shows work by Sandro Chia and other big names in the "Trans-Avantguardia" movement.

CAVALLINO
(Frezzeria 1725
Telephone 52.20.528)
Another important name on the international contemporary scene, Cavallino offers the work of prominent British and Italian artists with a number of Venetians and young newcomers. You'll also find a select group of books on international and video art for sale.

NAVIGLIO VENEZIA
(Calle di Piscina 1652,
near San Fantin
Telephone 52.27.634)
Venice branch of one of Milan's most noted galleries, the Naviglio is open only in summer, culminating with one important group show each September. Young and talented European artists are represented here in paintings and multimedia work, including books and even scarves.

Castello

T he *sestiere* of Castello offers the perfect chance to discover another side of Venice. Virtually next door to Piazza San Marco, it is a quiet residential neighborhood where women still play bingo in the street on summer evenings and laundry day is announced by fluttering tablecloths overhead. It is not a commercial area; stores consist of the typical fruit vendor and pharmacy. But there are some choice destinations for the intent shopper, and a few must-sees even for the uninterested, in particular the deconsecrated church that houses Jesurum's magnificent collection of Venetian needlework and lace. There are also some of the finest restaurants in the city, reached by a pleasant evening walk from Piazza San Marco past the Bridge of Sighs and along the broad, *caffè*-lined Riva degli Schiavoni. This waterside runway has become something of a swank boardwalk, serving as a prestigious address for Venice's best hotels.

The Schiavoni were merchants from Dalmatia, now part of Yugoslavia, who had engaged in trade with the Venetian Republic since early times. These Slavs founded a colony, and later a confraternity, in this area of Castello where they used to moor their boats. La Scuola di San Giorgio degli Schiavoni was their seat, and a series of masterpieces by the Venetian painter Carpaccio can be found there. A flourishing Greek

The quiet Castello sestiere is less inundated by the constant stream of tourism.

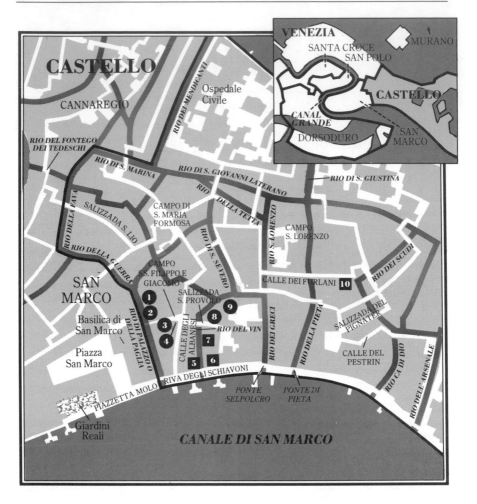

community also settled in Castello, and Venice's Orthodox residents still worship in their 16th-century church, San Giorgio dei Greci. But Castello's nucleus has always been the 12th-century Arsenale, once the world's largest and most sophisticated shipyards. The early residents of Castello belonged to a prosperous working class that sprang up around this shipbuilding center, quite different in character from the fishermen who live there today.

Beyond the Arsenale are the Giardini Pubblici (Public Gardens), site of one of the world's largest modern art shows, the celebrated Biennale. The Biennale is one of many cultural exhibitions that have kept alive an appreciation of the artistic and artisanal skills once again thriving in the city.

Pauly's location, once home of Doge Mozorini.

HOME

GLASS

One Hundred Years of Styles

1 PAULY & CO.
Ponte dei Consorzi
Tel. 70.98.99
Moderate; credit cards accepted
Open during lunch and Sunday morning

It's worth while to skip the three Pauly shops in Piazza San Marco and go directly to the firm's magnificent Palazzo of the Doge Mozorini. If you have little inclination to buy, consider this an educational tour through a century of vitreous art; that is the length of time Pauly has been involved with Murano's master glass artisans. If you are a potential purchaser interested in a particular style or period, ask for some direction upon entering, or you may spend hours wandering through the collec-

tion's 32 rooms. Extraordinarily elaborate chandeliers and ornate mirrors can be afforded by few, but take heart from the table glassware of every possible shape and form. Baroque-style glasses with hand-painted scenes and etched Liberty (art-deco) style pieces will capture the eye of the antiques-fancier. Avoid Pauly's contemporary collection, as you can find more handsome and extensive modern design elsewhere.

LACE, LINENS, & LINGERIE

Venetian Hand Embroidery

2 JESURUM 🍾🍾🍾🍾
Ponte Canonica 4310
Tel. 70.61.77
Expensive; credit cards accepted
Open during lunch

Venice will be forever indebted to Michelangelo Jesurum for reviving the local lace and needlework industry. Before his first efforts in 1868, this glorious Venetian patrimony had dwindled to barely a memory since its heyday centuries before. During the last 100 years, in this august converted 12th-century church, Jesurum has evolved into half-museum, half-boutique—and as much a local must-see as the Basilica of San Marco.

Intricate Venetian lace, appliquéd tablecloths, and embroidered place mats are magnificently displayed beneath vaulted ceilings and graceful arches. Room after room houses the precious old laces extinct elsewhere in the world, along with more modern and equally exquisite designs for the bath, boudoir and table. Pieces are available in every price range, from the antique and very expensive to the machine-made and affordable. You will always be told whether you are buying hand- or machine-made embroidery or lace. The fine machine embroidery is a complex, not-to-be-underrated craft, and is finished by hand. The making of lace in various traditional centers is flourishing anew, and particular styles represent different cities' or islands' production. If your circumstances do not permit sizable purchases, there are scores of delicate sachets and cushions, decorative pillowcases and handkerchiefs, baby bibs and collars whose prices are hard to resist.

Foreigners love Jesurum's new addition, resort wear (colorful yacht attire and bathing suits with coordinated après-swim robes and dresses. But aristocratic Venetian *signore* still come here to buy exquisite baptismal gowns for their precious babies, and embroidered clothing for their small children. Monograms can grace these items for those who have the patience to wait. Many a trousseau, too, is still labored over by Jesurum lace experts. And for the knowledgeable collector, director Eugenia Graziussi will lovingly bring out priceless lengths of antique lace and linen for table or bed in the privacy of a back room.

FASHION

CHILDREN'S

Designer Collections

3 AL GIROLONDO
Campo SS. Filippo e Giacomo 4292
Tel. 52.31.826
Expensive; credit cards accepted
Open during lunch

The bright and cheery windows here are real eye-grabbers for doting parents and grandparents. Inside, crea-

tive displays and a modern layout make for easy browsing among the fashion sportswear for children designed by Armani, Valentino, les Copains, Pepperino, Cacherel, Enrico Coveri and Blu Marine. The store takes its name from *al girondolo*, an Italian children's game something like Ring-Around-the-Rosy.

FASHION

MEN'S

Updated Classic

4 CERIELLO
Campo SS. Filippo e Giacomo 4275
Tel. 52.22.062
Expensive; credit cards accepted
Open during lunch

Menswear is classic and fashionable in the elegant ambiance of Ceriello, here since 1903. There is a wide selection of casual and office attire from Gianni Versace, Basile, Valentino, Brioni, St. Andrews and Ginochietti. With so many handsome outfits to choose from, only the impeccably demanding will want to take advantage of Ceriello's tailoring services and order a custom-made suit. Alterations on ready-made garments are of the same exceptional quality, and purchases can be shipped home.

SUSTENANCE

RISTORANTE/TRATTORIA

5 DANIELI TERRACE
Riva degli Schiavoni 4196
Tel. 26.480
Expensive to very expensive; credit cards
    accepted
Open seven days a week

Gracious dining on the Danieli Terrace.

You'll pass through the magnificent courtyard of the Danieli Hotel and enter into a lobby replete with Gothic staircase, ornate mirrors, cool marble and elaborate gilding on your way to the arched and canopied terrace restaurant on the fourth floor. No better place exists to watch the sun slide over the laguna and to sense the mystical element of Venice's character. The elegance of the table settings and the refined courtesy of the service foretell a very special dinner. The menu lists some international entries, but you'll do better to stick to the excellent risottos, the soups with seafood, or the house specialty, *fettuccine alla buranella* (with sole and shrimps in a cream sauce), followed by one of the innumerable varieties of fresh fish or shellfish (try the *scampi alla dogaressa* with sherry sauce). There is also an impressive array of desserts, including flaming crêpes.

SUSTENANCE

RISTORANTE/TRATTORIA

6 DO LEONI
Riva degli Schiavoni 4171
Tel. 25.032
Expensive; credit cards accepted
Closed Tuesday

For formal dining, the deluxe Londra Palace Hotel offers a handsome, wood-paneled and mirrored restaurant. Indoors, there are only ten linen-covered tables with antique etched Murano glassware, but in summer the outdoor terrace along the Canale Grande is just as lovely. The menu includes some excellently prepared Venetian specialties, but the reason to dine here is the nouvelle-influenced cuisine, whose imaginative presentations and moderate-sized portons are not typically Venetian. Try *l'orto ai ferri* (grilled seasonal vegetables served on a stone slab and a bed of rosemary); the excellent risottos made with fish, radicchio or herbs; scallops with saffron sauce or Kurdistan-style scampi with saffron rice. The wine list is compiled by renowned wine expert Luigi Veronelli. A light dessert to finish it all off is *macedonia al caramello* (fresh fruit salad with caramel sugar).

If some morning you're taken by an urge for an American breakfast, Do Leoni serves a daily brunch that includes bacon and eggs and cornflakes.

SUSTENANCE

RISTORANTE/TRATTORIA

7 MALAMOCCO
Campiello del Vin 4650
(near Campo San Provolo)
Tel. 27.438
Expensive; credit cards accepted
Closed Thursday

Malamocco, a well-known fish restaurant, has a romantic garden and a pleasant piano bar. Seafood specialties include *crespelle al lumache* (small crêpes with snails) and fresh fish *al cartoccio* (baked in a paper or foil envelope). Red meat finds its place on the menu with an excellent, paper-thin *carpaccio* and quality steaks. Tourists love the elegant and discreet décor, but there's also a regular clientele of Venice's high society. Malamocco offers a good lunch at a fixed but moderate price.

MASKS

8 MION-MARIE LACOMBE
Calle San Provolo 4719/A
No Telephone
Expensive; credit cards accepted
Open during lunch and Sunday

Far more original than the plethora of masks mass-produced for the ever-growing Carnival crowds are these hand-molded and hand-painted papier-mâché and leather creations. Some depict High Renaissance characters such as the court jester, others have ancient Roman models, while still others hint of African or Indian influence. Any of these pieces makes a collectible conversation-stopper to grace an empty wall.

LINENS & LINGERIE
Precious Hand Embroidery

9 MARIA MAZZARON
Fondamenta dell' Osmarin 4970
Tel. 52.21.392
Expensive; no credit cards accepted
By appointment only

Maria and Lina Mazzaron have been working wonders with lace since they went to study with the nuns at 14. These two charming, elderly sisters welcome you into their home on the first floor of what was once a patrician palazzo, today minus the maid-servants and private gondoliers. Two apprentices scuttle up and down ladders to bring out a wealth of extraordinary tablecloths and sheets; despite the flurry of confusion, Maria Mazzaron knows exactly where everything is. Among the very best of their generation of Venetian needlewomen, the Mazzaron sisters produce exquisite lace-trimmed everything, from linen tablecloths with scattered cobweb-like lace butterflies to linen sheets with a garland of bobbin lace around the border. Less expensive *servizi americani* (place mats with matching napkins) are made in fine white lace and can be trimmed to your specifications. The Mazzaron sisters will accommodate almost any whim within reason—as they have, for example, for Grace Kelly or for Barbra Streisand, "who wanted everything in pink."

It's a pleasant and easy stroll here after the commotion of Piazza San Marco, but it's best to call in advance and confirm that they'll be at home.

Castello, less commercial than San Marco.

BURANO, ISLAND OF LACE

Burano is the poor relation of the Venetian Lagoon, often overlooked by the tourist taking off from Piazza San Marco on his jaunt to Murano. It is hard to believe that from this island of poor fishermen came one of the most luxurious of fashion materials. Possibly because it was on the route of constant influences from the East, Burano became the cradle of lace-making in Europe in the early 1500s; it is a quaint little fishermen's island still.

Burano's colorful houses painted cobalt blue, russet red, green and pink (presumably to keep the flies away) look like an opera set. Behind billowing lace curtains in their parlors or sitting on the stoop in the day's strongest light, the Buranelle women (they do not consider themselves Venetian) sit in self-absorbed silence, tediously working away at their lace-making. *Tomboli* cushions held in their laps are used to create the airy delicacy of pillow or bobbin lace; it is made with twisted or plaited threads manipulated by dozens of bone or wooden bobbins. Another style, *punto ad ago* (openwork embroidery, also called *punto in aria*), is a needlepoint lace that elaborates decorative holes cut into fabric.

Today, 11 master lace-makers work in the Burano School of Lace (Scuola dei Merletti). Begun in 1872, it grew to 400 apprentices just before World War II, but closed on its 100th anniversary due to a lack of students. Thanks to the efforts of the Burano Lace Consortium, the school reopened in 1981; today it offers free courses to keep the art alive. The students' results are impressive, but pale next to some of the magnificent work of earlier periods exhibited in the school's museum. A visit there will help to train your eye; some of the lacegoods sold by fishermen's wives are actually imitations imported from the Orient, a curious turnabout from earlier times. At the school, you can buy from an exquisite array of modern and traditional table or bed linens, or commission directly from the school's lace-makers—probably some of the last handmade lacework of this quality to be found.

Scuola dei Merletti
Piazza B. Galuppi, Burano
Hours: 9:00 A.M. to 6:00 P.M.
(closed weekends and Tuesday)
Tel. 73.00.34

Directions: Burano is 5.5 miles northeast of Venice. The line 12 *vaporetto*, which also goes to Murano, leaves from the Fondamente Nuove roughly every hour and takes about 30 minutes.

RISTORANTE/TRATTORIA

10 ARCIMBOLDO
Calle dei Furlani 3219
(near Scuola di San Giorgio degli Schiavoni)
Tel. 86.569
Moderate; no credit cards accepted
Closed Tuesday

The name is an homage to the 16th-century painter Arcimboldo, whose peculiar depictions of people and scenes composed of flowers, fruits and vegetables, blown up to poster-size, decorate the restaurant's light-blue walls. Venetians love the cosmopolitan air of this restaurant, even though the young chef is one of the few in the city who do not offer fish. Vegetarians will appreciate the innovative use of vegetables, which are presented in exotic arrangements that reflect the painter's compositions. Carnivores will delight in the selec-

Sliding along quiet byways.

tion of meats; although the unusual mixtures of meat and fruit (chicken with grapefruit or veal with pineapple, for example) seem un-Venetian, it was Venetian Crusaders who first brought them back from the Orient.

Dorsoduro

*T*he quiet *sestiere* of Dorsoduro (literally "hard back") takes its name from the exceptionally firm clay subsoil of this southernmost section of Venice. In recent years this area has become the haunt of artists who snatched up open spaces in empty palazzi for their studios. But rents have now risen, and while many artisans have remained, community growth has temporarily slowed down.

Landmarks such as the Accademia and the Peggy Guggenheim Museum lend a note of prestige to the neighborhood. *Campi* such as the lively and picturesque Santa Margherita are both chic and unpretentious. Campo San Barnaba is smaller but also quaint; there you can buy fresh fruit and vegetables off a boat that arrives with mainland produce every morning. You'll find the same diversity in the following listings, from major glass firms and deluxe hotel restaurants to tiny artisan workshops.

There are few stores in Dorsoduro, but an impressive selection of monuments and sustenance stops. The Zattere (from the word for "rafts") is Venice's southernmost promenade, especially popular with families who spend Sunday afternoons strolling from *pizzeria* to *gelateria*. Of the many

At Campo Santa Margherita, a floating greengrocer pulls up with the day's produce.

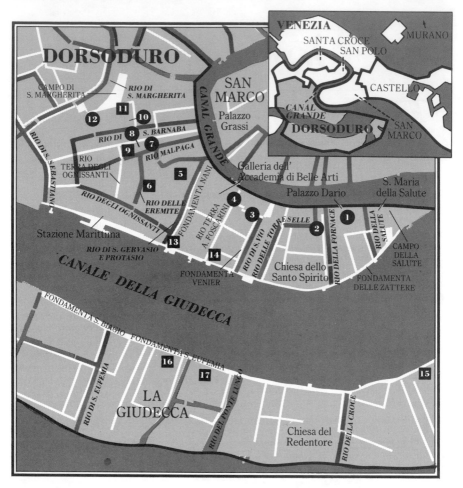

squeri (boatyards) that once supplied Venice with its beloved gondolas, a few still remain, including one picturesque cooperative in the San Trovaso area.

Dorsoduro includes the residential island of the Giudecca. Once heavily hit by attacking pirates, this island remained uninhabited for centuries. It probably takes its name from the Jewish population who lived there before being forced to move to the confines of the Ghetto in the *sestiere* of Cannaregio during the 16th century.

Salviati's landmark façade on the Grand Canal.

HOME

GLASS

One Hundred Years of Styles

1 SALVIATI & C.
San Gregorio 195
(on Grand Canal)
Tel. 52.22.532
Expensive; credit cards accepted
Open during lunch and Sunday morning

While boating along the Grand Canal, you will undoubtedly have noticed this magnificent palazzo whose façade is elaborately decorated with mosaic scenes. Here is housed the impressive Salviati glass collection. While two tiny Salviati stores in Piazza San Marco serve as advertisement, this setting is far more impressive. It is both a museum and a retail store for the respected firm that has helped put Murano back on the map with well over a century of award-winning glass design. Eight rooms are filled with endless varieties of glassware, from the meticulously etched to the baroque, from Roman to Renaissance replicas, from the clean and modern to the elaborately and colorfully molded. Salviati glass

is generally ornate and somewhat heavy in design, as are the company's lighting fixtures, which tend to be rather overblown by American standards. The shop will reliably package and ship your purchases home. There is a working furnace on the premises, one of the few outside Murano, and you can attend free demonstrations from 9:00 A.M. to 1:00 P.M. and from 3:00 to 5:00 P.M..

ANTIQUES & ENGRAVINGS

16th- to 19th-Century Engravings & Curios

2 ROSANNA BERTOTTO
Campiello Barbaro 364A
(Palazzo Dario)
Tel. 52.61.756
Moderate; credit cards accepted
Open during lunch

Browsing in this quaint and inviting shop crammed with objects and collectibles from the 16th to 19th centuries is not unlike visiting your Venetian grandmother's living room. There is also an interesting collection of original engravings, including a fascinating series of *Vedute di Venezia* (Scenes of Venice) by artists of the Venetian school. Remarkable photogravures of late-19th-century Venice

Some of Salviati's simpler models.

closely resemble the Venice we know today. The shop occupies two rooms of a low-ceilinged old building in a pretty little courtyard near the Peggy Guggenheim Museum.

FASHION

MEN'S & WOMEN'S

Discount Designer Names

3 SER ANGIÙ

Piscina del Forner 868
(near Campo San Vio)
Tel. 31.149
Moderate; no credit cards accepted
Open during lunch and Sunday

Don't misunderstand the slipshod nature of this boutique; the emphasis is on designer markdowns and close-outs, shown in a tiny, no-frills, rack-filled space. The garments here are grouped according to type and size, with labels left in, so the untrained eye can distinguish the Ferrè, Valentino, Basile or Coveri fashions. As is the case in such retail discount outlets (of which precious few exist in Italy), stock will vary erratically, from current or past seasons' leftovers to samples and garments less successful than anticipated.

You can find a second location for Ser Angiù in the San Marco neighborhood at Calle della Verona 3661 (telephone 70.81.28).

GALLERY

PRIMITIVE JEWELRY & ART

4 TOTEM—IL CANALE

Rio Terrà A. Foscarini 878/B
(Accademia)
Tel. 52.23.641
Moderate; credit cards accepted

Totem has recently moved to Dorsoduro from Mestre on the mainland, after earning a respected reputation as the first Italian gallery to deal seriously with primitive sculpture. Totem consists of two different spaces. The first is a store brimming with exotic African and primitive jewelry and objets d'art collected from around the world, as well as some pieces by Venetian artists who have been inspired by primitive styles. If you go through the shop you'll come into the second part of Totem, the gallery. Housed in a wing of the Palazzo Contarini dal Zaffo, a handsome Renaissance mansion that faces the Grand Canal, it displays a number of impressive sculptures.

SUSTENANCE

BAR/CAFFÈ

Pasticceria

5 VIO

Rio Terrà Toletta 1192
Tel. 57.451
Inexpensive; no credit cards accepted
Closed Tuesday

Right next to the Accademia is this small, stand-up *bar-caffè* that is as much a favorite with locals as with visiting strollers who are pulled in by a glimpse of the mouthwatering pastries. Light cream puffs, dense *sacher torte,* rich almond cake, colorful fruit tarts, and many other local classics have satisfied Venice's sweet tooth for untold centuries.

RISTORANTE/TRATTORIA

6 LOCANDA MONTIN
Fondamenta di Borgo 1147
(Campo San Barnaba)
Tel. 27.151
Moderate; credit cards accepted
Closed Wednesday

Reservations are a must at this big, informal inn whose walls are decorated with the artwork of renowned patrons. Artists and other regulars fill long, crowded tables attended by venerable white-aproned waiters. The atmosphere inside is noisy and upbeat, but Montin's is especially popular in the warm weather when you can linger in the spacious garden under cool trellises hung with grapes and flowering vines. The menu is predictably Venetian, with the traditional fresh fish and, as house specialties, *fegato alla veneziana* and *filetto* steak. Desserts not to be missed here are the *tiramisu* and the *torta di noci con panna* (hazlenut cake with whipped cream).

THE ULTIMATE SOUVENIR

However small, there *is* a foreign market for gondolas—Arab or Texan magnates who have realized that life is not complete without a sleek gondola floating in the backyard pool. If you don't have a pool —or a canal—it is still a fascinating experience to visit the *squero* of Signor Gastoni, who sells a handful of his prized vessels each year to foreigners.

Each gondola takes over two months to make and is made with seven different kinds of wood, including mahogany, cherry, oak, pine and elm, which are used for the various functions of strength, lightness and carving. The *squero* boatyards are today dangerously few in number, and skilled craftsmen like Signor Gastoni and his two sons are hard to come by. For their matchless labor, expect to pay approxi-

One of the world's few remaining squeri.

mately $12,000 for your standard model and an additional $5000 for the deluxe version. Signor Gastoni will arrange for shipping; rowing it home yourself is not recommended.
Cooperativa Gondolieri D. Manin
Campo San Trovaso 1097R
(in Dorsoduro)
Telephone 29.146

JEWELRY

7 ALDO OTTOCHIAN
Campo San Barnaba 2762
Tel. 24.181
Moderate; credit cards accepted

Young Aldo Ottochian creates beautiful and delicate gold jewelry. You can watch him at his workbench, fashioning intricate designs inspired by classic Roman and Etruscan styles. There's a profusion of rings set with small stones or with etched pieces of *paste di vetro,* an interesting material that simulates precious stones. These ersatz gems are also used on gold-trimmed leather bracelets and on grosgrain-ribbon necklaces. Ottochian offers good workmanship and value for moderate prices.

GIFTS

HAND-PAINTED WOOD PUZZLES

Unusual Venetian Souvenirs

8 SIGNOR BLUM
Calle Lunga 2864
(Campo San Barnaba)
Tel. 26.367
Moderate; credit cards accepted

Signor Blum's unusual wooden souvenirs.

This is the second location for Signor Blum, whose exquisite wood puzzles and panels you probably noticed in the display windows of his shop near the Piazza San Marco (see page 455). Just across the street from this store, you can glance into Signor Blum's fascinating woodcarving workshop.

SUSTENANCE

RISTORANTE/TRATTORIA

9 LA FURATOLA
Calle Lunga Barnaba 2870/A
(Campo San Barnaba)
Tel. 70.85.94
Moderate; no credit cards accepted
Closed Wednesday dinner and Thursday

At this unpretentious little restaurant that is a favorite in the neighborhood, there's not a steak to be found on the menu, just the freshest fish from the morning's fish market. A large table is laid out with each meal's offerings—marinated sardines, artichokes and various seafood appetizers. Pasta dishes are served with shrimp, mussels or clams, and entrées are a host of simple fish on the grill or fried.

MASKS

WORKSHOP/STUDIO

10 MONDONOVO
Rio Terrà Canal 3063
(Campo Santa Margherita)
Tel. 52.87.344
Moderate to expensive; credit cards
    accepted
Open Sunday

Giano Lovato is Venice's *mascheraio* par excellence. A consummate sculptor, he creates his own wooden shapes

Mondonovo, one of Venice's finest mask makers.

from which he then makes and hand-paints every mask in his shop. The mannequins at Mondonovo's door-step, masked in animal disguise, beckon you inside. Once you enter, you will find masks in 100 different styles: simple masks on a stick, numerous interpretations of the classic Commedia dell'Arte masks, and masks inspired by local frescoes and classical paintings that depict, among other things, the sun, the moon and mythical beasts.

Lovato is most attracted to unusual challenges. He often works with serious theatrical groups. If he is not pressed with other projects and is given sufficient time, he will custom-make a mask for you, guided by your facial measurements and fantasy.

SUSTENANCE

GELATERIA

11 IL DOGE
Campo Santa Margherita
Tel. 52.34.607
Inexpensive; no credit cards accepted
Open 7 days a week

The newest addition to the *campo*, this marble *gelateria* makes 24 delicious flavors of *propria produzione* (literally, "own production" or home-made). Fresh fruit in season is the biggest pull, but there are delicious chunky *straciatella* (chocolate chip) and Cointreau as well as traditional standbys.

GIFTS

CERAMICS

Modern

12 CAZANCO ART
Campo Santa Margherita 2899
Tel. 70.46.81
Inexpensive; credit cards accepted

This charming, homey little shop warrants a detour if you're interested in modern ceramics. If you are in the area near the Chiesa delle Carmini, come and watch young ceramist Emmanuela Zanoni at work. All of her pieces are handmade and hand-painted, using bright and modern abstract design in beautiful, innovative ways. Her tiny geometric shapes and naif patterns float randomly on pastel backgrounds. There are little boxes with lids, sugars and creamers, vases and pitchers. You can easily buy up a storm of lovely gifts, since Emmanuela's prices are reasonable and she is happy to ship.

GELATERIA

13 GELATERIA NICO
Zattere ai Gesuati 922
(Campo San Trovaso)
Tel. 25.293
Inexpensive; no credit cards accepted
Closed Thursday

This is a simple ice-cream parlor that produces a great assortment of flavors made fresh every day. Nico is almost everyone's favorite *gelateria* on the Zattere, although two other contenders are located nearby (one right next door), and it is not unusual for visitors to sample all three during a stroll before arriving at any conclusive decisions. *Giandiuotti di passeggio* is a slab of hazelnut-chocolate ice cream with fresh whipped cream "to go" for walking purposes, but if your feet are weary, there are indoor and outdoor tables where you can sit and relish an Olympic-sized *coppa olimpica* (sundae) or *tiramisu* creation.

PIZZERIA

14 PIZZERIA ALLE ZATTERE
Zattere ai Gesuati 795
(Campo San Agnese)
Tel. 70.42.24
Inexpensive; no credit cards accepted
Closed Tuesday

This is a popular family spot with the locals, as much for its lengthy list of pizzas as for its idyllic view of Giudecca Island from the outdoor tables set up on large floating rafts. True to form, one specialty is pizza with seafood combinations. There is also *pizza primavera* decorated with grilled vegetables, as well as an assortment of fresh pastas, *antipasti* and fresh seafood salads. You can continue the Venetian Sunday ritual you've innocently begun with a delicious pizza here and an ice cream at one of the Zattere's fine *gelaterie,* then stroll along the promenade in the warm sunshine.

RISTORANTE/TRATTORIA

15 CIPRIANI
Fondamenta San Giovanni 10
(La Giudecca)
Tel. 70.77.44
Very expensive; credit cards accepted
Open 7 days a week

One of Venice's singular luxuries, the Cipriani Hotel is also one of the newest. Today it is owned by the English owner of the Orient Express, who promises that dining at the Cipriani will be just as exotic as riding on that fabled train. A grand Venetian complex with beautiful gardens, the hotel offers a restful pool-side lunch featuring mouthwatering antipastos and towering club sandwiches. Dinner is served in the airy, *elegantissimo* dining room replete with Limoges china and Fortuny fabrics. Nor is any detail overlooked in the cuisine or its presentation. *Cannelloni con zucchini* (pasta with zucchini filling) and *penne con melanzane* (with eggplant) provide an exquisite break from the proliferation of pasta-cum-seafood offerings about town. Those are available as well, of course, together with fish and shellfish unsurpassed in its freshness and preparation.

If you haven't time for dinner, sip a sweet Bellini on the terrace or spend an enthralling hour at the piano bar, where the strains of Massimo will hold you captive. Classically trained but with an unlimited repertoire of popular standards, he plays Thursdays through Tuesdays from 7:30 until late night.

SUSTENANCE

RISTORANTE/TRATTORIA

16 HARRY'S DOLCI

Fondamenta Sant'Eufemia 673
(La Giudecca)
Tel. 52.24.844 or 70.76.32
Expensive; credit cards accepted
Closed Sunday afternoon and Monday

This is the newest addition to Harry Cipriani's restaurant dynasty. Far less expensive than Harry's Bar just across the waterway, this establishment (which translates as "Harry's Sweets") is just as chic and the menu just as delicious. It borrows many of Harry's superb classics such as *fegato alla veneziana, carpaccio,* hearty soup, fresh antipasto, and a "sandwich called club"—more like a puffy croissant with club-sandwich filling baked in. Canopy-covered waterfront dining is often reserved for the "beautiful people" regulars, but it's just as pleasant inside, where the décor resembles a yacht-turned-sleek-pastry-parlor. (If you call to reserve, specify your preference.) Although you can dine lightly, the name reminds you that sweets are the focus here, with a truly splendid assortment of rococo goodies such as the whipped-cream-mounded meringue, ultrachocolate cake, and rich homemade ice creams and sorbets. For sale are attractive jars of cookies, preserves, *carpaccio* sauce, and bottles of the house *aperitivo,* Cocktail Doge.

Water traffic is both practical and romantic.

SUSTENANCE

RISTORANTE/TRATTORIA

17 DUE MORI

Fondamenta del Ponte Piccolo 558
(La Giudecca)
Tel. 52.25.452
Moderate; no credit cards accepted
Closed Sunday

This is one of Venice's newest, most up-and-coming restaurants. Three talented professionals have recently escaped from Harry's Bar (including his chef of eight years, Giuseppe Trioli) to set up this large and comfortable restaurant. Informal paper tablecloths do little to foretell the expertise they've brought with them. Their wordly Venetian cuisine is not unlike Harry's. Excellent starters are *zuppa di pesce* and *crema di pioci* (cream of mussel soup). Traditional fish dishes are *sardelle in saor,* as well as an unusual *quaglie in saor* (marinated quail). Pizza, too, is a major attraction—crusty, light and with a range of fillings, including a vegetarian combination of zucchini, eggplant and peppers.

San Polo/ Santa Croce

*A*lthough they may pass through Santa Croce and San Polo when following the yellow-signed route from the train station to the Piazza San Marco, tourists and shoppers alike generally overlook these colorful and authentic *sestieri*. They are missing a hidden part of town that remains as Venice was centuries ago. It was considered "the other side of the Canal," even after being joined to the *sestiere* of San Marco in 1588 with the construction of the Rialto Bridge.

In this section we deal primarily with San Polo, while incorporating a number of nearby Santa Croce destinations that are too interesting to ignore. Stores in the vicinity of the Rialto Bridge and its famous open-air markets run the gamut from tawdry souvenir stalls to interesting modern boutiques and specialized establishments such as Emilio Ceccato, whose gondoliers' gear is purchased by foreign visitors and locals alike. Beyond the Rialto hub are a wealth of small artisans' workshops as well as the everyday shopping streets of Rio Terrà Secondo, Calle del Tintor and the Fondamenta Marin. You'll hear the old Venetian dialect spoken in this secluded neighborhood once frequented by the famous poet Gabriele D'Annunzio, who used it for his romantic trysts with Eleonora Duse.

Unusual for a city where space is a rarity, the broad Campo San Polo is a neighborhood hub.

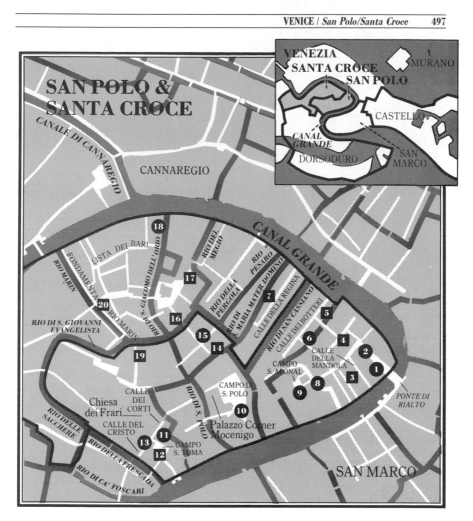

The *sestiere*'s name comes from an earthquake that occurred on the feast day of Saint Paul in 1343, destroying more than 100 buildings and causing the Grand Canal to dry up for two weeks. Today the Campo San Polo is the largest *campo* after Piazza San Marco and is a nucleus of social and neighborhood life. Its major historical attraction is the 14th-century Church of the Frari, the most important Gothic church in Venice and burial place of Titian. Carlo Goldoni, one of Italy's most celebrated playwrights, was born near the Goldoni Museum.

There are a number of enticing eating spots in the San Polo neighborhood, including the new and refined La Regina, the fashionable Caffè Orientale, and the popular Alle Oche Pizzeria. If you've made it as far as the Rialto Bridge from the Piazza San Marco, blaze ahead through the back streets of San Polo; it will add another dimension to your stay.

FASHION

MEN'S, WOMEN'S & CHILDREN'S

Gondoliers' Gear

1 EMILIO CECCATO

Sottoportico di Rialto 16–17
Tel. 22.700
Moderate; credit cards accepted
Open during lunch

The next best thing to bringing home a gondola is buying a gondolier's outfit from Emilio Ceccato. His small, crowded shop at the foot of the Rialto Bridge sells the real article: pure cotton navy-and-white-striped T-shirts and heavy white cotton jackets with sailor's collar, which come in sizes to fit the smallest of babies or the heftiest of gondoliers. Signor Ceccato also dresses Venice's waiters, clerks, and schoolchildren, as uniforms are his specialty.

LEATHERGOODS

BAGS & ACCESSORIES

Contemporary/Trendy

2 LA FURLA

Sottoportico di Rialto 53–54
Tel. 35.862
Moderate; credit cards accepted

Buried among some very touristy shops is this little breath of fresh air. Furla, a Bologna-based company, is always the first to pick up on a trend, if not to create one. Its leather bags are rather avant-garde, made of good-quality leathers often stamped or colored in the shades of the season, and most reasonably priced. The dramatic modern interior also highlights a collection of big belts and fashion jewelry to complete a Furla statement.

There's a second Furla shop in the San Marco neighborhood at Merceria San Salvador 4954 (telephone 52.30.611).

SUSTENANCE

RISTORANTE/TRATTORIA

3 ALLA MADONNA

Calle della Madonna 594
(Rialto)
Tel. 52.23.824
Moderate; credit cards accepted
Closed Wednesday

Lunch or dinner is fun at this big, noisy *trattoria* where the local Venetian businessmen mix with the tourists. Seasoned, amiable waiters are used to both, and will patiently wait as you check out the large refrigerator case displaying the day's fresh fish arrivals. This is a good place to try squid *in umido* (in its own ink), served with polenta; tiny squid fried whole; or *tartufi di mare* (sea truffles), a kind of clam from local waters. There are a few concessions to carnivores such as grilled and roast meats. A circular table is laden with *contorni* (side dishes), so you can see what's available. The upbeat atmosphere helps everyone feel at home.

SUSTENANCE

ENOTECA (WINE BAR)

4 DO MORI

Calle dei Due Mori 429
Tel. 52.25.401
Inexpensive; no credit cards accepted
Closed Sunday

This is the best of the old, traditional wine bars loyally patronized by the Venetians. A neighborhood watering hole since 1750, Do Mori is now under the expert guidance of owner/ sommelier Roberto Viscontin, who has amassed over 350 fine wines. You can also sample fresh *cicchetti* that include *coppa del toro* (smoked beef rolled up and speared on a toothpick), croquettes and great platters of local salami and prosciutto, although there's no place to sit. Old Venetian gentlemen stop by for their matinal regular when the bar first opens at 8:00 A.M. and, with the exception of a 2:00 to 4:30 P.M. siesta, you can sip and nibble away until 9:00 P.M. At least until you've finished reading this, there won't be a tourist in sight.

SUSTENANCE

RISTORANTE/TRATTORIA

5 POSTE VECIE
Pescheria 1608
Tel. 72.18.22
Moderate; credit cards accepted
Closed Tuesday

The name tells us it's near the old post office, and the street tells us it's near the daily fish market. A private bridge leads to this old Venice-styled inn with low ceilings and wooden beams, and there is garden dining in the summer. Although you are not obliged to choose from them, the restaurant has three different fixed-price menus (Business Lunch, Veneziano, or Grand Degustazione) and a good wine list if you want to sample something other than the very good house white wine. There's a splendid table of fresh antipasto, to be followed by scallops with *porcini* mushrooms, scallop ravioli or fish risotto. Perfectly grilled fish is Poste Vecie's specialty, but a handful of meat dishes are also offered.

Daily specialties at the Poste Vecie.

MASKS

WORKSHOP/STUDIO

6 TRAGICOMICA
Calle dei Botteri 1566
(Campo San Cassiano)
Tel. 72.11.02
Moderate; credit cards accepted

This is not your average mask atelier for tourists. Highly original and ornate masks are created by young artisans as you watch. As the name implies, both tragic and comical make up the large selection of papier-mâché Carnival masks. The workshop's owner and mentor, Gualtiero dell'Osto, a university professor in theater arts, supplied Verona's production of *Ballo in Maschera* with a number of theatrical masks. Here at the atelier, he is exceptionally earnest and enthusiastic about the fantasy he encourages from his talented artisans.

CARNIVAL, MASKS AND THE COMMEDIA DELL'ARTE

Europe was once full of Carnivals. Deriving its name from *carnem levare* ("to take meat away"), Carnival was the time for celebrating the last temptations of the flesh before enduring the rigorous period of Lent. Venice's particularly intemperate Carnival celebrations drew well-heeled crowds from all over the Continent. Unbridled merrymaking was further guaranteed by the masks behind which Venice sang and danced *con brio*. Exuberance grew so frenzied that Carnival went on for a ridiculously long time. Ironically, it was most popular during the 18th century—masking the final decline of the Venetian Republic.

Mask makers hand-paint labors of love.

The revelry generally begins in February or March and lasts for several weeks, building to a crescendo and culminating on Shrove Tuesday (Mardi Gras), the day before Lent begins on Ash Wednesday. If you're a seasoned survivor and don't mind the jostling, you'll find Carnival the quintessential theater *in situ,* with mimes, acrobats, and music filling every *campo* and *calle* and Venice as a perfect backdrop.

Masks were once so popular during Carnival time that they were worn for local feast days as well. Some even became a part of daily city attire, and allowed men impunity and women to circulate without chaperones. Adventurous husbands and frustrated wives took full advantage of the practice; a woman could not be accused of adultery if her cohort was wearing a mask, for she would insist she did not know the man was not her husband.

Today every store in town still carries a mask or two during Carnival time. The stores and workshops we have included specialize in handcrafted and painted masks offered all year round. Masks are perhaps the most Venetian of all souvenirs, be they fantasy masks of plumes and sequins or the classic and traditional. Many of the latter are derived from the 16th-century Commedia dell'Arte, an improvisational troupe of masked comics that traveled from court to court and theater to theater. Some of the timeless stock characters that have survived over the centuries and still appear *in maschera* today are *Arlecchino* (Harlequin), *Pierrot, Pulcinella* (Punch), and *Bauta*.

RISTORANTE/TRATTORIA

7 LA REGINA
Calle della Regina 2330 (near Campo San
    Cassiano in Santa Croce)
Tel. 52.41.402
Expensive; no credit cards accepted
Closed Tuesday

If all the simple grilled fish has left
you wanting something more imaginative, you'll like this lovely, new restaurant which excels in delicious Venetian *nuova cucina*. Its wood-
beamed dining rooms feature tables
with candlelight and fresh orchids.
One of the best Bellini cocktails in
town will mark the beginning of a
memorable meal. Try the *insalata di
mazzancolle* (jumbo shrimp salad
with warm, lemony mayonnaise), *tagliatelle al basilico con cape sante al
pomodoro fresco* (homemade basil
pasta with light, fresh tomato sauce
and barely cooked scallops), *San Pietro con peperoni* (John Dory fish with
julienne of sweet peppers and cream
sauce), or one of the many other fresh
fish on the menu; all are well prepared, lightly and wonderfully
sauced.

ENGRAVINGS & PRINTS

Contemporary Venetian Engravings

8 CADORE ART
Calle dell'Olio 1069
(Campo Sant'Aponal)
Tel. 52.31.108
Moderate; no credit cards accepted
Open during lunch

This tiny wood-paneled shop sells
quality prints from original engravings that depict dreamlike visions of
Venice. For more information, see the
listing for its sister shop BAC Art
Studio in San Marco (page 475).

MEN'S

Designer Collections

9 VOLPE
Campo Sant'Aponal 1228
Tel. 38.041
Expensive; credit cards accepted
Open during lunch

This is one of three locations in Venice for this elegant boutique of high-
fashion merchandise. Here you'll find
more casual sportswear for young-
minded tastes. See listing for the
other Volpe shops in San Marco (page
451).

Tomaso Pirredda's mask casts, before and after.

MASKS

WORKSHOP/STUDIO

10 TOMASO PIRREDDA
Campo San Polo 2008
Tel. 70.05.31
Moderate; no credit cards accepted
Open during lunch

One of Venice's true mask authorities, Tomaso Pirredda will sculpt an artistic mask to your features in papier-mâché or leather. Not all of his masks are personalized, however, and you're sure to find something just as wonderful among his ready-made creations of Carnival masks that border on the surreal. Tomaso considers himself foremost an artist , as well he should; he also makes elaborate theatrical masks for the Venice theater.

GIFTS

SILVER

Handcrafted

11 SFRISO
Campo San Tomà 2849
Tel. 23.558
Moderate; credit cards accepted

This surprisingly small shop near the

Some of Venice's great silversmiths.

16th-century Scuola di San Rocco is the exclusive outlet for two of Venice's leading silversmiths. The Sfriso brothers create their clean, tasteful designs in silverware, coffee and tea sets, picture frames, jewelry, letter openers, cigarette cases and sacred objects. They sign every piece. Tiny silver boxes with inlaid marble or miniature gondolas are bound to be unique gifts, and any Sfriso creation could become a collectible, for many believe that these artisans are the last of Venice's great silversmiths.

SUSTENANCE

PIZZERIA

12 TRATTORIA SAN TOMÀ
Campo San Tomà 2864
Tel. 52.38.819
Inexpensive; credit cards accepted
Closed Tuesday

If your wander-weary feet need a break, set up post at an outdoor table in front or in the quiet rear garden for a leisurely and delicious pizza. If it's just before lunch, you might see tables of homemade fresh pasta put out in the sun to dry—*linguine, tagliatelle, gnocchi* and *pappardelle.* You might want to try both pizza and pasta, knowing you'll walk it off by the end of the day. Ask for your favorite sauce even if it is not on the menu, and they'll most likely make it up for you. There's also the usual Venetian run of fresh fish fried or on the grill. It's interesting to know that this charming little neighborhood piazza was the center for the Scuola dei Calegheri, the religious fraternity or guild of cobblers whose 15th-century seat was in the white-faced marble church just across the *campo.*

ANTIQUE BOOKS & PRINTS

For Collectors

13 MANLIO PENSO

Calle del Mandoler 2916/A
(Campo San Tomà)
Tel. 52.38.215
Expensive; credit cards accepted

Here is a charming haunt for the
serious collector of precious volumes.
Signor Penso is an animated *appassionato* who will tirelessly guide you
through his renowned collection of
books and prints from the 1500s to
the 1700s. There are only originals,
no reproductions. A popular title with
those who have succumbed to the
city's spell is *Vedute di Venezia,* Venetian views as depicted by such masters as Canaletto, Tiepolo and Maries-
chi. Prints are sold framed and
unframed; a number of more affordable ones are from the 19th century.

SUSTENANCE

RISTORANTE/TRATTORIA

14 DA FIORE

Calle del Scaleter 2202
Tel. 37.208
Moderate; credit cards accepted
Closed Sunday and Monday

Da Fiore is a simple and elegant
Venetian inn of dignified local character. The freshest of fish and shellfish dishes are interpreted with flair,
and the impeccable service will delight even non-fisheaters. Succulent
risottos are made with shrimp, fish,
radicchio or squid in its ink or, if it's
the season, with scampi or asparagus.
For an entrée you're likely to find
moleche fritte (fried soft-shell crabs);
grilled *seppioline* (small cuttlefish) or

cannochie (shrimp) dressed with
extra-virgin olive oil and parsley; and
dati di mare (sea dates). There's
crusty homemade bread, studded
with whole green olives, to keep you
happy between courses, and a heavenly house specialty for dessert,
bavarese caramellato (creamy caramel bavarian with grated chocolate).

ENGRAVINGS & PRINTS

WORKSHOP/STUDIO

15 MARIO ROCCHI

Rio Terrà II 2309
(near Campo Sant'Agostin)
No telephone
Moderate; credit cards accepted

Mario Rocchi is known about town
for his beautiful aquatint engravings
of Venetian scenes. If you'd like some
tasteful artwork (not meant for the
serious collector) of this splendid city,
browse through prints large and
small. You can watch him at work in
his light, airy studio infused with
strains of opera.

SUSTENANCE

PIZZERIA

16 ALLE OCHE

Calle del Tintor 1552/A
(near Campo San Giacomo dell'Orio in
    Santa Croce)
Tel. 27.559
Inexpensive; credit cards accepted
Closed Monday

Young Venetians flock to Alle Oche
for a good pizza—and an incredible
41 varieties from which to choose. If
one of the outdoor tables is free, pull
up a seat to watch the runway of
neighborhood passersby. If not,

there's a convivial atmosphere with booths inside, or a pleasant rear garden. Accomplished fire-eaters should try the *mangiafuoco* (pizza with spicy *salame* and chili pepper); those with noble tastes, *pizza dello zar* (salmon and caviar). The *bosco* (forest) is made with three different kinds of wild mushrooms, and the *disco volante* (flying saucer) is two pizzas face-to-face, like a giant sandwich. There is also a regular *trattoria* menu of casual food—salads, pastas and simple fish dishes.

SUSTENANCE

RISTORANTE/TRATTORIA

17 LA ZUCCA
Calle del Megio 1762
(near Campo San Giacomo dell'Orio in
    Santa Croce)
Tel. 70.04.62
Moderate; no credit cards accepted
Closed Monday

This may be your only chance to eat pumpkin pasta—a tasty innovation from which this small, informal *osteria* takes its name. Some Venezuelan-inspired dishes employ avocados, and herbs and spices recall the adventurous days of Marco Polo's route to

Waterfront palazzos, once grand, now weathered.

Cathay. The original and light cuisine makes few concessions to red-meat lovers; fresh fish, chicken (try the version with a spicy avocado sauce) and salads are the most interesting offerings. The back windows overlook canal life, while up front a busy wine bar offers snacks and a few inviting tables outdoors.

FABRICS

FURNISHINGS

Antique Patterns

18 LUIGI BEVILACQUA
Campiello Comare 1320
(near Campo Zandegolà in Santa Croce)
Tel. 23.384
Expensive; no credit cards accepted

For over a century the inimitable Bevilacqua silk brocades, damasks and printed velvets have draped Europe's courts, the world's most luxurious hotels, the Vatican and, more currently, the White House. Less then ten hand looms are in operation in Venice today, a sad contrast to the 10,000 that functioned in the 15th century. At the Bevilacqua factory you can see a vast room containing over 30 period wooden hand looms. Third-generation owner Giulio Bevilacqua takes great pride in carrying on Venice's artistry in textile production, even though he has just one loom operating to produce (on special order only) exquisite brocades and the nearly extinct *soprarizzo* (cut velvet). Bevilacqua remains dedicated to the antique styles and techniques, which he feels will always be of value. His master weavers can take as much as eight hours to create half a yard. High prices are justified by unsurpassable quality. Over 1000 cardboard templates of antique designs from the 1500s to the 1800s can potentially be made up by Bevilacqua's second- and third-generation loom operators in either pure silk or a silk blend (silk and linen, silk and cotton). Signor Bevilacqua has planted one foot in the 20th century with a factory on the mainland where precision machinery produces classic brocades that will enhance any patrician home.

SUSTENANCE

RISTORANTE/TRATTORIA

19 CAFFÈ ORIENTALE
Calle dell'Olio 2426
(at Rio Marin in Santa Croce)
Tel. 71.98.04
Expensive; credit cards accepted
Closed Thursday

Two young brothers are the new proprietors of this, one of the most romantic restaurants in Venice. With Mama in the kitchen, the menu mirrors the past, offering such traditional specialties as *granseola* (giant crabmeat cocktail), *risi e zucca* (risotto made with golden winter squash), and mixed grilled seafood such as tuna, eel and monkfish. Soft lighting enhances a pastel-colored postmodern setting with artistic flower arrangements and modern Murano glassware. If you're lucky enough to procure a table on the terrace, watch complimentary glasses of wine being handed down to passing gondolas or water taxis on the narrow Rio Marin; the only finale sweeter than the delicious *tiramisu* (literally "pick-me-up") dessert is a ride home in one of the restaurant's slender, romantic gondolas.

Proud owner Gilda Vio in her spotless kitchen.

SUSTENANCE

BAR-CAFFÈ

Pasticceria

20 LA BOUTIQUE DEL DOLCE
Fondamenta Rio Marin 890
(near Campo Nazario Sauro in Santa Croce)
Tel. 71.85.23
Inexpensive; no credit cards accepted
Closed Wednesday

It's a bit out of the way, but if you'll settle for nothing less then Venice's best as your breakfast croissant, it's worth the walk. Gilda Vio's ultra-buttery croissants are delicious plain; they take on a turnover shape when filled with chocolate or whatever fresh fruit is in season, such as figs, blackberries or bananas. There's a stand-up bar where frothy cappuccino is made with the morning's fresh milk deliveries. Italian Oscars for uncompromising freshness and quality testify to such temptations of the palate as dark chocolate layer cake with meringue filling; three flavors of *tartufi; crostata* (tarts) with fresh pears, peaches or apricots; petit fours and a host of fresh cookies. Venetians come from far and wide to this picturesque area not far from the train station to enjoy Signora Gilda's wonders.

Murano

*M*urano is a group of five small islands just a 30-minute ferry ride from Venice. Unimpressed by the cheap glass trinkets that clutter the San Marco area, most tourists never come near Murano and its world-famous glass-blowing furnaces. But a breath of fresh air has been blown into Murano glass; some exquisite, contemporary glassware is now produced here, in addition to reproductions of traditional designs that made Murano the glass capital of the world centuries ago.

To sort out who's doing what, head for Murano's magnificent Museo Vetrario (Glass Museum) at Fondamenta Giustinian 8, an obligatory visit for glass collectors. You'll get a diversified view of the world's best modern glass design in a new division (Fondamenta Manin 1C/D) dedicated entirely to 20th-century work. For those with more classic tastes, the museum also exhibits over 4000 prize pieces that span 500 years of vitreous art; fortunately, many of these pieces are still being reproduced. The new museum addition and the recent renaissance of the glass-blowing art are the results of a collaboration between local authorities and a handful of Murano glass firms, led by two enterprising brothers, Carlo and Giovanni Moretti of the Carlo Moretti glassmaking house.

In a successful effort to keep alive their thousand-year-old craft, the Moretti brothers and their colleagues have founded the Consortium for the Promotion of Venetian Artistic Glass. Look for their VM trademark (Vetro Murano), a guarantee of authenticity and quality control. The 53 member companies produce articles for every taste and budget, from inexpensive collector objects and glass jewelry to museum-quality tableware.

Venetian glass blowing was already creating a name for itself in the 10th century, but it was only in 1292 that the Doge ordered all furnaces moved to the remote island of Murano for fire-hazard reasons. Since then, all glassware has been produced on Murano, despite the rash of "Furnace Demonstration" signs you'll see in downtown Venice. Many of the working furnaces remain closed to the public so that the secrets of special effects will not be disclosed. Only two demonstration (not production) furnaces in Venice are worth seeing: on Murano, behind the Domus store (see page 509) at Pescheria 15/A; the other at Salviati in Dorsoduro (see page 489).

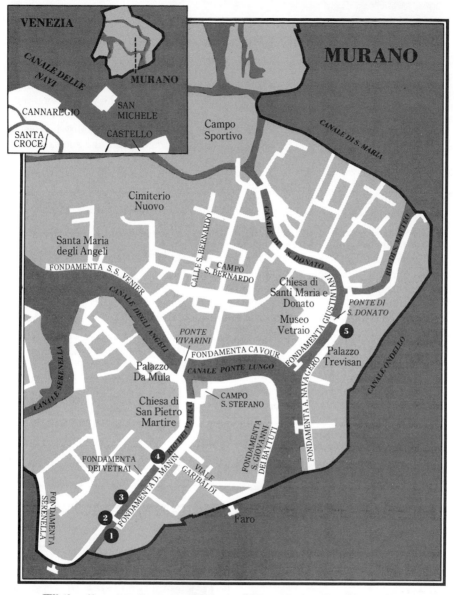

While all major firms produce on Murano, not all of them have retail outlets there. Salviati and Venini, for example, have wholesale showrooms on Murano, but you'll have to go to their respective locations in Dorsoduro and San Marco to buy. Conversely, many glass firms worth seeing, such as Foscarini and Barovier & Toso, sell only on Murano. These establishments, together with the Glass Museum and the pleasant *traghetto* (line 5 or 12), make Murano a delightful outing.

GLASS

LAMPS & LIGHTING SHOWROOM

Classic to Very Contemporary

1 FOSCARINI
Fondamenta Manin 1
Tel. 73.98.35
Expensive; credit cards accepted
Closed Saturday

At the beginning of the Fondamenta's strip of glass showrooms are Foscarini's large windows exhibiting a profusion of ceiling, tabletop and freestanding lighting fixtures. Murano's best house for lamps and fixtures made of mouth-blown glass, Foscarini has something for every taste. There are traditional Venetian crystal chandeliers of the kind that light the palazzi along the Grand Canal and the palaces of Europe, and also modern designs made for high-tech décor. Most models come in American voltage and cost considerably less than the Foscarini products sold abroad. Should you be looking for something unique, Foscarini will create custom-made chandeliers for you, as it does for major international hotels and banks.

GLASS

Small Gifts

2 GUGLIELMO SENT
Fondamenta dei Vetrai 8/A
Tel. 73.91.00
Moderate; credit cards accepted
Open during lunch and Sunday

Though Gugliemo Sent is not one of Venice's major glassmakers, this respected family-operated firm has an interesting retail shop that sells the glass designs of the father, Guglielmo,

and his daughter Susanna. Using a range of techniques, they produce both traditional and contemporary objects of decorated glass and multi-colored enamel. The contemporary interpretations of the young daughter are of particular interest—modern design and excellent quality in vases, tabletop accessories and such smaller glass gift items as pens and fake candies and fruits.

GLASS

Top-Name

3 BAROVIER & TOSO
Fondamenta dei Vetrai 28
Tel. 73.90.49
Expensive; credit cards accepted
Closed Saturday

Barovier & Toso is one of the great families of the Venetian glass industry, whose classical techniques are now applied chiefly to modern design. Classic and contemporary lighting fixtures include chandeliers, floor and table lamps, as well as wall lights that can be custom-made on special request. The special series of vases created for Barovier & Toso by Toni Zuccheri is called Gli Spacchi (The

Idle gondoliers await their next passage.

Slits): black opaque glass is slit at the rim and folded back, revealing the different-colored glass on the inner side. Rich infusions of color, marbleized effects and parallel stripes circling vases are among the characteristic features of the firm's other beautiful pieces, many of which are in the Murano Glass Museum.

GLASS

OBJECTS & JEWELRY

Showcase for Top Makers

4 DOMUS VETRI D'ARTE
Fondamenta dei Vetrai 82
Tel. 73.92.15
Moderate to expensive; credit cards accepted
Open during lunch and Sunday

Domus is the best shop on Murano in which to find a selection of fine glassware from the island's leading furnaces and glass masters. You'll see good representations of Carlo Moretti, Nason & Moretti, A.V. Mazzega, Toso Vetri d'Arte (with designs by Ettore Sottsass and Marco Zanini), Lidio Seguso, and Linio Tagliapietra for Effetre International. There is also an exceptionally large collection of innovative glass-beaded jewelry. Don't be mislead by the commerical look of this store; it is far superior to the rash of lesser-quality gift shops that populate Murano.

GLASS

Fine Contemporary Design

5 PAOLO MARTINUZZI
Fondamenta Navagero 56–57
Tel. 73.91.66
Expensive; credit cards accepted
Open during lunch

Lovely glassware at Paolo Martinuzzi.

This attractive boutique stands out from its myriad neighbors hawking tawdry glass trinkets. It is well worth the pleasant stroll or *traghetto* ride from the more trafficked Fondamenta dei Vetrai. In a setting that looks like a country antique store, Paolo Martinuzzi offers a select grouping of fine contemporary glassware made by Murano's masters. Showcased on old wooden tables and among antique furniture and curios are the resonant creations of Carlo Moretti—articles in clear glass of the purest design, such as his gold-rimmed series. If you're coming from Venice, you can arrive directly at Martinuzzi's by getting off at the Navagero *traghetto* stop.

INDEX TO STORES LISTED BY PRODUCT

The following index of stores in Venice is arranged by product category so that you can quickly find stores of particular interest to you. In each category, stores are grouped by neighborhood (SM = San Marco, C = Castello, DD = Dorsoduro, SP/SC = San Polo/Santa Croce, M = Murano); the number following this designation is the store's location code on the neighborhood map and also represents the order in which the store is listed. Page numbers are provided for reference to the stores' descriptions in the text. An asterisk (*) means the store is usually open during lunch.

General Index

W

Index to Stores, Markets & Eating Places

ALPHABETIZATION

Store names that begin with an Italian article (*la, le, il, lo, l', i* or *gli*) or with a contraction of the preposition *a* and an article (*alla, alle, al, allo, all', ai* or *agli*) are alphabetized under the word following the article or contraction; for example, "La Furla" is listed under the letter F and "Al Duca d'Aosta" can be found under the letter D.

Stores that are named for people, whether real or fictitious, are entered under both the first and last names; for example, Cesare Paciotti, the shoe boutique, can be found under the letter C (Cesare) as well as P (Paciotti). Stores with more than one location, however, such as Georgio Armani, are listed fully only under the last name, with a cross-reference appearing at the first-name entry.

CITIES & NEIGHBORHOOD CODES

Each entry includes geographical information about the store: both the city (or cities) in which it is located and a code number identifying its shopping neighborhood. For keys to the neighborhood codes, consult the Indexes to Stores Listed by Product for each city (Florence, p. 134; Milan, p. 295; Rome, p. 419; Venice, p. 510).

(Page numbers in **boldface** refer to special profiles of designers and shops.)

A

A. Caraceni *(Milan-B)*, 256
Achromatichic *(Rome-PN)*, 367–68
A. Codognato *(Venice-SM)*, 468–69
Adriana Mode *(Milan-S)*, 242
Aimo e Nadia *(Milan-VM)*, 283
Lionello Ajò *(Rome-PS)*, 329
Albanese-Mauri *(Milan-M)*, 232
L'Albero del Pane *(Rome-CF)*, 394–95
Alberta Ferretti *(Milan-M)*, 217–18
Alberto & Marina Menasci *(Rome-TB)*, 413
Alberto Martinangeli *(Rome-PN)*, 365
Giorgio Albertosi *(Florence-O)*, 128
Alberto Subert *(Milan-S)*, 242

Alberto Valese *(Venice-SM)*, 444–45
Albrizzi *(Milan-M)*, 226
Aldo Ottochian *(Venice-DD)*, 492
Aldrovandi *(Milan-M)*, 232
Alessi Paride *(Florence-CS)*, 67
Alex *(Florence-C)*, 90
Alexander-Nicolette *(Milan-M)*, 232
Alfio *(Milan-M)*, 230
Alimentari *(Florence-C)*, 89
Alinari Photo/Bookstore *(Florence-C)*, 91
Alivar *(Rome-CF)*, 404
Aloisia *(Florence-C)*, 91
L'Altro Calafuria *(Milan-B)*, 261
Amedeo Micocci *(Rome-PP)*, 387
A. Melozzi *(Florence-O)*, 118
American Bookstore *(Milan-VM)*, 280